evidence
that
demands
a verdict

historical evidences
for the Christian faith

Revised Edition

compiled
by
Josh
McDowell

Traveling Representative for
Campus Crusade for Christ International

EVIDENCE THAT DEMANDS A VERDICT
Revised Edition

A Campus Crusade for Christ Book
Published by
HERE'S LIFE PUBLISHERS, INC.
P.O. Box 1576
San Bernardino, CA 92402

Cloth Edition: ISBN 0-918956-57-9
                Product No. 40-099-4
Quality Paperback Edition: ISBN 0-918956-46-3
                Product No. 40-06-39
Library of Congress No. 78-75041

FOREWORD

Is Christianity credible?

Is there an intellectual basis for faith in Jesus Christ as the Son of God?

Scholars throughout the centuries, as well as millions of students and older adults, would answer such questions with a resounding, "Yes!" That is what *Evidence That Demands a Verdict,* by Josh McDowell, is all about.

Since 1964, Josh has served as a traveling representative with Campus Crusade for Christ International. Five million students and professors on more than 539 campuses in 53 countries have been enlightened, encouraged, helped and challenged by the inspired witness of Josh McDowell. His experience in speaking to student gatherings — large rallies and small, plus classroom lectures and hundreds of counseling sessions, plus a *magna cum laude* degree from Talbot Theological Seminary and his extensive research on the historical evidences of the Christian faith — have qualified Josh to speak and write with authority on the credibility of Christianity.

A lawyer once asked Jesus: "Sir, which is the most important commandment in the law of Moses?" To which He replied, "Love the Lord your God with all your heart, soul and mind. This is the first and greatest commandment." God created man with the ability to *think,* to acquire knowledge and to discern truth. *God wants us to use our minds.* The apostle Peter admonishes, "Sanctify Christ as Lord in your hearts, always being ready to make a defense to every one who asks you to give an account for the hope that is in you. . . ."

For this reason, the ministry of Campus Crusade for Christ has always given a special emphasis to training Christians how to experience and share the abundant, exciting life which is available to all who place their trust in Jesus Christ. Leadership Training Institutes, Lay Institutes for Evangelism, Institutes of Biblical Studies and other training programs have helped hundreds of thousands be prepared to give valid, convincing, historical, documented reasons for their faith in Jesus Christ.

In my own experience of more than 28 years of sharing the good news of the Savior with the academic world, I personally have never heard a single individual — who has honestly considered the evidence — deny that Jesus Christ is the Son of God and the Savior of men. The evidence confirming the deity of the Lord Jesus Christ is overwhelmingly conclusive to any honest, objective seeker after truth. However, not all — not even the majority — of those to whom I have spoken have accepted Him as their Savior and Lord. This is not because they were *unable* to believe — they were simply *unwilling* to believe! For example, a brilliant but confused psychiatrist who came to Arrowhead Springs for counsel frankly confessed to me that he had never been willing to consider honestly the claims of Christ in his own life for fear that he would be convinced and, as a result, would have to change his way of life. Other well-known professing atheists, including Aldous Huxley and Bertrand Russell, have refused to come to intellectual grips with the basic historical facts concerning the birth, life, teachings, miracles, death and resurrection of Jesus of Nazareth. Those who have, such as C. S. Lewis and C. E. M. Joad, have found the evidence so convincing that they have accepted the verdict that Jesus Christ truly is who He claimed to be — and who others have believed Him to be — the Son of God and their own Savior and Lord.

A careful and prayerful study of the material contained in this book will help the reader always to be prepared to make an intelligent and convincing presentation of the good news. However, there is one final word of caution and counsel: one should not assume that the average person has intellectual doubts about the deity of Jesus Christ. The majority in most countries do not need to be convinced of His deity, nor of their need of Him as Savior. Rather, they need to be told how to receive Him as Savior and follow Him as Lord.

Thus, it is the Christian who will derive the greatest benefit from reading *Evidence That Demands a Verdict*. It will not only strengthen his own faith in Christ, but it will also provide evidence that will enable him to share his faith more effectively with others.

"Then He said to Thomas, 'Reach here your finger, and see My hands; and reach here your hand, and put it into My side; and be not unbelieving, but believing.'

"Thomas answered and said to Him, 'My Lord and my God!'

"Jesus said to him, 'Because you have seen Me, have you believed? Blessed are they who did not see, and yet believed' " (John 20:27-29).

William R. Bright
President and Founder
Campus Crusade for Christ International
Arrowhead Springs
San Bernardino, CA 92414

PREFACE

WHAT? ANOTHER BOOK?

No, this is not a book. It is a compilation of my notes prepared for my lecture series on "Christianity: Hoax or History?"

There has been a definite shortage in the area of documentation of historical evidences for the Christian faith. Often students, professors and laymen have asked, "How can we document and use what you and others teach?"

WHY A REVISED EDITION?

Since the first edition of *Evidence That Demands a Verdict* was published in 1972, significant new discoveries have occurred which further confirm the historical evidence for the Christian faith. For example, the first edition of this text documented that more than 13,000 manuscript copies of portions of the New Testament were in existence. Today we know of more than 24,000 existing manuscript portions.

As another example, since 1974, archaeological excavations have unearthed some 17,000 tablets from the era of the Ebla Kingdom, once located in northern Syria. Study of these tablets has contributed valuable support for the Mosaic authorship and the historical reliability of the Pentateuch.

These and many other discoveries convinced me that a second edition of *Evidence That Demands a Verdict* was necessary to keep Christians informed of the most up-to-date information to substantiate our faith.

DO WHAT WITH IT?

It is my desire that these notes will help my brothers and sisters in Jesus Christ to write term papers, give speeches and inject into classroom dialogues their convictions about Christ, the Scriptures and the relevancy of Christianity in the 20th century.

Students have commented on how they have used the lecture notes in the universities.

One wrote: ". . . In my speech class, I used your lecture notes to prepare my three speeches before the class. The first was on the reliability of the Scriptures, the second on Jesus Christ, and the third on the resurrection."

Another student wrote: ". . . Your documentation has encouraged many of us here to speak up in our classes . . . the boldness of the Christian is beginning 'o be evident everywhere."

Still another said: "I used the notes in preparing a speech for an oratory contest. I won, and will be giving the same speech at graduation. Thanks a lot, brother."

WATCH YOUR ATTITUDE

The proper motivation behind the use of these lecture notes is to glorify and magnify Jesus Christ — not to win an argument. Evidence is not for proving the Word of God but simply for providing a basis for faith.

One should have a gentle and reverent spirit when using apologetics or evidences:
"But sanctify Christ as Lord in your hearts, always being ready to make a defense to every one who asks you to give an account for the hope that is in you, *yet with gentleness and reverence*" (I Peter 3:15).

These notes, used with a proper attitude, will help to motivate a person to consider Jesus Christ honestly and to get him back to the central and primary issue — the gospel (such as contained in the Four Spiritual Laws at the end of this book).

My philosophy has always been that after I share Christ with someone who has some honest doubts, I give him enough apologetics to answer his questions or satisfy his curiosity and then turn the conversation back to his relationship with Christ. The presentation of evidence (apologetics) should never be a substitute for using the Word of God.

WHY COPYRIGHTED?

The reason that these notes have been copyrighted is not to limit their use, but to protect their misuse and to safeguard the rights of the authors and publishers of the multitude of quotations I have used and documented.

WHY IN OUTLINE FORM?

Because the notes are in outline form and the transitions between various concepts are not extensively written out, the effective use of this material will result as a person spends time thinking through individual sections and developing his own convictions. Thus, it becomes his message and not the parroting of someone else's.

GODISNOWHERE

means

GOD IS NO WHERE? or GOD IS NOW HERE?

The outline structure of the notes can sometimes cause a person to misunderstand an illustration or concept. Be cautious in drawing conclusions one way or another when you do not clearly understand something. Study it further and investigate other sources.

A LIFETIME INVESTMENT

The following are books that I recommend a person buy for his library. Also, these would be good books to buy and donate to your university library. (Often university libraries will buy books if you fill out a request slip.)

1. Gleason Archer. *A Survey of Old Testament Introduction*. Moody Press.
2. F. F. Bruce. *The Books and the Parchments*. Fleming Revell.
3. F. F. Bruce. *The New Testament Documents: Are They Reliable?* Inter-Varsity Press.
4. Norman L. Geisler and William E. Nix. *A General Introduction to the Bible*. Moody Press.
5. Carl Henry (Ed.) *Revelation and the Bible*. Baker Book House.
6. K. A. Kitchen. *Ancient Orient and Old Testament*. Inter-Varsity Press.
7. Paul Little. *Know Why You Believe*. Inter-Varsity Press.
8. John Warwick Montgomery. *History and Christianity*. Inter-Varsity Press.
9. John Warwick Montgomery. *Shapes of the Past*. Edwards Brothers.

10. Clark Pinnock. *Set Forth Your Case*. Craig Press.
11. Bernard Ramm. *Protestant Christian Evidences*. Moody Press.
12. Wilbur Smith. *Therefore Stand*. Baker Book House.
13. Peter Stoner. *Science Speaks*. Moody Press.
14. John Stott. *Basic Christianity*. Inter-Varsity Press.
15. Griffith Thomas. *Christianity Is Christ*. Moody Press.

WHO SAID IT?

Approximately 5,000 man-hours were spent tracing down the primary source documentation. In the bibliographies at the end of each section, the reader has hundreds of documented sources that he can confidently use.

Working with me in compiling this research was a team of 11 students from nine universities. It all started when several of them approached me about working on the project so they could receive credit at their universities. (Since that time, they have all graduated.)

RESEARCH TEAM MEMBERS

Doug Wilder—	Michigan State University RESEARCH: The Lives of the Apostles
Phil Edwards—	Ohio State University RESEARCH: Messianic Concepts
Ron Lutjens—	Bowling Green University RESEARCH: Historic Reliability of the Old Testament
Wayne Trout—	Virginia Polytechnic Institute RESEARCH: Character of Christ
Brent Nelson—	Indiana University RESEARCH: Claims That Christ Made to Deity
David Sheldon—	Ohio State University RESEARCH: Messianic Prophecy
Frank Dickerson—	Ohio State University RESEARCH: The Resurrection
Steve Smith—	Virginia Polytechnic Institute RESEARCH: The Evidence of Changed Lives
James Davis—	Louisiana Polytechnic Institute RESEARCH: Prophecy
Linn Smith—	North Texas State University RESEARCH: Current Events
Stick Ustick—	Sacramento State University RESEARCH TEAM SUPPORTER

EXPLANATION OF GENERAL FORMAT

FOOTNOTES: After each quote there will be two sets of numbers divided by a diagonal (example 47/21-23). The number to the left of the diagonal is the reference to the source in the bibliography at the end of each chapter. The number on the right refers to the page or pages where the quote is located in the reference source.

BIBLIOGRAPHY: The entire bibliography is not placed at the back of the lecture notes. There are nine individual bibliographies placed at the end of the various divisions of the notes.

This enables a person to remove a section of the notes and have its bibliography with it to facilitate the locating of reference sources.

OUTLINE: I have chosen not to use the traditional method of outlining. Instead I am employing a method that is easy to use in locating specific references in printed notes while lecturing.

Traditional	Method Used Here
I.	1A.
A.	1B.
1.	1C.
a.	1D.
(1)	1E.
(a)	1F.

The outline at the beginning of each chapter is not the outline of that chapter but a sample outline that could be filled in from the chapter to facilitate the use of the material in writing papers and speeches.

INDEXES: Located at the back of the notes are two separate indexes to help you in using these notes: 1. Author Index; 2. Subject Index.

BIOGRAPHICAL SKETCHES: At the back of the book is a limited biography of various authors. This will give the reader a background on some of the authors quoted.

TABLE OF CONTENTS

FOREWORD
PREFACE
EXPLANATION OF GENERAL FORMAT
INTRODUCTION 1
    Bibliography 12

SECTION I. THE BIBLE—I TRUST IT 13
    Chapter 1. THE UNIQUENESS OF THE BIBLE 15
An intelligent person who is seeking truth would certainly read and consider a book that has the historical qualifications of the Bible. These unique qualifications separate the Scriptures from any book that has ever been written.

    Chapter 2. HOW WAS THE BIBLE PREPARED? 25
What materials were used? When did chapter and verse divisions come about? Why is the Bible divided the way it is?

    Chapter 3. THE CANON 29
Why do we have just 39 Old Testament books and 27 New Testament books? What about the Apocrypha? Why are the other books not included in the Bible?

    Chapter 4. THE RELIABILITY OF THE BIBLE 39
        Part 1—Confirmation of the Historical Text 39
The accusation that the Old and New Testaments are not reliable is dealt with here. Several tests for the reliability and accuracy of a piece of literature are outlined; these tests are applied to the Scriptures and then a comparison is made between the historicity of the Bible and classical literature. The logical conclusion based upon evidence is that if one rejects the Bible as being reliable, then, if he is consistent and uses the same tests, he must throw out all classical literature and disregard their historical testimony.

        Part 2—Confirmation by Archaeology 65
The trustworthiness of Scripture is confirmed by specific, documented, archaeological discoveries. Testimonies are given of skeptics who have had their attitudes toward the Bible radically changed as the result of archaeological investigation.
        Bibliography 74

SECTION II. THE ACADEMY AWARDS—
        IF JESUS WAS NOT GOD,
        THEN HE DESERVED AN OSCAR 79

    Chapter 5. JESUS — A MAN OF HISTORY 81
Documented sources of the historical person of Jesus of Nazareth apart from the Bible.
        Bibliography 87

Chapter 6.   JESUS — GOD'S SON 89
              An explanation of the character of Christ and His claims to
              deity, with an emphasis on secular and Jewish sources.

Chapter 7.   THE TRILEMMA — LORD, LIAR OR LUNATIC? 103
              This section deals with who Jesus was and rules out the
              possible conclusion that He was just a good man or great
              prophet.
              Bibliography 107

Chapter 8.   THE GREAT PROPOSITION 111
              The use of the "if . . . then" argument is applied to Christ. In
              other words, "If God became man, then what would He be
              like?" or "Did Jesus possess the characteristics of God?"
              Incorporates many quotations and observations of great
              men, Christians and non-Christians, about the person,
              character, life and death of Jesus of Nazareth and His
              impact on the world for 2,000 years.
              Bibliography 138

Chapter 9.   THE MESSIANIC PROPHECIES OF THE OLD
              TESTAMENT FULFILLED IN JESUS CHRIST 141
              This section contains several illustrations of the
              probabilities that all these prophecies could be fulfilled in
              one man to answer the critic who says, "It is all just a
              coincidence." There is a great emphasis on Jewish sources
              confirming these predictions as being Messianic to answer
              the accusation, "That's the way you Christians look at
              them, but what about the Jews?"
              Bibliography 176

Chapter 10.   THE RESURRECTION — HOAX OR HISTORY? 179
              This heavily documented section treats the proper
              historical approach to the resurrection, the positive
              evidence for it and a refutation of each theory set forth to
              explain away the miracle of the historical event of the
              resurrection of Christ.
              Bibliography 260

SECTION III. GOD AT WORK IN HISTORY AND HUMAN LIVES 265

Chapter 11.   PROPHECY FULFILLED IN HISTORY 267
              This unique section deals with one of the great proofs that
              there is a living God behind the Bible and history. Twelve
              prophecies are dealt with in detail. There is a listing of the
              prophecies, their dating, historical background, and an
              outlining of the historical fulfillment of each prediction.
              Bibliography 320

Chapter 12.   THE UNIQUENESS OF THE CHRISTIAN
              EXPERIENCE 325
              So often the Christian negates the authority of a
              transformed life as evidence of Christ's reality because it is
              a subjective experience or argument. This section shows
              that it is supported by an objective reality — the
              resurrection of Jesus Christ.
              Bibliography 359

HE CHANGED MY LIFE 363
   The testimony of how a relationship with Jesus Christ transformed the
   author's life.

ADDITIONAL HISTORICAL SOURCES OF CHRISTIANITY 369

BIOGRAPHICAL SKETCHES OF AUTHORS 371

AUTHOR INDEX 375

SUBJECT INDEX 379

THE FOUR SPIRITUAL LAWS 383
   These laws explain how an individual can know God personally and
   experience the abundant Christian life.

TO DOTTIE

My sweetheart, my best friend and my wife.

Without her patience, love and constructive criticism

this project could never have been completed.

introduction _____

1A. LET'S HAVE AN UNDERSTANDING

1B. Use of Apologetics

"But sanctify Christ as Lord in your hearts, always being ready to make a defense to every one who asks you to give an account for the hope that is in you, yet with gentleness and reverence. . . ." (I Peter 3:15).

The word "defense" (Gk. *apologia*) indicates "a defense of conduct and procedure." Wilbur Smith puts it this way: ". . . a verbal defense, a speech in defense of what one has done or of truth which one believes. . . ." 19/481

"*Apologia*" (basic English translation is apology) was used predominantly in early times "but it did not convey the idea of excuse, palliation or making amends for some injury done." 2/48

"*Apologia*" translated by the English word "defense" is used eight times (including I Peter 3:15 above) in the New Testament:

Acts 22:1
"Brethren and fathers, hear my *defense* which I now offer to you."

Acts 25:16
"And I answered them that it is not the custom of the Romans to hand over any man before the accused meets his accusers face to face, and has an opportunity to make his *defense* against the charges."

I Corinthians 9:3
"My *defense* to those who examine me is this. . . ."

II Corinthians 7:11
"For behold what earnestness this very thing, this godly sorrow, has produced in you, what vindication of yourselves [*defense*], what indignation, what fear, what longing, what zeal, what avenging of wrong! In everything you demonstrated yourselves to be innocent in the matter."

Philippians 1:7
". . . since both in my imprisonment and in the *defense* and confirmation of the gospel, you all are partakers of grace with me."

Philippians 1:16
". . . the latter do it out of love, knowing that I am appointed for the *defense* of the gospel. . . ."

II Timothy 4:16
"At my first *defense* no one supported me, but all deserted me; may it not
be counted against them."

The manner in which the word "defense" is used in I Peter 3:15 denotes
the kind of defense one would make to a police inquiry, "Why are you a
Christian?" A believer is responsible to give an adequate answer to that
question.

Paul Little quotes John Stott saying, "We cannot pander to a man's
intellectual arrogance, but we must cater to his intellectual integrity"
[And, I add, questions of honest inquiry must be answered]. 10/28

Beattie concludes that:

"Christianity is either EVERYTHING for mankind, or NOTHING. It is
either the highest certainty or the greatest delusion. . . . But if
Christianity be EVERYTHING for mankind, it is important for every
man to be able to give a good reason for the hope that is in him in regard to
the eternal verities of the Christian faith. To accept these verities in an
unthinking way, or to receive them simply on authority, is not enough for
an intelligent and stable faith." 2/37,38

The basic "apologetic" thesis of these notes is:

"There is an infinite, all-wise, all-powerful, all-loving God who has
revealed Himself by means natural and supernatural in creation, in the
nature of man, in the history of Israel and the Church, in the pages of Holy
Scripture, in the incarnation of God in Christ, and in the heart of the
believer by the gospel." 15/33

2B. Christianity Is a FACTual Religion

Christianity appeals to history, the facts of history, which P. Carnegie
Simpson calls, "the most patent and accessible of data." Simpson
continues that "He [Jesus] is a fact of history cognizable as any other."

J. N. D. Anderson records D. E. Jenkins' remark, "Christianity is based
on indisputable facts. . . ." 1/10

Clark Pinnock defines this type of facts:
"The facts backing the Christian claim are not a special kind of religious
fact. They are the cognitive, informational facts upon which all
historical, legal, and ordinary decisions are based." 14/6,7

One of the purposes of these "notes on Christian evidences" is to present
some of these "indisputable facts" and to inquire whether the Christian
interpretation of these facts is not by far the most logical. The objective of
apologetics is not to convince a man unwittingly, contrary to his will, to
become a Christian.

Clark Pinnock writes:

"It strives at laying the evidence for the Christian gospel before men in
an intelligent fashion, so that they can make a meaningful commitment
under the convicting power of the Holy Spirit. The heart cannot delight in
what the mind rejects as false." 14/3

THE BEST DEFENSE IS A . . .

3B. Good Offense

During a philosophical apologetics course in graduate school, I had to
write a paper on "The Best Defense of Christianity." The writing of it was
constantly being put off or avoided, not because I didn't have the
material, but rather because, in my thinking, I felt I was at odds with

what the professor was expecting (obviously something based on the ream of my lecture notes from his class).

Finally, I decided to voice my convictions. I started the paper with the phrase, "Some people say the best offense is a good defense, but I say unto you that the best defense is a good offense." Then I continued by explaining that I felt the best defense of Christianity is a "clear, simple presentation of the claims of Christ and who He is." I then wrote out "The Four Spiritual Laws" and recorded my testimony of how, on December 19, 1959, at 8:30 p.m., my second year in the university, I accepted Christ. I then concluded the paper with a presentation of the evidence for the resurrection.

The professor must have pondered it quite laboriously. However, he must have agreed, for I got a grade of 96.

William Tyndale was right when he believed that "a ploughboy with the Bible would know more of God than the most learned ecclesiastic who ignored it." In other words, an Arkansas farm boy sharing the gospel would be more effective in the long run than a Harvard scholar with his intellectual arguments.

HEBREWS 4:12

"For the word of God is living and active and sharper than any two-edged sword, and piercing as far as the division of soul and spirit, of both joints and marrow, and able to judge the thoughts and intentions of the heart."

We need a balance of the two above ramifications. We must preach the gospel but also "be ready to give an answer for the hope that is in [us]."

The Holy Spirit will convict men of the truth; one does not have to be hit over the head with it. "And a certain woman named Lydia, from the city of Thyatira, a seller of purple fabrics, a worshiper of God, was listening; and *the Lord opened her heart to respond to* the things spoken by Paul" (Acts 16:14).

Pinnock, an able apologist and witness for Christ, appropriately concludes:

"An intelligent Christian ought to be able to point up the flaws in a non-Christian position and to present facts and arguments which tell in favor of the gospel. If our apologetic prevents us from explaining the gospel to any person, it is an inadequate apologetic." 14/7

2A. LET'S LAY SOME CONCRETE

Before one approaches the various evidences for the Christian faith, he ought to have some misconceptions cleared up and understand several basic facts.

QUICK! I NEED AN ASPIRIN...

1B. Blind Faith

A rather common accusation sharply aimed at the Christian often goes like this: "You Christians make me sick! All you have is a 'blind faith.'" This would surely indicate that the accuser seems to think that to become a Christian, one has to commit "intellectual suicide."

Personally, "my heart cannot rejoice in what my mind rejects." My heart and head were created to work and believe together in harmony. Christ commanded us to ". . . love the Lord your God with all your heart, and with all your soul, and with all your *mind*" (Matthew 22:37).

When Jesus Christ and the apostles called upon a person to exercise faith, it was not a "blind faith" but rather an "intelligent faith." The apostle Paul said, "I *know* whom I have believed" (II Timothy 1:12). Jesus said, "You shall know [not ignore] the truth, and the truth shall make you free" (John 8:32).

The belief of an individual involves "the *mind,* emotions and the will." F. R. Beattie is quite right when he says, "The Holy Spirit does not work a blind and ungrounded faith in the heart. . . ." 2/25

"Faith in Christianity," Paul Little justifiably writes, "is based on evidence. It is reasonable faith. Faith in the Christian sense goes beyond reason but not against it." 10/30 Faith is the assurance of the heart in the adequacy of the evidence.

A POLITICAL MANEUVER
(Avoiding the Issue)

2B. The Christian Faith Is an Objective Faith

The Christian faith is an objective faith; therefore, it must have an object. The Christian concept of "saving" faith is a faith that establishes one's relationship with Jesus Christ (the object), and is diametrically opposed to the average "philosophical" use of the term faith in the classroom today. One cliche that is to be rejected is, "It doesn't matter what you believe, as long as you believe it enough."

Let me illustrate.

I had a debate with the head of the philosophy department of a midwestern university. In answering a question, I happened to mention the importance of the resurrection. At this point, my opponent interrupted and rather sarcastically said, "Come on, McDowell, the key issue is not whether the resurrection took place or not; it is 'do *you* believe it took place?'" What he was hinting at (actually boldly asserting) is that my believing was the most important thing. I retorted immediately, "Sir, it does matter what I as a Christian believe, because the value of Christian faith is not in the one believing, but in the one who is believed in, its object." I continued that "if anyone can demonstrate to me that Christ was not raised from the dead, I would not have the right to my Christian faith" (I Corinthians 15:14).

The Christian faith is faith *in* Christ. Its value or worth is not in the one believing, but in the one believed — not in the one trusting, but in the one trusted.

Immediately after the above debate a Moslem fellow approached me and, during our most edifying conversation, he said very sincerely, "I know many Moslems who have more faith in Mohammed than some Christians have in Christ." I said, "That may well be true, but the Christian is 'saved.' You see, it doesn't matter how much faith you have, but rather who is the object of your faith; that is important from the Christian perspective of faith."

Often I hear students say, "Some Buddhists are more dedicated and have more faith in Buddha (shows a misunderstanding of Buddhism) than Christians have in Christ." I can only reply, "Maybe so, but the Christian is saved."

Paul said, "I know *whom* I have believed." This explains why the Christian gospel centers on the person of Jesus Christ.

John Warwick Montgomery says:

"If our 'Christ of faith' deviates at all from the biblical 'Jesus of history,' then to the extent of that deviation, we also lose the genuine Christ of faith. As one of the greatest Christian historians of our time, Herbert Butterfield, has put it: 'It would be a dangerous error to imagine that the characteristics of an historical religion would be maintained if the Christ of the theologians were divorced from the Jesus of history.' " 12/145

The phrase, "Don't confuse me with the facts," is not appropriate for a Christian.

I SAW IT WITH MY OWN EYES

3B. Eyewitnesses

The writers of the New Testament either wrote as eyewitnesses of the events they described or recorded eyewitness firsthand accounts of the events.

II Peter 1:16
"For we did not follow cleverly devised tales when we made known to you the power and coming of our Lord Jesus Christ, but we were eyewitnesses of His majesty."

They certainly knew the difference between myth, legend and reality. A professor of a world literature class in which I was speaking asked the question, "What do you think of Greek mythology?" I answered with another question, "Do you mean, were the events of the life of Jesus, the resurrection, virgin birth, etc., just myth?" He said, "Yes." I replied that there is one obvious difference between these things applied to Christ and these things applied to Greek mythology that is usually overlooked. The similar events, such as the resurrection, etc, of Greek mythology were not applied to real, flesh and blood individuals, but rather to mythological characters. But, when it comes to Christianity, these events are attached to a person the writers knew in time-space dimension history, the historic Jesus of Nazareth whom they knew personally.

The professor replied, "You're right, I never realized that before."

S. Estborn in *Gripped by Christ* explains further the above. He relates that Anath Nath "studied both the Bible and the *Shastras*. Two biblical themes in particular deeply engaged his mind: first, the reality of the Incarnation, and second, the Atonement for human sin. These doctrines he sought to harmonize with Hindu Scriptures. He found a parallel to Christ's self-sacrifice in Prajapati, the Vedic creator-god. He saw, too, a vital difference. Whereas the Vedic Prajapati is a mythical symbol, which has been applied to several figures, Jesus of Nazareth is a historic person. 'Jesus is the true Prajapati,' he said, 'the true Saviour of the world.' " 6/43

J. B. Phillips, cited by Blaiklock, states, "I have read, in Greek and Latin, scores of myths but I did not find the slightest flavour of myth here. Most people who know their Greek and Latin, whatever their attitude to the New Testament narratives, would agree with him. . . .

"A myth may be defined as 'a pre-scientific and imaginative attempt to explain some phenomenon, real or supposed, which excites the curiosity of the mythmaker, or perhaps more accurately as an effort to reach a feeling of satisfaction in place of bewilderment concerning such phenomena. It often appeals to the emotions rather than the reason, and indeed, in its most typical forms, seems to date from an age when rational explanations were not called for.' " 3/47

EYEWITNESSES

I John 1:1-3
"What was from the beginning, what we have heard, what we have seen with our eyes, what we beheld and our hands handled, concerning the Word of Life — and the life was manifested, and we have seen and bear witness and proclaim to you the eternal life, which was with the Father and was manifested to us — what we have seen and heard we proclaim to you also, that you also may have fellowship with us; and indeed our fellowship is with the Father, and with His Son Jesus Christ."

Luke 1:1-3
"Inasmuch as many have undertaken to compile an account of the things accomplished among us, just as those who from the beginning were eyewitnesses and servants of the Word have handed them down to us, it seemed fitting for me as well, having investigated everything carefully from the beginning, to write it out for you in consecutive order, most excellent Theophilus."

The Cambridge Ancient History, writing about Luke's concern for accuracy, says:

"He is naturally concerned to state a good case for the religion he professes — and that not merely because he believed it to be true (and there was no inducement in those days to profess Christianity unless one was passionately convinced of its truth). . . ." 4/258

Acts 1:1-3
"The first account I composed, Theophilus, about all that Jesus began to do and teach, until the day when He was taken up, after He had by the Holy Spirit given orders to the apostles whom He had chosen. To these He also presented Himself alive, after His suffering, by many convincing proofs, appearing to them over a period of forty days, and speaking of the things concerning the kingdom of God."

I Corinthians 15:6-8
"After that He appeared to more than five hundred brethren at one time, most of whom remain until now, but some have fallen asleep; then He appeared to James, then to all the apostles; and last of all, as it were to one untimely born, He appeared to me also."

John 20:30,31
"Many other signs therefore Jesus also performed in the presence of the disciples, which are not written in this book; but these have been written that you may believe that Jesus is the Christ, the Son of God; and that believing you may have life in His name."

Acts 10:39-42
" 'And we are witnesses of all the things He did both in the land of the Jews and in Jerusalem. And they also put Him to death by hanging Him on a cross. God raised Him up on the third day, and granted that He should become visible, not to all the people, but to witnesses who were chosen beforehand by God, that is, to us, who ate and drank with Him after He arose from the dead. And He ordered us to preach to the people, and solemnly to testify that this is the One who has been appointed by God as Judge of the living and the dead.' "

I Peter 5:1
"Therefore, I exhort the elders among you, as your fellow-elder and witness of the sufferings of Christ, and a partaker also of the glory that is to be revealed."

Acts 1:9

"And after He had said these things, He was lifted up while they were looking on, and a cloud received Him out of their sight."

John Montgomery writes that "the inability to distinguish Jesus' claim for Himself from the New Testament writers' claim for Him should cause no dismay, since (1) the situation exactly parallels that for all historical personages who have not themselves chosen to write (e.g., Alexander the Great, Augustus Caesar, Charlemagne). We would hardly claim that in these cases we can achieve no adequate historical portraits. Also, (2) the New Testament writers . . . record eyewitness testimony concerning Jesus, and can therefore be trusted to convey an accurate historical picture of Him." 11/48

The apostles were witnesses of His resurrected life:

Luke 24:48	Acts 13:31
Acts 1:8	I Corinthians 15:4-9
Acts 2:32	I Corinthians 15:15
Acts 3:15	I John 1:2
Acts 4:33	Acts 22:15
Acts 5:32	Acts 23:11
Acts 10:39	Acts 26:16
Acts 10:41	

YES, YOU DID — YOU KNEW THAT . . .

4B. Firsthand Knowledge

The writers of the New Testament appealed to the firsthand knowledge of their readers or listeners concerning the facts and the evidence about the person of Jesus Christ.

The writers not only said, "Look, we saw this or we heard that . . .," but they turned the tables around and right in front of their most adverse critics said, "You also know about these things. . . . You saw them; you yourselves know about it."

One had better be careful when he says to his opposition, "You *know* this also," because if he is not right in the details, it will be "shoved right back down his throat."

Acts 2:22

"Men of Israel, listen to these words: Jesus the Nazarene, a man attested to you by God with miracles and wonders and signs which God performed through Him in your midst, just as you yourselves know. . . ."

Acts 26:24-28

"And while Paul was saying this in his defense, Festus said in a loud voice, 'Paul, you are out of your mind! Your great learning is driving you mad.' But Paul said, 'I am not out of my mind, most excellent Festus, but I utter words of sober truth. For the king knows about these matters, and I speak to him also with confidence, since I am persuaded that none of these things escape his notice; for this has not been done in a corner. King Agrippa, do you believe the Prophets? I know that you do.' And Agrippa replied to Paul, 'In a short time you will persuade me to become a Christian.' "

A CIVIL RIGHTS ISSUE . . .

5B. The Historical Prejudices

"If one were to study historically the life of Jesus of Nazareth, he would find a very remarkable man, not the Son of God." It is sometimes stated to me this way: "Following the 'modern historical' approach one would never discover the resurrection." Do you know, it is true. Before you jump to a conclusion, let me explain. For many today, the study of history is incorporated with the ideas that there is no God, miracles are not possible, we live in a closed system and there is no supernatural. With these presuppositions they begin their "critical, open and honest" investigation of history. When they study the life of Christ and read about His miracles or resurrection, they conclude that it was not a miracle or a resurrection because we know (not historically, but philosophically) that there is no God, we live in a closed system, miracles are not possible and there is no supernatural. Therefore, these things cannot be. What men have done is to rule out the resurrection of Christ even before they start an historical investigation of the resurrection.

These presuppositions are not so much historical biases but, rather, *philosophical prejudices.*

Their approach to history rests on the "rationalistic presupposition" that Christ could not have been raised from the dead. Instead of beginning with the historical data, they preclude it by "metaphysical speculation."

John W. Montgomery writes:

"The fact of the resurrection cannot be discounted on *a priori,* philosophical grounds; miracles are impossible only if one so defines them — but such definition rules out proper historical investigation." 12/139-144

I quote Montgomery quite extensively on this issue because he is the one who has stimulated my thinking about history.

Montgomery says:

"Kant conclusively showed that all arguments and systems begin with presuppositions; but this does not mean that all presuppositions are equally desirable. It is better to begin, as we have, with presuppositions of method (which will yield truth) rather than with presuppositions of substantive content (which assume a body of truth already). In our modern world we have found that the presuppositions of empirical method best fulfill this condition; but note that we are operating only with the presuppositions of scientific method, not with the rationalistic assumptions of Scientism ('the Religion of Science')." 12/144

Huizenga's comments are cited by Montgomery concerning historical skepticism ("De Historische Idee," in his *Verzamelde Werken,* VII [Haarlem, 1950], 134 ff.: quoted in translation in Fritz Stern [ed], *The Varieties of History* [New York: Meridian Books, 1956], p.302).

Huizenga states:

"The strongest argument against historical skepticism . . . is this: the man who doubts the possibility of correct historical evidence and tradition cannot then accept his own evidence, judgment, combination and interpretation. He cannot limit his doubt to his historical criticism, but is required to let it operate on his own life. He discovers at once that he not only lacks conclusive evidence in all sorts of aspects of his own life that he had quite taken for granted, but also that there is no evidence whatever. In short, he finds himself forced to accept a general philosophical skepticism along with his historical skepticism. And general philosophical skepticism is a nice intellectual game, but one cannot live by it." 12/139,140

Millar Burrows of Yale, the American expert on the Dead Sea Scrolls cited also by Montgomery, writes:

"There is a type of Christian faith . . . rather strongly represented today, [that] regards the affirmations of Christian faith as confessional statements which the individual accepts as a member of the believing community, and which are not dependent on reason or evidence. Those who hold this position will not admit that historical investigation can have anything to say about the uniqueness of Christ. They are often skeptical as to the possibility of knowing anything about the historical Jesus, and seem content to dispense with such knowledge. I cannot share this point of view. I am profoundly convinced that the historic revelation of God in Jesus of Nazareth must be the cornerstone of any faith that is really Christian. Any historical question about the real Jesus who lived in Palestine nineteen centuries ago is therefore fundamentally important." 11/15,16

Montgomery adds:

Historical events are "unique, and the test of their factual character can be only the accepted documentary approach that we have followed here. No historian has a right to a closed system of causation, for, as the Cornell logician Max Black has shown in a recent essay ["Models and Metaphors" (Ithaca: Cornell University Press, 1962), p. 16], the very concept of cause is 'a peculiar, unsystematic, and erratic notion,' and therefore 'any attempt to state a "universal law of causation" must prove futile.' " 11/76

The historian Ethelbert Stauffer can give us some suggestions on how to approach history:

"What do we [as historians] do when we experience surprises which run counter to all our expectations, perhaps all our convictions and even our period's whole understanding of truth? We say as one great historian used to say in such instances: 'It is surely possible.' And why not? For the critical historian nothing is impossible." 11/76

The historian Philip Schaff adds to the above:

"The purpose of the historian is not to construct a history from preconceived notions and to adjust it to his own liking, but to reproduce it from the best evidence and to let it speak for itself." 17/175

Robert M. Horn is very helpful in understanding people's biases in approaching history:

"To put it at its most obvious, a person who denies God's existence will not subscribe to belief in the Bible.

"A Muslim, convinced that God cannot beget, will not accept as the Word of God, a book that teaches that Christ is the only begotten Son of God.

"Some believe that God is not personal, but rather the Ultimate, the Ground of Being. Such will be predisposed to reject the Bible as God's personal self-revelation. On their premise, the Bible cannot be the personal word of 'I AM WHO I AM' (Exodus 3:14).

"Others rule out the supernatural. They will not be likely to give credence to the book which teaches that Christ rose from the dead.

"Still others hold that God cannot communicate His truth undistorted through sinful men; hence they regard the Bible as, at least in parts, no more than human." 8/10

A *basic* definition of history for me is "a knowledge of the past based on testimony." Some immediately say, "I don't agree." Then I ask, "Do you believe Lincoln lived and was President of the United States?" "Yes," is usually their reply. However, no one I've met has personally seen and observed Lincoln. The only way one knows is by testimony.

Precaution: When you give history this definition, you have to determine the trustworthiness of your witnesses. This will be dealt with in chapter four.

I MUST BE BLIND

6B. Which Leap?

Often the Christian is accused of taking a blind "leap into the dark." This idea often finds itself rooted in Kierkegaard.

For me, Christianity was not a "leap into the dark," but rather "a step into the light." I took the evidence that I could gather and put it on the scales. The scales tipped the way of Christ being the Son of God and resurrected from the dead. It was so overwhelmingly leaning to Christ that when I became a Christian, it was a "step into the light" rather than a "leap into the darkness."

If I had exercised "blind faith," I would have rejected Jesus Christ and turned my back on all the evidence.

Be careful. I did not prove beyond a shadow of a doubt that Jesus was the Son of God. What I did was investigate the evidence and weigh the pros and cons. The results showed that Christ must be who He claimed to be, and I had to make a decision, which I did. The immediate reaction of many is, "You found what you wanted to find." That is not the case. I confirmed through investigation what I wanted to refute. I set out to disprove Christianity. I had biases and prejudices not for Christ but contrary to Him.

Hume would say historic evidence is invalid because one cannot establish "absolute truth." I was not looking for absolute truth but rather "historical probability."

"Without an objective criterion," says John W. Montgomery, "one is at a loss to make a meaningful choice among *a prioris.* The resurrection provides a basis in historical probability for trying the Christian faith. Granted, the basis is only one of probability, not of certainty, but probability is the sole ground on which finite human beings can make any decisions. Only deductive logic and pure mathematics provide 'apodictic certainty,' and they do so because they stem from self-evident formal axioms (e.g., the tautology, if A then A) involving no matter of fact. The moment we enter the realm of fact, we must depend on probability; this may be unfortunate, but it is unavoidable." 12/141

At the conclusion of his four articles in *His* magazine, John W. Montgomery says, concerning history and Christianity, that he has ". . . tried to show that the weight of historical probability lies on the side of the validity of Jesus' claim to be God incarnate, the Savior of man, and the coming Judge of the world. If probability does in fact support these claims (and can we really deny it, having studied the evidence?), then we must act in behalf of them." 11/19

WILL THE REAL MR. EXCUSE PLEASE STAND UP?

7B. Intellectual Excuses

The rejection of Christ is often not so much of the "mind," but of the "will"; not so much "I can't," but "I won't."

I have met many people with intellectual excuses, but few with intellectual problems (however, I have met some).

Excuses can cover a multitude of reasons. I greatly respect a man who has taken time to investigate the claims of Christ and concludes he just can't believe. I have a rapport with a man who knows why he doesn't believe (factually and historically), for I know why I believe (factually and historically). This gives us a common ground (though different conclusions).

I have found that most people reject Christ for one or more of the following reasons:

1. Ignorance — Romans 1:18-23 (often self-imposed), Matthew 22:29
2. Pride — John 5:40-44
3. Moral problem — John 3:19, 20

I was counseling a person who was fed up with Christianity because she believed it was not historical and there was just nothing to it factually. She had convinced everyone that she had searched and found profound intellectual problems as the result of her university studies. One after another would try to persuade her intellectually and to answer her many accusations.

I listened and then asked several questions. Within 30 minutes she admitted she had fooled everyone and that she developed these intellectual doubts in order to excuse her moral life.

One needs to answer the basic problem or real question and not the surface detour that often manifests itself.

A student in a New England university said he had an intellectual problem with Christianity and just could not therefore accept Christ as Savior. "Why can't you believe?" I asked. He replied, "The New Testament is not reliable." I then asked, "If I demonstrate to you that the New Testament is one of the most reliable pieces of literature of antiquity, will you believe?" He retorted, "NO!" "You don't have a problem with your mind, but with your will," I answered.

A graduate student at the same university, after a lecture on "The Resurrection: Hoax or History?", was bombarding me with questions intermingled with accusations (later I found out he did it to most Christian speakers). Finally, after 45 minutes of dialogue, I asked him, "If I prove to you beyond a shadow of a doubt that Christ was raised from the dead and is the Son of God, will you consider Him?" The immediate and emphatic reply was, "NO!"

Michael Green cites Aldous Huxley, the atheist, who has destroyed the beliefs of many and has been hailed as a great intellect. Huxley admits his own biases (*Ends and Means*, pp. 270 ff.) when he says:

"I had motives for not wanting the world to have a meaning; consequently assumed that it had none, and was able without any difficulty to find satisfying reasons for this assumption. The philosopher who finds no meaning in the world is not concerned exclusively with a problem in pure metaphysics, he is also concerned to prove that there is no valid reason why he personally should not do as he wants to do, or why his friends should not seize political power and govern in the way that they find most advantageous to themselves. . . . For myself, the philosophy of meaninglessness was essentially an instrument of liberation, sexual and political." 8/36

Bertrand Russell is an example of an intelligent atheist who did not give careful examination to the evidence for Christianity. In his essay, *Why I Am Not a Christian*, it is obvious that he has not even considered the evidence of and for the resurrection of Jesus and, by his remarks, it is doubtful as to whether he has even glanced at the New Testament. It seems incongruous that a man would not deal with the resurrection in great detail since it is *the* foundation of Christianity. 8/36

John 7:17 assures one:

"If any man is willing to do His will, he shall know of the teaching, whether it is of God, or whether I speak from Myself."

If any man comes to the claims of Jesus Christ wanting to know if they are true, willing to follow His teachings if they are true, he will know. But one cannot come unwilling to accept and expect to find out.

Pascal, the French philosopher, writes:

"The evidence of God's existence and His gift is more than compelling, but those who insist that they have no need of Him or it will always find ways to discount the offer." 13/n.p.

BIBLIOGRAPHY

1. Anderson, J. N. D. *Christianity: A Witness of History.* Downers Grove: Inter-Varsity Press, 1970. Used by permission.

2. Beattie, F. R. *Apologetics.* Richmond: Presbyterian Committee of Publication, 1903.

3. Blaiklock, E. M. *Layman's Answer: An Examination of the New Theology.* London: Hodder and Stoughton, 1968.

4. *The Cambridge Ancient History.* Vol XI. Cambridge: at the University Press, 1965.

5. Carnell, E. J. *Christian Commitment.* New York: Macmillan Company, 1957.

6. Estborn, S. *Gripped by Christ.* London: Lutterworth Press, 1965.

7. Fisher, G. P. *The Grounds of Theistic and Christian Belief.* London: Hodder and Stoughton, 1902.

8. Green, Michael. *Runaway World.* Downers Grove: Inter-Varsity Press, 1968. Used by permission.

9. Horn, Robert M. *The Book That Speaks for Itself.* Downers Grove: Inter-Varsity Press, 1970. Used by permission.

10. Little, Paul. *Know Why You Believe.* Wheaton: Scripture Press Publications, 1967.

11. Montgomery, John Warwick, *History and Christianity.* Downers Grove: Inter-Varsity Press, 1972. Used by permission.

12. Montgomery, John Warwick. *The Shape of the Past.* Ann Arbor: Edwards Brothers, 1962.

13. Pascal, Blaise, *Pensee's* no. 430. (Translated by H. F. Stewart) New York: Random House, n.d.

14. Pinnock, Clark. *Set Forth Your Case.* Nutley: Craig Press, 1967.

15. Ramm, Bernard. *Protestant Christian Evidences.* Chicago: Moody Press, 1954. Used by permission.

16. Robertson, Austin. *Apologetics Defensively and Offensively Stated.* Unpublished Th.M. Thesis: Dallas Theological Seminary, 1961.

17. Schaff, Philip. *History of the Christian Church,* Vol. I, p. 175. Grand Rapids: William B. Eerdmans Publishing Co., 1962.

18. Simpson, Carnegie P. *The Fact of Christ.* Sixth edition. n.d., n.p.

19. Smith, Wilbur. *Therefore Stand.* Grand Rapids: Baker Book House, 1945.

20. Trueblood, Elton. *Philosophy of Religion.* New York: Harper & Row, 1957.

21. Van Til, C. Class Notes on Apologetics, 1953.

22. Van Til, C. *The Intellectual Challenge of the Gospel.* London: Tyndale Press, 1950.

section I_____

the
Bible
— I trust it

The purpose of this section is to build a working confidence in the Word of God. The Bible is reliable and will stand up under a thorough examination.

The following is an outline designed to aid you in effectively using this material.

1A. THE BIBLE IS UNIQUE
- 1B. In Its Continuity
- 2B. In Its Circulation
- 3B. In Its Translation
- 4B. In Its Survival
- 5B. In Its Teachings
- 6B. In Its Influence on Literature

2A. THE BIBLE IS TRUSTWORTHY
- 1B. The Bibliographical Test
- 2B. The Internal Evidence Test
- 3B. The External Evidence Test
- 4B. Its Confirmation by Archaeology

chapter 1

the
uniqueness
of the
Bible

1A. THE UNIQUENESS OF THE SCRIPTURE

1B. Introduction

Over and over again, like a broken record, I hear the phrase, "Oh, you don't read the Bible, do you?" Sometimes it is phrased, "Why, the Bible is just another book; you ought to read . . . etc." There is the student who is proud because his Bible is on the shelf with his other books, perhaps dusty, not broken in, but it is there with the other "greats."

Then there is the professor who degrades the Bible before his students and snickers at the thought of reading it, let alone of having it in one's library.

The above questions and observations bothered me when I tried, as a non-Christian, to refute the Bible as God's Word to man. I finally came to the conclusion that they were simply trite phrases from either biased, prejudiced or simply unknowledgeable, unread men and women.

The Bible should be on the top shelf all by itself. The Bible is "unique." That's it! The ideas I grappled with to describe the Bible are summed up by the word "unique."

Webster must have had this "Book of books" in mind when he wrote the definition for "unique": "1. one and only; single; sole. 2. different from all others; having no like or equal."

Professor M. Montiero-Williams, former Boden professor of Sanskrit, spent 42 years studying Eastern books and said in comparing them with the Bible:

"Pile them, if you will, on the left side of your study table; but place your own Holy Bible on the right side — all by itself, all alone — and with a wide gap between them. For, . . . there is a gulf between it and the so-called sacred books of the East which severs the one from the other utterly, hopelessly, and forever . . . a veritable gulf which cannot be bridged over by any science of religious thought." 18/314,315

2B. The Bible is Unique. It is the book "different from all others" in the following ways (plus a multitude more):

1C.   UNIQUE IN ITS CONTINUITY. Here is a book:

1. Written over a 1,500 year span.
2. Written over 40 generations.
3. Written by over 40 authors from every walk of life including kings, peasants, philosophers, fishermen, poets, statesmen, scholars, etc.:

    Moses, a political leader, trained in the universities of Egypt
    Peter, a fisherman
    Amos, a herdsman
    Joshua, a military general
    Nehemiah, a cupbearer
    Daniel, a prime minister
    Luke, a doctor
    Solomon, a king
    Matthew, a tax collector
    Paul, a rabbi

4. Written in different places:
    Moses in the wilderness
    Jeremiah in a dungeon
    Daniel on a hillside and in a palace
    Paul inside prison walls
    Luke while traveling
    John on the isle of Patmos
    Others in the rigors of a military campaign

5. Written at different times:
    David in times of war
    Solomon in times of peace

6. Written during different moods:
    Some writing from the heights of joy and others writing from the depths of sorrow and despair

7. Written on three continents:
    Asia, Africa and Europe

8. Written in three languages:
    Hebrew: Was the language of the Old Testament.
    >   In II Kings 18:26-28 called "the language of Judah."
    >   In Isaiah 19:18 called "the language of Canaan."

    Aramaic: Was the "common language" of the Near East until the time of Alexander the Great (6th century B.C. — 4th century B.C.) 32/218

    Greek: New Testament language. Was the international language at the time of Christ.

9. Its subject matter includes hundreds of controversial subjects. A controversial subject is one which would create opposing opinions when mentioned or discussed.

    Biblical authors spoke on hundreds of controversial subjects with harmony and continuity from Genesis to Revelation. There is one unfolding story: "God's redemption of man."

Geisler and Nix put it this way:

"The 'Paradise Lost' of the Genesis becomes the 'Paradise Regained' of Revelation. Whereas the gate to the tree of life is closed in Genesis, it is opened forevermore in Revelation." 32/24

F. F. Bruce observes: "Any part of the human body can only be properly explained in reference to the whole body. And any part of the Bible can only be properly explained in reference to the whole Bible." 15/89

Bruce concludes:

"The Bible, at first sight, appears to be a collection of literature — mainly Jewish. If we enquire into the circumstances under which the various Biblical documents were written, we find that they were written at intervals over a space of nearly 1400 years. The writers wrote in various lands, from Italy in the west to Mesopotamia and possibly Persia in the east. The writers themselves were a heterogeneous number of people, not only separated from each other by hundreds of years and hundreds of miles, but belonging to the most diverse walks of life. In their ranks we have kings, herdsmen, soldiers, legislators, fishermen, statesmen, courtiers, priests and prophets, a tentmaking Rabbi and a Gentile physician, not to speak of others of whom we know nothing apart from the writings they have left us. The writings themselves belong to a great variety of literary types. They include history, law (civil, criminal, ethical, ritual, sanitary), religious poetry, didactic treatises, lyric poetry, parable and allegory, biography, personal correspondence, personal memoirs and diaries, in addition to the distinctively Biblical types of prophecy and apocalyptic.

"For all that, the Bible is not simply an anthology; there is a unity which binds the whole together. An anthology is compiled by an anthologist, but no anthologist compiled the Bible." 15/88

10. Conclusion of continuity — a comparison with the *Great Books of the Western World.*

A representative of the *Great Books of the Western World* came to my house recruiting salesmen for their series. He spread out the chart of the *Great Books of the Western World* series. He spent five minutes talking to us about the *Great Books of the Western World* series, and we spent an hour and a half talking to him about the Greatest Book.

I challenged him to take just 10 of the authors, all from one walk of life, one generation, one place, one time, one mood, one continent, one language and just one controversial subject (the Bible speaks on hundreds with harmony and agreement).

Then I asked him: "Would they (the authors) agree?" He paused and then replied, "No!" "What would you have?" I retorted. Immediately he said, "A conglomeration."

Two days later he committed his life to Christ (the theme of the Bible).

Why all this? Very simple! Any person sincerely seeking truth would at least consider a book with the above unique qualifications.

2C.   UNIQUE IN ITS CIRCULATION

I am basically quoting figures of just the Bible Societies. Figures are from the *Encyclopaedia Britannica, Encyclopaedia Americana, One Thousand Wonderful Things About the Bible* (Pickering), *All About the Bible* (Collett), *Protestant Christian Evidences* (B. Ramm) and *A General Introduction to the Bible* (Geisler and Nix).

BIBLE PUBLICATION

Date	Bibles	New Testament	Portions (Individual books, etc.)
as of 1804 (Britain Bible Society)	409,000,000	X	X
in 1928 (Gideons of America)	965,000	X	X
(National Bible Society — Scotland)	88,070,068		
(Dublin Bible Society)	6,987,961		
(German Bible Society, 1927)	900,000		
in 1930	12,000,000		
as of 1932	1,330,213,815		
in 1947	14,108,436		
in 1951	952,666	1,913,314	13,135,965
in 1955	25,393,161		
1950 — 1960 (annually)	3,037,898	3,223,986	18,417,989
in 1963	54,123,820		
in 1964 (American Bible Society)	1,665,559		
Others	69,852,337	2,620,248	39,856,207
in 1965	76,953,369		
in 1966	87,398,961		

The Bible has been read by more people and published in more languages than any other book. There have been more copies produced of its entirety and more portions and selections than any other book in history. Some will argue that in a designated month or year more of a certain book was sold. However, over all there is absolutely no book that reaches or even begins to compare to the circulation of the Scriptures. The first major book printed was the Latin Vulgate. It was printed on Gutenberg's press. 38/478-480.

Hy Pickering says that about 30 years ago, for the British and Foreign Bible Society to meet its demands, it had to publish "one copy every three seconds day and night; 22 copies every minute day and night; 1,369 copies every hour day and night; 32,876 copies every day in the year. And it is deeply interesting to know that this amazing number of Bibles were dispatched to various parts of the world in 4,583 cases weighing 490 tons." 73/227

The Cambridge History of the Bible: "No other book has known anything approaching this constant circulation." 38/479

The critic is right: "This doesn't prove the Bible is the Word of God!" But it does factually show the Bible is unique.

3C.   UNIQUE IN ITS TRANSLATION

The Bible was one of the first major books translated (Septuagint: Greek translation of the Hebrew Old Testament, ca 250 B.C.). 99/1147

The Bible has been translated and retranslated and paraphrased more than any other book in existence.

Encyclopaedia Britannica says that "by 1966 the whole Bible had appeared . . . in 240 languages and dialects . . . one or more whole books of the Bible in 739 additional ones, a total of publication of 1,280 languages." 25/588

3,000 Bible translators between 1950-1960 were at work translating the Scriptures. 25/588

The Bible factually stands unique ("one of a kind") in its translation.

4C.   UNIQUE IN ITS SURVIVAL

1D.   Survival through time

Being written on material that perishes (see page 25), having to be copied and recopied for hundreds of years before the invention of the printing press, did not diminish its style, correctness nor existence. The Bible, compared with other ancient writings, has more manuscript evidence than any 10 pieces of classical literature combined. (See page 42.)

John Warwick Montgomery says that "to be skeptical of the resultant text of the New Testament books is to allow all of classical antiquity to slip into obscurity, for no documents of the ancient period are as well attested bibliographically as the New Testament." 64/29

Bernard Ramm speaks of the accuracy and number of biblical manuscripts:

"Jews preserved it as no other manuscript has ever been preserved. With their *massora (parva, magna,* and *finalis)* they kept tabs on every letter, syllable, word and paragraph. They had special classes of men within their culture whose sole duty was to preserve and transmit these documents with practically perfect fidelity — scribes, lawyers, massoretes. Who ever counted the letters and syllables and words of Plato or Aristotle? Cicero or Seneca?" 73/230,231

John Lea in *The Greatest Book in the World* compared the Bible with Shakespeare's writings:

"In an article in the *North American Review,* a writer made some interesting comparisons between the writings of Shakespeare and the Scriptures, which show that much greater care must have been bestowed upon the biblical manuscripts than upon other writings, even when there was so much more opportunity of preserving the correct text by means of printed copies than when all the copies had to be made by hand. He said:

" 'It seems strange that the text of Shakespeare, which has been in existence less than two hundred and eight years, should be far more uncertain and corrupt than that of the New Testament, now over eighteen centuries old, during nearly fifteen of which it existed only in manuscript. . . . With perhaps a dozen or twenty exceptions, the text of every verse in the New Testament may be said to be so far settled by general consent of scholars, that any dispute as to its readings must relate rather to the interpretation of the words than to any doubts respecting the words themselves. But in every one of Shakespeare's thirty-seven plays there are probably a hundred readings still in dispute, a large portion of which materially affects the meaning of the passages in which they occur.' " 56/15

2D.   Survival through persecution

The Bible has withstood vicious attacks of its enemies as no other book. Many have tried to burn it, ban it and "outlaw it from the days of Roman emperors to present-day Communist-dominated countries." 73/232

Sidney Collett in *All About the Bible* says, "Voltaire, the noted French infidel who died in 1778, said that in one hundred years from his time Christianity would be swept from existence and passed into history. But what has happened? Voltaire has passed into history, while the circulation of the Bible continues to increase in almost all parts of the world, carrying blessing wherever it goes. For example, the English Cathedral in Zanzibar is built on the site of the Old Slave Market, and the Communion Table stands on the very spot where the whipping-post once stood! The world abounds with such instances. . . . As one has truly said, 'We might as well put our shoulder to the burning wheel of the sun, and try to stop it on its flaming course, as attempt to stop the circulation of the Bible.' " 18/63

Concerning the boast of Voltaire on the extinction of Christianity and the Bible in 100 years, Geisler and Nix point out that "only fifty years after his death the Geneva Bible Society used his press and house to produce stacks of Bibles." 32/123,124 WHAT AN IRONY OF HISTORY!

In A.D. 303, Diocletian issued an edict (*Cambridge History of the Bible*, Cambridge University Press, 1963) to stop Christians from worshipping and to destroy their Scriptures: ". . . an imperial letter was everywhere promulgated, ordering the razing of the churches to the ground and the destruction by fire of the Scriptures, and proclaiming that those who held high positions would lose all civil rights, while those in households, if they persisted in their profession of Christianity, would be deprived of their liberty." 38/476; 26/259

The historic irony of the above edict to destroy the Bible is that Eusebius records the edict given 25 years later by Constantine, the emperor following Diocletian, that 50 copies of the Scriptures should be prepared at the expense of the government.

The Bible is unique in its survival. This does not prove the Bible is the Word of God. But it does prove it stands alone among books. Anyone seeking truth ought to consider a book that has the above unique qualifications.

3D.   Survival through criticism

H. L. Hastings, cited by John W. Lea, has forcibly illustrated the unique way the Bible has withstood the attacks of infidelity and skepticism:

"Infidels for eighteen hundred years have been refuting and overthrowing this book, and yet it stands today as solid as a rock. Its circulation increases, and it is more loved and cherished and read today than ever before. Infidels, with all their assaults, make about as much impression on this book as a man with a tack hammer would on the Pyramids of Egypt. When the French monarch proposed the persecution of the Christians in his dominion, an old statesman and warrior said to him, 'Sire, the Church of God is an anvil that has worn out many hammers.' So the hammers of infidels have been pecking away at this book for ages, but the hammers are worn out, and the anvil still endures. If this book had not been the book of God, men would have destroyed it long ago. Emperors and popes, kings and priests, princes and rulers have all tried their hand at it; they die and the book still lives." 56/17,18

Bernard Ramm adds: "A thousand times over, the death knell of the Bible has been sounded, the funeral procession formed, the inscription cut on the tombstone, and committal read. But somehow the corpse never stays put.

"No other book has been so chopped, knived, sifted, scrutinized, and villified. What book on philosophy or religion or psychology or *belles lettres* of classical or modern times has been subject to such a mass attack as the Bible? with such venom and skepticism? with such thoroughness and erudition? upon every chapter, line and tenet?

"The Bible is still loved by millions, read by millions, and studied by millions." 73/232,233

The phrase used to be "the assured results of higher criticism," but now the higher critics are falling by the wayside. Take, for example, the "Documentary Hypothesis." One of the reasons for its development, apart from the different names used for God in Genesis, was that the Pentateuch could *not* have been written by Moses because the "assured results of higher criticism" have proved that writing was not in existence at the time of Moses or, if it was in existence at that time, it was used sparingly. Therefore, it is obvious that it had to be of later authorship. The minds of the critics went to work: J, E, P, D writers put it all together. They went as far as to divide one verse into three authorships. They built great structures of criticisms. For an in-depth analysis of the Documentary Hypothesis see *More Evidence That Demands a Verdict.* (Campus Crusade for Christ, 1975.)

But then, some fellows discovered the "black stele." 99/444 It had wedge-shaped characters on it and contained the detailed laws of Hammurabi. Was it post-Moses? No! It was pre-Mosaic; not only that, but it preceded Moses' writings by at least three centuries. 99/444 Amazingly, it antedated Moses, who was supposed to be a primitive man without an alphabet.

What an irony of history! The "Documentary Hypothesis" is still taught, yet much of its original basis ("the assured results of higher criticism") has been eradicated and shown to be false.

The "assured results of higher criticism" said there were no
Hittites at the time of Abraham, for there were no other records of
them apart from the Old Testament. They must be myth. Well,
wrong again. As the result of archaeology, there are now hundreds
of references overlapping more than 1,200 years of Hittite
civilization. For further details on the Hittites, see the author's
book *More Evidence That Demands a Verdict*, pp. 309-311.

Earl Radmacher, president of Western Conservative Baptist
Seminary, quoting Nelson Glueck (pronounced Glek), former
president of the Jewish Theological Seminary in the Hebrew Union
College in Cincinnati and one of the three greatest archaeologists,
says: "I listened to him [Glueck] when he was at Temple
Emmanuel in Dallas, and he got rather red in the face and said,
'I've been accused of teaching the verbal, plenary inspiration of
the Scripture. I want it to be understood that I have never taught
this. All I have ever said is that in all of my archaeological
investigation I have never found one artifact of antiquity that
contradicts any statement of the Word of God.' " 71/50

Robert Dick Wilson, a man who was fluent in more than 45
languages and dialects, concluded after a lifetime of study in the
Old Testament:

"I may add that the result of my forty-five years of study of the
Bible has led me all the time to a firmer faith that in the Old
Testament we have a true historical account of the history of the
Israelite people." 103/42

The Bible is unique in facing its critics. There is no book in all of
literature like it. A person looking for truth would certainly
consider a book that has the above qualifications.

5C.   UNIQUE IN ITS TEACHINGS

1D.   Prophecy

Wilbur Smith, who compiled a personal library of 25,000 volumes,
concludes that "whatever one may think of the authority of and the
message presented in the book we call the Bible, there is
world-wide agreement that in more ways than one it is the most
remarkable volume that has ever been produced in these some five
thousand years of writing on the part of the human race.

"It is the only volume ever produced by man, or a group of men, in
which is to be found a large body of prophecies relating to
individual nations, to Israel, to all the peoples of the earth, to
certain cities, and to the coming of One who was to be the Messiah.
The ancient world had many different devices for determining the
future, known as divination, but not in the entire gamut of Greek
and Latin literature, even though they use the words prophet and
prophecy, can we find any real specific prophecy of a great historic
event to come in the distant future, nor any prophecy of a Savior to
arise in the human race. . . ."

"Mohammedanism cannot point to any prophecies of the coming of
Mohammed uttered hundreds of years before his birth. Neither
can the founders of any cult in this country rightly identify any
ancient text specifically foretelling their appearance." 86/9,10

2D.   History

From I Samuel through II Chronicles one finds the history of

Israel, covering about five centuries. *The Cambridge Ancient History*, (Vol. 1, p. 222) says: "The Israelites certainly manifest a genius for historical construction, and the Old Testament embodies the oldest history writing extant."

The distinguished archaeologist, Professor Albright, begins his classic essay, *The Biblical Period:*

"Hebrew national tradition excels all others in its clear picture of tribal and family origins. In Egypt and Babylonia, in Assyria and Phoenicia, in Greece and Rome, we look in vain for anything comparable. There is nothing like it in the tradition of the Germanic peoples. Neither India nor China can produce anything similar, since their earliest historical memories are literary deposits of distorted dynastic tradition, with no trace of the herdsman or peasant behind the demigod or king with whom their records begin. Neither in the oldest Indic historical writings (the Puranas) nor in the earliest Greek historians is there a hint of the fact that both Indo-Aryans and Hellenes were once nomads who immigrated into their later abodes from the north. The Assyrians, to be sure, remembered vaguely that their earliest rulers, whose names they recalled without any details about their deed, were tent dwellers, but whence they came had long been forgotten." 27/3

"The Table of Nations" in Genesis 10 is an astonishingly accurate historical account. According to Albright:

"It stands absolutely alone in ancient literature without a remote parallel even among the Greeks. . . . 'The Table of Nations' remains an astonishingly accurate document. . . . (It) shows such remarkably 'modern' understanding of the ethnic and linguistic situation in the modern world, in spite of all its complexity, that scholars never fail to be impressed with the author's knowledge of the subject." 7/70ff.

3D. **Personalities**

Lewis S. Chafer, founder and former president of Dallas Theological Seminary, puts it this way: "The Bible is not such a book a man would write if he could, or could write if he would."

The Bible deals very frankly with the sins of its characters. Read the biographies today, and see how they try to cover up, overlook or ignore the shady side of people. Take the great literary geniuses; most are painted as saints. The Bible does not do it that way. It simply tells it like it is:

The sins of the people denounced — Deuteronomy 9:24
Sins of the patriarchs — Genesis 12:11-13; 49:5-7
Evangelists paint their own faults and the faults of the apostles —
    Matthew 8:10-26; 26:31-56; Mark 6:52; 8:18; Luke 8:24,25;
    9:40-45; John 10:6; 16:32
Disorder of the churches — I Corinthians 1:11; 15:12;
    II Corinthians 2:4; etc.
Many will say, "Why did they have to put in that chapter about
    David and Bathsheba?" Well, the Bible has the habit of telling
    it like it is.

6C. **UNIQUE IN ITS INFLUENCE ON SURROUNDING LITERATURE**

Cleland B. McAfee writes in *The Greatest English Classic:* "If every Bible in any considerable city were destroyed, the Book could be restored in all its essential parts from the quotations on the shelves of the city public library. There are works, covering almost all the great literary writers, devoted especially to showing how much the Bible has influenced them." 60/134

The historian Philip Schaff (*The Person of Christ,* American Tract Society, 1913) vividly describes its uniqueness along with its Savior:

"This Jesus of Nazareth, without money and arms, conquered more millions than Alexander, Caesar, Mohammed, and Napoleon; without science and learning, He shed more light on things human and divine than all philosophers and scholars combined; without the eloquence of schools, He spoke such words of life as were never spoken before or since, and produced effects which lie beyond the reach of orator or poet; without writing a single line, He set more pens in motion, and furnished themes for more sermons, orations, discussions, learned volumes, works of art, and songs of praise than the whole army of great men of ancient and modern times."

Bernard Ramm adds:

"There are complexities of bibliographical studies that are unparalleled in any other science or department of human knowledge. From the Apostolic Fathers dating from A.D. 95 to the modern times is one great literary river inspired by the Bible — Bible dictionaries, Bible encyclopedias, Bible lexicons, Bible atlases, and Bible geographies. These may be taken as a starter. Then at random, we may mention the vast bibliographies around theology, religious education, hymnology, missions, the biblical languages, church history, religious biography, devotional works, commentaries, philosophy of religion, evidences, apologetics, and on and on. There seems to be an endless number." 73/239

Kenneth Scott Latourette, former Yale historian, says:

"It is evidence of his importance, of the effect that he has had upon history and presumably, of the baffling mystery of his being that no other life ever lived on this planet has evoked so huge a volume of literature among so many peoples and languages, and that, far from ebbing, the flood continues to mount." 55/44

3B. The Conclusion Is Obvious

The above does not prove the Bible is the Word of God, but to me it proves that it is unique ("different from all others; having no like or equal").

A professor remarked to me:

"If you are an intelligent person, you will read the one book that has drawn more attention than any other, *if* you are searching for the truth."

NOTE: The Bible is the first religious book to be taken into outer space (it was on microfilm). It is the first book read describing the source of the earth (astronauts read Genesis 1:1 — "In the beginning God . . ."). Just think, Voltaire said it would be extinct by 1850.

It is also one of the (if not the) most expensive books. Gutenberg's Latin Vulgate Bible sells for over $100,000. The Russians sold the Codex Sinaiticus (an early copy of the Bible) to England for $510,000. 73/227

And finally, the longest telegram in the world was the Revised Version New Testament sent from New York to Chicago. 73/227

chapter 2

how
was the Bible
prepared?

2A. PREPARATION OF THE SCRIPTURES

Many have questions about the background of the Bible, its divisions and the material used for its production. This section will familiarize you with its construction, and, I feel, will give the reader a greater appreciation of God's Word.

1B. Materials Used in Its Preparation

1C. WRITING MATERIAL

1D. *Papyrus.* Not being able to recover many of the ancient manuscripts (a MS is a handwritten copy of the Scriptures) is basically due to the perishable materials used for writing.

"All . . . autographs," writes F. F. Bruce, "have been long lost since. It could not be otherwise, if they were written on papyrus, since (as we have seen) it is only in exceptional conditions that papyrus survives for any length of time." 15/176

Kirsopp Lake points out that "it is hard to resist the conclusion that the scribes usually destroyed their exemplars when they copied the Sacred Books." 53/345,346

The most common ancient writing material was papyrus, made from the papyrus plant. This reed grew in the shallow lakes and rivers of Egypt and Syria. Large shipments of papyrus were sent through the Syrian port of Byblos. It is surmised that the Greek word for books (*Biblos*) is found in the name of this port. The English word "paper" comes from the Greek word for papyrus.

The Cambridge History of the Bible gives an account of how papyrus was prepared for writing:

"The reeds were stripped and cut lengthwise into thin narrow slices before being beaten and pressed together into two layers set at right angles to each other. When dried the whitish surface was polished smooth with a stone or other implement. Pliny refers to several qualities of papyri, and varying thicknesses and surfaces are found before the New Kingdom period when sheets were often very thin and translucent." 38/30

The oldest papyrus fragment known dates back to 2400 B.C. 37/19

The earliest MSS were on papyrus, and it was difficult for any to survive except in dry areas such as the sands of Egypt or in caves similar to those like the Qumran caves where the Dead Sea Scrolls were discovered.

Papyrus was enjoying popular use until about the third century A.D. 37/20

2D. *Parchment.* The name given to "prepared skins of sheep, goats, antelope and other animals." These skins were "shaved and scraped" in order to produce a more durable writing material.

F. F. Bruce writes that "the word 'parchment' comes from the name of the city of Pergamum, in Asia Minor, for the production of this writing material was at one time specially associated with that place." 15/11

3D. *Vellum.* This was the name given to calf skin. Often the vellum was dyed purple. Some of the MSS we have today are purple vellum. The writing on dyed vellum was usually gold or silver.

J. Harold Greenlee says the oldest leather scrolls date from around 1500 B.C. 37/21

4D. Other writing materials

  1E. *Ostraca.* This was unglazed pottery popular with the common people. The technical name is "potsherd" and has been found in abundance in Egypt and Palestine (Job 2:8).

  2E. Stones were inscribed on with an "*iron pen.*"

  3E. *Clay tablets* were engraved with a sharp instrument and then dried in order to make a permanent record (Jeremiah 17:13; Ezekiel 4:1). This was the cheapest and one of the most durable of the writing materials.

  4E. *Wax tablets.* A metal stylus was used on a piece of flat wood covered with a wax.

2C. WRITING INSTRUMENTS

  1D. *Chisel.* An iron instrument to engrave stones.

  2D. *Metal Stylus.* "A three-sided instrument with a leveled head, the stylus was used to make incursions into clay and wax tablets." 32/228

  3D. *Pen.* A pointed reed "was fashioned from rushes (*Juncus maritimis*) about 6-16 in. long, the end being cut to a flat chisel-shape to enable thick and thin strokes to be made with the broad or narrow sides. The reed-pen was in use from the early first millennium in Mesopotamia from which it may well have been adopted, while the idea of a quill pen seems to have come from the Greeks in the third century B.C." (Jeremiah 8:8). 38/31

  The pen was used on vellum, parchment and papyrus.

  4D. *Ink* was usually a compound of "charcoal, gum and water." 15/13

2B. Forms of Ancient Books

1C. ROLLS OR SCROLLS. These were made by gluing sheets of papyrus together and then winding these long strips around a stick. The size of the scroll was limited by the difficulty in using the roll. Writing was usually on only one side. A two-sided scroll is called an "Opisthograph" (Revelation 5:1). Some rolls have been known to be 144 feet long. The average scroll was about 20 to 35 feet.

It is no wonder that Callimachus, a professional cataloguer of books from Alexandria's library, said "a big book is a big nuisance." 62/5

2C. CODEX OR BOOK FORM. In order to make reading easier and less bulky, the papyrus sheets were assembled in leaf form and written on both sides. Greenlee says that Christianity was the prime reason for the development of the codex-book form.

The classical authors wrote on papyrus scrolls until about the third century A.D.

3B. Types of Writing

1C. UNCIAL WRITING used upper case letters which were deliberately and carefully executed. This was known as the "bookhand." Vaticanus and Sinaiticus are uncial MSS.

2C. MINUSCULE WRITING was "a script of smaller letters in a running hand [connected] . . . was created for the production of books." 62/9 This change was initiated in the ninth century. 62/9

The Greek manuscripts were written without any breaks between words. (Hebrew was written without vowels until 900 A.D. with the coming of the Massoretes.)

Bruce Metzger answers those who speak of the difficulty of a continuous text:

"It must not be thought, however, that such ambiguities occur very often in Greek. In that language it is the rule, with very few exceptions, that native Greek words can end only in a vowel (or a diphthong) or in one of three consonants, ν, ρ, and s, (Nu, Rho and Sigma). Furthermore, it should not be supposed that *scriptio continua* presented exceptional difficulties in reading, for apparently it was customary in antiquity to read aloud, even when one was alone. Thus despite the absence of spaces between words, by pronouncing to oneself what was read, syllable by syllable, one soon became used to reading *scriptio continua*." 62/13

4B. Divisions

1C. BOOKS (See page 30).

2C. CHAPTERS

The first divisions were made in 586 B.C. when the Pentateuch was divided into 154 groupings (sedarim)

Fifty years later it was further sectioned into 54 divisions (parashiyyoth) and into 669 smaller segments to assist in locating references. These were used in a one-year reading cycle.

The Greeks made divisions around 250 A.D. The oldest system of chapter division is from about 350 A.D. in the margins of Codex

Vaticanus. 62/22 Geisler and Nix write that "it was not until the 13th century that these sections were changed . . . Stephen Langton, a professor at the University of Paris, and afterward Archbishop of Canterbury, divided the Bible into the modern chapter divisions (ca 1227)." 32/231,232

3C.   VERSES. The first verse indicators varied from spaces between words to letters or numbers. They were not systematically used universally. The first standard verse divisions were around 900 A.D.

The Latin Vulgate was the first Bible to incorporate both verse and chapter divisions in both Old and New Testaments.

chapter 3
the
canon

3A. THE CANON

  1B. Introduction

    1C. MEANING OF THE WORD "CANON"

The word *canon* comes from the root word "reed" (English word "cane"; Hebrew form *ganeh* and Greek *Kanon*). The "reed" was used as a measuring rod and eventually meant "standard."

Origen used the word "canon to denote what we call the 'rule of faith,' the standard by which we are to measure and evaluate. . . ." Later it meant a "list" or "index." 15/95

The word "canon" applied to Scripture means "an officially accepted list of books." 23/31

One thing to keep in mind is that the church did not create the canon or books included in what we call Scripture. Instead, the church recognized the books that were inspired from their inception. They were inspired by God when written.

    2C. TESTS OF A BOOK FOR INCLUSION IN THE CANON

We don't know exactly what criteria the early church used to choose the canonical books. There were possibly five guiding principles used to determine whether or not a New Testament book is canonical or Scripture. Geisler and Nix record these five principles: 32/141

1. **Is it authoritative** — did it come from the hand of God? (Does this book come with a divine "thus saith the Lord"?)

2. **Is it prophetic** — was it written by a man of God?

3. **Is it authentic?** [The fathers had the policy of "if in doubt, throw it out." This enhanced the "validity of their discernment of canonical books."]

4. **Is it dynamic** — did it come with the life-transforming power of God?

5. **Was it received, collected, read and used** — was it accepted by the people of God?

Peter acknowledged Paul's work as Scripture parallel to Old Testament Scripture (II Peter 3:16).

  2B. Old Testament Canon

    1C. FACTORS DETERMINING NEED OF OLD TESTAMENT CANON

      1D. The Jewish sacrificial system was ended by the destruction of Jerusalem and the temple in 70 A.D. Even though the Old

Testament canon was settled in the Jewish mind long before 70 A.D., there was a need for something more definitive. The Jews were scattered and they needed to determine which books were the authoritative Word of God because of the many extra-scriptural writings and the decentralization. The Jews became a people of one Book and it was this Book that kept them together.

2D.   Christianity started to blossom and many writings of the Christians were beginning to be circulated. The Jews needed to expose them vividly and exclude them from their writings and use in the synagogues.

One needs to be careful that he separates the Hebrew canon of Scripture from the assortment of religious literature.

2C. THE HEBREW CANON

1D.   The following is the breakdown of the Jewish Old Testament canon (taken from my seminary notes but can be found in many books such as the modern editions of the Jewish Old Testament. Check *The Holy Scriptures,* according to the Massoretic Text and *Biblia Hebraica,* Rudolph Kittel, Paul Kahle [eds.]).

The Law
(Torah)
   1. Genesis
   2. Exodus
   3. Leviticus
   4. Numbers
   5. Deuteronomy

The Prophets (Nebhim)
  A. Former Prophets
   1. Joshua
   2. Judges
   3. Samuel
   4. Kings

  B. Latter Prophets
   1. Isaiah
   2. Jeremiah
   3. Ezekiel
   4. The Twelve

The Writings
(Kethubhim or Hagiographa [GK])
  A. Poetical Books
   1. Psalms
   2. Proverbs
   3. Job

  B. Five Rolls (*Megilloth*)
   1. Song of Songs
   2. Ruth
   3. Lamentations
   4. Esther
   5. Ecclesiastes

  C. Historical Books
   1. Daniel
   2. Ezra-Nehemiah
   3. Chronicles

Although the Christian church has the same Old Testament canon, the number of books differs because we divide Samuel, Kings, Chronicles, etc. into two books each; the Jews also consider the Minor Prophets as one book.

The order of books also differs. The Protestant Old Testament follows a topical order instead of an official order. 32/22

3C.   CHRIST'S WITNESS TO THE OLD TESTAMENT CANON

1D.   Luke 24:44. In the upper room Jesus told the disciples "that all things must be fulfilled, which were written in the law of Moses, and the Prophets, and the Psalms concerning Me." With these words "He indicated the three sections into which the Hebrew Bible was divided — the Law, the Prophets, and the 'Writings' (here called 'the Psalms' probably because the Book of Psalms is the first and longest book in this third section)." 15/96

2D. John 10:31-36; Luke 24:44. Jesus disagreed with the oral traditions of the Pharisees (Mark 7, Matthew 15), *not* with their concept of the Hebrew canon. 15/104 "There is no evidence whatever of any dispute between Him and the Jews as to the canonicity of any Old Testament book." 108/62

3D. Luke 11:51 (also Matthew 23:35): ". . . from the blood of Abel to the blood of Zechariah." Jesus here confirms His witness to the extent of the Old Testament canon. Abel, as everyone knows, was the first martyr (Genesis 4:8). Zechariah is the last martyr to be named (in the Hebrew Old Testament order. See listing above — 2C, 1D), having been stoned while prophesying to the people "in the court of the house of the Lord" (II Chronicles 24:21). Genesis was the first book in the Hebrew canon and Chronicles the last book. Jesus basically said "from Genesis to Chronicles," or, according to our order, "from Genesis to Malachi." 15/96

4C. EXTRA-BIBLICAL WRITERS' TESTIMONIES

1D. The earliest record of a three-fold division of the Old Testament is in the prologue of the book *Ecclesiasticus* (ca 130 B.C.). The prologue, written by the author's grandson, says: "The Law, and the Prophets and the other books of the fathers." There existed three definite divisions of Scripture. 108/71

2D. Josephus, the Jewish historian, (end of the first century A.D.) writes:

". . . and how firmly we have given credit to those books of our own nation is evident by what we do; for during so many ages as have already passed, no one has been so bold as either to add anything to them or take anything from them, or to make any change in them; but it becomes natural to all Jews, immediately and from their very birth, to esteem those books to contain divine doctrines, and to persist in them, and, if occasion be, willingly to die for them. For it is no new thing for our captives, many of them in number, and frequently in time, to be seen to endure racks and deaths of all kinds upon the theatres, that they may not be obliged to say one word against our laws, and the records that contain them. . . ." 45/609

3D. The Talmud

1E. Tosefta Yadaim 3:5 says: "The Gospel and the books of the heretics do not make the hands unclean; the books of Ben Sira and whatever books have been written since his time are not canonical." 70/63; 32/129

2E. Seder Olam Rabba 30 writes: "Up to this point [the time of Alexander the Great] the prophets prophesied through the Holy Spirit; from this time onward incline thine ear and listen to the sayings of the wise." 32/129

3E. Babylonian Talmud, Tractate "Sanhedrin" VII-VIII, 24: "After the latter prophets Haggai, Zechariah, and Malachi, the Holy Spirit departed from Israel."

4D. Melito, Bishop of Sardis, drew up the oldest list of the Old Testament canon that we can date (ca 170 A.D.).

Eusebius (*Ecclesiastical History IV. 26*) preserves his comments.

Melito said he had obtained the reliable list while traveling in
Syria. Melito's comments were in a letter to Anesimius, his friend:
"Their names are these . . . five books of Moses: Genesis, Exodus,
Numbers, Leviticus, Deuteronomy. Jesus Naue, Judges, Ruth.
Four books of Kingdoms, two of Chronicles, the Psalms of David,
Solomon's Proverbs (also called Wisdom), Ecclesiastes, Song of
Songs, Job. Of the Prophets: Isaiah, Jeremiah, the Twelve in a
single book, Daniel, Ezekiel, Ezra."

F. F. Bruce comments: "It is likely that Melito included
Lamentations with Jeremiah, and Nehemiah with Ezra (though it
is curious to find Ezra counted among the prophets). In that case,
his list contains all the books of the Hebrew canon (arranged
according to the Septuagint order), with the exception of Esther.
Esther may not have been included in the list he received from his
informants in Syria." 15/100

5D.   The threefold division of the present Jewish text (with 11 books in
      the Writings) is from the Mishnah (Baba Bathra tractate, fifth
      century A.D.). 32/20

5C.   THE NEW TESTAMENT WITNESS TO THE OLD TESTAMENT AS
      SACRED SCRIPTURE

      Matthew 21:42; 22:29; 26:54, 56
      Luke 24
      John 5:39; 10:35
      Acts 17:2, 11; 18:28
      Romans 1:2; 4:3; 9:17; 10:11; 11:2; 15:4; 16:26
      I Corinthians 15:3,4
      Galatians 3:8; 3:22; 4:30
      I Timothy 5:18
      II Timothy 3:16
      II Peter 1:20,21; 3:16

      ". . . As the *Scripture* said . . ." (John 7:38), without more specific
      identity there must have been a general understanding of the
      relationship of Scripture to various books.

6C.   THE COUNCIL OF JAMNIA

      Many students remark: "Sure, I know about the canon. The leaders
      got together in a council and decided which books best helped them
      and then forced the followers to accept them." This is about as far
      away from the truth as one can get. (But for some people, distance is
      no problem in the space age.)

      The comments of F. F. Bruce and H. H. Rowley are appropriate here:

      F. F. Bruce: "The chief reason for asking if the 'Writings' section was
      complete in our Lord's time is that we have records of discussions that
      went on among the Rabbis after the Fall of Jerusalem in A.D. 70 about
      some of the books in this section. When the destruction of the city and
      temple was imminent, a great Rabbi belonging to the school of Hillel
      in the Pharisaic party — Yochanan ben Zakkai by name — obtained
      permission from the Romans to reconstitute the Sanhedrin on a purely
      spiritual basis at Jabneh or Jamnia, between Joppa and Azotus
      (Ashdod). Some of the discussions which went on at Jamnia were
      handed down by oral transmission and ultimately recorded in the
      Rabbinical writings. Among their debates they considered whether

canonical recognition should be accorded to the books of Proverbs, Ecclesiastes, the Song of Songs and Esther. Objections had been raised against these books on various grounds; Esther, for example, did not contain the name of God, and Ecclesiastes was none too easy to square with contemporary orthodoxy. But the upshot of the Jamnia debates was the firm acknowledgement of all these books as Holy Scripture." 15/97

H. H. Rowley writes: "It is, indeed, doubtful how far it is correct to speak of the Council of Jamnia. We know of discussions that took place there amongst the Rabbis, but we know of no formal or binding decisions that were made, and it is probable that the discussions were informal, though none the less helping to crystallize and to fix more firmly the Jewish tradition." 80/170

7C.   THE OLD TESTAMENT APOCRYPHAL LITERATURE

1D.   Introduction

The term means "hidden or concealed" from the Greek word *apokruphos.*

In the fourth century Jerome was the first to call the group of literature "Apocrypha." The Apocrypha consists of the books added to the Old Testament by the Catholic church that Protestants say are not canonical.

2D.   Why not canonical?

Unger's Bible Dictionary gives reasons for their exclusion:

1. "They abound in historical and geographical inaccuracies and anachronisms.

2. "They teach doctrines which are false and foster practices which are at variance with inspired Scripture.

3. "They resort to literary types and display an artificiality of subject matter and styling out of keeping with inspired Scripture.

4. "They lack the distinctive elements which give genuine Scripture their divine character, such as prophetic power and poetic and religious feeling." 99/70

3D.   A summary of the individual books

Ralph Earle, in his excellent study guide, *How We Got Our Bible,* gives brief details of each book. I have chosen, because of its quality, to print his outline instead of producing another.

"*I Esdras* (about 150 B.C.) tells of the restoration of the Jews to Palestine after the Babylonian exile. It draws considerably from Chronicles, Ezra, and Nehemiah, but the author has added much legendary material.

"The most interesting item is the Story of the Three Guardsmen. They were debating what was the strongest thing in the world. One said, 'Wine'; another, 'the King'; the third, 'Woman and Truth.' They put these three answers under the king's pillow. When he awoke he required the three men to defend their answers. The unanimous decision was: 'Truth is greatly and supremely strong.' Because Zerubbabel had given this answer he was allowed, as a reward, to rebuild the Temple at Jerusalem.

"*II Esdras* (A.D. 100) is an apocalyptic work, containing seven visions. Martin Luther was so confused by these visions that he is said to have thrown the book into the Elbe River.

"*Tobit* (early 2nd cent. B.C.) is a short novel. Strongly Pharisaic in tone, it emphasizes the Law, clean foods, ceremonial washings, charity, fasting and prayer. It is clearly unscriptural in its statement that almsgiving atones for sin.

"*Judith* (about the middle of 2nd cent. B.C.) is also fictitious and Pharisaic. The heroine of this novel is Judith, a beautiful Jewish widow. When her city was besieged she took her maid, together with Jewish clean food, and went out to the tent of the attacking general. He was enamored of her beauty and gave her a place in his tent. Fortunately, he had imbibed too freely and sank into a drunken stupor. Judith took his sword and cut off his head. Then she and her maid left the camp, taking his head in their provision bag. It was hung on the wall of a nearby city and the leaderless Assyrian army was defeated.

"*Additions to Esther* (about 100 B.C.). Esther stands alone among the books of the Old Testament in having no mention of God. We are told that Esther and Mordecai fasted but not specifically that they prayed. To compensate for this lack, the Additions have long prayers attributed to these two, together with a couple of letters supposedly written by Artaxerxes.

"*The Wisdom of Solomon* (about A.D. 40) was written to keep the Jews from falling into skepticism, materialism, and idolatry. As in Proverbs, Wisdom is personified. There are many noble sentiments expressed in this book.

"*Ecclesiasticus,* or Wisdom of Sirach (about 180 B.C.), shows a high level of religious wisdom, somewhat like the canonical Book of Proverbs. It also contains much practical advice. For instance, on the subject of after-dinner speeches it says (32:8):

" 'Speak concisely; say much in few words. . . .'

" 'Act like a man who knows more than he says.'

And again (33:4):

" 'Prepare what you have to say,
    And then you will be listened to.'

"In his sermons John Wesley quotes several times from the Book of Ecclesiasticus. It is still widely used in Anglican circles.

"*Baruch* (about A.D. 100) represents itself as being written by Baruch, the scribe of Jeremiah, in 582 B.C. Actually, it is probably trying to interpret the destruction of Jerusalem in A.D. 70. The book urges the Jews not to revolt again, but to be in submission to the emperor. In spite of this the Bar-Cochba revolution against Roman rule took place soon after, in A.D. 132-35. The sixth chapter of Baruch contains the so-called 'Letter of Jeremiah,' with its strong warning against idolatry — probably addressed to Jews in Alexandria, Egypt.

"Our Book of Daniel contains 12 chapters. In the first century before Christ a thirteenth chapter was added, the story of *Susanna*. She was the beautiful wife of a leading Jew in Babylon, to whose house the Jewish elders and judges frequently came. Two of these became enamored of her and tried to seduce her. When she cried out, the two elders said they had found her in the arms of a young man. She was brought to trial. Since there were two witnesses who agreed in their testimony, she was convicted and sentenced to death.

"But a young man named Daniel interrupted the proceedings and began to cross-examine the witnesses. He asked each one separately under which tree in the garden they had found Susanna with a lover. When they gave different answers they were put to death and Susanna was saved.

"*Bel and the Dragon* was added at about the same time and called chapter 14 of Daniel. Its main purpose was to show the folly of idolatry. It really contains two stories.

"In the first, King Cyrus asked Daniel why he did not worship Bel, since that deity showed his greatness by daily consuming many sheep, together with much flour and oil. So Daniel scattered ashes on the floor of the Temple where the food had been placed that evening. In the morning the king took Daniel in to show him that Bel had eaten all the food during the night. But Daniel showed the king in the ashes on the floor the footprints of the priests and their families who had entered secretly under the table. The priests were slain and the temple destroyed.

"The story of the Dragon is just as obviously legendary in character. Along with Tobit, Judith, and Susanna, these stories may be classified as purely Jewish fiction. They have little if any religious value.

"The *Song of the Three Hebrew Children* follows Dan. 3:23 in the Septuagint and the Vulgate. Borrowing heavily from Psalms 148, it is antiphonal like Psalms 136, having 32 times the refrain: 'Sing praise to him and greatly exalt him forever.'

"The *Prayer of Manasseh* was composed in Maccabean times (2nd cent. B.C.) as the supposed prayer of Manasseh, the wicked king of Judah. It was obviously suggested by the statement in II Chron. 33:19 — 'His prayer also, and how God was entreated of him . . . behold, they are written among the sayings of the seers.' Since this prayer is not found in the Bible, some scribe had to make up the deficiency!

"*I Maccabees* (1st cent. B.C.) is perhaps the most valuable book in the Apocrypha. For it describes the exploits of the three Maccabean brothers — Judas, Jonathan, and Simon. Along with Josephus it is our most important source for the history of this crucial and exciting period in Jewish history.

"*II Maccabees* (same time) is not a sequel to I Maccabees, but a parallel account, treating only the victories of Judas Maccabeus. It is generally thought to be more legendary than I Maccabees." 23/37-41

4D. Historical testimony of their exclusion

Geisler and Nix give a succession of 10 testimonies of antiquity against accepting the Apocrypha:

1. "Philo, Alexandrian Jewish philosopher (20 B.C.-A.D. 40), quoted the Old Testament prolifically and even recognized the threefold division, but he never quoted from the Apocrypha as inspired.

2. "Josephus (A.D. 30-100), Jewish historian, explicitly excludes the Apocrypha, numbering the books of the Old Testament as 22. Neither does he quote these books as Scripture.

3. "Jesus and the New Testament writers never once quote the Apocrypha although there are hundreds of quotes and references to almost all of the canonical books of the Old Testament.

4.   "The Jewish scholars of Jamnia (A.D. 90) did not recognize the Apocrypha.

5.   "No canon or council of the Christian church for the first four centuries recognized the Apocrypha as inspired.

6.   "Many of the great Fathers of the early church spoke out against the Apocrypha, for example, Origen, Cyril of Jerusalem, Athanasius.

7.   "Jerome (340-420), the great scholar and translator of the Vulgate, rejected the Apocrypha as part of the canon. He disputed across the Mediterranean with Augustine on this point. He at first refused even to translate the Apocryphal books into Latin, but later he made a hurried translation of a few of them. After his death, and literally "over his dead body," the Apocryphal books were brought into his Latin Vulgate directly from the Old Latin Version.

8.   "Many Roman Catholic scholars through the Reformation period rejected the Apocrypha.

9.   "Luther and the Reformers rejected the canonicity of the Apocrypha.

10. "Not until A.D. 1546, in a polemical action at the Counter Reformation Council of Trent, did the Apocryphal books receive full canonical status by the Roman Catholic Church." 32/173

3B. The New Testament Canon

1C. TESTS FOR INCLUDING A BOOK IN THE NEW TESTAMENT CANON

The basic factor for determining New Testament canonicity was inspiration by God, and its chief test, apostolicity. 32/181

Geisler and Nix amplify the above:

"In New Testament terminology, the church was 'built upon the foundation of the apostles and prophets' (Eph. 2:20) whom Christ had promised to guide into 'all the truth' (John 16:13) by the Holy Spirit. The church at Jerusalem was said to have continued in the 'apostles' teaching and fellowship' (Acts 2:42). The term 'apostolic' as used for the test of canonicity does not necessarily mean 'apostolic authorship,' or 'that which was prepared under the direction of the apostles. . . .'

"It seems much better to agree with Gaussen, Warfield, Charles Hodge, and most Protestants that it is apostolic authority, or apostolic approval, that was the primary test for canonicity and not merely apostolic authorship." 32/183

N.B. Stonehouse writes that the apostolic authority "which speaks forth in the New Testament is never detached from the authority of the Lord. In the Epistles there is consistent recognition that in the church there is only one absolute authority, the authority of the Lord himself. Wherever the apostles speak with authority, they do so as exercising the Lord's authority. Thus, for example, where Paul defends his authority as an apostle, he bases his claim solely and directly upon his commission by the Lord (Gal. 1 and 2); where he assumes the right to regulate the life of the church, he claims for his word the Lord's authority, even when no direct word of the Lord has been handed down (I Cor. 14:37; cf. I Cor. 7:10). . . ." 88/117,118

"The only one who speaks in the New Testament with an authority that is underived and self-authenticating is the Lord." 67/18

2C. THE NEW TESTAMENT CANONICAL BOOKS

1D. Three reasons for a need to determine a New Testament canon: 23/41

1E. A heretic, Marcion (ca 140 A.D.), developed his own canon and began to propagate it. The church needed to offset his influence by determining what was the real canon of New Testament Scripture.

2E. Many Eastern churches were using books in services that were definitely spurious. It called for a decision concerning the canon.

3E. Edict of Diocletian (A.D. 303) declared the destruction of the sacred books of the Christians. Who wanted to die for just a religious book? They needed to know!

2D. Athanasius of Alexandria (A.D. 367) gives us the earliest list of New Testament books which is exactly like our present New Testament. This list was in a festal letter to the churches.

3D. Shortly after Athanasius, two writers, Jerome and Augustine, define the canon of 27 books. 15/112

4D. Polycarp (A.D. 115), Clement and others refer to the Old and New Testament books with the phrase "as it is said in these scriptures."

5D. Justin Martyr (A.D. 100-165), referring to the Eucharist, writes in his First Apology 1.67:

"And on the day called Sunday there is a gathering together to one place of all those who live in cities or in the country, and the memoirs of the apostles or the writings of the prophets are read, as long as time permits. Then when the reader has ceased the president presents admonition and invitation to the imitation of these good things."

He adds in his *Dialogue* with Trypho (pp. 49, 103, 105, 107) the formula "It is written," to quote from the Gospels. Both he and Trypho must have known to what "It is written" refers.

6D. Irenaeus (A.D. 180)

F. F. Bruce writes of the significance of Irenaeus:

"The importance of evidence lies in his link with the apostolic age and in his ecumenical associations. Brought up in Asia Minor at the feet of Polycarp, the disciple of John, he became Bishop of Lyons in Gaul, A.D. 180. His writings attest the canonical recognition of the fourfold Gospel and Acts, of Rom., 1 and 2 Cor., Gal., Eph., Phil., Col., 1 and 2 Thess., 1 and 2 Tim., and Titus, of I Peter and I John and of the Revelation. In his treatise, *Against Heresies,* III, ii, 8, it is evident that by A.D. 180 the idea of the fourfold Gospel had become so axiomatic throughout Christendom that it could be referred to as an established fact as obvious and inevitable and natural as the four cardinal points of the compass (as we call them) or the four winds." 15/109

7D. Ignatius (A.D. 50-115): "I do not wish to command you as Peter and Paul; they were apostles. . . ." Trall. 3. 3.

8D. The Church Councils. It is much the same situation as the Old Testament (see Chapter 3, 6C, The Council of Jamnia).

F. F. Bruce states that "when at last a Church Council — The Synod of Hippo in A.D. 393 — listed the twenty-seven books of the New Testament, it did not confer upon them any authority which they did not already possess, but simply recorded their previously established canonicity. (The ruling of the Synod of Hippo was re-promulgated four years later by the Third Synod of Carthage.)" 15/113

Since this time, there has been no serious questioning of the 27 accepted books of the New Testament by either Roman Catholics or Protestants.

3C. THE NEW TESTAMENT APOCRYPHA
32/200-205

Epistle of Pseudo-Barnabas (ca A.D. 70-79)

Epistle to the Corinthians (ca A.D. 96)

Ancient Homily, or the so-called *Second Epistle of Clement* (ca A.D. 120-140)

Shepherd of Hermas (ca A.D. 115-140)

Didache, Teaching of the Twelve (ca A.D. 100-120)

Apocalypse of Peter (ca A.D. 150)

The Acts of Paul and Thecla (A.D. 170)

Epistle to the Laodiceans (4th century?)

The Gospel According to the Hebrews (A.D. 65-100)

Epistle of Polycarp to the Philippians (ca A.D. 108)

The Seven Epistles of Ignatius (ca A.D. 100)

And many more.

chapter 4

the reliability of the Bible

PART 1 — Confirmation by Historical Text

4A. THE RELIABILITY AND TRUSTWORTHINESS OF SCRIPTURE

1B. Introduction

What we are establishing here is the historical reliability of the Scripture, not its inspiration.

The historical reliability of the Scripture should be tested by the same criteria that all historical documents are tested.

C. Sanders in *Introduction to Research in English Literary History*, lists and explains the three basic principles of historiography. They are the bibliographical test, the internal evidence test and the external evidence test. 81/143 ff.

2B. The Bibliographical Test for the Reliability of the New Testament

The bibliographical test is an examination of the textual transmission by which documents reach us. In other words, since we do not have the original documents, how reliable are the copies we have in regard to the number of manuscripts (MSS) and the time interval between the original and extant copy? 64/26

F. E. Peters points out that "on the basis of manuscript tradition alone, the works that made up the Christians' New Testament were the most frequently copied and widely circulated books of antiquity." 69/50

1C. MANUSCRIPT EVIDENCE OF THE NEW TESTAMENT

There are now more than 5,300 known Greek manuscripts of the New Testament. Add over 10,000 Latin Vulgate and at least 9,300 other early versions (MSS) and we have more than 24,000 manuscript copies of portions of the New Testament in existence today.

No other document of antiquity even begins to approach such numbers and attestation. In comparison, the *Iliad* by Homer is second with only 643 manuscripts that still survive. The first complete preserved text of Homer dates from the 13th century. 58/145

25,000	24,633 MSS
20,000	
15,000	
10,000	
5,000	
	■ 643 MSS
New Testament	Iliad

The following is a breakdown of the numbers of surviving manuscripts for the New Testament:

Greek

Uncials	267	
Minuscules	2,764	
Lectionaries	2,143	
Papyri	88	
Recent finds	47	
TOTAL	5,309	Extant Greek MSS

Latin Vulgate	10,000	plus
Ethiopic	2,000	plus
Slavic	4,101	
Armenian	2,587	
Syriac Pashetta	350	plus
Bohairic	100	
Arabic	75	
Old Latin	50	
Anglo Saxon	7	
Gothic	6	
Sogdian	3	
Old Syriac	2	
Persian	2	
Frankish	1	

Information for the preceding charts was gathered from the following sources: Kurt Aland's *Journal of Biblical Literature*, Vol. 87, 1968; Kurt Aland's *Kurzgefasste Liste Der Griechischen Handschriften Des Neven Testaments*, W. De Gruyter, 1963; Kurt Aland's "Neve Nevtestamentliche Papyri III," *New Testament Studies*, July, 1976; Bruce Metzger's *The Early Versions of the New Testament*, Clarendon Press, 1977; *New Testament Manuscript Studies*, (eds.) Merrill M. Parvis and Allen Wikgren, The University of Chicago Press, 1950; Eroll F. Rhodes' *An Annotated List of Armenian New Testament Manuscripts*, Tokyo, Ikeburo, 1959; *The Bible and Modern Scholarship*, (ed.) J. Phillip Hyatt, Abington Press, 1965.

John Warwick Montgomery says that "to be skeptical of the resultant text of the New Testament books is to allow all of classical antiquity to slip into obscurity, for no documents of the ancient period are as well attested bibliographically as the New Testament." 64/29

Sir Frederic G. Kenyon, who was the director and principal librarian of the British Museum and second to none in authority for issuing statements about MSS, says, ". . . besides number, the manuscripts of the New Testament differ from those of the classical authors, and this time the difference is clear gain. In no other case is the interval of time between the composition of the book and the date of the earliest extant manuscripts so short as in that of the New Testament. The books of the New Testament were written in the latter part of the first century; the earliest extant manuscripts (trifling scraps excepted) are of the fourth century — say from 250 to 300 years later.

"This may sound a considerable interval, but it is nothing to that which parts most of the great classical authors from their earliest manuscripts. We believe that we have in all essentials an accurate text of the seven extant plays of Sophocles; yet the earliest substantial manuscript upon which it is based was written more than 1400 years after the poet's death." 48/4

Kenyon continues in *The Bible and Archaeology:* "The interval then between the dates of original composition and the earliest extant evidence becomes so small as to be in fact negligible, and the last foundation for any doubt that the Scriptures have come down to us substantially as they were written has now been removed. Both the authenticity and the general integrity of the books of the New Testament may be regarded as finally established." 46/288

F. J. A. Hort rightfully adds that "in the variety and fullness of the evidence on which it rests the text of the New Testment stands absolutely and unapproachably alone among ancient prose writings." 43/561

J. Harold Greenlee states, ". . . the number of available MSS of the New Testament is overwhelmingly greater than those of any other work of ancient literature. In the third place, the earliest extant MSS of the N. T. were written much closer to the date of the original writing than is the case in almost any other piece of ancient literature." 37/15

2C. THE NEW TESTAMENT COMPARED WITH OTHER WORKS OF ANTIQUITY

1D. The manuscript comparison

F. F. Bruce in *The New Testament Documents* vividly pictures the comparison between the New Testament and ancient historical writings: "Perhaps we can appreciate how wealthy the New Testament is in manuscript attestation if we compare the textual material for other ancient historical works. For Caesar's Gallic Wars (composed between 58 and 50 B.C.) there are several extant MSS, but only nine or ten are good, and the oldest is some 900 years later than Caesar's day. Of the 142 books of the Roman history of Livy (59 B.C.-A.D. 17), only 35 survive; these are known to us from not more than 20 MSS of any consequence, only one of which, and that containing fragments of Books III-VI, is as old as the fourth century. Of the 14 books of the Histories of Tacitus (ca A.D. 100) only four and a half survive; of the 16 books of his Annals, 10 survive in full and two in part. The text of these extant portions of his two great historical works depends entirely on two MSS, one of the ninth century and one of the eleventh.

"The extant MSS of his minor works (Dialogus de Oratoribus, Agricola, Germania) all descend from a codex of the tenth century. The History of Thucydides (ca 460-400 B.C.) is known to us from eight MSS, the earliest belonging to ca A.D. 900, and a few papyrus scraps, belonging to about the beginning of the Christian era. The same is true of the History of Herodotus (B.C. 488-428). Yet no classical scholar would listen to an argument that the authenticity of Herodotus or Thucydides is in doubt because the earliest MSS of their works which are of any use to us are over 1,300 years later than the originals." 16/16,17

Greenlee writes in *Introduction to New Testament Textual Criticism* about the time gap between the original MS (the autograph) and the extant MS (the old copy surviving), saying that "the oldest known MSS of most of the Greek classical authors are dated a thousand years or more after the author's death. The time interval for the Latin authors is somewhat less, varying down to a minimum of three centuries in the case of Virgil. In the case of the N. T., however, two of the most important MSS were written within 300 years after the N. T. was completed, and some virtually complete N. T. books as well as extensive fragmentary MSS of many parts of the N. T. date back to one century from the original writings." 37/16

Greenlee adds that "since scholars accept as generally trustworthy the writings of the ancient classics even though the earliest MSS were written so long after the original writings and the number of extant MSS is in many instances so small, it is clear that the reliability of the text of the N. T. is likewise assured." 37/16

Bruce Metzger in *The Text of the New Testament* cogently writes of the comparison: *"The works of several ancient authors are preserved to us by the thinnest possible thread of transmission.* For example, the compendious history of Rome by Velleius Paterculus survived to modern times in only one incomplete manuscript, from which the *editio princeps* was made — and this lone manuscript was lost in the seventeenth century after being copied by Beatus Rhenanus at Amerbach. Even the *Annals* of the famous historian Tacitus is extant, so far as the first six books are concerned, in but a single manuscript, dating from the ninth century. In 1870 the only known manuscript of the *Epistle to Diognetus,* an early Christian composition which editors usually include in the corpus of Apostolic Fathers, perished in a fire at the municipal library in Strasbourg. *In contrast with these figures, the textual critic of the New Testament is embarrassed by the wealth of his material."* 62/34

F. F. Bruce says: "There is no body of ancient literature in the world which enjoys such a wealth of good textual attestation as the New Testament." 15/178

AUTHOR	When Written	Earliest Copy	Time Span	No. of Copies
Caesar	100-44 B.C.	900 A.D.	1,000 yrs.	10
Livy	59 B.C.-A.D. 17			20
Plato (*Tetralogies*)	427-347 B.C.	900 A.D.	1,200 yrs.	7
Tacitus (*Annals*)	100 A.D.	1100 A.D.	1,000 yrs.	20 (-)
also minor works	100 A.D.	1000 A.D.	900 yrs.	1
Pliny the Younger (*History*)	61-113 A.D.	850 A.D.	750 yrs.	7
Thucydides (*History*)	460-400 B.C.	900 A.D.	1,300 yrs.	8
Suetonius (*De Vita Caesarum*)	75-160 A.D.	950 A.D.	800 yrs.	8
Herodotus (*History*)	480-425 B.C.	900 A.D.	1,300 yrs.	8
Horace			900 yrs.	
Sophocles	496-406 B.C.	1000 A.D.	1,400 yrs.	193
Lucretius	Died 55 or 53 B.C.		1,100 yrs.	2
Catullus	54 B.C.	1550 A.D.	1,600 yrs.	3
Euripides	480-406 B.C.	1100 A.D.	1,500 yrs.	9
Demosthenes	383-322 B.C.	1100 A.D.	1,300 yrs.	200 *
Aristotle	384-322 B.C.	1100 A.D.	1,400 yrs.	49 †
Aristophanes	450-385 B.C.	900 A.D.	1,200 yrs.	10

*All from one copy.
†Of any one work.

2D.   The textual comparison

Bruce Metzger observes: "Of all the literary compositions by the Greek people, the Homeric poems are the best suited for comparison with the Bible." 61/144 He adds: "In the entire range of ancient Greek and Latin literature, the *Iliad* ranks next to the New Testament in possessing the greatest amount of manuscript testimony." 61/144

Metzger continues: "In antiquity men [1] memorized Homer as later they were to memorize the Scriptures. [2] Each was held in the highest esteem and quoted in defense of arguments pertaining to heaven, earth, and Hades. [3] Homer and the Bible served as primers from which different generations of school boys were taught to read. [4] Around both there grew up a mass of scholia and commentaries. [5] They were provided with glossaries. [6] Both fell into the hands of allegorists. [7] Both were imitated and supplemented — one with the Homeric Hymns and writings such as the Batrachomyomachia, and the other with apocryphal books. [8] Homer was made available in prose analyses; the Gospel of John was turned into epic hexameters by Nonnus of Panopolis. [9] The manuscripts of both Homer and the Bible were illustrated. [10] Homeric scenes appeared in Pompeian murals; Christian basilicas were decorated with mosaics and frescoes of Biblical episodes." 61/144,145

E. G. Turner points out that Homer was no doubt the most widely read author in antiquity. 92/97

WORK	WHEN WRITTEN	EARLIEST COPY	TIME SPAN	NO. OF COPIES
Homer (*Iliad*)	900 B.C.	400 B.C.	500 yrs.	643
New Testament	40-100 A.D.	125 A.D.	25 yrs.	over 24,000

Geisler and Nix make a comparison of the textual variations between the New Testament documents and ancient works: "Next to the New Testament, there are more extant manuscripts of the *Iliad* (643) than any other book. Both it and the Bible were considered 'sacred,' and both underwent textual changes and criticism of their Greek manuscripts. The New Testament has about 20,000 lines." 32/366

They continue by saying that "the *Iliad* [has] about 15,600. Only 40 lines (or 400 words) of the New Testament are in doubt whereas 764 lines of the *Iliad* are questioned. This five percent textual corruption compares with one-half of one percent of similar emendations in the New Testament.

"The national epic of India, the Mahabharata, has suffered even more corruption. It is about eight times the size of the *Iliad* and the *Odyssey* together, roughly 250,000 lines. Of these, some 26,000 lines are textual corruptions (10 percent)." 32/367

Benjamin Warfield in *Introduction to Textual Criticism of the New Testament* quotes Ezra Abbot's opinion about nineteen-twentieths of the New Testament textual variations, saying that they: ". . . have so little support . . . although there are various readings; and nineteen-twentieths of the remainder are of so little importance that their adoption or rejection would cause no appreciable difference in the sense of the passages where they occur." 100/14

Geisler and Nix make the following comment about how the textual variations are counted: "There is an ambiguity in saying there are some 200,000 variants in the existing manuscripts of the New Testament, since these represent only 10,000 places in the New Testament. If one single word is misspelled in 3,000 different manuscripts, this is counted as 3,000 variants or readings." 32/361

Although he was dealing with fewer manuscripts than we have today, *Philip Schaff* in *Comparison to the Greek Testament and the English Version* concluded that only 400 of the 150,000 variant readings caused doubt about the textual meaning, and only 50 of these were of great significance. Not one of the variations, Schaff says, altered "an article of faith or a precept of duty which is not abundantly sustained by other and undoubted passages, or by the whole tenor of Scripture teaching." 82/177

Fenton John Anthony Hort, whose life work has been with the MSS, says: "The proportion of words virtually accepted on all hands as raised above doubt is very great, not less, on a rough computation, than seven-eighths of the whole. The remaining eighth, therefore, formed in great part by changes of order and other comparative trivialities, constitutes the whole area of criticism.

"If the principles followed in this edition are sound, this area may be very greatly reduced. Recognizing to the full the duty of abstinence from peremptory decision in cases where the evidence leaves the judgment in suspense between two or more readings, we find that, setting aside differences of orthography, the words in our opinion still subject to doubt only make up about one-sixteenth of the whole New Testament. In this second estimate the proportion of comparatively trivial variations is beyond measure larger than in the former; so that the amount of what can in any sense be called substantial variation is but a small fraction of the whole residuary variation, and can hardly form more than a thousandth part of the entire text." 43/2

Geisler and Nix say, concerning the observations of Hort above, that "only about one-eighth of all the variants had any weight, as most of them are merely mechanical matters such as spelling or style. Of the whole, then, only about one-sixtieth rise above 'trivialities,' or can in any sense be called 'substantial variations.' Mathematically this would compute to a text that is 98.33 percent pure." 32/365

Warfield boldly declares that the facts show that the great majority of the New Testament "has been transmitted to us with no, or next to no, variation; and even in the most corrupt form in which it has ever appeared, to use the oft-quoted words of Richard Bentley, 'the real text of the sacred writers is competently exact; . . . nor is one article of faith or moral precept either perverted or lost . . . choose as awkwardly as you will, choose the worst by design, out of the whole lump of readings." 100/14; 85/163

Schaff quotes both Tregelles and Scrivener: "We possess so many MSS, and we are aided by so many versions, that we are never left to the need of conjecture as the means of removing errata." (Tregelles, *Greek New Testament,* "Protegomena," P.X.)

" 'So far,' says Scrivener, 'is the copiousness of our stores from causing doubt or perplexity to the genuine student of Holy Scripture, that it leads him to recognize the more fully its general integrity in the midst of partial variation. What would the thoughtful reader of Eschylus give for the like guidance through the obscurities which vex his patience and mar his enjoyment of that sublime poet?' " 82/182

F. F. Bruce in *The Books and the Parchments* writes that if no objective textual evidence is available to correct an obvious mistake, then "the textual critic must perforce employ the art of conjectural emendation — an art which demands the severest self-discipline. The emendation must commend itself as obviously right, and it must account for the way in which the corruption crept in. In other words, it must be both 'intrinsically probable' and 'transcriptionally probable.' It is doubtful whether there is any reading in the New Testament which requires it to be conjecturally emended. The wealth of attestation is such that the true reading i· almost invariably bound to be preserved by at least one of the thousands of witnesses." 15/179,180

That textual variations do not endanger doctrine is emphatically stated by Sir Frederic Kenyon (one of the great authorities in th· field of New Testament textual criticism): "One word of warni᷉ already referred to, must be emphasized in conclusion. No fundamental doctrine of the Christian faith rests on a disputed reading. . . .

"It cannot be too strongly asserted that in substance the text of the Bible is certain: Especially is this the case with the New Testament. The number of manuscripts of the New Testament, of early translations from it, and of quotations from it in the oldest writers of the Church, is so large that it is practically certain that the true reading of every doubtful passage is preserved in some one or other of these ancient authorities. *This can be said of no other ancient book in the world.*

"Scholars are satisfied that they possess substantially the true text of the principal Greek and Roman writers whose works have come down to us, of Sophocles, of Thucydides, of Cicero, of Virgil; yet our knowledge of their writings depends on a mere handful of manuscripts, whereas the manuscripts of the New Testament are counted by hundreds, and even thousands." 49/23

Gleason Archer, in answering the question about objective evidence, shows that variants or errors in transmission of the text do not affect God's revelation:

"A careful study of the variants (different readings) of the various earliest manuscripts reveals that none of them affects a single doctrine of Scripture. The system of spiritual truth contained in the standard Hebrew text of the Old Testament is not in the slightest altered or compromised by any of the variant readings found in the Hebrew manuscripts of earlier date found in the Dead Sea caves or anywhere else. All that is needed to verify this is to check the register of well-attested variants in Rudolf Kittel's edition of the Hebrew Bible. It is very evident that the vast majority of them are so inconsequential as to leave the meaning of each clause doctrinally unaffected." 10/25

Benjamin Warfield said, "If we compare the present state of the New Testament text with that of any other ancient writing, we must . . . declare it to be marvelously correct. Such has been the care with which the New Testament has been copied — a care which has doubtless grown out of true reverence for its holy words — such has been the providence of God in preserving for His

Church in each and every age a competently exact text of the Scriptures, that not only is the New Testament unrivalled among ancient writings in the purity of its text as actually transmitted and kept in use, but also in the abundance of testimony which has come down to us for castigating its comparatively infrequent blemishes." 100/12,13

The editors of the Revised Standard Version say: "It will be obvious to the careful reader that still in 1946, as in 1881 and 1901, no doctrine of the Christian faith has been affected by the revision, for the simple reason that, out of the thousands of variant readings in the manuscripts, none has turned up thus far that requires a revision of Christian doctrine." 34/42

Burnett H. Streeter believes that because of the great quantity of textual material for the New Testament, "the degree of security that . . . the text has been handed down to us in a reliable form is prima facie very high." 90/33

Frederic G. Kenyon continues in *The Story of the Bible:* "It is reassuring at the end to find that the general result of all these discoveries (of manuscripts) and all this study is to strengthen the proof of the authenticity of the Scriptures, and our conviction that we have in our hands, in substantial integrity, the veritable Word of God." 50/113

Millar Burrows of Yale says: "Another result of comparing New Testament Greek with the language of the papyri is an increase of confidence in the accurate transmission of the text of the New Testament itself." 17/52

Burrows also says that the texts "have been transmitted with remarkable fidelity, so that there need be no doubt whatever regarding the teaching conveyed by them." 17/2

I believe one can logically conclude from the perspective of literary evidence that the New Testament's reliability is far greater than any other record of antiquity.

3C. CHRONOLOGY OF IMPORTANT NEW TESTAMENT MANUSCRIPTS

Dating Procedure: Some of the factors that help determine the age of a MS are: 32/242-246

1. Materials	5. Ornamentation
2. Letter size and form	6. The color of the ink
3. Punctuation	7. The texture and color of parchment
4. Text divisions	

John Rylands' MS (130 A.D.) is located in The John Rylands Library of Manchester, England (oldest extant fragment of the New Testament). "Because of its early date and location (Egypt), some distance from the traditional place of composition (Asia Minor), this portion of the Gospel of John tends to confirm the traditional date of the composition of the Gospel about the end of the 1st century." 32/268

Bruce Metzger speaks of defunct criticism: "Had this little fragment been known during the middle of the past century, that school of New Testament criticism which was inspired by the brilliant Tubingen professor, Ferdinand Christian Baur, could not have argued that the Fourth Gospel was not composed until about the year 160." 62/39

Bodmer Papyrus II (150-200 A.D.) is located in the Bodmer Library of World Literature and contains most of John.

Bruce Metzger says that this MS was "the most important discovery of the N.T. manuscripts since the purchase of the Chester Beatty papyri. . . ." 62/39,40

In his article '*Zur Datierung des Papyrus Bodmer II* (P66),' *Anzeiger der osterreichischen Akademie der Wissenschaften,* phil.-hist, kl., 1960, Nr. 4, p. 12033, "Herbert Hunger, the director of the papyrological collections in the National Library at Vienna, dates 66 earlier, in the middle if not even in the first half of the second century; see his article." 62/39,40

Chester Beatty Papyri (200 A.D.) is located in C. Beatty Museum in Dublin and part is owned by the University of Michigan. This collection contains papyrus codices, three of them containing major portions of the New Testament. 15/182

In *The Bible and Modern Scholarship,* Sir Frederic Kenyon says, "The net result of this discovery — by far the most important since the discovery of the Sinaiticus — is, in fact, to reduce the gap between the earlier manuscripts and the traditional dates of the New Testament books so far that it becomes negligible in any discussion of their authenticity. No other ancient book has anything like such early and plentiful testimony to its text, and no unbiased scholar would deny that the text that has come down to us is substantially sound." 47/20

Diatessaron: meaning "a harmony of four parts." The Greek *dia Tessaron* literally means "through four." 15/195 This was a harmony of the Gospels done by Tatian (about 160 A.D.).

Eusebius in *Ecclesiastical History,* IV, 29 Loeb ed., 1, 397, wrote: ". . . Their former leader Tatian composed in some way a combination and collection of the Gospels, and gave this the name of *THE DIATESSARON,* and this is still extant in some places. . . ." It is believed that Tatian, an Assyrian Christian, was the first to compose a harmony of the Gospels; only a small portion is extant today. 32/318,319

Codex Vaticanus (325-350 A.D.), located in the Vatican Library, contains nearly all of the Bible.

Codex Sinaiticus (350 A.D.) is located in the British Museum. This MS, which contains almost all the New Testament and over half of the Old Testament, was discovered by Dr. Constantin Von Tischendorf in the Mount Sinai Monastery in 1859, presented by the Monastery to the Russian Czar and bought by the British Government and people from the Soviet Union for 100,000 pounds on Christmas Day, 1933.

The discovery of this manuscript is a fascinating story. Bruce Metzger relates the interesting background leading to its discovery:

"In 1844, when he was not yet thirty years of age, Tischendorf, a *Privatdozent* in the University of Leipzig, began an extensive journey through the Near East in search of Biblical manuscripts. While visiting the monastery of St. Catharine at Mount Sinai, he chanced to see some leaves of parchment in a waste-basket full of papers destined to light the oven of the monastery. On examination these proved to be part of a copy of the Septuagint version of the Old Testament, written in an early Greek uncial script. He retrieved from the basket no fewer than forty-three such leaves, and the monk casually remarked that two basket loads of similarly discarded leaves had already been burned up! Later, when Tischendorf was shown other portions of the same codex (containing all of Isaiah and I and II Maccabees), he warned the monks that such things were too valuable to be used to stoke their fires. The forty-three leaves which he was permitted to keep contained portions of I Chronicles, Jeremiah,

Nehemiah, and Esther, and upon returning to Europe he deposited them in the university library at Leipzig, where they still remain. In 1846 he published their contents, naming them the codex Frederico-Augustanus (in honour of the King of Saxony, Frederick Augustus, the discoverer's sovereign and patron)." 62/43

A second visit to the monastery by Tischendorf in 1853 produced no new manuscripts because the monks were suspicious as a result of the enthusiasm for the MS displayed during his first visit in 1844. During a third visit in 1859 under the direction of the Czar of Russia, Alexander II, shortly before leaving, Tischendorf gave the steward of the monastery an edition of the Septuagint that had been published by Tischendorf in Leipzig. "Thereupon the steward remarked that he too had a copy of the Septuagint, and produced from a closet in his cell a manuscript wrapped in a red cloth. There before the astonished scholar's eyes lay the treasure which he had been longing to see. Concealing his feelings, Tischendorf casually asked permission to look at it further that evening. Permission was granted, and upon retiring to his room Tischendorf stayed up all night in the joy of studying the manuscript — for, as he declared in his diary (which as a scholar he kept in Latin), *quippe dormire nefas videbatur* ('it really seemed a sacrilege to sleep')! He soon found that the document contained much more than he had even hoped; for not only was most of the Old Testament there, but also the New Testament was intact and in excellent condition, with the addition of two early Christian works of the second century, the Epistle of Barnabas (previously known only through a very poor Latin translation) and a large portion of the Shepherd of Hermas, hitherto known only by title." 62/44

Codex Alexandrinus (400 A.D.) is located in the British Museum; *Encyclopaedia Britannica* believes it was written in Greek in Egypt. It contains almost the entire Bible.

Codex Ephraemi (400's A.D.) is located in the Bibliotheque Nationale, Paris. The *Encyclopaedia Britannica* says that "its 5th century origin and the evidence it supplies make it important for the text of certain portions of the New Testament." 25/579; 15/183

Every book is represented in the MS except II Thessalonians and II John.

Codex Bezae (450 A.D. plus) is located in the Cambridge Library and contains the Gospels and Acts not only in Greek but also in Latin.

Codex Washingtonensis (or Freericanus) (ca 450) contains the four Gospels. 37/39

Codex Claromontanus (500's A.D.) contains the Pauline Epistles. It is a bilingual MS.

4C. MANUSCRIPT RELIABILITY SUPPORTED BY VARIOUS VERSIONS

Another strong support for textual evidence and accuracy is the ancient versions. For the most part, "ancient literature was rarely translated into another language." 37/45

Christianity from its inception has been a missionary faith.

"The earliest versions of the New Testament were prepared by missionaries to assist in the propagation of the Christian faith among peoples whose native tongue was Syriac, Latin, or Coptic." 62/67

Syriac and Latin versions (translations) of the New Testament were made around 150 A.D. This brings us back very near to the time of the originals.

A (original Text)

150 A.D.

Version (Syriac)

150-250 A.D.

**Various MSS
of Greek
now extant**

Version (Latin)

300-400 A.D.

**Various Copies
of version
now extant**

**Various Copies
of version
now extant**

There are more than 15,000 existing copies of various versions.

1D.   Syriac versions

Old Syriac Version contains four Gospels, copied about the fourth century. It needs to be explained that "Syriac is the name generally given to Christian Aramaic. It is written in a distinctive variation of the Aramaic alphabet." 15/193

Theodore of Mopsuestia (fifth century) wrote, "It has been translated into the tongue of the Syrians." 15/193

Syriac Peshitta. The basic meaning is "simple." It was the standard version, produced around 150-250 A.D. There are more than 350 extant MSS today from the 400's. 32/317

Palestinian Syriac. Most scholars date this version at about 400-450 A.D. (fifth century). 62/68-71

Philoxenian (508 A.D.). Polycarp translated a new Syriac New Testament for Philoxenas, bishop of Mabug. 37/49

Harkleian Syriac. 616 A.D. by Thomas of Harkel.

2D.   Latin versions

Old Latin. There are testimonies from the fourth century to the thirteenth century that in the third century an "old Latin version circulated in North Africa and Europe. . . ."

African Old Latin (Codex Babbiensis) 400 A.D. Metzger says that "E. A. Lowe shows palaeographical marks of it having been copied from a second century papyrus." 62/72-74

Codex Corbiensis (400-500 A.D.) contains the four Gospels.

Codex Vercellensis (360 A.D.).

Codex Palatinus (fifth century A.D.).

Latin Vulgate (meaning "common or popular"). Jerome was the secretary of Damasus, who was the Bishop of Rome. Jerome accomplished the bishop's request for a version between 366-384. 15/201

3D. Coptic (or Egyptian) versions

F. F. Bruce writes that it is probable that the first Egyptian version was translated in the third or fourth century. 15/214

Sahidic. Beginning of the third century. 62/79-80

Bohairic. The editor, Rodalphe Kasser, dates it about the fourth century. 37/50

Middle Egyptian. Fourth or fifth century.

4D. Other early versions

Armenian (400+ A.D.). Seems to have been translated from a Greek Bible obtained from Constantinople.

Gothic. Fourth century.

Georgian. Fifth century.

Ethiopic. Sixth century.

Nubian. Sixth century.

5C. MANUSCRIPT RELIABILITY SUPPORTED BY EARLY CHURCH FATHERS

The Encyclopaedia Britannica says: "When the textual scholar has examined the manuscripts and the versions, he still has not exhausted the evidence for the New Testament text. The writings of the early Christian fathers often reflect a form of text differing from that in one or another manuscript . . . their witness to the text, especially as it corroborates the readings that come from other sources, belongs to the testimony that textual critics must consult before forming their conclusions." 25/579

J. Harold Greenlee says that the quotations of the Scripture in the works of the early Christian writers "are so extensive that the N. T. could virtually be reconstructed from them without the use of New Testament manuscripts." 37/54

Bruce Metzger reiterates the above, in reference to the quotations in the commentaries, sermons, etc., by saying: "Indeed, so extensive are these citations that if all other sources for our knowledge of the text of the New Testament were destroyed, they would be sufficient alone for the reconstruction of practically the entire New Testament." 62/86

Sir David Dalrymple was wondering about the preponderance of Scripture in early writing when someone asked him, "Suppose that the New Testament had been destroyed, and every copy of it lost by the end of the third century, could it have been collected together again from the writings of the Fathers of the second and third centuries?"

After a great deal of investigation Dalrymple concluded:

"Look at those books. You remember the question about the New Testament and the Fathers? That question roused my curiosity, and as I possessed all the existing works of the Fathers of the second and third centuries, I commenced to search, and up to this time I have found the entire New Testament, except eleven verses." 58/35,36

A Precaution: Joseph Angus in *The Bible Handbook*, p. 56, gives several limitations of the early patristic writings:

1. Quotes are sometimes used without verbal accuracy.
2. Some copyists were prone to mistakes or to intentional alteration.

Clement of Rome (A.D. 95). Origen in *De Principus*, Book II, Chapter 3, calls him a disciple of the apostles. 8/28

Tertullian in *Against Heresies*, Chapter 23, writes that he [Clement] was appointed by Peter.

Irenaeus continues in *Against Heresies*, Book III, Chapter 3, that he "had the preaching of the Apostles still echoing in his ears and their doctrine in front of his eyes."

He quotes from:

Matthew	I Corinthians
Mark	I Peter
Luke	Hebrews
Acts	Titus

Ignatius (A.D. 70-110) was the Bishop of Antioch and was martyred. He knew well the apostles. His seven epistles contain quotations from:

Matthew	Ephesians	I and II Thessalonians
John	Philippians	I and II Timothy
Acts	Galatians	I Peter
Romans	Colossians	
I Corinthians	James	

Polycarp (A.D. 70-156), martyred at 86 years of age, was Bishop of Smyrna and a disciple of the apostle John.

Among others who quoted from the New Testament were Barnabas (ca A.D. 70), Hermas (ca A.D. 95), Tatian (ca A.D. 170), and Irenaeus (ca A.D. 170).

Clement of Alexandria (A.D. 150-212). 2,400 of his quotes are from all but three books of the New Testament.

Tertullian (A.D. 160-220) was a presbyter of the Church in Carthage and quotes the New Testament more than 7,000 times, of which 3,800 are from the Gospels.

Hippolytus (A.D. 170-235) has more than 1,300 references.

Justin Martyr (A.D. 133) battled the heretic Marcion.

Origen (A.D. 185-253 or 254). This vociferous writer compiled more than 6,000 works. He lists more than 18,000 New Testament quotes. 32/353

Cyprian (died A.D. 258) was bishop of Carthage. Uses approximately 740 Old Testament citations and 1,030 from the New Testament.

Geisler and Nix rightly conclude that "a brief inventory at this point will reveal that there were some 32,000 citations of the New Testament prior to the time of the Council of Nicea (325). These 32,000 quotations are by no means exhaustive, and they do not even include the fourth century writers. Just adding the number of references used by one other writer, Eusebius, who flourished prior to and contemporary with the Council at Nicea will bring the total citations of the New Testament to over 36,000." 32/353,354

To all the above you could add Augustine, Amabius, Laitantius, Chrysostom, Jerome, Gaius Romanus, Athanasius, Ambrose of Milan, Cyril of Alexandria, Ephraem the Syrian, Hilary of Poitiers, Gregory of Nyssa, etc., etc., etc.

Leo Jaganay, writing of the patristic quotations of the New Testament, writes: "Of the considerable volumes of unpublished material that Dean Burgon left when he died, of special note is his index of New Testament citations by the church fathers of antiquity. It consists of sixteen thick volumes to be found in the British Museum, and contains 86,489 quotations." 44/48

EARLY PATRISTIC QUOTATIONS OF THE NEW TESTAMENT*

WRITER	Gospels	Acts	Pauline Epistles	General Epistles	Revelation	Total
Justin Martyr	268	10	43	6	3 (266 allusions)	330
Irenaeus	1,038	194	499	23	65	1,819
Clement Alex.	1,017	44	1,127	207	11	2,406
Origen	9,231	349	7,778	399	165	17,922
Tertullian	3,822	502	2,609	120	205	7,258
Hippolytus	734	42	387	27	188	1,378
Eusebius	3,258	211	1,592	88	27	5,176
Totals	19,368	1,352	14,035	870	664	36,289

*14/357

6C. MANUSCRIPT RELIABILITY SUPPORTED BY LECTIONARIES

This is a greatly neglected area, and yet the second largest group of N. T. Greek MSS is the lectionaries.

Bruce Metzger gives the background of the lectionaries: "Following the custom of the synagogue, according to which portions of the Law and the Prophets were read at divine service each Sabbath day, the Christian Church adopted the practice of reading passages from the New Testament books at services of worship. A regular system of lessons from the Gospels and Epistles was developed, and the custom arose of arranging these according to a fixed order of Sundays and other holy days of the Christian year." 62/30

Metzger continues that 2,135 have been catalogued, but as of yet the majority still await critical analysis.

J. Harold Greenlee states that "the earliest lectionary fragments are from the sixth century, while complete MSS date from the eighth century and later." 37/45

The lectionaries usually were rather conservative and used older texts, and this makes them very valuable in textual criticism. 62/31

3B. The Bibliographical Test for the Reliability of the Old Testament

In the case of the O. T. we do not have the abundance of close MS authority as in the N. T. Until the recent discovery of the Dead Sea Scrolls, the oldest complete extant Hebrew MS was around 900 A.D. This made a time gap of 1,300 years (Hebrew O. T. completed about 400 B.C.). At first sight it would appear that the O. T. is no more reliable than other ancient literature. (See page 42.)

With the discovery of the Dead Sea Scrolls, a number of O. T. manuscripts have been found which scholars date before the time of Christ.

When the facts are known and compared, there is an overwhelming abundance of reasons for believing that the MSS we possess are trustworthy. We shall see, as Sir Frederic Kenyon put it, that "the Christian can take the whole Bible in his hand and say without fear or hesitation that he holds in it the true Word of God, handed down without essential loss from generation to generation throughout the centuries." 49/23

First, in order to see the uniqueness of the Scripture in its reliability, one needs to examine the extreme care in which the copyists transcribed the O. T. MSS.

1C. THE TALMUDISTS (A. D. 100-500)

During this period a great deal of time was spent in cataloging Hebrew civil and canonical law. The Talmudists had quite an intricate system for transcribing synagogue scrolls.

Samuel Davidson describes some of the disciplines of the Talmudists in regard to the Scriptures. These minute regulations (I am going to use the numbering incorporated by Geisler and Nix) are as follows: "[1] A synagogue roll must be written on the skins of clean animals, [2] prepared for the particular use of the synagogue by a Jew. [3] These must be fastened together with strings taken from clean animals. [4] Every skin must contain a certain number of columns, equal throughout the entire codex. [5] The length of each column must not extend over less than 48 or more than 60 lines; and the breadth must consist of thirty letters. [6] The whole copy must be first-lined; and if three words be written without a line, it is worthless. [7] The ink should be black, neither red, green, nor any other colour, and be prepared according to a definite recipe. [8] An authentic copy must be the exemplar, from which the transcriber ought not in the least deviate. [9] No word or letter, not even a yod, must be written from memory, the scribe not having looked at the codex before him . . . [10] Between every consonant the space of a hair or thread must intervene; [11] between every new parashah, or section, the breadth of nine consonants; [12] between every book, three lines. [13] The fifth book of Moses must terminate exactly with a line; but the rest need not do so. [14] Besides this, the copyist must sit in full Jewish dress, [15] wash his whole body, [16] not begin to write the name of God with a pen newly dipped in ink, [17] and should a king address him while writing that name he must take no notice of him." 21/89; 32/241

Davidson adds that "the rolls in which these regulations are not observed are condemned to be buried in the ground or burned; or they are banished to the schools, to be used as reading-books."

Why don't we have more old MSS? The very absence of ancient MSS, when the rules and accuracies of the copyists are considered, confirms the reliability of the copies we have today.

Gleason Archer, in comparing the manuscript variations of the Hebrew text with pre-Christian literature such as the Egyptian Book of the Dead, states that it is amazing that the Hebrew text does not have the phenomenon of discrepancy and MS change of other literature of the same age. He writes:

"Even though the two copies of Isaiah discovered in Qumran Cave 1 near the Dead Sea in 1947 were a thousand years earlier than the oldest dated manuscript previously known (A.D. 980), they proved to be word for word identical with our standard Hebrew Bible in more than 95 percent of the text. The 5 percent of variation consisted chiefly of obvious slips of the pen and variations in spelling. Even those Dead Sea fragments of Deuteronomy and Samuel which point to a different manuscript family from that which underlies our received Hebrew text do not indicate any differences in doctrine or teaching. They do not affect the message of revelation in the slightest." 10/25

The Talmudists were so convinced that when they finished transcribing a MS they had an exact duplicate, that they would give the new copy equal authority.

Frederic Kenyon in *Our Bible and the Ancient Manuscripts* expands on the above and the destruction of older copies: "The same extreme care which was devoted to the transcription of manuscripts is also at the bottom of the disappearance of the earlier copies. When a manuscript had been copied with the exactitude prescribed by the Talmud, and had been duly verified, it was accepted as authentic and regarded as being of equal value with any other copy. If all were equally correct, *age gave no advantage to a manuscript;* on the contrary, age was a positive disadvantage, since a manuscript was liable to become defaced or damaged in the lapse of time. A damaged or imperfect copy was at once condemned as unfit for use.

"Attached to each synagogue was a 'Gheniza,' or lumber cupboard, in which defective manuscripts were laid aside; and from these receptacles some of the oldest manuscripts now extant have in modern times been recovered. Thus, far from regarding an older copy of the Scriptures as more valuable, the Jewish habit has been to prefer the newer, as being the most perfect and free from damage. The older copies, once consigned to the 'Gheniza,' naturally perished, either from neglect or from being deliberately burned when the 'Gheniza' became overcrowded.

"The absence of very old copies of the Hebrew Bible need not, therefore, either surprise or disquiet us. If, to the causes already enumerated, we add the repeated persecutions (involving much destruction of property) to which the Jews have been subject, the disappearance of the ancient manuscripts is adequately accounted for, and those which remain may be accepted as preserving that which alone they profess to preserve — namely, the Massoretic text." 49/43

"Reverence for the Scriptures and regard for the purity of the sacred text did not first originate after the fall of Jerusalem." 36/173

One can go back as far as Ezra 7:6, 10 where Ezra is said to be "a ready scribe" (KJV). He was a professional, skilled in the Scripture.

2C.   THE MASSORETIC PERIOD (A.D. 500-900)

The Massoretes (from *massora*, "Tradition") accepted the laborious job of editing the text and standardizing it. Their headquarters was in Tiberias. The text which the Massoretes concluded with is called the "Massoretic" text. This resultant text had had vowel points added in order to insure proper pronunciation. This Massoretic text is the standard Hebrew text today.

The Massoretes were well disciplined and treated the text "with the greatest imaginable reverence, and devised a complicated system of safeguards against scribal slips. They counted, for example, the number of times each letter of the alphabet occurs in each book; they pointed out the middle letter of the Pentateuch and the middle letter of the whole Hebrew Bible, and made even more detailed calculations than these. 'Everything countable seems to be counted,' says Wheeler Robinson, and they made up mnemonics by which the various totals might be readily remembered." 15/117

Sir Frederic Kenyon says: "Besides recording varieties of reading, tradition, or conjecture, the Massoretes undertook a number of calculations which do not enter into the ordinary sphere of textual criticism. They numbered the verses, words, and letters of every book. They calculated the middle word and the middle letter of each. They enumerated verses which contained all the letters of the alphabet, or a certain number of them; and so on. These trivialities, as we may rightly consider them, had yet the effect of securing minute attention to the precise transmission of the text; and they are but an excessive manifestation of a respect for the sacred Scriptures which in itself deserves nothing but praise. The Massoretes were indeed anxious that not one jot nor tittle, not one smallest letter nor one tiny part of a letter, of the Law should pass away or be lost." 49/38

Flavius Josephus, the Jewish historian, writes: "We have given practical proof of our reverence for our own Scriptures. For, although such long ages have now passed, no one has ventured either to add, or to remove, or to alter a syllable; and it is an instinct with every Jew, from the day of his birth, to regard them as the decrees of God, to abide by them, and, if need be, cheerfully to die for them. Time and again ere now the sight has been witnessed of prisoners enduring tortures and death in every form in the theatres, rather than utter a single word against the laws and the allied documents." 45/179,180

Josephus continues by making a comparison between the Hebrew respect for Scripture and the Greek regard for their literature: "What Greek would endure as much for the same cause? Even to save the entire collection of his nation's writings from destruction he would not face the smallest personal injury. For to the Greeks they are mere stories improvised according to the fancy of their authors; and in this estimate even of the older historians they are quite justified, when they see some of their own contemporaries venturing to describe events in which they bore no part, without taking the trouble to seek information from those who know the facts." 45/181

3C.   QUOTATIONS AND OBSERVATIONS ON THE RELIABILITY OF THE OLD TESTAMENT

Robert Dick Wilson's brilliant observations take the veracity and trustworthiness of Scriptures back to Old Testament times: "In 144 cases of transliteration from Egyptian, Assyrian, Babylonian and Moabite into Hebrew and in 40 cases of the opposite, or 184 in all, the evidence shows that for 2300 to 3900 years the text of the proper names in the Hebrew Bible has been transmitted with the most minute accuracy. That the original scribes should have written them with such close conformity to correct philological principles is a wonderful proof of their thorough care and scholarship; further, that the Hebrew text should have been transmitted by copyists through so many centuries is a phenomenon unequaled in the history of literature." 102/71

Wilson adds: "There are about forty of these kings living from 2000 B.C. to 400 B.C. Each appears in chronological order '. . . with reference to the kings of the same country and with respect to the kings of other countries . . . no stronger evidence for the substantial accuracy of the Old Testament records could possibly be imagined, than this collection of kings.' Mathematically, it is one chance in 750,000,000,000,000,000,000,000,000,000 that this accuracy is mere circumstance." 102/70,71

Because of the evidence Wilson concludes:

"The proof that the copies of the original documents have been handed down with substantial correctness for more than 2,000 years cannot be denied. That the copies in existence 2,000 years ago had been in like manner handed down from the originals is not merely possible, but, as we have shown, is rendered probable by the analogies of Babylonian documents now existing of which we have both originals and copies, thousands of years apart, and of scores of papyri which show when compared with our modern editions of the classics that only minor changes of the text have taken place in more than 2,000 years and especially by the scientific and demonstrable accuracy with which the proper spelling of the names of kings and of the numerous foreign terms embedded in the Hebrew text has been transmitted to us." 102/85

F. F. Bruce states that "the consonantal text of the Hebrew Bible which the Massoretes edited had been handed down to their time with conspicuous fidelity over a period of nearly a thousand years." 15/178

William Green concludes that "it may safely be said that no other work of antiquity has been so accurately transmitted." 36/181

Concerning the accuracy of the transmission of the Hebrew text, Atkinson, who was Under-Librarian of the library at Cambridge University, says it is "little short of miraculous."

Rabbi Aquiba, second century A.D., with a desire to produce an exact text, is credited with saying that "the accurate transmission (Massoreth) of the text is a fence for the Torah." 40/211

4C.   THE HEBREW TEXT

Cairo Codex (A.D. 895) is located in the British Museum. It was produced by the Massoretic Moses ben Asher family. Contains both latter and former prophets. 15/115,116

Codex of the Prophets of Leningrad (A.D. 916) contains Isaiah, Jeremiah, Ezekiel and the twelve minor prophets.

The earliest complete MS of the Old Testament is the *Codex Babylonicus Petropalitanus* (A.D. 1008) located in Leningrad. It was prepared from a corrected text of Rabbi Aaron ben Moses ben Asher before 1000 A.D. 32/250

Aleppo Codex (A.D. 900+) is an exceptionally valuable MS. It once was thought lost, but in 1958 was rediscovered. It did not escape damage.

British Museum Codex (A.D. 950) contains part of Genesis through Deuteronomy.

Reuchlin Codex of the Prophets (A.D. 1105). The preparation of this text was done by the Massorete ben Naphtali.

5C.   THE WITNESS OF THE DEAD SEA SCROLLS TO THE RELIABILITY OF THE HEBREW SCRIPTURES

The big question was asked first by Sir Frederic Kenyon, "Does this

Hebrew text, which we call Massoretic, and which we have shown to descend from a text drawn up about A.D. 100, faithfully represent the Hebrew Text as originally written by the authors of the Old Testament books?" 49/47

The Dead Sea Scrolls give us the explicit and positive answer.

The problem before the discovery of the Dead Sea Scrolls was, "How accurate are the copies we have today compared to the text of the first century?" Because the text has been copied over many times, can we trust it?

What are the Dead Sea Scrolls?

The Scrolls are made up of some 40,000 inscribed fragments. From these fragments more than 500 books have been reconstructed.

Many extra-biblical books and fragments were discovered that shed light on the religious community of Qumran. Such writings as the "Zadokite documents," a "Rule of the Community" and the "Manual of Discipline" help us to understand the purpose of daily Qumran life. In the various caves are some very helpful commentaries on the Scriptures.

How were the Dead Sea Scrolls found?

Here I would like to quote Ralph Earle, who gives a vivid and concise answer to how the Scrolls were found:

"The story of this discovery is one of the most fascinating tales of modern times. In February or March of 1947 a Bedouin shepherd boy named Muhammad was searching for a lost goat. He tossed a stone into a hole in a cliff on the west side of the Dead Sea, about eight miles south of Jericho. To his surprise he heard the sound of shattering pottery. Investigating, he discovered an amazing sight. On the floor of the cave were several large jars containing leather scrolls, wrapped in linen cloth. Because the jars were carefully sealed, the scrolls had been preserved in excellent condition for nearly 1,900 years. (They were evidently placed there in A.D. 68.)

"Five of the scrolls found in Dead Sea Cave I, as it is now called, were bought by the archbishop of the Syrian Orthodox Monastery at Jerusalem. Meanwhile, three other scrolls were purchased by Professor Sukenik of the Hebrew University there.

"When the scrolls were first discovered, no publicity was given to them. In November of 1947, two days after Professor Sukenik purchased three scrolls and two jars from the cave, he wrote in his diary: 'It may be that this is one of the greatest finds ever made in Palestine, a find we never so much as hoped for.' But these significant words were not published at the time.

"Fortunately, in February of 1948, the archbishop, who could not read Hebrew, phoned the American School of Oriental Research in Jerusalem and told about the scrolls. By good providence, the acting director of the school at the moment was a young scholar named John Trever, who was also an excellent amateur photographer. With arduous, dedicated labor he photographed each column of the great Isaiah scroll, which is 24 feet long and 10 inches high. He developed the plates himself and sent a few prints by airmail to Dr. W. F. Albright of Johns Hopkins University, who was widely recognized as the dean of American biblical archaeologists. By return airmail Albright wrote: 'My heartiest congratulations on the greatest manuscript discovery of modern times! . . . What an absolutely incredible find! And there can happily not be the slightest doubt in the world about the genuineness of the manuscript.' He dated it about 100 B.C." 23/48,49

Trever quotes more of Albright's opinions: "There is no doubt in my mind that the script is more archaic than the Nash papyrus . . . I should prefer a date around 100 B.C. . . ." 32/260

The Value of the Scrolls

The oldest complete Hebrew MSS we possessed were from 900 A.D. on. How could we be sure of their accurate transmission since the time of Christ in 32 A.D.? Thanks to archaeology and the Dead Sea Scrolls, we now know. One of the scrolls found was a complete MS of the Hebrew text of Isaiah. It is dated by paleographers around 125 B.C. This MS is more than 1,000 years older than any MS we previously possessed.

The impact of this discovery is in the exactness of the Isaiah scroll (125 B.C.) with the Massoretic text of Isaiah (916 A.D.) 1,000 years later. This demonstrates the unusual accuracy of the copyists of the Scripture over a thousand-year period.

"Of the 166 words in Isaiah 53, there are only seventeen letters in question. Ten of these letters are simply a matter of spelling, which does not affect the sense. Four more letters are minor stylistic changes, such as conjunctions. The remaining three letters comprise the word 'light,' which is added in verse 11, and does not affect the meaning greatly. Furthermore, this word is supported by the LXX and IQ Is. Thus, in one chapter of 166 words, there is only one word (three letters) in question after a thousand years of transmission — and this word does not significantly change the meaning of the passage." 32/263

F. F. Bruce says, "An incomplete scroll of Isaiah, found along with the other in the first Qumran cave, and conveniently distinguished as 'Isaiah B,' agrees even more closely with the Massoretic text." 15/123

Gleason Archer states that the Isaiah copies of the Qumran community "proved to be word for word identical with our standard Hebrew Bible in more than 95 percent of the text. The 5 percent of variation consisted chiefly of obvious slips of the pen and variations in spelling." 10/19

Millar Burrows, cited by Geisler and Nix, concludes: "It is a matter of wonder that through something like a thousand years the text underwent so little alteration. As I said in my first article on the scroll, 'Herein lies its chief importance, supporting the fidelity of the Massoretic tradition.' " 32/261

6C. THE SEPTUAGINT SUBSTANTIATES THE GENUINENESS OF THE HEBREW TEXT

The Jews were scattered from their homeland and there was a need of the Scriptures in the common language of that day. Septuagint (meaning "seventy" and usually abbreviated by use of the Roman numerals LXX) was a name given to the Greek translation of the Hebrew Scriptures in the reign of King Ptolemy Philadelphia of Egypt (285-246 B.C.).

F. F. Bruce gives an interesting rendering of the origin of the name for this translation. Concerning a letter purporting to be written around 250 B.C. (more realistically a short time before 100 B.C.) by Aristeas, a court official of King Ptolemy, to his brother Philocrates, Bruce states:

"Ptolemy was renowned as a patron of literature and it was under him that the great library at Alexandria, one of the world's cultural wonders for 900 years, was inaugurated. The letter describes how

Demetrius of Phalerum, said to have been Ptolemy's librarian, aroused the king's interest in the Jewish Law and advised him to send a delegation to the high priest, Eleazar, at Jerusalem. The high priest chose as translators six elders from each of the twelve tribes of Israel and sent them to Alexandria, along with a specially accurate and beautiful parchment of the Torah. The elders were royally dined and wined, and proved their wisdom in debate; then they took up their residence in a house on the island of Pharos (the island otherwise famed for its lighthouse), where in seventy-two days they completed their task of translating the Pentateuch into Greek, presenting an agreed version as the result of conference and comparison." 15/146,147

The LXX, being very close to the Massoretic Text (A.D. 916) we have today, helps to establish the reliability of its transmission through 1,300 years. The greatest divergence of the LXX from the Massoretic text is Jeremiah.

The LXX and the scriptural citations found in the apocryphal books of Ecclesiasticus, the Book of Jubilees, etc., give evidence that the Hebrew text today is substantially the same as the text about 300 B.C.

Geisler and Nix, in their most helpful work, *A General Introduction to the Bible*, give four important contributions of the Septuagint. "[1] It bridged the religious gap between the Hebrew- and Greek-speaking peoples, as it met the needs of the Alexandrian Jews, [2] it bridged the historical gap between the Hebrew Old Testament of the Jews and the Greek-speaking Christians who would use it with their New Testament, [3] and it provided a precedent for missionaries to make translations of the Scriptures into various languages and dialects; [4] it bridges the textual criticism gap by its substantial agreement with the Hebrew Old Testament text (Aleph, A, B, C, et al.)." 32/308

F. F. Bruce gives several reasons why the Jews lost interest in the Septuagint:
1. ". . . From the first century A.D. onwards the Christians adopted it as their version of the Old Testament and used it freely in their propagation and defense of the Christian faith. 15/150
2. "Another reason for the Jews' loss of interest in the Septuagint lies in the fact that about A.D. 100 a revised standard text was established for the Hebrew Bible by Jewish scholars. . . ." 15/151

7C. SAMARITAN TEXT (fifth century B.C.)

This text contains the Pentateuch and is valuable to determine textual readings. Bruce says that "the variations between the Samaritan Pentateuch and the Massoretic edition [A.D. 916] of these books are quite insignificant by comparison with the area of agreement." 15/122

8C. THE TARGUMS (appear in written form — copies, about A.D. 500)

Basic meaning is "interpretation." They are paraphrases of the Old Testament.

After the Jews were taken into captivity, the Chaldean language took over for Hebrew. Therefore the Jews needed the Scriptures in the spoken language.

The chief Targums are (1) *The Targum of Onkelas* (60 B.C., some say by Onkelas, a disciple of the great Jewish scholar, Hillel). Contains Hebrew text of the Pentateuch. (2) *The Targum of Jonathon Ben Uzziel* (30 B.C.?). Contains the historical books and the Prophets.

F. F. Bruce gives more interesting background on the Targums:

". . . The practice of accompanying the public reading of the Scriptures in the synagogues by an oral paraphrase in the Aramaic vernacular grew up in the closing centuries B.C. Naturally, when Hebrew was becoming less and less familiar to the ordinary people as a spoken language, it was necessary that they should be provided with an interpretation of the text of Scripture in a language which they did know, if they were to understand what was read. The official charged with giving this oral paraphrase was called a methurgeman (translator or interpreter) and the paraphrase itself was called a targum.

". . . Methurgeman . . . was not allowed to read his interpretation out of a roll, as the congregation might mistakenly think he was reading the original Scriptures. With a view to accuracy, no doubt, it was further laid down that not more than one verse of the Pentateuch and not more than three verses of the Prophets might be translated at one time.

"In due course these Targums were committed to writing." 15/133

What value are the Targums?

J. Anderson in *The Bible, the Word of God* states their value saying: "The great utility of the earlier Targums consists in their vindicating the genuineness of the Hebrew text, by proving that it was the same at the period the Targums were made, as it exists among us at the present day." 8/17

9C.   THE MISHNAH (A.D. 200)

The meaning is "explanation, teaching." Contains a collection of Jewish traditions and exposition of the oral law. Written in Hebrew and often regarded as the Second Law. 32/306

The scriptural quotations are very similar to the Massoretic text and witness to its reliability.

10C.   THE GEMARAS (Palestinian A.D. 200; Babylonian A.D. 500)

These commentaries (written in Aramaic) that grew up around the Mishnah contribute to the textual reliability of the Massoretic text.

The Mishnah plus the Babylonian Gemara make up the *Babylonian Talmud.*

Mishnah + Bab. Gemara = Babylonian Talmud
Mishnah + Palest. Gemara = Palestinian Talmud

11C.   THE MIDRASH (100 B.C.-A.D. 300)

This was made up of doctrinal studies of the Old Testament Hebrew text. The Midrash quotations are substantially Massoretic.

12C.   THE HEXAPLA (sixfold)

Origen's (A.D. 185-254) production of a harmony of the Gospels in six columns: texts of the LXX, Aquila, Theodation, Symmachus, Hebrew in Hebrew letters and in Greek letters.

The Hexapla, plus writings of Josephus, Philo and the Zadokite Documents (Dead Sea Qumran community literature), "bear witness to the existence of a text quite similar to the Massoretic [text] from A.D. 40 to 100." 85/148

4B.   The Internal Test for Reliability of the Scriptures

1C.   BENEFIT OF THE DOUBT

On this test John Warwick Montgomery writes that literary critics still follow Aristotle's dictum that "the benefit of the doubt is to be given to the document itself, not arrogated by the critic to himself." 64/29

Therefore, "one must listen to the claims of the document under analysis, and not assume fraud or error unless the author disqualified himself by contradictions or known factual inaccuracies." 64/29

Horn amplifies this, saying: "Think for a moment about what needs to be demonstrated concerning a 'difficulty' in order to transfer it into the category of a valid argument against doctrine. Certainly much more is required than the mere appearance of a contradiction. First, we must be certain that we have correctly understood the passage, the sense in which it uses words or numbers. Second, that we possess all available knowledge in this matter. Third, that no further light can possibly be thrown on it by advancing knowledge, textual research, archaeology, etc.

"... Difficulties do not constitute objections," adds Robert Horn. "Unsolved problems are not of necessity errors. This is not to minimize the area of difficulty; it is to see it in perspective. Difficulties are to be grappled with and problems are to drive us to seek clearer light; but until such time as we have total and final light on any issue we are in no position to affirm, 'Here is a proven error, an unquestionable objection to an infallible Bible.' It is common knowledge that countless 'objections' have been fully resolved since this century began." 42/86,87

2C. PRIMARY SOURCE VALUE

They wrote as eyewitnesses or from first-hand information:

Luke 1:1-3 — "Inasmuch as many have undertaken to compile an account of the things accomplished among us, just as those who from the beginning were eyewitnesses and servants of the Word have handed them down to us, it seemed fitting for me as well, having investigated everything carefully from the beginning, to write it out for you in consecutive order, most excellent Theophilus."

II Peter 1:16 — "For we did not follow cleverly devised tales when we made known to you the power and coming of our Lord Jesus Christ, but we were eyewitnesses of His majesty."

I John 1:3 — "... What we have seen and heard we proclaim to you also, that you also may have fellowship with us; and indeed our fellowship is with the Father, and with His Son Jesus Christ."

Acts 2:22 — " 'Men of Israel, listen to these words: Jesus the Nazarene, a man attested to you by God with miracles and wonders and signs which God performed through Him in your midst, just as you yourselves know. . . .' "

John 19:35 — "And he who has seen has borne witness, and his witness is true; and he knows that he is telling the truth, so that you also may believe."

Luke 3:1 — "Now in the fifteenth year of the reign of Tiberius Caesar, when Pontius Pilate was governor of Judea, and Herod was tetrarch of Galilee, and his brother Phillip was tetrarch of the region of Ituraea and Trachonitis, and Lysanias was tetrarch of Abilene. . . ."

Acts 26:24-26 — "And while Paul was saying this in his defense, Festus said in a loud voice, 'Paul, you are out of your mind! Your great learning is driving you mad.' But Paul said, 'I am not out of my mind, most excellent Festus, but I utter words of sober truth. For the king knows about these matters, and I speak to him also with confidence, since I am persuaded that none of these things escape his notice; for this has not been done in a corner.' "

F. F. Bruce, the Rylands Professor of Biblical Criticism and Exegesis at the University of Manchester, says, concerning *the primary-source value of the New Testament records:*

"The earliest preachers of the gospel knew the value of . . . first-hand testimony, and appealed to it time and again. 'We are witnesses of these things,' was their constant and confident assertion. And it can have been by no means so easy as some writers seem to think to invent words and deeds of Jesus in those early years, when so many of His disciples were about, who could remember what had and had not happened.

"And it was not only friendly eyewitnesses that the early preachers had to reckon with; there were others less well disposed who were also conversant with the main facts of the ministry and death of Jesus. The disciples could not afford to risk inaccuracies (not to speak of willful manipulation of the facts), which would at once be exposed by those who would be only too glad to do so. On the contrary, one of the strong points in the original apostolic preaching is the confident appeal to the knowledge of the hearers; they not only said, 'We are witnesses of these things,' but also, 'As you yourselves also know' (Acts 2:22). Had there been any tendency to depart from the facts in any material respect, the possible presence of hostile witnesses in the audience would have served as a further corrective." 16/33, 44-46

3C. COMPETENT PRIMARY SOURCE MATERIAL

The New Testament must be regarded by scholars today as a competent primary source document from the first century. 64/34,35

CONSERVATIVE DATING

Paul's Letters	A.D. 50-66	(Hiebert)
Matthew	A.D. 70-80	(Harrison)
Mark	A.D. 50-60	(Harnak)
	A.D. 58-65	(T. W. Manson)
Luke	early 60's	(Harrison)
John	A.D. 80-100	(Harrison)

LIBERAL DATING

Paul's Letters	A.D. 50-100	(Kümmel)
Matthew	A.D. 80-100	(Kümmel)
Mark	A.D. 70	(Kümmel)
Luke	A.D. 70-90	(Kümmel)
John	A.D. 170	(Baur)
	A.D. 90-100	(Kümmel)

Figures on above charts are from the following sources: Werner Georg Kümmel's *Introduction to the New Testament*, translated by Howard Clark Kee, Abingdon Press, 1973; Everett Harrison's *Introduction to the New Testament*, William B. Eerdmans Publishing Co., 1971; D. Edmond Hiebert's *Introduction to the New Testament*, Vol. II, Moody Press, 1977; writings and lectures by T. W. Manson and F. C. Baur.

William Foxwell Albright, who was one of the world's foremost biblical archaeologists, said:

"We can already say emphatically that there is no longer any solid basis for dating any book of the New Testament after about A.D. 80, two full generations before the date between 130 and 150 given by the more radical New Testament critics of today." 7/136

He reiterates this in an interview for *Christianity Today,* 18 Jan. 1963: "In my opinion, every book of the New Testament was written by a baptized Jew between the forties and the eighties of the first century A.D. (very probably sometime between about A.D. 50 and 75)."

Albright concludes: "Thanks to the Qumran discoveries, the New Testament proves to be in fact what it was formerly believed to be: the teaching of Christ and his immediate followers between cir. 25 and cir. 80 A.D." 5/23

Many of the liberal scholars are being forced to consider earlier dates for the New Testament. Dr. John A. T. Robinson's conclusions in his new book *Redating the New Testament* are startlingly radical. His research led to the conviction that the whole of the New Testament was written before the Fall of Jerusalem in A.D. 70. 79

5B.   External Evidence Test for Reliability of Scripture

1C.   SUBSTANTIATING AUTHENTICITY

"Do other historical materials confirm or deny the internal testimony provided by the documents themselves?" 64/31

In other words, what sources are there apart from the literature under analysis that substantiate its accuracy, reliability and authenticity?

2C.   SUPPORTING EVIDENCE OF EXTRA-BIBLICAL AUTHORS

Eusebius, in his *Ecclesiastical History III.39,* preserves writings of Papias, the bishop of Heirapolis (130 A.D.) which Papias got from the Elder (apostle John):

"The Elder used to say this also: 'Mark, having been the interpreter of Peter, wrote down accurately all that he (Peter) mentioned, whether sayings or doings of Christ, not, however, in order. For he was neither a hearer nor a companion of the Lord; but afterwards, as I said, he accompanied Peter, who adapted his teachings as necessity required, not as though he were making a compilation of the sayings of the Lord. So then Mark made no mistake, writing down in this way some things as he (Peter) mentioned them; for he paid attention to this one thing, not to omit anything that he had heard, not to include any false statement among them.' "

Papias also comments about the Gospel of Matthew: "Matthew recorded the oracles in the Hebrew (i.e., Aramaic) tongue."

Irenaeus, Bishop of Lyons (A.D. 180), who was a student of Polycarp, Bishop of Smyrna; martyred in 156 A.D., had been a Christian for 86 years, and was a disciple of John the Apostle. He wrote:

"So firm is the ground upon which these Gospels rest, that the very heretics themselves bear witness to them, and, starting from these [documents], each one of them endeavours to establish his own particular doctrine" *(Against Heresies III).*

The four Gospels had become so axiomatic in the Christian world that Irenaeus can refer to it [fourfold Gospel] as an established and recognized fact as obvious as the four cardinal points of the compass:

"For as there are four quarters of the world in which we live, and four universal winds, and as the Church is dispersed over all the earth, and the gospel is the pillar and base of the Church and the breath of life, so it is natural that it should have four pillars, breathing immortality from every quarter and kindling the life of men anew. Whence it is manifest that the Word, the architect of all things, who sits upon the cherubim and holds all things together, having been manifested to men, has given us the gospel in fourfold form, but held together by one Spirit.

"Matthew published his Gospel," continues Irenaeus, "among the Hebrews (i.e. Jews) in their own tongue, when Peter and Paul were preaching the gospel in Rome and founding the church there. After their departure (i.e. death, which strong tradition places at the time of the Neronian persecution in 64), Mark, the disciple and interpreter of Peter, himself handed down to us in writing the substance of Peter's preaching. Luke, the follower of Paul, set down in a book the gospel preached by his teacher. Then John, the disciple of the Lord, who also leaned on His breast (this is a reference to John 13:25 and 21:20), himself produced his Gospel, while he was living at Ephesus in Asia."

Clement of Rome (ca A.D. 95) uses Scripture as being reliable and authentic.

Ignatius (A.D. 70-110). He was Bishop of Antioch and was martyred for his faith in Christ. He knew all the apostles and was a disciple of Polycarp, who was a disciple of the apostle John. 59/209

Elgin Moyer in *Who Was Who in Church History* writes that Ignatius "himself said, I would rather die for Christ than rule the whole earth. Leave me to the beasts that I may by them be partaker of God. He is said to have been thrown to the wild beasts in the colosseum at Rome. His Epistles were written during his journey from Antioch to his martyrdom." 66/209

Ignatius gave credence to the Scripture by the way he based his faith on the accuracy of the Bible. He had ample material and witnesses to discover scriptural trustworthiness.

Polycarp (A.D. 70-156) was a disciple of John and succumbed to martyrdom at 86 years of age because of his relentless devotion to Christ and the Scriptures. Polycarp's death demonstrated his trust in the accuracy of the Scripture. "About 155, in the reign of Antoninus Pius, when a local persecution was taking place in Smyrna and several of his members had been martyred, he was singled out as the leader of the Church, and marked for martyrdom. When asked to recant and live, he is reputed to have said, 'Eighty and six years have I served Him, and He hath done me no wrong. How can I speak evil of my King who saved me?' He was burned at the stake, dying a heroic martyr for his faith." 66/337 He certainly had ample contacts to know the truth.

Flavius Josephus — Jewish historian.

The differences between Josephus' account of the baptism of John the Baptist and that of the Gospel is that Josephus says that John's baptism was not for the remission of sin, while the Bible (Mark 1:4) says it was; and that John was killed for political reasons and not for his denunciation of Herod's marriage to Herodias. As Bruce points out, it is quite possible that Herod believed he could kill two birds with one stone by imprisoning John. In regard to the discrepancy over his baptism, Bruce says that the Gospels give a more probable account from the "religious-historical" point of view and that they are older than Josephus' work and, therefore, more accurate. However, the real point is that the general outline of Josephus' account confirms that of the Gospels. 16/107

In Ant. XVIII. 5.2, Josephus makes mention of John the Baptist. Because of the manner in which this passage is written, there is no ground for suspecting Christian interpolation. In this passage we read:

"Now some of the Jews thought that Herod's army had been destroyed by God, and that it was a very just penalty to avenge John, surnamed the Baptist. For Herod had killed him, though he was a good man, who bade the Jews practise virtue, be just one to another and pious toward God, and come together in baptism. He taught that baptism was acceptable to God provided that they underwent it not to procure remission of certain sins, but for the purification of the body, if the soul had already been purified by righteousness. And when the others gathered round him (for they were greatly moved when they heard his words), Herod feared that his persuasive power over men, being so great, might lead to a rising, as they seemed ready to follow his counsel in everything. So he thought it much better to seize him and kill him before he caused any tumult, than to have to repent of falling into such trouble later on, after a revolt had taken place. Because of this suspicion of Herod, John was sent in chains to Machaerus, the fortress which we mentioned above, and there put to death. The Jews believed that it was to avenge him that the disaster fell upon the army, God wishing to bring evil upon Herod." 16/106

Tatian (ca A.D. 170) organized the Scriptures in order to put them in the first "harmony of the Gospels" called the Diatessaron.

Part 2 — Confirmation by Archaeology

3C.   EVIDENCE FROM ARCHAEOLOGY

Nelson Glueck, the renowned Jewish archaeologist, wrote: "It may be stated categorically that no archaeological discovery has ever controverted a biblical reference." He continued his assertion of "the almost incredibly accurate historical memory of the Bible, and particularly so when it is fortified by archaeological fact." 33/31

William F. Albright, known for his reputation as one of the great archaeologists, states: "There can be no doubt that archaeology has confirmed the substantial historicity of Old Testament tradition." 1/176

Albright adds: "The excessive scepticism shown toward the Bible by important historical schools of the eighteenth and nineteenth centuries, certain phases of which still appear periodically, has been progressively discredited. Discovery after discovery has established the accuracy of innumerable details, and has brought increased recognition to the value of the Bible as a source of history." 2/127,128

John Warwick Montgomery exposes a typical problem of many scholars today: "[American] Institute [of Holy Land Studies] researcher Thomas Drobena cautioned that where archaeology and the Bible seem to be in tension, the issue is almost always dating, the most shaky area in current archaeology and the one at which scientistic A PRIORI and circular reasoning often replace solid empirical analysis." 63/47,48

Professor H. H. Rowley (cited by Donald F. Wiseman in *Revelation and the Bible*) claims that "it is not because scholars of today begin with more conservative presuppositions than their predecessors that they have a much greater respect for the Patriarchal stories than was formerly common, but because the evidence warrants it." 104/305

Merrill Unger states: "The role which archaeology is performing in New Testament research (as well as that of the Old Testament) in expediting scientific study, balancing critical theory, illustrating, elucidating, supplementing and authenticating historical and cultural backgrounds, constitutes the one bright spot in the future of criticism of the Sacred text." 98/25,26

Millar Burrows of Yale observes: "Archaeology has in many cases refuted the views of modern critics. It has shown in a number of instances that these views rest on false assumptions and unreal, artificial schemes of historical development (AS 1938, p. 182). This is a real contribution, and not to be minimized." 17/291

F. F. Bruce notes: "Where Luke has been suspected of inaccuracy, and accuracy has been vindicated by some inscriptional evidence, it may be legitimate to say that archaeology has confirmed the New Testament record." 14/331

Bruce adds that "for the most part the service which archaeology has rendered to New Testament studies is the filling in of the contemporary background, against which we can read the record with enhanced comprehension and appreciation. And this background is a first-century background. The New Testament narrative just will not fit into a second century background." 14/331

Merrill Unger summarizes: "Old Testament archaeology has rediscovered whole nations, resurrected important peoples, and in a most astonishing manner filled in historical gaps, adding immeasurably to the knowledge of biblical backgrounds." 98/15

William Albright continues: "As critical study of the Bible is more and more influenced by the rich new material from the ancient Near East we shall see a steady rise in respect for the historical significance of now neglected or despised passages and details in the Old and New Testament." 5/81

Burrows exposes the cause of much excessive unbelief: "The excessive skepticism of many liberal theologians stems not from a careful evaluation of the available data, but from an enormous predisposition against the supernatural." 95/176

The Yale archaeologist adds to his above statement: "On the whole, however, archaeological work has unquestionably strengthened confidence in the reliability of the Scriptural record. More than one archaeologist has found his respect for the Bible increased by the experience of excavation in Palestine." 17/1

"On the whole such evidence as archaeology has afforded thus far, especially by providing additional and older manuscripts of the books of the Bible, strengthens our confidence in the accuracy with which the text has been transmitted through the centuries." 17/42

Sir Frederic Kenyon says: "It is therefore legitimate to say that, in respect of that part of the Old Testament against which the disintegrating criticism of the last half of the nineteenth century was chiefly directed, the evidence of archaeology has been to re-establish its authority, and likewise to augment its value by rendering it more intelligible through a fuller knowledge of its background and setting. Archaeology has not yet said its last word; but the results already achieved confirm what faith would suggest, that the Bible can do nothing but gain from an increase of knowledge." 46/279

Archaeology has produced an abundance of evidence to substantiate the correctness of our Massoretic text. (See chapter 4, 2C, The Massoretic Period.)

Bernard Ramm writes of the *Jeremiah Seal:* "Archaeology has also given us evidence as to the substantial accuracy of our Massoretic text. The *Jeremiah Seal,* a seal used to stamp the bitumen seals of wine jars, and dated from the first or second century A.D., has Jeremiah 48:11 stamped on it and, in general, conforms to the Massoretic text. This seal '. . . attests the accuracy with which the text was transmitted between the time when the seal was made and the time when the manuscripts were written.' Furthermore, the *Roberts Papyrus,* which dates to the second century B.C., and the *Nash Papyrus,* dated by Albright before 100 B.C., confirm our Massoretic text." 72/8-10

William Albright affirms that "we may rest assured that the consonantal text of the Hebrew Bible, though not infallible, has been preserved with an accuracy perhaps unparalleled in any other Near-Eastern literature. . . . No, the flood of light now being shed on biblical Hebrew poetry of all periods by Ugaritic literature guarantees the relative antiquity of its composition as well as the astonishing accuracy of its transmission." 6/25

Archaeologist Albright writes concerning the accuracy of the Scriptures as the result of archaeology:

"The contents of our Pentateuch are, in general, very much older than the date at which they were finally edited; new discoveries continue to confirm the historical accuracy or the literary antiquity of detail after detail in it. . . . It is, accordingly, sheer hypercriticism to deny the substantially Mosaic character of the Pentateuchal tradition." 22/224

Albright comments on what the *critics used to say:* "Until recently it was the fashion among biblical historians to treat the patriarchal sagas of Genesis as though they were artificial creations of Israelite scribes of the Divided Monarchy or tales told by imaginative rhapsodists around Israelite campfires during the centuries following their occupation of the country. Eminent names among scholars can be cited for regarding every item of Gen. 11-50 as reflecting late invention, or at least retrojection of events and conditions under the Monarchy into the remote past, about which nothing was thought to have been really known to the writers of later days." 3/1,2

Now it has all been changed, says Albright: "Archaeological discoveries since 1925 have changed all this. Aside from a few die-hards among older scholars, there is scarcely a single biblical historian who has not been impressed by the rapid accumulation of data supporting the substantial historicity of patriarchal tradition. According to the traditions of Genesis the ancestors of Israel were closely related to the semi-nomadic peoples of Trans-Jordan, Syria, the Euphrates basin and North Arabia in the last centuries of the second millennium B.C., and the first centuries of the first millennium." 3/1,2

Millar Burrows continues: "To see the situation clearly we must distinguish two kinds of confirmation, general and specific. General confirmation is a matter of compatibility without definite corroboration of particular points. Much of what has already been discussed as explanation and illustration may be regarded also as general confirmation. The picture fits the frame; the melody and the accompaniment are harmonious. The force of such evidence is cumulative. The more we find that items in the picture of the past presented by the Bible, even though not directly attested, are compatible with what we know from archaeology, the stronger is our impression of general authenticity. Mere legend or fiction would inevitably betray itself by anachronisms and incongruities." 17/278

1D.   **Ebla Kingdom proofs**

An archaeological find that relates to biblical criticism is the recently discovered Ebla tablets. The discovery was made in northern Syria by two professors from the University of Rome, Dr. Paolo Matthiae, an archaeologist; and Dr. Giovanni Petinato, an epigrapher. The excavation of the site, Tell Mardikh, began in 1964; and in 1968 they uncovered a statue of King Ibbit-Lim. The inscription made a reference to Ishtar, the goddess who "shines brightly in Ebla." Ebla, at its height of power in 2300 B.C., had a population of 260,000 people. It was destroyed in 2250 B.C. by Naram-Sin, grandson of Sargan the Great.

Since 1974 17,000 tablets have been unearthed from the era of the Ebla Kingdom.

It will be quite a while before there can be any significant research done to determine the relationship of Ebla to the biblical world. However, valuable contributions have already been made to biblical criticism.

The proponents of the "Documentary Hypothesis" have taught in the past that the period described in the Mosaic narrative (1400 B.C., a thousand years after the Ebla Kingdom) was a time prior to all knowledge of writing (see author's *More Evidence That Demands a Verdict*, p. 63). But Ebla shows that a thousand years before Moses, laws, customs and events were recorded in writing in the same area of the world in which Moses and the patriarchs lived.

The higher critics have not only taught that it was a time prior to writing but also that the Priestly Code and legislation recorded in the Pentateuch were too far developed to have been written by Moses. It was alleged that the Israelites were too primitive at that time to have written them and that it wasn't until about the first half of the Persian period (538-331 B.C.) that such detailed legislation was recorded.

However, the tablets containing the law codes of Ebla have demonstrated elaborate judicial proceedings and case law. Many are very similar to the Deuteronomy law code (example: Deuteronomy 22:22-30) which critics have claimed has a *very* late date.

An additional example of the contribution of the Ebla discovery is in relation to Genesis 14, which for years has been considered to be historically unreliable. The victory of Abraham over Chedolaomer and the Mesopotamian kings has been described as fictitious and the five Cities of the Plain (Sodom, Gomorrah, Admah, Zeboiim and Zoar) as legendary (*More Evidence That Demands a Verdict*, pp. 79-83).

Yet the Ebla archives refer to all five Cities of the Plain and on one tablet the Cities are listed in the exact same sequence as Genesis 14. The milieu of the tablets reflect the culture of the patriarchal period and depict that, before the catastrophe recorded in Genesis 14, the area was a flourishing region experiencing prosperity and success, as recorded in Genesis.

2D.   **Old Testament examples of archaeological confirmation**

(For more information, see *More Evidence That Demands a Verdict*, Campus Crusade for Christ, 1975.)

1E. Genesis derives the ancestry of Israel from Mesopotamia. It is this fact with which archaeological findings concur. Albright says that it is "beyond reasonable doubt that Hebrew tradition was correct in tracing the Patriarchs directly back to the Balikh Valley in northwestern Mesopotamia." The evidence is based on the coincidence of biblical and archaeological findings tracing the movement of these people out of the land of Mesopotamia. 3/2

2E. According to Scripture, "The whole earth was of one language and one speech" (Genesis 11:1) before the Tower of Babel. After the building of the tower and its destruction, God confounded the language of all the earth (Genesis 11:9). Many modern day philologists attest to the likelihood of such an origin for the world's languages. Alfredo Trombetti says he can trace and prove the common origin of *all* languages. Max Mueller also attests to the common origin. And Otto Jespersen goes so far as to say that language was directly given to the first men by God. 29/47

3E. In the genealogy of Esau, there is mention made of the Horites (Genesis 36:20). It was at one time accepted that these people were "cave-dwellers" because of the similarity between Horite and the Hebrew word for cave — thus the idea that they lived in caves. Now, however, findings have shown that they were a prominent group of warriors living in the Near East in Patriarchal times. 29/72

4E. During the excavations of Jericho (1930-1936) Garstang found something so startling that a statement of what was found was prepared and signed by himself and two other members of the team. In reference to these findings Garstang says: "As to the main fact, then, there remains no doubt: the walls fell outwards so completely that the attackers would be able to clamber up and over their ruins into the city." Why so unusual? Because the walls of cities do not fall outwards, they fall inwards. And yet in Joshua 6:20 we read ". . . The wall fell down flat, so that the people went up into the city every man straight ahead, and they took the city." The walls were made to fall outward. 31/146

5E. We find that the genealogy of Abraham is definitely historical. However, there seems to be some question as to whether or not these names represent individuals or ancient cities. The one thing that is certain about Abraham is that he was an individual and that he did exist. As we hear from Burrows: "Everything indicates that here we have an historical individual. As noted above, he is not mentioned in any known archaeological source, but his name appears in Babylonia as a personal name in the very period to which he belongs." 17/258,259

Earlier attempts had been made to move the date of Abraham to the 15th or 14th century B.C., a time much too late for him. However, Albright points out that because of the data mentioned above and other evidence, we have "a great deal of evidence from personal and place names, almost all of which is against such unwarranted telescoping of traditional data." 31/9

6E. Although specific archaeological evidence for the stories of the Patriarchs may not be forthcoming, the social customs of the stories fit the period and region of the Patriarchs. 17/278,279

Much of this evidence came from excavations at Nuzu and Mari. Light was shed on Hebrew poetry and language from work at Ugarit. Mosaic legislation was seen in Hittite, Assyrian, Sumerian and Eshunna codes. Through these we are able to see the life of the Hebrew against the surrounding world, and as Albright says, "This is a contribution before which everything else must fade into insignificance." 6/28

The discoveries found thus far have led scholars, no matter what their religious opinion, to affirm the historical nature of the narratives related to the Patriarchs. 104/305

7E.   *Julius Wellhausen,* a well-known biblical critic of the 19th century, felt that the record of the laver made of brass mirrors was not an original entry into the Priestly Code. By stating so he puts the record of the tabernacle much too late for the time of Moses. However, there is no valid reason for employing the late dating (500 B.C.) of Wellhausen. There is specific archaeological evidence of such bronze mirrors in what is known as the Empire Period of Egypt's history (1500-1400 B.C.). Thus, we see that this period is contemporary with Moses and the Exodus (1500-1400 B.C.). 29/108

8E.   *Henry M. Morris* observes: "Problems still exist, of course, in the complete harmonization of archaeological material with the Bible, but none so serious as not to bear real promise of imminent solution through further investigation. It must be extremely significant that, in view of the great mass of corroborative evidence regarding the Biblical history of these periods, there exists today not one unquestionable find of archaeology that proves the Bible to be in error at any point." 65/95

3D.   New Testament examples

1E.   Luke's reliability as an historian is unquestionable. Unger tells us that archaeology has authenticated the Gospel accounts, especially Luke. In Unger's words, "The Acts of the Apostles is now generally agreed in scholarly circles to be the work of Luke, to belong to the first century and to involve the labors of a careful historian who was substantially accurate in his use of sources." 97/24

Sir William Ramsay is regarded as one of the greatest archaeologists ever to have lived. He was a student in the German historical school of the mid-19th century. As a result, he believed that the Book of Acts was a product of the mid-second century A.D. He was firmly convinced of this belief. In his research to make a topographical study of Asia Minor he was compelled to consider the writings of Luke. As a result he was forced to do a complete reversal of his beliefs due to the overwhelming evidence uncovered in his research. He spoke of this when he said: "I may fairly claim to have entered on this investigation without prejudice in favour of the conclusion which I shall now seek to justify to the reader. On the contrary, I began with a mind unfavourable to it, for the ingenuity and apparent completeness of the Tubingen theory had at one time quite convinced me. It did not then lie in my line of life to investigate the subject minutely; but more recently I found myself brought into contact with the Book of Acts as an authority for the topography, antiquities and society of Asia Minor. It was gradually borne upon me that in various details the narrative showed marvelous truth. In fact, beginning with a fixed idea that the work was essentially a second century composition, and never relying on its evidence as trustworthy for first century conditions, I gradually came to find it a useful ally in some obscure and difficult investigations." 13/36 quoted from Ramsay's book: *St. Paul the Traveler and the Roman Citizen.*

Concerning Luke's ability as a historian, Ramsay concluded after 30 years of study that "Luke is a historian of the first rank; not merely are his statements of fact trustworthy . . . *this author should be placed along with the very greatest of historians.*" 75/222

Ramsay adds: "Luke's history is unsurpassed in respect of its trustworthiness." 76/81

What Ramsay had done conclusively and finally was to exclude certain possibilities. As seen in the light of archaeological evidence, the New Testament reflects the conditions of the second half of the first century A.D., and does not reflect the conditions of any later date. Historically it is of the greatest importance that this should have been so effectively established. In all matters of external fact the author of Acts is seen to have been minutely careful and accurate as only a contemporary can be.

It was at one time conceded that Luke had entirely missed the boat in the events he portrayed as surrounding the birth of Jesus (Luke 2:1-3). Critics argued that there was no census, that Quirinius was not governor of Syria at that time and that everyone did not have to return to his ancestral home. 24/159,160; 29/285

First of all, archaeological discoveries show that the Romans had a regular enrollment of taxpayers and also held censuses every 14 years. This procedure was indeed begun under Augustus and the first took place in either 23-22 B.C. or in 9-8 B.C. The latter would be the one to which Luke refers.

Second, we find evidence that Quirinius was governor of Syria around 7 B.C. This assumption is based on an inscription found in Antioch ascribing to Quirinius this post. As a result of this finding, it is now supposed that he was governor twice — once in 7 B.C. and the other time in 6 A.D. (the date ascribed by Josephus). 24/160

Last, in regard to the practices of enrollment, a papyrus found in Egypt gives directions for the conduct of a census.

It reads: "Because of the approaching census it is necessary that all those residing for any cause away from their homes should at once prepare to return to their own governments in order that they may complete the family registration of the enrollment and that the tilled lands may retain those belonging to them." 24/159,160; 29/285

Archaeologists at first believed Luke's implication wrong that Lystra and Derbe were in Lycaonia and Iconium was not (Acts 14:6). They based their belief on the writings of Romans such as Cicero who indicated that Iconium was in Lycaonia. Thus, archaeologists said the Book of Acts was unreliable. However, in 1910, Sir William Ramsay found a monument that showed that Iconium was a Phrygian city. Later discoveries confirm this. 29/317

Among other historical references of Luke is that of Lysanias the Tetrarch of Abilene (Luke 3:1) at the beginning of John the Baptist's ministry in 27 A.D. The only Lysanias known to ancient historians was one who was killed in 36 B.C. However, an inscription found near Damascus speaks of "Freedman of Lysanias the Tetrarch" and is dated between 14 and 29 A.D. 14/321

In his Epistle to the Romans written from Corinth, Paul makes mention of the city treasurer, Erastus (Romans 16:23). During the excavations of Corinth in 1929, a pavement was found inscribed: ERASTVS PRO: AED: S: P: STRAVIT ("Erastus, curator of public buildings, laid this pavement at his own expense"). According to Bruce, the pavement quite likely existed in the first century A.D. and the donor and the man Paul mentions are probably one and the same. 16/95; 95/185

Also found in Corinth is a fragmentary inscription which is believed to have borne the words "Synagogue of the Hebrews." Conceivably it stood over the doorway of the synagogue Paul debated in (Acts 18:4-7). Another Corinthian inscription mentions the city "meat market" which Paul refers to in I Corinthians 10:25.

Thus, thanks to the many archaeological finds, most of the ancient cities mentioned in the Book of Acts have been identified. The journeys of Paul can now be accurately traced as a result of these finds. 16/95; 7/118

Luke writes of the riot of Ephesus and represents a civic assembly (*Ecclesia*) taking place in a theater (Acts 19:23 ff.). The facts are that it did meet there as borne out by an inscription which speaks of silver statues of Artemis (Diana in KJV) to be placed in the "theater during a full session of the *Ecclesia.*" The theater, when excavated, proved to have room for 25,000 people. 14/326

Luke also relates that a riot broke out in Jerusalem because Paul took a Gentile into the temple (Acts 21:28). Inscriptions have been found which read, in Greek and Latin, "No foreigner may enter within the barrier which surrounds the temple and enclosure. Anyone who is caught doing so will be personally responsible for his ensuing death." Luke is proved right again! 14/326

Also in doubt were Luke's usages of certain words. Luke refers to Philippi as a "part" or "district" of Macedonia. He uses the Greek word *meris* which is translated "part" or "district." F. J. A. Hort believed Luke wrong in this usage. He said that *meris* referred to a "portion" not a "district," thus, his grounds for disagreement. Archaeological excavations, however, have shown that this very word, *meris*, was used to describe the divisions of the district. Thus, archaeology has again shown the accuracy of Luke. 29/320

Other poor word usages were attached to Luke. He was not technically correct for referring to the Philippian rulers as *praetors*. According to the "scholars" two *duumuirs* would have ruled the town. However, as usual, Luke was right. Findings have shown that the title of *praetor* was employed by the magistrates of a Roman colony. 29/321

His choice of the word *proconsul* as the title for Gallio (Acts 18:12) is correct as evidenced by the Delphi inscription which states in part: "As Lucius Junius Gallio, my friend, and the Proconsul of Achaia. . . ." 95/180

The Delphi inscription (A.D. 52) gives us a fixed time period for establishing Paul's ministry of one and a half years in Corinth. We know this by the fact, from other sources, that Gallio took office on July 1 and that his proconsulship lasted only one year and that one year overlapped Paul's work in Corinth. 14/324

Luke gives to Publius, the chief man in Malta, the title "first man of the island" (Acts 28:7). Inscriptions have been unearthed which do give him the title of "first man." 14/325

Still another case is his usage of *politarchs* to denote the civil authorities of Thessalonica (Acts 17:6). Since *politarch* is not found in the classical literature, Luke was again assumed to be wrong. However, some 19 inscriptions have been found that make use of the title. Interestingly enough, five of these are in reference to Thessalonica. 14/325

In 1945, two ossuaries (receptacles for bones) were found in the vicinity of Jerusalem. These ossuaries exhibited graffiti which their discoverer, Eleazar L. Sukenik, claimed to be "the earliest records of Christianity." These burial receptacles were found in a tomb which was in use before 50 A.D. The writings read *lesous iou* and *lesous aloth*. Also present were four crosses. It is likely that the first is a prayer to Jesus for help and the second, a prayer for resurrection of the person whose bones were contained in the ossuary. 14/327,328

Is it no wonder that E. M. Blaiklock, professor of Classics in Auckland University, concludes that "Luke is a consummate historian, to be ranked in his own right with the great writers of the Greeks." 12/89

2E. *The Pavement.* For centuries there has been no record of the court where Jesus was tried by Pilate (named Gabbatha or the Pavement, John 19:13).

William F. Albright in *The Archaeology of Palestine* shows that this court was the court of the Tower of Antonia which was the Roman military headquarters in Jerusalem. It was left buried when the city was rebuilt in the time of Hadrian and not discovered until recently. 2/141

3E. *The Pool of Bethesda,* another site with no record of it except in the New Testament, can now be identified "with a fair measure of certainty in the northeast quarter of the old city (the area called Bezetha, or 'New Lawn') in the first century A.D., where traces of it were discovered in the course of excavations near the Church of St. Anne in 1888." 14/329

CONCLUSION

After trying to shatter the historicity and validity of the Scripture, I came to the conclusion that it is historically trustworthy. If one discards the Bible as being unreliable, then he must discard almost all literature of antiquity.

One problem I constantly face is the desire on the part of many to apply one standard or test to secular literature and another to the Bible. One needs to apply the same test, whether the literature under investigation is secular or religious.

Having done this, I believe one can hold the Scriptures in his hand and say, "The Bible is trustworthy and historically reliable."

This section can be appropriately summarized by the words of Sir Walter Scott in reference to the Scriptures:

> "Within that awful volume lies
> The mystery of mysteries
> Happiest they of human race
> To whom God has granted grace
> To read, to fear, to hope, to pray
> To lift the latch, and force the way;
> And better had they ne'er been born,
> Who read to doubt, or read to scorn." 84/140

BIBLIOGRAPHY

1. Albright, William F. *Archaeology and the Religions of Israel*. Baltimore: Johns Hopkins University Press, 1956.

2. Albright, William F. *The Archaeology of Palestine*. Rev. ed. Harmondsworth, Middlesex: Pelican Books, 1960.

3. Albright, William F. *The Biblical Period From Abraham to Ezra*. New York: Harper & Row, 1960.

4. Albright, William F. "The Elimination of King 'So.' " *The Bulletin of the American Schools of Oriental Research*. No. 171, October, 1963, p.66.

5. Albright, William F. *From the Stone Age to Christianity*. Baltimore: Johns Hopkins Press, 1946.

6. Albright, William F. "Old Testament and the Archaeology of the Ancient East." Found in *Old Testament and Modern Study* by Harold Henry Rowley. Oxford University Press, 1951.

7. Albright, William F. *Recent Discoveries in Bible Lands*. New York: Funk and Wagnalls, 1955. By courtesy of the publisher.

8. Anderson, J. *The Bible, the Word of God*. Brighton: n. p., 1905.

9. Anderson, J. N. D. *Christianity: The Witness of History*. London: Tyndale Press, 1969. Used by permission of Inter-Varsity Press, Downers Grove, IL 60515.

10. Archer, Gleason, *A Survey of the Old Testament*. Chicago: Moody Press, 1964. Used by permission.

11. Aristotle. *Aristotle's Art of Poetry; a Greek View of Poetry and Drama*. Oxford: Clarendon Press, 1961.

12. Blaiklock, Edward Musgrave. *The Acts of the Apostles*. Grand Rapids: William B. Eerdmans Publishing Co., 1959. Used by permission.

13. Blaiklock, Edward Musgrave. *Layman's Answer: An Examination of the New Theology*. London: Hodder and Stoughton, 1968.

14. Bruce, F. F. "Archaeological Confirmation of the New Testament." *Revelation and the Bible*. Edited by Carl Henry. Grand Rapids: Baker Book House, 1969.

15. Bruce, F. F. *The Books and the Parchments*. Rev. ed. Westwood: Fleming H. Revell Co., 1963.

16. Bruce, F. F. *The New Testament Documents: Are They Reliable?* Downers Grove; IL 60515: Inter-Varsity Press, 1964. Used by permission.

17. Burrows, Millar. *What Mean These Stones?* New York: Meridian Books, 1956.

18. Collett, Sidney. *All About the Bible*. Old Tappan: Revell, n.d.

19. Collier, Donald. "New Radiocarbon Method for Dating the Past." *Biblical Archaeologist Reader*. Edited by G. E. Wright and D. N. Freedman. New York: Doubleday & Co., 1961.

20. Culver, Robert D. "The Old Testament as Messianic Prophecy." *Bulletin of the Evangelical Theological Society*. Vol. VII, No. 3, 1964.

21. Davidson, Samuel. *Hebrew Text of the Old Testament*. 2nd ed., London: Samuel Bagster & Sons, 1859.

22. Dodd, C. H. *More New Testament Studies*. Manchester: University Press, 1968.

23. Earle, Ralph. *How We Got Our Bible*. Grand Rapids: Baker Book House, 1971.

24. Elder, John. *Prophets, Idols and Diggers*. Indianapolis, New York: Bobbs-Merrill, 1960.

25. *Encyclopaedia Britannica*. Vol. 3. Reprinted by permission, copyright by Encyclopaedia Britannica, 1970.

26. Eusebius. *Ecclesiastical History*. VIII, 2. Loeb. ed., II, 159.

27. Finkelstein, Louis (ed.). *The Jews, Their History, Culture, and Religion*. Vol. 1, 3rd ed. New York: Harper and Brothers, 1960.

28. Frank, Henry Thomas. *Bible, Archaeology and Faith*. Nashville: Abingdon Press, 1971.

29. Free, Joseph. *Archaeology and Bible History*. Wheaton: Scripture Press Publications, 1969.

30. Freedman, D. N. and J. C. Greenfield (eds.). *New Directions in Biblical Archaeology*. Garden City: Doubleday and Co., 1969.

31. Garstang, John. *The Foundations of Bible History; Joshua, Judges*. London: Constable, 1931.

32. Geisler, Norman L. and William E. Nix. *A General Introduction to the Bible*. Chicago: Moody Press, 1968.

33. Glueck, Nelson. *Rivers in the Desert; History of Negev*. Philadelphia: Jewish Publications Society of America, 1969.

34. Grant, F. C. An Introduction to the *Revised Standard Version of the New Testament*. 1946.

35. Green, Michael. *Runaway World*. Downers Grove, IL 60515: Inter-Varsity Press, 1968. Used by permission.

36. Green, William Henry. *General Introduction to the Old Testament – The Text*. New York: C. Scribner's Sons, 1899.

37. Greenlee, J. Harold. *Introduction to New Testament Textual Criticism*. Grand Rapids: William B. Eerdmans Publishing Co., 1964. Used by permission.

38. Greenslade, Stanley Lawrence (ed.). *Cambridge History of the Bible*. New York: Cambridge University Press, 1963.

39. Hall, F. W. "MS Authorities for the Text of the Chief Classical Writers." *Companion to Classical Text*. Oxford: Clarendon Press, 1913. Used by permission.

40. Harrison, R. K. *Introduction to the Old Testament*. Grand Rapids: William B. Eerdmans Publishing Co., 1969. Used by permission.

41. Heidel, Alexander. *The Babylonian Genesis*. Chicago: University of Chicago Press, 1963.

42. Horn, Robert M. *The Book That Speaks for Itself*. Downers Grove, IL 60515: Inter-Varsity Press, 1970. Used by permission.

43. Hort, Fenton John Anthony and Brooke Foss Westcott. *The New Testament in the Original Greek*. New York: Macmillan Co., 1881. Vol. 1.

44. Jaganay, Leo. *An Introduction to the Textual Criticism of the New Testament.* Trans. by B. V. Miller. London: Sands and Co., 1937.

45. Josephus, Flavius. "Flavius Josephus Against Apion." *Josephus, Complete Works.* Translated by William Whiston, Grand Rapids: Kregel Publications, 1960.

46. Kenyon, Frederic G. *The Bible and Archaeology.* New York: Harper & Row, 1940.

47. Kenyon, Frederic G. *The Bible and Modern Scholarship.* London: John Murray, 1948.

48. Kenyon, Frederic G. *Handbook to the Textual Criticism of the New Testament.* London: Macmillan and Company, 1901.

49. Kenyon, Frederic G. *Our Bible and the Ancient Manuscripts.* New York: Harper & Brothers, 1941.

50. Kenyon, Frederic G. *The Story of the Bible.* Grand Rapids: William B. Eerdmans Publishing Company, 1967. Used by permission.

51. Klausner, Joseph. *Jesus of Nazareth.* New York: The Macmillan Co., 1946.

52. Kline, M. G. *Treaty of the Great King.* Grand Rapids: William B. Eerdmans Publishing Co., 1963. Used by permission.

53. Lake, Kirsopp. "Caesarean Text of the Gospel of Mark." *Harvard Theological Review.* Vol. 21, 1928.

54. Lapp, Paul W. *Biblical Archaeology and History.* New York: World Publishing Co., 1969.

55. Latourette, Kenneth Scott. *A History of Christianity.* New York: Harper & Row, 1953.

56. Lea, John W. *The Greatest Book in the World.* Philadelphia: n.p., 1929.

57. Lea, John W. *The Book of Books.* Philadelphia: n.p., 1922.

58. Leach, Charles. *Our Bible. How We Got It.* Chicago: Moody Press, 1898.

59. Liplady, Thomas. *The Influence of the Bible.* New York: Fleming H. Revell, 1924.

60. McAfee, Cleland B. *The Greatest English Classic.* New York: n.p., 1912.

61. Metzger, Bruce. *Chapters in the History of New Testament Textual Criticism.* Grand Rapids: William B. Eerdmans Publishing Co., 1963.

62. Metzger, Bruce M. *The Text of the New Testament.* New York and Oxford: Oxford University Press, 1968.

63. Montgomery, John W. "Evangelicals and Archaeology." *Christianity Today.* August 16, 1968. Used by permission.

64. Montgomery, John W. *History and Christianity.* Downers Grove, IL 60515: Inter-Varsity Press, 1971. Used by permission.

65. Morris, Henry. *The Bible and Modern Science.* Rev. ed. Chicago: Moody Press, 1956.

66. Moyer, Elgin S. *Who Was Who in Church History.* Rev. ed. Chicago: Moody Press, 1968. Used by permission.

67. Murray, John. "The Attestation of Scripture." *The Infallible Word* (a symposium). Philadelphia: Presbyterian and Reformed Publishing Co., 1946.

68. Neill, Stephen. *The Interpretation of the New Testament.* 1861-1961. London: Oxford University Press, 1966.

69. Peters, S. E. *The Harvest of Hellenism.* New York: Simon and Schuster, 1971.

70. Pfeiffer, R. H. *Introduction to the Old Testament.* New York: Harper & Row, 1948.

71. Radmacher, Earl. Conversation with Dr. Earl Radmacher. Dallas, TX, June, 1972.

72. Ramm, Bernard. "Can I Trust My Old Testament?" *The King's Business.* Feb. 1949.

73. Ramm, Bernard. *Protestant Christian Evidences.* Chicago: Moody Press, 1957. Used by permission.

74. Ramsay, Sir W. M. *The Bearing of Recent Discovery on the Trustworthiness of the New Testament.* London: Hodder and Stoughton, 1915.

75. Ramsay, W. M. *The Bearing of Recent Discovery on the Trustworthiness of the New Testament.* Grand Rapids: Baker Book House, 1953.

76. Ramsay, W. M. *St. Paul the Traveller and the Roman Citizen.* Grand Rapids: Baker Book House, 1962.

77. Robertson, Archibald T. *An Introduction to the Textual Criticism of the New Testament.* London: n.p., 1907.

78. Robertson, A. T. *Introduction to the Textual Criticism of the New Testament.* Nashville: Broadman Press, 1925.

79. Robinson, John A. T. *Redating the New Testament.* London: SCM Press, 1976.

80. Rowley, H. H. *The Growth of the Old Testament.* London: Hutchinson's University Library, 1950.

81. Sanders, C. *Introduction in Research in English Literary History.* New York: Macmillan Co., 1952.

82. Schaff, Philip. *Companion to the Greek Testament and the English Version.* Rev. ed. New York: Harper Brothers, 1883.

83. Schaff, Philip. *History of the Christian Church.* Vol. 1 (8 vols.). Grand Rapids: William B. Eerdmans Publishing Co., 1960. Used by permission.

84. Scott, Sir Walter. *The Monastery.* Boston: Houghton Mifflin Co., 1913.

85. Skilton, John H. "The Transmission of the Scripture." *The Infallible Word* (a symposium). Philadelphia: Presbyterian and Reformed Publishing Co., 1946.

86. Smith, Wilbur M. *The Incomparable Book.* Minneapolis: Beacon Publications, 1961.

87. Souter, Alexander. *The Text and Canon of the New Testament.* New York: Charles Scribner's Sons, 1912.

88. Stonehouse, Ned B. "The Authority of the New Testament." *The Infallible Word* (a symposium). Philadelphia: Presbyterian and Reformed Publishing Co., 1946.

89. Stott, John R. W. *Basic Christianity.* Downers Grove, IL 60515: Inter-Varsity Press, 1971. Used by permission.

90. Streeter, Burnett Hillman. *The Four Gospels.* London: Macmillan & Co., 1930.

91. Tenney, Merrill C. "Reversals of New Testament Criticism." *Revelation and the Bible.* Edited by Carl Henry. Grand Rapids: Baker Book House, 1969.

92. Turner, E. G. *Greek Manuscripts of the Ancient World.* Princeton: Princeton University Press, 1971.

93. Turner, H. E. W. *The Historicity of the Gospels.* London: A. R. Mowbray, 1963.

94. Vardaman, Jerry. *Archaeology and the Living Word.* Nashville: Broadman Press, 1965.

95. Vos, Howard. *Can I Trust My Bible?* Chicago: Moody Press, 1963. Used by permission.

96. Vos, Howard. *Genesis and Archaeology.* Chicago: Moody Press, 1963. Used by permission.

97. Unger, Merrill F. *Archaeology and the New Testament.* (A companion volume to *Archaeology and the Old Testament.*) Grand Rapids: Zondervan Publishing House, 1962. Used by permission.

98. Unger, Merrill F. *Archaeology and the Old Testament*. Chicago: Moody Press, 1954. Used by permission.

99. Unger, Merrill F. *Unger's Bible Dictionary*. Rev. ed. Chicago: Moody Press, 1971. Used by permission.

100. Warfield, Benjamin B. *Introduction to Textual Criticism of the New Testament*. Seventh edition. London: Hodder and Stoughton, 1907.

101. Whitcomb, John C., Jr. *Darius the Mede*. Philadelphia: Presbyterian and Reformed Publishing Co., 1963.

102. Wilson, Robert Dick. *A Scientific Investigation of the Old Testament*. Chicago: Moody Press, 1959. Used by permission.

103. Wilson, Robert Dick. *Which Bible?* Ed. by David Otis Fuller.

104. Wiseman, Donald F. "Archaeological Confirmation of the Old Testament." *Revelation and the Bible*. Edited by Carl Henry. Grand Rapids: Baker Book House, 1969.

105. Wright, G. E. and D. N. Freedman. *Biblical Archaeologist Reader*. New York: Doubleday and Co., 1961.

106. Wright, G. E. *Biblical Archaeology*. Philadelphia: Westminster Press, 1957.

107. Wright, G. E. "Some Radiocarbon Dates." *Biblical Archaeologist Reader*. Edited by Wright and Freedman. Garden City: Doubleday and Co., 1961.

108. Young, Edward J. "The Authority of the Old Testament." *The Infallible Word* (a symposium). Philadelphia: Presbyterian and Reformed Publishing Co., 1946.

section II _____

the academy awards

-if Jesus was not God, then he deserved an Oscar

This section is extremely important because it deals with the person of Jesus Christ. Who is He? Is He God's Son? The answer is crucial because if He is who He claimed to be, the Messiah, the Son of God, then one's eternal relationship with God will depend upon his relationship with Christ in the world. These notes will show that Jesus was a SuperSavior, not a Superstar.

chapter 5

Jesus
-a man of history

1A. JESUS IS A MAN OF HISTORY

In a debate sponsored by the Associate Students of a midwestern university, my opponent, a congressional candidate for the Progressive Labor Party (Marxist) in New York, said in her opening remarks: "Historians today have fairly well dismissed Jesus as being historical. . . ." I couldn't believe my ears (but I was thankful she said it, because the 2,500 students were soon aware that historical homework was missing in her preparation). It just so happened that I had the following notes and documentation with me to use in my rebuttal. It is certainly not the historians (maybe a few economists) who propagate a Christ-myth theory of Jesus.

As F. F. Bruce, Rylands professor of biblical criticism and exegesis at the University of Manchester, has rightly said:

"Some writers may toy with the fancy of a 'Christ-myth,' but they do not do so on the ground of historical evidence. The historicity of Christ is as axiomatic for an unbiased historian as the historicity of Julius Caesar. It is not historians who propagate the 'Christ-myth' theories." 2/119

Otto Betz concludes that "no serious scholar has ventured to postulate the non-historicity of Jesus." 1/9

1B. Christian Sources for the Historicity of Jesus

1C. TWENTY-SEVEN DIFFERENT NEW TESTAMENT DOCUMENTS
(See page 39ff.)

John Montgomery asks:

"What, then, does a historian know about Jesus Christ? He knows, first and foremost, that the New Testament documents can be relied upon to give an accurate portrait of Him. And he knows that this portrait cannot be rationalized away by wishful thinking, philosophical presuppositionalism, or literary maneuvering." 6/40

2C. CHURCH FATHERS

Polycarp, Eusebius, Irenaeus, Ignatius, Justin, Origen, etc. (See page 50.)

2B. Non-biblical Sources for Historicity of Jesus

1C. CORNELIUS TACITUS (born A.D. 52-54)

A Roman historian, in 112 A.D., Governor of Asia, son-in-law of Julius Agricola who was Governor of Britain A.D. 80-84. Writing of the reign of Nero, Tacitus alludes to the death of Christ and to the existence of Christians at Rome:

"But not all the relief that could come from man, not all the bounties that the prince could bestow, nor all the atonements which could be presented to the gods, availed to relieve Nero from the infamy of being believed to have ordered the conflagration, the fire of Rome. Hence to suppress the rumor, he falsely charged with the guilt, and punished with the most exquisite tortures, the persons commonly called Christians, who were hated for their enormities. Christus, the founder of the name, was put to death by Pontius Pilate, procurator of Judea in the reign of Tiberius: but the pernicious superstition, repressed for a time broke out again, not only through Judea, where the mischief originated, but through the city of Rome also." *Annals* XV. 44

Tacitus has a further reference to Christianity in a fragment of his *Histories,* dealing with the burning of the Jerusalem temple in A.D. 70, preserved by Sulpicius Severus (Chron. ii. 30.6).

2C.   LUCIAN OF SAMOSATA

A satirist of the second century, who spoke scornfully of Christ and the Christians. He connected them with the synagogues of Palestine and alluded to Christ as: ". . . the man who was crucified in Palestine because he introduced this new cult into the world. . . . Furthermore, their first lawgiver persuaded them that they were all brothers one of another after they have transgressed once for all by denying the Greek gods and by worshipping that crucified sophist himself and living under his laws." *The Passing Peregrinus*

Lucian also mentions the Christians several times in his *Alexander the False Prophet,* sections 25 and 29.

3C.   FLAVIUS JOSEPHUS (born A.D. 37)

A Jewish historian, became a Pharisee at age 19; in A.D. 66 he was the commander of Jewish forces in Galilee. After being captured, he was attached to the Roman headquarters. He says in a hotly-contested quotation:

"Now there was about this time Jesus, a wise man, if it be lawful to call him a man, for he was a doer of wonderful works, a teacher of such men as receive the truth with pleasure. He drew over to him both many of the Jews, and many of the Gentiles. He was the Christ, and when Pilate, at the suggestion of the principal men among us, had condemned him to the cross, those that loved him at the first did not forsake him; for he appeared to them alive again the third day; as the divine prophets had foretold these and ten thousand other wonderful things concerning him. And the tribe of Christians so named from him are not extinct at this day." *Antiquities.* xviii.33. (Early second century)

The Arabic text of the passage is as follows: "At this time there was a wise man who was called Jesus. And his conduct was good, and (He) was known to be virtuous. And many people from among the Jews and the other nations became his disciples. Pilate condemned Him to be crucified and to die. And those who had become his disciples did not abandon his discipleship. They reported that He had appeared to them three days after his crucifixion and that He was alive; accordingly, He was perhaps the Messiah concerning whom the prophets have recounted wonders."

The above passage is found in the Arabic manuscript entitled: "Kitab Al-Unwan Al-Mukallal Bi-Fadail Al-Hikma Al-Mutawwaj Bi-Anwa Al-Falsafa Al-Manduh Bi-Haqaq Al-Marifa." The approximate translation would be: "Book of History Guided by All the Virtues of

Wisdom. Crowned with Various Philosophies and Blessed by the Truth of Knowledge."

The above manuscript composed by Bishop Apapius in the 10th century has a section commencing with: "We have found in many books of the philosophers that they refer to the day of the crucifixion of Christ." Then he gives a list and quotes portions of the ancient works. Some of the works are familiar to modern scholars and others are not. 8/n.p.

We also find from Josephus a reference to James the brother of Jesus. In *Antiquities* XX 9:1 he describes the actions of the high priest Ananus:

"But the younger Ananus who, as we said, received the high priesthood, was of a bold disposition and exceptionally daring; he followed the party of the Sadducees, who are severe in judgment above all the Jews, as we have already shown. As therefore Ananus was of such a disposition, he thought he had now a good opportunity, as Festus was now dead, and Albinus was still on the road; so he assembled a council of judges, and brought before it the brother of Jesus the so-called Christ, whose name was James, together with some others, and having accused them as law-breakers, he delivered them over to be stoned." 2/107

4C.   SUETONIUS (A.D. 120)

Another Roman historian, court official under Hadrian, annalist of the Imperial House, says: "As the Jews were making constant disturbances at the instigation of Chrestus (another spelling of Christus), he expelled them from Rome." *Life of Claudius* 25.4

He also writes: "Punishment by Nero was inflicted on the Christians, a class of men given to a new and mischievous superstition." *Lives of the Caesars*, 26.2

5C.   PLINIUS SECUNDUS, PLINY THE YOUNGER

Governor of Bithynia in Asia Minor (A.D. 112), Pliny was writing the emperor Trajan seeking counsel as to how to treat the Christians.

He explained that he had been killing both men and women, boys and girls. There were so many being put to death that he wondered if he should continue killing anyone who was discovered to be a Christian, or if he should kill only certain ones. He explained that he had made the Christians bow down to the statues of Trajan. He goes on to say that he also "made them curse Christ, which a genuine Christian cannot be induced to do." In the same letter he says of the people who were being tried:

"They affirmed, however, that the whole of their guilt, or their error, was, that they were in the habit of meeting on a certain fixed day before it was light, when they sang in alternate verse a hymn to Christ as to a god, and bound themselves to a solemn oath, not to any wicked deeds, but never to commit any fraud, theft, adultery, never to falsify their word, not to deny a trust when they should be called upon to deliver it up." *Epistles* X.96

6C.   TERTULLIAN

Jurist-theologian of Carthage, in a defense of Christianity (A.D. 197) before the Roman authorities in Africa, mentions the exchange between Tiberius and Pontius Pilate:

"Tiberius accordingly, in those days the Christian name made its entry into the world, having himself received intelligence from the truth of Christ's divinity, brought the matter before the senate, with his own decision in favor of Christ. The senate, because it had not given the approval itself, rejected his proposal. Caesar held to his opinion, threatening wrath against all the accusers of the Christians" (*Apology*, V.2). Some historians doubt the historicity of this passage. Also, Cr. Justin Martyr, *Apology*, 1.35.

7C. THALLUS, THE SAMARITAN-BORN HISTORIAN

One of the first Gentile writers who mentions Christ is Thallus, who wrote in 52 A.D. However, his writings have disappeared and we only know of them from fragments cited by other writers. One such writer is Julius Africanus, a Christian writer about 221 A.D. One very interesting passage relates to a comment from Thallus. Julius Africanus writes:

" 'Thallus, in the third book of his histories, explains away this darkness as an eclipse of the sun — unreasonably, as it seems to me' (unreasonably, of course, because a solar eclipse could not take place at the time of the full moon, and it was at the season of the Paschal full moon that Christ died)."

Thus, from this reference we see that the Gospel account of the darkness which fell upon the land during Christ's crucifixion was well known and required a naturalistic explanation from those non-believers who witnessed it. 2/113

8C. PHLEGON, A FIRST CENTURY HISTORIAN

His *Chronicles* have been lost, but a small fragment of that work, which confirms the darkness upon the earth at the crucifixion, is also mentioned by Julius Africanus. After his (Africanus') remarks about Thallus' unreasonable opinion of the darkness, he quotes Phlegon that "during the time of Tiberius Caesar an eclipse of the sun occurred during the full moon." 7/IIB, sect. 256 f16, p. 1165

Phlegon is also mentioned by Origen in *Contra Celsum*, Book 2, sections 14, 33, 59.

Philopon (De. opif. mund. II 21) says: "And about this darkness . . . Phlegon recalls it in the *Olympiads* (the title of his history)." He says that "Phlegon mentioned the eclipse which took place during the crucifixion of the Lord Christ, and no other (eclipse), it is clear that he did not know from his sources about any (similar) eclipse in previous times . . . and this is shown by the historical account itself of Tiberius Caesar." 4/II B, sect. 257 f16, c, p. 1165

9C. LETTER OF MARA BAR-SERAPION

F. F. Bruce records that there is:

" . . . in the British Museum an interesting manuscript preserving the text of a letter written some time later than A.D. 73, but how much later we cannot be sure. This letter was sent by a Syrian named Mara Bar-Serapion to his son Serapion. Mara Bar-Serapion was in prison at the time, but he wrote to encourage his son in the pursuit of wisdom, and pointed out that those who persecuted wise men were overtaken by misfortune. He instances the deaths of Socrates, Pythagoras and Christ:

" 'What advantage did the Athenians gain from putting Socrates to death? Famine and plague came upon them as a judgment for their crime. What advantage did the men of Samos gain from burning Pythagoras? In a moment their land was covered with sand. What advantage did the Jews gain from executing their wise King? It was just after that that their kingdom was abolished. God justly avenged these three wise men: the Athenians died of hunger; the Samians were overwhelmed by the sea; the Jews, ruined and driven from their land, live in complete dispersion. But Socrates did not die for good; he lived on in the teaching of Plato. Pythagoras did not die for good; he lived on in the statue of Hera. Nor did the wise King die for good; He lived on in the teaching which He had given.' " 2/114

10C. JUSTIN MARTYR

About A.D. 150, Justin Martyr, addressing his *Defence of Christianity* to the Emperor Antoninus Pius, referred him to Pilate's report, which Justin supposed must be preserved in the imperial archives. But the words, "They pierced my hands and my feet," he says, "are a description of the nails that were fixed in His hands and His feet on the cross; and after He was crucified, those who crucified Him cast lots for His garments, and divided them among themselves; and that these things were so, you may learn from the 'Acts' which were recorded under Pontius Pilate." Later he says: "That He performed these miracles you may easily be satisfied from the 'Acts' of Pontius Pilate." *Apology* 1.48.

Elgin Moyer, in *Who Was Who in Church History,* describes Justin as a:

". . . philosopher, martyr, apologist, born at Flavia Neapolis. Well educated, seems to have had sufficient means to lead a life of study and travel. Being an eager seeker for truth, knocked successively at the doors of Stoicism, Aristotelianism, Pythagoreanism and Platonism, but hated Epicureanism. In early days became somewhat acquainted with the Jews, but was not interested in their religion. Platonism appealed to him the most and he thought he was about to reach the goal of his philosophy — the vision of God — when one day in a solitary walk along the seashore, the young philosopher met a venerable old Christian of pleasant countenance and gentle dignity. This humble Christian shook his confidence in human wisdom, and pointed him to the Hebrew prophets, 'men more ancient than all those who were esteemed philosophers, whose writings and teachings foretold the coming of Christ. . . .' Following the advice of the old gentleman, this zealous Platonist became a believing Christian. He said, 'I found this philosophy alone to be safe and profitable.' After conversion, which occurred in early manhood, he devoted himself wholeheartedly to the vindication and spread of the Christian religion." 7/227

11C. THE JEWISH *TALMUDS* (See page 53.)

Tol'doth Yeshu. Jesus is referred to as "Ben Pandera."

Babylonian Talmud. (Giving opinion of the Amorian) writes ". . . and hanged him on the eve of Passover."

Talmud title referring to Jesus: "Ben Pandera (or 'Ben Pantere')" and "Jeshu ben Pandera." Many scholars say "pandera" is a play on words, a travesty on the Greek word for virgin "parthenos," calling him a "son of a virgin." Joseph Klausner, a Jew, says "the illegitimate birth of Jesus was a current idea among the Jews. . . ."

Comments in the *Baraila* are of great historical value:

"On the eve of Passover they hanged Yeshu (of Nazareth) and the herald went before him for forty days saying (Yeshu of Nazareth) is going forth to be stoned in that he hath practiced sorcery and beguiled

and led astray Israel. Let everyone knowing aught in his defence come
and plead for him. But they found naught in his defence and hanged
him on the eve of Passover" (Babylonia *Sanhedrin* 43a). — "Eve of
Passover."

The Amoa 'Ulla' ("Ulla" was a disciple of R. Youchanan and lived in
Palestine at the end of the third century.) adds:

"And do you suppose that for (Yeshu of Nazareth) there was any right
of appeal? He was a beguiler, and the Merciful One hath said: 'Thou
shalt not spare neither shalt thou conceal him.' It is otherwise with
Yeshu, for he was near to the civil authority."

The Jewish authorities did not deny that Jesus performed signs and
miracles (Matthew 9:34; 12:24; Mark 3:22) but they attributed them
to acts of sorcery. 5/23

"The *Talmud*," writes the Jewish scholar Joseph Klausner, "speaks of
hanging in place of crucifixion, since this horrible Roman form of
death was only known to Jewish scholars from Roman trials, and not
from the Jewish legal system. Even Paul the Apostle (Gal. iii. 13)
expounds the passage 'for a curse of God is that which is hanged'
(Deut. xxi. 23) as applicable to Jesus." 5/28

Sanhedrin 43a also makes references to the disciples of Jesus.

Yeb. IV 3; 49a:

"R. Shimeon ben Azzai said [concerning Jesus]: 'I found a
genealogical roll in Jerusalem wherein was recorded, Such-an-one is
a bastard of an adulteress.' "

Klausner adds to the above:

"Current editions of the *Mishnah* add: 'To support the words of R.
Yehoshua' (who, in the same *Mishnah*, says: What is a bastard?
Everyone whose parents are liable to death by the Beth Din). That
Jesus is here referred to seems to be beyond doubt. . . ." 5/35

An early *Baraita,* in which R. Eliezer is the central figure, speaks of
Jesus by name. The brackets are within the quote. Eliezer speaking:
"He answered, Akiba, you have reminded me! Once I was walking
along the upper market (*Tosefta* reads 'street') of Sepphoris and found
one [of the disciples of Jesus of Nazareth] and Jacob of Kefar Sekanya
(*Tosefta* reads 'Sakkanin') was his name. He said to me, It is written in
your Law, 'Thou shalt not bring the hire of a harlot, etc.' What was to
be done with it — a latrine for the High Priest? But I answered nothing.
He said to me, so [Jesus of Nazareth] taught me (*Tosefta* reads, 'Yeshu
ben Pantere'): 'For of the hire of a harlot hath she gathered them, and
unto the hire of a harlot shall they return'; from the place of filth they
come, and unto the place of filth they shall go. And the saying pleased
me, and because of this I was arrested for *Minuth.* And I transgressed
against what is written in the Law; 'Keep thy way far from here' —
that is *Minuth;* 'and come not nigh the door of her house' — that is the
civil government." 5/38

The above brackets are found in *Dikduke Sof'rim* to *Abada Zara*
(Munich Manuscript, ed. Rabinovitz).

Klausner, commenting on the above passage, says:

"There can be no doubt that the words, 'one of the disciples of Jesus of
Nazareth,' and 'thus Jesus of Nazareth taught me,' are, in the present
passage both early in date and fundamental in their bearing on the
story; and their primitive character cannot be disputed on the
grounds of the slight variations in the parallel passages; their

variants ('Yeshu ben Pantere' or 'Yeshu ben Pandera,' instead of 'Yeshu of Nazareth') are merely due to the fact that, from an early date, the name 'Pantere,' or 'Pandera,' became widely current among the Jews as the name of the reputed father of Jesus." 5/38

12C. ENCYCLOPAEDIA BRITANNICA

The latest edition of the *Encyclopaedia Britannica* uses 20,000 words in describing this person, Jesus. His description took more space than was given to Aristotle, Cicero, Alexander, Julius Caesar, Buddha, Confucius, Mohammed or Napoleon Bonaparte.

Concerning the testimony of the many independent secular accounts of Jesus of Nazareth, it records:

"These independent accounts prove that in ancient times even the opponents of Christianity never doubted the historicity of Jesus, which was disputed for the first time and on inadequate grounds by several authors at the end of the 18th, during the 19th, and at the beginning of the 20th centuries." 3/145

BIBLIOGRAPHY

1. Betz, Otto. *What Do We Know About Jesus?* SCM Press, 1968.
2. Bruce, F. F. *The New Testament Documents: Are They Reliable?* 5th revised edition. Downers Grove: Inter-Varsity Press, 1972. Used by permission.
3. *Encyclopaedia Britannica.* 15th edition, 1974.
4. Jacoby, Felix. *Die Fragmente der Griechischen Historiker.* Berlin: Wiedmann, 1923.
5. Klausner, Joseph. *Jesus of Nazareth.* New York: The Macmillan Company, 1925.
6. Montgomery, John Warwick. *History and Christianity.* Downers Grove: Inter-Varsity Press, 1964. Used by permission.
7. Moyer, Elgin. *Who Was Who in Church History.* Chicago: Moody Press, 1968.
8. Pines, Shlomo, Professor of Philosophy at Hebrew University, Jerusalem; David Flusser, professor at Hebrew University, New York Times press release, Feb. 12, 1972, carried by *Palm Beach Post-Times,* Sunday, Feb. 13, 1972, "CHRIST DOCUMENTATION: Israeli Scholars Find Ancient Document They Feel Confirms the Existence of Jesus."

chapter 6 _____

Jesus-
God's
son

The following is an outline designed to aid you in effectively using this
material.

1A.   HIS DIRECT CLAIMS TO DEITY
>   1B.   His Trial
>   2B.   His Personal Claims
>   3B.   His Acceptance of Worship as God
>   4B.   His Claims Confirmed by Others

2A.   HIS INDIRECT CLAIMS TO DEITY
>   1B.   Forgiveness of Sin
>   2B.   Immutable
>   3B.   Life
>   4B.   Judgment

3A.   HIS TITLES OF DEITY
>   1B.   YHWH
>   2B.   Son of God
>   3B.   Son of Man
>   4B.   Abba, Father

1A. DIRECT CLAIMS

1B. Introduction

"Obviously *who* is Christ, is as important as what He did." 20/11 So we ask
who is Christ? What type of person is He?

As *Albert Wells* puts it, "One marvels at the way in which He draws
attention to Himself, placing Himself at the center of every situation that
arises." 33/51

As we see, He certainly does not fit the mold of other religious leaders,
writes Thomas Schultz:

"Not one *recognized* religious leader, not Moses, Paul, Buddha,
Mohammed, Confucius, etc., has ever claimed to be God; that is, with the
exception of Jesus Christ. Christ is the only religious leader who has ever
claimed to be deity and the only individual ever who has convinced a
great portion of the world that He is God." 38/209

How could a "man" make others think He was God? We hear first from F. J. Meldau:

"His teachings were ultimate, final — above those of Moses and the prophets. He never added any afterthoughts or revisions; He never retracted or changed; He never guessed, 'supposed,' or spoke with any uncertainty. This is all so contrary to human teachers and teachings." 24/5

Add to this the testimony of Foster:

"But the reason overshadowing all others, which led directly to the ignominious execution of the Teacher of Galilee, was His incredible claim that He, a simple carpenter's son among the shavings and sawdust of His father's workshop, was in reality God in the flesh!" 2/49

One may well say, "Of course Jesus is presented this way in the Bible because it was written by His associates who desired to make an everlasting memorial to Him." However, to disregard all the Bible is not to disregard all the evidence, as we have seen from historical records.

William Robinson states: "However, if one takes a historically objective approach to the question, it is found that even secular history affirms that Jesus lived on earth and that He was worshipped as God. He founded a church which has worshipped Him for 1,900 years. He changed the course of the world's history." 32/29

2B. The Trial

Mark 14:61-64

"But He held his peace, and answered nothing. Again the high priest asked Him, and said unto Him, Art Thou the Christ, the Son of the Blessed? And Jesus said, I am: and ye shall see the Son of man sitting on the right hand of power, and coming in the clouds of heaven. Then the high priest rent his clothes, and saith, what need we any further witnesses? Ye have heard the blasphemy: what think ye? And they all condemned Him to be guilty of death" (KJV).

Judge Gaynor, the accomplished jurist of the New York bench, in his address upon the trial of Jesus, takes the ground that blasphemy was the one charge made against Him before the Sanhedrin. He says: "It is plain from each of the gospel narratives, that the alleged crime for which Jesus was tried and convicted was blasphemy: . . . Jesus had been claiming supernatural power, which in a human being was blasphemy" (citing John 10:33). His reference is to Jesus' "making Himself God," not to what He said concerning the Temple. 6/118,119

To the questions of the Pharisees, A. T. Robertson says, "Jesus accepts the challenge and admits that He claims to be all three (the Messiah, the Son of Man, the Son of God). Ye say *(Humeis legete),* is just a Greek idiom for 'Yes' (compare 'I AM' in Mark 14:62 with 'Thou hast said' in Matthew 26:64)." 31/277

It was to Jesus' reply that the high priest rent his garments. H. B. Swete explains the significance of this: "The law forbade the High Priest to rend his garment in private troubles (Lev. x.6, xxi, 10), but when acting as a judge, he was required by custom to express in this way his horror of any blasphemy uttered in his presence. The relief of the embarrassed judge is manifest. If trustworthy evidence was not forthcoming, the necessity for it had now been superseded: the Prisoner had incriminated Himself." 43/339

We begin to see that this is no ordinary trial. Irwin Linton, a lawyer, brings this out when he states:

"Unique among criminal trials is this one in which not the actions but the identity of the accused is the issue. The criminal charge laid against Christ, the confession or testimony or, rather, act in presence of the court, on which He was convicted, the interrogation by the Roman governor and the inscription and proclamation on His cross at the time of execution all are concerned with the one question of Christ's real identity and dignity. 'What think ye of Christ? Whose son is he?' " 20/7

In this same regard we hear from the one-time skeptic, Frank Morison, "Jesus of Nazareth was condemned to death, not upon the statements of His accusers, but upon an admission extorted from Him under oath." 27/25

Also from Hilarin Felder (Christ and the Critics) we hear, "This inspection of the trial of Jesus should be sufficient to give us the invincible conviction that the Saviour confessed His true divinity before His judges." 7/299,300

Simon Greenleaf, a one-time professor at the Harvard School of Law, and himself a great lawyer, said regarding Jesus' trial:

"It is not easy to perceive on what ground His conduct could have been defended before any tribunal unless upon that of His superhuman character. No lawyer, it is conceived, would think of placing His defence upon any other basis." 10/562

Even though Jesus' answers to His judges take different form in each of the Synoptics, we see, as Morison tells us, that they all are equal in meaning:

". . . These answers are really identical. The formulae 'Thou hast said' or 'Ye say that I am,' which to modern ears sound evasive, had no such connotation to the contemporary Jewish mind. 'Thou sayest' was the traditional form in which a cultivated Jew replied to a question of grave or sad import. Courtesy forbade a direct 'yes' or 'no.' " 27/26

To be certain that Jesus made these implications from His answers, C. G. Montefiore analyzes His statement which follows His profession of deity: "The two expressions 'Son of Man' (frequently on his lips) and 'at the right hand of power' . . . (a peculiar Hebrew expression for the Deity) show that the answer is perfectly in accord with Jesus' spirit and manner of speech." 26/360

It is perfectly clear then that this is the testimony that Jesus wanted to bear of Himself. We also see that the Jews must have understood His reply as a claim to His being God. There were two alternatives to be faced then; that His assertions were pure blasphemy or that He was God. His judges had to see the issue clearly — so clearly, in fact, that they crucified Him and then taunted Him because, "He trusted in God . . . for He said, 'I am the Son of God' " (Matthew 27:43). 40/125

Thus, we see that Jesus was crucified for being who He really was, for being the Son of God. An analysis of His testimony will bear this out. His testimony affirmed that:

1. He was the Son of the Blessed.
2. He was the one who would sit at the right hand of power.
3. He was the Son of Man who would come on the clouds of heaven.

William Childs Robinson then concludes from this that "each of these [three] affirmations is distinctly Messianic. Their cumulative Messianic effect is 'stunningly significant.' " 33/65

Herschel Hobbs then goes on to reiterate:

"The Sanhedrin caught all three points. They summed them up in one question. 'Art thou then the Son of God?' Their question invited an affirmative answer. It was the equivalent of a declarative statement on their part. So Jesus simply replied, 'Ye say that I am.' Therefore, He made them admit to His identity before they formally found Him guilty of death. It was a clever strategy on Jesus' part. He would die not merely upon His own admission to deity but also upon theirs.

"According to them there was need for no other testimony. For they had heard Him themselves. So they condemned Him by the words 'of his own mouth.' But He also condemned them by their words. They could not say that they did not proclaim the Son of God guilty of death." 12/322

Robert Anderson says:

"But no confirmatory evidence is more convincing than that of hostile witnesses, and the fact that the Lord laid claim to Deity is incontestably established by the action of His enemies. We must remember that the Jews were not a tribe of ignorant savages, but a highly cultured and intensely religious people; and it was upon this very charge that, without a dissentient voice, His death was decreed by the Sanhedrin — their great national Council, composed of the most eminent of their religious leaders, including men of the type of Gamaliel and his great pupil, Saul of Tarsus." 2/5

From Hilarin Felder we have this statement which brings more light on the judgment the Pharisees actually impose on themselves:

"But since they condemn the Saviour as a blasphemer by reason of his own confession, the judges prove officially and on oath that Jesus confessed not only that he was the theocratical Messiah-King and human son of God, but also that he was the divine Messiah and the essential Son of God, and that He on account of this confession was put to death." 7/306, Vol. 1

As a result of our study, we may then safely conclude that Jesus claimed deity for Himself in a way that all could recognize. These claims were regarded as blasphemous by the religious leaders and resulted in His crucifixion because "He made Himself out to be the Son of God" (John 19:7). 21/45

3B.   Other Claims

1C.   EQUALITY WITH THE FATHER

1D.   John 10:30-33. Did Jesus claim to be God in other parts of the narratives? The Jews said He did, as we see in this passage:

"I and *My* Father are one. Then the Jews took up stones again to stone Him. Jesus answered them, Many good works have I shewed you from My Father; for which of those works do ye stone Me? The Jews answered Him, saying, For a good work we stone Thee not; but for blasphemy; and because Thou, being a man, makest Thyself God" (KJV). 22/409

An interesting and strengthening implication arises when the Greek wording is studied. From A. T. Robertson we find:

"One *(hen)*. Neuter, no masculine *(heis)*. Not one person (cf. *heis* in Gal. 3:28), but one essence or nature."

Robertson then adds:

"This crisp statement is the climax of Christ's claims concerning the relation between the Father and Himself (the Son). They stir the Pharisees to uncontrollable anger." 31/186,187

It is very evident then that in the minds of those who heard this statement, there was no doubt that Jesus claimed before them that He was God. Thus:

"The Jews could regard Jesus' word only as blasphemy, and they proceeded to take the judgment into their own hands. It was laid down in the Law that blasphemy was to be punished by stoning (Lev. 24:16). But these men were not allowing the due processes of law to take their course. They were not preparing an indictment so that the authorities could take the requisite action. In their fury they were preparing to be judges and executioners in one. 'Again' will refer back to their previous attempt at stoning (John 8:59)." 3/524

Their reply rejects any chance that Jesus is threatened with stoning for His good works. Rather, it is the "blasphemy." They definitely understood His teaching but, one may ask, did they stop to consider whether His claims were true or not?

2D.   John 5:17,18

"But Jesus answered them, My Father worketh hitherto, and I work. Therefore the Jews sought the more to kill Him, because He not only had broken the sabbath, but said also that God was His Father, making Himself equal with God" (KJV).

A word study from A. T. Robertson's *Word Pictures of the New Testament* gives some interesting insights:

"Jesus distinctly says, 'My Father' (*ho pater mou*). Not 'our Father,' claim to peculiar relation to the Father. Worketh even until now (*heos arti ergazetai*). . . . Jesus put himself on a par with God's activity and thus justifies his healing on the Sabbath." 31/82,83

It is also worthy of note that the Jews did not refer to God as "My Father." If they did, they would qualify the statement with "in heaven." However, this Jesus did not do. He made a claim that the Jews could not misinterpret when He called God "My Father." 28/309

Jesus also implies that while God is working, He, the Son, is working, too. 29/1083 Again, the Jews understood the implication that He was God's Son. Resulting from this statement, the Jews' hatred has grown. Even though they are seeking, mainly, to persecute Him, they are growing in their desire to kill Him. 17/376

2C.   "I AM"

John 8:58: "Jesus said unto them, Verily, verily, I say unto you, Before Abraham was, I am" (KJV).

"He said unto them, 'Verily, verily, I say unto you . . .' Prefaced by a double Amen — the strongest oath — our Lord claims the incommunicable name of the Divine Being. The Jews recognize His meaning, and, horrified, they seek to stone Him." 39/54

How did the Jews receive this statement? As Henry Alford tells us, ". . . All unbiased exegesis of these words must recognize in them a declaration of the essential pre-existence of Christ." 1/801,802

Marvin Vincent in his *Word Studies of the New Testament* writes that Jesus' statement is "the formula for *absolute*, timeless 'I AM' (*eimi*)." 44/181. Vol. 2

By relying on Old Testament references, we can find out the significance of I AM. A. G. Campbell makes this inference for us:

"From such Old Testament references as Ex. 3:14, Deuteronomy 32:39 and Isaiah 43:10 it is clear that this is no new idea which Jesus is presenting. The Jews were quite familiar with the idea that the Jehovah of the Old Testament is the eternally existent One. That which is new to the Jews is the identification of this designation with Jesus." 4/12

From the reactions of the surrounding Jews we have proof that they understood His reference as a claim to absolute deity. Their insights prompted them to set about to fulfill the Mosaic law for blasphemy by stoning Jesus (Leviticus 24:13-16).

Campbell speaks on the above point for the non-Jew:

"That we must also understand the expression 'I am' *(eimi)* as intended to declare the full deity of Christ is clear from the fact that Jesus did not attempt an explanation. He did not try to convince the Jews that they had misunderstood Him, but rather He repeated the statement several times on various occasions." 4/12,13

3C.   JESUS IS DUE THE SAME HONOR AS THAT GIVEN TO GOD

John 5:23,24

"That all men should honour the Son, even as they honour the Father. He that honoureth not the Son honoureth not the Father which hath sent him. Verily, verily, I say unto you, He that heareth My word, and believeth on Him that sent Me, hath everlasting life, and shall not come into condemnation; but is passed from death unto life" (KJV).

In the last part of this verse Jesus thrusts a warning at those who accuse Him of blasphemy. He tells them that by hurling abuse at Him, they are actually hurling it at God and that it is God who is outraged by their treatment of Jesus. 8/174. Vol. 2

We also see that Jesus claims the right to be worshipped as God. And from this it follows, as previously stated, that to dishonor Jesus is to dishonor God. 31/86

Wordsworth (cited by J. C. Ryle, *Expository Thoughts on the Gospels*) remarks, "They who profess zeal for the one God do not honour Him aright, unless they honour the Son as they honour the Father." 34/291. Vol. 1

4C.   TO KNOW ME

John 8:19

"Then said they unto Him, Where is Thy Father? Jesus answered, Ye neither know Me, nor My Father: if ye had known Me, ye should have known My Father also" (KJV).

5C.   BELIEVE IN ME

John 14:1

"Let not your heart be troubled: ye believe in God, believe also in Me" (KJV). Merrill Tenney explains:

"He was doomed to death, the death that overtakes all men. Nevertheless, He had the audacity to demand that they make Him an object of faith. He made Himself the key to the question of destiny, and clearly stated that their future depended on His work. He promised to prepare a place for them, and to return to claim them." 43/213

6C. HE WHO HAS SEEN ME . . .

John 14:9

"Jesus saith unto him, Have I been so long time with you, and yet hast thou not known Me, Philip? He that hath seen Me hath seen the Father; and how sayest thou then, Shew us the Father?" (KJV).

7C. I SAY UNTO YOU . . .

Matthew 5:20,22,26,28,etc.

In this Scripture we find Jesus teaching and speaking in His own name. By doing so, He elevated the authority of His words directly to heaven. Instead of repeating the prophets by saying, "Thus saith the Lord," Jesus repeated, "Verily, verily, I say unto you."

As Karl Scheffrahn and Henry Kreyssler tell us:

"He never hesitated nor apologized. He had no need to contradict, withdraw or modify anything he said. He spoke the unequivocal words of God (John 3:34). He said, 'Heaven and earth will pass away, but My Words will not pass away' " (Mark 13:31). 37/11

4B. He asked for and accepted worship as God

1C. WORSHIP RESERVED FOR GOD ONLY

1D. To fall down in homage is the greatest act of adoration and worship which can be performed for God (John 4:20-22; Acts 8:27).

2D. Adoration in spirit and truth (John 4:24).

3D. "Thou shalt worship the Lord thy God" (Matthew 4:10; Luke 4:8).

2C. JESUS RECEIVED WORSHIP AS GOD AND *ACCEPTED* IT

1D. "There came a leper and worshipped Him . . ." (Matthew 8:2).

2D. The man born blind, after being healed, "falls down and worships Him" (John 9:35-39).

3D. The disciples "worshipped Him, saying: 'Indeed Thou art the Son of God' " (Matthew 14:33).

4D. "Then He said to Thomas, 'Reach here your finger, and see My hands; and reach here your hand, and put it into My side; and be not unbelieving, but believing.'

"Thomas answered and said to Him, 'My Lord and my God!'

"Jesus said to him, 'Because you have seen Me, have you believed? Blessed are they who did not see, and yet believed' " (John 20:27-29).

3C. JESUS CONTRASTED WITH OTHERS

1D. The centurion Cornelius falls at the feet of Peter and "adores him," and Peter reproves him saying, "Stand up; I myself also am a man" (Acts 10:25,26, KJV).

2D. Before the angel of the Apocalypse, John fell at his feet to "adore him," and the angel told him that he was a "fellow servant" and that John was to "adore God" (Revelation 19:10).

4C. As we see, Jesus commanded and accepted worship as God. It was this fact that led Thiessen to write: "If He is a deceiver, or is self-deceived, and, in either case, if He is not God He is not good (*Christus si non Deus, non bonus*)." [Thiessen, *Outline of Lectures in Systematic Theology*, p. 65]

5B. What Others Said

1C. PAUL

1D. Philippians 2:9-11

"Wherefore God also hath highly exalted Him, and given Him a name which is above every name: That at the name of Jesus every knee should bow, of things in heaven, and things in earth, and things under the earth; and that every tongue should confess that Jesus Christ is Lord, to the glory of God the Father" (KJV).

2D. Titus 2:13

"Looking for that blessed hope, and the glorious appearing of the great God and our Saviour Jesus Christ . . ." (KJV).

2C. JOHN THE BAPTIST

"And the Holy Ghost descended in a bodily shape like a dove upon Him, and a voice came from heaven, which said, Thou art My beloved Son; in Thee I am well pleased" (Luke 3:22, KJV).

3C. PETER

1D. Probably Peter's most famous affirmation is found in Matthew 16:15-17: "He saith unto them, But whom say ye that I am? And Simon Peter answered and said, Thou art the Christ, the Son of the living God. And Jesus answered and said unto him, Blessed art thou, Simon Bar-jona: for flesh and blood hath not revealed it unto thee, but My Father which is in heaven" (KJV).

Of this, Scheffrahn and Kreyssler write that "instead of rebuking for his brashness (as Jesus always did when confronted by error), Jesus blesses Peter for his confession of faith. Throughout His ministry Jesus accepted prayers and worship as rightfully belonging to Himself." 37/10

2D. Peter again affirms his belief in Acts 2:36:

"Therefore let all the house of Israel know assuredly, that God hath made that same Jesus, whom ye have crucified, both Lord and Christ" (KJV).

4C. THOMAS

"The Doubter" bears the following witness found in John 20:28: "And Thomas answered and said unto Him, 'My Lord and my God'" (KJV).

John Stott in *Basic Christianity* expounds on Thomas' exclamation:

"The Sunday following Easter Day, incredulous Thomas is with the other disciples in the upper room when Jesus appears. He invites Thomas to feel His wounds, and Thomas, overwhelmed with wonder, cries out, 'My Lord and my God!' (John 20:26-29). Jesus accepts the designation. He rebukes Thomas for his unbelief, but not for his worship." 41/28

5C. FROM THE WRITER OF HEBREWS

Hebrews 1:8

"But unto the Son he saith, 'Thy throne, O God, is for ever and ever: a sceptre of righteousness is the sceptre of Thy kingdom" (KJV).

Thomas Schultz writes that "the vocative . . . in 'thy throne, O God' is preferred to the nominative where it would be translated 'God is thy throne' or 'thy throne is God.' Once again the evidence is conclusive — Jesus Christ is called God in the Scriptures." 38/180

6C. STEPHEN

Acts 7:59

"And they stoned Stephen, calling upon God, and saying, Lord Jesus, receive my spirit" (KJV).

Stephen here precisely asks of Jesus what Jesus had asked of God while He was on the cross. Stephen thereby ascribes to Jesus the qualities of deity.

6B. Conclusion

William Biederwolf draws a very apt conclusion from the evidence. That is:

"A man who can read the New Testament and not see that Christ claims to be more than a man, can look all over the sky at high noon on a cloudless day and not see the sun." 23/50

We quote the words of the "Beloved Apostle" John:

"And many other signs truly did Jesus in the presence of His disciples, which are not written in this book: But these are written, that ye might believe that Jesus is the Christ, the Son of God; and that believing ye might have life through His name" (John 20:30, 31, KJV).

2A. INDIRECT CLAIMS

Jesus, in many cases, indirectly made known His deity. Below is a listing of many of these references with a few of His direct claims as well.

JESUS IS JEHOVAH		
Of Jehovah	Mutual Title or Act	Of Jesus
Isa. 40:28	Creator	John 1:3
Isa. 45:22; 43:11	Savior	John 4:42
I Sam. 2:6	Raise dead	John 5:21
Joel 3:12	Judge	John 5:27, cf. Matt. 25:31 ff.
Isa. 60:19-20	Light	John 8:12
Exodus 3:14	I Am	John 8:58, cf. 18:5,6
Ps. 23:1	Shepherd	John 10:11
Isa. 42:8; cf. 48:11	Glory of God	John 17:1,5
Isa. 41:4; 44:6	First and Last	Rev. 1:17; 2:8
Hosea 13:14	Redeemer	Rev. 5:9
Isa. 62:5 (and Hosea 2:16)	Bridegroom	Rev. 21:2, cf. Matt. 25:1ff.
Ps. 18:2	Rock	I Cor. 10:4
Jer. 31:34	Forgiver of Sins	Mark 2:7,10
Ps. 148:2	Worshiped by Angels	Heb. 1:6
Throughout O. T.	Addressed in Prayer	Acts 7:59
Ps. 148:5	Creator of Angels	Col. 1:16
Isa. 45:23	Confessed as Lord	Phil. 2:11

[Norman Geisler, *Christ: The Theme of the Bible*, Moody Press, 1969, ed., p. 48]

It is our feeling that some of these claims require further explanation. That is the purpose of this section.

1B.   He Claimed to Be Able to Forgive Sins as Evidenced in Mark 2:5 and Luke 7:48

By Jewish law this was only for God to do, as only God could forgive sins.

This is seen from Mark 2:7. The scribes, in their discontent with Jesus, ask in verse 7, "Why does this man speak that way? He is blaspheming; who can forgive sins but God alone?"

In Matthew 9:5,6, Jesus has just healed a paralytic by forgiving his sins. Once again He is confronted by the religious leaders.

In these verses Jesus asks which would be easier, to say "your sins are forgiven" or to say "rise and walk." According to the Wycliffe Commentary this is "an unanswerable question. The statements are equally simple to pronounce; but to say either, with accompanying performance requires divine power. An imposter, of course, in seeking to avoid detection, would find the former easier. Jesus proceeded to heal the illness that men might *know* that He had *authority* to deal with its cause. . . ." 29/944

At this He was accused of blasphemy by the scribes and Pharisees. "The charge by the scribes and Pharisees . . . condemned Him for taking to Himself the prerogatives of God." 29/943

C. E. Jefferson tells that ". . . He forgave sins, He spoke as one having authority. Even the worst sinners when penitent at His feet received from Him authoritative assurance of forgiveness." 14/330

From L. S. Chafer we are told that "none on earth has either authority or right to forgive sin. None could forgive sin save the One against whom all have sinned. When Christ forgave sin, as He certainly did, He was not exercising a human prerogative. Since none but God can forgive sins, it is conclusively demonstrated that Christ, since He forgave sins, is God, and being God, is from everlasting." 5/21, Vol. 5

Not only did He forgive sins committed against Himself, but He forgave the sins of one individual against another, which, up to that time, was unheard of. John Stott reminds us: "We may forgive the injuries which others do to us; but the sins we commit against God only God Himself can forgive." 41/29 And Jesus does just that.

Thus, we see that Jesus' power to forgive sin is the "climactic exhibition of a power that belongs to God alone." (*The Jerome Biblical Commentary*, Vol. 2. Prentice Hall, 1968)

2B.   Jesus Is Immutable

Lewis S. Chafer says that "the unchangeableness of Deity is ascribed to Christ. All else is subject to change." 5/18, Vol. 5. Hebrews 13:8 compares with Malachi 3:6.

3B.   Jesus Claimed to Be "Life"

In John 14:6 Jesus claimed to be "life." "I am the . . . life. . . ."

In analyzing this statement, Merrill Tenney tells us that "He did not say He knew the way, the truth, and the life, nor that He taught them. He did not make Himself the exponent of a new system; He declared Himself to be the final key to all mysteries." 43/215

4B.   In Him Is Life

"And the witness is this, that God has given us eternal life, and this life is in His Son. He who has the Son has the life; he who does not have the Son of God does not have the life" (I John 5:11, 12).

Speaking of this life, John Stott (*Basic Christianity*) writes:

"He likened His followers' dependence on Him to the sustenance derived from the vine by its branches. He stated that God hàd given Him authority over all flesh, that He should give life to as many as God gave Him. . . ." 41/29

5B. Jesus Has Authority

"And He [God] gave Him [Jesus] authority to execute judgment, because He [Jesus] is the Son of Man" (John 5:27).

In claiming that He will judge the world, Jesus will Himself arouse the dead, He will gather the nations before Himself, He will sit on a throne of glory and He shall judge the world. Some, on the basis of His judgment, will inherit heaven, others, hell.

3A. TITLES

1B. YHWH — Lord

1C.   SACRED TO THE JEWS

The more literal translation of *YHWH* is *Yahweh*.

"The precise meaning," writes Herbert F. Stevenson, "of the name is obscure. In the Hebrew, it was originally composed of four consonants YHWH — known to theologians as 'the tetragrammaton' — to which the vowels of *Adonai* were afterwards added (except when the name is joined to *Adonai:* then the vowels of *Elohim* are used). The Jews came to regard the name as too sacred to pronounce, however, and in the public reading of the Scriptures they substituted *Adonai* for it — Jehovah was indeed to them 'the incommunicable name.' " 40/20

". . . the Jewish people out of sheer reverence refused even to pronounce this name. . . ." 5/264, Vol. I

"The avoidance," writes L. S. Chafer (*Systematic Theology*), "of the actual pronouncement of this name may be judged as mere superstition; but plainly it was an attempt at reverence however much misguided, and doubtless this practice, with all its confusing results, did serve to create a deep impression on all as to the ineffable character of God." 5/264, Vol. 1

The *Jewish Encyclopedia* (ed., Isidore Singer, Funk and Wagnalls, Vol. 1, 1904) indicates that the translation of YHWH by the word "Lord" can be traced to the Septuagint. "About the pronunciation of the Shem ha Metorash, the 'distinctive name' YHWH, there is no authentic information." Beginning from the Hellenistic period, the name was reserved for use in the Temple.

"From Sifre to Num. vi. 27, Mishnah Tamid, vii.2, and Sotah vii.6 it appears that the priests were allowed to pronounce the name at the benediction only in the Temple; elsewhere they were obliged to use the appellative name (*kinnuy*) 'Adonai.' "

The *Jewish Encyclopedia* goes on to quote from Philo and Josephus.

Philo: "The four letters may be mentioned or heard only by holy men whose ears and tongues are purified by wisdom, and by no others in any place whatsoever" ["Life of Moses," iii, 41].

Josephus: "Moses besought God to impart to him the knowledge of His name and its pronunciation so that he might be able to invoke Him by name at the sacred acts, whereupon God communicated His name, hitherto unknown to any man; and it would be a sin for me to mention it" [*Antiquities*. ii 12, par. 4].

2C.   CHRIST SPEAKS OF HIMSELF AS THE JEHOVAH

Scotchmer, cited by W. C. Robinson: "The identification of our Lord Jesus Christ with the Lord of the Old Testament results in an explicit doctrine of His Deity." 33/118

"Yahweh" (Exodus 3:14) basically means "He who is," or "I am who I am," and declares the divine Self-existence [Unger's Bible Dictionary, p. 409].

Kreyssler and Scheffrahn say: "He claimed the covenant of YHWH — or Jehovah. In the 8th Chapter of John's Gospel we find: 'Unless you believe that I AM, you shall die in your sins.' V. 24; 'When you lift up (i.e., on the cross) the Son of Man, then you will know that I AM. . . .' V. 28; 'Truly, truly, I say to you, before Abraham was, I AM,' V. 58. His use of the I Am connects with Exodus 3:14 where God reveals Himself to Moses: 'I AM Who I AM.' And He said, 'Say this to the people of Israel, I AM has sent me to you.' Thus the name of God in Hebrew is YHWH or I AM." 37/11

In Matthew 13:14,15, Christ identifies Himself with the "Lord" (Adonai) of the Old Testament (Isaiah 6:8-10). 24/15

Clark Pinnock in *Set Forth Your Case* says that "His teachings rang with the great I AM statements which are divine claims in structure and content" (Exodus 3:14; John 4:26; 6:35; 8:12; 10:9; 11:25). 30/60

In John 12:41, Christ is described as the one seen by Isaiah in Isaiah 6:1. Also Isaiah writes, says William C. Robinson, of the forerunner of Jehovah: "Prepare ye the way of the Lord . . ." (Isaiah 40:3, KJV). Christ endorsed the claim of the Samaritans who said, "We . . . know that this is indeed the Christ, the Saviour of the world" (John 4:42, KJV). From the Old Testament this can only designate the Jehovah-God. Hosea 13:4 declares: "I am the Lord thy God . . . thou shalt know no god but Me: for there is no saviour besides Me" (KJV). 33/117,118

2B.   Son of God

Hilarin Felder relates that "Gustav Dalman sees himself forced to this confession: 'Nowhere do we find that Jesus proclaimed Himself to be the Son of God in such a way that merely a religious and ethical relation to God is meant, which others also could and should also in reality possess. . . . Jesus has given men unmistakably to understand that He is not only 'a,' but 'the Son of God.' " [*Die Worte Jesu, mit Beruecksichtigung des nachkanonischen juedischen Schrifttums und der aramaeischen Sprache eroertert*, i, 230,235 (Leipzig, 1898).] 7/269

H. F. Stevenson comments that "it is true that the term 'sons of God' is used of men (Hosea 1:10) and of angels, in the Old Testament (Gen. 6:2; Job 1:6; 38:7). But in the New Testament, the title 'Son of God' is used of, and by, our Lord in quite a different way. In every instance the term implies that He is the one, only-begotten Son; co-equal, co-eternal with the Father." 40/123

In the repeated uses of the term "Son" in juxtaposition to "the Father," they declare His explicit claim of equality with the Father and formulate the truth of the Trinity (John 10:33-38; 3:35; 5:19-27; 6:27; 14:13; Mark 13:32; Matthew 23:9,10).

Jesus complimented Peter on his knowledge of Him as the Son of God when Peter confessed at Caesarea Philippi: "Thou art the Christ, the Son of the living God." He replied, "Blessed art thou, Simon Bar-jona: for flesh and blood hath not revealed it unto thee, but My Father which is in heaven" (Matthew 16:16,17, KJV). 40/124

Felder writes on Christ's concept of God being His Father: "As often as Jesus speaks of His relations with His Father He uses constantly and without exception the expression 'My Father'; and as often as He calls the attention of the disciples to their childlike relation to God, there is the equally definite characterization, 'Your Father.' Never does He associate Himself with the disciples and with men by the natural form of speech, 'Our Father.' "

Felder continues: "Even on those occasions in which Jesus unites Himself with the disciples before God, and when therefore it would be certainly expected that He would use the collective expression, 'Our Father,' there stands, on the contrary, 'My Father': 'I will not drink henceforth of this fruit of the vine until that day when I shall drink it with *you* new in the kingdom of *My Father*' (Matt. xxvi, 29). 'And I send the promise of *My Father* upon *you*' (Luke xxiv, 49). 'Come, ye blessed of *My Father,* possess you the kingdom prepared for *you* from the foundation of the world' (Matt. xxv, 34). Thus and similarly does Jesus distinguish unequivocally between His divine sonship and that of the disciples and men in general." 7/268,269

Scotchmer concludes that "His disciples and His enemies understand from their Jewish background that the real import of the term 'Son of God' was Deity. One hundred and four times, Christ refers to God as 'Father' or 'the Father.' " 7/300

3B. Son of Man

Jesus makes use of the title "Son of Man" in three distinctive ways:

1. Concerning His earthly ministry
   1) Matthew 8:20
   2) Matthew 9:6
   3) Matthew 11:19
   4) Matthew 16:13
   5) Luke 19:10
   6) Luke 22:48

2. When foretelling His passion
   1) Matthew 12:40
   2) Matthew 17:9, 22
   3) Matthew 20:18

3. In His teaching regarding His coming again
   1) Matthew 13:41
   2) Matthew 24:27, 30
   3) Matthew 25:31
   4) Luke 18:8
   5) Luke 21:36

Stevenson attaches a special significance to the title " 'Son of man,' because this was the designation which our Lord habitually used concerning Himself. It is not found in the New Testament on any other lips than His own — except when His questioners quoted His words (John 12:34), and in the one instance of Stephen's ecstatic exclamation in the moment of his martyrdom, 'Behold, I see the heavens opened, and the Son of man standing on the right hand of God' (Acts 7:56, KJV). It is clearly a Messianic title, as the Jews recognized" (John 12:34). 40/120

Kreyssler and Scheffrahn write that "Jesus clearly believed Himself to be the fulfillment of the Old Testament prophecies of the Messiah. In referring to Himself He continually used the title 'The Son of Man' from Daniel's vision" (Daniel 7: 13,14). 30/9,10

In Mark 14: 61-64 Jesus applies Daniel 7: 13,14 and, alongside of it, Psalms 110: 1 to Himself as something that is going to transpire before their eyes.

C. G. Montefiore adds: "If Jesus said these words we can hardly think that He distinguished between Himself, the Son of man, and the Messiah. The Son of man must be the Messiah, and both must be Himself." 26/361

Montefiore continues by quoting Professor Peak:

"In spite of the 'perplexing use of the Son of man alongside of the first person singular, it is difficult to resist the conclusion that in this context Jesus means to identify the two. He could scarcely in one breath have affirmed His identity with the Messiah and implied His distinction from the Son of man. This is not to say that the Son of man is necessarily equivalent to Messiah; but if the ideas are distinct Jesus was conscious that both were fulfilled in Him, just as He was at once both Messiah and Servant of Yahweh' " [*Messiah and the Son of Man* (1924), p. 26]. 26/362

4B. Abba — Father

Michael Green, in his book *Runaway World*, writes that Christ "asserted that He had a relationship with God which no one had ever claimed before. It comes out in the Aramaic word *Abba* which He was so fond of using, especially in prayer. Nobody before Him in all the history of Israel had addressed God by this word. . . . To be sure, Jews were accustomed to praying to God as Father: but the word they used was *Abhinu,* a form of address which was essentially an appeal to God for mercy and forgiveness. There is no appeal to God for mercy in Jesus' mode of address, *Abba.* It is the familiar word of closest intimacy. That is why He differentiated between His own relationship with God as Father and that of other people." 9/99,100

It is interesting that even David, with his closeness to the Father, did not speak to God as Father but said that "like as a father . . . so the Lord" (Psalms 103: 13, KJV).

Jesus Christ used the word "Father" often in prayer. "The Pharisees, of course, realized the implications of it, and charged Him with blasphemy (John 5: 18) '. . . but [He] also called God His Father, making Himself equal with God' (RSV). And indeed unless He were equal with God His words were blasphemous." 40/97

chapter 7 _____

the trilemma-
lord, liar or lunatic?

The following is an outline designed to aid you in effectively using this material:

1A. JESUS CLAIMED TO BE GOD
     (See Chapter 6.)
2A. THREE ALTERNATIVES
     1B. Was He a Liar?
     2B. Was He a Lunatic?
     3B. Was He Lord?

1A. THE QUESTION: WHO IS JESUS OF NAZARETH?

Jesus considered *who* men believed Him to be of fundamental importance. C. S. Lewis, who was a professor at Cambridge University and once an agnostic, wrote: "I am trying here to prevent anyone saying the really foolish thing that people often say about Him: 'I'm ready to accept Jesus as a great moral teacher, but I don't accept His claim to be God.' That is the one thing we must not say. A man who was merely a man and said the sort of things Jesus said would not be a great moral teacher. He would either be a lunatic — on a level with the man who says he is a poached egg — or else he would be the Devil of Hell. You must make your choice. Either this man was, and is, the Son of God: or else a madman or something worse." 18/40,41

C. S. Lewis adds: "You can shut Him up for a fool, you can spit at Him and kill Him as a demon; or you can fall at His feet and call Him Lord and God. But let us not come up with any patronising nonsense about His being a great human teacher. He has not left that open to us. He did not intend to." 18/40,41

F. J. A. Hort has written: "His words were so completely parts and utterances of Himself, that they had no meaning as abstract statements of truth uttered by Him as a Divine oracle or prophet. Take away Himself as the primary (though not the ultimate) subject of every statement and they all fall to pieces." 13/207

In the words of Kenneth Scott Latourette, the great historian of Christianity at Yale University: "It is not His teachings which make Jesus so remarkable, although these would be enough to give Him distinction. It is a combination of the teachings with the man Himself. The two cannot be separated. . . ." 15/44

"It must be obvious to any thoughtful reader of the Gospel records that Jesus regarded Himself and His message as inseparable. He was a great teacher, but He was more. His teachings about the kingdom of God, about human conduct, and about God were important, but they could not be divorced from Him without, from His standpoint, being vitiated." 15/48

JESUS CLAIMS TO BE GOD

(TWO ALTERNATIVES)

Claims were FALSE	Claims were TRUE
(Two Alternatives)	He is LORD

He KNEW His Claims Were FALSE	He DID NOT KNOW His Claims Were FALSE

(Two Alternatives)

	You can ACCEPT	You can REJECT

He made a DELIBERATE MISREPRESENTATION

He was a LIAR	
He was a HYPOCRITE	He was SINCERELY DELUDED
He was a DEMON	He was a LUNATIC
He was a FOOL for He died for it	

2A. IS JESUS CHRIST GOD?

Jesus claimed to be God. He did not leave any other options. His claim to be God must be either true or false and is something that should be given serious consideration. Jesus' question to His disciples, "But who do you say that I am?" (Mark 8:29) is also asked of us today.

Jesus' claim to be God must be either true or false. If Jesus' claims are true, then He is the Lord, and we must either accept or reject His lordship. We are "without excuse."

First, consider that His claim to be God was false. If it was false then we have two and only two alternatives. He either knew it was false or He did not know it was false. We will consider each one separately and examine the evidence.

3A. WAS HE A LIAR?

If, when Jesus made His claims He knew that He was not God, then He was lying. But, if He was a liar, then He was also a hypocrite because He told others to be honest, whatever the cost, while Himself teaching and living a colossal lie.

And, more than that, He was a demon, because He told others to trust Him for their eternal destiny. If He could not back up His claims and knew it, then He was unspeakably evil.

Last, He would also be a fool, because it was His claims to being God that led to His crucifixion.

Mark 14: 61-64

"But He kept silent, and made no answer. Again the high priest was questioning Him, and saying to Him, 'Are You the Christ, the Son of the Blessed *One*?'

"And Jesus said, 'I am; and you shall see the SON OF MAN SITTING AT THE RIGHT HAND OF POWER, and COMING WITH THE CLOUDS OF HEAVEN.'

"And tearing his clothes, the high priest said, 'What further need do we have of witnesses?

" 'You have heard the blasphemy; how does it seem to you?' And they all condemned Him to be deserving of death."

John 19: 7

"The Jews answered him, 'We have a law, and by that law He ought to die because He made Himself out *to be* the Son of God.' "

J. S. Mill, the philosopher, skeptic and antagonist of Christianity, wrote: "About the life and sayings of Jesus there is a stamp of personal originality combined with profundity of insight in the very first rank of men of sublime genius of whom our species can boast. When this pre-eminent genius is combined with the qualities of probably the greatest moral reformer and martyr to that mission who ever existed upon earth, religion cannot be said to have made a bad choice in pitching upon this man as the ideal representative and guide of humanity; nor even now would it be easy, even for an unbeliever, to find a better translation of the rule of virtue from the abstract into the concrete than to endeavour to live so that Christ would approve of our life." 11/34

William Lecky, one of Great Britain's most noted historians and a dedicated opponent of organized Christianity, in *History of European Morals from Augustus to Charlemagne* wrote: "It was reserved for Christianity to present to the world an ideal character which through all the changes of eighteen centuries has inspired the hearts of men with an impassioned love; has shown itself capable of acting on all ages, nations, temperaments and conditions; has been not only the highest pattern of virtue, but the strongest incentive to its practice. . . . The simple record of these three short years of active life has done more to regenerate and soften mankind than all the disquisitions of philosophers and all the exhortations of moralists." 16/8; 11/34

Philip Schaff, the Christian historian, said: "This testimony, if not true, must be downright blasphemy or madness. The former hypothesis cannot stand a moment before the moral purity and dignity of Jesus, revealed in His every word and work, and acknowledged by universal consent. Self-deception in a matter so momentous, and with an intellect in all respects so clear and so sound, is equally out of the question. How could He be an enthusiast or a madman who never lost the even balance of His mind, who sailed serenely over all the troubles and persecutions, as the sun above the clouds, who always returned the wisest answer to tempting questions, who calmly and deliberately predicted His death on the cross, His resurrection on the third day, the outpouring of the Holy Spirit, the founding of His Church, the destruction of Jerusalem — predictions which have been literally fulfilled? A character so original, so complete, so uniformly consistent, so perfect, so human and yet so high above all human greatness, can be neither a fraud nor a fiction. The poet, as has been well said, would in this case be greater than the hero. It would take more than a Jesus to invent a Jesus." 35/109

Elsewhere Schaff (*The Person of Christ*) gives very convicting evidence: "The hypothesis of imposture is so revolting to moral as well as common sense, that its mere statement is its condemnation. It was invented by the Jews who crucified the Lord to cover their crime, but has never been seriously carried out, and no scholar of any decency and self-respect would now dare to profess it openly. How, in the name of logic, common sense, and experience, could an impostor — that is a deceitful, selfish, depraved man — have invented, and consistently maintained from the beginning to end, the purest and noblest character known in history with the most perfect air of truth and reality? How could he have conceived and successfully carried out a plan of unparalleled beneficence, moral magnitude, and sublimity, and sacrificed his own life for it, in the face of the strongest prejudices of his people and ages?" 36/94,95

Someone who lived as Jesus lived, taught as Jesus taught and died as Jesus died could not have been a liar. What other alternatives are there?

4A. LUNATIC?

If it is inconceivable for Jesus to be a liar, then could not He actually have thought Himself to be God, but been mistaken? After all, it is possible to be both sincere and wrong.

But we must remember that for someone to think that He is God, especially in a culture that is fiercely monotheistic, and then to tell others that their eternal destiny depends on believing in Him is no slight flight of fantasy but the thoughts of a lunatic in the fullest sense. Was Jesus Christ such a person?

C. S. Lewis has written: "The historical difficulty of giving for the life, saying and influence of Jesus any explanation that is not harder than the Christian explanation is very great. The discrepancy between the depth and sanity of His moral teaching and the rampant megalomania which must lie behind His theological teaching unless He is indeed God has never been satisfactorily explained. Hence the non-Christian hypotheses succeed one another with the restless fertility of bewilderment." 19/113

Napoleon (cited by *Vernon C. Grounds, The Reason for Our Hope*) said: "I know men; and I tell you that Jesus Christ is not a man. Superficial minds see a resemblance between Christ and the founders of empires, and the gods of other religions. That resemblance does not exist. There is between Christianity and whatever other religions the distance of infinity. . . . Everything in Christ astonishes me. His spirit overawes me, and His will confounds me. Between Him and whoever else in the world, there is no possible term of comparison. He is truly a being by Himself. His ideas and sentiments, the truth which He announces, His manner of convincing, are not explained either by human organization or by the nature of things. . . . The nearer I approach, the more carefully I examine, everything is above me — everything remains grand, of a grandeur which overpowers. His religion is a revelation from an intelligence which certainly is not that of man. . . . One can absolutely find nowhere, but in Him alone, the imitation or the example of His life. . . . I search in vain in history to find the similar to Jesus Christ, or anything which can approach the gospel. Neither history, nor humanity, nor the ages, nor nature, offer me anything with which I am able to compare it or to explain it. Here everything is extraordinary." 11/37

Even Channing, the Unitarian writer, speaking of the lunatic theory (cited by P. Schaff) said: "The charge of an extravagant, self-deluding enthusiasm is the last to be fastened on Jesus. Where can we find the traces of it in His history? Do we detect them in the calm authority of His precepts? in the mild, practical and beneficent spirit of His religion; in the unlabored simplicity of the language with which He unfolds His high powers and the sublime truths of religion; or in the good sense, the knowledge of human nature, which He always discovers in His estimate and treatment of the different classes of men with whom He acted? Do we discover this enthusiasm in the singular fact, that whilst He claimed power in the future world, and always turned men's minds to heaven, He never indulged His own imagination, or stimulated that of His disciples, by giving vivid pictures or any minute description of that unseen state? The truth is, that, remarkable as was the character of Jesus, it was distinguished by nothing more than by calmness and self-possession. This trait pervades His other excellences. How calm was His piety! Point me, if you can, to one vehement, passionate expression of His religious feelings. Does the Lord's Prayer breathe a feverish enthusiasm? . . . His benevolence, too, though singularly earnest and deep, was composed and serene. He never lost the possession of Himself in His sympathy with others; was never hurried into the impatient and rash enterprises of an enthusiastic philanthropy; but did good with the tranquility and constancy which mark the providence of God." 36/98,99

Philip Schaff, the historian, wrote: "Is such an intellect — clear as the sky, bracing as the mountain air, sharp and penetrating as a sword, thoroughly healthy and vigorous, always ready and always self-possessed — liable to a radical and most serious delusion concerning His own character and mission? Preposterous imagination!" 36/97,98

5A. LORD!!

Who you decide Jesus Christ is must not be an idle intellectual exercise. You cannot put Him on the shelf as a great moral teacher. That is not a valid option. He is either a liar, a lunatic or the Lord. You must make a choice. "But," as the apostle John wrote, "these have been written that you may believe that Jesus is the Christ, the Son of God"; and more important, "that believing you may have life in His Name" (John 20:31).

The evidence is clearly in favor of Jesus as Lord. However, some people reject the clear evidence because of moral implications involved. There needs to be a moral honesty in the above consideration of Jesus as either a liar, lunatic or Lord and God.

BIBLIOGRAPHY

1. Alford, Henry. *The Greek Testament.* Cambridge: Deighton, Bell, and Co., 1868.

2. Anderson, Robert. *The Lord from Heaven.* London: James Nisbet and Co., Ltd., 1910.

3. Bruce, F. F. (ed.) *The New International Commentary on the New Testament.* Grand Rapids: William B. Eerdmans Publishing Co., 1971. Used by permission.

4. Campbell, A. Glen. *The Greek Terminology for the Deity of Christ.* Unpublished Th.M. Thesis: Dallas Theological Seminary, Dallas, Texas, Jan. 1948.

5. Chafer, Lewis Sperry. *Systematic Theology.* Dallas Theological Seminary Press, 1947.

6. Deland, Charles Edmund. *The Mis-Trials of Jesus.* Boston: Richard G. Badger, 1914.

7. Felder, Hilarin. *Christ and the Critics.* Translated by John L. Stoddard. London: Burns Oates and Washburn Ltd., 1924.

8. Godet, F. *Commentary on the Gospel of St. John.* Edinburgh: T. & T. Clark, 1892.

9. Green, Michael. *Runaway World.* Downers Grove: Inter-Varsity Press, 1968. Used by permission.

10. Greenleaf, Simon. *The Testimony of the Evangelists.* Grand Rapids: Baker Book House, 1965.

11. Grounds, Vernon C. *The Reason for Our Hope.* Chicago: Moody Press, 1945. Used by permission.

12. Hobbs, Herschel. *An Exposition of the Gospel of Luke.* Grand Rapids: Baker Book House, 1966.

13. Hort, F. J. A. *Way, Truth and the Life.* New York: Macmillan and Co., 1894.

14. Jefferson, Charles Edward. *The Character of Jesus.* New York: Thomas Y. Crowell Co., 1908. Copyright renewed by Charles E. Jefferson, 1936. Used by permission.

15. Latourette, Kenneth Scott. *A History of Christianity.* New York: Harper & Row, 1953.

16. Lecky, William E. *History of European Morals from Augustus to Charlemagne.* New York: D. Appleton and Co., 1903.

17. Lenski, R. C. H. *The Interpretation of St. John's Gospel.* Columbus: Lutheran Book Concern, 1942.

18. Lewis, C. S. *Mere Christianity.* New York: The Macmillan Company, 1952.

19. Lewis, C. S. *Miracles: A Preliminary Study.* New York: The Macmillan Company, 1947.

20. Linton, Irwin H. *The Sanhedrin Verdict.* New York: Loizeaux Brothers, Bible Truth Depot, 1943.

21. Little, Paul. *Know What You Believe.* Wheaton: Scripture Press Publications, Inc., 1970.

22. Marshall, Alfred. *The Interlinear Greek-English New Testament.* Rev. ed. Grand Rapids: Zondervan Publishing House, 1969.

23. Mead, Frank (ed.). *The Encyclopedia of Religious Quotations.* Westwood: Fleming H. Revell, n.d.

24. Meldau, Fred John. *101 Proofs of the Deity of Christ from the Gospels.* Denver: The Christian Victory Publishing Co., 1960.

25. Mill, John S. *Three Essays of Religion.* Westport: Greenwood Press, 1970. (Reprinted from 1874 edition.)

26. Montefiore, C. G. *The Synoptic Gospels.* London: Macmillan and Co., Ltd., 1909, 1927 (two volumes).

27. Morison, Frank. *Who Moved the Stone?* London: Faber and Faber Ltd., 1958.

28. Morris, Leon. *New International Commentary, the Gospel According to John.* Grand Rapids: William B. Eerdmans Publishing Co., 1971. Used by permission.

29. Pfeiffer, Charles F. and Everett F. Harrison (eds.). *The Wycliffe Bible Commentary.* Chicago: Moody Press, 1962. Used by permission.

30. Pinnock, Clark H. *Set Forth Your Case.* Nutley: The Craig Press, 1967.

31. Robertson, Archibald Thomas. *Word Pictures in the New Testament.* Vol. I-V. Nashville: Broadman Press, 1930.

32. Robinson, William Childs. *Our Lord.* Grand Rapids: William B. Eerdmans Publishing Co., 1937. Used by permission.

33. Robinson, William Childs (ed.). *Who Say Ye That I Am?* Grand Rapids: William B. Eerdmans Publishing Co., 1949.

34. Ryle, J. C. *Expository Thoughts on the Gospels.* (St. Mark). New York: Robert Carter and Brothers, 1866.

35. Schaff, Philip. *History of the Christian Church.* 8 vols. Grand Rapids: William B. Eerdmans Publishing Co., 1910 (reprint from original, 1962). Used by permission.

36. Schaff, Philip. *The Person of Christ.* New York: American Tract Society, 1913. Used by permission.

37. Scheffrahn, Karl and Henry Kreyssler. *Jesus of Nazareth: Who Did He Claim to Be?* Dallas: Pat Booth, 1968.

38. Schultz, Thomas. *The Doctrine of the Person of Christ with an Emphasis upon the Hypostatic Union.* Unpublished dissertation. Dallas Theological Seminary, May, 1962.

39. Spurr, Frederick C. *Jesus is God.* London: A. H. Stockwell & Co., 1899.

40. Stevenson, Herbert F. *Titles of the Triune God.* Westwood: Fleming H. Revell Co., 1956.

41. Stott, J. R. W. *Basic Christianity.* Downers Grove: Inter-Varsity Press, 1971. Used by permission.

42. Swete, Henry Barclay. *The Gospel According to St. Mark.* London: Macmillan and Co., Ltd., 1898.

43. Tenney, Merrill C. *John: The Gospel of Belief.* Grand Rapids: William B. Eerdmans Publishing Co., 1948. Used by permission.

44. Vincent, Marvin R. *Word Studies in the New Testament.* 4 vols. New York: Charles Scribner's Sons, 1924.

chapter 8 _____

the
great
proposition

INTRODUCTION

"If God became man THEN what would He be like?" Or *"Did Jesus possess the attributes of God?"* To begin to answer this question we must first answer another question, namely, why would God become man? We will use an ant illustration. Imagine you are watching a farmer plow a field. You notice an ant hill will be plowed under by the farmer on his next time around. Because you are an ant lover, you run to the ant hill to warn them. First you shout to them the impending danger, but they continue with their work. You then try sign language and finally resort to everything you can think of, but nothing works. Why? Because you are not communicating with them. What is the best way to communicate with them? Only by becoming an ant can you communicate with them so they will understand.

Now, if God wanted to communicate with us, what would be the best way? We see that in order for Him to communicate with us, He could best do so by becoming a man and thus, reach us directly.

We can begin to answer our primary question now. If God did become man, who or what would He be like? He would possess the attributes of God, He would have an unusual entrance into this world, He would perform feats of the supernatural, He would be sinless; a lasting and universal impression would be left by Him and many more things. It is my feeling that God came to earth in the person of Jesus Christ, and in Jesus we see manifest the attributes of God and the characteristics that would accompany a God-man.

This section will encompass the philosophical argument, "If . . . then." I first read of this applied to Christ in Bernard Ramm's Book, *Protestant Christian Evidences,* Chapter 6, "The Verification of Christianity by the Supernatural Character of its Founder."

The following is an outline designed to aid you in effectively using this material.

IF GOD BECAME MAN, THEN WE WOULD EXPECT HIM TO:

1. Have an unusual entrance into life.
2. Be without sin.
3. Manifest the supernatural in the form of miracles.
4. Have an acute sense of difference from other men.
5. Speak the greatest words ever spoken.
6. Have a lasting and universal influence.

7. Satisfy the spiritual hunger in man.

8. Exercise power over death.

1A. IF GOD BECAME MAN, THEN WE WOULD EXPECT HIM TO HAVE AN UNUSUAL ENTRANCE INTO THIS LIFE

The virgin birth of Christ is evidence of this point.

1B. Testimony Concerning the Virgin Birth

The main body of testimony concerning the virgin birth occurs in the Gospels of Matthew and Luke. Thus, a study of their reliability and their agreement is very important in considering the miraculous birth of Jesus.

1C. THE CONCEPT

The concept of the virgin birth of Jesus must concur with the prescribed mode of entrance granted the Messiah in the Old Testament.

The first prophecy concerning Christ's coming is in Genesis 3:15. In this verse God says that the seed of woman shall crush the head of the serpent. Thus, the Deliverer would come of the woman's seed, not of man's seed as is biologically accepted.

A clearer prophecy occurs in Isaiah 7:14 which states that ". . . a virgin shall conceive, and bear a son, and shall call His name Immanuel" (KJV). This is very specific in that the reference is to a virgin. This, most logically, refers to the woman in Genesis 3:15.

Henry Morris writes: "Although its exact meaning has been debated, its usage is always consistent with the meaning 'virgin,' and in some cases this is the only possible meaning. The scholars who translated the Old Testament into the Greek Septuagint version used the standard Greek word for 'virgin' in translating Isaiah 7:14. So did Matthew when he quoted this prophecy (Matt. 1:23) as being fulfilled in the virgin birth of Christ." 30/36

Also, in Isaiah 7:14, the birth is said to be a "sign" from the "Lord Himself." This is certainly unique in that this could be no ordinary birth. Thus, we can see that the doctrine of the virgin birth presented in the Gospel is in accord with earlier Scripture teachings.

2C. RELIABILITY

The reliability of the Gospel accounts should also be based on their historical accuracy.

The historicity of the Gospel accounts is attested to by the time at which each writer places the events of Jesus' birth and the events themselves. There are alleged discrepancies in Luke's account of the birth dealing with the census ordered by Quirinius. It was at first believed that Quirinius was governor only in 8 A.D. Thus, this would have put him and his census after the birth of Christ and also Herod's death. However, some now believe that Quirinius served two terms of office, the first of these being 10-7 B.C., which would put his first census at the time, roughly, of Christ's birth shortly before Herod's death in 4 B.C. 39/113-115

3C. AGREEMENT IN TESTIMONIES

For something to be true, those who are bearing witness of it must agree in their testimonies.

In regard to the accounts in Matthew and Luke, Orr states that although they are told from different points of view and originate from different sources, they agree on one central fact, "that Jesus, conceived by the Holy Ghost, was born of Mary, a Virgin betrothed to Joseph, with his full knowledge of the cause. . . ." 34/35

1D.   Agreement versus discrepancy of the narratives

"The critics speak of the discrepancies of the narratives. Much more remarkable, it seems to me, are their agreements, and the subtle harmonies that pervade them. The agreements, if we study them carefully, prove to be far more numerous than may at first strike us. Here, e.g., is a list of 12 points, which lie really on the surface of the narratives, yet give very clearly the gist of the whole story.

   1E.   Jesus was born in the last days of Herod (Matt. 2:1,13; Luke 1:5).

   2E.   He was conceived by the Holy Ghost (Matt. 1:18,20; Luke 1:35).

   3E.   His mother was a virgin (Matt. 1:18,20,23; Luke 1:27,34).

   4E.   She was betrothed to Joseph (Matt. 1:18; Luke 1:27; 2:5).

   5E.   Joseph was of the house and lineage of David (Matt. 1:16,20; Luke 1:27; 2:4).

   6E.   Jesus was born at Bethlehem (Matt. 2:1; Luke 2:4,6).

   7E.   By divine direction He was called Jesus (Matt. 1:21; Luke 1:31).

   8E.   He was declared to be a Savior (Matt. 1:21; Luke 2:11).

   9E.   Joseph knew beforehand of Mary's condition and its cause (Matt. 1:18-20; Luke 2:5).

   10E.   Nevertheless, he took Mary as wife and assumed full paternal responsibilities for her child (Matt. 1:20,24,25; Luke 2:5ff.).

   11E.   The annunciation and birth were attended by revelations and visions (Matt. 1:20, etc.; Luke 1:26,27, etc.).

   12E.   After the birth of Jesus, Joseph and Mary dwelt in Nazareth (Matt. 2:23; Luke 2:39)." 34/36,37

One apparent discrepancy in the accounts involves the family lineage of Jesus. There are two genealogies of Christ given in the Bible. Upon examination they appear to contradict. However, the one listed in Matthew is that of Joseph and the one in Luke is that of Mary. 30/37 Since Joseph was descended from Jechonias, Jesus could not rightly claim the throne (see Jeremiah 22:30; Coniah, Jechonias, II Kings 24, and Jechonias in Matthew 1:11 are the same person). However, the lineage of Mary does not include Jechonias, and since Joseph did not father Jesus, He had claim to the throne as "the seed" of the woman, Mary (Luke 3:23).

2D.   The Witness of Mark, John and Paul:

An argument often used by critics is that there is no reference in the New Testament to the virgin birth except in Matthew and Luke. Therefore, it is often concluded that the doctrine was not vital to the message of the New Testament church.

William Childs Robinson, the emeritus professor of historical theology at Columbia Theological Seminary, points out that "what is explicit in Matthew and Luke is implicit in Paul and John." 38

Robert Gromacki writes that "it is not tenable to argue from silence to disbelief or from silence to an ignorance of the doctrine.

The apostles did not record everything that they taught or knew (cf. John 20:30). In fact, the so-called silence argument of the liberal can boomerang on him. Since Paul did not mention any human father for the person Jesus, does that mean that he believed that Jesus had no human father? Most regard silence as assent. If Paul and the others did not believe in the virgin birth, should they not have corrected the earlier birth narratives? The argument of silence can be used both ways. Actually, no confession or denial should ever be based upon the argument from silence." 12/183

It can also be argued that ". . . while it is true that it appears at the beginning of both the first and third Gospels, it is absent from that of St. Mark, or, as it is commonly put, St. Mark 'knows nothing about it,' though his was the first to be written and was used by the other two. St. Mark's Gospel, we have it on good authority, was his account of what he had heard St. Peter preach. He was his 'interpreter.' It represents what St. Peter found useful or necessary in preaching in public, just as St. Paul preached on the Areopagus at Athens, or at Jerusalem, Antioch, and Rome.

"Now, for obvious reasons, the question of our Lord's birth would not have been a subject to be discussed on such occasions, especially so long as His Mother was still alive, and was, possibly, personally known to those listening. The main appeal was to be teaching that Christ gave, the signs that He had wrought, and, above all, as we see from the place it occupies, the events of His Passion." 39/99-101

It is possible that the fourth writer infers a miraculous birth to Jesus by his use of the word "begotten" in John 3:16.

As John R. Rice states: "Jesus repeatedly referred to Himself as God's 'only begotten Son.' Now the word 'begat' is a word of human genealogies, a term referring to the male part in procreating or generating a child. It refers to the physical birth. Jesus insisted that He was not begotten of Joseph but was begotten of God. The same word, *monogenes*, is used six times in the New Testament about Jesus as the only-begotten of God, and twice Jesus Himself used it about Himself! Note that Jesus does not claim to be simply one who is begotten of God. Rather, He claims to be the only one ever born who was so begotten. He is the *only* begotten Son of God. No one else was ever born of a virgin. In a spiritual sense, it may be said that Christians are 'begotten . . . again unto a lively hope' (I Peter 1:3), but in the sense in which Jesus was begotten of God, no one else ever was. Clearly Jesus was claiming that He was physically begotten of God and not by any human father." 37/22,23

The apostle John's genealogy is essentially "in the beginning," and therefore doesn't deal with the virgin birth. "In the beginning was the Word. . . . and the Word became flesh" (John 1:1,14).

Likewise in regard to Paul: "St. Paul knew St. Luke quite well. He was his companion for a long time in his travels, and was with him at Rome, and St. Luke is our chief authority for the story of our Lord's birth. St. Paul must have known it, and it is quite natural that, knowing it, he should have spoken of our Lord as he does when he says: 'God sent forth His Son born of a woman.' " Clement F. Rogers 39/101

2B.   Historical Evidence Surrounding the Virgin Birth Other Than the Gospel Accounts

1C. TIME

An important consideration concerning the Gospel accounts is the time they were written. Due to the early dating of the Gospel writings, no adequate time was left for the growth of a myth surrounding the birth of Christ. Thus, we should see evidence of the teaching of the virgin birth in the early church. In relation to this are two questions:

1D. How did the concept of a virgin birth arise so soon if it was not based on fact?

2D. If the Gospels were not historical, how were they accepted so universally at such an early date?

In regard to the early church belief in the virgin birth, Gresham Machen writes:

"Even . . . if there were not a word about the subject in the New Testament, the second-century testimony would show that the belief in the virgin birth must have arisen, to say the least, well before the first century was over." 25/44

In the very early days of the church, there was a group called the Ebionites. They objected to the church's use of the passage in Isaiah concerning the virgin bearing a son (Isaiah 7:14). They said that the verse should be translated "a young woman." 39/105 The important point is that the church believed in the virgin birth.

To this thought James Orr writes:

"*. . . Apart from the Ebionites . . . and a few Gnostic sects, no body of Christians in early times is known to have existed who did not accept as part of their faith the birth of Jesus from the Virgin Mary; while . . . we* have the amplest evidence that *this belief was part of the general faith of the Church.*" 34/138

In speaking of the early church, Aristides says, "Everything that we know of the dogmatics of the early part of the second century agrees with the belief that at that period the virginity of Mary was a part of the formulated Christian belief." 2/25

2C. WITNESS OF EARLY CHURCH FATHERS

Very important in the history of the early church's belief in the virgin birth is the testimony of its early fathers. In 110 A.D. Ignatius wrote in his *Epistle to the Ephesians*, "For our God Jesus Christ was . . . conceived in the womb of Mary . . . by the Holy Ghost." 55/18:2

"Now the virginity of Mary, and He who was born of her . . . are the mysteries most spoken of throughout the world, yet done in secret by God." 52/19:1 Ignatius received his information from his teacher, John the apostle.

"We have further evidence," writes Clement F. Rogers, "which shows that the belief in Ignatius' time was no new one. For we know that the belief of Christians in the Virgin Birth was attacked by those outside. Cerinthus, for example, was the contemporary and opponent of St. John. It was said that the Evangelist, meeting him in the public baths, cried out, 'Let us flee lest the bath fall in while Cerinthus, the enemy of the truth, is here.' He [Cerinthus] taught, Irenaeus tells us, that our Lord was born of Joseph and Mary like other men." 39/105

Another of the post-apostolic writers, Aristides in 125 A.D., speaks of the virgin birth: "He is Himself Son of God on high, who was manifested of the Holy Spirit, came down from heaven, and being born of a Hebrew virgin took on His flesh from the virgin. . . . He it is who was according to the flesh born of the race of Hebrews, by the God-bearing virgin Miriam." 2/32

Justin Martyr in 150 A.D. gives ample evidence to the concept of Jesus' miraculous birth. ". . . Our Teacher Jesus Christ, who is the first-begotten of God the Father, was not born as a result of sexual relations . . . the power of God descending upon the virgin overshadowed her, and caused her, while still a virgin, to conceive . . . For, by God's power He was conceived by a virgin . . . in accordance with the will of God, Jesus Christ, His Son, has been born of the Virgin Mary." (Apology 1:21-33; Dialogue with Trypho the Jew)

"The first great Latin-speaking Christian was the converted lawyer Tertullian. He tells us that not only there was in his days (ca A.D. 200) a definite Christian creed on which all churches agree, but he also tells us, its technical name was a *tessera*. Now things only get technical names when they have been established for some time. He quotes this creed four times. It includes the words *'ex virgine Maria'* (of the Virgin Mary)." 39/103

3C.   THE EARLY JEWISH WITNESS

As should be expected, there are negative arguments concerning the virgin birth also. These were brought forth by the Jews. Our purpose here is to show that in the very early days of the church there was outside controversy concerning the birth of Jesus, and that for this controversy to have originated, the church must have been teaching Christ's miraculous birth.

Ethelbert Stauffer says that,

"In a genealogical table dating from before A.D. 70 Jesus is listed as 'the bastard of a wedded wife.' Evidently the Evangelist Matthew was familiar with such lists and was warring against them. Later rabbis bluntly called Jesus the son of an adulteress. They also claimed to know precisely the 'unknown father's name: Panthera.' In old rabbinical texts we find frequent mention of Jesus ben Panthera, and the eclectic Platonist Celsus around 160 details all sorts of gossipy anecdotes about Mary and the legionary Panthera." 47/17

In the *Toldoth Jeschu,* the Jewish history of Christ, it is taught that Jesus is of "illegitimate origin, through the union of his mother with a soldier named Panthera." 34/146

Hugh Schonfield, the Jewish skeptic, relates: "R. Shimeon ben Azzai said: 'I found a genealogical scroll in Jerusalem, and therein was written, 'so-and-so, bastard son of an adulteress.' " 42/139f.

R. Shimeon lived at the end of the first and beginning of the second century A.D. According to Schonfield, this document must have been in existence at the time of the capture of Jerusalem in 70 A.D. In the older Jewish records, Jesus' name is represented by "so and so."

Schonfield then goes on to say that "there would be no object in making it unless the Christian original (genealogy) made some claim that the birth of Jesus was not normal." 44/139,140

Due to the reference of R. Shimeon, Schonfield says that the charge against Jesus "that he was the bastard son of an adulteress, goes back to an early date." 44/140

Origen in his *Contra Celsum* states: "Let us return, however, to the words put into the mouth of the Jew, where the *mother of Jesus* is described as having been *turned out by the carpenter who was betrothed to her, as she had been convicted of adultery and had a child by a certain soldier named Panthera.* Let us consider whether those who fabricated the myth that the virgin and Panthera committed adultery and that the carpenter turned her out, were not blind when they concocted all this to get rid of the miraculous conception by the Holy Spirit. For on account of its highly miraculous character they could have falsified the story in other ways without, as it were, unintentionally admitting that Jesus was not born of an ordinary marriage. It was inevitable that those who did not accept the miraculous birth of Jesus would have invented some lie. But the fact that they did not do this convincingly, but kept as part of the story that the virgin did not conceive Jesus by Joseph, makes the lie obvious to people who can see through fictitious stories and show them up. Is it reasonable that a man who ventured to do such great things for mankind in order that, so far as in the universe, should have had, not a miraculous birth, but a birth more illegitimate and disgraceful than any? . . . It is therefore probably that this soul, which lived a more useful life on earth than many men (to avoid appearing to beg the question by saying 'all' men), needed a body which was not only distinguished among human bodies, but was also superior to all others." 33/1:32,33

Even in the Gospels this controversy is brought out, in Mark 6:3: " 'Is not this the carpenter, the son of Mary, and brother of James, and Joses, and Judas, and Simon? Are not His sisters here with us?' And they took offense at Him."

"This account," writes Ethelbert Stauffer, "which appears only in Mark does full justice to the situation. The Jews had strict rules governing name-giving. A Jew was named after his father (Jochanan ben Sakkai, for example) even if his father had died before his birth. He was named after his mother only when the father was unknown." 47/16

4C. THE KORAN

1D. In the *Koran* we find Jesus referred to regularly as Isa ibn Maryam — Jesus, the son of Mary. Stauffer writes, "Abdullah al-Baidawi, the classical commentator on the Koran, remarks with full understanding of the Semitic practice in nomenclature: The name of the mother is borne when the father is unknown. But this name and explanation are here intended in a thoroughly positive sense. In Islam Jesus is regarded as the Son of the Virgin Mary who was begotten by the creative Word of God." 47/17,18

"In the *Logia* we learn that Jesus was berated for being a 'glutton and drunkard.' There must have been some grounds for this charge. For it fits in with all that we know about the attitude of Jesus and about his Pharisaical groups' reaction to it. Now, among Palestinian Jews this particular insult would be flung at a person born of an illegitimate connection who betrayed by his mode of life and his religious conduct the stain of his birth. This was the sense in which the Pharisees and their followers employed the phrase against Jesus. Their meaning was: 'he is a bastard.' " 47/16

As a result of the early Jewish aversions to the illegitimacy of Christ (before A.D. 70), they are acknowledging the fact that there was doubt as to His parentage. The very early Christian church, at most forty years after his death, must have been teaching some doctrine about His birth, i.e., the virgin birth.

2D. We find reference to Jesus' birth in the *Koran* (Mary v. 20). When it was announced to Mary that she would bear a son, she replied,

"How can this be, for I am a virgin and no mortal has ever touched me." The account goes on to say that "it is easy for Me (the Lord)." He then "breathed on her His Spirit." 4/6

3B. Summation by Various Writers

On the basis of the available evidence, it is important to see what some of the world's authors say about it.

W. H. Griffith Thomas writes: "The chief support for the doctrine is the necessity of accounting for the uniqueness of the life of Jesus." 50/125

Henry Morris states: "It is altogether fitting that the One who performed many miracles during His life, who offered Himself on the cross as an atoning sacrifice for the sins of men, and who then rose bodily from the dead in vindication of all His claims, should have begun such a unique life by a unique entrance into that life." 30/38

"If He is truly our Savior, He must be far more than a mere man, though also He is truly the Son of man. To die for our sins, He must Himself be free from any sin of His own. To be sinless in practice, He must first be sinless in nature. He could not have inherited a human nature, bound under the Curse and the bondage of sin as it must have been, as do all other sons of men. His birth, therefore, must have been a miraculous birth. The 'seed of the woman' was implanted in the virgin's womb when, as the angel said: 'The Holy Ghost shall come upon thee, and the power of the Highest shall overshadow thee; therefore also that holy thing which shall be born of thee shall be called the Son of God' " (Luke 1:35). 30/38

"Not only is the Virgin Birth true because it is clearly taught in the Bible, but also because it is the only type of birth consistent with the character and mission of Jesus Christ and with God's great plan of salvation for a lost world." 30/38

"To say that such a miracle is impossible is to deny the existence of God or else to deny that He can control His creation." 30/38

In summing up the evidence of Jesus' birth, *J. Gresham Machen* states: "Thus there is good ground, we think, to hold that the reason why the Christian Church came to believe in the birth of Jesus without a human father was simply that He was as a matter of fact so born." 25/269

Clement Rogers concludes that: "All the evidence there is goes to prove the miraculous birth of Christ." 39/115

2A. IF GOD BECAME MAN, THEN WE WOULD EXPECT HIM TO BE WITHOUT SIN

1B. First of All, We Look at His Witness of Himself

John 8:46

"Which one of you convicts Me of sin?"

He received no answer. When He invited them to accuse Him, He could stay and bear their scrutiny. He was without sin; thus He was able to open Himself in such a manner.

He also said, "I always do the things that are pleasing to Him" (John 8:29). He seems to have lived in unbroken communion with God.

Christ's self-conscious purity is astonishing in that it is totally unlike the experience of the other believers. Every Christian knows that the nearer he approaches God, the more aware he becomes of his sin. However, with Christ this is not the case. Jesus lived more closely to God than anyone else and was free from all sense of sin.

Along this same line of thought, we are told of the temptations of Jesus (Luke 4) but never of His sins. We never hear of Him confessing or asking forgiveness of His sins, although He tells His disciples to do so. It appears that He had no sense of guilt that accompanies a sin nature.

2B. The Witness of His Friends

Throughout the Bible, the inconsistencies of all persons are brought out. None of the great Jewish heroes are presented without blemish, not even David or Moses. Even in the New Testament, the shortcomings of the apostles are written about in almost every book, and yet nowhere do we find mention of one sin in Christ's life.

First of all, we must establish why we would study the accounts of His disciples. We see that their witness must be studied for the following reasons:

1C. THEY LIVED IN CLOSE CONTACT WITH JESUS FOR ABOUT THREE YEARS

2C. THEY WERE JEWS AND SINCE BIRTH HAD BEEN MADE AWARE OF THEIR OWN SIN NATURE AND THAT OF OTHERS

3C. THEIR TESTIMONY TO HIS SINLESSNESS IS INDIRECT

They do not set out to prove He was sinless; rather, their remarks on the subject are such that they acknowledge His sinlessness.

Of their writings A. E. Garvie states: ". . . It seems absolutely incredible that any one of the disciples could have first invented and then depicted the personality of Jesus as it appears in the Gospels." 10/98

In their close contact with Him, they never saw in Him the sins they saw in themselves. They got on one another's nerves, they grumbled and argued, but never did they see this in Jesus. Because of their strict Jewish background, they would be hardset to say that Jesus was without sin unless He really was sinless.

His closest associates, Peter and John, attest to His being without sin.

I Peter 1:19

"But with the precious blood of Christ, as of a lamb without blemish and without spot" (KJV).

I Peter 2:22

"Who did no sin, neither was guile found in His mouth" (KJV).

I John 3:5

"And ye know that He was manifested to take away our sins; and in Him is no sin" (KJV).

John went so far as to say that if anyone declares himself to be without sin, he is a liar and he is calling God a liar also. However, John also gave testimony to the sinless character of Jesus when he said that in Christ "there is no sin" (I John 3:5).

Even the one responsible for His death recognized His innocence and piety. Judas, after betraying Jesus, saw His righteousness and fell into deep remorse because he had "betrayed innocent blood" (Matthew 27:3,4).

The apostle Paul also bore witness of Jesus' sinlessness in his epistles (II Corinthians 5:21).

3B.   More Important, Perhaps, Than the Witness of His Friends Is That of His Enemies

One of the men crucified with Jesus gives testimony to His sinlessness. In Luke 23:41, one of the robbers rebuked the other robber, saying, ". . . This man has done nothing wrong."

Pilate's own testimony of Jesus' sinlessness was, "What evil has this man done?" (Luke 23:22).

The centurion at the cross proclaimed, "Certainly this man was innocent" (Luke 23:47).

It is also evident that His enemies would try to bring forth some accusation to convict Him of wrong. However, they could not (Mark 14:55,56).

In reference to this: Mark assembles four criticisms that His enemies brought forth (in 2:1-3:6). First, they accused Him of blasphemy because He had forgiven a man's sins. However, if He was divine, He had every power to grant forgiveness. Second, they were appalled by His evil associations — sinners, publicans, harlots, etc. The religious leaders of that day thought it righteous to avoid contact with such people. To these accusations He refers to Himself as a physician to the sinners (Mark 2:17). Third, He was accused of retaining a frivolous religion in that He did not fast like the Pharisees. However, there is no doubt that He did take His religion seriously. Last, they were upset by His sabbath-breaking (healing, picking grain, etc.). Yet no one can doubt that He was submissive to the law of God. Because He was "Lord of the Sabbath," He chose to destroy false traditions and give God's law its true interpretation.

4B.   Last, We Have Available the Witness of History

He is seen as sinless in the religion of Islam. In the *Koran,* (Mary, V. 19), the angel Gabriel came to Mary and told her that her son, Jesus, would be "without fault," i. e., sinless.

Philip Schaff assures us: "Here is the Holy of Holies of humanity. . . ." 42/107

"There never lived a more harmless being on earth. He injured nobody, He took advantage of nobody. He never spoke an improper word, He never committed a wrong action." 43/36,37

"The first impression which we receive from the life of Jesus is that of perfect innocency and sinlessness in the midst of a sinful world. He, and He alone, carried the spotless purity of childhood untarnished through His youth and manhood. Hence the lamb and the dove are His appropriate symbols." 43/35

"It is, in one word, the absolute perfection which raises His character high above the reach of all other men and makes it an exception to a universal rule, a moral miracle in history." 42/107

"He is the living incarnation of the ideal standard of virtue and holiness, and the highest model for all that is pure and good and noble in the sight of God and man." 43/44

"Such was the Jesus of Nazareth, — a true man in body, soul, and spirit, yet differing from all men; a character unique and original from tender childhood to ripe manhood, moving in unbroken union with God, overflowing with love to man, free from every sin and error, innocent and holy, devoted to the noblest ends, teaching and practising all virtues in perfect harmony, sealing the purest life with the sublimest death, and ever acknowledged since as the one and only perfect model of goodness and holiness." 43/73

John W. Stott contributes: "This utter disregard of self in the service of God and man is what the Bible calls love. There is no self-interest in love. The essence of love is self-sacrifice. The worst of men is adorned by an occasional flash of such nobility, but the life of Jesus irradiated it with a never-fading incandescent glow. Jesus was sinless because He was selfless. Such selflessness is love. And God is love." 48/44,45

Another writer, *Wilbur Smith*, states: "The outstanding characteristic of Jesus in His earthly life was the one in which all of us acknowledge we fall so short, and yet which at the same time all men recognize as the most priceless characteristic any man can have, namely, *absolute* goodness, or, to phrase it otherwise, perfect *purity*, genuine *holiness*, and in the case of Jesus, nothing less than *sinlessness*." 46/7

C. E. Jefferson writes: "The best reason we have for believing in the sinlessness of Jesus is the fact that He allowed His dearest friends to think that He was. There is in all His talk no trace of regret or hint of compunction or suggestion of sorrow for shortcoming, or slightest vestige of remorse. He taught other men to think of themselves as sinners, He asserted plainly that the human heart is evil, He told His disciples that every time they prayed they were to pray to be forgiven, but He never speaks or acts as though He Himself has the faintest consciousness of having ever done anything other than what was pleasing to God." 17/225

In this regard *Philip Schaff* states: "It is an indisputable fact, then, both from His mission and uniform conduct, and His express dedication, that Christ *knew* Himself free from sin and guilt. The only rational explanation of this fact is that Christ *was* no sinner." 43/40

Another testimony is that of *A. E. Garvie:* "If there were any secret sin in Him, or even the memory of sins in the past, this would show a moral insensibility in irreconcilable contrast with the moral discernment His teaching shows." 10/97

C. E. Jefferson states: "There is nothing in Jesus' consciousness which indicates that He was guilty of any sin." 17/328

Jesus' personality betrayed His thoughts and beliefs, as Stott tells us: "It is clear then that Jesus believed Himself to be sinless, as He believed Himself to be the Messiah and the Son of God." 48/39

Kenneth Scott Latourette, the famous historian, testifies: "Another quality which has often been remarked was the absence of any sense of having committed sin or of a basic corruption of Himself. . . . It is highly significant that in one as sensitive morally as was Jesus and who taught His followers to ask for the forgiveness of their sins there is no hint of any need of forgiveness for Himself, no asking of pardon, either from those about Him or of God." 21/47

"The Sermon on the Mount is Christ's biography. Every syllable He had already written down in deeds. The sermon merely translated His life into language." *Thomas Wright* 29/60

Henry Morris writes: "If God Himself, incarnate in His only Son, could not measure up to the standard of His own holiness, then it is utterly futile to search elsewhere for meaning and salvation in the universe." 30/34

Bernard Ramm says: ". . . Jesus led the one perfect life of piety and personal holiness on the sole consideration that He was God-incarnate." 36/169

Of this *Griffith Thomas* writes: ". . . Not for a single instant did the faintest shadow come between Him and His heavenly Father. He was without sin." 50/17

Griffith Thomas again states: "If Christ's own life had not been sinless, it is obvious that He could not be the Redeemer of mankind from sin." 50/17

From *Philip Schaff* we hear: "The better and holier a man is, the more he feels his need of pardon, and how far he falls short of his own imperfect standard of excellence. But Jesus, with the same nature as ours and tempted as we are, never yielded to temptation; never had cause for regretting any thought, word, or action; He never needed pardon, or conversion, or reform; He never fell out of harmony with His heavenly Father. His whole life was one unbroken act of self-consecration to the glory of God and the eternal welfare of His fellow-men." 42/107

"I know of no sincere enduring good but the moral excellency which shines forth in Jesus Christ." *William Ellery Channing* 29/51

Wilbur Smith observes: "Fifteen million minutes of life on this earth, in the midst of a wicked and corrupt generation — every thought, every deed, every purpose, every work, privately and publicly, from the time He opened His baby eyes until He expired on the cross, were all approved of God. Never once did our Lord have to confess any sin, for He had no sin." 46/8,9

5B. **With the Witness of History We Find the Testimonies of Some of the World's Most Renowned Skeptics**

Rousseau stated: "When Plato describes his imaginary righteous man, loaded with all the punishments of guilt, yet meriting the highest rewards of virtue, he describes exactly the character of Jesus Christ. . . ." 43/134

The famous writer, *John Stuart Mill,* asks: "But who among his disciples or among their proselytes was capable of inventing the saying ascribed to Jesus, or imagining the life and character revealed in the Gospels?" 43/145

"Jesus is the most perfect of all men that have yet appeared." *Ralph Waldo Emerson* 29/52

The historian *William Lecky* states, "He . . . has been not only the highest pattern of virtue, but the strongest incentive to its practice. . . ." 22/8

"Even *David Strauss,*" writes Wilbur Smith, "the bitterest of all opponents of the supernatural elements of the Gospels, whose works did more to destroy faith in Christ than the writings of any other man in modern times — even Strauss, with all his slashing, brilliant, vicious criticisms and his sweeping denials of everything partaking of the miraculous, was forced to confess, toward the end of his life, that in Jesus there is moral perfection. 'This Christ . . . is *historical,* not mythical; is an *individual,* no mere symbol. . . . He remains the highest model of religion within the reach of our thought; and no perfect piety is possible without His presence in the heart.' " 46/11

To conclude, *Bernard Ramm* writes: "Sinless perfection and perfect sinlessness is what we would expect of God-incarnate, and this we do find in Jesus Christ. The hypothesis and the facts concur." 36/169

3A. IF GOD BECAME MAN, THEN WE WOULD EXPECT HIM TO MANIFEST THE SUPERNATURAL IN THE FORM OF MIRACLES

1B. **The Scriptural Witness**

"Go and report to John what you have seen and heard: the blind receive sight, the lame walk, the lepers are cleansed, and the deaf hear, the dead are raised up, the poor have the gospel preached to them" (Luke 7:22).

Thus we see that His miracles demonstrated a great variety of power: power over nature, power over disease, power over demons, powers of creation and power over death. This was also an appeal to prophecy and its messianic fulfillment in Christ.

A listing of these would include:

MIRACLES OF PHYSICAL HEALING

A leper, Matthew 8:2-4; Mark 1:40-45; Luke 5:12-15
A paralytic, Matthew 9:2-8; Mark 2:3-12; Luke 5:18-26
Fever (Peter's mother-in-law), Matthew 8:14-17; Mark 1:29-31
Nobleman's son healed, John 4:46-53
Physical infirmity, John 5:1-9
A withered hand, Matthew 12:9-13; Mark 3:1-6; Luke 6:6-11
Deafness and dumbness, Mark 7:31-37
Blindness at Bethsaida, Mark 8:22-25; in Jerusalem, John 9;
    Bartimaeus, Mark 10:46-52
Ten lepers, Luke 17:11-19
Malchus' severed ear, Luke 22:47-51
Hemorrhage, Matthew 9:20-22; Mark 5:25-34; Luke 8:43-48
Dropsy, Luke 14:2-4

MIRACLES IN THE NATURAL REALM

Water converted to wine at Cana, John 2:1-11
Stilling of a storm, Matthew 8:23-27; Mark 4:35-41; Luke 8:22-25
Supernatural catch of fish, Luke 5:1-11; John 21:6
Multiplying food: 5,000 fed, Matthew 14:15-21; Mark 6:34-44; Luke
    9:11-17; John 6:1-14; 4,000 fed, Matthew 15:32-39; Mark 8:1-9
Walking on water, Matthew 14:22,23; Mark 6:45-52; John 6:19
Money from a fish, Matthew 17:24-27
Fig tree dried up, Matthew 21:18-22; Mark 11:12-14

MIRACLES OF RESURRECTION

Jairus' daughter, Matthew 9:18-26; Mark 5:35-43; Luke 8:41-56
Widow's son, Luke 7:11-15
Lazarus of Bethany, John 11:1-44 48/500

2B.   **Comments and Quotes on His Miracles**

"Christ demonstrated a power over natural forces that could belong only to God, the author of these forces." 24/56

With this are the words of C. S. Lewis: "All the essentials of Hinduism would, I think, remain unimpaired if you subtracted the miraculous, and the same is almost true of Muhammadanism, but you cannot do that with Christianity. It is precisely the story of a great Miracle. A naturalistic Christianity leaves out all that is specifically Christian." 23/83

Another purpose of the miracles is stated by Bernard Ramm: "Miracles are believed in non-Christian religions because the religion is already believed, but in the Biblical religion, miracles are part of the means of establishing the true religion. This distinction is of immense importance. Israel was brought into existence by a series of miracles, the law was given surrounded by supernatural wonders, and many of the prophets were identified as God's spokesmen by their power to perform miracles. Jesus came not only preaching but performing miracles, and the apostles from time to time worked wonders. It was the miracle authenticating the religion at every point." 37/142f.

Philip Schaff states that Christ's miracles were "in striking contrast with deceptive juggler works and the useless and absurd miracles of apocryphal fiction. They were performed without any ostentation, with such simplicity and ease as to be called simply His works." 42/105

To continue this thought, *Griffith Thomas* relates: "It is noteworthy that one of the words very frequently used of these miracles in the Gospels is the ordinary term, works (*erga*). They were the natural and necessary outcome of His life, the expression in act of what He Himself was." 50/50 was." 50/50

They also mirrored the character of their worker.

Griffith Thomas continues: "The inquiry resolves itself simply into this: granted such a supernatural Person, were supernatural deeds congruous with His life? The character of the works attributed to Him, their beneficence, the restraint under which they were worked, the comparatively insignificant place they occupied in His ministry, and the constant stress laid by Him on spiritual kinship as primary — these are all entirely congruous with the manifestation and working of so miraculous and superhuman a Person as Jesus is seen to be." 50/54

Philip Schaff tells us: "All His miracles are but natural manifestations of His person, and hence they were performed with the same ease with which we perform our ordinary daily works." 43/76,77

Again, from *Philip Schaff:* "His miracles were, without exception, prompted by the purest motives and aimed at the glory of God and the benefit of men; they are miracles of love and mercy, full of instruction and significance and in harmony with His character and mission." 43/91

F. H. Chase states: "The motive and scope of the Lord's miracles recorded in the Gospels are ever the same. The notices of the miracles are scattered up and down over the Gospels. But when they are considered in relation to each other, we discover in them an undesigned unity. Together they cover the whole ground of our Lord's work as the Saviour, renewing each element in man's complex being and restoring peace in the physical order. They are not presented in the Gospels as primarily designed to enhance His dignity and His power. If they had been the invention of pious fancy, yearning to illustrate by imposing stories of His greatness and His glory, it is a moral impossibility that this subtle unity of purpose should have been so consistently and so unobtrusively observed." 6/404

"The miracles," writes *A. E. Garvie*, "are harmonious with the character and consciousness of Jesus; they are not external confirmations but internal constituents of the revelation of the Heavenly Father's love, mercy, and grace, given in Him, the beloved Son of God, and the compassionate Brother of men." 11/51,52

Thomas concludes: "For us today the Person of Christ is the great miracle, and the true line of thought is to argue from Christ to miracles rather than from miracles to Christ." 50/49

Islam even recognizes His ability to perform miracles as we see that the *Koran* (the *Table* V110) bears reference to them. It speaks of healing the blind, the lepers and raising the dead.

3B. Early Jewish Witness

"We find many references," writes *Ethelbert Stauffer* in *Jesus and His Story,* "to Jesus' miracles in the Jewish law books and histories."

"Around A.D. 95 Rabbi Eliezer ben Hyrcanus of Lydda speaks of Jesus' magic arts." 47/9

"Around the same period (A.D. 95-110) we encounter the ritual denunciation: 'Jesus practiced magic and led Israel astray' " [Sanhedrin 43a]. 47/10

"Around 110 we hear of a controversy among Palestinian Jews centering upon the question of whether it is permissible to healed in the name of Jesus." 47/10

"Now, miraculous healings in the name of Jesus imply that Jesus Himself performed such miracles." 47/10

We also have a roundabout reference from Julian the Apostate, Roman Emperor from 361-363, who was one of the most gifted of the ancient adversaries to Christianity. In his work against Christianity, he states:

"Jesus . . . has now been celebrated about three hundred years; having done nothing in his lifetime worthy of fame, unless anyone thinks it a very great work to heal lame and blind people and exorcise demoniacs in the villages of Bethsaida and Bethany." 43/133 He unwittingly ascribes to Christ the power to perform miracles.

4B. To Silence the Critic

"If miracles," says *Bernard Ramm*, "are capable of sensory perception, they can be made matters of testimony. If they are adequately testified to, then the recorded testimony has the same validity for evidence as the experiences of beholding the events." 36/140

Thus, many of His miracles were performed before the public for open scrutiny and investigation by skeptics. First let us look at the biblical account of Jesus raising Lazarus from the dead.

Bernard Ramm observes: "If the raising of Lazarus was actually witnessed by John and recorded faithfully by him when still in soundness of faculties and memory, for purposes of evidence it is the same as if we were there and saw it." 36/140,141

In reference to raising Lazarus from the dead, it is significant that His adversaries did not deny the miracle, but, rather, tried to kill Him before all men believed in Him (John 11:48).

Thus, Jesus' contemporaries, His enemies included, attested to His ability to perform miracles. However, this power was attributed to Satan by His enemies and to God by His friends (Matthew 12:24).

In answer to the charge Jesus said, "Any kingdom divided against itself is laid waste; and any city or house divided against itself shall not stand. And if Satan casts out Satan, he is divided against himself: how then shall his kingdom stand?" (Matthew 12:25,26).

On the basis of the evidence and testimonies available we see that the Gospel miracles cannot be discounted because of the extravagant and superstitious claims of pagan miracles. Just because some miracles are counterfeit is no proof that all are fraudulent.

Miracles are often discounted because they are against natural law. However, laws cannot cause anything to happen. Therefore, when the miracles of Jesus are discussed they must be observed as God coming in and altering the ordinary course of things.

We can see then that miracles are an inherent part of God's communication with us. Thus, the whole question depends ultimately on the existence of God.

On this thought, *Griffith Thomas* says, "If, therefore, we are to allow the scientific doctrine of the uniformity and continuity of nature to bar the way, we shall inevitably come to the conclusion that miracles are impossible, and from this would follow, as it usually does follow, the conclusion that a miraculous Christ is impossible. The question is thus really decided on *a priori* grounds before the evidence is even looked at." 50/52

Paul Little states the fact that "science can only say miracles do not occur in the ordinary course of nature. Science cannot 'forbid' miracles because natural laws do not cause, and therefore cannot forbid, anything." 24/125

Also in regard to natural law we hear from *Philip Schaff.* "True miracles are above nature, not *against* nature. . . . They are manifestation of a higher law, which the lower laws must obey." 43/92

In conclusion are two quotes, the first from *John A. Broadus* and the second from *A. E. Garvie.*

"Take the Gospels as they stand . . . and if Jesus of Nazareth did not perform supernatural works, He many times spoke falsely. Either He who spake as never man spake, and in whose character no criticism can discern a fault . . . either He did perform supernatural works or He spoke falsely." 10/72

Garvie states: ". . . A Christ who being Son of God, and seeking to become Saviour of men, (and) wrought no miracle, would be less intelligible and credible than the Jesus whom the Gospel records so consistently present to us." 10/73

4A. IF GOD BECAME MAN, THEN WE WOULD EXPECT HIM TO HAVE AN ACUTE SENSE OF DIFFERENCE FROM OTHER MEN

1B. The Witness of Friends

Jesus' influence has been such that men have "to take sides for or against Him. Indifference has always been impossible." In the *Koran* (Al-Imran, V. 45) Jesus is referred to as "the greatest above all in this world and in the world to come." Pascal said, "Who has taught the evangelists the qualities of a perfectly heroic soul, that they paint it so perfectly in Jesus Christ." 56/29

"Jesus, in every respect, was truly human and also more than human." 45/27

Channing, cited by Frank Ballard in *The Miracles of Unbelief,* stated: "I know not what can be added to heighten the wonder, reverence, and the love which are due to Jesus." 3/252

A. M. Fairbairn in *Philosophy of the Christian Religion* says: "Jesus, in a word, was Deity manifested in humanity and under the conditions of time. Now this is in itself an extraordinary conception, and it is made more extraordinary by the marvelous way in which it is embodied in a personal history. There never was a loftier idea. . . ." 8/326

"His life was holy; His word was true; His whole character was the embodiment of truth. There never has been a more real or genuine man than Jesus of Nazareth." *G. Thomas* 50/11

W. R. Gregg affirms that "Jesus had one of those gifted natures rarely met with, never in equal perfection, the purity and absolute harmony of whose mental and moral elements confer a clearness of vision which almost rises to the quality of prophecy." 3/152

Hausrath, cited by Frank Ballard, thinks: "There is no other noble life known to human record encumbered with so little that is earthy, transitory, local; no other that can be put to purposes so high and universal." 3/252

John Young in *Christ of History* asks: ". . . How it has come to pass, that of all men He alone has risen to spiritual perfection? What God did for piety and virtue on the earth at one time and in one case, God certainly could have done at other times and in other cases. If Jesus was man only, God could have raised up, in successive ages, many such living examples of sanctified humanity as He was, to correct, instruct, and quicken the world. But He did not. . . ." 57/243

Carnegie Simpson wrote: "Instinctively we do not class Him with others. When one reads His name in a list beginning with Confucius and ending with Goethe we feel it is an offense less against orthodoxy than against decency. Jesus is not one of the group of the world's great. Talk about Alexander the Great and Charles the Great and Napoleon the Great if you will . . . Jesus is apart. He is not the Great; He is the Only. He is simply Jesus. Nothing could add to that. . . . He is beyond our analyses. He confounds our canons of human nature. He compels our criticism to overleap itself. He awes our spirits." 98/36 (Quoted by John Stott in *Basic Christianity.*)

From *Philip Schaff:* "His zeal never degenerated into passion, nor His constancy into obstinacy, nor His benevolence into weakness, nor His tenderness into sentimentality. His unworldliness was free from indifference and unsociability, His dignity from pride and presumption, His affectibility from undue familiarity, His self-denial from moroseness, His temperance from austerity. He combined child-like innocency with manly strength, absorbing devotion to God with untiring interest in the welfare of man, tender love to the sinner with uncompromising severity against sin, commanding dignity with winning humility, fearless courage with wise caution, unyielding firmness with sweet gentleness." 43/63

In a conversation between Robert Browning and *Charles Lamb,* cited by John R. W. Stott, Lamb was talking about the reaction they would experience if someone from the dead walked in. When asked what he would do if Christ entered the room, Lamb replied ". . . If Shakespeare was to come into this room we should all rise up to meet him, but if that Person was to come into it, we should all fall down and try to kiss the hem of his garment." 48/36

Griffith Thomas states: "He represents a definite, divine intervention on behalf of man, at a particular moment of time in the world's history, and on this great miracle of the Person of Christ we take our stand. . . ." 50/53

"He embraces all the good elements which mark other men, and it is not too much to say that there is no element missing which men think desirable in the human character." 50/11

Klausner, a Jewish scholar, says, "Jesus was the most Jewish of Jews; even more Jewish than Hillel." 19/1249

"It is universally admitted . . . that Christ taught the purest and sublimest system of ethics, one which throws the moral precepts and maxims of the wisest men of antiquity far into the shade." 43/44

Joseph Parker writes in *Ecce Deus:* "Only a Christ could have conceived a Christ." 27/57

Johann Gottfried Von Herder declares: "Jesus Christ is in the noblest and most perfect sense the realized ideal of humanity." 29/53

Napoleon Bonaparte has said: "I know men and I tell you that Jesus Christ is no mere man. Between Him and every other person in the world there is no possible term of comparison. Alexander, Caesar, Charlemagne, and I have founded empires. But on what did we rest the creations of our genius? Upon force. Jesus Christ founded His empire upon love; and at this hour millions of men would die for Him." 29/56

Theodore Parker, a famous Unitarian, avows that "Christ unites in Himself the sublimest principles and divinest practices, thus more than realizing the dream of prophets and sages, rises free from all prejudices of his age, nation, or sect, and pours out a doctrine beautiful as the light, sublime as heaven, and true as God. Eighteen centuries have passed since the sun of humanity rose so high in Jesus. What man, what sect has mastered His thought, comprehended His method, and fully applied it to life?" 3/252

Ralph Waldo Emerson had this to say: "Jesus astonishes and overpowers sensual people. They cannot unite Him to history or reconcile Him with themselves." 29/52

"The latest edition of the *Encyclopaedia Britannica*," writes Wilbur Smith, "gives twenty thousand words to this person Jesus, and does not even hint that He did not exist — more words, by the way, than are given to Aristotle, Alexander, Cicero, Julius Caesar, or Napoleon Bonaparte." 46/5

Phillips Brooks: "Jesus Christ, the condescension of divinity, and the exaltation of humanity." 29/56

2B.   What the Antagonists Say

"And *Goethe*," cites historian Philip Schaff, "another commanding genius, of very different character, but equally above suspicion of partiality for religion, looking in the last years of his life over the vast field of history, was constrained to confess that 'if ever the Divine appeared on earth, it was in the Person of Christ,' and that 'the human mind, no matter how far it may advance in every other department, will never transcend the height and moral culture of Christianity as it shines and glows in the Gospels.' " 42/110

"I esteem the Gospels to be thoroughly genuine, for there shines forth from them the reflected splendour of a sublimity, proceeding from the person of Jesus Christ, and of as Divine a kind as was ever manifested upon earth." 3/251

H. G. Wells, the noted historian, writes a fascinating testimony to Jesus Christ:

"He was too great for his disciples. And in view of what he plainly said, is it any wonder that all who were rich and prosperous felt a horror of strange things, a swimming of their world at his teaching? Perhaps the priests and the rulers and the rich men understood him better than his followers. He was dragging out all the little private reservations they had made from social service into the light of a universal religious life. He was like some terrible moral huntsman digging mankind out of the snug burrows in which they had lived hitherto. In the white blaze of this kingdom of his there was to be no property, no privilege, no pride and precedence; no motive indeed and no reward but love. Is it any wonder that men were dazzled and blinded and cried out against him? Even his disciples cried out when he would not spare them the light. Is it any wonder that the priests realized that between this man and themselves there was no choice but that he or the priestcraft should perish? Is it any wonder that the Roman soldiers, confronted and amazed by something soaring over their comprehension and threatening all their disciplines, should take refuge in wild laughter, and crown him with thorns and robe him in purple and make a mock Caesar of him? For to take him seriously was to enter upon a strange and alarming life, to abandon habits, to control instincts and impulses, to essay an incredible happiness. . . .

"Is it any wonder that to this day this Galilean is too much for our small hearts?" 52/535,536

When *Wells* was asked which person has left the most permanent impression on history, he replied that judging a person's greatness by historical standards, "By this test Jesus stands first." 36/163

"Whatever may be the surprises of the future, Jesus will never be surpassed." *Ernest Renan* 41/146

Thomas Carlyle refers to Jesus as ". . . our divinest symbol. Higher has the human thought not yet reached. A symbol of quite perennial, infinite character; whose significance will ever demand to be anew inquired into, and anew made manifest." 43/139

Rousseau asks, "Can the Person whose history the Gospels relate be Himself a man? What sweetness, what purity in His manners! What affecting goodness in His instructions! What sublimity in His maxims! What profound wisdom in His discourses! What presence of mind, what ingenuity of justice in His replies! Yes, if the life and death of Socrates are those of a philosopher, the life and death of Jesus Christ are those of a God." 3/251

To conclude, we hear first from *Bernard Ramm* and then from *G. A. Ross*: "Jesus Christ as the God-man is the greatest *personality* that ever lived, and therefore His personal impact is the greatest of any man that ever lived." Ramm 36/173

"Have we ever thought of the peculiar position occupied by Jesus with respect to the ideals of the sexes? No man has ever dared to call Jesus, in any opprobrious sense, sexless: yet in character He stands above, and if one may use the term, midway between the sexes — His comprehensive humanity a veritable storehouse of the ideals we associate with both the sexes. No woman has ever had any more difficulty than men have had in finding in Him the realized ideal. Whatever there is in men of strength, justice, and wisdom, whatever there is in women of sensibility, purity, and insight, is in Christ without the conditions which hinder among us the development of contrasted virtues in one person." 41/23

5A. IF GOD BECAME MAN, THEN CERTAINLY HIS WORDS WOULD BE THE GREATEST EVER SPOKEN

1B. Jesus Himself said, "Heaven and earth will pass away, but My words will not pass away" (Luke 21:33).

Luke 4:32 tells us that "they were continually amazed at His teaching. . . ."

From the officers of the guard we hear, "Never did a man speak the way this man speaks" (John 7:46).

2B. The Greatest Words Ever Spoken

Many of today's scholars feel that Jesus' words are the greatest ever spoken: one such man is Bernard Ramm. He feels their greatness lies in their ability to deal authoritatively and clearly with the greatest burdens and problems man faces; namely, those dealing with his relationship to God.

Sholem Ash wrote:

"Jesus Christ is the outstanding personality of all time. . . . No other teacher — Jewish, Christian, Buddhist, Mohammedan — is *still* a teacher whose teaching is such a guidepost for the world we live in. Other teachers may have something basic for an Oriental, an Arab, or an Occidental; but every act and word of Jesus has value for all of us. He became the Light of the World. Why shouldn't I, a Jew, be proud of that?" 29/49

G. J. Romanes tells us:

"For when we consider what a large number of sayings are recorded of — or at least attributed to — Him, it becomes most remarkable that in literal truth there is no reason why any of His words should ever pass away in the sense of becoming obsolete. . . . Contrast Jesus Christ in this respect with other thinkers of like antiquity. Even Plato, who, though some four hundred years before Christ in point of time, was greatly in advance of Him in respect of philosophic thought, is nowhere in this respect as compared with Christ. Read the *Dialogues,* and see how enormous is the contrast with the Gospels in respect of errors of all kinds, reaching even to absurdity in respect of reason, and to sayings shocking to the moral sense. Yet this is confessedly the highest level of human reason on the lines of spirituality when unaided by alleged revelation." 41/157

"For two thousand years, He *has* been the Light of the World, and His words have *not* passed away." *Morris* 30/28

The great personality behind His words is reason for the greatness of His words, according to *Ramm.* 36/173

From *F. J. A. Hort:*

"His words were so completely parts and utterances of Himself, that they had no meaning as abstract statements of truth uttered by Him as a Divine oracle or prophet. Take away Himself as the primary (though not the ultimate) subject of every statement and they all fall to pieces." 14/207

"But Jesus' words and acts are impressively integral, and we trust those sayings we judge to be authentically His as revelatory of His person. When Jesus uses the personal pronoun, 'I' ('But *I* say to you,' 'Amen, *I* say to you'), He stands in back of every word with personal fidelity and personal intentionality. If His words and acts are messianic in character, *it is because He intends them to be,* and if He intends them to be, He is thinking of Himself in messianic terms." *Gruenler* 13/97

"Christ's words are of permanent value because of His person; they endure because He endures." *Griffith Thomas* 50/44

Joseph Parker states: "After reading the doctrines of Plato, Socrates or Aristotle, we feel the specific difference between their words and Christ's is the difference between an inquiry and a revelation." 29/57

In the words of *Bernard Ramm:* "Statistically speaking, the Gospels are the greatest literature ever written. They are read by more people, quoted by more authors, translated into more tongues, represented in more art, set to more music, than any other book or books written by any man in any century in any land. But the words of Christ are not great on the grounds that they have such a statistical edge over anybody else's words. They are read more, quoted more, loved more, believed more, and translated more because they are the greatest words ever spoken. And where is their greatness? Their greatness lies in the pure, lucid spirituality in dealing clearly, definitively, and *authoritatively* with the greatest problems that throb in the human breast; namely, Who is God? Does He love Me? What should I do to please Him? How does He look at my sin? How can I be forgiven? Where will I go when I die? How must I treat others? No other man's words have the appeal of Jesus' words because no other man can answer these fundamental human questions as Jesus answered them. They are the kind of words and the kind of answers we would expect God to give, and we who believe in Jesus' deity have no problem as to why these words came from His mouth." 36/170,171

"Never did the Speaker seem to stand more utterly alone than when He uttered this majestic utterance. Never did it seem more improbable that it should be fulfilled. But as we look across the centuries we see how it has been realized. His words have passed into law, they have passed into doctrines, they have passed into proverbs, they have passed into consolations, but they have *never* 'passed away.' What human teacher ever dared to claim an eternity for his words?" *G. F. Maclean 26*/149

"Systems of human wisdom will come and go, kingdoms and empires will rise and fall, but for all time to come Christ will remain 'the Way, the Truth, and the Life.' " *Philip Schaff* 42/111

Christ's teachings are complete in every point, from the regulation of thought to control of the will. Because of this, *Thomas* points out that Christ's message is "'inexhaustible." Each generation finds it new and exciting. 50/36

Mark Hopkins affirms: "No revolution that has ever taken place in society can be compared to that which has been produced by the words of Jesus Christ." 29/53

W. S. Peake: "It is sometimes said, 'Everything that Jesus said has been said before Him by others.' Let us grant that it is true, what then? Originality may or may not be a merit. If the truth has already been uttered, the merit lies in repeating it, and giving it new and fuller application. But there are other considerations to be borne in mind. We have no other teacher who so completely eliminated the trivial, the temporal, the false from his system, no one who selected just the eternal and the universal, and combined them in a teaching where all these great truths found their congenial home. These parallels from the teaching of others to that of Christ are brought together from this quarter and from that; how is it that none of these teachers furnishes us with any parallel to the teachings of Christ? As a whole, while each of them gives us such truths as He expresses mingled with a mass of what is trivial and absurd? How was it that a carpenter, of no special training, ignorant of the culture and learning of the Greeks, born of a people whose great teachers were narrow, sour, intolerant, pedantic legalists, was the supreme religious Teacher the world has known, whose supremacy here makes Him the most important figure in the world's history?" 35/226,227

Griffith Thomas concludes: "Although without formal rabbinical training, He showed no timidity or self-consciousness, no hesitation as to what He felt to be truth. Without any thought of Himself or His audience, He spoke out fearlessly on every occasion, utterly heedless of the consequences to Himself, and only concerned for truth and the delivery of His Father's message. The power of His teaching was also deeply felt. 'His word was with power' (Luke 4:32). The spiritual force of His personality expressed itself in His utterances and held His hearers in its enthralling grasp. And so we are not surprised to read of the impression of uniqueness made by Him. 'Never man spake like this man' (John 7:46). The simplicity and charm and yet the depth, the directness, the universality, and the truth of His teaching made a deep mark on His hearers, and elicited the conviction that they were in the presence of a Teacher such as man had never known before. And thus the large proportion of teaching in the Gospels, and the impressions evidently created by the Teacher Himself, are such that we are not at all surprised that years afterward the great Apostle of the Gentiles should recall these things and say, 'Remember the words of the Lord Jesus' (Acts 20:35). The same impression has been made in every age since the days of Christ and His immediate followers, and in any full consideration of His Person as the substance of Christianity great attention must necessarily be paid to His teaching." 50/32

6A. IF GOD BECAME MAN, THEN WE WOULD EXPECT HIM TO HAVE A LASTING AND UNIVERSAL INFLUENCE

To be sure, the personality of Jesus Christ has made such an impact on humanity that even after 2,000 years the impact has not worn off. Each day, there are persons who have revolutionary experiences with Jesus.

The great historian, *Kenneth Scott Latourette,* said: "As the centuries pass the evidence is accumulating that, measured by His effect of history, *Jesus is the most influential life ever lived on this planet.* That influence appears to be mounting." 20/272

Philip Schaff adds:

"This Jesus of Nazareth, without money and arms, conquered more millions than Alexander, Caesar, Mohammed, and Napoleon; without science and learning, He shed more light on things human and divine than all philosophers and scholars combined; without the eloquence of schools, He spoke such words of life as were never spoken before or since and produced effects which lie beyond the reach of orator or poet; without writing a single line, He set more pens in motion, and furnished themes for more sermons, orations, discussions, learned volumes, works of art, and songs of praise, than the whole army of great men of ancient and modern times." 43/33

"The influence of Jesus on mankind is today as strong as it was when He dwelt among men." *Martin Scott* 45/29

"That ministry lasted only three years — and yet in these three years is condensed the deepest meaning of the history of religion. No great life ever passed so swiftly, so quietly, so humbly, so far removed from the noise and commotion of the world; and no great life after its close excited such universal and lasting interest." *Philip Schaff* 42/103

"When Jesus Christ left this earth," *Griffith Thomas* writes, "He told His disciples that after His departure they should do greater works than He had done, and the centuries of Christianity have borne out the truth of this statement. Works greater in kind have been done — are being done. Jesus Christ is doing more wonderful things today than ever He did when on earth, redeeming souls, changing lives, transforming characters, exalting ideals, inspiring philanthropies, and making for the best, truest, and highest in human life and progress."

Griffith Thomas continues: "We are therefore justified in calling attention to the influence of Christ through the ages as one of the greatest, most direct, and most self-evident proofs that Christianity is Christ, and that Christ has to be accounted for. It is impossible to consider this question solely as one of history; it touches life at every point today." 50/121

William Lecky, the skeptic, states in *History of European Morals from Augustus to Charlemagne:*

"The Platonist exhorted men to imitate God; the Stoic, to follow reason; the Christian, to the love of Christ. The later Stoics had often united their notions of excellence in an ideal sage, and Epictetus had even urged his disciples to set before them some man of surpassing excellence, and to imagine him continually near them; but the utmost the Stoic ideal could become was a model for imitation, and the admiration it inspired could never deepen into affection. It was reserved for Christianity to present to the world an ideal character, which through all the changes of eighteen centuries has inspired the hearts of men with an impassioned love; has shown itself capable of acting on all ages, nations, temperaments, and conditions; has been not only the highest pattern of virtue, but the strongest incentive to its practice; and has exercised so deep an influence that it may be truly said that the simple record of three short years of active life has done more to regenerate and soften mankind than all the disquisitions of philosophers and all the exhortations of moralists. This has indeed been the wellspring of whatever is best and purest in the Christian life. Amid all the sins and failings, amid all the priestcraft and persecution and fanaticism that have defaced the Church, it has preserved in the character and example of its Founder, an enduring principle of regeneration." 22/8

"Yet thousands and millions today, as in all ages, are testifying to the power and glory of Christianity in dealing with their sin and wickedness. These are facts which stand the test of examination and carry their own conclusion to all who are willing to learn." G. Thomas 50/119

". . . He is the greatest influence in the world today. There is, as it has been well said, a fifth Gospel being written — the work of Jesus Christ in the hearts and lives of men and nations." G. Thomas 50/117

Napoleon said: "Christ alone has succeeded in so raising the mind of man towards the unseen that it becomes insensible to the barriers of time and space. Across the chasm of eighteen hundred years Jesus Christ makes a demand which is beyond all others difficult to satisfy. He asks for that which a philosophy may often seek in vain at the hands of his friends, or a father of his children, or a bride of her spouse, or a man of his brother. He asks for the human heart; He will have it entirely to Himself; He demands it unconditionally, and forthwith His demand is granted. Its powers and faculties become an annexation to the empire of Christ. All who sincerely believe in Him experience that supernatural love towards Him. This phenomenon is unaccountable, it is altogether beyond the scope of man's creative powers. Time, the great destroyer, can neither exhaust its strength nor put a limit to its range." 3/265

E. Y. Mullins in Why Is Christianity True? says:

"But, it may be asked, 'Is this lofty religion one which can be appropriated by men universally?' Does it appeal, as we have declared, to man as man regardless of race, climate or condition? Does it reach the ignorant and learned? May its principles be grasped by all men everywhere?" 31/407

Wherever He is, He is Master. When He asks men to make sacrifices, they make them. His call is not that of a fanatic. However, it leads men to deeds of great quality and personal sacrifice.

Again from Napoleon: "The nature of Christ's existence is mysterious, I admit; but this mystery meets the wants of man — reject it and the world is an inexplicable riddle; believe it, and the history of our race is satisfactorily explained." 29/56

One cannot "fail to see . . . that since the days of Christ, in spite of all the progress of thought, not a single new ethical ideal has been given to the world." G. Thomas 15/35

R. G. Gruenler says: "The kerygma of the community is the proclamation that Jesus is of universal relevance. Wherever and whenever He is proclaimed, men are confronted by His concreteness, His humanness, and are brought into the presence of God." 13/25

From Griffith Thomas we have: "Other religions have had their ethical ideal of duty, opportunity, and even of love, but nowhere have they approached those of Christ, either in reality or in attractiveness or in power. Christ's message is remarkable for its universal adaptation. Its appeal is universal; it is adapted to all men from the adult down to the child; it makes its appeal to all times and not merely to the age in which it was first given. And the reason is that it emphasizes a threefold ethical attitude toward God and man which makes a universal appeal as nothing else does or perhaps can do. Christ calls for repentance, trust and love." 50/35

"The most marvelous and astonishing thing in nineteen centuries of history is the power of His life over the members of the Christian Church." 50/104

George Bancroft said: "I find the name of Jesus Christ written on the top of every page of modern history." 29/50

"It is true that there have been other religions with millions of adherents, but it is also true that the existence and progress of the Church is something unique in history to say nothing of the fact that Christianity has attracted to itself the profoundest thinkers of the human race, and is in no way hindered by the ever-advancing tide of human knowledge." *G. Thomas* 50/103

A. M. Fairbairn has said, "The most remarkable fact in the history of His religion is the continuous and ubiquitous activity of His person. He has been the permanent and efficient factor in its extension and progress. Under all its forms, in all its periods, and through all its divisions, the one principle alike of reality and unity has been and is devotion to Him." 7/380

Even after 1,800 years, *David Strauss* is forced to say: "He remains the highest model of religion within the reach of our thought; and no perfect piety is possible without His presence in the heart." 43/142

William E. Channing said it this way: "The sages and heroes of history are receding from us, and history contracts the record of their deeds into a narrower and narrower page. But time has no power over the name and deeds and words of Jesus Christ." 29/51

From *Ernest Renan* we have the following two quotes: "Jesus was the greatest religious genius that ever lived. His beauty is eternal, and His reign shall never end. Jesus is in every respect unique, and nothing can be compared with Him." 29/57

"All history is incomprehensible without Christ." 29/57

"That a Galilean carpenter should so claim to be the Light of the world, and be so recognized after so many centuries, is best explained on the ground of His divinity." *Bernard Ramm* 36/177

In a *Life Magazine* article, *George Buttrick* wrote:

"Jesus gave history a new beginning. In every land He is at home: everywhere men think His face is like their best face — and like God's face. His birthday is kept across the world. His death-day has set a gallows against every city skyline. Who is He?" 29/51

The famous essay, "One Solitary Life," states:

"Here is a man who was born in an obscure village, the child of a peasant woman. He grew up in another village. He worked in a carpenter shop until He was thirty, and then for three years He was an itinerant preacher. He never owned a home. He never wrote a book. He never held an office. He never had a family. He never went to college. He never put his foot inside a big city. He never traveled two hundred miles from the place where He was born. He never did one of the things that usually accompany greatness. He had no credentials but Himself. . . . While still a young man, the tide of popular opinion turned against Him. His friends ran away. One of them denied Him. He was turned over to His enemies. He went through the mockery of a trial. He was nailed upon a cross between two thieves. While He was dying His executers gambled for the only piece of property He had on earth — his coat. When He was dead, He was taken down and laid in a borrowed grave through the pity of a friend.

"Nineteen long centuries have come and gone, and today He is the centerpiece of the human race and the leader of the column of progress. I am far within the mark when I say that all the armies that ever marched, all the navies that ever were built; all the parliaments that ever sat and all the kings that ever reigned, put together, have not affected the life of man upon this earth as powerfully as has that one solitary life."

"The Incomparable Christ," another vivid essay:

"More than nineteen hundred years ago there was a Man born contrary to the laws of life. This Man lived in poverty and was reared in obscurity. He did not travel extensively. Only once did He cross the boundary of the country in which He lived; that was during His exile in childhood.

"He possessed neither wealth nor influence. His relatives were inconspicuous, and had neither training nor formal education. In infancy He startled a king; in childhood He puzzled doctors; in manhood He ruled the course of nature, walked upon the billows as if pavements, and hushed the sea to sleep. He healed the multitudes without medicine and made no charge for His service.

"He never wrote a book, and yet all the libraries of the country could not hold the books that have been written about Him. He never wrote a song, and yet He has furnished the theme for more songs than all the songwriters combined.

"He never founded a college, but all the schools put together cannot boast of having as many students.

"He never marshaled an army, nor drafted a soldier, nor fired a gun; and yet no leader ever had more volunteers who have, under His orders, made more rebels stack arms and surrender without a shot fired.

"He never practiced psychiatry, and yet He has healed more broken hearts than all the doctors far and near. Once each week the wheels of commerce cease their turning and multitudes wend their way to worshipping assemblies to pay homage and respect to Him.

"The names of the past proud statesmen of Greece and Rome have come and gone. The names of the past scientists, philosophers, and theologians have come and gone; but the name of this Man abounds more and more. Though time has spread nineteen hundred years between the people of this generation and the scene of His crucifixion, yet He still lives. Herod could not destroy Him, and the grave could not hold Him.

"He stands forth upon the highest pinnacle of heavenly glory, proclaimed of God, acknowledged by angels, adored by saints, and feared by devils, as the living, personal Christ, our Lord and Saviour." 16/

7A. IF GOD BECAME MAN, THEN WE WOULD EXPECT HIM TO SATISFY THE SPIRITUAL HUNGER IN MAN

"Blessed are those who hunger and thirst for righteousness, for they shall be satisfied" (Matthew 5:6).

"If any man is thirsty, let Him come to Me and drink" (John 7:37).

"But whoever drinks of the water that I shall give him shall never thirst" (John 4:14).

"Peace I leave with you; My peace I give to you; not as the world gives, do I give to you. Let not your heart be troubled, nor let it be fearful" (John 14:27).

"I am the bread of life; he who comes to Me shall not hunger, and he who believes in Me shall never thirst" (John 6:35).

"Come to Me, all who are weary and heavy-laden, and I will give you rest" (Matthew 11:28).

"I came that they might have life, and might have it abundantly" (John 10:10).

Otto Rauk in *Beyond Psychology* says that "man needs to be in touch with something more than himself."

The major religions testify to man's need. The pyramids of Mexico and the shrines of India are examples of man's spiritual search.

Mark Twain wrote of men's emptiness: ". . . From his cradle to his grave a man never does a single thing which has any first and foremost objective save one — to secure peace of mind — spiritual comfort for himself."

Fisher, the historian, said, ". . . There is a cry in the soul, to which no response comes from the world."

Thomas Aquinas exclaimed, "The soul's restless thirst [is] for happiness, yet it is a thirst to be satisfied in God alone."

Bernard Ramm states that the "Christian experience alone provides man with an experience commensurate with his nature as free spirit. . . . Anything less than God leaves the spirit of man thirsty, hungry, restless, frustrated, and incomplete." 36/215

From *Philip Schaff* we read: "He rose above the prejudices of party and sect, above the superstitions of His age and nation. He addressed the naked heart of man and touched the quick of the conscience." 42/104,105

George Schweitzer, in his personal testimony, says: "Man has changed his world in a remarkable way, but has not been able to alter himself. Since this problem is basically a spiritual one, and since man is naturally bent toward evil (as history attests), the sole way that man can be changed is by God. Only if a man commits himself to Christ Jesus and submits himself to the Holy Spirit for guidance can he be changed. Only in this miraculous transformation rests hope for the atom-awed, radio-activity-ruffled world of our day and its inhabitants." 49/n.p.

The Director of Scientific Relations at Abbott Laboratories, *E. J. Matson,* writes: "No matter how exacting, how tiring my life as scientist, business man, citizen, husband or father, I had only to return to this center to meet Jesus Christ, demonstrating His keeping power as well as His saving power." 49/n.p.

A coed at the University of Pittsburgh says: "Whatever joys and gladness, all put together of my past experience, these can never equal that special joy and peace that the Lord Jesus Christ has given me since that time when He entered into my life to rule and to guide." 32/n.p.

R. L. Mixter, professor of zoology at Wheaton College: "When he follows the creed of his profession, a scientist believes what he does because of the evidence he can find. I became a Christian because I found in myself a need which could be satisfied only by Jesus Christ. I needed forgiveness and He gave it. I needed companionship and He was a Friend. I needed encouragement and He provided it." 49/n.p.

Paul H. Johnson: "God has shaped a peculiar vacuum inside us — a vacuum shaped like God. Nothing satisfies that vacuum except God Himself. You can put money, homes, wealth, power, fame, or anything you want into the vacuum, but it doesn't fit. Only God fills it, fits it and satisfies it." 18/n.p.

Walter Hearn of Ohio State College: "Often I am absorbed in a kind of philosophical quest . . . knowing Christ means life itself to me, but a new kind of life, the 'abundant life' He promised." 49/n.p.

A public relations and advertising man, *Frank Allnutt* relates: "Then I asked Jesus to come into my life and dwell there. For the first time in my life I experienced complete peace. The lifetime of emptiness I had known was removed, and I have never felt alone since." 1/22

J. C. Martin, former major league baseball catcher, says: "I have found happiness and the fulfillment of all I have desired in Jesus Christ." 27/n.p.

8A. IF GOD BECAME MAN, THEN WE WOULD EXPECT HIM TO EXERCISE POWER OVER DEATH

1B. Death

It is seen that Jesus was not forced to give up His life. As evidenced in Matthew 26:53,54, He had the power available to Him to do whatever He pleased. It is in John 10:18 that we find the answer: "No one has taken it (My life) away from Me, but I lay it down on My own initiative. I have authority to lay it down, and I have authority to take it up again. This commandment I received from My Father." We see that Christ willingly died for the sins of man.

W. H. Griffith Thomas feels:

"It was not the death of a suicide, for did He not say, 'I lay down My life of Myself.' The death was purely voluntary. *We* have to suffer: He need not have suffered. A word from Him might have saved His life. Nor was it an accidental death, for the obvious reason that it was foreseen, foretold, and prepared for in a variety of ways. Again, it was certainly not the death of a criminal, for no two witnesses could be found to agree together as to the charge against Him. Pilate declared that he found no fault in Him, and even Herod had not a word to say against Him. This, then, was no ordinary execution." 50/61

Another important fact of His death is related by *W. C. Robinson:* "For no mere man in all history has ever had the power to dismiss his spirit of his own volition as did our Lord Jesus (Luke 23:46).... Luke and John use verbs which can only be interpreted as meaning that Jesus miraculously ... handed over His spirit to God when He had paid the full price for sin. There was a miracle on Calvary on Friday as well as a miracle in the garden on Easter morning. ..." 38/85,86

2B. Burial

"And when it was evening, there came a rich man from Arimathea, named Joseph, who himself had also become a disciple of Jesus. This man came to Pilate and asked for the body of Jesus. Then Pilate ordered it to be given over to him" (Matthew 27:57,58).

"And Nicodemus came also, who had first come to Him by night; bringing a mixture of myrrh and aloes, about a hundred pounds weight" (John 19:39).

"And Joseph bought a linen sheet, took Him down, wrapped Him in the linen sheet, and laid Him in a tomb which had been hewn out in the rock; and he rolled a stone against the entrance of the tomb. And Mary Magdalene and Mary the mother of Jesus were looking on to see where He was laid" (Mark 15:46,47).

"And they returned and prepared spices and perfumes. And on the Sabbath they rested according to the commandment" (Luke 23:56).

"And they (the Pharisees' guard) went and made the grave secure, and along with the guard they set a seal on the stone" (Matthew 27:66).

3B. Resurrection

"Indeed, taking all the evidence together," *B. F. Westcott* writes, "it is not too much to say that there is no historic incident better or more variously supported than the resurrection of Christ. Nothing but the antecedent assumption that it must be false could have suggested the idea of deficiency in the proof of it." 54/4-6

From *Henry Morris* we read: "The fact of His resurrection is the most important event of history and therefore, appropriately, is one of the most certain facts in all history." 30/46

Jesus not only predicted His death, but He also predicted His bodily resurrection. In John 2:19 He says, "Destroy this temple, and in three days I will raise it up." Here, temple refers to His body.

Again *Morris* writes: "He alone, of all men who ever lived, conquered death itself. By all rules of evidence, His bodily resurrection from the grave can be adjudged the best-proved fact of all history. 'I am the resurrection and the life,' He said. 'Because I live, ye shall live also' " (John 11:25; 14:19). 30/28

"The resurrection of Christ is *the seal of our resurrection*. The healing of sick people does not warrant us in believing that Christ will heal each of us today, nor did the resuscitation of Lazarus guarantee our immortality. It is the resurrection of Christ as *firstfruits* which alone opens the grave — in anticipation — to the believer and unto life eternal. Because He arose, we shall arise" (Romans 8:11). *Ramm* 36/185,186

After Jesus' resurrection, the apostles were able to raise the dead through His power (Acts 9:40,41). Thus, He gave life to others after His death. It follows then that Jesus is alive (Hebrews 13:8) and that "This Jesus, who has been taken up from you into heaven, will come in just the same way as you have watched Him go into heaven" (Acts 1:11).

"But Jesus Christ, the eternal Son of God and the world's promised Redeemer, has conquered death. . . ." 30/46

BIBLIOGRAPHY

1. Allnutt, Frank. *Contact.* Vol. 30, No. 5, May 1972.
2. *The Apology of Aristides.* Translated and edited by Rendel Harris. London: Cambridge University Press, 1893.
3. Ballard, Frank. *The Miracles of Unbelief.* Edinburgh: T & T Clark, 1908.
4. Box, Hubert S. *Miracles and Critics.* London: Faith Press, Ltd., 1935.
5. Broadus, John A. *Jesus of Nazareth.* Grand Rapids: Baker Book House, 1963.
6. Chase, F. H. *Essays on Some Theological Questions of the Day.* H. B. Swelt, ed. London: Macmillan & Co., 1905.
7. Fairbairn, A. M. *Christ in Modern Theology.* London: Hodder and Stoughton, 1893.
8. Fairbairn, A. M. *Philosophy of the Christian Religion.* London: Hodder and Stoughton, 1908.
9. Fuller, Reginald H. *Interpreting the Miracles.* London: SCM Press, Ltd., 1963.
10. Garvie, A. E. *Handbook of Christian Apologetics.* London: Duckworth and Co., 1923.
11. Garvie, A. E. *Studies in the Inner Life of Christ.* New York: Hodder and Stoughton, 1907.
12. Gromacki, Robert Glenn. *The Virgin Birth.* New York: Thomas Nelson, Inc., 1974.
13. Gruenler, Royce Gordon. *Jesus, Persons and the Kingdom of God.* St. Louis: United Church Press, 1967.
14. Hort, F. J. A. *Way, Truth and the Life.* New York: Macmillan and Co., 1894.

15. Hunter, A. M. *The Work and Words of Jesus*. Philadelphia: Westminster Press, 1950.

16. "The Incomparable Christ." Oradell, N. J.: American Tract Society. Used by permission.

17. Jefferson, Charles Edward. *The Character of Jesus*. New York: Thomas Y. Crowell Company, 1908. Copyright renewed by Charles E. Jefferson, 1936. Used by permission.

18. Johnson, Paul H. "Master Plan." Westchester: Good News Publishers, n.d.

19. Klausner. *Yeschu Hanostri*. Quoted by Lapide in *Christian Century*. Vol. 87, Oct. 1970, p. 1249.

20. Latourette, Kenneth Scott. *American Historical Review*. LIV, January, 1949.

21. Latourette, Kenneth Scott. *A History of Christianity*. New York: Harper and Row, 1953.

22. Lecky, William Edward Hatpole. *History of European Morals from Augustus to Charlemagne*. New York: D. Appleton and Co., 1903.

23. Lewis, C. S. *Miracles*. New York: Macmillan and Co., 1947.

24. Little, Paul E. *Know Why You Believe*. Wheaton: Scripture Press Publications, Inc., 1967.

25. Machen, J. Gresham. *The Virgin Birth of Christ*. Grand Rapids: Baker Book House, 1965.

26. Maclean, G. F. *Cambridge Bible for Schools, St. Mark*. London: Cambridge University Press, 1893.

27. Martin, J. C. "Converted Catcher." Oradell, N.J.: American Tract Society, Sports Division, n.d. Used by permission.

28. Martyr, Justin. *Apologies and Dialogue with Trypho, Fathers of the Church*. Translated by Thomas Falls. New York: Christian Heritage Inc., 1948.

29. Mead, Frank (ed.). *The Encyclopedia of Religious Quotations*. Westwood: Fleming H. Revell, n.d.

30. Morris, Henry M. *The Bible Has the Answer*. Grand Rapids: Baker Book House, 1971.

31. Mullins, E. Y. *Why Is Christianity True?* Chicago: Christian Culture Press, 1905.

32. Ordonez, Rose Marie. *I Was Blind But Now I See*. Colorado Springs: International Students, Inc., n.d.

33. Origen. *Contra Celsum*. Translated by Henry Chadwick. London: Cambridge University Press, 1953.

34. Orr, James. *The Virgin Birth of Christ*. New York: Charles Scribner's Sons, 1907.

35. Peake, W. S. *Christianity, Its Nature and Its Truths*. London: Duckworth and Co., 1908.

36. Ramm, Bernard. *Protestant Christian Evidences*. Chicago: Moody Press, 1957. Used by permission.

37. Rice, John R. *Is Jesus God?* 4th rev. ed. Murfreesboro: Sword of the Lord Publishers, 1966.

38. Robinson, William Childs. *Who Say Ye That I Am?* Grand Rapids: William B. Eerdmans Publishing Co., 1949. Used by permission.

39. Rogers, Clement F. *The Case for Miracles*. London: Society for Promoting Christian Knowledge, 1936. Used by permission.

40. Romanes, G. J. *Thoughts on Religion*. Chicago: Open Court Publishing Co., 1898.

41. Ross, G. A. Johnston. *The Universality of Jesus*. New York: Fleming H. Revell Co., 1906.

42. Schaff, Philip. *History of the Christian Church*. Grand Rapids: William B. Eerdmans Publishing Co., 1910. Reprinted from original, 1962. Used by permission.

43. Schaff, Philip. *The Person of Christ*. New York: American Tract Society, 1913. Used by permission.

44. Schonfield, Hugh. *According to the Hebrews*. London: Gerald Duckworth & Co., 1937.

45. Scott, Martin J. *Jesus as Men Saw Him*. New York: P.J. Kennedy and Sons, 1940.

46. Smith, Wilbur. *Have You Considered Him?* Downers Grove: Inter-Varsity Press, 1970. Used by permission.

47. Stauffer, Ethelbert. *Jesus and His Story*. Translated by Richard and Clara Winston. New York: Alfred A. Knopf, 1960.

48. Stott, John R. W. *Basic Christianity*. Downers Grove: Inter-Varsity Press, 1971. Used by permission.

49. *Ten Scientists Look at Life*. Westchester: Good News Publishers (tract).

50. Thomas, W. H. Griffith. *Christianity Is Christ*. Chicago: Moody Press, 1965. Used by permission.

51. Unger, Merrill F. *Unger's Bible Handbook*. Chicago: Moody Press, 1967. Used by permission.

52. Wells, H. G. *Outline of History*. Garden City: Garden City Publishing Co., 1931.

53. Westcott, B. F. *Gospel of Life*. London: Macmillan and Co., 1903.

54. Westcott, B. F. *Gospel of the Resurrection*. London: Macmillan and Co., 1868.

55. William of Canterbury (trans.). *Genuine Epistles of the Apostolical Fathers*. London: Samuel Bagster, 1840.

56. Wolff, Richard. *The Son of Man, Is Jesus Christ Unique?* Lincoln: Back to the Bible Broadcast, 1960.

57. Young, John. *Christ of History*. London: Strahan & Co., 1868.

chapter 9

the
messianic
prophecies

OF THE OLD TESTAMENT
FULFILLED IN JESUS CHRIST

The apostles throughout the New Testament appealed to two areas of the life of Jesus of Nazareth to establish His Messiahship. One was the resurrection and the other was fulfilled messianic prophecy. The Old Testament, written over a 1,000-year period, contains several hundred references to the coming Messiah. All of these were fulfilled in Jesus Christ, and they establish a solid confirmation of His credentials as the Messiah.

1A. INTRODUCTION

1B. Purpose of Messianic Prophecy

1C. GOD IS THE ONLY TRUE GOD WHOSE KNOWLEDGE IS INFINITE AND WHOSE WORD IS NEVER BROKEN

"God is not a man, that He should lie,
Nor a son of man, that He should repent;
Has He said, and will He not do it?
Or has He spoken, and will He not make it good?"

Numbers 23:19

2C. ALL THINGS ARE SUBJECT TO GOD'S DIVINE WILL

"Remember the former things long past,
For I am God, and there is no other;
I am God, and there is no one like Me,
Declaring the end from the beginning
And from ancient times things which have not been done,
Saying, 'My purpose will be established,
And I will accomplish all My good pleasure.'"

Isaiah 46:9,10

3C. MESSIAH WILL ABSOLUTELY BE KNOWN, BASED UPON HIS CREDENTIALS

"I declared the former things long ago
And they went forth from My mouth, and I proclaimed them.
Suddenly I acted, and they came to pass.
Therefore I declared them to you long ago,
Before they took place I proclaimed them to you,
Lest you should say, 'My idol has done them,

And my graven image and my molten image have commanded them.' "

Isaiah 48:3,5

"Which He promised beforehand through His prophets in the holy Scriptures, concerning His Son, who was born of the seed of David according to the flesh, who was declared with power to be the Son of God by the resurrection from the dead, according to the Spirit of holiness, Jesus Christ our Lord.' "

Romans 1:2-4

2B. Appeal to Messianic Prophecy

1C. JESUS

"Do not think that I came to abolish the Law or the Prophets; I did not come to abolish, but to fulfill."

Matthew 5:17

"And beginning with Moses and with all the prophets, He explained to them the things concerning Himself in the Scriptures."

Luke 24:27

"Now He said to them, 'These are My words which I spoke to you while I was still with you, that all things which are written about Me in the Law of Moses and the Prophets and the Psalms must be fulfilled.' "

Luke 24:44

"You search the Scriptures, because you think that in them you have eternal life; and it is these that bear witness of Me;
and you are unwilling to come to Me, that you may have life.
For if you believed Moses, you would believe Me; for he wrote of Me.
But if you do not believe his writings, how will you believe My words?"

John 5:39,40,46,47

"And in their case the prophecy of Isaiah is being fulfilled, which says,
'You will keep on hearing, but will not understand;
And you will keep on seeing, but will not perceive.' "

Matthew 13:14 (on parables)

"This is the one about whom it was written,
'Behold, I send My messenger before Your face,
Who will prepare Your way before You.' "

Matthew 11:10 (on John the Baptist)

"Jesus said to them, 'Did you never read in the Scriptures,
"The stone which the builders rejected,
This became the chief corner stone . . ."?' "

Matthew 21:42

"But all this has taken place that the Scriptures of the prophets may be fulfilled."

Matthew 26:56

"And then they shall see the Son of Man coming in clouds with great power and glory."

Mark 13:26 (refer to Daniel 7:13,14)

"And He closed the book, and gave it back to the attendant, and sat down; and the eyes of all in the synagogue were fixed upon Him. And

He began to say to them, 'Today this Scripture has been fulfilled in your hearing.' "

Luke 4:20,21

"For I tell you, that this which is written must be fulfilled in Me, 'And He was numbered with transgressors'; for that which refers to Me has its fulfillment."

Luke 22:37

"But they have done this in order that the word may be fulfilled that is written in their Law, 'They hated Me without a cause.' "

John 15:25

2C. NEW TESTAMENT WRITERS APPEAL TO PROPHECIES FULFILLED IN JESUS

"But the things which God announced beforehand by the mouth of all the prophets, that His Christ should suffer, He has thus fulfilled."

Acts 3:18

"Of Him all the prophets bear witness that through His name every one who believes in Him has received forgiveness of sins."

Acts 10:43

"And when they had carried out all that was written concerning Him, they took Him down from the cross and laid Him in a tomb."

Acts 13:29

"And according to Paul's custom, he went to them, and for three Sabbaths reasoned with them from the Scriptures, explaining and giving evidence that the Christ had to suffer and rise again from the dead, and saying, 'This Jesus whom I am proclaiming to you is the Christ.' "

Acts 17:2,3

"For I delivered to you as of first importance what I also received, that Christ died for our sins according to the Scriptures, and that He was buried, and that He was raised on the third day according to the Scriptures."

I Corinthians 15:3,4

"Which He promised beforehand through His prophets in the holy Scriptures."

Romans 1:2

"You also, as living stones, are being built up as a spiritual house for a holy priesthood, to offer up spiritual sacrifices acceptable to God through Jesus Christ. For this is contained in Scripture: 'Behold I lay in Zion a choice stone, a precious corner stone, And he who believes in Him shall not be disappointed.' "

I Peter 2:5,6

"And gathering together all the chief priests and scribes of the people, he began to inquire of them where the Christ was to be born. And they said to him, 'In Bethlehem of Judea, for so it has been written by the prophet,
"And you, Bethlehem, land of Judah,
Are by no means least among the leaders of Judah;
For out of you shall come forth a Ruler,
Who will shepherd My people Israel." ' "

Matthew 2:4-6

3C. IN THE WORK AND PERSON OF CHRIST THERE IS A FULFILLMENT OF THE LEVITICAL FEASTS 13/41

The Feast (Leviticus 23)	The Fulfillment in Christ
Passover (April)	Death of Christ (I Cor. 5:7)
Unleavened Bread (April)	Holy Walk (I Cor. 5:8)
First Fruits (April)	Resurrection (I Cor. 15:23)
Pentecost (June)	Outpouring of Spirit (Acts 1:5; 2:4)
Trumpets (Sept.)	Israel's Regathering (Matt. 24:31)
Atonement (Sept.)	Cleansing by Christ (Rom. 11:26)
Tabernacles (Sept.)	Rest and Reunion with Christ (Zech. 14:16-18)

3B. Significance of Predictive Prophecy

1C. CONCLUDES THAT THERE IS A DIVINE INTELLECT BEHIND THE OLD AND NEW TESTAMENTS

2C. ESTABLISHES THE FACT OF GOD

3C. AUTHENTICATES THE DEITY OF JESUS

4C. DEMONSTRATES THE INSPIRATION OF THE BIBLE

2A. THE OLD TESTAMENT CONTAINS OVER 300 REFERENCES TO THE MESSIAH THAT WERE FULFILLED IN JESUS

1B. Objection

The prophecies were written at or after the time of Jesus, and therefore fulfill themselves.

2B. Answer

If you are not satisfied with 450 B.C. as the historic date for the completion of the Old Testament, then take into consideration the following: The Septuagint, the Greek translation of the Hebrew Scriptures, was initiated in the reign of Ptolemy Philadelphus (285-246 B.C.). It is rather obvious that if you have a Greek translation initiated in 250 B.C., then you had to have the Hebrew text from which it was written. This will suffice to indicate that there was *at least* a 250-year gap between the prophecies being written down and their fulfillment in the person of Christ.

3A. CREDENTIALS OF JESUS AS THE MESSIAH THROUGH FULFILLED PROPHECY

1B. Prophecies Concerning His Birth:

1. BORN OF THE SEED OF WOMAN

PROPHECY	FULFILLMENT
"And I will put enmity Between you and the woman And between your seed and her seed; He shall bruise you on the head, And you shall bruise him on the heel." Genesis 3:15	"But when the fulness of the time came, God sent forth His Son, born of a woman, born under the Law." Galatians 4:4 (Also see Matthew 1:20.)

Jewish source: *Targum Onkelos* on Genesis 3:15 says, "And I will put enmity between thee and between the woman, and between thy son and her son. He will remember thee, what thou didst to him (at) from the beginning, and thou shalt be observant unto him at the end." 10/41

Jewish source: *Targum Pseudo Jonathan* on Genesis 3:15 states, "And I will put enmity between thee and the woman, and between the seed of your offspring and the seed of her offspring; and it shall be that when the offspring of the woman keep the commandments of the Law, they will aim right (at you) and they will smite you on the head; but when they abandon the commandments of the Law, you will aim right (at them), and you will wound them in the heel. However, for them there will be a remedy, but for you there will be none, and in the future they will make peace with the heel in the days of the king, Messiah." 3/122

The following is an interesting observation of David L. Cooper:

"In Gen. 3:15 we find the first prediction relative to the Saviour of the world, called 'the seed of the women.' In the original oracle God foretold the age-long conflict which would be waged between 'the seed of the woman' and 'the seed of the serpent' and which will eventually be won by the former. This primitive promise indicates a struggle between the Messiah of Israel, the Saviour of the world, on one hand, and Satan, the adversary of the human soul, on the other. It foretells complete victory eventually for the Messiah. Some commentators believe that an echo of this promise and Eve's understanding of it is found in Genesis 4:1 — the statement of Eve when Cain, her first son, was born. 'I have gotten a man even Jehovah.' She correctly understood this primitive prediction but misapplied it in her interpreting it as being fulfilled in Cain, her son. It is clear that Eve believed that the child of promise would be Jehovah Himself. Some old Jewish commentators used to interpolate the word 'angel' in this passage and say that Eve claimed that her son was 'the angel of Jehovah.' There is no ground for this assertion." 5/8,9

The New American Standard Bible renders Genesis 4:1: ". . . she said, 'I have gotten a manchild with *the help of* the Lord.' "

2. BORN OF A VIRGIN

PROPHECY	FULFILLMENT
"Therefore the Lord Himself will give you a sign: Behold, a virgin will be with child and bear a son, and she will call His name Immanuel." Isaiah 7:14	". . . She was found to be with child by the Holy Spirit. And Joseph . . . kept her a virgin until she gave birth to a Son; and he called His name Jesus." Matthew 1:18,24,25 (Also see Luke 1:26-35.)

Virgin is denoted by two words in Hebrew:
1. *bethulah* – proper meaning denotes a virgin maiden. (Genesis 24:16; Leviticus 21:13; Deuteronomy 22:14,23,28; Judges 11:37; I Kings 1:2) Joel 1:8 is, according to Unger, not an exception because it "refers to the loss of one betrothed, not married."
2. *almah* (veiled) — young woman of marriageable age. This is the word used in Isaiah 7:14. "The Holy Spirit through Isaiah did not use *bethulah,* because both the ideas of virginity and marriageable age had to be combined in one word to meet the immediate historical situation and the prophetic aspect centering in a virgin-born Messiah." 28/1159

Virgin is denoted in Greek by: *parthenos* — a virgin, marriageable maiden or young married woman, pure virgin. (Matthew 1:23; 25:1,7,11; Luke 1:27; Acts 21:9; I Corinthians 7:25, 28,33; II Corinthians 11:2) 28/1159

When the translators of the Septuagint translated Isaiah 7:14 into Greek they used the Greek word *parthenos*. To them Isaiah 7:14 denoted that the Messiah would be born of a virgin.

3. SON OF GOD

PROPHECY

"I will surely tell of the decree of the Lord: He said to Me, 'Thou art My Son, Today I have begotten Thee.' "
　　　Psalms 2:7 (Also see
　　　I Chronicles 17:11-14;
　　　II Samuel 7:12-16.)

FULFILLMENT

". . . And behold, a voice out of the heavens, saying, 'This is My beloved Son, in whom I am well-pleased.' "
　　　Matthew 3:17
　　　(Also see Matthew 16:16;
　　　Mark 9:7; Luke 9:35; 22:70;
　　　Acts 13:30-33; John 1:34,49.)

Mark 3:11 — The demons realized His Sonship.

Matthew 26:63 — Even the high priest realized His Sonship.

E. W. Hengstenberg says:

"It is an undoubted fact, and unanimously admitted even by the recent opposers of its reference to Him, that the Psalm (Psalm 2) was universally regarded by the ancient Jews as foretelling the Messiah." 15/43

"At the incarnation the First-begotten was brought into the world (Heb. 1:6). But it was only at and by His resurrection that His Divinity, as the Only-begotten of the Father, was manifested and openly attested by God. 'Made of the seed of David according to the flesh,' He was then 'declared to be the Son of God with power, according to the Spirit of holiness, by the resurrection from the dead' " (Romans 1:4). 11/107

4. SEED OF ABRAHAM

PROPHECY

"And in your descendants [lit., seed] all the nations of the earth shall be blessed, because you have obeyed My voice."
　　　Genesis 22:18
　　　(See also Genesis 12:2,3.)

FULFILLMENT

"The book of the genealogy of Jesus Christ, the son of David, the son of Abraham."
　　　Matthew 1:1

"Now the promises were spoken to Abraham and to his seed. He does not say, 'And to seeds,' as referring to many, but rather to one, 'And to your seed,' that is, Christ."
　　　Galatians 3:16

The importance of the event in Genesis 22:18 is established when we realize that it is the only time that God swears by Himself in His relationship with the patriarchs.

Matthew Henry says about Genesis 22:18, "In thy Seed, one particular person that shall descend from thee (for he speaks not of many, but of one, as the apostle observes, Gal. 3:16), shall all the nations of the earth be blessed, or shall bless themselves, as the phrase is, Isa. 65:16." 16/82

The above passage determines that the Messiah would come from the Hebrew race.

5. SON OF ISAAC

PROPHECY

"But God said to Abraham . . . through Isaac your descendants shall be named [lit., your seed will be called]."
    Genesis 21:12

FULFILLMENT

"Jesus, . . . the son of Isaac. . . ."
    Luke 3:23,34
    (Also see Matthew 1:2.)

Abraham had two sons, Isaac and Ishmael. Now God eliminates one-half of the lineage of Abraham.

6. SON OF JACOB

PROPHECY

"I see him, but not now;
I behold him, but not near;
A star shall come forth from Jacob,
And a scepter shall rise from Israel,
And shall crush through the forehead of Moab,
And tear down all the sons of Sheth."
    Numbers 24:17
    (Also see Genesis 35:10-12.)

FULFILLMENT

"Jesus . . . the son of Jacob. . . ."
    Luke 3:23,34
    (Also see Matthew 1:2 and Luke 1:33.)

Jewish source: *Targum Jonathan* on Genesis 35:11, 12 says, "And the Lord said to him, I am El Shaddai: spread forth and multiply; a holy people, and a congregation of prophets and priests, shall be from thy sons whom thou hast begotten, and two kings shall yet from thee go forth. And the land which I gave to Abraham and to Izhak will I give unto thee, and to thy sons after thee will I give the land." 10/279

Jewish source: *Targum Onkelos* on Numbers 24:17 states, "I see him, but not now; I behold him, but not nigh. When a king shall arise out of Jakob, and the Meshiha be anointed from Israel. . . ." 10/309

In the above *Targums* we can see that the Jews gave Messianic import to the passages. Likewise, the *Midrash Bamidbar Rabbah* gives a Messianic meaning to this text. Paul Heinisch relates that "at the time of Hadrian (132 A.D.) the Jews revolted against the Roman yoke, they called their leader Barkochba, 'The Son of the Star.' For they believed that Balaam's oracle on the star from Jacob was then being fulfilled and that through him God would utterly destroy the Romans." 14/44,45

Hengstenberg, in his *Christology of the Old Testament,* points out that "by this Ruler, the Jews from the earliest times have understood the Messiah, either exclusively, or else principally, with a secondary reference to David. Either its exclusive relation to the Messiah was maintained, or it was allowed to refer indeed, in the first instance, to David; but then both himself and his temporal victories were regarded as typical of Christ, and His spiritual triumphs, which (according to this exposition) the prophet had especially in view." 15/34

Isaac had two sons, Jacob and Esau. Now God eliminates one-half of the lineage of Isaac.

7. TRIBE OF JUDAH

PROPHECY	FULFILLMENT
"The scepter shall not depart from Judah, Nor the ruler's staff from between his feet, Until Shiloh comes, And to him shall be the obedience of the peoples." Genesis 49:10 (Also see Micah 5:2.)	"Jesus . . . the son of Judah. . . ." Luke 3:23,33 (Also see Matthew 1:2 and Hebrews 7:14.)

Jewish source: *Targum Jonathan* on Genesis 49:10,11a says, "Kings shall not cease, nor rulers, from the house of Jehuda, nor sapherim teaching the law from his seed, till the time that the King, the Meshiha, shall come, the youngest of his sons; and on account of him shall the peoples flow together. How beauteous is the King, and Meshiha who will arise from the house of Jehuda!" 10/331

Jewish source: *Targum Pseudo Jonathan* on Genesis 49:11a states, "How noble is the King, Messiah, who is going to rise from the house of Judah." 3/278

Jacob had 12 sons out of which developed the 12 tribes of the Hebrew nation. Now God eliminates eleven-twelfths of the tribes of Israel. Joseph had no tribe named after him, but his two sons Ephraim and Manasseh did become heads of tribes.

8. FAMILY LINE OF JESSE

PROPHECY	FULFILLMENT
"Then a shoot will spring from the stem of Jesse, And a branch from his roots will bear fruit." Isaiah 11:1 (Also see Isaiah 11:10.)	"Jesus . . . the son of Jesse. . . ." Luke 3:23,32 (Also see Matthew 1:6.)

Jewish source: *Targum Isaiah* states, "And a King shall come forth from the sons of Jesse, and an Anointed One (or Messiah) from his son's sons shall grow up. And there shall rest upon him a spirit from before the Lord, the spirit of wisdom and understanding, the spirit of counsel and might, the spirit of knowledge, and of the fear of the Lord." 26/40

Delitzsch comments, "Out of the stumps of Jesse, i.e., out of the remnant of the chosen royal family which has sunk down to the insignificance of the house from which it sprang, there comes forth a twig (*choter*), which promises to supply the place of the trunk and crown; and down below, in the roots covered with earth, and only rising a little above it, there shows itself a *netzer*, i.e., a fresh green shoot (from *natzer*, to shine or blossom). In the historical account of the fulfillment, even the ring of the words of the prophecy is noticed: the *netzer*, at first so humble and insignificant, was a poor despised Nazarene" (Matthew 2:23). 6/281,282

9. HOUSE OF DAVID

PROPHECY

" 'Behold, the days are coming.'
declares the Lord, 'When I shall
raise up for David a righteous
Branch;
And He will reign as king and act
wisely
And do justice and righteousness
in the land.' "
  Jeremiah 23:5
  (Also see II Samuel 7:12-16;
  Psalms 132:11.)

FULFILLMENT

"Jesus . . . the son of David. . . ."
  Luke 3:23,31
  (Also see Matthew 1:1; 9:27;
  15:22; 20:30,31; 21:9,15;
  22:41-46; Mark 9:10;
  10:47,48; Luke 18:38,39;
  Acts 13:22,23;
  Revelation 22:16.)

Jewish source: The Messiah as being referred to as the "Son of David" is
scattered throughout the Talmuds.

Driver says about II Samuel 7:11b, "Here Nathan comes to the main
subject of his prophecy — the promise relating not to David himself, but
to his posterity, and the declaration that it is not David who will build a
house for Yahweh, but Yahweh who will build a house (i.e., a family) for
David." 7/275

Jacob Minkin, in his book titled *The World of Moses Maimonides,* gives the
view of this learned Jewish scholar: "Dismissing the mystical
speculations concerning the Messiah, his origin, activity, and the
marvellous superhuman powers ascribed to him, Maimonides insisted
that he must be regarded as a mortal human being, differing from his
fellow-men only in the fact that he will be greater, wiser, and more
resplendent than they. He must be a descendant of the House of David and
like him, occupy himself with the Study of the Torah and observance of its
commandments." 24/63

"Behold, the days are coming" is a common expression which is used in
reference to the entrance of the Messianic era (see Jeremiah 31:27-34).
19/189

Jesse had *at least* eight sons (see I Samuel 16:10, 11). Now God eliminates
all of Jesse's sons except one, David.

10. BORN AT BETHLEHEM

PROPHECY

"But as for you, Bethlehem
Ephrathah,
Too little to be among the
clans of Judah,
From you One will go forth for Me
to be ruler in Israel.
His goings forth are from long ago,
From the days of eternity."
  Micah 5:2

FULFILLMENT

". . . Jesus was born in Bethlehem
of Judea. . . ."
  Matthew 2:1
  (Also see John 7:42;
  Matthew 2:4-8;
  Luke 2:4-7.)

In Matthew 2:6 the scribes tell Herod with great assurance that the Christ
would be born in Bethlehem. It was well known among the Jews that the
Christ would come from Bethlehem (see John 7:42). It is only fitting that

Bethlehem, meaning the house of bread, should be the birthplace of the one who is the Bread of Life. 16/1414

God now eliminates all the cities in the world, save one, for the entrance of His incarnate Son.

11. PRESENTED WITH GIFTS

PROPHECY

"Let the kings of Tarshish and of the islands bring presents; The kings of Sheba and Seba offer gifts."
          Psalms 72:10
          (Also see Isaiah 60:6.)

FULFILLMENT

". . . Magi from the east arrived in Jerusalem . . . and they fell down and worshiped Him; and opening their treasures they presented to Him gifts. . . ."
          Matthew 2:1,11

The historic application of this passage is to Solomon. The Messianic application is amplified in verses 12-15 (Psalms 72).

The inhabitants of Seba and Sheba, the Sabeans, lived in Arabia. 25/941,1006 Matthew Henry says about Matthew 2:1,11 that the wise men were "men of the east, who were noted for their soothsaying (Isa. 2:6). Arabia is called the land of the east (Gen. 25:6) and the Arabians are called, Men of the east (Judg. 6:3). The presents they brought were the products of that country. . . ." 16/16

12. HEROD KILLS CHILDREN

PROPHECY

"Thus says the Lord, 'A voice is heard in Ramah, Lamentation and bitter weeping. Rachel is weeping for her children; She refuses to be comforted for her children, Because they are no more.' "
          Jeremiah 31:15

FULFILLMENT

"Then when Herod saw that he had been tricked by the magi, he became very enraged, and sent and slew all the male children who were in Bethlehem and in all its environs, from two years old and under, according to the time which he had ascertained from the magi."
          Matthew 2:16

The dispersion and extermination of Israel is spoken of in Jeremiah 31:17,18. What does Herod murdering the infants of Bethlehem have to do with the deportation? Was Matthew mistaken when he viewed Jeremiah's prophecy being fulfilled in Herod's atrocities (Matthew 2:17,18) or the murder of the innocents as a type of the destruction of Israel or Judah? Laetsch says, "No. Certainly not. The entire context of ch. 31, beginning ch. 30:20 and continuing to ch. 33:26, is Messianic. The four chapters speak of the approach of the Lord's salvation, of the coming of Messiah to re-establish the Kingdom of David in the form of a new covenant, of which forgiveness of sins is to be the foundation (ch. 31:31-34); a kingdom in which every weary and sorrowful soul shall be fully comforted (vv. 12-14,25). As an example of this comfort the Lord introduces the consolation to be extended to mothers who had suffered great loss for the sake of Christ, the cruel murder of their infant sons." 19/250

2B.   Prophecies Concerning His Nature:

13.   HIS PRE-EXISTENCE

PROPHECY

"But as for you, Bethlehem
Ephrathah,
Too little to be among the clans
of Judah,
From you One will go forth for
Me to be ruler in Israel.
His goings forth are from long
ago,
From the days of eternity."
        Micah 5:2
        (Also see Isaiah 9:6,7; 41:4;
        44:6; 48:12; Psalms
        102:25; Proverbs 8:22,23.)

FULFILLMENT

"And He is before [or, has
existed prior to] all things, and in
Him all things hold together."
        Colossians 1:17
        (Also see John 1:1,2; 8:58;
        17:5,24; Revelation
        1:17; 2:8; 22:13.)

Jewish source: *Targum Isaiah* says, "The prophet saith to the house of
David, A child has been born to us, a son has been given to us; and He has
taken the law upon Himself to keep it, and His name has been called from
of old, Wonderful counsellor, Mighty God, He who lives forever, the
Anointed one (or Messiah), in whose days peace shall increase upon us"
(Isaiah 9:6). 26/32

Jewish source: *Targum Isaiah* states, "Thus saith the Lord, the King of
Israel, and his saviour the Lord of hosts; I am He, I am He that is from of
old; yea, the everlasting ages are mine, and beside me there is no God"
(Isaiah 44:6). 26/148

Hengstenberg says about Micah 5:2, "The existence of the Messiah in
general, before His temporal birth at Bethlehem, is asserted; and then
His eternity in contrast with all time is mentioned here." 15/573

14.   HE SHALL BE CALLED LORD

PROPHECY

"The Lord says to my Lord:
'Sit at My right hand,
Until I make Thine enemies
a footstool for Thy feet.' "
        Psalms 110:1
        (Also see Jeremiah 23:6.)

FULFILLMENT

"For today in the city of David there
has been born for you a Savior, who
is Christ the Lord."
        Luke 2:11
"He said to them, 'Then how
does David in the Spirit call
Him "Lord," saying,
"The Lord said to my Lord, 'Sit at
My right hand, until I put Thine
enemies beneath Thy feet.' " If
David then calls Him "Lord," how
is He his son?' "
        Matthew 22:43-45

Jewish source: The *Midrash Tehillim,* Commentary on Psalms, 200-500
A.D., says on Psalms 21:1: "God calls King Messiah by His own name.
But what is His name? Answer: Jehovah is a man of war" (Exodus 15:3).
19/193

Jewish source: *Echa Rabbathi*, 200-500 (Lamentations in Large
Commentary on Pentateuch and five scrolls), on Lamentations 1:16:

" 'What is the name of Messiah?' R. Abba ben Cahana (200-300 A.D.) has said: Jehovah is His name, and this is proved by 'This is His name' " (Jeremiah 23:6). 19/193

"The Lord said unto my Lord. 'Jehovah said unto Adonai,' or 'my Lord,' — i.e., the Lord of David, not in his merely personal capacity, but as representative of Israel, literal and spiritual. It is because he addresses Him as Israel's and the Church's Lord, that Christ in the three Gospels quotes it. 'David calls Him Lord,' not 'His Lord.' " 11/346

15. SHALL BE IMMANUEL (God With Us)

PROPHECY

"Therefore the Lord Himself will give you a sign: Behold, a virgin will be with child and bear a son, and she will call His name Immanuel."

Isaiah 7:14

FULFILLMENT

" 'Behold, the virgin shall be with child, and shall bear a Son, and they shall call His name Immanuel,' which translated means, 'God with us.' "

Matthew 1:23

(Also see Luke 7:16.)

Jewish source: *Targum Isaiah* on Isaiah 7:14 says, "Therefore the Lord himself shall give you a sign; Behold a damsel is with child, and shall bear a son, and shall call His name Immanuel." 26/24

Delitzsch says about Isaiah 9:6 the following, "There is no reason why we should take El in this name of the Messiah in any other sense than in Immanu-El; not to mention the fact that El in Isaiah is always a name of God, and that the prophet was ever strongly conscious of the antithesis between El and Adam, as ch. 31:3 (cf. Hosea 11:9) clearly shows." 6/252

16. SHALL BE A PROPHET

PROPHECY

"I will raise up a prophet from among their countrymen like you, and I will put My words in his mouth, and he shall speak to them all that I command him."

Deuteronomy 18:18

FULFILLMENT

"And the multitudes were saying, 'This is the prophet Jesus, from Nazareth in Galilee.' "

Matthew 21:11

(Also see Luke 7:16; John 4:19; 6:14; 7:40.)

Jewish source: The Jewish scholar, Maimonides, in a letter to the community of Yemen, denounces a purporter of the Messiahship by writing: "The Messiah will be a very great Prophet, greater than all the Prophets with the exception of Moses our teacher . . . His status will be higher than that of the Prophets and more honourable, Moses alone excepted. The Creator, blessed be He, will single him out with features wherewith He had not singled out Moses; for it is said with reference to him, 'And his delight shall be in the fear of the Lord; and he shall not judge after the sight of his eyes, neither decide after the hearing of his ears' " (Isaiah 11:3). 4/221

Christ compared to Moses:
1. He was delivered from a violent death in His infancy.
2. He was willing to become Redeemer of His people (Exodus 3:10).
3. He worked as mediator between Yahweh and Israel (Exodus 19:16; 20:18).
4. He made intercession on behalf of sinful people (Exodus 32:7-14, 33; Numbers 14:11-20).

"Sir, I perceive that Thou art a prophet" (John 4:19, KJV).

Kligerman says, "The use of the term 'prophet' by the Jews of Jesus' day shows not only that they expected the Messiah to be a prophet in accordance with the promise in Deuteronomy eighteen, but also that He who performed these miracles was indeed the Promised Prophet." 18/22,23

"For the law was given through Moses; grace and truth were realized through Jesus Christ" (John 1:17).

17. PRIEST

PROPHECY

"The Lord has sworn and will not change His mind, 'Thou art a priest forever according to the order of Melchizedek.' "
    Psalms 110:4

FULFILLMENT

"Therefore, holy brethren, partakers of a heavenly calling, consider Jesus, the Apostle and High Priest of our confession."
    Hebrews 3:1

"So also Christ did not glorify Himself so as to become a high priest, but He who said to Him, 'Thou art My Son, today I have begotten Thee'; just as He says also in another passage, 'Thou art a priest forever according to the order of Melchizedek.' "
    Hebrews 5:5,6

"The final victory of Messiah's people over the world and Satan is . . . certain. The oath of God did not accompany the Aaronic priesthood, as it does our Melchizedek-like Priest, who 'is made not after the law of a carnal commandment, but after the power of an endless life.' 'After the order of Melchizedek' is explained, Heb. 7:15, 'after the similitude of Melchizedek.' The oath of covenant on the part of the Father to the Son is for the comfort of Messiah's people. Uzziah's punishment for his usurpation of the functions of priest shows that David cannot be the King-Priest here described (II Chron. 26:16-21). The extraordinary oath of God shows that the King-Priesthood here is something unparalleled. David died, but this Melchizedek-like Priest lives forever. Zech. 6:9-15, especially 13, similarly describes Messiah — 'He shall sit and rule upon His throne, and He shall be a Priest upon His throne.' " 11/347

18. JUDGE

PROPHECY

"For the Lord is our judge, The Lord is our lawgiver, The Lord is our king; He will save us. . . ."
    Isaiah 33:22

FULFILLMENT

"I can do nothing on My own initiative. As I hear, I judge; and My judgment is just, because I do not seek My own will, but the will of Him who sent Me."
    John 5:30
    (Also see II Timothy 4:1.)

Jewish source: *Targum Isaiah* on Isaiah 33:22 says, "For the Lord is our judge, who brought us out of Egypt by his might; the Lord is our teacher, who gave us the instruction of his law from Sinai; the Lord is our King, he shall deliver us, and execute a righteous vengeance for us on the armies of Gog." 26/110

"... Judge ... lawgiver ... King — perfect ideal of the theocracy, to be realized under Messiah alone: the judicial, legislative, and administrative functions as King, to be exercised by Him in person (Isaiah 11:4; 32:1; James. 4:12)." 11/666

19. KING

PROPHECY

"But as for Me, I have installed My King upon Zion, My holy mountain."
Psalms 2:6
(Also see Zechariah 9:9;
Jeremiah 23:5.)

FULFILLMENT

"And they put up above His head the charge against Him which read, 'This is Jesus the King of the Jews.'"
Matthew 27:37
(Also see Matthew 21:5;
John 18:33-38.)

20. SPECIAL ANOINTMENT OF HOLY SPIRIT

PROPHECY

"And the Spirit of the Lord will rest on Him,
The spirit of wisdom and understanding,
The spirit of counsel and strength,
The spirit of knowledge and the fear of the Lord."
Isaiah 11:2
(Also see Psalms 45:7;
Isaiah 42:1; 61:1,2.)

FULFILLMENT

"And after being baptized, Jesus went up immediately from the water; and behold, the heavens were opened, and he saw the Spirit of God descending as a dove, and coming upon Him, and behold, a voice out of the heavens, saying, 'This is My beloved Son, in whom I am well-pleased.'"
Matthew 3:16,17
(Also see Matthew 12:17-21;
Mark 1:10,11; Luke 4:15-21,
43; John 1:32.)

Jewish source: *Targum Isaiah* on Isaiah 11:1-4a says, "And a king shall come forth from the sons of Jesse, and an Anointed One (or, Messiah) from his sons' sons shall grow up. And there shall rest upon him a spirit from before the Lord, the spirit of wisdom and understanding, the spirit of counsel and might, the spirit of knowledge, and of the fear of the Lord: and the Lord shall bring him to his fear: and not according to the sight of his eyes shall he judge, nor exercise judgement according to the hearing of his ears. But he shall judge with truth the poor, and adjudge with faithfulness the needy among the people." 26/40

Jewish source: In the *Babylonian Talmud,* the *Sanhedrin II* says, "The Messiah — as it is written, And the spirit of the Lord shall rest upon him, the spirit of wisdom and understanding, the spirit of counsel and might, the spirit of knowledge of the fear of the Lord. And shall make him of quick understanding [*wa-hariho*] in the fear of the Lord. R. Alexandri said: This teaches that he loaded him with good deeds and suffering as a mill [is laden]." 25/626,627

21.   HIS ZEAL FOR GOD

PROPHECY

"For zeal for Thy house has
consumed me,
And the reproaches of those who
reproach Thee have fallen on me."
Psalms 69:9

FULFILLMENT

"And He made a scourge of cords,
and drove them all out of the
temple . . . and . . . He said, 'Take
these things away; stop making My
Father's house a house of
merchandise.'"
John 2:15-17

A. R. Fausset says: "For the zeal of thine house hath eaten me up —
consumes me like a flame with its very intensity (Ps. 119:139). The
expansion of 'for thy sake' (v. 7): cf. John 2:17 as a specimen of Messiah's
zeal for the honour of the house of God. And the reproaches of them that
reproached thee are fallen upon me — in consequence of my glowing
'zeal' for thine honour, the reproaches aimed at thee fall upon me." 11/245

3B.   Prophecies Concerning His Ministry

22.   PRECEDED BY MESSENGER

PROPHECY

"A voice is calling, 'Clear the way
for the Lord in the wilderness;
Make smooth in the desert a high-
way for our God.'"
Isaiah 40:3
(Also see Malachi 3:1.)

FULFILLMENT

". . . John the Baptist came,
preaching in the wilderness of
Judea, saying, 'Repent, for the
kingdom of heaven is at hand.'"
Matthew 3:1,2
(Also see Matthew 3:3;
11:10; John 1:23;
Luke 1:17.)

Jewish source: *Targum Isaiah* on Isaiah 40:3 says, "The voice of one that
crieth, Prepare ye a way in the wilderness before the people of the Lord,
tread down paths in the desert before the congregation of our God."
26/130

23.   MINISTRY TO BEGIN IN GALILEE

PROPHECY

"But there will be no more gloom
for her who was in anguish; in
earlier times He treated the
land of Zebulun and the land
of Napthtali with contempt,
but later on He shall make it
glorious, by the way of the sea,
on the other side of Jordan,
Galilee of the Gentiles."
Isaiah 9:1

FULFILLMENT

"Now when He heard that John
had been taken into custody,
He withdrew into Galilee; and
leaving Nazareth, He came and
settled in Capernaum, which is
by the sea, in the region of
Zebulun and Naphtali.
From that time Jesus began to
preach and say, 'Repent, for
the kingdom of heaven is at
hand.'"
Matthew 4:12,13,17

24. MINISTRY OF MIRACLES

PROPHECY

"Then the eyes of the blind will
be opened,
And the ears of the deaf will be
unstopped.
Then the lame will leap like a
deer,
And the tongue of the dumb will
shout for joy."
> Isaiah 35: 5, 6a
> (Also see Isaiah 32: 3,4.)

FULFILLMENT

"And Jesus was going about all the
cities and the villages, teaching in
their synagogues, and proclaiming
the gospel of the kingdom, and
healing every kind of disease and
every kind of sickness."
> Matthew 9: 35
> (Also see Matthew
> 9: 32,33; 11: 4-6;
> Mark 7: 33-35; John 5: 5-9;
> 9: 6-11; 11: 43,44,47.

25. TEACHER OF PARABLES

PROPHECY

"I will open my mouth in a
parable; I will utter dark
sayings of old. . . ."
> Psalms 78: 2

FULFILLMENT

"All these things Jesus spoke to
the multitudes in parables, and
He was not talking to them
without a parable. . . ."
> Matthew 13: 34

26. HE WAS TO ENTER THE TEMPLE

PROPHECY

". . . And the Lord, whom you
seek, will suddenly come to His
temple. . . ."
> Malachi 3: 1

FULFILLMENT

"And Jesus entered the temple
and cast out all those who were
buying and selling in the
temple. . . ."
> Matthew 21: 12

27. HE WAS TO ENTER JERUSALEM ON DONKEY

PROPHECY

"Rejoice greatly, O daughter of
Zion! Shout in triumph,
O daughter of Jerusalem!
Behold, your king is coming to
you; He is just and endowed
with salvation, humble,
and mounted on a donkey,
Even on a colt, the foal of
a donkey."
> Zechariah 9: 9

FULFILLMENT

"And they brought it to Jesus,
and they threw their garments
on the colt, and put Jesus on it.
And as He was going, they were
spreading their garments in
the road. And as He was now
approaching, near the descent
of the Mount of Olives. . . ."
> Luke 19: 35,36,37a
> (Also see Matthew 21: 6-11.)

28. "STONE OF STUMBLING" TO JEWS

PROPHECY

"The stone which the builders
rejected
Has become the chief cornerstone."
> Psalms 118: 22
> (Also see Isaiah 8: 14; 28: 16.)

FULFILLMENT

"This precious value, then, is for
you who believe, but for those who
disbelieve, 'the stone which the
builders rejected, this became the
very cornerstone.' "
> I Peter 2: 7
> (Also see Romans 9: 32,33.)

Jewish source: *Targum Isaiah* on Isaiah 8:13-15 says, "The Lord of hosts, him shall ye call holy; and let him be your fear and let him be your strength. And if ye will not hearken, his Memra shall be amongst you for vengeance and for a stone of smiting, and for a rock of offence to the two houses of the princes of Israel, for a breaking, and for a stumbling, because the house of Israel hath been separated from them of the house of Judah who dwell in Jerusalem. And many shall stumble against them, and shall fall, and be broken and be snared, and be taken." 26/28

29. "LIGHT" TO GENTILES

PROPHECY

"And nations will come to your light,
And kings to the brightness of your rising."
      Isaiah 60:3
      (Also see Isaiah 49:6.)

FULFILLMENT

" 'For thus the Lord has commanded us, "I have placed you as a light for the Gentiles, that you should bring salvation to the end of the earth." '
And when the Gentiles heard this, they began rejoicing and glorifying the word of the Lord. . . ."
      Acts 13:47,48a
      (Also see Acts 26:23;
        28:28.)

4B. Prophecies Concerning Events After His Burial

30. RESURRECTION

PROPHECY

"For Thou wilt not abandon my soul to Sheol;
Neither wilt Thou allow Thy Holy One to see the pit."
      Psalms 16:10
      (Also see Psalms 30:3; 41:10;
        118:17; Hosea 6:2.)

FULFILLMENT

". . . He was neither abandoned to Hades, nor did His flesh suffer decay."
      Acts 2:31
      (Also see Acts 13:33;
        Luke 24:46; Mark 16:6;
        Matthew 28:6.)

Jewish source: Friedlaender says, "Ibn Ezra frequently takes occasion to assert his firm belief in the resurrection of the dead." 12/100

Jewish source: The *Sanhedrin II, Babylonian Talmud* states the following: "Mishnah. All Israel have a portion in the world to come, for it is written, 'Thy people are all righteous; they shall inherit the land forever, the branch of My planting, the work of My hands, that I may be glorified.' But the following have no portion there-in: He who maintains that resurrection is not a Biblical doctrine, the Torah was not divinely revealed." 25/601

31. ASCENSION

PROPHECY

"Thou hast ascended on high. . . ."
      Psalms 68:18a

FULFILLMENT

". . . He was lifted up while they were looking on, and a cloud received Him out of their sight."
      Acts 1:9

32. SEATED AT RIGHT HAND OF GOD

PROPHECY

"The Lord says to my Lord:
'Sit at My right hand,
Until I make Thine enemies a
footstool for Thy feet.' "
Psalms 110:1

FULFILLMENT

". . . When He had made
purification of sins, He sat down
at the right hand of the Majesty
on high."
Hebrews 1:3
(See also Mark 16:19;
Acts 2:34,35.)

5B. Prophecies Fulfilled in One Day

The following 29 prophecies from the Old Testament, which speak of the
betrayal, trial, death and burial of our Lord Jesus Christ, were spoken at
various times by many different voices during the five centuries from
1000-500 B.C., and yet all of them were literally fulfilled in Jesus in one
24-hour period of time.

33. BETRAYED BY A FRIEND

PROPHECY

"Even my close friend, in whom I
trusted,
Who ate my bread,
Has lifted up his heel against me."
Psalms 41:9
(Also see Psalms
55:12-14.)

FULFILLMENT

". . . Judas Iscariot, the one who
betrayed Him."
Matthew 10:4
(Also see Matthew
26:49,50; John 13:21).

Psalms 41:9— "lit., 'the man of my peace'; he who saluted me with the
kiss of peace, as Judas did" (Matthew 26:49: cf. the type, Jeremiah
20:10). 11/191

34. SOLD FOR 30 PIECES OF SILVER

PROPHECY

"And I said to them, 'If it is good
in your sight, give me my wages;
but if not, never mind!' So they
weighed out thirty shekels of
silver as my wages."
Zechariah 11:12

FULFILLMENT

". . . 'What are you willing to give
me to deliver Him up to you?' And
they weighed out to him thirty
pieces of silver."
Matthew 26:15
(Also see Matthew 27:3.)

35. MONEY TO BE THROWN IN GOD'S HOUSE

PROPHECY

". . . So I took the thirty shekels of
silver and threw them to the potter
in the house of the Lord."
Zechariah 11:13b

FULFILLMENT

"And he threw the pieces of silver
into the sanctuary and
departed. . . ."
Matthew 27:5a

36. PRICE GIVEN FOR POTTER'S FIELD

PROPHECY

". . . So I took the thirty shekels of silver and threw them to the potter in the house of the Lord."
Zechariah 11:13b

FULFILLMENT

"And they counseled together and with the money bought the Potter's Field as a burial place for strangers."
Matthew 27:7

In the previous four prophecies we find in both prophecy and fulfillment the following:

1. Betrayed
2. By a friend
3. For 30 pieces (not 29)
.4 Of silver (not gold)
5. Thrown down (not placed)
6. In the House of the Lord
7. Money used to buy potter's field

37. FORSAKEN BY HIS DISCIPLES

PROPHECY

". . . Strike the Shepherd that the sheep may be scattered. . . ."
Zechariah 13:7

FULFILLMENT

"And they all left Him and fled."
Mark 14:50
(Also see Matthew 26:31; Mark 14:27.)

Laetsch says Zechariah 13:7 is "a clear prophecy of the offense taken by the disciples when Christ was smitten. So Christ Himself interprets these words (Matthew 26:31; Mark 14:27). They were fulfilled (see Matthew 26:56; Mark 14:50ff.). Yet the Lord would not forsake the sheep. The Lord Himself, acting in and through the person of His 'Fellow' (John 5:19f.,30), will turn His hand upon (Gr.N.), come to the aid of the little ones (Gr.N.), His despondent, terrified disciples (Luke 24:4f.,11,17ff.,37; John 20:2,11ff.,19,26). These weaklings and deserters became the courageous, invincible heralds of the Messiah's kingdom." 20/491,492

38. ACCUSED BY FALSE WITNESSES

PROPHECY

"Malicious witnesses rise up; They ask me of things that I do not know."
Psalms 35:11

FULFILLMENT

"Now the chief priests and the whole Council kept trying to obtain false testimony against Jesus, in order that they might put Him to death; and they did not find it, even though many false witnesses came forward."
Matthew 26:59,60

39. DUMB BEFORE ACCUSERS

PROPHECY

"He was oppressed and He was afflicted, Yet He did not open His mouth. . . ."
Isaiah 53:7

FULFILLMENT

"And while He was being accused by the chief priests and elders, He made no answer."
Matthew 27:12

40. WOUNDED AND BRUISED

PROPHECY

"But He was pierced through for
  our transgressions,
  He was crushed for our iniquities;
  The chastening for our well-being
  fell upon Him,
  And by His scourging we are
  healed."
          Isaiah 53:5
          (Also see Zechariah 13:6.)

FULFILLMENT

"Then he released Barabbas for
  them; but Jesus he scourged and
  delivered over to be crucified."
          Matthew 27:26

"— A bodily wound: not mere mental sorrow; *mecholal,* from *chalal* —
literally pierced; minutely appropriate to Messiah, whose hands, feet,
and side were pierced (Psalms 22:16)." 11/730

". . . But from the crown of the head, which was crowned with thorns, to
the soles of his feet, which were nailed to the cross, nothing appeared but
wounds and bruises." 16/826

41. SMITTEN AND SPIT UPON

PROPHECY

"I gave My back to those who
  strike Me,
  And My cheeks to those who
  pluck out the beard;
  I did not cover My face from
  humiliation and spitting."
          Isaiah 50:6
          (Also see Micah 5:1.)

FULFILLMENT

"Then they spat in His face and
  beat Him with their fists; and
  others slapped Him."
          Matthew 26:67
          (Also see Luke 22:63.)

Jewish source: *Targum Isaiah* on Isaiah 50:6 says, "I gave my back to the
smiters, and my cheeks to them that pluck out the hair; I hid not my face
from humiliation and spitting." 26/170

Henry states, "In this submission, He resigned Himself, (1.) To be
scourged; . . . (2.) To be buffeted; . . . (3.) To be spit upon; . . . All this
Christ underwent for us, and voluntarily, to convince us of His willingness
to save us." 16/816

42. MOCKED

PROPHECY

"All who see me sneer at me;
  They separate with the lip, they
  wag the head, saying,
  'Commit yourself to the Lord;
  let Him deliver him;
  Let Him rescue him, because He
  delights in him.' "
          Psalms 22:7,8

FULFILLMENT

"And after they had mocked
  Him, they took His robe off and
  put His garments on Him, and led
  Him away to crucify Him."
          Matthew 27:31

43.   FELL UNDER THE CROSS

PROPHECY

"My knees are weak from fasting;
And my flesh has grown lean,
    without fatness.
I also have become a reproach
    to them;
When they see me, they wag
    their head."
            Psalms 109: 24,25

FULFILLMENT

"They took Jesus therefore; and
He went out, bearing His own
cross. . . ."
            John 19: 17
"And when they led Him away,
they laid hold of one Simon, a
Cyrenian, coming in from the
country, and placed on him the
cross to carry behind Jesus."
            Luke 23: 26
            (Also see Matthew
            27: 31,32.)

Evidently Jesus was so weak that, under the weight of the heavy cross,
His knees were giving way, so they had to place it on another.

44.   HANDS AND FEET PIERCED

PROPHECY

". . . They pierced my hands
    and my feet."
            Psalms 22: 16
            (Also see Zechariah 12: 10.)

FULFILLMENT

"And when they came to the
place called The Skull, there they
crucified Him. . . ."
            Luke 23: 33
            (Also see John 20: 25.)

Jesus was crucified in the usual Roman manner; the hands and feet were
pierced by large dull spikes which attached the body to the wooden cross
or stake.

45.   CRUCIFIED WITH THIEVES

PROPHECY

". . . Because He poured out
    Himself to death,
And was numbered with the
    transgressors. . . ."
            Isaiah 53: 12

FULFILLMENT

"At that time two robbers were
crucified with Him, one on the
right and one on the left."
            Matthew 27: 38
            (Also see Mark 15: 27,28.)

Blinzler states, "Crucifixion was unknown in Jewish criminal law. The
hanging on a gibbet, which was prescribed by Jewish law for idolaters
and blasphemers who had been stoned, was not a death penalty, but an
additional punishment after death designed to brand the executed person
as one accursed of God, in accordance with Deut. 21: 23 (LXX): 'For he is
accursed of God that hangeth on a tree.' The Jews applied these words
also to one who had been crucified. If crucifixion was the most shameful
and degrading death penalty even in the eyes of the pagan world, the
Jews in the time of Jesus regarded a person so executed as being, over
and above, accursed of God." 2/247,248

The Encyclopedia Americana records:

"The history of crucifixion as a mode of punishment for crime must be
studied as a part of the Roman system of jurisprudence. . . . The
Hebrews, for example, adopted or accepted it only under Roman

compulsion: under their own system, before Palestine became Roman territory, they inflicted the death penalty by stoning." 8/253

"... In 63 B.C., Pompey's legions cut their way into the Judean capital. Palestine became a Roman province, though nominally a puppet Jewish dynasty survived." 29/262

Thus, the type of death pictured in Isaiah 53 and Psalms 22 did not come into practice under the Jewish system until hundreds of years after the account was written.

46. MADE INTERCESSION FOR HIS PERSECUTORS

PROPHECY

"... Yet He Himself bore the
sin of many,
And interceded for the
transgressors."
Isaiah 53:12

FULFILLMENT

"... Father, forgive them; for
they do not know what they are
doing...."
Luke 23:34

"This office He began on the cross (Luke 23:34), and now continues in heaven..." (Heb. 9:24; I John 2:1). 11/733

47. REJECTED BY HIS OWN PEOPLE

PROPHECY

"He was despised and forsaken
of men,
A man of sorrows, and
acquainted with grief;
And like one from whom men
hide their face.
He was despised, and we did
not esteem Him."
Isaiah 53:3
(Also see Psalms 69:8;
118:22.)

FULFILLMENT

"For not even His brothers were
believing in Him.
No one of the rulers or Pharisees
has believed in Him, has he?"
John 7:5,48
(Also see John 1:11;
Matthew 21:42,43.)

"This was fulfilled in Christ, whose brethren did not believe on Him (John 7:5), who came to His own, and His own received Him not (John 1:11), and who was forsaken by His disciples, whom He had been free with as His brethren." 16/292

48. HATED WITHOUT A CAUSE

PROPHECY

"Those who hate me without a
cause are more than the hairs
of my head...."
Psalms 69:4
(Also see Isaiah 49:7.)

FULFILLMENT

"But they have done this in order
that the word may be fulfilled
that is written in their Law, 'They
hated Me without a cause.' "
John 15:25

49. FRIENDS STOOD AFAR OFF

PROPHECY

"My loved ones and my friends stand aloof from my plague; And my kinsmen stand afar off."

Psalms 38:11

FULFILLMENT

"And all His acquaintances and the women who accompanied Him from Galilee, were standing at a distance, seeing these things."

Luke 23:49
(Also see Mark 15:40; Matthew 27:55,56.)

"At the very time when my affliction would have required them to stand nearer and more steadily by me than ever, they are afraid of the danger that they would incur by seeming to take part with me. While the enemies are near, the friends are far. So in the case of Messiah" (Matthew 26:56; 27:55; Luke 23:49; John 16:32). 11/184

50. PEOPLE SHOOK THEIR HEADS

PROPHECY

"I also have become a reproach to them; When they see me, they wag their head."

Psalms 109:25
(Also see Psalms 22:7.)

FULFILLMENT

"And those who were passing by were hurling abuse at Him, wagging their heads. . . ."

Matthew 27:39

" — A gesture implying that there is no hope for the sufferer, at whom they contemptuously sneer" (Job 16:4; Psalms 44:14). 10/148

" — As though it was all over with me: and I and my cause were irretrievably ruined" (Psalms 22:7; Matthew 27:39). 10/345

51. STARED UPON

PROPHECY

"I can count all my bones. They look, they stare at me."

Psalms 22:17

FULFILLMENT

"And the people stood by, looking on. . . ."

Luke 23:35

52. GARMENTS PARTED AND LOTS CAST

PROPHECY

"They divide my garments among them, And for my clothing they cast lots."

Psalms 22:18

FULFILLMENT

"The soldiers therefore, when they had crucified Jesus, took His outer garments and made four parts, a part to every soldier and also the tunic; now the tunic was seamless, woven in one piece. They said . . . 'Let us not tear it, but cast lots for it, to decide whose it shall be. . . .' "

John 19:23,24

The Old Testament statement in Psalms almost seems to be contradictory until we look at the account at the scene of the cross. The garments were parted among the soldiers, but the vesture was awarded to one by the casting of lots.

53.   TO SUFFER THIRST

PROPHECY

". . . And for my thirst they gave me vinegar to drink."
>   Psalms 69:21
>   (Also see Psalms 22:15.)

FULFILLMENT

"After this, Jesus . . . said, 'I am thirsty.' "
>   John 19:28

54.   GALL AND VINEGAR OFFERED HIM

PROPHECY

"They also gave me gall for my food,
And for my thirst they gave me vinegar to drink."
>   Psalms 69:21

FULFILLMENT

"They gave Him wine to drink mingled with gall; and after tasting it, He was unwilling to drink."
>   Matthew 27:34
>   (Also see John
>   19:28,29.)

A. R. Fausset writes:

"His bitter sufferings might have been expected to soften even His enemies, who had caused those sufferings; but instead of cordials, they gave Him gall and vinegar. Twice vinegar was offered to the Saviour on the cross — first vinegar mixed with gall (Matthew 27:34), and myrrh (Mark 15:23); but when He had tasted it, He would not drink it; for He would not meet His sufferings in a state of stupefaction, which is the effect of myrrh. As given to criminals, it was a kindness; as given to the righteous Sin-bearer, it was an insult. Next, in order to fulfil this Scripture, He cried 'I thirst,' and vinegar was given Him to drink" (John 19:28; Matthew 27:48). 11/246

55.   HIS FORSAKEN CRY

PROPHECY

"My God, my God, why hast Thou forsaken me?"
>   Psalms 22:1a

FULFILLMENT

"And about the ninth hour Jesus cried out with a loud voice, saying, 'Eli, Eli lama sabachthani?' that is, 'My God, My God, why hast Thou forsaken Me?' "
>   Matthew 27:46

Psalms 22 — "The expressive repetition twice (v. 1) of the cry, 'my God,' implies that the Sufferer clung firmly to this truth, that God was still His God, in spite of all appearances to the contrary. This was His antidote to despair, and the pledge that God would yet interpose as His Deliverer." 11/148

This cry turned the attention of the people back to Psalms 22. Christ was quoting the first verse of the psalm, and that psalm is a clear prophecy of the crucifixion.

56. COMMITTED HIMSELF TO GOD

PROPHECY

"Into Thy hand I commit my
spirit."
Psalms 31:5

FULFILLMENT

"And Jesus, crying out with a
loud voice, said, 'Father, into
Thy hands I commit My spirit.'"
Luke 23:46

57. BONES NOT BROKEN

PROPHECY

"He keeps all his bones;
Not one of them is broken."
Psalms 34:20

FULFILLMENT

". . . But coming to Jesus, when
they saw that He was already
dead, they did not break His
legs."
John 19:33

Although not stated in Scripture, there are two other prophecies which
concern His bones that undoubtedly had an exact fulfillment.
1. And all my bones are out of joint (Psalms 22:14). The disjointing of
bones while hanging on the cross by the hands and feet could easily
come about, especially when we note that His body was attached to the
cross while it was lying on the ground.
2. I can count all my bones. They look, they stare at me (Psalms 22:17).
All His bones could easily be seen while He was left hanging on the
cross. The extension of His body during crucifixion would tend to make
the bones more prominent than usual.

58. HEART BROKEN

PROPHECY

"My heart is like wax;
It is melted within me."
Psalms 22:14

FULFILLMENT

". . . But one of the soldiers
pierced His side with a spear,
and immediately there came
out blood and water."
John 19:34

The blood and water which came forth from His pierced side are
evidences that the heart had literally burst.

59. HIS SIDE PIERCED

PROPHECY

". . . They will look on Me
whom they have pierced. . . ."
Zechariah 12:10

FULFILLMENT

". . . But one of the soldiers
pierced His side with a
spear. . . ."
John 19:34

Theodore Laetsch writes:
"Now a remarkable statement is added. The Lord Jehovah speaks of
Himself as having been pierced by men who shall look upon Him and shall
mourn for Him.

"The word pierce — thrust through — occurs nine times as a thrust by a
sword or spear (Num. 25:8; Judg. 9:54; I Sam. 31:4; I Chron. 10:4; Is.
13:15; Jer. 37:10, 'wounded'; 51:4; Zech. 12:10; 13:3); it occurs once as

pierced by pangs of hunger described as more painful than a sword thrust" (Lamentations 4:9). 20/483

60.   DARKNESS OVER THE LAND

PROPHECY

" 'And it will come about in that day,' declares the Lord God,
'That I shall make the sun go down at noon
And make the earth dark in broad daylight.' "
Amos 8:9

FULFILLMENT

"Now from the sixth hour darkness fell upon all the land until the ninth hour."
Matthew 27:45

Because the Jews reckoned 12 hours from sunrise to sunset, it would make the sixth hour near noon and the ninth hour about three o'clock.

61.   BURIED IN RICH MAN'S TOMB

PROPHECY

"His grave was assigned to be with wicked men,
Yet with a rich man in His death. . . ."
Isaiah 53:9

FULFILLMENT

". . . There came a rich man from Arimathea, named Joseph . . . and asked for the body of Jesus. . . . And Joseph took the body and wrapped it in a clean linen cloth, and laid it in his own new tomb. . . ."
Matthew 27:57-60

4A.   PROPHECIES FULFILLED COMFIRM JESUS AS THE MESSIAH, THE CHRIST, THE SON OF GOD

1B.   Objection: Fulfilled Prophecy in Jesus Was Deliberate

Answer: The above objection might seem plausible until we realize that many of the prophecies concerning the Messiah were totally beyond the human control of Jesus, such as —

1. Place of birth (Micah 5:2).
2. Time of birth (Daniel 9:25; Genesis 49:10).
3. Manner of birth (Isaiah 7:14).
4. Betrayal.
5. Manner of death (Psalms 22:16).
6. People's reactions (mocking, spitting, staring, etc.).
7. Piercing.
8. Burial.

2B.   Objection: Fulfilled Prophecy in Jesus Was Coincidental, an Accident

"Why, you could find some of these prophecies fulfilled in Kennedy, King, Nasser, etc.," replies the critic.

Answer: Yes, one could possibly find one or two prophecies fulfilled in other men, but not all 61 major prophecies! In fact, if you can find someone, other than Jesus, either living or dead, who can fulfill only half of the predictions concerning Messiah which are given in *Messiah in Both Testaments* by Fred John Meldau, the Christian Victory Publishing Company of Denver is ready to give you a $1,000 reward. There are a lot of men in the universities who could use some extra cash!

H. Harold Hartzler, of the American Scientific Affiliation, Goshen College, in the foreword of Stoner's book writes: "The manuscript for *Science Speaks* has been carefully reviewed by a committee of the American Scientific Affiliation members and by the Executive Council of the same group and has been found, in general, to be dependable and accurate in regard to the scientific material presented. The mathematical analysis included is based upon principles of probability which are thoroughly sound and Professor Stoner has applied these principles in a proper and convincing way."

The following probabilities are taken from Peter Stoner in *Science Speaks* to show that coincidence is ruled out by the science of probability. Stoner says that by using the modern science of probability in reference to eight prophecies (*1.* — No. 10; *2.* — No. 22; *3.* — No. 27; *4.* — No. 33 & 44; *5.* — No. 34; *6.* — No. 35 & 36; *7.* — No. 39; *8.* — No. 44 & 45 [crucified]), ". . . We find that the chance that any man might have lived down to the present time and fulfilled all eight prophecies is 1 in 10^{17}." That would be 1 in 100,000,000,000,000,000. In order to help us comprehend this staggering probability, Stoner illustrates it by supposing that "we take 10^{17} silver dollars and lay them on the face of Texas. They will cover all of the state two feet deep. Now mark one of these silver dollars and stir the whole mass thoroughly, all over the state. Blindfold a man and tell him that he can travel as far as he wishes, but he must pick up one silver dollar and say that this is the right one. What chance would he have of getting the right one? Just the same chance that the prophets would have had of writing these eight prophecies and having them all come true in any one man, from their day to the present time, providing they wrote them in their own wisdom.

"Now these prophecies were either given by inspiration of God or the prophets just wrote them as they thought they should be. In such a case the prophets had just one chance in 10^{17} of having them come true in any man, but they all came true in Christ.

"This means that the fulfillment of these eight prophecies alone proves that God inspired the writing of those prophecies to a definiteness which lacks only one chance in 10^{17} of being absolute." 27/100-107

Stoner considers 48 prophecies and says, ". . . We find the chance that any one man fulfilled all 48 prophecies to be 1 in 10^{157}.

"This is really a large number and it represents an extremely small chance. Let us try to visualize it. The silver dollar, which we have been using, is entirely too large. We must select a smaller object. The electron is about as small an object as we know of. It is so small that it will take 2.5 times 10^{15} of them laid side by side to make a line, single file, one inch long. If we were going to count the electrons in this line one inch long, and counted 250 each minute, and if we counted day and night, it would take us 19,000,000 years to count just the one-inch line of electrons. If we had a cubic inch of these electrons and we tried to count them it would take us, counting steadily 250 each minute, 19,000,000 times 19,000,000 times 19,000,000 years or 6.9 times 10^{21} years.

"With this introduction, let us go back to our chance of 1 in 10^{157}. Let us suppose that we are taking this number of electrons, marking one, and thoroughly stirring it into the whole mass, then blindfolding a man and letting him try to find the right one. What chance has he of finding the right one? What kind of a pile will this number of electrons make? They make an inconceivably large volume." 27/109,110

Such is the chance of any one man fulfilling 48 prophecies.

3B.   The Time of Messiah's Coming

1C.   THE REMOVAL OF THE SCEPTER

> "The scepter shall not depart from Judah,
> Nor the ruler's staff from between his feet,
> Until Shiloh comes,
> And to him shall be the obedience of the peoples."
>
> Genesis 49:10

The word which is best translated "scepter" in this passage means a "tribal staff." Each of the 12 tribes of Israel had its own particular "staff" with its name inscribed on it. Therefore, the "tribal staff" or "tribal identity" of Judah was not to pass away before Shiloh came. For centuries Jewish and Christian commentators alike have taken the word "Shiloh" to be a name of the Messiah.

We remember that Judah had been deprived of its national sovereignty during the 70-year period of the Babylonian captivity; however, it never lost its "tribal staff" or "national identity" during this time. They still possessed their own lawgivers or judges even while in captivity (see Ezra 1:5,8).

Thus, according to this Scripture and the Jews of their time, two signs were to take place soon after the advent of the Messiah:

1. Removal of the scepter or identity of Judah.
2. Suppression of the judicial power.

The first visible sign of the beginning of the removal of the scepter from Judah came about when Herod the Great, who had no Jewish blood, succeeded the Maccabean princes, who belonged to the tribe of Levi and who were the last Jewish kings to have their reign in Jerusalem (Sanhedrin, folio 97, verso.) (*Maccabees*, Book 2).

Magath, in his book *Jesus Before the Sanhedrin*, titles his second chapter: "The legal power of the Sanhedrin is restricted twenty-three years before the trial of Christ." This restriction was the loss of the power to pass the death sentence.

This occurred after the deposition of Archelaus, who was the son and successor of Herod, 11 A.D., or 7 V.E. (Josephus, *Ant.*, Book 17, Chap. 13, 1-5). The procurators, who administered in the Augustus name, took the supreme power of the Sanhedrin away so they could exercise the *jus gladii* themselves; that is, the sovereign right over life and death sentences. All the nations which were subdued by the Roman Empire were deprived of their ability to pronounce capital sentences. Tacitus says, ". . . The Romans reserved to themselves the right of the sword, and neglected all else."

The Sanhedrin, however, retained certain rights:

1. Excommunication (John 9:22).
2. Imprisonment (Acts 5:17,18).
3. Corporeal punishment (Acts 16:22).

The *Talmud* itself admits that "a little more than forty years before the destruction of the Temple, the power of pronouncing capital sentences was taken away from the Jews." (*Talmud*, Jerusalem, Sanhedrin, fol. 24, recto.) However, it hardly seems possible that the *jus gladii* remained in the Jewish hands until that time. It probably had ceased at the time of Coponius, 7 A.D. (*Essai sur l'histoire et la geographie de la Palestine, d'apres les Talmuds et la geographie de la Palestine, d'apres les Talmuds et les autres sources Rabbinique*, p. 90: Paris, 1867.) Rabbi Rachmon says, "When the members of the

Sanhedrin found themselves deprived of their right over life and death, a general consternation took possession of them; they covered their heads with ashes, and their bodies with sackcloth, exclaiming: 'Woe unto us, for the scepter has departed from Judah, and the Messiah has not come!' " 21/28-30

Josephus, who was an eye-witness of this decadent process, says, "After the death of the procurator Festus, when Albinus was about to succeed him, the high-priest Ananus considered it a favorable opportunity to assemble the Sanhedrin. He therefore caused James the brother of Jesus, who was called Christ, and several others, to appear before this hastily assembled council, and pronounced upon them the sentence of death by stoning. All the wise men and strict observers of the law who were at Jerusalem expressed their disapprobation of this act. . . . Some even went to Albinus himself, who had departed to Alexandria, to bring this breach of the law under his observation, and to inform him that Ananus had acted illegally in assembling the Sanhedrin without the Roman authority" (Josephus, *Ant.*, 20, Chap. 9, 1).

The Jews, in order to save face, made up various reasons for eliminating the death penalty. For example, the *Talmud* (Bab., *Aboda Zarah,* or *Of Idolatry,* fol. 8, recto.) states, "The members of the Sanhedrin, having noticed that the number of murderers had increased to such an extent in Israel that it became impossible to condemn them all to death, they concluded among themselves [and said], 'It will be advantageous for us to change our ordinary place of meeting for another, so that we may avoid the passing of capital sentences.' To this, Maimonides adds in the Const. Sanhedrin, Chap. 14, that "forty years before the destruction of the second Temple criminal sentences ceased in Israel, although the Temple was still standing. This was due to the fact that the members of the Sanhedrin quitted the Hall Of Hewn Stones and held their sessions there no longer." 21/30-33

Lightfoot, in *Evangelium Matthaei, horoe hebraicoe,* p. 275, 276, Cambridge, 1658, adds that "the members of the Sanhedrin . . . had taken the resolution not to pass capital sentences as long as the land of Israel remained under the government of the Romans, and the lives of the children of Israel were menaced by them. To condemn to death a son of Abraham at a time when Judea is invaded on all sides, and is trembling under the march of the Roman legions, would it not be to insult the ancient blood of the patriarchs? Is not the least of the Israelites, by the very fact that he is a descendant of Abraham, a superior being to the Gentiles? Let us, therefore, quit the hall of hewn stones, outside of which no one can be condemned to death, and in protestation of which let us show by our voluntary exile and by the silence of justice that Rome, although ruling the world, is nevertheless mistress over neither the lives nor the laws of Judea." 21/33,34,38

The *Talmud* (Bab., Sanhedrin, Chap. 4, fol. 51b) says, "Since the Sanhedrin no longer had jurisdiction in capital offenses, there is no practical utility in this ruling, which can become effective only in the days of the Messiah." 25/346

Once the judicial power was suppressed, the Sanhedrin ceased to be. Yes, the scepter was removed and Judah lost its royal or legal power. And the Jews knew it themselves! "Woe unto us, for the scepter has been taken from Judah, and the Messiah has not appeared!" (*Talmud,*

Bab., Sanhedrin, Chap. 4, fol. 37, recto.). Little did they realize their Messiah was a young Nazarene walking in the midst of them.

2C.   THE DESTRUCTION OF THE TEMPLE

". . . And the Lord, whom you seek, will suddenly come to His temple. . . ."

Malachi 3:1

This verse, along with four others (Psalms 118:26; Daniel 9:26; Zechariah 11:13; Haggai 2:7-9), demands that the Messiah come while the temple at Jerusalem is still standing. This is of great significance when we realize that the temple was destroyed in 70 A.D. and has not since been rebuilt!

"Then after the sixty-two weeks the Messiah will be cut off and have nothing, and the people of the prince who is to come will destroy the city and the sanctuary. . . ."

Daniel 9:26

This is a remarkable statement! Chronologically:

1. Messiah comes (assumed).
2. Messiah cut off (dies).
3. Destruction of city (Jerusalem) and sanctuary (the temple). The temple and city were destroyed by Titus and his army in 70 A.D.; therefore, either Messiah had already come or this prophecy was a lie.

4B. Fulfilled Prophecy

In Daniel 9:24-27, a prophecy is given in three specific parts concerning the Messiah. The first part states that at the end of 69 weeks, the Messiah will come to Jerusalem. (The 7 and 62 weeks are understood as 69 seven-year periods.) The starting point of the 69 weeks is the decree to restore and rebuild Jerusalem.

The second part states that after the Messiah comes, He will be cut off (idiom for His death). Then the prince to come will destroy Jerusalem and the temple.

All of the above, according to Daniel 9:24-26, takes place *after* the 69 weeks of years. But Daniel 9:24 mentions 70 weeks (7+62+1), not just 69. The final week is described in 9:27. Many scholars believe 9:27 discusses a different person and time than that of 9:26. Even though the author refers to the prince, the reference is probably to another prince who is to come later in history. (Double references are somewhat common in prophecy. For example, a reference may refer to King David and also later to Christ.) This is supported by their actions: The prince in 9:27 forces Jewish temple practices to stop, but the prince in 9:26 has just destroyed the temple! So probably this prince comes later after the temple is rebuilt, which has yet to occur. Anyway, no matter which way one interprets the 70th week (the last seven years of the prophecy), the first two parts of the prophecy still can be examined historically. For further study on this prophecy in Daniel, see *Chronological Aspects of the Life of Christ.* 17

1C. THE TEXT

"Seventy weeks have been decreed for your people and your holy city, to finish the transgression, to make an end of sin, to make atonement for iniquity, to bring in everlasting righteousness, to seal up vision and prophecy, and to anoint the most holy place.

"So you are to know and discern that from the issuing of a decree to restore and rebuild Jerusalem until Messiah the Prince there will be seven weeks and sixty-two weeks; it will be built again, with plaza and moat, even in times of distress.

"Then after the sixty-two weeks the Messiah will be cut off and have nothing, and the people of the prince who is to come will destroy the city and the sanctuary. And its end will come with a flood; even to the end there will be war; desolations are determined.

"And he will make a firm covenant with the many for one week, but in the middle of the week he will put a stop to sacrifice and grain offering; and on the wing of abominations will come one who makes desolate, even until a complete destruction, one that is decreed, is poured out on the one who makes desolate."

Daniel 9:24-27

2C. INTERPRETATION OF THE PROPHECY

1D. Main features of this prophecy

(Taken from Dr. James Rosscup's class notes, Talbot Theological Seminary, California)

Concerns Daniel's people, Israel, and Daniel's city, Jerusalem (v.24)

Two princes mentioned:
1. Messiah (v.25)
2. Prince to come (v.26)

Time period of 70 weeks (v.24)
1. As a unit (v.24)
2. As a division of three periods: 7 weeks, 62 weeks, and 1 week (vs. 25,27)

Specified beginning of the 70 weeks (v.25)

Messiah appears at end of 69 weeks (v.25)

Destruction of city and sanctuary by people of prince to come (v.26)

Covenant made between Israel and the coming prince at the beginning of last week (v.27); this covenant is broken mid-week (v.27)

At end of the 70 weeks, Israel will have everlasting righteousness (v.24)

2D. Time measure indicated by 70 weeks:

Jewish concept of week

1. The Hebrew word for "week" is *shabua* and literally means a "seven." (We should disassociate any English concept of week with the concept intended by Gabriel.) Then, in Hebrew, the idea of 70 weeks is "seventy sevens."

2. The Jews were familiar with a "seven" of both days and years. "It was, in certain respects, even more important." 22/13

3. Leviticus 25:2-4 illustrates the above fact. Leviticus 25:8 shows that there was a multiple of a week of years.

Remembering what has been said previously, there are several reasons for believing that the 70 weeks mentioned in Daniel are 70 sevens of years.

1. Daniel had been thinking in terms of years and multiples of seven earlier in the chapter (Daniel 9:1,2).

2. Daniel knew that the Babylonian captivity was based on violation of the Sabbatic year, and since they were in captivity for 70 years, evidently the Sabbatic year was violated 490 years (Leviticus 26:32-35; II Chronicles 36:21 and Daniel 9:24).

3. The context is consistent and makes sense when we understand the 70 weeks as years.

4. *Shabua* is found in Daniel 10:2,3. Context demands it to mean "weeks" of days. It is literally "three sevens of days." If Daniel meant days in 9:24-27, why don't we find the same form of expression as that in chapter 10? Obviously, years are meant in chapter 9.

3D.   Length of prophetic year

The calendar year used in the Scriptures must be determined from the Scriptures themselves.

1. Historically — Compare Genesis 7:11 with Genesis 8:4, and the two of these with Genesis 7:24 and Genesis 8:3.

2. Prophetically — Many Scriptures refer to the great tribulation under various terms, but all have a common denominator of a 360-day year.

    Daniel 9:27 — "Midst" of the 70th week (obviously 3½ years) (KJV)

    Daniel 7:24,25 — "a time and times and the dividing of time" (KJV) (literally 3½ times)

    Revelation 13:4-7 — "forty and two months" (3½ years) (KJV)

    Revelation 12:13,14 — "a time, and times, and half a time" (KJV)

    Revelation 12:6 — "a thousand two hundred and three score days" (KJV) (1,260 days or 3½ years)

4D.   Beginning of 70 weeks

There are several commandments or decrees in Israel's history which have been suggested as the *terminus a quo* (beginning) of the 70 weeks. These are:

1. The decree of Cyrus, 539 B.C. (Ezra 1:1-4).
2. The decree of Darius, 519 B.C. (Ezra 5:3-7).
3. The decree of Artaxerxes to Ezra, 457 B.C. (Ezra 7:11-16).
4. The decree of Artaxerxes to Nehemiah, 444 B.C. (Nehemiah 2:1-8). 17/131ff.

However, the only one that appears to fit the data accurately is number four, the decree of Artaxerxes to Nehemiah.

J. D. Wilson comments on the starting point of the prophecy: "The . . . decree is referred to in Neh. ii. It was in the twentieth year of Artaxerxes. The words of the decree are not given, but its subject matter can easily be determined. Nehemiah hears of the desolate condition of Jerusalem. He is deeply grieved. The King asks the reason. Nehemiah replies, 'the city, the place of my fathers' sepulchres, lieth waste, and the gates thereof are consumed with fire.' The King bids him make request. He does so promptly, asking an order from the King that 'I be sent to the city that I may build it.'

And, as we read, he was sent, and he rebuilt Jerusalem.

"This decree then is the 'commandment to restore and rebuild Jerusalem.' There is no other decree authorizing the restoration of the city. This decree authorizes the restoration and the book of Nehemiah tells how the work was carried on. The exigencies of their various theories have led men to take some other decree for the *terminus a quo* of their calculations, but it is not apparent how any could have done so without misgivings. This decree of Neh. ii is the commandment to restore and rebuild Jerusalem; no other decree gives any permission to restore the city. All other decrees refer to the building of the temple and the temple only." 29/141,142

This decree was given in 444 B.C., based on the following:

1. ". . . In the month Nisan, in the twentieth year of King Artaxerxes" (Nehemiah 2:1).
2. Artaxerxes' accession was in 465 B.C.
3. There is no date specified, so according to the Jewish custom, the date is understood as the first day of the month, which would be Nisan 1, 444 B.C.
4. March 5, 444 B.C. is our corresponding calendar date.

5D. Way-mark of the first seven weeks

1. It took 49 years to restore the city (v.25).
2. The close of Hebrew prophecy and of the Old Testament canon in Malachi is noteworthy, marked 49 years after 444 B.C.

If Daniel is correct, the time from the edict to restore and rebuild Jerusalem (Nisan 1, 444 B.C.) to the coming of the Messiah to Jerusalem is 483 years (69 x 7), each year equaling the Jewish prophetic year of 360 days (173,880 days).

The terminal event of the 69 weeks is the presentation of Christ Himself to Israel as the Messiah as predicted in Zechariah 9:9. H. Hoehner, who has thoroughly researched this prophecy in Daniel and the corresponding dates, calculates the date of this event: "Multiplying the sixty-nine weeks by seven years for each week by 360 days gives a total of 173,880 days. The difference between 444 B.C. and A.D. 33 then is 476 solar years. By multiplying 476 by 365.24219879 or by 365 days, 5 hours, 48 minutes, 45.975 seconds [there are 365¼ days in a year], one comes to 173,855 days, 6 hours, 52 minutes, 44 seconds, or 173,855 days. This leaves only 25 days to be accounted for between 444 B.C. and A.D. 33. By adding the 25 days to March 5 (of 444 B.C.), one comes to March 30 (or A.D. 33) which was Nisan 10 in A.D. 33. This is the triumphal entry of Jesus into Jerusalem." 17/138

6D. Interval between weeks 69 and 70

After the termination of the 69 weeks and before the commencement of the 70th week, two events had to occur.

1. The 'cutting off' of the Messiah (Daniel 9:26).

   Christ was crucified April 3, A.D. 33, the Friday following His triumphal entry into Jerusalem.

2. The destruction of Jerusalem and the temple (Daniel 9:26).

Wilson discusses this part of the prophecy: "After that, the Roman prince [Titus] sent an army which utterly destroyed the city and temple of Jerusalem.

"That destruction was complete. The temple was not simply polluted, as it was by Antiochus Epiphanes — it was destroyed. It has not been reared in Jerusalem since. The Jewish ritual was ended. It has never been restored, and it never can be. It has had no priesthood since Jerusalem fell; for every son of Aaron was slain. There can be no more priestly sacrifices, nor atonement by high priest; for in that dire disaster, the older covenant passed away. Its vitality and validity had ceased when the Lamb of God was offered upon Calvary; but for forty years the outward shell remained. That shell was removed in the destruction of Jerusalem, 70 A.D." 29/148,149

3C. SUMMARY
Time line:

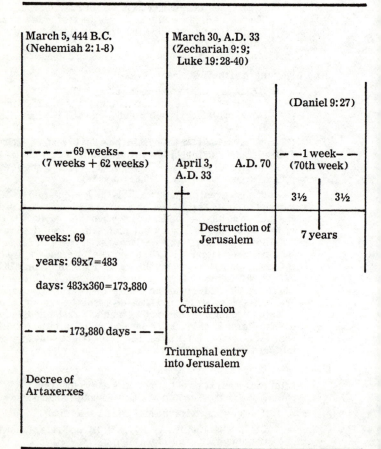

March 5, 444 B.C.
(Nehemiah 2:1-8)

March 30, A.D. 33
(Zechariah 9:9;
Luke 19:28-40)

(Daniel 9:27)

– – – – 69 weeks– – – –
(7 weeks + 62 weeks)

April 3,   A.D. 70
A.D. 33

– –1 week– –
(70th week)

3½   3½

weeks: 69

years: 69x7=483

days: 483x360=173,880

Destruction of
Jerusalem

7 years

Crucifixion

– – – –173,880 days– – –

Triumphal entry
into Jerusalem

Decree of
Artaxerxes

So Daniel prophesies accurately concerning the Messiah in his prophecy of the 70 weeks. Even if the 165 B.C. date of authorship is correct, all these events took place at least 200 years later.

They include:
1. The coming of the Messiah.
2. The death of the Messiah.
3. The destruction of Jerusalem and the temple.

The third part of the prophecy pertaining to the 70th week is yet to occur.

4A. OLD TESTAMENT PREDICTIONS WHICH WERE LITERALLY FULFILLED IN CHRIST

Floyd Hamilton in *The Basis of Christian Faith* (a modern defense of the Christian religion, revised and enlarged edition; New York: Harper and Row, 1964, p. 160) says: "Canon Liddon is authority for the statement that there are in the Old Testament 332 distinct predictions which were literally fulfilled in Christ."

1B. His First Advent

The fact. Genesis 3:15; Deuteronomy 18:15; Psalms 89:20; Isaiah 9:6; 28:16; 32:1; 35:4; 42:6; 49:1; 55:4; Ezekiel 34:24; Daniel 2:44; Micah 4:1; Zechariah 3:8.

The time. Genesis 49:10; Numbers 24:17; Daniel 9:24; Malachi 3:1.

His Divinity. Psalms 2:7,11; 45:6,7,11; 72:8; 102:24-27; 89:26,27; 110:1; Isaiah 9:6; 25:9; 40:10; Jeremiah 23:6; Micah 5:2; Malachi 3:1.

Human Generation. Genesis 12:3; 18:18; 21:12; 22:18; 26:4; 28:14; 49:10; II Samuel 7:14; Psalms 18:4-6,50; 22:22,23; 89:4; 29:36; 132:11; Isaiah 11:1; Jeremiah 23:5; 33:15.

2B. His Forerunner

Isaiah 40:3; Malachi 3:1; 4:5.

3B. His Nativity and Early Years

The Fact. Genesis 3:15; Isaiah 7:14; Jeremiah 31:22.

The Place. Numbers 24:17,19; Micah 5:2.

Adoration by Magi. Psalms 72:10,15; Isaiah 60:3,6.

Descent into Egypt. Hosea 11:1

Massacre of Innocents. Jeremiah 31:15.

4B. His Mission and Office

Mission. Genesis 12:3; 49:10; Numbers 24:19; Deuteronomy 18:18,19; Psalms 21:1; Isaiah 59:20; Jeremiah 33:16.

Priest like Melchizedek. Psalms 110:4.

Prophet like Moses. Deuteronomy 18:15.

Conversion of Gentiles. Isaiah 11:10; Deuteronomy 32:43; Psalms 18:49; 19:4; 117:1; Isaiah 42:1; 45:23; 49:6; Hosea 1:10; 2:23; Joel 2:32.

Ministry in Galilee. Isaiah 9:1,2.

Miracles. Isaiah 35:5,6; 42:7; 53:4.

Spiritual Graces. Psalms 45:7; Isaiah 11:2; 42:1; 53:9; 61:1,2.

Preaching. Psalms 2:7; 78:2; Isaiah 2:3; 61:1; Micah 4:2.

Purification of Temple. Psalms 69:9.

5B. His Passion

Rejection by Jews and Gentiles. Psalms 2:1; 22:12; 41:5; 56:5; 69:8; 118:22, 23; Isaiah 6:9,10; 8:14; 29:13; 53:1; 65:2.

Persecution. Psalms 22:6; 35:7,12; 56:5; 71:10; 109:2; Isaiah 49:7; 53:3.

Triumphal Entry into Jerusalem. Psalms 8:2; 118:25,26; Zechariah 9:9.

Betrayal by Own Friend. Psalms 41:9; 55:13; Zechariah 13:6.

Betrayal for Thirty Pieces of Silver. Zechariah 11:12.

Betrayer's Death. Psalms 55:15,23; 109:17.

Purchase of Potter's Field. Zechariah 11:13.

Desertion by Disciples. Zechariah 13:7.

False Accusation. Psalms 27:12; 35:11; 109:2; Psalms 2:1,2.

Silence under Accusation. Psalms 38:13; Isaiah 53:7.

Mocking. Psalms 22:7,8,16; 109:25.

Insult, Buffeting, Spitting, Scourging. Psalms 35:15,21; Isaiah 50:6.

Patience Under Suffering. Isaiah 53:7-9.

Crucifixion. Psalms 22:14,17.

Offer of Gall and Vinegar. Psalms 69:21.

Prayer for Enemies. Psalms 109:4.

Cries Upon the Cross. Psalms 22:1; 31:5.

Death in Prime of Life. Psalms 89:45; 102:24.

Death With Malefactors. Isaiah 53:9,12.

Death Attested by Convulsions of Nature. Amos 5:20; Zechariah 14:4,6.

Casting Lots for Vesture. Psalms 22:18.

Bones Not to Be Broken. Psalms 34:20.

Piercing. Psalms 22:16; Zechariah 12:10; 13:6.

Voluntary Death. Psalms 40:6-8.

Vicarious Suffering. Isaiah 53:4-6,12; Daniel 9:26.

Burial With the Rich. Isaiah 53:9.

6B. His Resurrection

Psalms 16:8-10; 30:3; 41:10; 118:17; Hosea 6:2.

7B. His Ascension

Psalms 16:11; 24:7; 68:18; 110:1; 118:19.

8B. His Second Advent

Psalms 50:3-6; Isaiah 9:6,7; 66:18; Daniel 7:13,14; Zechariah 12:10; 14:4-8.

Dominion Universal and Everlasting. I Chronicles 17:11-14; Psalms 72:8; Isaiah 9:7; Daniel 7:14; Psalms 2:6-8; 8:6; 110:1-3; 45:6,7.

BIBLIOGRAPHY

1. Berean Mission, Inc. St. Louis, Mo. Used by permission.

2. Blinzler, Josef. *The Trial of Jesus*. Translated by Isabel and Florence McHugh. Westminster, Md.: The Newman Press, 1959.

3. Bowker, John. *The Targums and Rabbinic Literature*. London: Cambridge University Press, 1969.

4. Cohen, A. *The Teachings of Maimonides.* London: George Routledge & Sons, Ltd., 1927.

5. Cooper, David L. "God and Messiah." Los Angeles: Biblical Research Society.

6. Delitzsch, Franz. *Biblical Commentary on the Prophecies of Isaiah.* Vol. 1. Translated by James Martin. Grand Rapids: William B. Eerdmans Publishing Company, 1950. Used by permission.

7. Driver, S. R. *Notes on the Hebrew Text and the Topography of the Books of Samuel.* Oxford: Clarendon Press, 1966. Used by permission.

8. *The Encyclopedia Americana.* Vol. 8. Americana Corporation, 1960. Used by permission.

9. *The Encyclopedia Americana.* Vol. 16. Americana Corporation, 1960. Used by permission.

10. Ethridge, J. W. *The Targums of Onkelos and Jonathan Ben Ussiel on the Pentateuch.* Vols. 1,2. New York: KTAV Publishing House, Inc., 1968.

11. Fausset, A. R. *A Commentary Critical, Experimental and Practical on the Old and New Testaments.* Vol III. Grand Rapids: William B. Eerdmans Publishing Company, 1961. Used by permission.

12. Friedlaender, M. *Essays on the Writings of Abraham Ibn Ezra.* Vol. IV. London: Trubner and Company, n.d.

13. Geisler, Norman. *Christ: The Theme of the Bible.* Chicago: Moody Press, 1969. Used by permission.

14. Heinisch, Paul. *Christ in Prophecy.* The Liturgical Press, 1956.

15. Hengstenberg, E. W. *Christology of the Old Testament and a Commentary on the Messianic Predictions.* Grand Rapids: Kregel Publications, 1970.

16. Henry, Matthew. *Matthew Henry's Commentary on the Whole Bible.* Vols. I,II. Wilmington: Sovereign Grace Publishers, 1972.

17. Hoehner, Harold. *Chronological Aspects of the Life of Christ.* Grand Rapids: Zondervan Publishing House, 1977.

18. Kligerman, Aaron Judah. *Messianic Prophecy in the Old Testament.* Grand Rapids: Zondervan Publishing House, 1957. Used by permission.

19. Laetsch, Theodore. *Bible Commentary: Jeremiah.* St. Louis: Concordia Publishing House, 1953.

20. Laetsch, Theodore. *Bible Commentary: The Minor Prophets.* St. Louis: Concordia Publishing House, 1970.

21. LeMann, M. M. *Jesus Before the Sanhedrin.* Translated by Julius Magath. Nashville: Southern Methodist Publishing House, 1886.

22. McClain, Alva J. *Daniel's Prophecy of the Seventy Weeks.* Grand Rapids: Zondervan Publishing House, 1972. Used by permission.

23. McDowell, Josh. Class notes.

24. Minkin, Jacob S. *The World of Moses Maimonides.* New York: Thomas Yoseloff, 1957.

25. Nezikin, Seder. *The Babylonian Talmud.* Translated by I. Epstein. London: The Soncino Press, 1935.

26. Stenning, J. F. (ed.). *The Targum of Isaiah.* London: Clarendon Press, 1949. Used by permission.

27. Stoner, Peter W. *Science Speaks.* Chicago: Moody Press, 1963. Used by permission.

28. Unger, Merrill F. *Unger's Bible Dictionary.* Chicago: Moody Press, 1971. Used by permission.

29. Wilson, Joseph D. *Did Daniel Write Daniel?* New York: Charles C. Cook, n.d.

chapter 10

the resurrection-
hoax or
history?

After more than 700 hours of studying this subject, and thoroughly investigating its foundation, I have come to the conclusion that the resurrection of Jesus Christ is one of the "*most wicked, vicious, heartless hoaxes ever foisted upon the minds of men,* or it is the most fantastic fact of history."

Jesus has three basic credentials: (1) The impact of His life upon history; (2) Fulfilled prophecy in His life; and (3) His resurrection. The resurrection of Jesus Christ and Christianity stand or fall together. A student at the University of Uruguay said to me: "Professor McDowell, why can't you refute Christianity?" I answered: "For a very simple reason: I am not able to explain away an event in history — the resurrection of Jesus Christ."

THE RESURRECTION ACCOUNT IN MATTHEW 28:1-11
(See also Mark 16, Luke 24, John 20-21)

1 Now late on the Sabbath, as it began to dawn toward the first day of the week, Mary Magdalene and the other Mary came to look at the grave.

2 And behold, a severe earthquake had occurred, for an angel of the Lord descended from heaven and came and rolled away the stone and sat upon it.

3 And his appearance was like lightning, and his garment as white as snow;

4 and the guards shook for fear of him, and became like dead men.

5 And the angel answered and said to the women, "Do not be afraid; for I know that you are looking for Jesus who has been crucified.

6 "He is not here, for He has risen, just as He said. Come, see the place where He was lying.

7 "And go quickly and tell His disciples that He has risen from the dead; and behold, He is going before you into Galilee, there you will see Him; behold, I have told you."

8 And they departed quickly from the tomb with fear and great joy and ran to report it to His disciples.

9 And behold, Jesus met them and greeted them. And they came up and took hold of His feet and worshiped Him.

10 Then Jesus said to them, "Do not be afraid; go and take word to

My brethren to leave for Galilee, and there they shall see Me."

11 Now while they were on their way, behold, some of the guards came into the city and reported to the chief priests all that had happened.

The following is an outline designed to aid you in effectively using this material.

1A.	**THE IMPORTANCE OF THE RESURRECTION**
2A.	**THE CLAIMS OF CHRIST THAT HE WOULD BE RAISED FROM THE DEAD**
	1B. The importance of the claims
	2B. The claims as given by Jesus
3A.	**THE HISTORICAL APPROACH**
	1B. A time-space dimension event
	2B. The testimony of history and law
	3B. The testimony of early church fathers
4A.	**THE RESURRECTION SCENE**
	1B. Jesus was dead
	2B. The tomb
	3B. The burial
	4B. The stone
	5B. The seal
	6B. The guard
	7B. The disciples
	8B. The post-resurrection appearances

1A. IMPORTANCE OF THE RESURRECTION OF CHRIST

All but four of the major world religions are based on mere philosophical propositions. Of the four that are based on personalities rather than a philosophical system, only Christianity claims an empty tomb for its founder. Abraham, the father of Judaism, died about 1900 B.C., but no resurrection was ever claimed for him.

Wilbur M. Smith says in *Therefore Stand:* "The original accounts of Buddha never ascribe to him any such thing as a resurrection; in fact, in the earliest accounts of his death, namely, the *Mahaparinibbana Sutta,* we read that when Buddha died it was 'with that utter passing away in which nothing whatever remains behind.' " 60/385

"*Professor Childers* says, 'There is no trace in the *Pali* scriptures or commentaries (or so far as I know in any Pali book) of Sakya Muni having existed after his death or appearing to his disciples.' Mohammed died June 8, 632 A.D., at the age of sixty-one, at Medina, where his tomb is annually visited by thousands of devout Mohammedans. All the millions and millions of Jews, Buddhists, and Mohammedans agree that their founders have never come up out of the dust of the earth in resurrection." 60/385

Theodosus Harnack says: "Where you stand with regard to the fact of the Resurrection is in my eyes no longer Christian theology. To me Christianity stands or falls with the Resurrection." 60/437

Professor William Milligan states: "While speaking of the positive evidence of the Resurrection of our Lord, it may be further urged that the fact, if true, harmonizes all the other facts of His history." 43/71

Wilbur M. Smith concludes: "If our Lord said, frequently, with great definiteness and detail, that after He went up to Jerusalem He would be put to death, but on the third day He would rise again from the grave, and this prediction came to pass, then it has always seemed to me that everything else that our Lord ever said must also be true." 60/419

It is further stated by *W. J. Sparrow-Simpson:*

"If it be asked how the resurrection of Christ is a proof of His being the Son of God, it may be answered, first, because He rose by His own power. He had power to lay down His life, and He had power to take it again, John x.18. This is not inconsistent with the fact taught in so many other passages, that He was raised by the power of the Father, because what the Father does the Son does likewise; creation, and all other external works, are ascribed indifferently to the Father, Son and Spirit. But in the second place, as Christ had openly declared Himself to be the Son of God, His rising from the dead was the seal of God to the truth of that declaration. Had He continued under the power of death, God would thereby have disallowed His claim to be His Son; but as He raised Him from the dead, He publicly acknowledged Him; saying, 'Thou art My Son, this day have I declared Thee such.' " 60/583; 62/287,288

Also, Peter's sermon on the day of Pentecost is "wholly and entirely founded on the Resurrection. Not merely is the Resurrection its principal theme, but if that doctrine were removed there would be no doctrine left. For the Resurrection is propounded as being (1) the explanation of Jesus' death; (2) prophetically anticipated as the Messianic experience; (3) apostolically witnessed; (4) the cause of the outpouring of the Spirit, and thus accounting for religious phenomena otherwise inexplicable; and (5) certifying the Messianic and Kingly position of Jesus of Nazareth. Thus the whole series of arguments and conclusions depends for stability entirely upon the Resurrection. Without the Resurrection the Messianic and Kingly position of Jesus could not be convincingly established. Without it the new outpouring of the Spirit would continue a mystery unexplained. Without it the substance of the apostolic witness would have disappeared. All that would be left of this instruction would be the Messianic exposition of Psalm xvi.; and that, only as a future experience of a Messiah who had not yet appeared. The Divine Approval of Jesus as certified by His works would also remain; but apparently as an approval extended only to His life; a life ending like that of any other prophet whom the nation refused to tolerate any longer. Thus the first Christian sermon is founded on the position of Jesus as determined by His Resurrection." 60/230

Even *Adolf Harnack,* who rejects the Church's belief in the resurrection, admits: "The firm confidence of the disciples in Jesus was rooted in the belief that He did not abide in death, but was raised by God. That Christ was risen was, in virtue of what they had experienced in Him, certainly only after they had seen Him, just as sure as the fact of His death, and became the main article of their preaching about Him" (*History of Dogma,* Chapter II). 13/3

H. P. Liddon says: "Faith in the resurrection is the very keystone of the arch of Christian faith, and, when it is removed, all must inevitably crumble into ruin." 60/577

The resurrection of Christ has always been categorically the central tenet of the Church. As *Wilbur Smith* puts it:

"From the first day of its divinely bestowed life, the Christian church has unitedly borne testimony to its faith in the Resurrection of Christ. It is what we may call one of the great fundamental doctrines and convictions of the church, and so penetrates the literature of the New Testament, that if you lifted out every passage in which a reference is made to the Resurrection, you would have a collection of writings so mutilated that what remained could not be understood. The Resurrection entered intimately into the life of the earliest Christians; the fact of it appears on their tombs, and in the drawings found on the walls of the catacombs; it entered deeply into Christian hymnology; it became one of the most vital themes of the great apologetic writings of the first four centuries; it was the theme constantly dwelt upon in the preaching of the ante-Nicene and post-Nicene period. It entered at once into the creedal formulae of the church; it is in our Apostles' Creed; it is in all the great creeds that followed.

"All evidence of the New Testament goes to show that the burden of the good news or gospel was not 'Follow this Teacher and do your best,' but, 'Jesus and the Resurrection.' You cannot take that away from Christianity without radically altering its character and destroying its very identity." 60/369,370

Professor Milligan says: "It thus appears that from the dawn of her history the Christian Church not only believed in the Resurrection of her Lord, but that her belief upon the point was interwoven with her whole existence." 43/70

W. Robertson Nicoll quotes Pressensé as saying: "The empty tomb of Christ has been the cradle of the Church. . . ." 60/580

W. J. Sparrow-Simpson says: "If the Resurrection is not historic fact, then the power of death remains unbroken, and with it the effect of sin; and the significance of Christ's Death remains uncertified, and accordingly believers are yet in their sins, precisely where they were before they heard of Jesus' name." 25/514

R. M'Cheyne Edgar, in his work, *The Gospel of a Risen Saviour*, has said:

"Here is a teacher of religion and He calmly professes to stake His entire claims upon His ability, after having been done to death, to rise again from the grave. We may safely assume that there never was, before or since, such a proposal made. To talk of this extraordinary test being *invented* by mystic students of the prophecies, and inserted in the way it has been into the gospel narratives, is to lay too great a burden on our credulity. He who was ready to stake everything on His ability to come back from the tomb stands before us as the most original of all teachers, one who shines in His own self-evidencing life!" 60/364

The following is found in the *Dictionary of the Apostolic Church:*

"D. F. Strauss, e.g., the most trenchant and remorseless of her critics in dealing with the Resurrection, acknowledges that it is the 'touchstone not of lives of Jesus only, but of Christianity itself,' that it 'touches all Christianity to the quick,' and is 'decisive for the whole view of Christianity' (*New Life of Jesus,* Eng. tr., 2 vols., London, 1865, i. 41, 397). If this goes, all that is vital and essential in Christianity goes; if this remains, all else remains. And so through the centuries, from Celsus onwards, the Resurrection has been the storm centre of the attack upon the Christian faith." 24/330

"Christ Himself," as *B. B. Warfield* puts it, "deliberately staked His whole claim to the credit of men upon His resurrection. When asked for a sign He pointed to this sign as His single and sufficient credential." 2/103

Ernest Kevan says of the famous Swiss theologian, Frederick Godet: "In his *Lectures in Defence of the Christian Faith* [1883, p. 41], [he] speaks of the importance of the resurrection of Christ, and points out that it was this miracle, and this alone, to which Christ referred as the attestation of His claims and authority." 32/3

Michael Green makes the point well: "Christianity does not hold the resurrection to be one among many tenets of belief. Without faith in the resurrection *there would be no Christianity at all*. The Christian church would never have begun; the Jesus-movement would have fizzled out like a damp squib with His execution. Christianity stands or falls with the truth of the resurrection. Once disprove it, and you have disposed of Christianity.

"Christianity is a historical religion. It claims that God has taken the risk of involving Himself in human history, and the facts are there for you to examine with the utmost rigour. They will stand any amount of critical investigation. . . ." 19/61

John Locke, the famous British philosopher, said concerning Christ's resurrection: "Our Saviour's resurrection . . . is truly of great importance in Christianity; so great that His being or not being the Messiah stands or falls with it: so that these two important articles are inseparable and in effect make one. For since that time, believe one and you believe both; deny one of them, and you can believe neither." 60/423

As *Philip Schaff,* the church historian, concludes: "The resurrection of Christ is therefore emphatically a test question upon which depends the truth or falsehood of the Christian religion. It is either the greatest miracle or the greatest delusion which history records." 56/173

Wilbur M. Smith, noted scholar and teacher, says: "No weapon has ever been forged, and . . . none ever will be, to destroy rational confidence in the historical records of this epochal and predicted event. The resurrection of Christ is the very citadel of the Christian faith. This is the doctrine that turned the world upside down in the first century, that lifted Christianity preeminently above Judaism and the pagan religions of the Mediterranean world. If this goes, so must almost everything else that is vital and unique in the Gospel of the Lord Jesus Christ: 'If Christ be not risen, then is your faith vain' " (I Cor. 15:17). 59/22

2A. THE CLAIMS OF CHRIST THAT HE WOULD BE RAISED FROM THE DEAD

1B. The Importance of the Claims

Wilbur M. Smith asserts:

"It was this same Jesus, the Christ who, among many other remarkable things, said and repeated something which, proceeding from any other being would have condemned him at once as either a bloated egotist or a dangerously unbalanced person. That Jesus said He was going up to Jerusalem to die is not so remarkable, though all the details He gave about that death, weeks and months before He died, are together a prophetic phenomenon. But when He said that He himself *would rise again from the dead,* the third day after He was crucified, He said something that only a fool would dare say, if he expected longer the devotion of any disciples, unless — He was sure He was going to rise. No founder of any world religion known to men ever dared say a thing like that!" 57/10,11

Christ predicted His resurrection in an unmistakable and straightforward manner. While His disciples simply couldn't understand it, the Jews took His assertions quite seriously.

Concerning the above point, *J. N. D. Anderson* makes the following observation:

"Not so very long ago there was in England a young man barrister, or what you would call a trial lawyer, by the name of Frank Morison. He was an unbeliever. For years he promised himself that one day he would write a book to disprove the resurrection finally and forever. At last he got the leisure. He was an honest man and he did the necessary study. Eventually [after accepting Christ] he wrote a book that you can buy as a paperback, *Who Moved the Stone?* Starting from the most critical possible approach to the New Testament documents he concludes *inter alia* that you can explain the trial and the conviction of Jesus only on the basis that He Himself had foretold His death and resurrection." 3/9

Smith says further: "If you or I should say to any group of friends that we expected to die, either by violence or naturally, at a certain time, but that, three days after death, we would rise again, we would be quietly taken away by friends, and confined to an institution, until our minds became clear and sound again. This would be right, for only a foolish man would go around talking about rising from the dead on the third day, only a foolish man, *unless* he knew that this was going to take place, and no one in the world has ever known that about himself except One Christ, the Son of God." 60/364

Bernard Ramm remarks: "Taking the Gospel record as faithful history there can be no doubt that Christ Himself anticipated His death and resurrection, and plainly declared it to His disciples. . . . The gospel writers are quite frank to admit that such predictions really did not penetrate their minds till the resurrection was a fact (John 20:9). But the evidence is there from the mouth of our Lord that He would come back from the dead after three days. He told them that He would be put to death violently, through the cause of hatred, and would rise the third day. All this came to pass." 52/191

John R. W. Stott writes:

"Jesus Himself never predicted His death without adding that He would rise, and described His coming resurrection as a 'sign.' Paul, at the beginning of his letter to the Romans, wrote that Jesus was 'designated Son of God in power . . . by His resurrection from the dead,' and the earliest sermons of the apostles recorded in the Acts repeatedly assert that by the resurrection God has reversed man's sentence and vindicated His Son." 63/47

2B. **The Claims as Given by Jesus:**

Jesus not only predicted His resurrection but also emphasized His rising from the dead would be the "sign" to authenticate His claims to be the Messiah (Matthew 12; John 2).

Matthew 12:38-40; 16:21; 17:9; 17:22,23; 20:18,19; 26:32; 27:63
Mark 8:31-9:1; 9:10; 9:31; 10:32-34; 14:28,58
Luke 9:22-27
John 2:18-22; 12:34; Chps. 14-16

Matthew 16:21 — "From that time Jesus Christ began to show His disciples that He must go to Jerusalem, and suffer many things from the elders and chief priests and scribes, and be killed, and be raised up on the third day."

Matthew 17:9 — "And as they were coming down from the mountain, Jesus commanded them, saying, 'Tell the vision to no one until the Son of Man has risen from the dead.' "

Matthew 17:22,23 — "And while they were gathering together in Galilee, Jesus said to them, 'The Son of Man is going to be delivered into the hands of men; and they will kill Him, and He will be raised again on the third day.' And they were deeply grieved."

Matthew 20:18,19 — "Behold, we are going up to Jerusalem; and the Son of Man will be delivered up to the chief priests and scribes, and they will condemn Him to death, and will deliver Him up to the Gentiles to mock and scourge and crucify Him, and on the third day He will be raised up."

Matthew 26:32 — "But after I have been raised, I will go before you to Galilee."

Mark 9:10 — "And they seized upon that statement, discussing with one another what rising from the dead might mean."

Luke 9:22-27 — " '. . . The Son of Man must suffer many things, and be rejected by the elders and chief priests and scribes, and be killed, and be raised up on the third day.' And He was saying to them all, 'If anyone wishes to come after Me, let him deny himself, and take up his cross daily, and follow Me. For whoever wishes to save his life shall lose it, but whoever loses his life for My sake, he is the one who will save it. For what is a man profited if he gains the whole world, and loses or forfeits himself? For whoever is ashamed of Me and My words, of him will the Son of Man be ashamed when He comes in His glory, and the glory of the Father and of the holy angels. But I tell you truly, there are some of those standing here who shall not taste death until they see the kingdom of God.' "

John 2:18-22 — "The Jews therefore answered and said to Him, 'What sign do You show to us, seeing that You do these things?' Jesus answered and said to them, 'Destroy this temple, and in three days I will raise it up.' The Jews therefore said, 'It took forty-six years to build this temple, and will you raise it up in three days?' But He was speaking of the temple of His body. When therefore He was raised from the dead, His disciples remembered that He said this; and they believed the Scripture, and the word which Jesus had spoken."

3A. THE HISTORICAL APPROACH

1B. The Resurrection of Christ as a Time-Space Dimension Event in History
(See pages 7-10.)

The resurrection of Christ is an event in history wherein God acted in a definite time-space dimension. Concerning this, Wilbur Smith says, "The *meaning* of the resurrection is a theological matter, but the fact of the resurrection is a historical matter; the nature of the resurrection body of Jesus may be a mystery, but the fact that the body disappeared from the tomb is a matter to be decided upon by historical evidence.

"The place is of geographical definiteness, the man who owned the tomb was a man living in the first half of the first century; that tomb was made out of rock in a hillside near Jerusalem, and was not composed of some mythological gossamer, or cloud-dust, but is something which has geographical significance. The guards put before that tomb were not aerial beings from Mt. Olympus; the Sanhedrin was a body of men meeting frequently in Jerusalem. As a vast mass of literature tells us, this person, Jesus, was a living person, a man among men, whatever else He was, and the disciples who went out to preach the risen Lord were men among men, men who ate, drank, slept, suffered, worked, died. What is there 'doctrinal' about this? This is a historical problem." 60/386

Ignatius (ca 50-115 A.D.), Bishop of Antioch, a native of Syria, a pupil of the apostle John, is said to have "been thrown to the wild beasts in the colosseum at Rome. His *Epistles* were written during his journey from Antioch to his martyrdom." At a time when he would undoubtedly have been very sober of mind, he says of Christ: "He was crucified and died under Pontius Pilate. He really, and not merely in appearance, was crucified, and died, in the sight of beings in heaven, and on earth, and under the earth.

"He also rose again in three days. . . . On the day of the preparation, then, at the third hour, He received the sentence from Pilate, the Father permitting that to happen; at the sixth hour He was crucified; at the ninth hour He gave up the ghost; and before sunset He was buried. During the

Sabbath He continued under the earth in the tomb in which Joseph of Arimathaea had laid Him.

"He was carried in the womb, even as we are, for the usual period of time; and was really born, as we also are; and was in reality nourished with milk, and partook of common meat and drink, even as we do. And when He had lived among men for thirty years, He was baptized by John, really and not in appearance; and when He had preached the gospel three years, and done signs and wonders, He who was Himself the Judge was judged by the Jews, falsely so called, and by Pilate the governor; was scourged, was smitten on the cheek, was spit upon; He wore a crown of thorns and a purple robe; He was condemned: He was crucified in reality, and not in appearance, not in imagination, not in deceit. He really died, and was buried, and rose from the dead. . . ." 47/209; 29/199-203

The brilliant historian *Alfred Edersheim* speaks of the particular time of Christ's death and resurrection:

"The brief spring-day was verging towards the 'evening of the Sabbath.' In general, the Law ordered that the body of a criminal should not be left hanging unburied over night. Perhaps in ordinary circumstances the Jews might not have appealed so confidently to Pilate as actually to ask him to shorten the sufferings of those on the Cross, since the punishment of crucifixion often lasted not only for hours but days, ere death ensued. But here was a special occasion. The Sabbath about to open was a 'high-day' — it was both a Sabbath and the second Paschal Day, which was regarded as in every respect equally sacred with the first — nay, more so, since the so-called Wavesheaf was then offered to the Lord." 15/612,613

As *Wilbur Smith* put it: "Let it simply be said that we know more about the details of the hours immediately before and the actual death of Jesus, in and near Jerusalem, than we know about the death of any other one man in all the ancient world." 60/360

"*Justin Martyr* (ca 100-165) philosopher, martyr, apologist. . . . Being an eager seeker for truth, knocked successively at the doors of Stoicism, Aristotelianism, Pythagoreanism and Platonism, but hated Epicureanism. . . . This zealous Platonist became a believing Christian. He said, 'I found this philosophy alone to be safe and profitable.' " 47/227

Indeed, Justin Martyr came to realize that while the philosophical systems of the world offered intellectual propositions, Christianity alone offered God Himself intervening in time and space through Jesus Christ. In a very straight-forward manner he asserts: ". . . Christ was born one hundred and fifty years ago under Cyrenius, and subsequently, in the time of Pontius Pilate. . . ." 40/46

Tertullian (ca 160-220) of Carthage, North Africa, says: "But the Jews were so exasperated by His teaching, by which their rulers and chiefs were convicted of the truth, chiefly because so many turned aside to Him, that at last they brought Him before Pontius Pilate, at the time Roman governor of Syria, and, by the violence of their outcries against Him, extorted a sentence giving Him up to them to be crucified." 67/94

Of Christ's ascension Tertullian asserts: It is "a fact more certain far than the assertions of your Proculi concerning Romulus" [Proculus was a Roman senator, who affirmed that Romulus had appeared to him after his death].

All these things Pilate did to Christ: and now "in fact a Christian in his own convictions, he sent word of Him to the reigning Caesar, who was at the time Tiberius. Yes, and the Caesars too would have believed on Christ, if either the Caesars had not been necessary for the world, or if

Christians could have been Caesars. His disciples also spreading over the world, did as their Divine Master bade them; and after suffering greatly themselves from the persecutions of the Jews, and with no unwilling heart, as having faith undoubting in the truth, at last by Nero's cruel sword sowed the seed of Christian blood at Rome." 67/95

Josephus, a Jewish historian, writing at the end of the first century A.D., has this fascinating passage in *Antiquities,* 18.3.3: "Now there was about this time Jesus, a wise man, if it be lawful to call him a man; for he was a doer of wonderful works, a teacher of such men as receive the truth with pleasure. He drew over to him many Jews, and also many of the Greeks. This man was the Christ. And when Pilate had condemned him to the cross, upon his impeachment by the principal man among us, those who had loved from the first did not forsake him, for he appeared to them alive on the third day, the divine prophets having spoken these and thousands of other wonderful things about him. And even now, the race of Christians, so named from him, has not died out."

Attempts have been made to show that Josephus could not have written this. (See page 82.) However, "this passage," writes Michael Green in *Man Alive,* "was in the text of Josephus used by Eusebius in the fourth century." Also, it is "reiterated by the most recent Loeb edition of his works. And it is all the more remarkable when we remember that, so far from being sympathetic to Christians, Josephus was a Jew writing to please the Romans. This story would not have pleased them in the slightest. He would hardly have included it if it were not true." 19/35,36

Professor Leaney says concerning the historical nature of the faith of the early Church: "The New Testament itself allows absolutely no escape from putting the matter as follows: Jesus was crucified and buried. His followers were utterly dejected. A very short time afterwards they were extremely elated and showed such reassurance as carried them by a sustained life of devotion through to a martyr's death. If we ask them through the proxy of writings dependent upon them, what caused this change, they do not answer, 'the gradual conviction that we were marked out by death but the crucified and buried one was alive' but 'Jesus who was dead appeared to some of us alive after his death and the rest of us believed their witness.' It may be worth noting that this way of putting the matter is a historical statement, like the historical statement, 'The Lord is risen indeed,' which has influenced men and women toward belief." 21/108

Speaking of the forensic nature of the New Testament narratives, *Bernard Ramm* says: "In Acts 1, Luke tells us that Jesus showed Himself alive by many infallible proofs (*en pollois tekmeriois*), an expression indicating the strongest type of legal evidence." 52/192

Clark Pinnock also states: "The certainty of the apostles was founded on their experiences in the factual realm. To them Jesus showed Himself alive 'by many infallible proofs' (Acts 1:3). The term Luke uses is *tekmerion,* which indicates a demonstrable proof. The disciples came to their Easter faith through inescapable empirical evidence available to them, and available to us through their written testimony. It is important for us, in an age that calls for evidence to sustain the Christian claim, to answer the call with appropriate historical considerations. For the resurrection stands within the realm of historical factuality, and constitutes excellent motivation for a person to trust Christ as Saviour." 4/11

Professor Ernest Kevan further establishes the evidential quality of these witnesses:

"The Book of the *Acts of the Apostles* was written by Luke sometime between A.D. 63 and the fall of Jerusalem in A.D. 70. He explains in the preface to his Gospel that he gathered his information from eye-witnesses, and this, it may be concluded, was also the way in which he prepared the Book of the *Acts.* Further as certain sections in the history show, by the use of the pronoun 'we,' Luke was himself a participator in some of the events which he narrates. He was in the midst of the early preaching, and took a share in the great happenings of the early days. Luke is, therefore, a contemporary and first-hand witness. . . . It is impossible to suppose that the Early Church did not know its own history; and the very fact of the acceptance by the Church of this book is evidence of its accuracy." 32/4,5

Quoting a noted Christian scholar, Kevan points out: "As the Church is too holy for a foundation of rottenness, so she is too real for a foundation of myth." 32/4,5

"For the establishment of an alleged historical fact no documents are esteemed to be more valuable than contemporary letters." 32/6

Professor Kevan says of the epistles of the New Testament, ". . . There is the unimpeachable evidence of the contemporary letters of Paul the Apostle. These epistles constitute historical evidence of the highest kind. The letters addressed to the *Galatians,* the *Corinthians,* and the *Romans,* about the authenticity and date of which there is very little dispute, belong to the time of Paul's missionary journeys, and may be dated in the period A.D. 55-58. This brings the evidence of the resurrection of Christ still nearer to the event: the interval is the short span of twenty-five years. Since Paul himself makes it plain that the subject of his letter was the same as that about which he had spoken to them when he was with them, this really brings back the evidence to a still earlier time." 32/6

Bernard Ramm says that even "the most cursory reading of the Gospels reveals the fact that the Gospels deal with the death and resurrection of Christ in far greater detail than any other part of the ministry of Christ. The details of the resurrection must not be artificially severed from the passion account." 52/191,192

Christ made many appearances after His resurrection. These appearances occurred at specific times in the lives of specific individuals and were further restricted to specific places.

For further information concerning the appearances of Christ after His resurrection, see pages 223,224.

Wolfhart Pannenberg, "professor of systematic theology at the University of Munich, Germany, studied under Barth and Jaspers, and has been concerned primarily with questions of the relation between faith and history. With a small group of dynamic theologians at Heidelberg, he has been forging a theology that considers its primary task the scrutiny of the historical data of the origins of Christianity." 4/9

The brilliant scholar says, "Whether the resurrection of Jesus took place or not is a historical question, and the historical question at this point is inescapable. And so the question has to be decided on the level of historical argument." 4/10

The New Testament scholar, *C. H. Dodd,* writes, "The resurrection remains an event within history. . . ." 64/3

J. N. D. Anderson, citing Cambridge professor *C. F. D. Moule,* asserts, "From the very first the conviction that Jesus had been raised from death has been that by which their very existence has stood or fallen. There was no other motive to account for them, to explain them. . . . At no point within the New Testament is there any evidence that the Christians stood for an original philosophy of life or an original ethic. Their sole function is to bear witness to what they claim as an event — the raising of Jesus from among the dead. . . . The one really distinctive thing for which the Christians stood was their declaration that Jesus had been raised from the dead according to God's design, and the consequent estimate of Him as in a unique sense Son of God and representative man, and the resulting conception of the way to reconciliation." 2/100,101

W. J. Sparrow-Simpson says: "The Resurrection of Christ is *the foundation of Apostolic Christianity,* and this for dogmatic just as truly as for evidential reasons. . . . Their consciousness of its basal character is shown in the position it occupies in their witness. An Apostle is ordained to be a witness of the Resurrection (Acts 1:22). The content of St. Paul's Christianity is thought at Athens to be 'Jesus and the resurrection' (17:18). The early sections in the Acts reiterate the statement, 'This Jesus hath God raised up, whereof we all are witnesses' (2:32).

"As a historic fact, it has been His Resurrection which has enabled men to believe in His official exaltation over humanity. It is not a mere question of the moral influence of His character, example, and teaching. It is that their present surrender to Him as their Redeemer has been promoted by this belief, and could not be justified without it. Indeed, those who deny His Resurrection consistently deny as a rule His Divinity and His redemptive work in any sense that St. Paul would have acknowledged." 25/513,514

2B.   The Testimony of History and Law

When an event takes place in history and there are enough people alive who were eyewitnesses of it or had participated in the event, and when the information is published, one is able to verify the validity of an historical event (circumstantial evidences).

William Lyon Phelps, for more than 40 years Yale's distinguished professor of English literature, author of some 20 volumes of literary studies, public orator of Yale, says:

"In the whole story of Jesus Christ, the most important event is the resurrection. Christian faith depends on this. It is encouraging to know that it is explicitly given by all four evanglists and told also by Paul. The names of those who saw Him after His triumph over death are recorded; and it may be said that the historical evidence for the resurrection is stronger than for any other miracle anywhere narrated; for as Paul said, if Christ is not risen from the dead then is our preaching in vain, and your faith is also vain." 57/18

"Professor Ambrose Fleming, emeritus professor of Electrical Engineering in the University of London, honorary fellow of St. John's College, Cambridge, receiver of the Faraday medal in 1928, . . . one of England's outstanding scientists . . ." says of the New Testament documents:

"We must take this evidence of experts as to the age and authenticity of this writing, just as we take the facts of astronomy on the evidence of astronomers who do not contradict each other. This being so, we can ask ourselves whether it is probable that such book, describing events that occurred about thirty or forty years previously, could have been accepted and cherished if the stories of abnormal events in it were false or mythical. It is impossible, because the memory of all elderly persons regarding events of thirty or forty years before is perfectly clear.

"No one could now issue a biography of Queen Victoria, who died thirty-one years ago, full of anecdotes which were quite untrue. They would be contradicted at once. They would certainly not be generally accepted and passed on as true. Hence, there is a great improbability that the account of the resurrection given by Mark, which agrees substantially with that given in the other Gospels, is a pure invention. This mythical theory has had to be abandoned because it will not bear close scrutiny. . . ." 60/427,428

Ambrose Fleming asserts that there is nothing in the Gospels that would cause a man of science to have problems with the miracles contained therein, and concludes with a challenge to intellectual honesty, asserting that if such a ". . . study is pursued with what eminent lawyers have called a willing mind, it will engender a deep assurance that the Christian Church is not founded on fictions, or nourished on delusions, or, as St. Peter calls them, 'cunningly devised fables,' but on historical and actual events, which, however strange they may be, are indeed the greatest events which have ever happened in the history of the world." 60/427,428

In a book which has become a best-seller, *Who Moved the Stone?, Frank Morison,* a lawyer, "tells us how he had been brought up in a rationalistic environment, and had come to the opinion that the resurrection was nothing but a fairy tale happy ending which spoiled the matchless story of Jesus. Therefore, he planned to write an account of the last tragic days of Jesus, allowing the full horror of the crime and the full heroism of Jesus to shine through. He would, of course, omit any suspicion of the miraculous, and would utterly discount the resurrection. But when he came to study the facts with care, he had to change his mind, and he wrote his book on the other side. His first chapter is significantly called, 'The Book that Refused to Be Written,' and the rest of his volume consists of one of the shrewdest and most attractively written assessments I have ever read. . . ." 19/54,55

The noted scholar, *Professor Edwin Gordon Selwyn,* says: "The fact that Christ rose from the dead on the third day in full continuity of body and soul — that fact seems as secure as historical evidence can make it." 57/14

Many impartial students who have approached the resurrection of Christ with a judicial spirit have been compelled by the weight of the evidence to belief in the resurrection as a fact of history. An example may be taken from a letter written by Sir Edward Clarke, K. C. to the Rev. E. L. Macassey:

"As a lawyer I have made a prolonged study of the evidences for the events of the first Easter Day. To me the evidence is conclusive, and over and over again in the High Court I have secured the verdict on evidence not nearly so compelling. Inference follows on evidence, and a truthful witness is always artless and disdains effect. The Gospel evidence for the resurrection is of this class, and as a lawyer I accept it unreservedly as the testimony of truthful men to facts they were able to substantiate." 63/47

"To one's amazement, though no department of Columbia University in this generation has been noted for its defense of the Christian faith, nor for praise offered to Jesus of Nazareth, yet its great *Encyclopedia,* the most important single volume of an encyclopedic nature in the English world, says, without apology, 'The Gospels do not leave Jesus in His grave. On the first day of the week some of the women going to the tomb found it opened, and the body of Jesus gone. An angel at the tomb told them that He had risen from the dead. Soon they saw Him and talked with Him, and His disciples met Him, and many others as well.' " 57/14

Professor Thomas Arnold, cited by Wilbur Smith, was for 14 years the famous headmaster of Rugby, author of a famous three-volume *History of*

Rome, appointed to the chair of Modern History at Oxford, and certainly a man well acquainted with the value of evidence in determining historical facts. This great scholar said:

"The evidence for our Lord's life and death and resurrection may be, and often has been, shown to be satisfactory; it is good according to the common rules for distinguishing good evidence from bad. Thousands and tens of thousands of persons have gone through it piece by piece, as carefully as every judge summing up on a most important cause. I have myself done it many times over, not to persuade others but to satisfy myself. I have been used for many years to study the histories of other times, and to examine and weigh the evidence of those who have written about them, and I know of no one fact in the history of mankind which is proved by better and fuller evidence of every sort, to the understanding of a fair inquirer, than the great sign which God hath given us that Christ died and rose again from the dead." 60/425,426

Wilbur Smith writes of a great legal authority of the last century. He refers to *John Singleton Copley,* better known as Lord Lyndhurst (1772-1863), recognized as one of the greatest legal minds in British history, the Solicitor-General of the British government in 1819, attorney-general of Great Britain in 1824, three times High Chancellor of England, and elected in 1846, High Steward of the University of Cambridge, thus holding in one lifetime the highest offices which a judge in Great Britain could ever have conferred upon him. When Chancellor Lyndhurst died, a document was found in his desk, among his private papers, giving an extended account of his own Christian faith, and in this precious, previously-unknown record, he wrote: "I know pretty well what evidence is; and I tell you, such evidence as that for the Resurrection has never broken down yet."

"This statement of Lord Lyndhurst was sent to Mr. E. H. Blakeney, of Winchester College, by the late Bishop H. C. G. Moule. Reference to the correspondence appeared in a British periodical, *Dawn,* some few years ago. I have since had it confirmed in a letter from Mr. Blakeney. In Marty Amoy's *The Domestic and Artistic Life of John Copley and Reminiscences of His Son, Lord Lyndhurst, High Chancellor of Great Britain* occurs the interesting note — 'A record of Lyndhurst's belief in the truth of religion, and his view of the scheme of redemption, was found in his own handwriting after his death, in the drawer of his writing table.' (Lord Lyndhurst died October 11, 1863, at the age of 91.)" 60/425,584

Simon Greenleaf (1783-1853) was the famous Royall Professor of Law at Harvard University, and succeeded Justice Joseph Story as the Dane Professor of Law in the same university, upon Story's death in 1846. 60/423

H. W. H. Knott says of this great authority in jurisprudence: "To the efforts of Story and Greenleaf is to be ascribed the rise of the Harvard Law School to its eminent position among the legal schools of the United States." 60/423

Greenleaf produced a famous work entitled *A Treatise on the Law of Evidence* which "is still considered the greatest single authority on evidence in the entire literature of legal procedure." 60/423

In 1846, while still Professor of Law at Harvard, Greenleaf wrote a volume entitled *An Examination of the Testimony of the Four Evangelists by the Rules of Evidence Administered in the Courts of Justice.* In his classic work the author examines the value of the testimony of the apostles to the resurrection of Christ. The following are this brilliant jurist's critical observations:

"The great truths which the apostles declared, were, that Christ had risen from the dead, and that only through repentance from sin, and faith in Him, could men hope for salvation. This doctrine they asserted with one voice, everywhere, not only under the greatest discouragements, but in the face of the most appalling errors that can be presented to the mind of man. Their master had recently perished as a malefactor, by the sentence of a public tribunal. His religion sought to overthrow the religions of the whole world. The laws of every country were against the teachings of His disciples. The interests and passions of all the rulers and great men in the world were against them. The fashion of the world was against them. Propagating this new faith, even in the most inoffensive and peaceful manner, they could expect nothing but contempt, opposition, revilings, bitter persecutions, stripes, imprisonments, torments, and cruel deaths. Yet this faith they zealously did propagate; and all these miseries they endured undismayed, nay, rejoicing. As one after another was put to a miserable death, the survivors only prosecuted their work with increased vigor and resolution. The annals of military warfare afford scarcely an example of the like heroic constancy, patience, and unblenching courage. They had every possible motive to review carefully the grounds of their faith, and the evidences of the great facts and truths which they asserted; and these motives were pressed upon their attention with the most melancholy and terrific frequency. It was therefore impossible that they could have persisted in affirming the truths they have narrated, had not Jesus actually risen from the dead, and had they not known this fact as certainly as they knew any other fact. If it were morally possible for them to have been deceived in this matter, every human motive operated to lead them to discover and avow their error. To have persisted in so gross a falsehood, after it was known to them, was not only to encounter, for life, all the evils which man could inflict, from without, but to endure also the pangs of inward and conscious guilt; with no hope of future peace, no testimony of a good conscience, no expectation of honor or esteem among men, no hope of happiness in this life, or in the world to come.

"Such conduct in the apostles would moreover have been utterly irreconcilable with the fact that they possessed the ordinary constitution of our common nature. Yet their lives do show them to have been men like all others of our race; swayed by the same motives, animated by the same hopes, affected by the same joys, subdued by the same sorrows, agitated by the same fears, and subject to the same passions, temptations, and infirmities, as ourselves. And their writings show them to have been men of vigorous understandings. If then their testimony was not true, there was no possible motive for its fabrication." 20/28-30

John Locke was probably the greatest philosopher of his century. This British scholar says in his work, *A Second Vindication of the Reasonableness of Christianity, Works,* cited by Wilbur Smith:

"There are some particulars in the history of our Saviour, allowed to be so peculiarly appropriated to the Messiah, such innumerable marks of Him, that to believe them of Jesus of Nazareth was in effect the same as to believe Him to be the Messiah, and so are put to express it. The principal of these is His Resurrection from the dead; which being the great and demonstrative proof of His being the Messiah, it is not at all strange that those believing His Resurrection should be put forth for believing Him to be the Messiah; since the declaring His Resurrection was declaring Him to be the Messiah." 60/422,423

Brooke Foss Westcott (1825-1901), English scholar who was appointed regius professor at Cambridge in 1870, said: "Indeed, taking all the evidence together, it is not too much to say that there is no historic incident better or more variously supported than the resurrection of Christ. Nothing but the antecedent assumption that it must be false could have suggested the idea of deficiency in the proof of it." 38/70

Clifford Herschel Moore, professor at Harvard University, well said, "Christianity knew its Saviour and Redeemer not as some god whose history was contained in a mythical faith, with rude, primitive, and even offensive elements. . . . Jesus was a historical not a mythical being. No remote or foul myth obtruded itself of the Christian believer; his faith was founded on positive, historical, and acceptable facts." 57/48

Benjamin Warfield of Princeton expressed in his article, "The Resurrection of Christ an Historical Fact, Evinced by Eye-Witnesses":

"The Incarnation of an Eternal God is Necessarily a Dogma; no human eye could witness His stooping to man's estate, no human tongue could bear witness to it as a fact and yet, if it be not a fact, our faith is vain, we are yet in our sins. On the other hand the Resurrection of Christ is a fact, an external occurrence within the cognizance of man, to be established by other testimonies and yet which is the cardinal doctrine of our system: on it all other doctrines hang." 60/361,362

Wilbur Smith introduces an outstanding scholar of this century: "One of the greatest physiologists of our generation is *Dr. A. C. Ivy,* of the Department of Chemical Science of the University of Illinois (Chicago Campus), who served as head of the Division of Physiology in Chicago Professional Colleges, 1946-1953. President of the American Physiological Society from 1939-1949 and author of many scientific articles, his words are wholesome:

" 'I believe in the bodily resurrection of Jesus Christ. As you say, this is a "personal matter," but I am not ashamed to let the world know what I believe, and that I can intellectually defend my belief. . . . I cannot prove this belief as I can prove certain scientific facts in my library which one hundred years ago were almost as mysterious as the resurrection of Jesus Christ. On the basis of historical evidence of existing biological knowledge, the scientist who is true to the philosophy of science can doubt the bodily resurrection of Jesus Christ, but he cannot deny it. Because to do so means that he can prove that it *did not* occur. I can only say that present-day biological science cannot resurrect a body that has been dead and entombed for three days. To deny the resurrection of Jesus Christ on the basis of what biology now knows is to manifest an unscientific attitude according to my philosophy of the true scientific attitude.' " 59/6,22

Michael Green says that ". . . two able young men, Gilbert West and Lord Lyttleton, went up to Oxford. They were friends of Dr. Johnson and Alexander Pope, in the swim of society. They were determined to attack the very basis of the Christian faith. So Lyttleton settled down to prove that Saul of Tarsus was never converted to Christianity, and West to demonstrate that Jesus never rose from the tomb.

"Some time later, they met to discuss their findings. Both were a little sheepish. For they had come independently to similar and disturbing conclusions. Lyttleton found, on examination, that Saul of Tarsus *did* become a radically new man through his conversion to Christianity; and West found that the evidence pointed unmistakably to the fact that Jesus did rise from the dead. You may still find his book in a large library. It is entitled *Observations on the History and Evidences of the Resurrection of Jesus Christ,* and was published in 1747. On the fly-leaf he has had printed his telling quotation from Ecclesiasticus 11:7, which might be adopted with profit by any modern agnostic: *'Blame not before thou hast examined the truth.'* " 19/55,56

"The evidence points unmistakably to the fact that on the third day Jesus rose. This was the conclusion to which a former Chief Justice of England, Lord Darling, came. At a private dinner party the talk turned to the truth of Christianity, and particularly to a certain book dealing with the resurrection. Placing his fingertips together, assuming a judicial attitude, and speaking with a quiet emphasis that was extraordinarily impressive, he said, 'We, as Christians, are asked to take a very great deal on trust; the teachings, for example, and the miracles of Jesus. If we had to take all on trust, I, for one, should be sceptical. The crux of the problem of whether Jesus was, or was not, what He proclaimed Himself to be, must surely depend upon the truth or otherwise of the resurrection. On that greatest point we are not merely asked to have faith. In its favour as living truth there exists such overwhelming evidence, positive and negative, factual and circumstantial, that no intelligent jury in the world could fail to bring in a verdict that the resurrection story is true.' " 19/53,54

Armand Nicholi, of Harvard Medical School, speaks of J. N. D. Anderson as ". . . a scholar of international repute and one eminently qualified to deal with the subject of evidence. He is one of the world's leading authorities on Islamic law. . . . He is dean of the faculty of law in the University of London, chairman of the department of Oriental law at the School of Oriental and African Studies, and director of the Institute of Advanced Legal Studies in the University of London." 3/4

This outstanding British scholar who is today influential in the field of international jurisprudence says: "The evidence for the historical basis of the Christian faith, for the essential validity of the New Testament witness to the person and teaching of Christ Himself, for the fact and significance of His atoning death, and for the historicity of the empty tomb and the apostolic testimony to the resurrection, is such as to provide an adequate foundation for the venture of faith." 2/106

3B. The Testimony of the Early Church Fathers

Professor W. J. Sparrow-Simpson says that "next to Christology, the Resurrection is undoubtedly the doctrine which held the chief place in early Christian literature.

"The sub-apostolic age presents many references, but the second century yields treatises exclusively devoted to it; as, for instance, Athenagoras, and the work ascribed to Justin Martyr." 62/339

Professor Bernard Ramm comments: "In both ecclesiastical history and creedal history the resurrection is affirmed from the earliest times. It is mentioned in Clement of Rome, *Epistle to the Corinthians* (A.D. 95), the earliest document of church history and so continuously throughout all of the patristic period. It appears in all forms of the *Apostles' Creed* and is never debated." 52/192

Sparrow-Simpson says:

"The substance of Ignatius' Gospel [ca 50–ca 115] is Jesus Christ, and the Christian religion consists in 'faith in Him and love toward Him, in His Passion and Resurrection.' He enjoins upon Christians to 'be fully convinced of the birth and passion and resurrection.'

"Jesus Christ is described as 'our hope through the Resurrection.' The Resurrection of Jesus is the promise of our Resurrection also.

"Ignatius further declares that the Church 'rejoices in the Passion of our Lord and in His Resurrection without wavering.' The main facts upon which he dwells are Christ's Cross and Death and Resurrection. These he groups together. Speaking of certain heretics, he says: 'They withhold themselves from Eucharist and prayer, because they confess not that the Eucharist is the flesh of our Saviour Jesus Christ, which flesh suffered for our sins, and which in His lovingkindness the Father raised up.' Again, he says that the Resurrection 'was both of the flesh and the spirit.' " 62/339

Sparrow-Simpson adds:

"In the Epistle of S. Polycarp to the Philippians (about A.D. 110) the writer speaks of our Lord Jesus Christ having 'endured to come so far as to death for our sins, whom God raised, having loosed the pains of death.' He says that God 'raised our Lord Jesus Christ from the dead and gave Him glory and a throne on His right hand, to Whom were subjected all things in heaven and on earth.' The Risen Jesus 'is coming as Judge of quick and dead.' And 'He that raised Him from the dead will raise us also, if we do His will and walk in His commandments.'

"To S. Polycarp the exalted Jesus is 'the Eternal High Priest.' And the saintly bishop's final prayer before his martyrdom was that he 'might take a portion in the number of the martyrs in the cup of Christ, to the resurrection of eternal life both of soul and body in the incorruption of the Holy Ghost.' " 62/341

Professor Sparrow-Simpson says of Justin Martyr's treatise on the resurrection (ca 100-165): It ". . . deals with distinctively Christian doctrine. Contempory opposition to the faith asserted that the Resurrection was impossible; undesirable, since the flesh is the cause of sins; inconceivable, since there can be no meaning in the survival of existing organs. They further maintained that the Resurrection of Christ was only in physical appearance and not in physical reality. To these objections and difficulties Justin . . . [made reply]. . . ." 62/342

Elgin Moyer in *Who Was Who in Church History* mentions another church father, Quintus Septimius Florens Tertullian:

"(ca 160-220) Latin church father and apologist, born in Carthage, North Africa. . . . Thorough education prepared him for successful writing in both Greek and Latin, as well as for politics, the practice of law, and forensic eloquence. For thirty or forty years lived in licentiousness. In about 190 he embraced Christianity with deep conviction. The rest of his life faithfully devoted to defending the Christian faith against heathen, Jew, and heretic. He was . . . a strong defender of the faith." 47/401

Bernard Ramm concludes: "Unbelief has to deny all the testimony of the Fathers. . . . It must assume that these men either did not have the motivation or the historical standards to really investigate the resurrection of Christ. The Fathers, considered by the Eastern Orthodox Catholic Church and by the Roman Catholic Church and Anglican Church as authoritative or highly authoritative, respected by the Reformers, and given due weight by all theologians, *are written off the record by unbelief.* They are deemed trustworthy for data about apostolic or near-apostolic theology, yet in matters of fact they are not granted a shred of evidential testimony. But this must be, or unbelief cannot make its case stick." 52/206

4A. THE CIRCUMSTANCES AT THE SCENE OF THE TOMB

1B. The Pre-resurrection Scene

1C. JESUS WAS DEAD

Mark records the following narrative of the events after Jesus' trial:

"And wishing to satisfy the multitude, Pilate released Barabbas for them, and after having Jesus scourged, he delivered Him over to be crucified. And the soldiers took Him away into the palace (that is, the Praetorium), and they called together the whole Roman cohort. And they dressed Him up in purple, and after weaving a crown of thorns, they put it on Him; and they began to acclaim Him, 'Hail, King of the Jews!' And they kept beating His head with a reed, and spitting at Him, and kneeling and bowing before Him. And after they had mocked Him, they took the purple off Him, and put His garments on Him. And they led Him out to crucify Him" (Mark 15:15-20).

The whipping of a victim prior to crucifixion is described by *John Mattingly:*

"The adjudged criminal was usually first forcefully stripped of his clothes, and then tied to a post or pillar in the tribunal. Then the awful and cruel scourging was administered by the lictors or scourgers. Although the Hebrews limited by their law the number of strokes in a scourging to forty, the Romans set no such limitation; and the victim was at the mercy of his scourgers.

"The brutal instrument used to scourge the victim was called a flagrum. Of this device Mattingly comments: 'It can readily be seen that the long, lashing pieces of bone and metal would greatly lacerate human flesh.' " 42/21

Bishop Eusebius of Caesarea, the church historian of the third century, said (*Epistle of the Church in Smyrna*) concerning the Roman scourging inflicted on those to be executed: the sufferer's "veins were laid bare, and . . . the very muscles, sinews, and bowels of the victim were open to exposure." 42/73

John Mattingly, citing *John Peter Lange,* says of Christ's sufferings: "It has been conjectured that [His] scourging even surpassed the severity of the normal one. Although the normal scourging was administered by lictors, Lange concludes that since there were no lictors at Pilate's disposal, he used the soldiers. Thus, from the very character of these low, vile soldiers, it may be supposed that they exceeded the brutality meted out by the lictors." 42/33

After suffering the most intense forms of physical punishment, Christ also had to endure the journey to the place of crucifixion — Golgotha. Of this stage of Christ's sufferings Mattingly relates:

1. "Even the preparation for the journey must have been a source of acute agony. Matthew 27:31 reads: 'And when they had mocked Him, they took the robe off from Him and put His own raiment on Him, and led Him away to crucify Him.' The rude stripping of the mock royal garments and the replacing of His own garments, undoubtedly on contact with the cut and bruised skin from the scourging, resulted in great pain." 42/35

2. "The phrase 'And they bring unto the place of Golgotha' (Mark 15:22a) would also indicate that Christ, unable to walk under His own power, had to be literally brought or borne along to the place of execution. Thus, the revolting and horrifying pre-cross sufferings were brought to a close, and the actual act of crucifying began." 42/36

Mark records the following narrative of Christ's crucifixion:

"And they brought Him to the place Golgotha, which is translated, Place of a Skull. And they tried to give Him wine mixed with myrrh; but He did not take it. And they crucified Him, and divided up His garments among themselves, casting lots for them, to decide what each should take. And it was the third hour when they crucified Him. And the inscription of the charge against Him read, 'THE KING OF THE JEWS.' And they crucified two robbers with Him; one on the right and one on the left. And those passing by were hurling abuse at Him, wagging their heads, and saying, 'Ha! You who were going to destroy the temple and rebuild it in three days, save Yourself, and come down from the cross!' In the same way the chief priests along with the scribes were also mocking Him among themselves and saying, 'He saved others: He cannot save Himself. Let this Christ, the King of Israel, now come down from the cross, so that we may see and believe!' And those who were crucified with Him were casting the same insult at Him. And when the sixth hour had come, darkness fell over the whole land until the ninth hour. And at the ninth hour Jesus cried out with a loud voice, 'Eloi, Eloi, lama sabachthani?' which is translated, 'My God, My God, why hast Thou forsaken Me?' And when some of the bystanders heard it, they began saying, 'Behold, He is calling for Elijah.' And someone ran and filled a sponge with sour wine, put it on a reed, and gave Him a drink, saying, 'Let us see whether Elijah will come to take Him down.' And Jesus uttered a loud cry, and breathed His last. And the veil of the temple was torn in two from top to bottom. And when the centurion, who was standing right in front of Him, saw the way He breathed His last, he said, 'Truly this man was the Son of God!' " (Mark 15: 22-27, 29-39).

Of the crucifixion itself, Mattingly says: "It cannot be overemphasized that the sufferings endured on the cross were extremely intense and severe. The abominableness of this torture was realized by Rome's most famous orator, Marcus Tullius Cicero, who said, 'Even the mere word, cross, must remain far not only from the lips of the citizens of Rome, but also from their thoughts, their eyes, their ears' [Marcus Tullius Cicero, *Pro Rabirio*, V, 16]." 42/26

Michael Green says of Jesus' physical sufferings: "After a sleepless night, in which He was given no food, endured the mockery of two trials, and had His back lacerated with the cruel Roman cat-o'-nine-tails, He was led out to execution by crucifixion. This was an excruciatingly painful death, in which every nerve in the body cried aloud in anguish." 19/32

Farrar gives a vivid description of death by crucifixion: "For indeed a death by crucifixion seems to include all that pain and death *can* have of horrible and ghastly — dizziness, cramp, thirst, starvation, sleeplessness, traumatic fever, tetanus, shame, publicity of shame, long continuance of torment, horror of anticipation, mortification of untended wounds — all intensified just up to the point at which they can be endured at all, but all stopping just short of the point which would give to the sufferer the relief of unconsciousness.

"The unnatural position made every movement painful; the lacerated veins and crushed tendons throbbed with incessant anguish; the wounds, inflamed by exposure, gradually gangrened; the arteries — especially at the head and stomach — became swollen and oppressed with surcharged blood; and while each variety of misery went on gradually increasing, there was added to them the intolerable pang of a burning and raging thirst; and all these physical complications caused an internal excitement and anxiety, which made the prospect of death itself — of death, the unknown enemy, at whose approach man usually shudders most — bear the aspect of a delicious and exquisite release." 18/440

Professor E. H. Day relates: "It is St. Mark who lays stress upon Pilate's wonder at hearing that Christ was already dead, and upon his personal questioning of the centurion before he would give leave for the removal of the body from the Cross. The Roman soldiers were not unfamiliar with the evidences of death, or with the sight of death following upon crucifixion." 13/46-48

As *Michael Green* points out, crucifixions were "not uncommon in Palestine." 19/32

Pilate required certification of Christ's death. Of this Green remarks: "Four executioners came to examine him, before a friend, Joseph of Arimathea, was allowed to take away the body for burial." 19/32

Green says of these four specialists who were accustomed to dealing with death: "They knew a dead man when they saw one — and their commanding officer had heard the condemned man's death cry himself and certified the death to the governor, Pontius Pilate. . . ." ["And when the centurion, who was standing right in front of Him, saw the way He breathed His last, he said, 'Truly this man was the Son of God' (Mark 15:39)!" "And Pilate wondered if He was dead by this time, and summoning the centurion, he questioned him as to whether He was already dead (Mark 15:44)."] 19/32,33

John R. W. Stott writes: "Pilate was indeed surprised that Jesus was already dead, but he was sufficiently convinced by the centurion's assurance to give Joseph permission to remove the body from the cross." 63/49

Professor Day observes that "the account in St. Matthew's Gospel of the guarding of the sepulchre is clear evidence that the Jews, for their part, believed that Jesus was dead." 13/46-48

Day further points out that none "of those who were occupied with the taking down of the body, and its laying in the grave, [had] any suspicion that life remained." 13/46-48

Professor Day, speaking of the volume *The Physical Cause of the Death of Christ,* says of its author, *James Thompson:* He "demonstrates that the death of Christ was due, not to physical exhaustion, or to the pains of crucifixion, but to agony of mind producing rupture of the heart. His energy of mind and body in the act of dissolution proves beyond contradiction that His death was not the result of exhaustion; the soldier's spear was the means to exhibiting to the world that His death was due to a cardiac rupture." 13/48,49

Samuel Houghton, M.D., the great physiologist from the University of Dublin, relates his view on the physical cause of Christ's death:

"When the soldier pierced with his spear the side of Christ, He was already dead; and the flow of blood and water that followed was either a natural phenomenon explicable by natural causes or it was a miracle. That St. John thought it, if not to be miraculous, at least to be unusual, appears plainly from the comment he makes upon it, and from the emphatic manner in which he solemnly declares his accuracy in narrating it.

"Repeated observations and experiments made upon men and animals have led me to the following results —

"When the left side is freely pierced after death by a large knife, comparable in size with a Roman spear, three distinct cases may be noted:

"1st. No flow of any kind follows the wound, except a slight trickling of blood.

"2nd. A copious flow of blood only follows the wound.

"3rd. A flow of water only, succeeded by a few drops of blood, follows the wound.

"Of these three cases, the first is that which usually occurs; the second is found in cases of death by drowning and by strychnia, and may be demonstrated by destroying an animal with that poison, and it can be proved to be the natural case of a crucified person; and the third is found in cases of death from pleurisy, pericarditis, and rupture of the heart. With the foregoing cases most anatomists who have devoted their attention to this subject are familiar; but the two following cases, although readily explicable on physiological principles, are not recorded in the books (except by St. John). Nor have I been fortunate enough to meet with them.

"4th. A copious flow of water, succeeded by a copious flow of blood, follows the wound.

"5th. A copious flow of blood, succeeded by a copious flow of water, follows the wound.

" . . . Death by crucifixion causes a condition of blood in the lungs similar to that produced by drowning and strychnia; the fourth case would occur in a crucified person who had previously to crucifixion suffered from pleuritic effusion; and the fifth case would occur in a crucified person, who had died upon the cross from rupture of the heart. The history of the days preceding our Lord's crucifixion effectually excludes the supposition of pleurisy, which is also out of the question if blood first and water afterwards followed the wound. There remains, therefore, no supposition possible to explain the recorded phenomenon except *the combination of the crucifixion and rupture of the heart.*

"That rupture of the heart was the cause of the death of Christ is ably maintained by Dr. William Stroud; and that rupture of the heart actually occurred I firmly believe. . . ." 11/349,350

The apostle John records a minutely detailed description of his observations at Golgotha. Houghton concludes:

"The importance of this is obvious. It [shows] that the narrative in St. John xix. could never have been invented; that the facts recorded must have been seen by an *eye-witness;* and that the eye-witness was so astonished that he apparently thought the phenomenon miraculous." 11/349,350

Michael Green writes of Christ's death: "We are told on eyewitness authority that 'blood and water' came out of the pierced side of Jesus (John 19: 34,35). The eyewitness clearly attached great importance to this. Had Jesus been alive when the spear pierced His side, strong spouts of blood would have emerged with every heart beat. Instead, the observer noticed semi-solid dark red clot seeping out, distinct and separate from the accompanying watery serum. This is evidence of massive clotting of the blood in the main arteries, and is exceptionally strong medical proof of death. It is all the more impressive because the evangelist could not possibly have realized its significance to a pathologist. The 'blood and water' from the spear-thrust is proof positive that Jesus was already dead." 19/33

Samuel Chandler says: "All the Evangelists agree, that *Joseph had begged* the body of *Jesus* off *Pilate;* who finding from the Centurion, who guarded the Cross, that He had been . . . *sometime dead,* gave it to him." 8/62,63

Professor Chandler then asserts that "the remarkable Circumstance of *wrapping up the dead Body in Spices*, by *Joseph* and *Nicodemus*, *according to the Manner of the Jews in burying*, is full Proof that Jesus *was dead*, and known to be dead. Had there indeed been *any Remains* of Life in Him, when taken down from the Cross, the *pungent Nature* of the Myrrh and Aloes, their strong Smell, their Bitterness, their being wrapped round His Body in Linens with *a Roller*, and over His Head *and Face* with a Napkin, *as was the Custom of the Jews to bury*, must have entirely extinguished them." 8/62,63

Paulus of Heidelberg, at the beginning of the last century, made a futile attempt to explain away the resurrection of Christ by asserting that Jesus didn't really die, but merely swooned or fainted on the cross. However, as *Bishop E. LeCamus* of La Rochelle, France, charges: "Medical science, which he invoked to sustain his thesis, was the first to destroy his system. He was informed that if Jesus had been taken down from the cross while still alive, He must have died in the tomb, as the contact of the body with the cold stone of the sepulchre would have been enough to bring on a syncope through the congelation of the blood, owing to the fact that the regular circulation was already checked. Besides, a man in a swoon is not revived ordinarily by being shut up in a cave, but by being brought out into the open air. The strong odour of aromatics in a place hermetically sealed would have killed a sick person whose brain was already seized with the most unyielding swoon. In our days, rationalists of every stripe reject this hypothesis, which is as absurd as it is odious, and all agree that the Crucified Jesus really died on Friday." 34/485,486

As *Professor Albert Roper* puts it, "Jesus was crucified by Roman soldiers, crucified according to the laws of Rome, which the soldiers had to the very last degree faithfully carried out." 54/33

In conclusion, we can agree with the statement made by the apostle John concerning his observations of Christ's death as he validated his testimony of the event:
"He who has seen has born witness, and his witness is true; and he knows that he is telling the truth. . . ." (John 19:35).

2C.   THE TOMB

Wilbur M. Smith observes that "the word for *tomb* or *sepulcher* occurs thirty-two times in these four Gospel records of the resurrection. . . ." 58/38

The tomb of Joseph of Arimathea on Easter morning was indeed a subject of much interest to the Gospel writers.

Concerning the burial given Christ, *W. J. Sparrow-Simpson* makes the following observation: "The Roman practice was to leave the victim of crucifixion hanging on the cross to become the prey of birds and beasts. But who would dream of saying that there were no exceptions to this rule? Josephus [*Autobiography*, ch. 75; *Wars of the Jews*, IV, v. 2] induced the Emperor Titus to take down from the cross three crucified persons while still alive. Would any one argue that this cannot be historic because the rule was otherwise? The Jewish practice, no doubt, was the burial of the condemned. This was the Jewish law. But Josephus assures us that even the Jews themselves broke the law of burial at times. In the 'Wars of the Jews,' he writes: 'They proceeded to that degree of impiety as to cast away their dead bodies without burial, although the Jews used to take so much care of the burial of men, that they took down those that were condemned and crucified, and buried them before the going down of the sun.'

"Loisy thinks that relatives might obtain permission for burial of one condemned. No relative, however, obtained it for Jesus' body: nor any of the Twelve. The three crucified men whom Josephus induced the imperial authority to take down from the cross were not relatives; they were only friends. He 'remembered them as his former acquaintances.' A strong case might be made out against the likelihood of Josephus' request, still more of its being granted. No one, however, appears to doubt the facts. They are constantly quoted as if they were true. Why should not Joseph of Arimathea make a similar request to Pilate?" 62/21,22

Henry Latham in *The Risen Master* gives the following information concerning Jesus' burial. He first cites ". . . the description of the Sepulchre of our Lord when it was supposed to have been newly discovered by the Empress Helena. The account is that of Eusebius of Caesarea — the father of Church History. It is taken from his *Theophania* — a work recovered during this century, and of which a translation was published by Dr. Lee at Cambridge in 1843.

"The grave itself was a cave which had evidently been hewn out; a cave that had now been cut out in the rock, and which had experienced (the reception of) no other body. For it was necessary that it, which was itself a wonder, should have the care of that corpse only. For it is astonishing to see even this rock, standing out erect, and alone on a level land, and having only one cavern within it; lest had there been many, the miracle of Him who overcame death should have been obscured.

"Extract from the *Architectural History of the Holy Sepulchre,* by Prof. Willis, formerly Jacksonian Professor in the University of Cambridge. *The Holy City:* G. Williams, Vol. I, p. 150.

" 'In many instances the sarcophagus, couch, or other resting-place, is hewn out of the solid rock, and thus must have been left standing out from the floor, or projecting from the sides, when this apartment was first excavated. When the stone couch was employed, its surface was either level, or merely hollowed out an inch or two in depth, to afford a resting-place; and a raised part is often left at the head, to serve as a pillow, or a round cavity cut for the same purpose. Such couches are found in the Etruscan rock-tombs, and in those of Greece and Asia Minor. . . . In the Jewish tombs of Syria the recess in the side of the chambers appears to have been always employed. But even this admits of great variety. In its simplest form, it is a rectangular opening or cavity in the face of the rocky side of the tomb, the bottom of it being usually higher than the floor of the chamber; and its length and depth just sufficient to admit of a human body being deposited in it. Often its upper surface or soffit is curved into an arch, which is either segmental or semicircular; and this, too, is its usual form when a sarcophagus is deposited in it.' " 33/87,88

Professor Guignebert, in his work, *Jesus,* p. 500, makes the following utterly unfounded statement: "The truth is that we do not know, and in all probability the disciples knew no better, where the body of Jesus had been thrown after it had been removed from the cross, probably by the executioners. It is more likely to have been cast into the *pit* for the executed than laid in a new *tomb.*" 60/372

1D. Professor Guignebert makes these assertions with absolutely no supporting evidence for his claims.

2D. He totally disregards the testimony to the events as preserved in the secular and ecclesiastical literature of the first three centuries.

3D. He completely ignores the perfectly straightforward narrative of the Gospel records:

1E. Why are the following accounts given if Christ's body was not actually taken by Joseph of Arimathea?

"And when it was evening, there came a rich man from Arimathea, named Joseph, who himself had also become a disciple of Jesus. This man came to Pilate and asked for the body of Jesus. Then Pilate ordered it to be given over to him" (Matthew 27:57,58).

"And when evening had already come, because it was the Preparation Day, that is, the day before the Sabbath, Joseph of Arimathea came, a prominent member of the Council, a man who was himself waiting for the kingdom of God; and he gathered up courage and went in before Pilate, and asked for the body of Jesus. And Pilate wondered if He was dead by this time, and summoning the centurion, he questioned him as to whether He was already dead. And ascertaining this from the centurion, he granted the body to Joseph" (Mark 15:42-45).

"And behold, a man named Joseph, who was a member of the Council, a good and righteous man, (he had not consented to their plan and action) a man from Arimathea, a city of the Jews, who was waiting for the kingdom of God, this man went to Pilate and asked for the body of Jesus" (Luke 23:50-52).

"And after these things Joseph of Arimathea, being a disciple of Jesus, but a secret one, for fear of the Jews, asked Pilate that he might take away the body of Jesus; and Pilate granted permission. He came therefore, and took away His body" (John 19:38).

The records speak for themselves; the body of Christ was anything but thrown into a pit for the executed!

2E. What about the accounts of the burial preparations?

"And Joseph took the body and wrapped it in a clean linen cloth . . ." (Matthew 27:59).

"And Joseph brought a linen sheet, took Him down, wrapped Him in the linen sheet . . ." (Mark 15:46).

"And when the Sabbath was over, Mary Magdalene, and Mary the mother of James, and Salome, bought spices, that they might come and anoint Him" (Mark 16:1).

"And they [the women who had come with Him out of Galilee] returned and prepared spices and perfumes" (Luke 23:56a).

"He [Joseph of Arimathea] came . . . and Nicodemus came also . . . bringing a mixture of myrrh and aloes, about a hundred pounds weight. And so they took the body of Jesus, and bound it in linen wrappings with the spices, as is the burial custom of the Jews" (John 19:38b-40).

Why are these accounts recorded if such preparations did not take place?

3E. What of the women who watched while Joseph of Arimathea and Nicodemus prepared and entombed Jesus' body? They had:

". . . followed after, and saw the tomb . . ." (Luke 23:55), and were ". . . sitting opposite the grave" (Matthew 27:61), and ". . . were looking on to see where He was laid" (Mark 15:47).

These women surely knew there was a tomb. The records make this point very obvious.

4E. How can one ignore the observations recorded concerning the tomb itself?

"And Joseph took the body . . . and laid it in his own new tomb . . ." (Matthew 27:59,60).

". . . which had been hewn out in the rock . ." (Mark 15:46).

". . . where no one had ever lain" (Luke 23:53).

which was located ". . . in the place where He was crucified . . . in the garden . . ." (John 19:41).

Professor Alford, the Greek scholar, states his observations on the evidence contained in the Gospel accounts:

"Matthew alone relates that it was Joseph's *own* tomb. John, that it was *in a garden*, and *in the place where he was crucified*. All, except Mark, notice the *newness* of the tomb. John does not mention that it *belonged to Joseph*. . . ." 1/298,299

Of Joseph of Arimathea, he says: "His reason for the body being laid there is that *it was near*, and the preparation rendered haste necessary." 1/298,299

Concluding from Alford's comments, then, the evidence "that we can determine respecting the sepulchre from the data here furnished, is (1) That it was not a *natural* cave, but an *artificial excavation in the rock*. (2) That it was not cut *downwards*, after the manner of a grave with us, but *horizontally or nearly so*, into the face of the rock." 1/298,299

5E. Why did the Jews ask Pilate to place a guard at Christ's tomb, if no such sepulcher existed?

"Now on the next day, which is the one after the preparation, the chief priests and the Pharisees gathered together with Pilate, and said, 'Sir, we remember that when he was still alive that deceiver said, "After three days I am to rise again." Therefore, give orders for the grave to be made secure until the third day, lest the disciples come and steal Him away and say to the people, "He has risen from the dead," and the last deception will be worse than the first.' Pilate said to them, 'You have a guard; go, make it as secure as you know how.' And they went and made the grave secure, and along with the guard they set a seal on the stone" (Matthew 27:62-66).

Indeed, the truth of the matter is plain, as Professor Major so clearly puts it: "Had the body of Christ merely been thrown into a common grave and left unattended, there would have been no possible reason for the anxiety of His enemies to spread the report that the body had been stolen." 60/578

6E. What are we to think of the visit of the women to the tomb after the Sabbath?

"Now late on the Sabbath, as it began to dawn toward the first day of the week, Mary Magdalene and the other Mary came to look at the grave" (Matthew 28:1).

"And very early on the first day of the week, they came to the tomb when the sun had risen" (Mark 16:2).

". . . On the first day of the week, at early dawn, they [the women who had come with Him out of Galilee] came to the tomb, bringing the spices which they had prepared" (Luke 24:1).

"Now on the first day of the week Mary Magdalene came early to the tomb, while it was still dark, and saw the stone already taken away from the tomb" (John 20:1).

If Jesus hadn't actually been entombed in Joseph's grave, records of such a visit would not appear in the Gospel narratives.

7E. What are we to think of Peter's and John's visit to the tomb after hearing the women's report?

"But Peter arose and ran to the tomb; stooping and looking in, he saw the linen wrappings only; and he went away to his home, marveling at that which had happened" (Luke 24:12).

"Peter therefore went forth, and the other disciple [John], and they were going to the tomb. And the two were running together; and the other disciple ran ahead faster than Peter, and came to the tomb first; and stooping and looking in, he saw the linen wrappings lying there; but he did not go in. Simon Peter therefore also came, following him, and entered the tomb; and he beheld the linen wrappings lying there, and the face-cloth, which had been on His head, not lying with the linen wrappings, but rolled up in a place by itself. Then entered in therefore the other disciple also, who had first come to the tomb, and he saw, and believed" (John 20:3-8).

The evidence of this narrative is likewise ignored.

8E. Wilbur M. Smith makes the following statement concerning Guignebert's hypothesis:

"He denies the fact which the four Gospels clearly set forth, that the body of Jesus was placed in the tomb of Joseph of Arimathea. Denying this he presents no evidence to contradict it, but makes a statement which proceeds out of his own imagination. In fact, one would say his statement about the body of Jesus proceeds not alone from his imagination, but from his preconceived [philosophical, not historical, prejudice] determination. . . ." 60/372

The evidence clearly speaks for itself, but Professor Guignebert refuses to acknowledge the evidence because it does not agree with his world view that the miraculous is not possible. The French professor draws his conclusions in spite of the evidence, not because of it. Indeed, as Smith says of his theory: "We dismiss it, as being utterly without historical foundation, and for this reason not deserving further consideration, in studying the four *historical* documents we have in front of us, known as the Gospels." 60/372

3C. THE BURIAL

In discussing the records of Jesus' entombment in Joseph of Arimathea's sepulcher, *Wilbur Smith* writes: "We know more about the burial of the Lord Jesus than we know of the burial of any single character in all of ancient history. We know infinitely more about His burial than we do the burial of any Old Testament character, of any king of Babylon, Pharaoh of Egypt, any philosopher of Greece, or triumphant Caesar. We know who took His body from the cross; we know something of the wrapping of the body in spices, and burial clothes; we know the very tomb in which this body was placed, the name of the man who owned it, Joseph, of a town known as Arimathaea. We know even where this tomb was located, in a garden nigh to the place where He was crucified, outside the city walls. We have four records of this burial of our Lord, all of them in amazing agreement, the record of Matthew, a disciple of Christ who was there when Jesus was crucified; the record of Mark, which some say was written within ten years of our Lord's ascension; the record of Luke, a companion of the apostle Paul, and a great historian; and the record of John, who was the last to leave the cross, and, with Peter, the first of the Twelve on Easter to behold the empty tomb." 60/370,371

The historian, *Alfred Edersheim,* gives these details of the burial customs of the Jews:

"Not only the rich, but even those moderately well-to-do, had tombs of their own, which probably were acquired and prepared long before they were needed, and treated and inherited as private and personal property. In such caves, or rock-hewn tombs, the bodies were laid, having been anointed with many spices, with myrtle, aloes, and, at a later period, also with hyssop, rose-oil, and rose-water. The body was dressed and, at a later period, wrapped, if possible, in the worn cloths in which originally a Roll of the Law had been held. The 'tombs' were either 'rock-hewn,' or natural 'caves' or else large walled vaults, with niches along the sides." 15/318,319

Of Christ's burial Edersheim says: "The proximity of the holy Sabbath, and the consequent need of haste, may have suggested or determined the proposal of Joseph to lay the Body of Jesus in his own rock-hewn new tomb, wherein no one had yet been laid. . . .

"The Cross was lowered and laid on the ground; the cruel nails drawn out, and the ropes unloosed. Joseph, with those who attended him, 'wrapped' the Sacred Body 'in a clean linen cloth,' and rapidly carried It to the rock-hewn tomb in the garden close by. Such a rock-hewn tomb or cave (*Meartha*) had niches (*Kukhin*), where the dead were laid. It will be remembered, that at the entrance to 'the tomb' — and within 'the rock' — there was 'a court,' nine feet square, where ordinarily the bier was deposited, and its bearers gathered to do the last offices for the Dead." 15/617

Edersheim next mentions: ". . . that other Sanhedrist, Nicodemus . . . [who] now came, bringing 'a roll' of myrrh and aloes, in the fragrant mixture well known to the Jews for purposes of anointing or burying.

"It was in 'the court' of the tomb that the hasty embalmment — if such it may be called — took place." 15/617

It was customary in Christ's time to use great quantities of spices for embalming the dead, especially for those held in high esteem.

Michael Green relates the following concerning the burial preparation given Jesus' remains:

"The body was placed on a stone ledge, wound tightly in strips of cloth, and covered with spices. St. John's Gospel tells us that some seventy-pounds were used, and that it is likely enough. Joseph was a rich man, and no doubt wanted to make up for his cowardliness during the lifetime of Jesus by giving him a splendid funeral. The amount, though great, has plenty of parallels. Rabbi Gamaliel, a contemporary of Jesus, was buried with eighty pounds of spices when he died." 19/33

Flavius Josephus, the Jewish historian of the first century, mentions the funeral of Aristobulus, who was "murdered, being not eighteen years old, and having kept the high priesthood one year only" [*Antiquities of the Jews,* XV, iii, 3].

At his funeral Herod "took care [that it] should be very magnificent, by making great preparation for a sepulchre to lay his [Aristobulus] body in, and providing a great quantity of spices, and burying many ornaments together with him" [*Antiquities of the Jews,* XVII, viii, 3].

Professor James Hastings says concerning the grave clothes found in Christ's empty tomb: "As far back as Chrysostom's time [the 4th century A.D.] attention was called to the fact that the myrrh was a drug which adheres so closely to the body that the grave clothes would not easily be removed" (Joan. Hom. 85). 25/507

Merrill Tenney explains the graveclothes as follows: "In preparing a body for burial according to Jewish custom, it was usually washed and straightened, and then bandaged tightly from the armpits to the ankles in strips of linen about a foot wide. Aromatic spices, often of a gummy consistency, were placed between the wrappings or folds. They served partially as a preservative and partially as a cement to glue the cloth wrappings into a solid covering. . . . John's term 'bound' (Gr. *edesan*) is in perfect accord with the language of Lk. 23:53, where the writer says that the body was *wrapped* . . . in linen. . . . On the morning of the first day of the week the body of Jesus had vanished, but the graveclothes were still there. . . ." 66/117

Professor George B. Eager in *The International Standard Bible Encyclopedia* says of Christ's burial: "It was in strict accordance with such customs and the provision of the Mosaic law (Deut. 21:23) ["His corpse shall not hang all night on the tree, but you shall surely bury him on the same day (for he who is hanged is accursed of God), so that you do not defile your land which the Lord your God gives you as an inheritance."] (cf. Gal. 3:13) ["Christ redeemed us from the curse of the Law, having become a curse for us — for it is written, 'CURSED IS EVERYONE WHO HANGS ON A TREE.' "], as well as in compliance with the impulses of true humanity, that Joseph of Arimathea went to Pilate and begged the body of Jesus for burial on the very day of the crucifixion (Matthew 27:58ff.)." 48/529

Professor Eager further observes: "Missionaries and natives of Syria tell us that it is still customary to wash the body (cf. John 12:7; 19:90; Mark 16:1; Luke 24:1), swathe hands and feet in gravebands, usually of linen (John 19:40), and cover the face or bind it about with a napkin or handkerchief (John 11:44b). It is still common to place in the wrappings of the body aromatic spices and other preparations to retard decomposition . . . we are . . . told that after the burial of Jesus, Nicodemus brought 'a mixture of myrrh and aloes, about a hundred pounds,' and that they 'took the body of Jesus, and bound it in linen wrappings with the spices, as the custom of the Jews is to bury,' and that Mary Magdalene and two other women brought spices for the same purpose (Mark 16:1; Luke 23:56)." 48/529

Henry Latham gives the following details concerning Christ's burial:

"We can make out . . . from ancient authorities, that the body was borne to burial without coffin or enclosure of any kind; it was carried on men's shoulders on a bier, and was either attired in the ordinary garb, bound round with grave-bands, in order, perhaps, to keep in the spices, or else it was swathed in linen cloths. 'The face of the dead body,' says Dr. Edersheim (Vol. I. p. 556), 'was uncovered. The body lay with its face turned upwards, and its hands folded on the breast.' I believe, judging from existing usage . . . that the neck and the upper surface of the shoulders were commonly left bare as well as the face.

"The Lord's body, we read (S. John xix. 38-41), was prepared for the tomb in great haste by Nicodemus and Joseph of Arimathaea. I suppose it to have been wrapped in three or four lengths of linen cloth, with abundant spices between each fold, and the napkin to have been twirled round the head, with its ends interlaced. When the body was laid in the tomb, the head would have rested upon the raised portion of the ledge at the far end which served for a pillow.

"I now come to the matter of the spices. Neither in S. John's Gospel, nor in any of the others, is it said that any spices were seen in the tomb. This makes a significant feature in my case. My contention is that the spice lay between the folds of the linen wrappers. That the amount of spice, named by S. John as brought by Nicodemus for the preparation of the body for the tomb, is extremely large, has been commonly noticed: the quantity, however, is of less importance to me than the fact, which seems to be established by the best authorities, that the spices were dry, and would therefore fall to the ground in a heap if the body were placed in an erect posture, or the cerements were removed. A quantity that weighed a hundred pounds would be conspicuous by its bulk. What is here called 'aloes' was a fragrant wood pounded or reduced to dust, while the myrrh was an aromatic gum, morsels of which were mixed with the powdered wood. It was also the practice, so we gather, to anoint the body with a semi-liquid unguent such as nard. One effect of this would be to cause the powder immediately about the body to adhere to it, but the great bulk of it would remain dry. The head and hair were also anointed with this unguent. I do not find that the powdered spice was applied to the face or head. When, however, our Lord's body was hurriedly prepared for the tomb, there would be no time for anointing the body or for any elaborate process, because sunset was fast approaching and with it the Sabbath would come. The body would be simply embedded in the powdered spice. It may have been that the women desired to repair this omission as far as they could, and that what they brought on the Sunday morning was nard, or some costly unguent, in order to complete the anointing. S. John speaks only of myrrh and aloes, but S. Luke says that the women prepared spices and *ointments,* and in S. Mark we have 'they bought sweet spices that they might come and *anoint* him' (chap. xvi. I). Possibly they did not intend to disturb the grave-clothes, but only to anoint the head and neck with the unguents." 33/35-37

4C.   THE STONE

Concerning that which covered the opening of Jesus' tomb, *A. B. Bruce* says:

"The Jews called the stone *golel.*" 6/334

H. W. Holloman, citing G. M. Mackie, says: "The opening to the central chamber was guarded by a large and heavy disc of rock which could roll along a groove slightly depressed at the centre, in front of the tomb entrance." 28/38

Professor T. J. Thorburn mentions that this stone was used "as a protection against both men and beasts." He further observes: "This stone is often mentioned by the Talmudists. According to Maimonides, a structure *ex lingo, alia Materia* was also used." Of the enormous size of such a stone Dr. Thorburn comments: "It usually required several men to remove it." Since the one rolled to the entrance of Jesus' tomb was intended to prevent an expected theft, it was probably even larger than what would normally have been used! 68/97,98

Indeed, concerning the tremendous weight of the rock, Thorburn remarks: "A gloss in Cod. Bez. [a phrase written in parenthesis, within the text of Mark 16:4 as found in a [fourth] century manuscript (Codex Bezae in the Cambridge Library)] adds, 'And when he was laid there, he (Joseph) put against the tomb a stone which twenty men could not roll away.' " The significance of Dr. Thorburn's observation is realized when one considers the rules for transcribing manuscripts. It was the custom that if a copier was emphasizing his own interpretation, he would write his thought in the margin and not include it within the text. One might conclude, therefore, that the insert in the text was copied from a text even closer to the time of Christ, perhaps a first century manuscript. The phrase, then, could have been recorded by an eye-witness who was impressed with the enormity of the stone which was rolled against Jesus' sepulchre. Gilbert West of Oxford also brings out the importance of this portion of the Bezae Codex on pp. 37,38 of his work, *Observations on the History and Evidences of the Resurrection of Jesus Christ.* 68/1,2

Professor Samuel Chandler says: "The Witnesses here all agree, that when the Women came, *they found the Stone rolled or* taken away. The Women could not do it, the Stone being *too large* for them to move." 8/33

Professor Edersheim, the Hebrew-Christian who is an exceptionally good source for the historical background of the New Testament times, relates the following concerning Jesus' burial: "And so they laid Him to rest in the niche of the rock-hewn new tomb. And as they went out, they rolled, as was the custom, a 'great stone' — the *Golel* — to close the entrance to the tomb, probably leaning against it for support, as was the practice, a smaller stone — the so-called *Dopheg.* It would be where the one stone was laid against the other, that on the next day, the Sabbath though it was, the Jewish authorities would have affixed the seal, so that the slightest disturbance might become apparent." 15/618

Professor Frank Morison, commenting on the visit of Mary and her friends to Jesus' tomb that early Sunday morning, says:

"The question as to how they were to remove this stone must of necessity have been a source of considerable perplexity to the women. Two of them at least had witnessed the interment and knew roughly how things stood. The stone, which is known to have been large and of considerable weight, was their great difficulty. When, therefore, we find in the earliest record, the Gospel of St. Mark, the words: 'Who shall roll us away the stone from the door of the tomb?' we can hardly avoid feeling that this preoccupation of the women with the question of the stone is not only a psychological necessity of the problem, but a definitely historical element in the situation right up to the moment of their arrival at the grave." 46/76

Morison calls the stone at Jesus' tomb "the one silent and infallible witness in the whole episode — and there are certain facts about this stone which call for very careful study and investigation." 46/147

"Let us begin by considering first its size and probable character. . . . no doubt . . . the stone was large and consequently very heavy. This fact is asserted or implied by all the writers who refer to it. St. Mark says it was 'exceeding great.' St. Matthew speaks of it as 'a great stone.' Peter says, 'for the stone was great.' Additional testimony on this point is furnished by the reported anxiety of the women as to how they should move it. If the stone had not been of considerable weight the combined strength of three women should have been capable of moving it. We receive, therefore, a very definite impression that it was at least too weighty for the women to remove unaided. All this has a very definite bearing upon the case. . . ." 46/147

5C.   THE SEAL

Matthew 27:66 states: "And they went and made the grave secure, and along with the guard they set a seal on the stone."

A. T. Robertson says that the method of sealing the stone at Jesus' tomb was ". . . probably by a cord stretched across the stone and sealed at each end as in Dan. 6:17 ['And a stone was brought and laid over the mouth of the den; and the king sealed it with his own signet ring and with the signet rings of his nobles, so that nothing might be changed in regard to Daniel.']. The sealing was done in the presence of the Roman guards who were left in charge to protect this stamp of Roman authority and power. They did their best to prevent theft and the resurrection (Bruce), but they overreached themselves and provided additional witness to the fact of the empty tomb and the resurrection of Jesus (Plummer)." 53/239

A. B. Bruce observed that "the participial clause [sealing the stone] is a parenthesis pointing to an additional precaution, sealing the stone, with a thread over it and sealed to the tomb at either end. The worthy men did their best to prevent theft, and — the resurrection!" 6/335

Henry Sumner Maine, ". . . member of the Supreme Council of India; formerly Reader on Jurisprudence and the Civil Law at the Middle Temple, and Regius Professor of the Civil Law in the University of Cambridge," speaks of the legal authority attached to the Roman seal. He points out that it was actually "considered as a mode of authentication." 37/203

In the area of jurisprudence, Maine continues, "We may observe, that the seals of Roman Wills and other documents of importance did not only serve as the index of the presence or assent of the signatory, but were also literally fastenings which had to be broken before the writing could be inspected." 39/203,204

Considering in like manner the securing of Jesus' tomb, the Roman seal affixed thereon was meant to prevent any attempted vandalizing of the sepulcher. Anyone trying to move the stone from the tomb's entrance would have broken the seal and thus incurred the wrath of Roman law.

Professor Henry Alford says, "The sealing was by means of a cord or string passing across the stone at the mouth of the sepulchre, and fastened at either end to the rock by sealing-clay." 1/301

Marvin Vincent comments: "The idea is that they sealed the stone in the presence of the guard, and then left them to keep watch. It would be important that the guard should witness the sealing. The sealing was performed by stretching a cord across the stone and fastening it to the rock at either end by means of sealing clay. Or, if the stone at the door happened to be fastened with a cross beam, this latter was sealed to the rock." 70/147

Professor D. D. Whedon says: "The door could not be opened, therefore, without breaking the seal; which was a crime against the authority of the proprietor of the seal. The guard was to prevent the duplicity of the disciples; the seal was to secure against the collusion of the guard. So in Dan. vi, 17: 'A stone was brought, and laid upon the mouth of the den; and the king sealed it with his own signet and with the signet of his lord.' " 72/343

John Chrysostom, Archbishop of Constantinople in the fourth century, records the following observations concerning the security measures taken at Jesus' tomb:

"See, at any rate, these words bearing witness to every one of these facts. 'We remember,' these are the words, 'that that deceiver said, when He was yet alive,' (He was therefore now dead), 'After three days I rise again. Command therefore that the sepulchre be sealed,' (He was therefore buried), 'lest His disciples come and steal Him away.' So that if the sepulchre be sealed, there will be no unfair dealing. For there could not be. So then the proof of His resurrection has become incontrovertible by what ye have put forward. For because it was sealed, there was no unfair dealing. But if there was no unfair dealing, and the sepulchre was found empty, it is manifest that He is risen, plainly and incontrovertibly. Seest thou, how even against their will they contend for the proof of the truth?" 9/525

6C.   THE GUARD AT THE TOMB

1D.   The narrative of Matthew 27: 62-66 reads as follows: "Now on the next day, which is the one after the preparation, the chief priests and the Pharisees gathered together with Pilate, and said, 'Sir, we remember that when He was still alive that deceiver said, "After three days I am to rise again." Therefore, give orders for the grave to be made secure until the third day, lest the disciples come and steal Him away and say to the people, "He has risen from the dead," and the last deception will be worse than the first.' Pilate said to them. 'You have a guard; go, make it as secure as you know how.' And they went and made the grave secure, and along with the guard they set a seal on the stone."

Commenting on this passage, *Albert Roper* in *Did Jesus Rise from the Dead?* makes the following observations:

"Led by Annas and Caiaphas, their chief priests, a deputation of Jewish leaders sought out Pilate, to request that the tomb wherein Jesus was buried be sealed and that a Roman guard be stationed around it, giving as their motive their fear that the friends of Jesus might come stealthily by night and steal His body in order to make it appear that a resurrection had taken place.

"To this request the acquiescent Pilate responded: 'Ye shall have a guard; go your way; make it secure according to your wish.' They went their way, attended by a guard of Roman soldiers numbering from ten to thirty who, under their direction, sealed the tomb of Joseph of Arimathaea with the Imperial Seals of Rome, affixing thereto in wax the official stamp of the procurator himself which it would be a high crime even to deface. Thus did these zealous enemies of Jesus unwittingly prepare in advance an unanswerable challenge to their subsequent explanation of the resurrection — an explanation which did not, and could not, in the very nature of things explain [it]. . . ." 54/23,24

Professor Albert Roper continues: "Commanding the guard was a centurion designated by Pilate, presumably one in which he had full confidence, whose name according to tradition was Petronius.

"It is, therefore, reasonable to assume that these representatives of the Emperor could have been trusted to perform their duty to guard a tomb quite as strictly and as faithfully as they had executed a crucifixion. They had not the slightest interest in the task to which they were assigned. Their sole purpose and obligation was rigidly to perform their duty as soldiers of the empire of Rome to which they had dedicated their allegiance. The Roman seal affixed to the stone before Joseph's tomb was far more sacred to them than all the philosophy of Israel or the sanctity of her ancient creed. Soldiers cold-blooded enough to gamble over a dying victim's cloak are not the kind of men to be hoodwinked by timid Galileans or to jeopardize their Roman necks by sleeping on their post." 54/33

2D.   There has been much discussion concerning the phrase in Matthew 27:65, "You have a guard." The question is whether this term speaks of the "temple police" or a "Roman guard."

Professor Alford says the phrase can be translated "either (1), indicative, *Ye have:* — but then the question arises, *What guard* had they? and if they had one, why go to Pilate? Perhaps we must understand some detachment placed at their disposal during the feast — but there does not seem to be any record of such a practice . . . or (2) . . . imperative; . . . and the sense . . . would be, *Take a body of men for a guard*." 1/301

Mgr. E. Le Camus says: "Some think that Pilate here means ministers of the Temple whom the chief priests had in their service, and whom they might employ with advantage in guarding a tomb. It would be easier to explain the corruption of the latter than that of Roman soldiers in inducing them to declare that they had slept when they should have kept watch. Nevertheless, the word . . . [*koustodia*] borrowed from the Latin, would seem to indicate a *Roman* guard, and the mention of the captain . . . (St. Matt. xxviii, 14) ought to make this opinion prevail." 34/392

A. T. Robertson, the noted Greek scholar, says that the phrase " 'Have a guard' (*echete koustodian*) [is] present imperative [and refers to] a guard of Roman soldiers, not mere temple police." 53/239

Robertson further observes that "the Latin term *koustodia* occurs in an Oxyrhynchus papyrus of A. D. 22." 53/239

Professor T. J. Thorburn remarks: "It is generally assumed that Matthew means it to be understood that the guard referred to consisted of *Roman* soldiers. . . . However . . . the priests had a Jewish Temple guard, which would probably not be allowed by the Romans to discharge any duties outside those precincts. Pilate's reply, therefore, which may read either, 'Take a guard,' or '*Ye have a guard*' (a polite form of refusal, if the request was for Roman soldiers), may be understood in either sense. If the guard were Jewish it would explain the fact that Pilate overlooked the negligence. Ver. 14 ['And if this should come to the governor's ears, we will win him over and keep you out of trouble.'], however, seems against this view. . . ." 68/179-182

A. B. Bruce says of the phrase "You have": ". . . probably imperative, not indicative — have your watch, the ready assent of a man who thinks there is not likely to be much need for it, but has no objections to gratify their wish in a small matter." 6/335

Arndt and Gingrich (*A Greek-English Lexicon of the New Testament,* University of Chicago Press, 1952) cite the following sources wherein the word for guard, *Koustodia,* is found:

"POxy.294,20 [22 ad]; PRyl.189,2; BGU 341,3; cf. Hahn 233,6; 234,7 w. lit. Lat. loanw., custodia, also in rabb.). . . ." 5/448

They define it as being "*a guard* composed of soldiers" Matthew 27:66; 28:11 . . . "*take a guard*" 27:65. 5/448

Professor Harold Smith in *A Dictionary of Christ and the Gospels* gives the following information on the Roman guard:

"*GUARD.*—1. RV rendering of [Koustodia] (Lat. *custodia*), Mt 27:65,66; 28:11, AV 'watch'; obtained by the chief priests and Pharisees from Pilate to guard the sepulchre. The need of Pilate's authorization and the risk of punishment from him (Mt. 28:14) show that this guard must have consisted, not of the Jewish Temple police, but of soldiers from the Roman cohort at Jerusalem; possibly, though not probably, the same as had guarded the cross. . . . [You have] is probably imperative, 'have (take) a guard.' " 25/694

Lewis and Short record the following in their Latin dictionary: "*Custodia*, ae. f. [id], *a watching, watch, guard, care, protection.* 1. Usu in *plur.* and in milit. lang., *persons who serve as guards, a guard, watch, sentinel.*" 36/504,505

The context of Matthew 27 and 28 seems to corroborate the view that it was a "Roman guard" which was used to secure Jesus' tomb. If Pilate had told them to use the "temple police" just to get rid of them, then the guard would be responsible to the chief priests only and not to Pilate. However, if Pilate gave them a "Roman guard" to protect the tomb, then the guard would be responsible to Pilate and not the chief priests. The key lies in verses 11 and 14 of chapter 28.

In verse 11 it says that the guard came and reported to the Chief Priest. At first glance it seems that they are responsible to the Chief Priest. But, if some of the guards had reported to Pilate they would have been put to death immediately, as will be explained below. Verse 14 confirms the view that they were a Roman guard and directly responsible to Pilate.

"And if this should come to the governor's ears, we will win him over and keep you out of trouble." If they were the "temple police," why worry about Pilate hearing about it? There is no indication that he would have jurisdiction over them. The writer feels this is what happened: They were a "Roman guard" to which Pilate had given instructions to secure the grave, in order to satisfy and keep peace with all the religious hierarchy. The chief priests cautiously had sought a "Roman guard" in Matthew 27:64; "Therefore, give orders for the grave to be made secure. . . ."

If the priest had wanted to post temple police at the tomb, they would not have needed the orders of the governor to do it. As it happened, the Roman soldiers came to the chief priests for protection, because they knew that they would have influence over Pilate and would keep them from being executed: ". . . we will win him [the governor, Pilate] over and keep you out of trouble" (Matthew 28:14b).

3D. The military discipline of the Romans

George Currie, in speaking of the discipline of the Roman guard, says, "The punishment for quitting post was death, according to the laws (Dion. Hal, *Antiq. Rom.* VIII.79). The most famous discourse on the strictness of camp discipline is that of Polybius

VI.37-38 which indicates that the fear of punishments produced faultless attention to duty, especially in the night watches. It carries weight from the prestige of the author, who was describing what he had an opportunity to see with his own eyes. His statements are duplicated in a general way by others." 12/41-43

Professor Currie, citing Polybius, says: "Running a gauntlet [sic.] of cudgels . . . is referred to as punishment for faulty night watches, stealing, false witnessing, and injuring one's own body; decimation for desertion of the ranks because of cowardice is also mentioned." 12/43,44

Currie continues, "Vegetius speaks of daily attention to strictness of discipline by the prefect of the legion (*Military Institutes* 11.9). And Vegetius certainly maintains (*Military Institutes* 1.21) that the earlier Romans [at the time of Christ] disciplined more strictly than those of his day." 12/43,44

Currie, in speaking of Vegetius' comments on the Roman army, says: "The system he described provided for the severest punishment. The classicum was the signal blown on the trumpet to announce an execution (11.22). Daily attention to strictness of discipline was the duty of the prefect of the legion (11.9)." 12/49,50

Currie points out: "In the various writers of [Justinian's] Digest 49.16, eighteen offenses of soldiers are mentioned punishable by death. They are as follows: a scout remaining with the enemy (-3.4), desertion (-3.11; -5. 1-3), losing or disposing of one's arms (-3.13), disobedience in war time (-3.15), going over the wall or rampart (-3.17), starting a mutiny (-3.19), refusing to protect an officer or deserting one's post (-3.22), a drafted man hiding from service (-4.2), murder (-4.5), laying hands on a superior or insult to a general (-6.1), leading flight when the example would influence others (-6.3), betraying plans to the enemy (-6.4; -7), wounding a fellow soldier with a sword (-6.6), disabling self or attempting suicide without reasonable excuse (-6.7), leaving the night watch (-10.1), breaking the centurion's staff or striking him when being punished (-13.4), escaping guard house (-13.5), and disturbing the peace (-16.1)." 12/49,50

Professor Currie documents the following examples from the annals of Roman military history which reflect the type of disciplinary measures employed in the Roman army: "In 418, standard bearer lagging in battle, slain by general's own hand; in 390, asleep on duty, hurled from the cliff of the Capitolium [Dig. 49.16.3.6.; - 10.1], in 252, negligence, beaten and rank reduced; in 218, negligence, punished; in 195, lagging, struck with weapon; . . . . The types of punishment above mentioned would justify the word 'strict' as descriptive of them." 12/33

Currie further comments: "Since the death penalty was assessed in 40 cases out of 102 where the punishment is mentioned, it is clear that punishment in the Roman army was severe in comparison with that in modern armies." Currie speaks of the Roman army as "an instrument for conquest and domination" and, concerning its strict discipline, writes: "Valerius Maximus . . . refers to sharp observation of camp discipline and military theory (11.8 intro.; 11.9 intro.) [as being the primary reasons for] the extensive conquests and power of Rome." 12/33,38,43,44

T. G. Tucker gives the following vivid description of the weaponry a Roman soldier would carry:

"In his right hand he will carry the famous Roman pike. This is a stout weapon, over 6 feet in length, consisting of a sharp iron head fixed in a wooden shaft, and the soldier may either charge with it as with a bayonet, or he may hurl it like a javelin and then fight at close quarters with his sword. On the left arm is a large shield, which may be of various shapes. One common form is curved inward at the sides like a portion of a cylinder some 4 feet in length by 2½ in width: another is six-sided — a diamond pattern, but with the points of the diamond squared away. Sometimes it is oval. In construction it is of wickerwork or wood, covered with leather, and embossed with a blazon in metal-work, one particularly well known being that of a thunderbolt. The shield is not only carried by means of a handle, but may be supported by a belt over the right shoulder. In order to be out of the way of the shield, the sword — a thrusting rather than a slashing weapon, approaching 3 feet in length — is hung at the right side by a belt passing over the left shoulder. Though this arrangement may seem awkward to us, it is to be remembered that the sword is not required until the right hand is free of the pike, and that then, before drawing, the weapon can easily be swung around to the left by means of the suspending belt. On the left side the soldier wears a dagger at his girdle." 69/342-344

4D.   What was a Roman guard?

Professor William Smith in *Dictionary of Greek and Roman Antiquities* gives us some information about the number of men in a Roman "guard." According to Dr. Smith, the maniple (a sub-division of the Roman legion) consisting of either 120 or 60 men "furnished . . . for the tribune to whom it was specially attached . . . two guards . . . of four men each, who kept watch, some in front of the tent and some behind, among the horses. We may remark in passing, that four was the regular number for a Roman guard . . . of these one always acted as a sentinel, while the others enjoyed a certain degree of repose, ready, however, to start up at the first alarm." 61/250,251

Professor Harold Smith relates: "A watch usually consisted of four men (Polyb. vi.33), each of whom watched in turn, while the others rested beside him so as to be roused by the least alarm; but in this case the guards may have been more numerous." 25/694

Professor Whedon says of a watch: "Probably a guard of four soldiers. Such certainly was the number who watched the crucifixion. John xix, 23. . . ." 72/343

5D.   What was the temple guard?

The Jewish historian, *Alfred Edersheim,* gives us the following information concerning the "temple guard": "At night guards were placed in twenty-four stations about the gates and courts. Of these twenty-one were occupied by Levites alone; the other innermost three jointly by priests and Levites. Each guard consisted of ten men; so that in all two hundred and forty Levites and thirty priests were on duty every night. The Temple guards were relieved by day, but not during the night, which the Romans divided into four, but the Jews, properly, into three watches, the fourth being really the morning watch." 16/147-149

The Mishnah (translated by Herbert Danby, Oxford University Press, 1933) relates the following concerning the temple guard: "The priests kept watch at three places in the Temple: at the

Chamber of Abtinas, at the Chamber of the Flame, and at the Chamber of the Hearth; and the levites at twenty-one places: five at the five gates of the Temple Mount, four at its four corners inside, five at five of the gates of the Temple Court, four at its four corners outside, and one at the Chamber of Offerings, and one at the Chamber of the Curtain, and one behind the place of the Mercy Seat." 44/Middoth

Professor P. Henderson Aitken records: "The duty of this 'captain of the mount of the Temple' was to keep order in the Temple, visit the stations of the guard during the night, and see that the sentries were duly posted and alert. He and his immediate subalterns are supposed to be intended by the 'rulers'   mentioned in Ezra 9:? and Nehemiah. . . ." 25/271

6D.   The military discipline of the temple guard

Alfred Edersheim gives us this description of the tight discipline under which the temple police worked: "During the night the 'captain of the Temple' made his rounds. On his approach the guards had to rise and salute him in a particular manner. Any guard found asleep when on duty was beaten, or his garments were set on fire — a punishment, as we know, actually awarded. Hence the admonition to us who, as it were, are here on Temple guard, 'Blessed is he that watcheth, and keepeth his garments' [Rev. 16: 15]." 16/147-149

The Mishnah shows the treatment given anyone found asleep during the watch:

"The officer of the Temple Mount used to go round to every watch with lighted torches before him, and if any watch did not stand up and say to him, 'O officer of the Temple Mount, peace be to thee!' and it was manifest that he was asleep, he would beat him with his staff, and he had the right to burn his raiment. And they would say, 'What is the noise in the Temple Court?' 'The noise of some levite that is being beaten and having his raiment burnt because he went to sleep during his watch.' R. Eliezer b. Jacob said: 'They once found my mother's brother asleep and burnt his raiment.' " 44/Middoth

The Jewish Encyclopedia comments concerning "the sacred premises within [the temple]," those who were on watch therein "were not allowed to sit down, much less to sleep. The captain of the guard saw that every man was alert, chastising a priest if found asleep at his post, and sometimes even punishing him by burning his shirt upon him, as a warning to others (Mid. k.I)." 31/81

7D.   Conclusions

Mgr. E. Le Camus says in reference to the tight security measures taken at Jesus' sepulcher: "Never had a criminal given so much worry after his execution. Above all never had a crucified man had the honour of being guarded by a squad of soldiers." 34/396,397

Professor G. W. Clark concludes: "So everything was done that human policy and prudence could, to prevent a Resurrection, which these very precautions had the most direct tendency to indicate and establish." 10/Matt. 27:35

7C.   THE DISCIPLES WENT THEIR OWN WAY

Matthew shows us the cowardice of the disciples in his Gospel (26:56).

Jesus had been arrested in the garden of Gethsemane and ". . . then all the disciples left Him and fled."

Mark says in his Gospel (14:50): "And they all left Him and fled."

Professor George Hanson remarks: "They were not naturally either very brave or large-minded. In the most cowardly fashion, when their Master was arrested, they 'all forsook Him' and fled, leaving Him to face His fate alone." 22/24-26

Professor Albert Roper speaks of Simon Peter's "cringing under the taunt of a maid in the court of the high priests and denying with a curse that he knew 'this man of whom ye speak.' " 54/50

He asserts that "fear, abject fear for his own personal safety brought Peter to reject the Man he truly loved. Fear, craven fear, made him recreant to the One who had called him from his nets to become a fisher of men." 54/52

Concerning the character of the disciples, Roper comments:

"They are Galileans, for the most part fisher-folk, all of them more or less strangers to cities and to the ways of city life. One by one, they had become adherents of the young Teacher from Nazareth and devoted to His way of life. They had followed Him gladly and reverently until the hour of crisis came. When He was arrested on the outskirts of the Garden of Gethsemane, they all fell back and away, awed by the torches and the clamor and the rattling sabers.

"[The disciples] secreted themselves in their lodgings and nothing is heard of them until the startling news is brought to them by the Magdalene on the morning of the third day. Thereupon, two — and two only — have the temerity to venture forth to learn for themselves if the news brought to them by Mary could be as reported by her or was as they themselves believed, just 'idle talk.' The whole demeanor of the disciples is one of abject fright and self-preservation." 54/34,35

Alfred Edersheim asks: "What thoughts concerning the Dead Christ filled the minds of Joseph of Arimathea, of Nicodemus, and of the other disciples of Jesus, as well as of the Apostles and of the pious women?" 15/623

To this question he answers: "They believed Him to be dead, and they did not expect Him to rise again from the dead — at least, in our accepted sense of it. Of this there is abundant evidence from the moment of His Death, in the burial-spices brought by Nicodemus, in those prepared by the women (both of which were intended as against corruption), in the sorrow of the women at the empty tomb, in their supposition that the Body had been removed, in the perplexity and bearing of the Apostles, in the doubts of so many, and indeed in the express statement: 'For as yet they knew not the Scripture, that He must rise again from the dead.' " 15/623

2B. The Post-resurrection Scene

1C.   THE EMPTY TOMB

W. J. Sparrow-Simpson points out that the empty tomb by itself did not cause the disciples to believe. Of John it is said: ". . . he saw, and believed" (John 20:8). This, however, was probably because he remembered that Christ had foretold His resurrection. Neither Mary Magdalene, nor the women, nor even Peter were brought to believe by the testimony of the empty tomb. 25/506

It was Christ's post-resurrection appearances which assured His followers that He had actually risen from the dead. The empty tomb stood as a historical fact, verifying the appearances as being nothing less than Jesus of Nazareth, resurrected in flesh and blood. 25/506

J. N. D. Anderson, lawyer and professor of oriental law at the University of London, asks:

"Have you noticed that the references to the empty tomb all come in the Gospels, which were written to give the Christian community the facts they wanted to know? In the public preaching to those who were not believers, as recorded in the Acts of the Apostles, there is an enormous emphasis on the fact of the resurrection but not a single reference to the empty tomb. Now, why? To me there is only one answer: There was no point in arguing about the empty tomb. Everyone, friend and opponent, knew that it was empty. The only questions worth arguing about were why it was empty and what its emptiness proved." 3/4-9

In other writings, Anderson says:

"The empty tomb stands, a veritable rock, as an essential element in the evidence for the resurrection. To suggest that it was not in fact empty at all, as some have done, seems to me ridiculous. It is a matter of history that the apostles from the very beginning made many converts in Jerusalem, hostile as it was, by proclaiming the glad news that Christ had risen from the grave — and they did it within a short walk from the sepulchre. Any one of their hearers could have visited the tomb and come back again between lunch and whatever may have been the equivalent of afternoon tea. Is it conceivable, then, that the apostles would have had this success if the body of the one they proclaimed as risen Lord was all the time decomposing in Joseph's tomb? Would a great company of the priests and many hard-headed Pharisees have been impressed with the proclamation of a resurrection which was in fact no resurrection at all, but a mere message of spiritual survival couched in the misleading terms of a literal rising from the grave?" 2/95,96

Paul Althus, cited by Wolfhart Pannenberg, says: " 'In Jerusalem, the place of Jesus' execution and grave, it was proclaimed not long after his death that he had been raised. The situation *demands* that within the circle of the first community one had a reliable testimony for the fact that the grave had been found empty.' The resurrection Kerygma [proclamation] 'could have not been maintained in Jerusalem for a single day, for a single hour, if the emptiness of the tomb had not been established as a fact for all concerned.' " 50/100

Professor E. H. Day comments:

"If it be asserted that the tomb was in fact not found to be empty, several difficulties confront the critic. He has to meet, for example, the problem of the rapid rise of the very definite tradition, never seriously questioned, the problem of the circumstantial nature of the accounts in which the tradition is embodied, the problem of the failure of the Jews to prove that the Resurrection had not taken place by producing the body of Christ, or by an official examination of the sepulchre, a proof which it was to their greatest interest to exhibit." 15/25,26

The English barrister, *Frank Morison*, comments:

"In all the fragments and echoes of this far-off controversy which have come down to us we are nowhere told that any responsible person asserted that the body of Jesus was still in the tomb. We are only given reasons why it was not there. Running all through these ancient documents is the persistent assumption that the tomb of Christ was vacant.

"Can we fly in the face of this cumulative and mutually corroborative evidence? Personally, I do not think we can. The sequence of coincidences is too strong." 46/115

Michael Green cites a secular source of early origin which bears testimony to Jesus' empty tomb. This piece of evidence ". . . is called the Nazareth Inscription, after the town where it was found. It is an imperial edict, belonging either to the reign of Tiberius (AD 14-37) or of Claudius (AD 41-54). And it is an invective, backed with heavy sanctions, against meddling around with tombs and graves! It looks very much as if the news of the empty tomb had got back to Rome in a garbled form (Pilate would have had to report: and he would obviously have said that the tomb had been rifled). This edict, it seems, is the imperial reaction." 19/36

Green concludes: "There can be no doubt that the tomb of Jesus was, in fact, empty on the first Easter day." 19/36

Matthew 28: 11-15 records the attempt of the Jewish authorities to bribe the Roman guard to say the disciples stole Jesus' body. *The Dictionary of the Apostolic Church* comments: "This fraudulent transaction proceeds upon the admission by the enemies of Christianity that the grave was empty — an admission which is enough to show that the evidence for the empty grave was 'too notorious to be denied.' " 24/340

W. J. Sparrow-Simpson writes: "The emptiness of the grave is acknowledged by *opponents* as well as affirmed by disciples. The narrative of the guards attempts to account for the fact as a fraudulent transaction (Matthew 28: 11-15). 'But this Jewish accusation against the Apostles takes for granted that the grave was empty. What was needed was an explanation.' . . . This acknowledgment by the Jews that the grave was vacated extends to all subsequent Jewish comments on the point." 25/507,508

Sparrow-Simpson supports this point by citing as an example ". . . a 12th century version of the empty grave circulated by the Jewish anti-Christian propaganda. The story is that when the queen heard that the elders had slain Jesus and had buried Him, and that He was risen again, she ordered them within three days to produce the body or forfeit their lives. 'Then spake Judas, "Come and I will show you the man whom ye seek: for it was I who took the fatherless from his grave. For I feared lest his disciples should steal him away, and I have hidden him in my garden and led a waterbrook over the place." ' And the story explains how the body was produced." 25/507,508

Sparrow-Simpson concludes: "It is needless to remark that this daring assertion of the actual production of the body is a mediaeval fabrication, but it is an assertion very necessary to account for facts, when the emptiness of the grave was admitted and yet the Resurrection denied." 25/507,508

Ernest Kevan cites as evidence what he describes as ". . . the indisputable fact of the *empty tomb*. The tomb was empty; and the foes of Christ were unable to deny it." 32/14

He asserts, ". . . The fact of the empty tomb deals a mortal blow to all the hypotheses which are set up against the Christian testimony. This is the stone over which all specious theories stumble, and it is therefore not surprising to discover that reference to the empty tomb is studiously avoided by many of the counter-arguments which are brought forward." 32/14

W. J. Sparrow-Simpson, citing Julius Wellhausen, the famous German scholar who is noted for his higher criticism of the Old Testament, gives this testimony concerning the resurrection of Christ: "It is admitted that with the Resurrection the body of Jesus also had vanished from the grave, and it will be impossible to account for this on natural grounds." 25/508

Why did Jesus' sepulcher not become an object of veneration?

J. N. D. Anderson comments that "it is also significant that no suggestion has come down to us that the tomb became a place of reverence or pilgrimage in the days of the early church. Even if those who were convinced Christians might have been deflected from visiting the sepulchre by their assurance that their Master had risen from the dead, what of all those who had heard His teaching, and even known the miracle of His healing touch, without joining the Christian community? They, too, it would seem, knew that His body was not there, and must have concluded that a visit to the tomb would be pointless." 2/97

Frank Morison in his book, *Who Moved the Stone?* makes an interesting observation: "Consider first the small but highly significant fact that not a trace exists in the Acts, or the Missionary Epistles or in any apocryphal document of indisputably early date, of anyone going to pay homage at the shrine of Jesus Christ. It is remarkable — this absolutely unbroken silence concerning the most sacred place in Christian memory. Would no woman, to whom the Master's form was a hallowed recollection, ever wish to spend a few moments at that holy site? Would Peter and John and Andrew never feel the call of a sanctuary that held all that was mortal of the Great Master? Would Saul himself, recalling his earlier arrogance and self-assurance, not have made one solitary journey and shed hot tears of repentance for his denial of the Name? If these people really knew that the Lord was buried there, it is very, very strange." To a critic of the resurrection, this extraordinary silence of antiquity concerning the later history of the grave of Jesus produces, I'm sure, a feeling of profound disquiet and unrest. 46/137

2C.   THE GRAVE CLOTHES

In the following narrative, John shows the significance of the grave clothes as evidence for the resurrection:

"Peter therefore went forth, and the other disciple, and they were going to the tomb. And the two were running together; and the other disciple ran ahead faster than Peter, and came to the tomb first; and stooping and looking in, he saw the linen wrappings lying there; but he did not go in. Simon Peter therefore also came, following him, and entered the tomb; and he beheld the linen wrappings lying there; but he did not go in. Simon Peter therefore also came, following him, and entered the tomb; and he beheld the linen wrappings lying there, and the face cloth, which had been on His head, not lying with the linen wrappings, but rolled up in a place by itself. Then entered in therefore the other disciple also, who had first come to the tomb, and he saw, and believed. For as yet they did not understand the Scripture, that He must rise again from the dead" (John 20:3-9).

Commenting on John's narrative, *J. N. D. Anderson* says of the empty tomb:

". . . It seems that it wasn't really empty. You remember the account in John's Gospel of how Mary Magdalene ran and called Peter and John and how the two men set out to the tomb. John, the younger, ran on quicker than Peter and came first to the tomb. He stooped down, 'peeped' inside (which I believe is the literal meaning of the Greek), and saw the linen clothes and the napkin that had been about the head. And then Simon Peter came along and, characteristically, blundered straight in, followed by John; and they took note of the linen clothes and the napkin, which was not lying with the linen clothes but was apart, wrapped into one place. The Greek there seems to suggest that the linen clothes were lying, not strewn about the tomb, but where the body had been, and that there was a gap where the neck of Christ had lain — and that the napkin which had been about His head was not with the linen clothes but apart and wrapped in its own place, which I suppose means still done up, as though the body had simply withdrawn itself. We are told that when John saw that, he needed no further testimony from man or angel; he saw and believed, and his testimony has come down to us." 3/7,8

Cyril of Alexandria (376-444) suggests that from the manner in which the grave clothes lay folded, the apostles were led to the idea of the resurrection. (*Migne,* 7.683)

Professor E. H. Day says of John's narrative: "It is characterized throughout by the personal touch, it has all the marks of the evidence not only of an eyewitness, but of a careful observer. . . . The running of the disciples, the order of their arrival at the sepulchre and their entry; the fact that St. John first stooped down and looking through the low doorway saw the linen clothes lying, while St. Peter, more bold, was the first to enter; the exact word, . . . [*theorei*], which is used for St. Peter's careful observation (even examination may perhaps be implied in it) of the grave-clothes; the description of the position of the linen clothes and the napkin, a description not laboured, but minutely careful in its choice of words; the subsequent entry of St. John, and the belief which followed upon the sight of the grave-clothes — this can surely be nothing else than the description of one who actually *saw,* upon whose memory the scene is still impressed, to whom the sight of the empty grave and the relinquished grave-clothes was a critical point in faith and life." 13/16,17

John R. W. Stott makes the following observations:

"It is a remarkable fact that the narratives which say that the body of Jesus had gone also tell us that the graveclothes had not gone. It is John who lays particular emphasis on this fact, for he accompanied Peter on that dramatic early morning race to the tomb. The account he gives of this incident (20:1-10) bears the unmistakable marks of first-hand experience. He outran Peter, but on arrival at the tomb he did not more than look in, until Peter came and entered it. 'Then the other disciple, who reached the tomb first, also went in, and he saw and believed.' The question is: What did he see which made him believe? The story suggests that it was not just the absence of the body, but the presence of the graveclothes and, in particular, their undisturbed condition.

". . . John tells us (19:38-42) that while Joseph begged Pilate for the body of Jesus, Nicodemus 'came bringing a mixture of myrrh and aloes, about a hundred pounds' weight.' Then together 'they took the body of Jesus, and bound it in linen cloths with the spices, as is the burial custom of the Jews.' That is to say, as they wound the linen 'bandages' round His body, they sprinkled the powdered spices into the folds.

"Now supposing we had been present in the sepulchre when the resurrection of Jesus actually took place. What should we have seen? . . . We should suddenly have noticed that the body had disappeared. . . . the body cloths, under the weight of 100 lbs. of spices, once the support of the body had been removed, would have subsided or collapsed, and would now be lying flat. A gap would have appeared between the body cloths and the head napkin, where His face and neck had been. And the napkin itself, because of the complicated criss-cross pattern of the bandages, might well have retained its concave shape, a crumpled turban, but with no head inside it.

"A careful study of the text of John's narrative suggests that it is just these three characteristics of the discarded graveclothes which he saw. First, he saw the cloths 'lying.' The word is repeated twice, and the first time it is placed in an emphatic position in the Greek sentence. We might translate, 'He saw, as they were lying (or 'collapsed'), the linen cloths.' Next, the head napkin was 'not . . . with the linen cloths but . . . in a place by itself.' This is unlikely to mean that it had been bundled up and tossed into a corner. It lay still on the stone slab, but was separated from the body cloths by a noticeable space. Third, this same napkin was 'not lying . . . but wrapped together. . . .' This last word has been translated 'twirled.' The Authorized Version 'wrapped together' and the Revised Standard Version 'rolled up' are both unfortunate translations. The world aptly describes the rounded shape which the empty napkin still preserved.

"It is not hard to imagine the sight which greeted the eyes of the apostles when they reached the tomb: the stone slab, the collapsed graveclothes, the shell of the head-cloth and the gap between the two. No wonder they 'saw and believed.' A glance at these graveclothes proved the reality, and indicated the nature, of the resurrection. They had been neither touched nor folded nor manipulated by any human being. They were like a discarded chrysalis from which the butterfly has emerged.

"That the state of the graveclothes was intended to be visible, corroborative evidence for the resurrection is further suggested by the fact that Mary Magdalene (who had returned to the tomb after bringing the news to Peter and John) 'stooped to look into the tomb; and she saw two angels in white, sitting where the body of Jesus had lain, one at the head and one at the feet.' Presumably this means that they sat on the stone slab with the graveclothes between them. Both Matthew and Mark add that one of them said, 'He is not here; for He has risen, as He said. Come, see the place where He lay.' Whether or not the reader believes in angels, these allusions to the place where Jesus had lain, emphasized by both the position and the words of the angels, at least confirms what the understanding of the evangelists was: the position of the clothes and the absence of the body were concurrent witnesses to His resurrection." 63/52-54

Henry Latham says: ". . . It seems clear to me that S. John's account indicates that a change came over the two Apostles owing to what they saw. . . ." Why? 31/45

Latham describes what the disciples saw in Jesus' tomb:

"In . . . [the] recess, on the lower part of the ledge, lay the grave-clothes. They were in no disorder, they were just as they were when Joseph and others had wrapped them round the body of the Lord, only they were lying flat, fold over fold, for the body was gone. On the raised part of the ledge at the far end, all by itself, was the napkin that had gone round the head; this was not lying flat, but was standing up a little, retaining the twirled form which had been given it when it had been twined round the head of the Lord. Nothing in the place gave any sign of the touch of human hands: the body had been embedded in the powdered aloes and myrrh, but of this there was not a trace; the spice remained enclosed by the 'cloths' between which it had been placed when the body was laid on the slab. Something which the scene conveyed may have gone to the hearts of Peter and John; at any rate we can see that when they went out, they were not in the frame of mind that they had been in when they reached the tomb. I think that the impression stole over them, as they scrutinized what they saw, that 'God was in that place.' " 33/34

Professor Latham writes of the face cloth which had covered Jesus' head:

"The words 'not lying with the linen cloths' yield me something . . .; they tell me incidentally that the linen cloths were all in one place. If they were lying, as I take them to have done, all upon the lower part of the ledge, the expression is perfectly clear; but if the linen cloths had been lying, one here and one there, as though they had been thrown hastily aside, there would have been no meaning in saying that the napkin was 'not lying with the linen cloths,' for the 'linen cloths' would not have defined any particular spot. We again note the introduction of the word 'lying' when it is not absolutely required. The napkin was not lying flat, as the linen cloths were, and S. John, perhaps, marks the difference." 33/44

Latham continues: ". . . The napkin, which had been twisted round the top of the head, would remain on . . . [the] elevated slab; there it would be found 'rolled up in a place by itself.' " 33/36

Dr. Latham says that the phrase " 'rolled up' is ambiguous, the twisted napkin I suppose formed a ring like the roll of a turban loosened, without the central part." 33/36

Professor Latham concludes:

"There lie the clothes, — they are fallen a little together, but are still wrapped fold over fold, and no grain of spice is displaced. The napkin, too, is lying on the low step which serves as a pillow for the head of the corpse; it is twisted into a sort of wig, and is all by itself. The very quietude of the scene makes it seem to have something to say. It spoke to those who saw it, and it speaks to me when I conjure it before my mind's eye, with the morning light from the open doorway streaming in.

"What it says, I make out to be this:

" 'All that was Jesus of Nazareth has suffered its change and is gone. We, — grave-clothes, and spices, and napkin, — belong to the earth and remain.' " 33/11

3C.   THE SEAL

Professor A. T. Robertson comments: "The sealing was done in the presence of the Roman guard who were left in charge to protect this stamp of Roman authority and power." 53/239

D. D. Whedon says: "The door could not be opened, therefore, without breaking the seal; which was a crime against the authority of the proprietor of the seal." 72/343

The seal was broken when the stone was rolled away. The person or persons who were responsible for breaking the seal would have the provincial governor and his agencies to answer to. Indeed, at the time of Christ's resurrection everyone feared the breaking of the Roman seal.

4C.   THE ROMAN GUARD

Matthew makes the following observations:

"And behold, a severe earthquake had occurred, for an angel of the Lord descended from heaven and came and rolled away the stone and sat upon it. And his appearance was like lightning, and his garment as white as snow; and the guards shook for fear of him, and became like dead men.

"Now while they were on their way, behold, some of the guard came into the city and reported to the chief priests all that had happened. And when they had assembled with the elders and counseled together, they gave a large sum of money to the soldiers, and said, 'You are to say, "His disciples came by night and stole Him away while we were asleep." And if this should come to the governor's ears, we will win him over and keep you out of trouble.' And they took the money and did as they had been instructed; and this story was widely spread among the Jews, and is to this day" (Matthew 28:2-4, 11-15).

Understanding who these guards were makes the narrative of Matthew 28 very impressive.

The sight which coincided with Jesus' resurrection was frightening enough to cause rugged soldiers to "become like dead men" (Matthew 28:4).

Professor Roper gives this description of the guard: "They had not the slightest interest in the task to which they were assigned. Their sole purpose and obligation was rigidly to perform their duty as soldiers of the empire of Rome to which they had dedicated their allegiance. The Roman seal affixed to the stone before Joseph's tomb was far more sacred to them than all the philosophy of Israel or the sanctity of her ancient creed. [They were] . . . cold-blooded enough to gamble over a dying victim's cloak. . . ." 54/33

T. G. Tucker describes in great detail (see page 214) the armor and weapons which a centurion would have worn. The picture he gives is of a human fighting machine. 69/342-344

For furthur information on the Roman guard, see page 214.

Thomas Thorburn tells us that the guard which had kept the watch was in dire straits. After the stone had been rolled away and the seal broken, they were as good as court-martialed. Thorburn writes: "The soldiers cannot have alleged they were asleep, for they well knew that the penalty of sleeping upon a watch was death — always rigorously enforced." 68/179-182

Thorburn continues: "Here the soldiers would have practically no other alternative than to trust to the good offices of the priests. The body (we will suppose) was *gone,* and their negligence in *any* case would (under ordinary circumstances) be punishable by death (cp. Acts xii. 19)." 68/179-182

5C.   JESUS WAS ALIVE — POST-RESURRECTION APPEARANCES

1D.   Importance of the appearances

Professor C. S. Lewis, in speaking of the importance of Christ's post-resurrection appearances, says: "The first fact in the history of Christendom is a number of people who say they have seen the Resurrection. If they had died without making anyone else believe this 'gospel' no gospels would ever have been written." 37/149

J. N. D. Anderson writes of the testimony of the appearances:

"The most drastic way of dismissing the evidence would be to say that these stories were mere fabrications, that they were pure lies. But, so far as I know, not a single critic today would take such an attitude. In fact, it would really be an impossible position. Think of the number of witnesses, over 500. Think of the character of the witnesses, men and women who gave the world the highest ethical teaching it has ever known, and who even on the testimony of their enemies lived it out in their lives. Think of the psychological absurdity of picturing a little band of defeated cowards cowering in an upper room one day and a few days later transformed into a company that no persecution could silence — and then attempting to attribute this dramatic change to nothing more convincing than a miserable fabrication they were trying to foist upon the world. That simply wouldn't make sense." 3/5,6

John Warwick Montgomery comments:

"Note that when the disciples of Jesus proclaimed the resurrection, they did so as eyewitnesses and they did so while people were still alive who had had contact with the events they spoke of. In 56 A.D. Paul wrote that over 500 people had seen the risen Jesus and that most of them were still alive (I Corinthians 15:6 ff.). It passes the bounds of credibility that the early Christians could have manufactured such a tale and then preached it among those who might easily have refuted it simply by producing the body of Jesus." 45/78

Bernard Ramm writes:

"If there were no resurrection it must be admitted by radical critics that Paul deceived the apostles of an actual appearance of Christ to him, and they in turn deceived Paul about the appearances of a risen Christ to them. How difficult it is to impugn the evidence of the Epistles at this point when they have such strong validation as authentic!" 52/203

2D. The appearances of Christ in the lives of individuals:

To Mary Magdalene, John 20:14, Mark 16:9
To women returning from the tomb, Matthew 28:9,10
To Peter later in the day, Luke 24:34; I Corinthians 15:5
To the Emmaus disciples, Luke 24:13-33
To the apostles, Thomas absent, Luke 24:36-43; John 20:19-24
To the apostles, Thomas present, John 20:26-29
To the seven by the Lake of Tiberias, John 21:1-23
To a multitude of 500-plus believers on a Galilean mountain,
    I Corinthians 15:6
To James, I Corinthians 15:7
To the eleven, Matthew 28:16-20; Mark 16:14-20; Luke 24:33-52;
    Acts 1:3-12
At the ascension, Acts 1:3-12
To Paul, Acts 9:3-6; I Corinthians 15:8
To Stephen, Acts 7:55
To Paul in the temple, Acts 22:17-21; 23:11
To John on Patmos, Revelation 1:10-19

6C.   THE ENEMIES OF CHRIST GAVE NO REFUTATION OF THE
      RESURRECTION

1D.   **They were silent**

In Acts 2, Luke records Peter's sermon on the day of Pentecost.
There was no refutation given by the Jews to his bold proclamation
of Christ's resurrection. Why? Because the evidence of the empty
tomb was there for anyone to examine if they wanted to disclaim it.
However, everyone knew that the grave no longer held the body of
Jesus Christ.

In Acts 25, we see Paul imprisoned in Caesarea. Festus "took his
seat on the tribunal and ordered Paul to be brought. And after he
had arrived, the Jews who had come down from Jerusalem stood
around him, bringing many serious charges against him which
they could not prove." Just what was it about Paul's gospel that so
irritated the Jews? What point did they totally avoid in making
their accusations? Festus, in explaining the case to King Agrippa,
describes the central issue as concerning "a certain dead man,
Jesus, whom Paul asserted to be alive" (Acts 25:19). The Jews
could not explain the empty tomb.

They made all kinds of personal attacks on Paul, but avoided the
objective evidence for the resurrection. They were reduced to
subjective name-calling and avoided discussing the silent witness
of the empty grave.

The silence of the Jews speaks louder than the voice of the
Christians, or as Fairbairn says:

"The silence of the Jews is as significant as the speech of the
Christians" (Fairbairn, *Studies in the Life of Christ, 357).*

Professor Day says, "The simple disproof, the effective
challenging, of the fact of the Resurrection would have dealt a
death-blow to Christianity. And they had every opportunity of
disproof, if it were possible." 13/33-35

W. Pannenberg, cited by J. N. D. Anderson, states:

"The early Jewish polemic against the Christian message about
Jesus' resurrection, traces of which have already been left in the
Gospels, does not offer any suggestion that Jesus' grave had
remained untouched. The Jewish polemic would have had to have
every interest in the preservation of such a report. However, quite
to the contrary, it shared the conviction with its Christian
opponents that Jesus' grave was empty. It limited itself to
explaining this fact in its own way. . . ." 2/96

The Church was founded on the resurrection, and disproving it
would have destroyed the whole Christian movement. However,
instead of any such disproof, throughout the first century,
Christians were threatened, beaten, flogged and killed because of
their faith. It would have been much simpler to have silenced them
by producing Jesus' body, but this was never done.

John R. W. Stott has well said, the silence of Christ's enemies "is as
eloquent a proof of the resurrection as the apostles' witness." 63/51

2D.   **They mocked**

1E.   In Athens

When Paul spoke to the Athenians about Christ, they had no
answer for his claims: "Now when they heard of the

resurrection of the dead, some began to sneer" (Acts 17:32). They merely laughed it off, because they could not understand how a man could rise from the dead. They did not even attempt to make a defense for their position. They, in essence, said: "Don't confuse me with the facts, my mind is already made up."

Why did Paul see such unbelief in Greece unlike that in Jerusalem? Because while in Jerusalem the fact of the empty tomb was indisputable (it was right there for people to examine), in Athens the evidence was far away, so that the emptiness of the tomb was not common knowledge. Paul's hearers had not checked the story out for themselves, and rather than go to any trouble to investigate, they were satisfied to jest in ignorance. Intellectual suicide best describes their stand.

2E. Before Agrippa and Festus in Caesarea

Paul told Agrippa and everyone in the court that Christ was "by reason of His resurrection from the dead . . . the first to proclaim light both to the Jewish people and to the Gentiles. And while Paul was saying this in his defense, Festus said in a loud voice, 'Paul, you are out of your mind! Your great learning is driving you mad.' But Paul said, 'I am not out of my mind, most excellent Festus, but I utter words of sober truth. For the king [Agrippa] knows about these matters, and I speak to him also with confidence, since I am persuaded that none of these things escape his notice; for this has not been done in a corner. King Agrippa, do you believe the Prophets? I know that you do.' And Agrippa replied to Paul, 'In a short time you will persuade me to become a Christian' " (Acts 26:23-28).

Again, just as in Athens, Paul met with unbelief. His message was again, "His resurrection from the dead" (Acts 26:23), and again no evidence to the contrary was presented in rebuttal. Only vain mockery came from Festus. Paul's defense was uttered in words "of sober truth" [marginal reading of truth and rationality] (Acts 26:25). Paul stressed the empirical nature of his case saying, "This has not been done in a corner" (Acts 26:26). He challenged Agrippa and Festus with the evidence, but Festus, like the Athenians, could only laugh it off. This incident took place in Caesarea, where it would not have been known by everyone that the tomb was empty. A trip to Jerusalem would have confirmed the fact.

3B. Established Historical Fact

The empty tomb is that silent testimony to the resurrection of Christ which has never been refuted. The Romans and Jews could not produce Christ's body or explain where it went, but nonetheless, they refused to believe. Not because of the insufficiency of evidence but in spite of its sufficiency do men still reject the resurrection.

Professor E. H. Day writes: "In that empty tomb Christendom has always discerned an important witness to the reasonableness of belief. Christians have never doubted that as a matter of fact it was found empty on the third day; the Gospel narratives agree in emphasizing it; it [the burden of proof] . . . rests not upon those who hold the tradition, but upon those who either deny that the tomb was found empty, or explain the absence of the Lord's body by some rationalistic theory." 13/25

Professor James Denney, cited by Smith, says:

". . . The empty grave is not the product of a naive apologetic spirit, a spirit not content with the evidence for the Resurrection contained in the fact that the Lord had appeared to His own and had quickened them unto new victorious life; . . . it is an original, independent and unmotived part of the apostolic testimony." 60/374

4B.   Established Psychological Facts

1C.   THE TRANSFORMED LIVES OF THE DISCIPLES

1D.   *John R. W. Stott* says: "Perhaps the transformation of the disciples of Jesus is the greatest evidence of all for the resurrection. . . ." 63/58,59

2D.   *Dr. Simon Greenleaf,* the Harvard attorney, says of the disciples: "It was therefore impossible that they could have persisted in affirming the truths they have narrated, had not Jesus actually risen from the dead, and had they not known this fact as certainly as they knew any other fact.

"The annals of military warfare afford scarcely an example of the like heroic constancy, patience, and unflinching courage. They had every possible motive to review carefully the grounds of their faith, and the evidences of the great facts and truths which they asserted. . . ." 20/29

3D.   *Paul Little* asks: "Are these men, who helped transform the moral structure of society, consummate liars or deluded madmen? These alternatives are harder to believe than the fact of the Resurrection, and there is no shred of evidence to support them." 38/63

4D.   Look at the changed life of James, the brother of Jesus. Before the resurrection he despised all that his brother stood for. He thought Christ's claims were blatant pretention and served only to ruin the family name. After the resurrection, though, James is found with the other disciples preaching the gospel of their Lord. His epistle describes well the new relationship that he had with Christ. He describes himself as "a bond-servant of God and of the Lord Jesus Christ . . ." (James 1:1). The only explanation for this change in his life is that which Paul gives: "Then He [Jesus] appeared to James . . ." (I Corinthians 15:7).

5D.   *George Matheson* says that "the scepticism of Thomas comes out in the belief that the death of Jesus would be the death of His kingdom. 'Let us go, that we may die with Him.' The man who uttered these words had, at the time when he uttered them, no hope of Christ's resurrection. No man would propose to die with another if he expected to see him again in a few hours. Thomas, at that moment, had given up all intellectual belief. He saw no chance for Jesus. He did not believe in His physical power. He had made up his mind that the forces of the outer world would be too strong for Him, would crush Him." 41/140

6D.   However, Jesus made Himself known to Thomas also. The result was recorded in John's Gospel where Thomas exclaimed: "My Lord and my God!" (John 20:28). Thomas made an about-face after seeing his Lord risen from the grave and went on to die a martyr's death.

7D.   The following description of the change that occurred in the lives of the apostles after the resurrection is an interesting poetic portrayal:

"On the day of the crucifixion they were filled with sadness; on the first day of the week with gladness. At the crucifixion they were hopeless; on the first day of the week their hearts glowed with certainty and hope. When the message of the resurrection first came they were incredulous and hard to be convinced, but once they became assured they never doubted again. What could account for the astonishing change in these men in so short a time? The mere removal of the body from the grave could never have transformed their spirits, and characters. Three days are not enough for a legend to spring up which would so affect them. Time is needed for a process of legendary growth. It is a psychological fact that demands a full explanation.

"Think of the character of the witnesses, men and women who gave the world the highest ethical teaching it has ever known, and who even on the testimony of their enemies lived it out in their lives. Think of the psychological absurdity of picturing a little band of defeated cowards cowering in an upper room one day and a few days later transformed into a company that no persecution could silence — and then attempting to attribute this dramatic change to nothing more convincing than a miserable fabrication they were trying to foist upon the world. That simply wouldn't make sense." 3/5,6

2C.   THE TRANSFORMED LIVES OF 1,900 YEARS OF HISTORY

Just as Jesus Christ transformed the lives of His disciples, so men throughout the past 1,900 years have also had the same experience. For further evidence concerning the witness of transformed lives, see the chapter titled "The Uniqueness of Christian Experience."

3C.   THE VERDICT

The established psychological fact of changed lives, then, is a credible reason for believing in the resurrection. It is subjective evidence bearing witness to the objective fact that Jesus Christ arose on the third day. For only a risen Christ could have such transforming power in a person's life.

5B.   Established Sociological Facts

1C.   AN INSTITUTION: THE CHRISTIAN CHURCH

1D.   A basic foundation of the establishing of the Church was the preaching of Christ's resurrection:

Acts 1:21,22 — "It is therefore necessary that of the men who have accompanied us all the time that the Lord Jesus went in and out among us — beginning with the baptism of John, until the day that He was taken up from us — one of these should become a witness with us of His resurrection."

Acts 2:23,24 — "This Man, delivered up by the predetermined plan and foreknowledge of God, you nailed to a cross by the hands of godless men and put Him to death. And God raised Him up again, putting an end to the agony of death, since it was impossible for Him to be held in its power."

Acts 2:31,32 — "He looked ahead and spoke of the resurrection of the Christ, that He was neither abandoned to Hades, nor did His flesh suffer decay. This Jesus God raised up again, to which we are all witnesses."

Acts 3:14,15 — "But you disowned the Holy and Righteous One, and asked for a murderer to be granted to you, but put to death the Prince of life, the one whom God raised from the dead, a fact to which we are witnesses."

Acts 3:26 — "For you first, God raised up His Servant, and sent Him to bless you by turning every one of you from your wicked ways."

Acts 4:10 — "Let it be known to all of you, and to all the people of Israel, that by the name of Jesus Christ the Nazarene, whom you crucified, whom God raised from the dead — by this name this man stands here before you in good health."

Acts 5:30 — "The God of our fathers raised up Jesus, whom you had put to death by hanging Him on a cross."

Acts 10:39-41 — "And we are witnesses of all the things He did both in the land of the Jews and in Jerusalem. And they also put Him to death by hanging Him on a cross. God raised Him up on the third day, and granted that He should become visible, not to all the people, but to witnesses who were chosen beforehand by God, that is, to us, who ate and drank with Him after He arose from the dead."

Acts 13:29-39 — "And when they had carried out all that was written concerning Him, they took Him down from the cross and laid Him in a tomb. But God raised Him from the dead; and for many days He appeared to those who came up with Him from Galilee to Jerusalem, the very ones who are now His witnesses to the people. And we preach to you the good news of the promise made to the fathers, that God has fulfilled this promise to our children in that He raised up Jesus, as it is also written in the second Psalm, 'Thou art My Son; today I have begotten Thee.' And as for the fact that He raised Him up from the dead, no more to return to decay, He has spoken in this way: 'I will give you the holy and sure blessings of David.' Therefore He also says in another Psalm, 'Thou wilt not allow Thy Holy One to undergo decay.' For David, after he had served the purpose of God in his own generation, fell asleep, and was laid among his fathers, and underwent decay; but He whom God raised did not undergo decay. Therefore let it be known to you, brethren, that through Him forgiveness of sins is proclaimed to you, and through Him everyone who believes is freed from all things, from which you could not be freed through the Law of Moses."

Acts 17:30,31 — "Therefore having overlooked the times of ignorance, God is now declaring to men that all everywhere should repent, because He has fixed a day in which He will judge the world in righteousness through a Man whom He has appointed, having furnished proof to all men by raising Him from the dead."

Acts 26:22,23 — "And so, having obtained help from God, I stand to this day testifying both to small and great, stating nothing but what the Prophets and Moses said was going to take place; that the Christ was to suffer, and that by reason of His resurrection from the dead He should be the first to proclaim light both to the Jewish people and to the Gentiles."

2D.   The Church is a fact of history

The explanation for the existence of the Church is its faith in the resurrection. Throughout its early years, this institution suffered much persecution from the Jews and Romans. Individuals suffered torture and death for their Lord only because they knew that He had arisen from the grave.

Wilbur Smith says that even the rationalist, Dr. Guignebert, is forced to the following admission: "There would have been no Christianity if the belief in the resurrection had not been founded and systematized. . . . The whole of the soteriology and the essential teaching of Christianity rests on the belief of the Resurrection, and on the first page of any account of Christian dogma must be written as a motto, Paul's declaration: 'And if Christ be not risen, then is our preaching vain, and your faith is also vain.' From the strictly historical point of view, the importance of the belief in the resurrection is scarcely less. . . . By means of that belief, faith in Jesus and in His mission became the fundamental element of a new religion which, after separating from, became the opponent of Judaism, and set out to conquer the world." 57/20,21

Paul Little points out that the Church which was founded around 32 A.D. did not just happen, but had a definite cause. It was said of the Christians at Antioch in the early days of the Church that they turned the world upside down (Acts 17:6). The cause of this influence was the resurrection. 38/62

H. D. A. Major, principal of Ripon Hall, Oxford, (cited by Smith) says: "Had the crucifixion of Jesus ended His disciples' experience of Him, it is hard to see how the Christian church could have come into existence. That church was founded on faith in the Messiahship of Jesus. A crucified messiah was no messiah at all. He was one rejected by Judaism and accursed of God. It was the Resurrection of Jesus, as St. Paul declares in Romans 1:4, which proclaimed him to be the Son of God with power." 60/368

Kenneth S. Latourette, cited by Straton, says: "It was the conviction of the resurrection of Jesus which lifted His followers out of the despair into which His death had cast them and which led to the perpetuation of the movement begun by Him. But for their profound belief that the crucified had risen from the dead and that they had seen Him and talked with Him, the death of Jesus and even Jesus Himself would probably have been all but forgotten." 64/3

2C.   THE PHENOMENON OF THE CHRISTIAN SUNDAY

The Jews' original day of rest and worship was Saturday because it was said that God had finished His creation and rested on the seventh day. It was written into their holy laws. The Sabbath is one of the supporting columns of Judaism. One of the most reverent things in the life of a Jew was the keeping of the Sabbath. The Christians met for worship on the first day of the Jewish week in acknowledgment of the resurrection of Jesus. These Christians actually succeeded in changing this age-old and theologically-backed day of rest and worship to Sunday. Yet remember, THEY WERE JEWS THEMSELVES! Keeping in mind what they thought would happen if they were wrong, we must recognize that this was probably one of the biggest decisions any religious body of men have ever made!! How are we to explain the change from Saturday to Sunday worship without the resurrection? 19/51

J. N. D. Anderson observes that the majority of the first Christians were of Jewish background and had been fanatically attached to their Sabbath. It took, therefore, something extremely significant to change this habit; it took the resurrection to do it! 3/9

3C.   THE PHENOMENON OF CHRISTIAN SACRAMENTS

1D.   Communion — Acts 2:46; John 6; Matthew 26:26; Mark 14:22; Luke 22:19; I Corinthians 11:23,24.

The Lord's Supper is a remembrance of His death, but we read in Acts 2:46 that it was a time of joy. Now, if there was not a resurrection, how could there be joy? The memory of the meal which led directly to the betrayal and crucifixion of Jesus, their Lord, would have been an unbearable pain. What changed the anguish of the Last Supper into a communion of joy the world over?

Michael Green comments: "They *met* Him in this sacrament. He was not dead and gone, but risen and alive. And they would celebrate this death of His, in the consciousness of His risen presence, until His longed for return at the end of history (I Corinthians 11:26). We possess a short eucharistic prayer from the earliest Christian community, from the original Aramaic-speaking church (I Corinthia' 16:22 and *Didache,* 10). Here it is. *Maranatha!* It means, 'Our Lord, come!' How that could have been the attitude of the early Christians as they met to celebrate the Lord's Supper among themselves is quite inexplicable, unless He did indeed rise from the dead on the third day." 19/53

2D.   Baptism — Colossians 2:12; Romans 6:1-6

The Christians had an initiation ceremony — baptism. This is where they dared to differ again with Judaism. The Jews continued in circumcision and the Christians followed their Lord's command about baptism. A man had to repent of his sins, believe in the risen Lord and be baptized. Now, what did baptism symbolize? There is little doubt about this! Paul explains that a man in baptism is united to Christ in His death and resurrection. When he enters the water he is dying to his old sin nature, and he rises out of the water to share a new resurrected life of Christ. There is nothing in Christianity older than the sacraments, and yet they are directly linked to the death and resurrection of Christ. How is one to account for the meaning of Christian baptism if the resurrection never took place?

4C.   THE HISTORICAL PHENOMENON OF THE CHURCH

The institution of the Church, then, is an historical phenomenon, explained only by Jesus' resurrection. Those sacraments which Christianity observes serve also as a continual evidence of the Church's origin.

L. L. Morris comments of the first believers who witnessed Christ's resurrection: "They were Jews, and Jews have a tenacity in clinging to their religious customs. Yet these men observed the Lord's day, a weekly memorial of the resurrection, instead of the Sabbath. On that Lord's day they celebrated the holy communion, which was not a commemoration of a dead Christ, but a thankful remembrance of the blessings conveyed by a living and triumphant Lord. Their other sacrament, baptism, was a reminder that believers were buried with Christ and raised with Him (Colossians 2:12). The resurrection gave significance to all that they did." 14/1088

5A. INADEQUATE THEORIES CONCOCTED TO EXPLAIN AWAY THE RESURRECTION
("Futility of futilities! All is futility." Ecclesiastes 1:2b)

The following is a compilation of the most popular theoretical explanations that have been put forth to explain away the resurrection of Christ. Each theory will be considered in turn with the corresponding refutation. It becomes apparent with research that every objection to the resurrection has a reasonable alternative for belief.

J. N. D. Anderson, the British attorney, is quite aware of the importance of good evidence in judging a case's veracity. Concerning the testimony which history gives to the resurrection, he writes: "A point which needs stressing is that the evidence must be considered as a whole. It is comparatively easy to find an alternative explanation for one or another of the different strands which make up this testimony. But such explanations are valueless unless they fit the other strands in the testimony as well. A number of different theories, each of which might conceivably be applicable to part of the evidence but which do not themselves cohere into an intelligible pattern, can provide no alternative to the one interpretation which fits the whole." 4/105

Such will be the approach taken in considering the following theories.

1B. The Swoooooon Theory

   1C.   THE VIEW — CHRIST NEVER ACTUALLY DIED ON THE CROSS, BUT ONLY *SWOONED*

   When He was placed in the tomb of Joseph of Arimathea, He was still alive. After several hours, He was revived by the cool air of the tomb, arose and departed.

   Professor J. N. D. Anderson says of this theory that it was ". . . first put forward by a man named Venturini a couple of centuries or so ago. It has been resuscitated in recent years in a slightly different form by a heterodox group of Muslims called the Ahmadiya, who used to have their main headquarters at a place called Qadian and who have their English headquarters in a part of London called Putney.

   "Their explanation runs like this: Christ was indeed nailed to the cross. He suffered terribly from shock, loss of blood, and pain, and He swooned away; but He didn't actually die. Medical knowledge was not very great at that time, and the apostles thought He was dead. We are told, are we not, that Pilate was surprised that He was dead already. The explanation assertedly is that He was taken down from the cross in a state of swoon by those who wrongly believed Him to be dead, and laid in the sepulcher. And the cool restfulness of the sepulcher so far revived Him that He was eventually able to issue forth from the grave. His ignorant disciples couldn't believe that this was a mere resuscitation. They insisted it was a resurrection from the dead." 2/7

   Professor Kevan says of the swoon theory that also responsible for Christ's resuscitation was the ". . . reviving effects of the spices with which He had been embalmed. . . ." 32/9

   2C.   THE REFUTATION —

   Anderson comes to the conclusion: ". . . This theory does not stand up to investigation. . . ." 4/95

   W. J. Sparrow-Simpson says that it is ". . . now quite obsolete. . . ." 17/510

   I am confident that the following points will show why these men came to such conclusions.

1D.   Christ did die on the cross, according to the judgment of the
soldiers, Joseph and Nicodemus.

Paul Little says in reference to the swoon theory: "It is significant
that not a suggestion of this kind has come down from antiquity
among all the violent attacks which have been made on
Christianity. All of the earliest records are emphatic about Jesus'
death." 38/65

Professor T. J. Thorburn mentions the following as what Christ
suffered at the hands of Pilate: ". . . the Agony in the Garden, the
arrest at midnight, the brutal treatment in the hall of the High
Priest's palace and at the praetorium of Pilate, the exhausting
journeys backwards and forwards between Pilate and Herod, the
terrible Roman scourging, the journey to Calvary, during which
He fell exhausted by the strain upon His powers, the agonizing
torture of the Crucifixion, and the thirst and feverishness which
followed." 68/183-185

Thorburn observes: "It would be difficult to imagine even the most
powerful of men, after enduring all these, not succumbing to death.
Moreover, it is recorded that the victims of crucifixion seldom
recovered, even under the most favourable circumstances."
68/183-185

He concludes: "We cannot state the insuperable objections to this
theory better than in . . . [these] words. . . . 'Then,' says Keim,
'there is the most impossible thing of all; the poor, weak Jesus,
with difficulty holding Himself erect, in hiding, disguised, and finally
dying — this Jesus an object of faith, of exalted emotion, of the
triumph of His adherents, a risen conqueror, and Son of God! Here, in
fact, the theory begins to grow paltry, absurd, worthy only of
rejection.' " 68/183-185

Professor F. Godet, cited by Kevan, says: "Jesus, before His
crucifixion, had already suffered much, both in body and soul. He
had passed through the anticipation of His death in Gethsemane.
He had undergone the frightful pain of a Roman scourging, which
left deep scars on the back of the sufferer, and which is almost
equivalent to capital punishment. Then they had pierced His hands
and feet with nails. The small amount of strength which He might
still have had left had been worn away by the six hours of frightful
suffering which He had already passed through. Consumed with
thirst and completely exhausted, He had at last breathed out His
soul in that last cry recorded by the evangelists. Again, a Roman
soldier had pierced His heart with a spear. With no food or drink,
with no one to dress His wounds or alleviate His suffering in any
way, He had passed a whole day and two nights in the cave in which
He was laid. And yet, on the morning of the third day behold Him
reappearing, active and radiant!" 32/9,10

J. N. D. Anderson remarks of the hypothesis that Jesus did not die: "Well
. . . it's very ingenious. But it won't stand up to investigation. To begin
with, steps were taken — it seems — to make quite sure that Jesus was
dead; that surely is the meaning of the spear-thrust in His side. But
suppose for argument's sake that He was not quite dead. Do you really
believe that lying for hour after hour with no medical attention in a
rock-hewn tomb in Palestine at Easter, when it's quite cold at night,
would so far have revived Him, instead of proving the inevitable end to
His flickering life, that He would have been able to loose Himself from
yards of graveclothes weighted with pounds of spices, roll away a stone

that three women felt incapable of tackling, and walk miles on wounded feet?" 3/7

As *John R. W. Stott* asks, are we to believe "that after the rigours and pains of trial, mockery, flogging and crucifixion He could survive thirty-six hours in a stone sepulchre with neither warmth nor food nor medical care? That He could rally sufficiently to perform the superhuman feat of shifting the boulder which secured the mouth of the tomb, and this without disturbing the Roman guard? That then, weak and sickly and hungry, He could appear to the disciples in such a way as to give them the impression that He had vanquished death? That He could go on to claim that He had died and risen, could send them into all the world and promise to be with them unto the end of time? That He could live somewhere in hiding for forty days, making occasional surprise appearances, and then finally disappear without any explanation? Such credulity is more incredible than Thomas' unbelief." 63/48,49

Of modern rationalists who deny the resurrection of Christ, *E. Le Camus* writes:

"They say: 'If He is risen, He was not dead, or if He died, He is not risen.'

"Two facts, one as certain as the other, throw light on this dilemma. The first is that on Friday evening Jesus was dead; and the second, that He appeared full of life on Sunday and on the days that followed.

"That He was dead on Friday evening no one has doubted; neither in the Sanhedrin, nor in the Praetorium, nor on Calvary. Pilate alone was astonished that He had so soon given up the ghost, but his astonishment only called forth new testimony corroborating the assertion of those who asked for His body.

"Therefore, friends and enemies, looking on the Crucified, saw clearly that He was no more. To prove it the better, the centurion pierced Him with his lance, and the corpse made no motion. From the wound came forth a mixture of water and of blood, which revealed a rapid decomposition of the vital elements. Bleeding, they say, is fatal in syncope. Here it has not killed Him Who is already dead. For the circumstances in which it occurred prove that Jesus had ceased to live some moments before. And it does not occur to the most intelligent of His enemies, such as the chief priests, to cast a doubt on the reality of His death. All that they fear is fraud on the part of the disciples, who may remove the body, but not on the part of Jesus Whom they have seen expire. He was taken down from the cross, and just as He had shown no sign of life at the stroke of the soldier's spear, so now He lies still and cold in the loving arms that lift Him up, take Him away, embalm, enshroud, and lay Him in the tomb, after covering Him with proofs of their desolation and their love. Can we imagine a more complete swoon than this or one more suitably timed? Let us add that this would indeed be a most fortuitous ending of a life already, in itself, so prodigious in its sanctity and so fecund in its influence. This were an impossible coincidence! It were more miraculous even than the Resurrection itself!" 34/485,486

For further information on Jesus' death, see page

2D.   Jesus' disciples did not perceive Him as having merely revived from a swoon.

The skeptic, *David Friedrich Strauss* — himself certainly no believer in the resurrection — gave the deathblow to any thought that Jesus revived from a swoon. Here are his words: "It is impossible that a being who had stolen half-dead out of the sepulchre, who crept about weak and ill, wanting medical treatment, who required bandaging, strengthening and indulgence, and who still at last yielded to his sufferings, could have given to the disciples the impression that he was a Conqueror over death and the grave, the Prince of Life, an impression which lay at the bottom of their future ministry. Such a resuscitation could only have weakened the impression which he had made upon them in life and in death, at the most could only have given it an elegiac voice, but could by no possibility have changed their sorrow into enthusiasm, have elevated their reverence into worship." 65/412

William Milligan, in describing Jesus' appearances to His disciples, says they were ". . . not those of a sick chamber, but of health and strength and busy preparation for a great work to be immediately engaged in." He continues: "Despondency has given place to hope, despair to triumph, prostration of all energy to sustained and vigorous exertion." 43/76,77

He continues: "When the first fears of the disciples were dispelled, it was one of joy, of boldness, and of enthusiasm; we see none of those feelings of pity, of sympathy with suffering, of desire to render help, that must have been called forth by the appearance of a person who had swooned away through weariness and agony, who had continued in unconsciousness from Friday afternoon to Sunday morning, and who was now only in the first moments of recovery." 43/76,77

Professor E. H. Day says: "In the narratives of the various appearances of the risen Christ there is no hint of any such physical weakness as would have been inevitable if Christ had revived from apparent death. The disciples in fact saw in their risen Master not One recovering against all expectation from acute sufferings, but One Who was the Lord of life and the Conqueror of death, and Who was no longer fettered as they had known Him to be in the days of His ministry, by physical limitations." 13/49,50

3D.   Those who propose the swoon theory also have to say that Jesus, once He had revived, was able to perform a miracle of wiggling out of the graveclothes which were wound tightly about all the curves of His body and leave without disarranging these at all.

Merrill C. Tenney explains the graveclothes: "In preparing a body for burial according to Jewish custom, it was usually washed and straightened, and then bandaged tightly from the armpits to the ankles in strips of linen about a foot wide. Aromatic spices, often of a gummy consistency, were place between the wrappings or folds. They served partially as a preservative and partially as a cement to glue the cloth wrappings into a solid covering. . . . John's term 'bound' (Gr. *edesan*), is in perfect accord with the language of Luke 23:53, where the writer says that the body was *rolled* . . . in linen. . . .

"On the morning of the first day of the week the body of Jesus had vanished, but the graveclothes were still there. . . .

"The wrappings were in position where the head had been, separated from the others by the distance from armpits to neck. The shape of the body was still apparent in them, but the flesh and bone had disappeared. . . . How was the corpse extricated from the wrappings, since they would not slip over the curves of the body when tightly wound around it?" 60/116,117

For further information on Jesus' burial, see page 204.

4D.   "Those who hold this theory," says *James Rosscup,* "have to say that Christ, in a weakened condition, was able to roll back the stone at the entrance of the tomb — a feat which historians say would take several men — step out of the sepulchre without awaking any one of the soldiers (if we assume for argument's sake that they were asleep, and we know they were certainly not!), step over the soldiers and escape." 55/3

Professor E. H. Day comments on this point: "The physical improbabilities of the supposition are indeed overwhelming. Even if we were to reject the account of the guarding of the sepulchre (in obedience to the dictates of a criticism which finds in it an inconvenient incident) there remains the difficulty of supposing that One but just recovered from a swoon could have rolled away the stone from the door of the sepulchre, 'for it was very great.' " 13/48,49

Concerning the enormous size of that stone at Jesus' tomb, see page 207.

It is absurd to suppose that Jesus could have fought off the Roman guard even if He had managed to roll away the stone. Such men as would have kept the watch should scarcely have had difficulty in dealing with "a being who had stolen half-dead out of the sepulchre," as Strauss described Jesus. Also, the punishment for falling asleep while on watch was death, so the guard would have been wide awake.

For further information of the Roman guard with whom Jesus would have had to fight, see page 214.

5D.   If Jesus had merely revived from a swoon, the long walk ". . . to a village named Emmaus, which was about seven miles from Jerusalem" (Luke 24:13), would have been impossible.

Professor Day says, "A long walk, followed by the appearance to the disciples at Jerusalem, is inconceivable in the case of one recovered from a swoon caused by wounds and exhaustion." 13/48,49

Professor E. F. Kevan makes the following comments on this point:

"On His feet, which had been pierced through and through only two days back, He walks without difficulty the two leagues between Emmaus and Jerusalem. He is so active, that during the repast He disappears suddenly out of sight of His fellow-travellers, and when they return to the capital to announce the good news to the apostles, they find Him there again! He has overtaken them. With the same quickness which characterizes all His movements, He presents Himself suddenly in the room in which the disciples are assembled. . . . Are these the actions of a man who had just been taken down half-dead from the cross, and who has been laid in a grave in a condition of complete exhaustion? No." 32/9,10

6D.   If Jesus had merely revived from a deathlike swoon, He would have explained His condition to the disciples. Remaining silent, He would have been a liar and deceiver, allowing His followers to spread a resurrection proclamation that was really a resurrection fairy tale.

E. Le Camus writes: "Let us say, moreover, that if Jesus had only swooned, He could not, without injury to His character, allow any one to believe that He had been dead. Instead of presenting Himself as one *risen again*, He should have said simply *preserved* by chance. In fact, here as everywhere else in the Gospel, we encounter this unsurmountable dilemma: either Jesus was the Just One, the Man of God, or among men He is the greatest of criminals. If He presented Himself as one from the dead, whereas He was not such, He is guilty of falsehood, and must be denied even the most common honesty." 34/485,486

Paul Little comments that such a theory requires us to believe that "Christ Himself was involved in flagrant lies. His disciples believed and preached that He was dead but became alive again. Jesus did nothing to dispel this belief, but rather encouraged it." 38/66

John Knox, the New Testament scholar, quoted by Straton, says, "It was not the fact that a man had risen from the dead but that a particular man had done so which launched the Christian movement. . . . The character of Jesus was its deeper cause." 64/3

Jesus would have had no part in perpetrating the lie that He had risen from the grave if He had not. Such an allegation is unreservedly impugned as one examines His spotless character.

7D. If Christ did not die at this time, then when did He die, and under what circumstances?

Professor E. H. Day says: ". . . If the swoon-theory be accepted, it is necessary to eliminate from the Gospels and the Acts the whole of the Ascension narrative, and to account for the sudden cessation of Christ's appearances by the supposition that He withdrew Himself from them completely, to live and die in absolute seclusion, leaving them with a whole series of false impressions concerning His Own Person, and their mission from Him to the world." 13/50

William Milligan says that if Christ merely swooned on the cross and later revived, "He must have retired to some solitary retreat unknown even to the most attached of His disciples. While His Church was rising around Him, shaking the old world to its foundations, and introducing everywhere amidst many difficulties a new order of things — while it was torn by controversies, surrounded by temptations, exposed to trials, placed in short in the very circumstances that made it most dependent on His aid — He was absent from it, and spending the remainder of His days, whether few or many, in what we can describe by no other term than ignoble solitude. And then at last He must have died — no one can say either where, or when, or how! There is not a ray of light to penetrate the darkness; and these early Christians, so fertile, we are told, in legends, have not a single legend to give us help." 43/79

3C. CONCLUSION

With *George Hanson*, one can honestly say of the swoon theory: "It is hard to believe that this was the favourite explanation of eighteenth-century rationalism." The evidence speaks so much to the contrary of such a hypothesis that it is now obsolete. 22/19

2B. The Theft Theory

    1C.   THE VIEW — THE DISCIPLES STOLE THE BODY

        1D.   Matthew records the following as the theory which prevailed at his time to explain away the resurrection of Christ:

            "Now while they were on their way, behold, some of the guard came into the city and reported to the chief priests all that had happened. And when they had assembled with the elders and counseled together, they gave a large sum of money to the soldiers, and said, 'You are to say, "His disciples came by night and stole Him away while we were asleep." And if this should come to the governor's ears, we will win him over and keep you out of trouble.' And they took the money and did as they had been instructed; and this story was widely spread among the Jews, and is to this day" (Matthew 28:11-15).

        2D.   That the theft theory as recorded in Matthew was popular among the Jews for some time is seen in the writings of Justin Martyr, Tertullian and others.

            Professor Thorburn makes the following observations:

            "In Justin's *Dialogue Against Trypho* 108, the Jew speaks of 'one Jesus, a Galilean deceiver, whom we crucified; but his disciples stole him by night from the tomb, where he was laid when unfastened from the cross, and now deceive men by asserting that he has risen from the dead and ascended into heaven.'

            "So also Tertullian (*Apology* 21) says: 'The grave was found empty of all but the clothes of the buried one. But, nevertheless, the leaders of the Jews, whom it nearly concerned both to spread abroad a lie, and keep back a people tributary and submissive to them from the faith, gave it out that the body of Christ had been stolen by his followers.' And, again, with a fine scorn he says [*De Spectac.* 30.], 'This is he whom his disciples secretly stole away that it might be said that he had risen again, or the gardener had taken away, in order that his lettuces might not be damaged by the crowds of visitors!'

            "This statement we find repeated in Jewish mediaeval literature [Jewish book in Eisenmenger, i. pp. 189 ff., etc.]. Reimarus repeats the same story: 'The disciples of Jesus,' he says, 'purloined the body of Jesus before it had been buried twenty-four hours, played at the burial-place the comedy of the empty grave, and delayed the public announcement of the resurrection until the fiftieth day, when the decay of the body had become complete.'

            "The statements and arguments of this very old theory were fully answered by Origen [*Contr. Cels.*]." 68/191,192

        3D.   *John Chrysostom* of Antioch (347-407 A.D.) said of the theft theory:

            "For indeed even this establishes the resurrection, the fact I mean of their saying, that the disciples stole Him. For this is the language of men confessing, that the body was not there. When therefore they confess the body was not there, but the stealing it is shown to be false and incredible, by their watching by it, and by the seals, and by the timidity of the disciples, the proof of the resurrection even hence appears incontrovertible." 10/531

2C.   THE REFUTATION

1D.   The empty tomb has to be explained somehow.

Professor E. F. Kevan says that while the empty tomb does not necessarily prove the resurrection, it does, however, present two distinct alternatives. Kevan writes, "Those alternatives are that the empty tomb was either a Divine work or a human one." Both of these choices must be objectively considered and the one with the highest probability of being true must be accepted. 32/14

Kevan continues: "No difficulty presents itself, however, when the decision has to be made between such alternatives as these. The enemies of Jesus had no motive for removing the body; the friends of Jesus had no power to do so. It would have been to the advantage of the authorities that the body should remain where it was; and the view that the disciples stole the body is impossible. The power that removed the body of the Saviour from the tomb must therefore have been Divine." 32/14

Le Camus puts it this way: "If Jesus, who had been laid in the tomb on Friday, was not there on Sunday, either He was removed or He came forth by His own power. There is no other alternative. Was He removed? By whom? By friends or by enemies? The latter had set a squad of soldiers to guard Him, therefore they had no intention of causing Him to disappear. Moreover, their prudence could not counsel this. This would have made the way too easy for stories of the resurrection which the disciples might invent. The wisest course was for them to guard Him as a proof. Thus they could reply to every pretension that might arise: 'Here is the corpse, He is not risen.'

"As for His friends, they had neither the intention nor the power to remove Him." 34/482

Wilbur Smith says: ". . . These soldiers did not know how to explain the empty tomb; they were told what to say by the Sanhedrin and bribed that they might repeat in fear this quickly concocted tale." 57/22,23

A. B. Bruce remarks: "The report to be sent abroad assumes that there is a fact to be explained, the disappearance of the body. And it is implied that the statement to be given out as to that was known by the soldiers to be false." 6/337,338

2D.   That the disciples stole Christ's body is not a reasonable explanation for the empty tomb.

1E.   The guard's testimony was not questioned. Matthew records that ". . . some of the guard came into the city and reported to the chief priests all that had happened" (Matthew 28:11).

Professor R. C. H. Lenski remarks that the message of Jesus' resurrection was delivered to the high priests through their own witnesses, "the soldiers they themselves had posted, the most unimpeachable witnesses possible." The testimony of the guard was accepted as being entirely true; they knew the guard had no reason to lie. 35/1161,1162

Wilbur M. Smith writes: "It should be noticed first of all that the Jewish authorities never questioned the report of the guards. They did not themselves go out to see if the tomb was empty, because they knew it was empty. The guards would never have come back with such a story as this on their lips, unless they were reporting actual, indisputable occurrences, as far as they were able to apprehend them. The story which the Jewish authorities told the soldiers to repeat was a story to explain how the tomb became *empty*." 60/375,376

Professor Albert Roper, speaking of Annas and Caiaphas, says: "Their hypocritical explanation of the absence of the body of Jesus from the tomb proclaims the falsity of their allegation, else why should they have sought to suborn the perjured testimony of the soldiers?" 54/37

The Jews, then, by not questioning the veracity of the guard's testimony, give tacit assent to the emptiness of Christ's tomb. Their concocted tale that the disciples stole Jesus' body is only a lame excuse, put forth for lack of anything better.

2E.   Much precaution was taken in securing the tomb against the theft. To the disciples, such measures would have been an insurmountable obstacle in any plan of grave robbery.

Professor Albert Roper says: "Let us be fair. We are confronted with an explanation which to reasonable minds cannot and does not explain; a solution which does not solve. When the chief priests induced Pilate to 'command . . . that the sepulchre be made sure until the third day,' the factual record justifies the conclusion that the sepulchre was in very truth made 'sure.' Reasoning, therefore, from that record, we are inescapably faced with the conclusion that the measures taken to prevent the friends of Jesus from stealing His body now constitute unimpeachable proof that they could not and did not steal it." 54/34

Fallow's Encyclopedia says, "The disciples could not resist Roman power. How could soldiers be armed, and on guard, suffer themselves to be overreached by a few timorous people?" 17/1452

John Chrysostom, in speaking of the women who came early Sunday morning to Jesus' tomb, writes: "They considered that no man could have taken Him when so many soldiers were sitting by Him, unless He raised up Himself." 9/527

3E.   The depression and cowardice of the disciples is a hard-hitting argument that they could not have suddenly become so brave and daring as to face a detachment of soldiers at the tomb and steal the body. They were in no mood to try anything like that.

Wilbur M. Smith says: ". . . The disciples who had fled from Jesus when He was being tried, neither had the courage nor the physical power to go up against a group of soldiers." 57/22,23

Smith continues: ". . . These disciples were in no mood to go out and face Roman soldiers, subdue the entire guard, and snatch that body out of the tomb. I think, myself, if they had attempted it, they would have been killed, but they certainly were in no mood even to try it. On Thursday night of that week Peter had proved himself such a coward, when a maid twitted him in the lower hall of the palace of the high priest, accusing him of belonging to the condemned Nazarene, that, to save his own skin, he denied his Lord, and cursed and swore. What could have happened to Peter within those few hours to change him from such a coward to a man rushing out to fight Roman soldiers?" 60/376,377

Concerning the theft theory, Fallow writes in his encyclopedia: "It is probable they would not, and it is next to certain they [the disciples] could not [rob Jesus' grave].

"How could they have undertaken to remove the body? Frail and timorous creatures, who fled as soon as they saw Him taken into custody; even Peter, the most courageous, trembled at the voice of a servant girl, and three times denied that he knew Him. People of this character, would they have dared to resist the authority of the governor? Would they have undertaken to oppose the determination of the Sanhedrin, to force a guard, and to elude or overcome soldiers armed and aware of danger? If Jesus Christ were not risen again (I speak the language of unbelievers), He had deceived His disciples with vain hopes of His resurrection. How came the disciples not to discover the imposture? Would they have hazarded themselves by undertaking an enterprise so perilous in favor of a man who had so cruelly imposed on their credulity? But were we to grant that they formed the design of removing the body, how could they have executed it?" 17/1452

Professor A. Roper says: "There is not one of that little band of disciples who would have dared to violate that sealed tomb even if there were no Roman soldiers guarding it. The thought that one of them could accomplish such an undertaking in the face of the preventive measures which had been adopted is utterly fantastic." 54/37

See pages 212-214 on the Roman guard to understand further why the disciples would have been afraid of the watch.

4E.   If the soldiers were sleeping, how could they say the disciples stole the body?

The following commentary on the theft theory appears in *Fallow's Encyclopedia:* " 'Either,' says St. Augustine, 'they were asleep or awake; if they were awake, why should they suffer the body to be taken away? If asleep, how could they know that the disciples took it away? How dare they then depose that it was stolen?' " 17/1452

A. B. Bruce says of the Roman guard: ". . . They were perfectly aware that they had not fallen asleep at their post and that no theft had taken place. The lie for which the priests paid so much money is suicidal; one half destroys the other. Sleeping sentinels could not know what happened." 6/337,338

Professor David Brown remarks: "If anything were needed to complete the proof of the reality of Christ's resurrection, it would be the silliness of the explanation which the guards were bribed to give of it. That a whole guard should go to sleep on their watch at all, was not very likely; that they should do it in a case like this, where there was such anxiety on the part of the authorities that the grave should remain undisturbed, was in the last degree improbable. . . ." 30/133

Paul Little says of the theory concocted by the Jews: "They gave the soldiers money and told them to explain that the disciples had come at night and stolen the body while they were asleep. That story is so obviously false that Matthew does not even bother to refute it! What judge would listen to you if you said that while you were asleep, your neighbor came into your house and stole your television set? Who knows what goes on while he's asleep? Testimony like this would be laughed out of any court." 38/63,64

5E.   The soldiers would not have fallen asleep while on watch — to do so would have meant death from their superior officers.

Professor A. B. Bruce writes: "The ordinary punishment for falling asleep on the watch was death. Could the soldiers be persuaded by any amount of money to run such a risk? Of course they might take the money and go away laughing at the donors, meaning to tell their general the truth. Could the priests expect anything else? If not, could they propose the project seriously? The story has its difficulties." 6/337,338

Edward Gordon Selwyn, cited by Wilbur Smith, comments on the possibility of the guards' falling asleep: "That without an exception *all* should have fallen asleep when they were stationed there for so extraordinary a purpose, to see that the body was not stolen . . . is not credible: especially when it is considered that these guards were subjected to the severest discipline in the world. It was death for a Roman sentinel to sleep at his post. Yet these guards were not executed; nor were they deemed culpable even by the rules, woefully chagrined and exasperated as they must have been by failure of their plan for securing the body. . . . That the Jewish rulers did not believe what they instructed and bribed the soldiers to say, is almost self-evident. If they did, why were not the disciples at once arrested and examined? For such an act as was imputed to them involved a serious offence against the existent authorities. Why were they not compelled to give up the body? Or, in the event of their being unable to exculpate themselves from the charge, why were they not punished for their crime? . . . It is nowhere intimated that the rulers even attempted to substantiate the charge." 60/578,579

William Paley, the English theologian and philosopher, writes: "It has been rightly, I think, observed by Dr. Townshend (Dis. upon the Res. p. 126), that the story of the guards carried collusion upon the fact of it: — 'His disciples came by night, and stole him away, while we slept.' Men in their circumstances would not have made such an acknowledgment of their negligence, without previous assurances of protection and impunity." 49/196

For further information on the kind of punishment given those (either Roman guard or temple police) who fell asleep while on watch, see pages 212-215.

6E.   The stone at the tomb was extremely large (see page 207). Even if the soldiers were asleep and the disciples did try to steal the body, the noise caused while moving such a rock would surely have awakened them.

Professor Wilbur Smith says: "Surely these soldiers would have been awakened by the rolling back of a heavy stone, and the taking out of the body of Jesus." 57/22,23

David Brown writes: ". . . But — even if it could be supposed that so many disciples should come to the grave as would suffice to break the seal, roll back the huge stone, and carry off the body — that the guards should all sleep soundly enough and long enough to admit of all this tedious and noisy work being gone through at their very side without being awoke." 30/133

7E.   The graveclothes give a silent testimony to the impossibility of theft. (For a comprehensive discussion of the Jewish custom of burial, see pages 204-207.)

Merrill Tenney remarks: "No robbers would ever have rewound the wrappings in their original shape, for there would not have been time to do so. They would have flung the cloths down in disorder and fled with the body. Fear of detection would have made them act as hastily as possible." 66/119

Professor Albert Roper says:

"Such orderliness is inconsistent with grave desecration and body-snatching. One brash enough to undertake such a mission, if one could have been found, would assuredly not have practiced such orderliness, such leisureliness, such calm. It is certainly not in keeping with similar felonious acts with which we are familiar that criminals practice such studious care to leave in a meticulously neat and tidy condition premises which they have looted or vandalized. On the contrary, disorder and disarray are the earmarks of a prowling visitor. Such acts, in the very nature of things, are not performed in a leisurely manner. Their perpetration calls for haste in which tidiness plays no part. The very orderliness of the tomb, testified to by John, proclaims the absurdity of the charge that the body of Jesus was stolen by His disciples." 54/35-37

Gregory of Nyssen, writing 1,500 years ago, commenting on these facts, says "that the disposition of the clothes in the sepulchre, the napkin that was about our Saviour's head, not lying with the linen clothes, but wrapped together in a place by itself, did not bespeak the terror and hurry of thieves, and, therefore, refutes the story of the body being stolen" (cited in Whitworth). 73/64,65

Chrysostom, also a fourth century author, writes in like manner: "And what mean also the napkins that were stuck on with the myrrh; for Peter saw these lying. For if they had been disposed to steal, they would not have stolen the body naked, not because of dishonoring it only, but in order not to delay and lose time in stripping it, and not to give them that were so disposed opportunity to awake and seize them. Especially when it was myrrh, a drug that adheres so to the body, and cleaves to the clothes, whence it was not easy to take the clothes off the body, but they that did this needed much time, so that from this again, the tale of the theft is improbable.

"What? did they not know the rage of the Jews? and that they would vent their anger on them? And what profit was it at all to them, if He had not risen again?" 9/530,531

Simon Greenleaf, the famous Harvard professor of law, says:

"The grave-clothes lying orderly in their place, and the napkin folded together by itself, made it evident that the sepulchre had not been rifled nor the body stolen by violent hands; for these garments and spices would have been of more value to thieves, than merely a naked corpse; at least, they would not have taken the trouble thus to fold them together. The same circumstances showed also that the body had not been removed by friends; for they would not thus have left the graveclothes behind. All these considerations produce in the mind of John the germ of a belief that Jesus was risen from the dead." 20/542

Henry Latham, who gives a good description of the grave-clothes, remarks that they were in one spot, and makes further observations on ". . . the hundred pounds' weight of spice. This spice was dry; the quantity mentioned is large; and if the clothes had been unwrapped, the powdered myrrh and aloes would have fallen on the slab, or on the floor, in a very conspicuous heap. Peter, when from the inside of the tomb he described to John, with great particularity, what he saw, would certainly have not passed this by. Mr. Beard bears the spice in mind, and speaks of it as weighing down the grave-clothes, but he misses the point, — to me so significant, — that if the clothes had been unfolded the spice would have dropped out and made a show. That nothing is said about the spice favours the supposition that it remained between the wrappers where it was originally laid, and consequently was out of sight." 33/9

8E.   The disciples would not have moved Christ's body.

Wilbur Smith comments: ". . . The disciples had absolutely no reason for taking away the body, which had been honorably buried. They could do no more for the body of their Lord than had been done. Joseph of Arimathea never told them to remove the body from its first burial place; it was not suggested by anyone else; and therefore, if they *had* undertaken such a task, it would only be, not for the honor of the Lord, or for their own preservation, but for the purpose of deceiving others; in other words, to foist a lie concerning Jesus upon the people of Palestine. Now whatever else these disciples were, who had followed the Lord for three years, they were not liars, with the exception of Judas, who was already dead. They were not mean men given to deceit. It is inconceivable that the eleven, after having companioned with the Holy Son of God who, Himself, condemned falsehood and ever exalted the truth, after hearing Him preach a gospel of more exalted righteousness than had ever been heard anywhere in the world before, it is inconceivable that these eleven disciples should all suddenly agree to enter into such a vile conspiracy as this." 60/377

9E.   They did not realize the truth of the resurrection as yet and so would not have been seeking to make it come true (cf. Luke 24).

As *John F. Whitworth* observes, ". . . They did not seem to understand that He was to rise the third day; they certainly were surprised when they found that He had risen. These circumstances negate the thought that they would even contemplate stealing the body to create the impression that He had risen." 73/64

Professor A. B. Bruce writes: "The disciples, even if capable of such a theft, so far as scruples of conscience were concerned, were not in a state of mind to think of it, or to attempt it. They had not spirit left for such a daring action. Sorrow lay like a weight of lead on their hearts, and made them almost as inanimate as the corpse they are supposed to have stolen. Then the motive for the theft is one which could not have influenced them then. Steal the body to propagate a belief in the resurrection! What interest had they in propagating a belief which they did not entertain themselves? 'As yet they knew not the Scriptures, that He must rise again from the dead': nor did they remember aught that their Master had said on this subject before His decease." 7/494

10E.   "The disciples were men of honor," says *James Rosscup*, "and could not have foisted a lie upon the people. They spent the rest of their lives proclaiming the message of the resurrection, as cowards transformed into men of courage. They were willing to face arrest, imprisonment, beating, and horrible deaths, and not one them ever denied the Lord and recanted of his belief that Christ had risen." 55/4

Paul Little, in discussing the theft theory, remarks: "Furthermore, we are faced with a psychological and ethical impossibility. Stealing the body of Christ is something totally foreign to the character of the disciples and all that we know of them. It would mean that they were perpetrators of a deliberate lie which was responsible for the misleading and ultimate death of thousands of people. It is inconceivable that, even if a few of the disciples had conspired and pulled off this theft, they would never have told the others." 38/63,64

J. N. D. Anderson, the British lawyer, in commenting on the idea that the disciples stole Christ's body, says: "This would run totally contrary to all we know of them: their ethical teaching, the quality of their lives, their steadfastness in suffering and persecution. Nor would it begin to explain their dramatic transformation from dejected and dispirited escapists into witnesses whom no opposition could muzzle." 2/92

Concerning the theft theory, Kevan writes: "It is here that even the opponents of the Christian view come to its help, for Strauss [1808-1874], the skeptic, rejects the hyposthesis of imposture on the part of the disciples as morally impossible. 'The historian,' says Strauss, 'must acknowledge that the disciples firmly believed that Jesus was risen' " (*Leben Jesu*, 1864, p. 289). 32/9

Wilbur Smith says, "Even many orthodox Jewish scholars today utterly repudiate this story, including Klausner himself, who will have none of it, and who himself admits that the disciples were too honorable to perform any piece of deception like this" (*Jesus of Nazareth; His Life, Times, and Teaching,* New York, 1925, p. 414). 57/22,23

Was it a "stolen body" that gave Peter boldness in his refutation in Acts 4: 8?

"Then Peter, filled with the Holy Spirit, said to them, 'Rulers and elders of the people, if we are on trial today for a benefit done to a sick man, as to how this man has been made well, let it be known to all of you, and to all the people of Israel, that by the name of Jesus Christ the Nazarene, whom you crucified, whom God raised from the dead, — by this name this man stands here before you in good health. He is the stone which was rejected by you, the builders, but which became the very corner stone. And there is salvation in no one else; for there is no other name under heaven that has been given among men, by which we must be saved' " (Acts 4: 8-12).

Wilbur Smith explains: "The power of God so came down upon Peter on the day of Pentecost that on that one day, in a sermon occupied, for the most part, with the truth of the Resurrection of Christ, three thousand souls were won to the Lord. One thing is true: *Peter was at least preaching what he believed:* that God had raised Christ from the dead. You cannot conscientiously preach lies with power like this. The disciples went on preaching the Resurrection, until the whole world was turned upside down by faith in this glorious truth. No, the disciples did not and could not have stolen the body of our Lord." 60/377,378

Each of the disciples, except John, died a martyr's death. They were persecuted because they tenaciously clung to their beliefs and statements. As *Paul Little* writes: "Men will die for what they *believe* to be true, though it may actually be false: They do not, however, die for what they *know* is a lie." If the disciples had stolen Jesus' body, they would have known that their resurrection proclamation was false. However, they "constantly referred to the Resurrection as the basis for their teaching, preaching, living and — significantly — dying." The theory that the disciples stole the body, then, is utterly absurd! 36/62,64

I agree with *John R. W. Stott:* The theory that the disciples stole Christ's body "simply does not ring true. It is so unlikely as to be virtually impossible. If anything is clear from the Gospels and the Acts, it is that the apostles were sincere. They may have been deceived, if you like, but they were not deceivers. Hypocrites and martyrs are not made of the same stuff." 63/50

3D.   The theory that the Jews, the Romans, or Joseph of Arimathea moved Christ's body is no more reasonable an explanation for the empty tomb than theft by the disciples.

1E.   Did the Jews move the body?

J. N. D. Anderson says, "Within seven short weeks [after Christ's resurrection] — if the records are to be believed at all, and I cannot see any possible reason for Christian writers to have invented that difficult gap of seven weeks — within seven short weeks Jerusalem was seething with the preaching of the resurrection. The apostles were preaching it up and down the city. The chief priests were very much upset about it. They said that the apostles were trying to bring this man's blood upon them. They were being accused of having crucified the Lord of glory. And they were prepared to go to almost any lengths to nip this dangerous heresy in the bud." 3/6

If the Jews had issued on official order to have the body moved, why, when the apostles were preaching the resurrection in Jerusalem, didn't they explain:

"Wait! We moved the body — Christ didn't rise from the grave."

If such a rebuttal failed, why didn't they explain exactly where His body lay?

If this failed, why didn't they recover the corpse, put it on a cart, and wheel it through the center of Jerusalem? Such an action would have destroyed Christianity — not in the cradle, but in the womb!

William Paley, the English theologian and philosopher, says, ". . . It is evident that, if His body could have been found, the Jews would have produced it, as the shortest and completest answer possible to the whole story. For, notwithstanding their precaution, and although thus prepared and forewarned; when the story of the resurrection of Christ came forth, as it immediately did; when it was publicly asserted by His disciples, and made the ground and basis of their preaching in His name, and collecting followers to His religion; the Jews had not the body to produce. . . ." 49/196-198

John Whitworth writes of the Jews' silence as to the whereabouts of Jesus' body: "While this story [of the theft] was afterwards commonly reported among the Jews, yet, as Dr. Gilmore observes, 'not once is it adverted to on those trials of the Apostles which soon took place at Jerusalem, on account of their bold and open proclamation of their Master's resurrection.' Though the Apostles were cited before that very body who had given currency to the report of the disciples' theft, they are not even once taxed with the crime; not even a whisper escapes the lips of the Sanhedrin on the subject; and the story was soon abandoned as untenable and absurd." 73/66

2E. Did the Romans move the body?

It would have been to the governor's advantage to keep the body in its grave. Pilate's main interest was to keep things peaceful. Moving the body would have caused unwanted agitation to arise from the Jews and the Christians.

J. N. D. Anderson says of Pilate: "He . . . was upset about this strange teaching. If he had had the body moved, it seems incredible that he wouldn't have informed the chief priests when they were so upset." 3/6

Pilate merely wanted peace.

3E. Did Joseph of Arimathea move the body?

Joseph was a secret disciple and as such would not have moved the body without consulting the other disciples first.

If Joseph had ventured to move Christ's body without consulting the rest, he surely would have told the other disciples afterward, when the resurrection message was being published, what he had done.

4E. In conclusion, the facts of the case speak loudly against the theory that Christ's body was moved.

As *George Hanson* says: "The simple faith of the Christian who believes in the Resurrection is nothing compared to the credulity of the sceptic who will accept the wildest and most improbable romances rather than admit the plain witness of historical certainties. *The difficulties of belief may be great; the absurdities of unbelief are greater.*" 22/24

3B. The Hallucination Theory

1C. THE VIEW — ALL OF CHRIST'S POST-RESURRECTION APPEARANCES WERE REALLY ONLY SUPPOSED APPEARANCES. WHAT REALLY HAPPENED WAS THIS: PEOPLE HAD HALLUCINATIONS.

2C. THE REFUTATION

1D. Were Christ's appearances that important?

C. S. Lewis says: "In the earliest days of Christianity an 'apostle' was first and foremost a man who claimed to be an eye-witness of the Resurrection. Only a few days after the Crucifixion when two candidates were nominated for the vacancy created by the treachery of Judas, their qualification was that they had known Jesus personally both before and after His death and could offer first-hand evidence of the Resurrection in addressing the outer world (Acts 1:22). A few days later St. Peter, preaching the first Christian sermon, makes the same claim — 'God raised Jesus, of which we all (we Christians) are witnesses' (Acts 2:32). In the first *Letter to the Corinthians* St. Paul bases his claim to apostleship on the same ground — 'Am I not an apostle? Have I not seen the Lord Jesus?' " 37/148

2D. Would it matter if Christ's post-resurrection appearances were visions?

Considering Lewis' definition, if the view which regards all of Christ's appearances to have been mere hallucinations were true, then the value of the apostolic office would be nil.

If true, it means, in *Gresham Machen's* words, ". . . that the Christian Church is founded upon a pathological experience of certain persons in the first century of our era. It means that if there had been a good neurologist for Peter and the others to consult, there never would have been a Christian Church." 32/10,11

J. N. D. Anderson, in speaking of "the credibility of the apostolic witness . . . ," says that it will either "stand or fall by the validity of their testimony. . . ." 4/100

3D. What is a vision?

Professor Wilbur Smith says, "The most satisfying *definition* of a vision I have seen is the one by Weiss: 'The scientific meaning of this term is that an apparent act of vision takes place for which there is no corresponding external object. The optic nerve has not been stimulated by any outward waves of light or vibrations of the ether, but has been excited by a purely inner physiological cause. At the same time the sense-impression of sight is accepted by the one who experiences the vision as completely as if it were wholly "objective"; he fully believes the object of his vision to be actually before him.' " 60/581

4D. Were Christ's post-resurrection appearances visions?

Mere visions were not the experience of the disciples; the testimony of the New Testament totally opposes such a hypothesis.

As *Hillyer Straton* has said: ". . . Men who are subject to hallucinations never become moral heroes. The effect of the resurrection of Jesus in transformed lives was continuous, and most of these early witnesses went to their deaths for proclaiming this truth." 64/4

5D. The hallucination theory is not plausible because it contradicts certain laws and principles to which psychiatrists say visions must conform.

1E. Generally, only particular kinds of people have hallucinations. 3/4-9; 38/67-69; 51/97-99

They are those whom one would describe as "high-strung," highly imaginative and very nervous.

The appearances that Christ made were not restricted to persons of any particular psychological make-up.

John R. W. Stott says, ". . . There was a variety in mood. . . .

"Mary Magdalene was weeping; . . .

". . . the women were afraid and astonished; . . .

". . . Peter was full of remorse, . . .

". . . and Thomas of incredulity.

"The Emmaus pair were distracted by the events of the week. . . .

". . . and the disciples in Galilee by their fishing. . . .

"It is impossible to dismiss these revelations of the divine Lord as hallucinations of deranged minds." 63/57

2E. Hallucinations are linked in an individual's subconscious to his particular past experiences. 3/4-9; 38/67-69; 51/97-99

1F. They are very individualistic and extremely subjective.

Heinrich Kluerer in *Psychopathology of Perception* cites a famous neurobiologist: "[Raoul] Mourgue, in his fundamental treatise on the neurobiology of hallucinations, reached the conclusion that variability and inconstancy represent the most constant features of hallucinatory and related phenomena. For him the hallucination is not a static phenomenon but essentially a dynamic process, the instability of which reflects the very instability of the factors and conditions associated with its origin." 27/18

It is extremely unlikely, then, that two persons would have the same hallucination at the same time.

2F. The appearances that Christ made were seen by many people.

Thomas J. Thorburn asserts: "It is absolutely inconceivable that as many as (say) five hundred persons, of average soundness of mind and temperament, in various numbers, at all sorts of times, and in divers situations, should experience all kinds of sensuous impressions — visual, auditory, tactual — and that all these manifold experiences should rest entirely upon subjective hallucination. We say that this is incredible, because if such a theory were applied to any other than a 'supernatural' event in history, it would be dismissed forthwith as a ridiculously insufficient explanation." 68/158,159

Theodore Christlieb, cited by Wilbur Smith, says: "We do not deny that science can tell us of cases in which visions were seen by whole assemblies at once; but where this is the case, it has always been accompanied by a *morbid excitement of the mental life,* as well as by a morbid bodily condition, especially by nervous affections. Now, even if one or several of the disciples had been in this morbid state, we should by no means be justified in concluding that all were so. They were surely men of most varied temperament and constitution. And yet, one after another is supposed to have fallen into this morbid condition; not only the excited women, but even Peter, that strong and hardy fisherman who was assuredly as far from nervousness as any one, James, the two on their way to Emmaus, and so on down to the sober, doubting Thomas, aye, and all eleven at once, and even *more than five hundred brethren together.* All of these are supposed to have fallen suddenly into some self-deception, and that, be it noticed, at the most different times and places, and during

the most varied occupations (in the morning by the grave; in conversation by the wayside; in the confidential circle of friends at work on the lake); in which their frames of mind most assuredly have been very varied and their internal tendency to visions most uneven. And could they, all of them, have agreed to announce these visions to the world as bodily appearances of the risen Christ? Or had they done so, could it have been pure self-deception and intentional deceit? Surely, some one or other of them must afterwards seriously have asked himself whether the image he had seen was a reality. Schleiermacher says most truly, 'Whoever supposes that the disciples deceived themselves and mistook the internal for the external, accuses them of such mental weakness as must invalidate their entire testimony concerning Christ and make it appear as though Christ Himself, when He chose such witnesses, did not know what was in man. Or, if He Himself had willed and ordained that they should mistake inward appearances for outward perceptions, He would have been the author of error, and all moral ideas would be confounded if this were compatible with His high dignity.' "
60/396,397

3E. According to two noted psychiatrists, *L. E. Hinisie and J. Shatsky,* "[An illusion is] an erroneous perception, a false response to a sense-stimulation. . . .

". . . But in a normal individual this false belief usually brings the desire to check often another sense or other senses may come to the rescue and satisfy him that it is merely an illusion."
26/280

The appearances that Christ made could not have been "erroneous" perceptions:

Wilbur Smith writes of Luke's observations. He describes him as "a man accustomed to scientifically considering any subject which he is studying. Luke says at the beginning of his second book, the Acts of the Apostles, that our Lord showed Himself alive after His Passion 'by many infallible proofs,' or more literally, 'in many proofs.' " 60/400

Smith continues: ". . . The very kind of evidence which modern science, and even psychologists, are so insistent upon for determining the reality of any object under consideration is the kind of evidence that we have presented to us in the Gospels regarding the Resurrection of the Lord Jesus, namely, the things that are seen with the human eye, touched with the human hand, and heard by the human ear. This is what we call empirical evidence." 60/389,390

W. J. Sparrow-Simpson says that "the Appearances of the Risen Master may be analyzed according to the human senses to which they appealed, whether the sense of sight, or of hearing, or of touch. The different phenomena may be conveniently grouped together under these divisions" 62/83

Sparrow-Simpson continues: "And first as to the sense of sight. This is naturally first, as the initial form of gaining their attention. It is described in the Gospels by various expressions:

" 'Jesus met them.'
" 'They saw Him,' but this seeing

included those who doubted.
" 'They knew Him.'
" 'They . . . supposed that they beheld a
spirit.'   Matthew 28: 9
" 'See . . . My hands and My feet, that   Matthew 28: 17
it is I Myself; handle Me and see, for a
spirit hath not flesh and bones as ye
behold . . . Me having. And when He had   Luke 24: 31
said this He shewed unto them . . . His   Luke 24: 37
hands and His feet.'   Luke 24: 39

"Similarly also in the fourth Evangelist: John 20: 18
'I have seen the Lord.'
" 'He shewed unto them His hands and
His side.'   John 20: 20
" 'They saw the Lord.'   John 20: 20
" 'Except I shall see in His hands the
print of the nails.'   John 20: 25
" 'Because thou hast seen Me.'   John 20: 29
" 'And none of His disciples durst
inquire of Him, Who art Thou? knowing
that it was the Lord.'   John 21: 12
" 'Appearing unto them by the space of
forty days.'   Acts 1: 3

"Appeal is made by the Risen Lord in
these Appearances to the marks of the
wounds inflicted in the Passion.

"St. Luke speaks of the hands and
the feet.   Luke 24: 29-40
"St. Matthew mentions neither.
"St. John mentions 'His hands and His   John 20: 20-25,
side.' " 62/183,184   27

"The appearances of the risen Christ are
reported also as appeals to the sense of
touch.

"By far the most emphatic words in this
respect are those in St. Luke: 'Handle Me
and see; for a spirit hath not flesh and
bones, as ye behold Me having. . . .'   Luke 24: 39

" 'And they gave Him a piece of a
broiled fish. And He took it, and did
eat before them.' " 62/92,93   Luke 24: 42,43

Professor Thomas Thorburn says:

" . . . The 'hallucinatory' vision at the
tomb in Mark has an *auditory*
experience: the angel tells the women
to go and announce the fact to the
disciples.   Mark 16: 5-7

"Similarly in Matthew (who drew largely
from the same sources as Mark) the
women both see *and* hear Jesus, and *also*
touch Him." 68/133   Matthew 28: 9,10

4E.   Hallucinations are usually restricted as to when and where they
        occur. 3/4-9; 38/67-69; 51/97-99

They usually are experienced:

In a place with a nostalgic atmosphere.

Or at a time which particularly brings the person to a reminiscing mood.

The times of Christ's appearances and their locations did not conduce the witnesses to hallucinate. No fancied events were dreamed up because of familiar surroundings.

John R. W. Stott remarks that ". . . the outwardly favourable circumstances were missing. . . ." 63/57

Stott continues: "If the appearances had all taken place in one or two particularly sacred places, which had been hallowed by memories of Jesus . . ." and if ". . . their mood had been expectant . . ." then ". . . our suspicions might well be aroused." 63/57

Stott concludes: "If we had only the story of the appearances in the upper room, we should have cause to doubt and question. If the eleven had been gathered in that special place where Jesus had spent with them some of His last earthly hours, and they had kept His place vacant, and were sentimentalizing over the magic days of the past, and had remembered His promises to return, and had begun to wonder if He might return and to hope that He would, until the ardour of their expectation was consummated by His sudden appearance, we might indeed fear that they had been mocked by a cruel delusion." 63/57

W. Robertson Nicoll, cited by Kevan, says: "Let it be remembered that the disciples thought not only that they saw Christ, but that they conversed with Him, that the interviews were held in various circumstances, and that there were many witnesses." 30/10

James Orr considers the time factor, saying that the appearances "were not fleeting glimpses of Christ but 'prolonged interviews' " [*The Resurrection of Jesus,* p. 145 (cited by Ramm)]. 52/186

Consider the great variety of times and places:

Matthew 28:9,10 — The early morning appearance to the women at the tomb.

Luke 24:13-33 — The appearance on the road to Emmaus one afternoon.

Luke 24:34; I Corinthians 15:7 — A couple of private interviews in broad daylight.

John 21:1-23 — By the lake, early one morning.

I Corinthians 15:6 — On a Galilean mountain by 500-plus believers.

(For a complete list of Christ's post-resurrection appearances, see pages 223,224.)

Indeed, there is almost a studied variety in the times and places of Christ's appearances — a variance that defies the hypothesis that they were mere visions.

5E.   Hallucinations require of people an anticipating spirit of hopeful expectancy which causes their wish to become father of the thought. 3/4-9; 38/67-69; 51/97-99

1F. The following principles are characteristic of hallucinations. *Professor William Milligan* states that the subject of the vision must be characterized by "belief in the idea that it expresses, and excited expectation that the idea will somehow be realized." 43/93-95

    1G. "In order to have an experience like this, one must so intensely *want* to believe that he projects something that really isn't there and attaches reality to his imagination." 38/68

    2G. *Professor E. H. Day* observes that ". . . the seeing of visions, the perception of exceptional phenomena subjectively by large numbers of persons at the same time, necessitates a certain amount of 'psychological preparation,' extending over an appreciably long period." 13/51-53

    3G. *Paul Little* writes: "For instance, a mother who has lost a son in the war remembers how he used to come home from work every evening at 5:30 o'clock. She sits in her rocking chair every afternoon musing and meditating. Finally, she thinks she sees him come through the door, and has a conversation with him. At this point she has lost contact with reality." 38/68

2F. In the case of His post-resurrection appearances, Christ's followers were:

Caused to believe *against their wills.*

W. J. Sparrow-Simpson writes: "The phenomena, therefore, suggest that the Appearances were rather forced upon the mind's attention from without rather than created from within." 62/88

Alfred Edersheim says that ". . . such visions presuppose a previous expectancy of the event, which, as we know, is the opposite of the fact." 15/626

Professor E. H. Day writes in objection to the hallucination theory: ". . . We may recognize the slowness with which the disciples arrive at a conviction to which only the inexorable logic of facts led them." 13/53,54

Concerning the absence of "psychological preparation," Day observes:

"The first appearance of the Lord found the various disciples in very various mental attitudes, but the states of expectancy, anticipation, or preparedness to see Him are conspicuously absent from the category."

And that ". . . the faith of all had been shaken by the catastrophe of the shameful death, a death recalling so vividly the word of the Jewish Law, 'He that is hanged is accursed of God' (Deut. xxi. 23). The theory of subjective visions might seem a plausible one if there had been among the disciples a refusal to believe the worst. But the hopes of the disciples were so far shattered that recovery was very slow." 15/53,54

Paul Little explains that the general disposition of Christ's followers was not like what one would find in victims of an hallucinatory experience: "Mary came to the tomb on the first Easter Sunday morning with spices in her hands. Why? To anoint the dead body of the Lord she loved. She was obviously not expecting to find Him risen from the dead. In fact, when she first saw Him she mistook Him for the gardener! When the Lord finally appeared to the disciples, they were frightened and thought they were seeing a ghost!" 38/68,69

Alfred Edersheim comments: ". . . Such a narrative as that recorded by St. Luke seems almost designed to render the 'Vision-hypothesis' impossible. We are expressly told, that the appearance of the Risen Christ, so far from meeting their anticipations, had affrighted them, and that they had thought it spectral, on which Christ had reassured them, and bidden them handle Him, for 'a spirit hath not flesh and bones, as ye behold Me having.' " 15/628

Continuing, Edersheim says: "*Reuss* well remarks, that if this fundamental dogma of the Church had been the outcome of invention, care would have been taken that the accounts of it should be in the strictest and most literal agreement." 15/628

C. S. Lewis says that ". . . any theory of hallucination breaks down on the fact (and if it is invention it is the oddest invention that ever entered the mind of man) that on three separate occasions this hallucination was not immediately recognized as Jesus (Luke xxiv. 13-31; John xx. 15, xxi. 4). Even granting that God sent a holy hallucination to teach truths already widely believed without it, and far more easily taught by other methods, and certain to be completely obscured by this, might we not at least hope that He would get the fact of the hallucination *right*? Is He who made all faces such a bungler that He cannot even work up a recognizable likeness of the Man who was Himself?" 37/153

Writing of Jesus' manifestation to His disciples, *T. J. Thorburn* relates, ". . . If it had been mere subjective imagination, originating a similar train of equally unreal conceptions in the others, tradition would surely have given us a more highly elaborated account of it. . . ." 68/29-31

6E.   Hallucinations usually tend to recur over a long period of time with noticeable regularity. 3/4-9; 38/67-69; 51/97-99

They either recur more frequently until a point of crisis is reached, or they occur less frequently until they fade away.

Notice the following observations concerning Christ's appearances:

Professor C. S. Lewis writes: "All the accounts suggest that the appearances of the Risen Body came to an end; some describe an abrupt end six weeks after the death. . . . A phantom can just fade away, but an objective entity must go somewhere — something must happen to it." 37/153,154

He concludes: "If it were a vision then it was the most systematically deceptive and lying vision on record. But if it were real, then something happened to it after it ceased to appear. You cannot take away the Ascension without putting something else in its place." 37/154

Hastings' *Dictionary of the Apostolic Church* records that "the theory is inconsistent with the fact that the visions came so suddenly to an end. After the forty days no appearance of the Risen Lord is recorded, except that to St. Paul, the circumstances and object of which were altogether exceptional. It is not thus that imagination works. As Keim says, 'The spirits that men call up are not so quickly laid.' " 24/360

Professor Kevan asks, "But if the visions of the risen Saviour were hallucinations, why did they stop so suddenly? Why, after the Ascension, does one not find others still seeing the coveted vision? By the law of development, says Dr. Mullins, 'hallucinations should have become chronic after five hundred had been brought under their sway. But now hallucination gives place to a definite and conquering programme of evangelisation.' " 32/11

3C.   WHAT CONCLUSIONS CAN WE DRAW?

John R. W. Stott writes: "The disciples were not gullible, but rather cautious, sceptical and 'slow of heart to believe.' They were not susceptible to hallucinations. Nor would strange visions have satisfied them. Their faith was grounded upon the hard facts of verifiable experience." 63/57

Hallucinations have never, writes *T. J. Thorburn*, "stimulated people to undertake a work of enormous magnitude, and, while carrying it out, to lead lives of the most rigid and consistent self-denial, and even suffering. In a word, . . . we are constrained to agree with Dr. Sanday, who says, 'No apparition, no mere hallucination of the senses, ever yet moved the world.' " 68/136

4B.   **That the Women, and Subsequently Everyone Else, Went to the Wrong Tomb**

1C.   THE VIEW

Professor Lake says: "It is seriously a matter for doubt whether the women were really in a position to be quite certain that the tomb which they visited was that in which they had seen Joseph of Arimathea bury the Lord's body. The neighborhood of Jerusalem is full of rock tombs, and it would not be easy to distinguish one from another without careful notes. . . . It is very doubtful if they were close to the tomb at the moment of burial. . . . It is likely that they were watching from a distance, and that Joseph of Arimathea was a representative of the Jews rather than of the disciples. If so, they would have had but a limited power to distinguish between one rock tomb and another close to it. The possibility, therefore, that they came to the wrong tomb is to be reckoned with, and it is important because it supplies the natural explanation of the fact that whereas they had seen the tomb closed, they found it open. . . .

"If it were not the same, the circumstances all seem to fall into line. The women came in the early morning to a tomb which they thought was the one in which they had seen the Lord buried. They expected to find a closed tomb, but they found an open one; and a young man . . . guessed their errand, tried to tell them that they had made a mistake in the place. 'He is not here,' said he, 'see the place where they laid him,' and probably pointed to the next tomb. But the women were frightened at the detection of their errand, and fled . . ." (Kirsopp Lake, *The Historical Evidence for the Resurrection of Jesus Christ*).

2C.   **THE REFUTATION**

The women's visit to the empty tomb on Sunday morning is one of the best attested events in the New Testament narratives. Kirsopp Lake's theory assumes its historicity.

Frank Morison, the British lawyer, says, "The story of the women's adventure is in the earliest authentic document we possess, the Gospel of St. Mark. It is repeated by St. Matthew and St. Luke, it is confirmed so far as Mary Magdalene herself is concerned by St. John, it is in the Apocryphal Gospel of Peter; and, perhaps even more significantly, it is in that very ancient and independent fragment, preserved by St. Luke in chapter xxiv., verses 13-34, the journey to Emmaus." 46/98

Professor Lake accepts the visit as historical, but he is wrong in his speculations as to what happened at the tomb.

1D.   These women had carefully noted where the body of Jesus was interred less than 72 hours before:

"And Mary Magdalene was there, and the other Mary, sitting opposite the grave" (Matthew 27:61).

"And Mary Magdalene and Mary the mother of Joses were looking on to see where He was laid" (Mark 15:47).

"Now the women who had come with Him out of Galilee followed after, and saw the tomb and how His body was laid" (Luke 23:55).

Do you think that you or I or these women or any other rational person would forget so quickly the place where a dearly loved one was laid to rest just 72 hours earlier?

2D.   The women reported what they had experienced to the disciples, and later Peter and John also found the tomb empty.

"And so she ran and came to Simon Peter, and to the other disciple whom Jesus loved, and said to them, 'They have taken away the Lord out of the tomb, and we do not know where they have laid Him.' Peter therefore went forth, and the other disciple, and they were going to the tomb. And the two were running together; and the other disciple ran ahead faster than Peter, and came to the tomb first; and stooping and looking in, he saw the linen wrappings lying there; but he did not go in. Simon Peter therefore also came, following him, and entered the tomb; and he beheld the linen wrappings lying there, and the face-cloth, which had been on His head, not lying with the linen wrappings, but rolled up in a place by itself. Then entered in therefore the other disciple also, who had first come to the tomb, and he saw, and believed" (John 20:2-8).

Is it to be argued that Peter and John also went to the wrong tomb?

Paul Little remarks, ". . . It is inconceivable that Peter and John would succumb to the same mistake. . . ." 38/65

3D.   Furthermore, an angel, sitting here on a stone said, "Come see the place where the Lord lay" (Matthew 28:6).

Did the angel make a mistake, too?

Wilbur Smith says, "Someone has suggested, in trying to force this theory of the mistaken tomb, that the angel's words really meant, 'You are in the wrong place, come over here to see where the Lord's body was placed.'

"Well, in nineteen hundred years of the study of the New Testament, it took our modern, sophisticated age to find *that* in the

Gospel records, and no trustworthy commentary on any of the Gospels entertains such a foolish interpretation as that." 60/381,382

4D.   If the women went to the wrong tomb (an empty sepulchre), then the Sanhedrin could have gone to the *right* tomb and produced the body (if Jesus did not rise). This would have shut the disciples up forever!

The high priests and the other enemies of Christ would certainly have gone to the right tomb!

5D.   Even if the women, the disciples, the Romans and the Jews *all* went to the wrong tomb, one thing is sure:

As *Paul Little* says: ". . . Certainly Joseph of Arimathea, owner of the tomb, would have solved the problem." 38/65

6D.   The narrative in Mark reads: "And entering the tomb, they saw a young man sitting at the right, wearing a white robe; and they were amazed. And he said to them, 'Do not be amazed; you are looking for Jesus the Nazarene, who has been crucified. He has risen; He is not here; behold, here is the place where they laid Him' " (Mark 16: 5,6).

Professor Lake's citing of Mark 16: 6 is incomplete. He quotes only part of what the young man said and ignores the key part of the narration. The phrase, "He has risen," is conspicuously absent in Lake's citing of the verse. Notice the following comparison:

Lake's Version	Actual Version
". . . He is not here, see the place where they laid Him. . . ."	". . . He has risen; He is not here; behold, here is the place where they laid Him."

J. N. D. Anderson says of Lake's misquote: ". . . For [it] I can see no scholarly justification whatever." 3/7

If the text is quoted correctly, then Lake's theory cannot stand!

7D.   Anderson points out another problem for those who hold to the Lake theory: When the women went back to the disciples, these men would have done one of two things:

They would have gone to the tomb to verify the women's report;

Or they would have immediately begun proclaiming the resurrection. 3/7

Such preaching, however, does not occur until seven weeks later.

Anderson says: "I cannot see any possible motive for Christian writers to have invented that seven-week gap. So we're asked to believe that the women didn't tell the apostles this story for quite a long time. Why not? Because the apostles had supposedly run away to Galilee." 3/7

Concerning this point, *Frank Morison* says that the "interdependence of the women upon the men very seriously embarrasses Prof. Lake's theory at its most vital point." Morison concludes the major problems:

"Prof. Lake is compelled to keep the women in Jerusalem until Sunday morning, because he firmly believes that they really went to the tomb.

"He is also compelled to get the disciples out of Jerusalem before sunrise on Sunday because he holds that the women kept silence.

"Finally, to harmonize this with the fact that they did subsequently tell the story, with all its inevitable and logical results, he finds it necessary to keep the women in Jerusalem for several weeks while the disciples returned to their homes, had certain experiences, and came back to the capital." 46/10

8D.   *John R. W. Stott* mentions the attitude of the women. They were not blinded by tears of remorse, but had a practical purpose for their early morning visit.

Stott says: "They had bought spices and were going to complete the anointing of their Lord's body, since the approach of the sabbath had made the work so hasty two days previously. These devoted and business-like women were not the kind to be easily deceived or to give up the task they had come to do." 63/48

9D.   This was not a public cemetery, but a private burying ground. There was no other tomb there which would allow them to make such a mistake. *Wilbur Smith,* in commenting on this point, says: "The whole idea is so utterly fantastic that Professor A. E. J. Rawlinson, no conservative, in his epochal commentary on St. Mark's Gospel, felt compelled to say of Lake's suggestion, 'That the women went by mistake to the wrong tomb, and that the attempt of a bystander to direct them to the right one was misunderstood, is rationalization which is utterly foreign to the spirit of the narrative.' " 60/382

10D. *Merrill Tenney* says, "Lake fails to explain why the 'young man' [Mark 16:5] would have been present either in a public cemetery or in a private garden at such an early hour." 66/115,116

He asks, "What conceivable motive would have drawn a stranger there?

"If He were not a stranger, but one of the disciples making an independent investigation, why should his presence have frightened the women?" 66/115,116

Tenney further comments that "Mark's account, on which Lake relies, states that he was seated *inside* the tomb [vs. 5], so that he could scarcely have meant that they were at the wrong place . . ., but that Jesus was no longer there; they could see where He had been laid, but the body had vanished." 66/115,116

11D. Some identify the "young man" as a gardener. However, Frank Morison says that ". . . this theory, despite its appearance of rationality, has one peculiar weakness." 46/97

". . . If it was so dark that the women accidentally went to the wrong tomb, it is exceedingly improbable that the gardener would have been at work. If it was late enough and light enough for the gardener to be at work, it is improbable that the women would have been mistaken. The theory just rests upon the synchronization of two very doubtful contingencies. This is, however, only part of the improbability and intellectual difficulty which gathers around it." 46/97

Also, if the "young man" was the gardener, as some people assert, why didn't the priests secure his testimony as evidence that Christ's body was still in the grave? 46/101,102

He was not the gardener, but was an angel from heaven (Matthew 28:1-10).

Everyone *knew* that Christ's grave was empty — the real issue was *how* did it get that way?

12D. What are we to think of Professor Lake's theory that the people went to wrong tomb?

George Hanson says: "If I had any doubts about the Resurrection, Professor Lake's book would provide a most salutary counteractive to my scepticism. After reading it I am more than ever of the opinion expressed by De Wette in his 'Historical Criticism of the Evangelical History' (p. 229): 'The *fact* of the Resurrection, although a darkness which cannot be dissipated rests on the way and manner of it, cannot be doubted.' " 22/8

Wilbur Smith cites the verdict of the British scholar, Professor Morse: "Their theory that the women were approaching the wrong tomb arises, not from any evidence, but from disbelief in the possibility of the supernatural emptying of our Lord's tomb." 60/382

6A. CONCLUSION: HE IS RISEN, HE IS RISEN INDEED

John Warwick Montgomery says: "The earliest records we have of the life and ministry of Jesus give the overwhelming impression that this man went around not so much 'doing good' but making a decided nuisance of Himself.

"The parallel with Socrates in this regard is strong: Both men infuriated their contemporaries to such an extent that they were eventually put to death. But where Socrates played the gadfly on the collective Athenian rump by demanding that his hearers 'know themselves' — examine their unexamined lives — Jesus alienated His contemporaries by continually forcing them to think through their attitude to Him personally. 'Who do men say that I the Son of man am? . . . Who do you say that I am?' 'What do you think of Christ? Whose son is He?' These were the questions Jesus asked." 45/12

Christ made it very clear who He was. He told Thomas: "I am the way, and the truth, and the life; no one comes to the Father, but through Me" (John 14:6).

The apostle Paul said that Christ ". . . was declared with power to be the Son of God by the resurrection from the dead . . ." (Romans 1:4).

Simon Greenleaf, famous Harvard professor of law, says: "All that Christianity asks of men . . . is, that they would be consistent with themselves; that they would treat its evidences as they treat the evidence of other things; and that they would try and judge its actors and witnesses, as they deal with their fellow men, when testifying to human affairs and actions, in human tribunals. Let the witnesses be compared with themselves, with each other, and with surrounding facts and circumstances; and let their testimony be sifted, as if it were given in a court of justice, on the side of the adverse party, the witness being subjected to rigorous cross-examination. The result, it is confidently believed, will be an undoubting conviction of their integrity, ability, and truth." 20/46

As *G. B. Hardy* has said, "Here is the complete record:

Confucius' tomb	—	occupied
Buddha's tomb	—	occupied
Mohammed's tomb	—	occupied
Jesus' tomb	—	EMPTY." 23

The decision is now yours to make; the evidence speaks for itself. It says very clearly —

CHRIST IS RISEN INDEED.

BIBLIOGRAPHY

1. Alford, Henry. *The Greek Testament: With a Critically Revised Text: A Digest of Various Readings: Marginal References to Verbal and Idiomatic Usage: Prolegomena: And a Critical and Exegetical Commentary.* Vol. I. Sixth edition. London: Deighton, Bell, and Co., 1868.

2. Anderson, J. N. D. *Christianity: The Witness of History,* copyright Tyndale Press 1970. Used by permission of Inter-Varsity Press.

3. Anderson, J. N. D. "The Resurrection of Jesus Christ" (copyright). *Christianity Today.* March 29, 1968. Used by permission.

4. Anderson, J. N. D., Wolfhart Pannenberg and Clark Pinnock. "A Dialogue on Christ's Resurrection." *Christianity Today.* April 12, 1968. Used by permission.

5. Arndt, William F. and F. Wilbur Gingrich. *A Greek-English Lexicon of the New Testament and Other Early Christian Literature.* Chicago: The University of Chicago Press, 1952.

6. Bruce, Alexander Balmin. *The Expositors Greek New Testament.* Vol. I — *The Synoptic Gospels.* London: Hodder and Stoughton, 1903.

7. Bruce, A. B. *The Training of the Twelve.* Grand Rapids: Kregel Publications, 1971.

8. Chandler, Samuel. *Witnesses of the Resurrection of Jesus Christ.* London: n.p., 1744.

9. Chrysostom. *Homilies on the Gospel of Saint Matthew.* Found in *A Select Library of the Nicene and Post-Nicene Fathers of the Christian Church.* Vol. X. Edited by Philip Schaff. New York: The Christian Literature Company, 1888.

10. Clark, G. W. *The Gospel of Matthew.* Philadelphia: American Baptist Publication Society, 1896.

11. Cook, Frederick Charles (ed.). *Commentary on the Holy Bible.* London: John Murray, 1878.

12. Currie, George. *The Military Discipline of the Romans from the Founding of the City to the Close of the Republic.* An abstract of a thesis published under the auspices of the Graduate Council of Indiana University, 1928.

13. Day, E. Hermitage. *On the Evidence for the Resurrection.* London: Society for Promoting Christian Knowledge, 1906.

14. Douglas, J. D. (ed.). *The New Bible Dictionary.* Grand Rapids: William B. Eerdmans Publishing Co., 1962. Used by permission.

15. Edersheim, Alfred. *The Life and Times of Jesus the Messiah.* Vol. II. Grand Rapids: William B. Eerdmans Publishing Co., 1962. Used by permission.

16. Edersheim, Alfred. *The Temple: Its Ministry and Services.* Grand Rapids: William B. Eerdmans Publishing Co., 1958. Used by permission.

17. Fallow, Samuel (ed.). *The Popular and Critical Bible Encyclopedia and Scriptural Dictionary.* Vol. III. Chicago: The Howard Severance Co., 1908.

18. Farrar, Frederick W. *The Life of Christ.* Dutton, Dovar: Cassell and Co., 1897.

19. Green, Michael. *Man Alive.* Downers Grove: Inter-Varsity Press, 1968. Used by permission.

20. Greenleaf, Simon. *Testimony of the Evangelists, Examined by the Rules of Evidence Administered in Courts of Justice.* Grand Rapids: Baker Book House, 1965 (reprinted from 1847 edition).

21. Hanson, Anthony (ed.). *Vindications: Essays on the Historical Basis of Christianity.* New York: Morehouse-Barlow Co., 1966.

22. Hanson, George. *The Resurrection and the Life.* London: William Clowes & Sons, Ltd., 1911.

23. Hardy, G. B. *Countdown.* Chicago: Moody Press, 1970.

24. Hastings, James. *Dictionary of the Apostolic Church.* Vol. II. Edinburgh: T. & T. Clark, 1918.

25. Hastings, James, John A. Selbie, and John C. Lambert (eds.). *A Dictionary of Christ and the Gospels.* Vol. II. New York: Charles Scribner's Sons, 1909.

26. Hinsie, L. E. and J. Shatsky. *Psychiatric Dictionary.* New York: Oxford University Press, 1948.

27. Hoch, Paul H., Joseph Zubin and Grhune Stratton (eds.). *Psychopathology of Perception.* New York: n.p., 1965.

28. Holloman, Henry W. *An Exposition of the Post-Resurrection Appearances of Our Lord.* Unpublished Th.M. Thesis: Dallas Theological Seminary, May 1967.

29. Ignatius' Epistle to Trallians. Found in *Ante-Nicene Christian Library: Translations of the Writings of the Fathers.* Alexander Roberts and James Donaldson (eds.). Vol. I. Edinburgh: T. & T. Clark, 1867.

30. Jamieson, Robert, A. R. Fausset and David Brown (eds.). *A Commentary Critical, Experimental, and Practical on the Old and New Testaments.* Vol. V. Grand Rapids: William B. Eerdmans Publishing Co., 1948. Used by permission.

31. *The Jewish Encyclopedia.* New York: Funk and Wagnalls Company, n.d.

32. Kevan, Ernest F. *The Resurrection of Christ.* London: The Campbell Morgan Memorial Bible Lectureship, Westminster Chapel, Buckingham Gate, S. W. I., June 14, 1961.

33. Latham, Henry. *The Risen Master.* Cambridge: Deighton, Bell, and Co., 1904.

34. Le Camus, E. *The Life of Christ.* Vol. III. New York: The Cathedral Library Association, 1908.

35. Lenski, R. C. H. *The Interpretation of St. Matthew's Gospel.* Columbus: The Wartburg Press, 1943.

36. Lewis, Charlton T. and Charles Short (eds.) *A Latin Dictionary.* Oxford: Clarendon Press, n.d. Used by permission.

37. Lewis, C. S. *Miracles, A Preliminary Study.* New York: The Macmillan Company, 1947.

38. Little, Paul E. *Know Why You Believe.* Wheaton: Scripture Press Publications, Inc., 1967. Used by permission.

39. Maine, Henry Sumner. *Ancient Law.* New York: Henry Holt and Company, 1888.

40. Martyr, Justin. Found in *Ante-Nicene Christian Library: Translations of the Writings of the Fathers.* Alexander Roberts and James Donaldson (eds.). Vol. II. Edinburgh: T. & T. Clark, 1867.

41. Matheson, George. *The Representative Men of the New Testament.* London: Hodder and Stoughton, 1904.

42. Mattingly, John P. *Crucifixion: Its Origin and Application to Christ.* Unpublished Th. M. Thesis: Dallas Theological Seminary, May 1961.

43. Milligan, William. *The Resurrection of Our Lord.* New York: The Macmillan Company, 1927.

44. *The Mishnah.* Translated by Herbert Danby, London: Geoffrey Cumberlege, Oxford University Press, 1933.

45. Montgomery, John Warwick, *History and Christianity.* Downers Grove. Inter-Varsity Press, 1964. Used by permission.

46. Morison, Frank. *Who Moved the Stone?* London: Faber and Faber, 1967.

47. Moyer, Elgin S. (ed.) *Who Was Who in Church History.* Chicago: Moody Press, 1962. Used by permission.

48. Orr, James, John L. Nielson and James Donalson (eds.). *The International Standard Bible Encyclopedia,* Vol. I. Edinburgh: T. & T. Clark, 1867.

49. Paley, William, *A View of the Evidences of Christianity.* 14th ed. London: S. Hamilton, Weybridge, 1811.

50. Pannenburg, Wolfhart. *Jesus – God and Man.* Translated by L. L. Wilkins and D. A. Priche. Philadelphia: Westminster Press, copyright MCMLXVIII. Used by permission.

51. Peru, Paul William. *Outline of Psychiatric Case-Study.* New York: Paul B. Hoeger, Inc. 1939.

52. Ramm, Bernard. *Protestant Christian Evidences.* Chicago: Moody Press, 1957. Used by permission.

53. Robertson, A. T. *Word Pictures in the New Testament.* New York: R. R. Smith, Inc., 1931.

54. Roper, Albert. *Did Jesus Rise from the Dead?* Grand Rapids: Zondervan Publishing House, copyright 1965. Used by permission.

55. Rosscup, James. Class Notes. La Mirada, CA.: Talbot Theological Seminary, 1969.

56. Schaff, Philip. *History of the Christian Church.* Vol. I. Grand Rapids, William B. Eerdmans Publishing Co., 1962. Used by permission.

57. Smith, Wilbur M. *A Great Certainty in This Hour of World Crises.* Wheaton: Van Kampen Press, 1951.

58. Smith, Wilbur M. "The Indisputable Fact of the Empty Tomb." *Moody Monthly.* May, 1971. Used by permission.

59. Smith, Wilbur M. "Scientists and the Resurrection." *Christianity Today.* April 15, 1957. Used by permission.

60. Smith, Wilbur M. *Therefore Stand: Christian Apologetics.* Grand Rapids: Baker Book House, 1965.

61. Smith, William (ed.). *Dictionary of Greek and Roman Antiquities.* Rev. ed. London: James Walton and John Murray, 1870.

62. Sparrow-Simpson, W. J. *The Resurrection and the Christian Faith.* Grand Rapids: Zondervan Publishing House, 1968 (reprinted from 1911 edition of Langsmans Green, and Co., published under the title, *The Resurrection and Modern Thought*). Used by permission.

63. Stott, John R. W. *Basic Christianity.* Downers Grove: Inter-Varsity Press, 1971. Used by permission.

64. Straton, Hillyer H. "I Believe: Our Lord's Resurrection." *Christianity Today.* March 31, 1968. Used by permission.

65. Strauss, David Friedrich. *The Life of Jesus for the People.* Vol. I. 2d ed. London: Williams and Norgate, 1879.

66. Tenney, Merrill C. *The Reality of the Resurrection.* Chicago: Moody Press, 1963. Used by permission.

67. Tertulliaus. Writings of Quintus Sept. Flor. Tertulliaus. Found in *Ante-Nicene Christian Library: Translations of the Writings of the Fathers.* Alexander Roberts and James Donaldson. Vol. XI. Edinburgh: T & T. Clark, 1867.

68. Thorburn, Thomas James. *The Resurrection Narratives and Modern Criticism.* London: Kegan Paul, Trench, Trubner & Co., Ltd., 1910.

69. Tucker, T. G. *Life in the Roman World of Nero and St. Paul.* New York: The Macmillan Company, 1910.

70. Vincent, Marvin R. *Word Studies in the New Testament.* Vol. I. New York: Charles Scribner's Sons, 1900.

71. Vine, W. E. *Expository Dictionary of New Testament Words.* Vol. II. London: Edinburgh, 1939.

72. Whedon, D. D. *Commentary of the Gospels Matthew-Mark.* Vol. 9. New York: Hunt and Eaton, 1888.

73. Whitworth, John F. *Legal and Historical Proof of the Resurrection of the Dead.* Harnsburg: Publishing House of the United Evangelical Church, 1912.

section III

God at work in history and human lives

If God is and is alive today, then one should be able to see His influence in the course of history as well as in individual lives. The account of God's continued influence is seen in fulfilled prophecies and in the transformation of lives throughout the centuries.

chapter 11

prophecy
fulfilled in history

The purpose of this section, fulfilled historic and geographic prophecies, is mainly to illustrate the power of God through fulfillments of seemingly impossible predictions directly grounded in the course of human events.

Rarely does a researcher have the opportunity to investigate such a fascinating line of study. Clearly God's hand is on the shoulder of these prophets as they present the Word to those who would hear. Prophecy gives clear practical lessons in the omniscience and omnipotence of the God of us all, as well as food for thought in areas like inspiration of Scripture, etc.

The prophecies in this section have been divided into 12 areas of prophecy. Each area involves a specific prophetic theme (i.e., certain towns, cities, nations, etc.).

There is certain preliminary groundwork which must be covered before we begin with the specific prophecies.

The following is an outline designed to aid you in effectively using this material.

1A. INTRODUCTION
    1B.   Definition of Prophecy
    2B.   Tests of a Prophet
    3B.   Objection to Predictive Prophecy
    4B.   Specific Fulfillment of Prophecy
2A. THE PROPHECIES
    1. Tyre
    2. Sidon
    3. Samaria
    4. Gaza-Ashkelon
    5. Moab-Ammon
    6. Petra-Edom
    7. Thebes-Memphis
    8. Nineveh
    9. Babylon
    10. Chorazin-Bethsaida-Capernaum
    11. Jerusalem's Enlargement
    12. Palestine
3A. PROPHETIC PROBABILITY

1A. INTRODUCTION

  1B. Definition of Prophecy

    1C.   EXTRA-BIBLICAL DEFINITION:

        The Encyclopaedia Britannica says: "The literary records of Hebrew prophecy in Isaiah make clear that Prophecy means in the first instance and primarily a word or spoken message, proclaiming through a chosen messenger the will of God for those addressed. The predictive element of threat or promise is conditioned by the hearers' response (i, 18-20), or is offered as a 'sign' of what is coming (vii, 14), because all that happens is finally subordinate to the purpose of God's will." 15/xii. 656,657

Encyclopaedia Britannica continues that "Isaiah makes much of the importance of Babylon's gods, in contrast to Yahweh, to declare in advance what they intend to do and to do it (xii, 21-24; xlviii, 3). The predictions of the prophets are announcements of the purpose of a living God rather than of man's predetermined fate." 15/xii. 656,657

2C.   SCRIPTURAL DEFINITION:

The definition of "prophet" is someone who tells God's will and the future to the people as divine inspiration leads. 54/890

Merrill F. Unger in *Unger's Bible Dictionary* says: "In addition to the declaration of God's will, the enunciation of His judgments, the defense of truth and righteousness, and bearing testimony to the superiority of the moral to the ritual, prophecy had an intimate relation to God's gracious purpose toward Israel" (Mic. 5:4, 7:20; Isa. 60:3; 65:25). 54/891

The prophets' purpose, in addition to prediction, was moral, which, according to Charles Elliot, reveals the existence of God as He really is and shows that He works "according to the purpose of His will." This, in short, reveals God to man, and with that revelation, God's will and workings. 54/892

All writers, prophets included, have a distinctive style of writing, just as they have a style of speaking and presenting themselves. Each person maintains individuality, therefore, through his own style, yet in certain ways these men are set apart from non-biblical writers. Although their individualities remain, time and sense seem to fade as the Spirit completes control. 54/893

The impression most people have of a prophet is that he is a person who presents predictive prophecy. True, this is a large part of the prophet's message, but the great prophets were active reformers in social and political areas, yet constantly preaching righteousness and revival, as well as predicting judgments and awards. The prophet always spoke in a spiritual manner, reflecting God's will and urging obedience. 54/893

Although it sometimes arose (cf. Deut. 18:22), the predictive part of the message was not for sensationalism. The prophecies were pronounced because of (not in spite of) the conditions surrounding the prophet. Virtually every chapter pronouncing doom will have a chapter explaining precisely why the message of destruction was uttered. 54/863

The first prophecy goes all the way back to Adam and Eve with the predicted and promised Divine Redeemer of Genesis 3:15,16. From there, we can, and will, trace the speaking of God's words all the way to Revelation. Some of the early prophets were Enoch, Abraham and Moses (Num. 12:6-8; Deut. 18:18; John 6:14; 7:40). 54/893

Also, prophecy was of "divine origin," as I Samuel 9:9 and II Samuel 24:11 show. 54/893

The Bible is very clear that predictive prophecy is a sign of God's power and glory and presents the supernatural nature of His word. It is not only a demonstration of God's power, but also of His answer to man's prayers and needs. Since God reveals the future, a task no man is so capable of doing, we can know that He sees the future and sees all things even before they reach the present. Christians everywhere should rest assured that nothing will occur which the Father has not foreseen. 54/894

2B. Tests of a Prophet

According to the *New Bible Dictionary* article, "Prophecy, Prophets" by J. A. Motyer, vice-principal of Clifton Theological College in Bristol, certain points may be made about the question of true and false prophets.

There have been many episodes in the Bible which have caused conflict as to who was a true prophet and who was a false prophet (I Kings 22; Jer. 28; I Kings 13:18-22). The solution to this is very practical and important rather than simply academic. We have certain characteristics which we can examine and apply to see the falseness or truth in a prophet. 14/1041

One area to examine for false prophets is in what Prof. Motyer called "prophetic ecstasy." This state of ecstasy seemed to occur without forewarning or was caused by certain conditions, especially certain forms of music. Such unusual and suspicious conditions arose as total expulsion of all self-consciousness, and no sensitivity or fear of pain was evident. This was wide-spread in Canaan, especially with Baalism. Naturally this is not the only grounds for passing an unfavorable conclusion. One must also realize that this quality was not wholly divorced from the true prophets. Both Isaiah (in his temple experience) and Ezekiel (roughly overall) were ecstatic at times. 14/1041

Another observation to make is in the area of status. The false prophets were usually on a paid staff under the king. These men "prophesied" what the king desired to hear. This again is not a final test. Samuel, Nathan (under Daniel) and even Amos were considered professional prophets to a greater or lesser extent, yet were clearly not false prophets. These paid staff-prophets were usually found in groups, much like the ecstatics (see Dan. 2:2). 14/1041

The Old Testament records three noteworthy passages down this line (Deut. 13 and 18; Jer. 23; Ezek. 12:21-14:11). Deuteronomy 18 claims that what does not become fulfilled is not true prophecy. It should be remembered that this is a negative criterion, thus what *does* become fulfilled is still not necessarily from God. When a false prophet makes a fulfilled prediction, this may be a test of God's people. Deuteronomy 13 deals theologically and strikes a clear and ringing blow; if the prophet uses other gods removed from the true God (v. 2), then he is obviously not of Yahweh. Through Moses, the theme was sealed on all future prophecy by setting the norm of the theology by which all future prophets must accept. If a prophet presented fulfilled predictive prophecy, yet claimed theology out of keeping with the norm set down through Moses, the people had a false prophet. 14/1041, 1042

Jeremiah 23, the second passage dealing with the false prophets, expounds on the Deuteronomy 13 passage by painting a false prophet as immoral (v. 10-14) and condoning others' immorality (v. 17); he preaches of peace, not a God-like peace, but an artificial, manufactured peace. The true prophet presents a message of conviction and repentance (v. 29) and calls the people to righteousness and obedience (v. 22). 14/1042

It is very important, however, to remember the reason for the severe words of the prophets. One of the reasons the books of the prophets have been carved up so much by the critics is because of the mistaken impression that true prophets have only one message — doom. This is not the whole case. The reason these prophets do not begin with a message of peace is because God-like peace comes only through holiness, righteousness and repentance. The theme of the prophet has been set by Moses, which is the theme of God's Law. False prophets, according to Jeremiah, steal the name of the Lord, use their own authority in His name and claim their own self-exalted status (v. 30-32). The true prophet is commissioned by Yahweh, and speaks in His name, with His authority (v. 18, 21, 22, 28, 32). 14/1042

The third passage on this topic is in Ezekiel (12:21-14:11), which resembles Jeremiah. He is clear to say false prophets guide their own path and drum up their own prophecies (13:2,3). Consequently, they lead the people with false assurance (13:4-7). Their signature is a message of a false peace (again) and fragile optimism (13:10-16), devoid of building spiritual, righteous holiness (13:22). The true prophet digs directly to the soul and challenges his hearers head-on to examine themselves (14:4-5) for the quality of life which they already know God demands (14:7,8). "We see again that the true prophet is the Mosaic prophet." He does not speak quietly, but with all the boldness of the God of the Exile, repeating in new, fresh tones the truths that have never been improved and never been changed. 14/1042

3B. Objection to Predictive Prophecy — Postdating

1C. DATING OF PROPHECIES

As far as the question of dating of prophecies goes, many people will attack predictive prophecy from the standpoint of post-dating, that is, placing the time of the prophecy *after* the event of the fulfillment rather than before. Unfortunately for the critic, these prophets make their prophecies very clear — the tenses are very obvious. They claim to be exercising the miracle of predictive prophecy.

Unger's Bible Dictionary places either the various prophets' ministries or the dating of the various books as follows:

Amos	2nd qtr. of 8th cent. B.C.	p. 46
Daniel	605-538 B.C.	p. 491
Ezekiel	592-570 B.C.	p. 336
Hosea	748-690 B.C.	p. 501
Isaiah	783-738 B.C., 1st	
	735-719 B.C., 2nd	
	719-704 B.C., 3rd	p. 534
Jeremiah	626-aft. 586 B.C.	p. 568-570
Joel	before 300 B.C.	p. 1149
Leviticus (Moses)	1520-1400 B.C.	p. 760-762
Matthew	50 A.D.	p. 706
Micah	ab. 738-690 B.C.	p. 726
Nahum	aft. 661-bef. 612 B.C.	p. 774
Obadiah	before 300 B.C.	p. 1185
Zephaniah	betw. 640-621 B.C.	p. 1185

These dates are in some cases uncertain. This is because Unger's uses the contents of the prophets' writings themselves to determine the dating of the various books. Sometimes, the prophet did not clearly indicate the exact time of his writing. Joel and Obadiah are the only books in the list in which we are simply not supplied with concrete information by the authors to establish a firm date.

All of the Old Testament prophets were translated into Greek in the Greek Septuagint by about 280-250 B.C. Therefore, we can assume that all of the prophets (including Joel and Obadiah) were written before this time.

2C. DATING OF EZEKIEL

Ezekiel will be used more than any other prophet in this book, and so the book will be touched on briefly with the dating of the book at 570 B.C. We will begin with *The Encyclopaedia Britannica:*

"There is a wide variety of opinion regarding the unity and date of the Book of Ezekiel. According to the book itself, the prophet's career extended from 592 to 570, but one scholar (James Smith) places him in the 7th century at the time of Manasseh and another (N. Messel) after the time of Nehemiah, around 400 B.C. Most, however, accept the general chronology of the book." 15/ix. 17

"Two fragments of the text of Ezekiel IV, 16-vol. I were found among the Dead Sea Scrolls in Qumran Cave I, and fragments of two manuscripts of Ezekiel were reported from Cave IV." 15/ix. 16

"Oft repeated typical words and phrases give a strong impression of literary unity to the book: 'Then they will know that I am the Lord' (more than 50 times), 'As I live, says the Lord God' (13 times), 'my sabbaths' (12 times), 'countries' (24 times), 'idols' (. . . about 40 times), 'walking in my statutes' (11 times), etc." 15/ix. 17

Joseph P. Free in his book *Archaeology and Bible History* says that when he "first took a course in Biblical Criticism . . . I was told that the critics had not touched the book of Ezekiel, and that the validity of the book was accepted. . . . However, in recent years the book has been attacked . . . but, as W. F. Albright has pointed out, this critical attitude is not justified in the least, and to his way of thinking there seems to be every reason for going back to a more conservative attitude." 18/226

Free continues: "One of C. C. Torrey's (professor at Yale University) principal arguments against the authenticity of the book concerned the unusual dating of events by the years 'of king Jehoiachin's captivity' (AOTA, 164). This method of dating, however, now turns out to be an 'inexpugnable argument' (AOTA, 164) in favor of the genuineness of Ezekiel, as shown by archaeological discoveries. From the seal impression on three jar handles (For a description of these jar handles, see Free's *Archaeology and Bible History,* section on 'Archaeological Confirmation of Jehoiachin's Exile in Babylon.') bearing the reference to 'Eliakim steward of Jehoiachin,' it was deduced that Eliakim was the administrator of the crown property which still belonged to Jehoiachin while he was in exile. Evidently Jehoiachin was still considered as king by the people of Judah, and Zedekiah was regarded as king only in the sense of being regent for his captive nephew, Jehoiachin. Thus it was quite in harmony with the attitude of the Jewish people for Ezekiel to date events according to the reign of Jehoiachin, even though he was in exile." 18/226

The conclusion is striking. Joseph P. Free sums it up by saying: "The unusual system of dating in the book of Ezekiel, then, is not an evidence of its lack of authenticity, but, in the light of the archaeological evidence, 'proves its authenticity in a most striking way' " (AOTA, 165.) 18/227

E. J. Young, a highly respected scholar, made these observations on Ezekiel: "The above survey will show how varied are the views of recent negative criticism with respect to the book of Ezekiel. The so-called problems of the book are best solved upon the basis of the traditional view, namely, that Ezekiel himself composed the entire book." 60/237

Young continues with references to H. H. Rowley and S. R. Driver: "In 1953 H. H. Rowley defended the essential unity of the book and pointed out in a most convincing manner that the '. . . theories that transfer either the prophet himself or his literary creator to a post-exilic age are unconvincing' (p. 182). This work of Rowley's is an excellent introduction to the study of modern criticism of Ezekiel." 60/237

"And Driver," adds E. J. Young, "wrote, 'No critical question arises in connection with the authorship of the book, the whole from beginning to end bearing unmistakably the stamp of a single mind.' Indeed, the reasons for holding to the authorship of the entire book by Ezekiel are rather strong. The book is autobiographical — the first person singular is employed throughout. The book does make the strong impression that it is the work of a single personality. Further, many of the prophecies are dated and localized. The similarity of thought and arrangement throughout make it clear that the entire book is the work of one mind. Hence, we may with confidence hold to the view that Ezekiel was the author. And it is quite interesting to note that one of the latest scholarly commentaries, that by *Cooke*, holds that Ezekiel is the basic author of the book." 60/234

3C.   PROPHECIES OF SPECIFIC PLACES

Peter Stoner in *Science Speaks* made these comments about the prophecies of Tyre, Samaria, Gaza-Ashkelon, Jerusalem Enlargement, Palestine, Moab-Ammon, Petra-Edom, Babylon:

"No human being has ever made predictions which hold any comparison to those we have considered, and had them accurately come true. The span of time between the writing of these prophecies and their fulfillment is so great that the most severe critic cannot claim that the predictions were made after the events happened." 53/115 And further, "Others may say that these accounts in the Bible are not prophecies, but historical accounts written after the events happened. This is absurd, for all of these prophecies are found in the Old Testament, and everyone will date its writing before Christ. One of these prophecies was completely fulfilled before Christ. Two had small parts fulfilled before Christ and the remaining parts after Christ. All other prophecies considered were completely fulfilled after Christ. If we were to strike out all estimates given for parts of prophecies fulfilled before Christ, our probability number would still be so large that the strength of its argument could not be comprehended." 53/96

H. Harold Hartzler, Ph.D., the Secretary-Treasurer of the American Scientific Affiliation of Goshen College, Indiana, writes in the foreword of Peter Stoner's book:

"The manuscript for *Science Speaks* has been carefully reviewed by a committee of the American Scientific Affiliation members and by the Executive Council of the same group and has been found, in general, to be dependable and accurate in regard to the scientific material presented. The mathematical analysis included is based upon principles of probability which are thoroughly sound and Professor Stoner has applied these principles in a proper and convincing way." 53/4

Bernard Ramm in *Protestant Christian Evidence* made the following comment about the prophecies in his book:

"Furthermore, in practically every case we have given the radical the benefit of the doubt in dating the prophecies, so that the examples of fulfilled predictions *lie outside the dates of the passages set by the radical critic.*" 48/96

4C. PRE-SUPPOSITIONS OF CRITICS

The problems of most critics of predictive prophecy are their pre-suppositions that we live in a closed system, there is no God, miracles are not possible, and therefore there can be no predictive prophecy. So what happens is that they read a book containing prophetic utterances and see the fulfillment at a much later date, and therefore conclude that the so-called prophetic utterance had to be at a later date. The conclusion of the coinciding of the prophecy with its fulfillment is a result of the pre-suppositions and not the evidence of archaeology or the facts of history.

James Davis, a former student at Louisiana Tech., who did research in this area for these lecture notes, says that concerning many critics of prophecy he:

". . . used to wonder if what these men say really is true. I don't any more; not since I began seeing how these contentions were disproven again and again by archaeology and science. I finally saw that the skeptics are the real enemies of the truth. They are the ones who have the biased attitudes and the dogmatic premises. They gave all their accusations at first and never quit repeating them. However, one by one, their accusations began to dwindle in number and potency as archaeology continued to objectively search and find facts. Eventually, I refused to even give critics the benefit of doubt and gave up confidence in them completely."

4B. Specific Fulfillment of Prophecy

For each prophecy treated, this section will quote the Scriptures containing the prophecies alongside the comments of their historical fulfillment in order to assist the reader in realizing the impact of predictive prophecy. Thomas Urquhart in *The Wonders of Prophecy* (C. C. Cook, n.d.) succinctly states: "The seeker after certainty in religion will be grateful for the multiplicity, as well as for the minuteness and distinctness, of Scripture prophecy." 55/93

Urquhart says that the prophecies:

". . . contain what I may call prophetic pictures. They do not merely indicate one feature among the many after-characteristics of peoples and of countries: they describe one feature after another till their condition is fully portrayed. With the fulfillment of one, or perhaps two, of these it might be imagined that chance had had to do, but, as one after another is added, the suspicion becomes more and more unreasonable, till, before the accumulating evidence, it is swept away completely and forever." 55/44

Henry Morris, in *The Bible and Modern Science,* makes a superb point about problems with archaeological findings when he writes:

"Problems still exist, of course, in the complete harmonization of archaeological material with the Bible, but none so serious as not to bear real promise of imminent solution through further investigation." 39/95

Bernard Ramm, in his *Protestant Christian Evidences,* made a good analysis of the position a Christian apologist is in when he sets forth the case for the faith through fulfilled prophecy: "The enemy of Christianity must silence all our guns: we need to fire only one of them. Therefore, all the potentially fulfilled prophecies must be explained away on this basis or the objection is futile." 48/88

1. TYRE

1A. INTRODUCTION AND SCRIPTURE

One of the most unusual prophecies in the Bible is that concerning the ancient city of Tyre. Probably all books in defense of Christianity will use this example, and with good reason. Soon this reason will be clear.

Ezekiel 26:   (592-570 B.C.)

3. Therefore, thus says the Lord God, "Behold, I am against you, O Tyre, and I will bring up many nations against you, as the sea brings up its waves.

4. "And they will destroy the walls of Tyre and break down her towers; and I will scrape her debris from her and make her a bare rock."

7. For thus says the Lord God, "Behold, I will bring upon Tyre from the north Nebuchadnezzar king of Babylon, king of kings, with horses, chariots, cavalry, and a great army.

8. "He will slay your daughters on the mainland with the sword; and he will make siege walls against you, cast up a mound against you, and raise up a large shield against you.

12. "Also they will make a spoil of your riches and a prey of your merchandise, break down your walls and destroy your pleasant houses, and throw your stones and your timbers and your debris into the water.

14. "And I will make you a bare rock; you will be a place for the spreading of nets. You will be built no more, for I the Lord have spoken," declares the Lord God.

21. "I shall bring terrors on you, and you will be no more; though you will be sought, you will never be found again," declares the Lord God.

2A. PREDICTIONS

1B. **Nebuchadnezzar will destroy the mainland city of Tyre (26:8).**

2B. **Many nations against Tyre (26:3).**

3B. **Make her a bare rock; flat like the top of a rock (26:4).**

4B. **Fishermen will spread nets over the site (26:5).**

5B. **Throw the debris into the water (26:12).**

6B. **Never be rebuilt (26:14).**

7B. **Never to be found again (26:21).**

The predictions previously mentioned seem to be self explanatory. This is the type of prophecy which sounds contradictory — fortunately history is not contradictory, so all one must do is see the story of Tyre and then compare the prophecies to it.

3A. FULFILLMENT

A secular source made this observation: "Ezekiel's denunciation (especially 27:27) shows how important ancient Tyre was in the eyes of the Hebrew prophet and how varied and enriching was her trade." 24/1

1B. Nebuchadnezzar

Nebuchadnezzar laid siege to mainland Tyre three years after the prophecy. The *Encyclopaedia Britannica* says: "After a 13-year siege (585-573 B.C.) by Nebuchadnezzar II, Tyre made terms and acknowledged Babylonian suzerainty. In 538 B.C. Tyre, with the rest of Phoenicia, passed to the suzerainty of Achaemenid Persia." 15/xxii. 452

When Nebuchadnezzar broke the gates down, he found the city almost empty. The majority of the people had moved by ship to an island about one-half mile off the coast and fortified a city there. The mainland city was destroyed in 573 (Prediction 1B), but the city of Tyre on the island remained a powerful city for several hundred years.

2B. Alexander the Great

The next incident was with Alexander the Great.

"In his war on the Persians," writes the *Encyclopaedia Britannica*, "Alexander III, after defeating Darius III at the Battle of Issus (333), marched southward toward Egypt, calling upon the Phoenician cities to open their gates, as it was part of his general plan to deny their use to the Persian fleet. The citizens of Tyre refused to do so, and Alexander laid siege to the city. Possessing no fleet, he demolished old Tyre, on the mainland, and with the debris built a mole 200 ft. (60m.) wide across the straits separating the old and new towns, erecting towers and war engines at the farther end." (Prediction 5B) 15/xxii. 452

Curtius, an ancient writer (Loeb Classical Library: *Quintius Curtius* IV. 2. 18-19) wrote concerning the construction of the causeway by Alexander. He says much material was available from Mount Libanus (trees for beams) and the Old City of Tyre supplied stones and dirt. (Prediction 5B)

We can see very clearly from Arrian, a Greek historian, in *History of Alexander and Indica* II. 18, 19, 20 (Harvard University Press, 1954), how this great feat of conquering Tyre was accomplished. Tyre was one city divided between the mainland and an Alcatraz-like island fortress. Nebuchadnezzar took the mainland city but passed by the island city. Alexander planned, as Arrian related, to take all of Tyre. It would obviously be a massive undertaking. The island was completely surrounded by powerful walls, reaching to the very edges of the sea. The Tyrians and Alexander's enemy, the Persians under Darius, had control of the sea, but this Greek general decided to build a land peninsula out to the island. Work went well at first, but the depth increased as they progressed, as did also the harassment from the Tyrians. From their high walls, the islanders could do much damage, especially when one remembers that the workers were prepared for work and not war; they wore work-clothes, not armor. Occasionally the Tyrians would stage raids on the causeway which greatly retarded progress. Arrian continues that this activity was countered by the Greeks with two tall towers built and manned directly on the mole (causeway) for protection.

The Tyrians countered here with a full-scale raid on the whole operation which was very successful; they made use of fire-ships to start the towers burning and then swarmed over the mole after the Greeks were routed. General destruction of the mole was made to as great an extent as the raiding party was capable. Arrian progressed to the sea struggle. Alexander realized he needed ships. He began pressuring and mustering conquered subjects to make ships available for this operation. Alexander's navy grew from cities and areas as follows: Sidon, Aradus, Byblus (these contributed about 80 sails), 10 from Rhodes, three from

Soli and Mallos, 10 from Lycia, a big one from Macedon, and 120 from Cyprus. (Prediction 2B)

With this now superior naval force at Alexander's disposal, the conquest of Tyre through completion of the land bridge was simply a question of time. How long would this take? Darius III, Alexander's Persian enemy, was not standing idle at this time, but finally the causeway was completed, the walls were battered down, and mop-up operations began.

"The causeway still remains," writes Philip Myers, "uniting the rock with the mainland. When at last the city was taken after a siege of seven months, eight thousand of the inhabitants were slain and thirty thousand sold into slavery." 40/153

The Tyrians had given good reason to arouse the hatred of the Greeks. These defenders tried every ethical and not-so-ethical tactic to repulse the siege. John C. Beck says concerning her defeat: "It was lamentable that Tyre had resisted and endured so thorough a defeat at the hands of the Greek conqueror." 4/13

Philip Myers made an interesting quote here; he is a secular historian (not a theologian), and this is found in a history textbook:

"Alexander the Great . . . reduced it to ruins (332 B.C.). She recovered in a measure from this blow, but never regained the place she had previously held in the world. The larger part of the site of the once great city is now bare as the top of a rock (Prediction 3B) — a place where the fishermen that still frequent the spot spread their nets to dry." (Prediction 4B) 40/55

John C. Beck keeps the history of the island city of Tyre in the proper perspective: "The history of Tyre does not stop after the conquest of Alexander. Men continue to rebuild her and armies continue to besiege her walls until finally, after sixteen hundred years, she falls never to be rebuilt again." 4/41

3B. Antigonus

"Returning from successful wars in Babylonia," observes Nina Jidejian (*Tyre Through the Ages,* Dar El-Mashreq, Publishers, 1969), "Antigonus easily reduced the cities of Phoenicia but met with firm resistance from Tyre. Eighteen years had passed since Alexander had seized Tyre and the city had recovered rapidly. . . . After a siege of fifteen months Tyre was reduced by Antigonus." 24/80, 81

Antigonus is dated 314 B.C., arithmetically. According to the *International Standard Bible Encyclopedia* (p. 2499), Ptolemy II (Philadelphus) reigned from 285-247 B.C.

"However when Ptolemy Philadelphus built the harbor of Berenice on the Red Sea and made a road with stations and watering places to Coptos and reopened the canal which joined the Pelusiac branch of the Nile to the Gulf of Suez, Tyre suffered a great and permanent loss. Traffic of the Red Sea and the Indian Ocean which had formerly passed through the port of Eloth to Rhinocolura in Phoenicia by way of Petra and thence to all parts of the Mediterranean by vessels of Tyre, now passed by way of the canal to Alexandria. The wealth that formerly had flowed into Tyre now found its way to Alexandria." 24/81, 82

Jidejian relates the Persian traveler Nasir-i-Khusrau's visit and description at 1047 A.D. 22/122. "They have built the city on a rock (that is in the sea) after such a manner that the town hall for one hundred yards only, is upon the dry land, and the remainder rises up from the very water. The walls are built of hewn stone, their joints being set in bitumen in order to keep the water out. I estimated the area of the town to be a thousand arsh [18 inches] square, and its caravanserais are built of five and six stories, set one above the other. There are numerous fountains of water, bazaars are very clean; also great is the quantity of wealth exposed. This city of Tyre is, in fact, renowned for wealth and power among all the maritime cities of Syria. They have erected a Mash-had (a shrine or place of martyrdom) at the city gate, where one may see great quantities of carpets and hangings and lamps and lanterns of gold and silver. The town itself stands on an eminence. Water is brought thereto from the mountain; and leading up to the town-gate they have built arches (for the aqueduct) along which the water comes into the city." 41/11, 12

4B. The Moslems

The city was unfortunately captured by the Moslems which caused the Crusaders to fight for it, which they did, and successfully retake the island. This place became an important base during the Crusades, but according to Joseph Michaud, it was retaken. Michaud describes the event:

"After the taking and the destruction of Ptolemais, the sultan sent one of his emirs with a body of troops to take possession of the city of Tyre; this city, seized with terror, opened its gates without resistance. . . . These cities, which had not afforded the least succour to Ptolemais, in the last great struggle, and which believed themselves protected by a truce, beheld their population massacred, dispersed, and led into slavery; the fury of the Mussulmans extended even to the stones, they seemed to wish to destroy the very earth which the Christians had trod upon; their houses, their temples, the monuments of their piety, their valour and their industry, everything was condemned to perish with them by the sword or by fire." (Prediction 6B) 38/213

LeStrange quotes Abu'l fiela who, in 1321 [A.D.] wrote: "The city was reconquered by the Moslems in 690 (1291), at the same time as Acre and other coast towns, and was then laid in ruins, as it remains down to the present day" (i.e., 1321 A.D.). 24/139

LeStrange (p. 345) lists Ibn Batutah as visiting the ruins and commenting (1355), "It was formerly proverbial for its strength, being washed on three sides by the sea. Of the ancient walls and port traces remain, and of old there was a chain across the mouth of the port." (Prediction 6B) 24/139

Pliny the Elder makes a great summation, quoted here from Jidejian (p. 17), "Tyre . . . formerly famous as the mother-city from which sprang the cities of Leptis, Utica and the great rival of Rome's empire in coveting world sovereignty, Carthage, and also Cadiz, which she founded outside the confines of the world; but the entire renown of Tyre now consists in a shellfish and a purple dye." (Prediction 7B) 24/5, 17, 76

5B. The Present Situation

We will now see Tyre at present, as described by Nina Jidejian: "The 'Sidonian' port of Tyre is still in use today. Small fishing vessels lay at anchor there. An examination of the foundations reveals granite columns of the Roman period which were incorporated as binders in the walls by the Crusaders. The port has become a haven today for fishing boats and a place for spreading nets." 24/139

"The destiny of Tyre according to the prophet is a place where fishermen would spread their nets. The existence of a small fishing village [There is a city of Tyre today, but it is not the original city, but is built down the coast from the original site of Tyre.] upon the site of the ancient city of

Tyre does not mean that the prophecy is not fulfilled but is the final confirmation that the prophecy was fulfilled. Tyre, the mistress of the seas, the trade and commercial center of the world for centuries, passed away never to rise (re-build) again. The fishermen drying their nets upon the rocks that once formed the foundation of that ancient metropolis are the last link in the chain of prophecy that Ezekiel gave over twenty-five hundred years ago." (Prediction 4B) 4/47, 48

Jidejian concludes in her excellent book that Tyre's "stones may be found as far away as Acre and Beirut. Yet evidences of a great past are abundant and recent excavations have revealed successive levels of this proud Phoenician seaport. . . . [22/xvi] The great ancient city of Tyre lay buried under accumulated debris. The ruins of an aqueduct and a few scattered columns and the ruins of a Christian basilica were the only remains found above ground. . . . [22/2] Looking down into the water one can see a mass of granite columns and stone blocks strewn over the sea bottom. Until recently the ruins of Tyre above water were few." 24/xvi

4A. SPECIFIC FULFILLMENT

Thus was the story of the ancient city of Tyre.

Now for specific fulfillment.

1B. Nebuchadnezzar did destroy the old (mainland) city of Tyre.

2B. Many nations were against Tyre.

This fact can be seen even in this very brief history by John C. Beck: "Because a characteristic of waves is that they come in succession with their destructive force due to their repetition and continuous pounding, this author understands Ezekiel to be referring to a succession of invaders extending over a prolonged period of time.

"With this understanding, this summary of Ezekiel (verses 3-6) unfolds. First, 'they will destroy the walls of Tyre and break down her towers' (Nebuchadnezzar's siege). Next, 'I will also scrape her dust from her and make her a bare rock' (Alexander's siege). And finally, 'she shall become a spoil to the nations' (history following the siege of Alexander)." 4/11, 12

3B. Alexander scraped the old site of Tyre clean when he made the causeway out to the island and left a "bare rock."

4B. Numerous references have been previously made (some by secular observers) to the spreading of nets. Nina Nelson observes during a visit: "Pale turquoise fishing nets were drying on the shore. . . ." 42/220

Hans-Wolf Rackl, describing the present situation of the site of ancient Tyre, writes: "Today hardly a single stone of the old Tyre remains intact. . . . Tyre has become a place 'to dry fish nets,' as the prophet predicted." 47/179

5B. Alexander threw the debris into the water in order to make the causeway.

"Ezekiel's prophecy," writes Joseph Free, "concerning the laying of the stones, the timber, and the dust in 'the midst of the water' (Ezek. 26:12b) was specifically fulfilled when Alexander's engineers built the mole, and used the remains of the ancient land city of Tyre, laying them in the midst of the water." 18/263, 264

Nina Nelson in *Your Guide to Lebanon* writes: "The ruins of ancient Tyre are different from all the others — situated . . . in the heart of the sea." 42/220

6B. The city was never to be rebuilt.

As for 6B, "never to be rebuilt," Floyd Hamilton in, *The Basis of the Christian Faith* states: "It is also written, 'thou shalt be built no more' (XXVI:14). Other cities destroyed by enemies had been rebuilt; Jerusalem was destroyed many times, but always has risen again from the ruins; what reason was there for saying that Old Tyre might not be rebuilt? But twenty-five centuries ago a Jew in exile over in Babylonia looked into the future at the command of God and wrote the words, 'thou shalt be built no more!' The voice of God has spoken and Old Tyre today stands as it has for twenty-five centuries, a bare rock, uninhabited by man! Today anyone who wants to see the site of the old city, can have it pointed out to him along the shore, but there is not a ruin to mark the spot. It has been scraped clean and has never been rebuilt." 20/299

"The great freshwater springs of Reselain are at the site of the mainland city of Tyre, and no doubt supplied the city with an abundance of fresh water. These springs are still there and still flow, but their water runs into the sea. The flow of these springs was measured by an engineer, and found to be about 10,000,000 gallons daily. It is still an excellent site for a city and would have free water enough for a large modern city, yet it has never been rebuilt. Thus item [6B] of the prophecy has stood true for more than 2,500 years." 53/76, 77

7B. The city was never to be found again.

Most commentators say that the actual site of the ancient city would be forgotten or lost because of destruction. A better interpretation of this verse is that the seeking by men would be for the purpose of elevating Tyre to her former position of wealth and splendor. It is difficult to believe that the actual location of the city could be lost when it formerly occupied completely the island with walls built to the water's edge." 4/47

Some people may still have trouble accepting fulfillment of the never-be-rebuilt prediction, in light of the fishing village which is now occupying the site of ancient Tyre. No one should deny the fact of the village any more than the fact of predictive prophecy, but recall the entire prophecy, if you will. The site would be the place for spreading of nets, which it is. We must have fishermen to have the nets to have the spreading of nets. The fishermen must live somewhere, and if they spread nets on the site of the ancient city (which the prophecy says must happen), they aren't going to live 10 miles down the coast; they will live where they have their nets.

Tyre was destroyed in 1291 and then it died forever and never was rebuilt. Something grew up from the same site, but it was no more the ancient city of Tyre than it was the city of Seattle.

Nina Nelson observes, "I went to visit Tyre on a summer's day. The town was sleepy, the harbor still. Fishing boats were putting out to sea. Pale turquoise fishing nets were drying on the shore." 42/220

Hans-Wolf Rackl, in *Archeology Underwater,* notes, "Today hardly a single stone of the old Tyre is intact. . . . Later settlers used the remaining building stones in the erection of their own modest dwellings. Tyre has become a place 'to dry fish nets' as the prophet had predicted." 47/179

Philip Ward in *Touring Lebanon* acknowledges: "Since then [1261], agriculture and fishing, twin exercises of peaceful frugal men, have turned Tyre for the first time into a backwater." 57/68

Peter Stoner's seven predictions regarding this miracle were like the ones here — except for my last one, which he did not use, and one of his which is omitted. Stoner evaluates the miracle in the following manner:

"If Ezekiel had looked at Tyre in his day and had made these seven predictions in human wisdom, these estimates mean that there would have been only one chance in 75,000,000 of their all coming true. They all came true in the minutest detail." 53/80

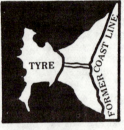

2. SIDON

1A. SCRIPTURE AND DATING

Ezekiel made another prophecy concerning Tyre's sister-city, Sidon.

Ezekiel 28:   (592-570 B.C.)

> 22. And say, "Thus says the Lord God,
> 'Behold, I am against you, O Sidon,
> And I shall be glorified in your midst.'
> 'Then they will know that I am the Lord, when I
>   execute judgments in her,
> And I shall manifest My holiness in her.
>
> 23. 'For I shall send pestilence to her
> And blood to her streets,
> And the wounded will fall in her midst
> By the sword upon her on every side;
> Then they will know that I am the Lord.' "

2A. EXPLANATIONS AND PREDICTIONS

There are three predictions which will be investigated.

1B. **No mention of her destruction.**

2B. **Blood in the streets (28:23).**

3B. **Sword on every side (28:23).**

George Davis strikes a good contrast between Tyre and Sidon in his book, *Fulfilled Prophecies that Prove the Bible*. He says that "the prophecy against Sidon is very different from that concerning Tyre. It was foretold that Tyre would be destroyed, made bare like a rock, and built no more. The prediction against Sidon is that blood will be in her streets, her wounded shall fall in the midst of her, and the sword is to be on her every side. But there is no doom of extinction pronounced against her as was the case with Tyre." 12/16, 18

For many centuries, the relative position politically of Sidon and Tyre was understood. The author of a history text, Philip Van Ness Myers, states in *General History for Colleges and High Schools* that "from the eleventh to the fourth century B.C. Tyre controlled, almost without dispute on the part of Sidon, the affairs of Phoenicia. During this time the maritime enterprise and energy of her Tyre merchants spread the fame of the little island capital throughout the world. She was queen and mistress of the Mediterranean." 40/55

Floyd Hamilton explains what happened in the fourth century B.C. when, "in 351 B.C. the Sidonians, who had been vassals of the Persian king, rebelled, and successfully defended their city against his attacks. At last their own king, in order to save his own life, betrayed the city to the enemy. Well knowing what the vengeance of the Persian king would be, 40,000 of the citizens shut themselves up in their homes, set fire to their own houses and perished in the flames rather than submit to the torture of their enemies! Blood indeed was sent into the streets." (Prediction 3B) 20/300

Mr. Davis explains that "not once but many times blood has been in her (Sidon's) streets, her wounded have fallen in the midst of her and the sword has been 'upon her every side.' " (Predictions 2B, 3B) 12/19

In *The Basis of the Christian Faith*, Floyd Hamilton cites another time Sidon was destroyed and writes that Sidon "was soon rebuilt, however, and though it has been captured over and over again, its citizens butchered and houses razed time after time, the city has always been rebuilt, and is today [1927] a town of about 15,000 inhabitants. Blood has flowed in the streets again and again, but the city stayed in existence and stands today, a monument to fulfilled prophecy." 20/300

George Davis records:

"In the days of the Crusades it (Sidon) was taken and retaken again and again by opposing forces. Three times it was captured by the Crusaders, and three times it fell before the Moslem armies." 10/18, 19

And he further notes that "even in modern times tribulation has continued to be meted out to the city. It has been the scene of conflicts between the Druses and the Turks, and between the Turks and the French. In 1840 Sidon 'was bombarded by the combined fleets of England, France, and Turkey.' " 12/19

Morris explains:

"No fate of extinction was foretold for Sidon and even today it is a city of about 20,000 [1956]. However, it has had one of the bloodiest histories any city ever had." (Predictions 1B, 2B) 39/113

4A. CONCLUSIONS

George Davis concludes with a chilling claim: "No human mind could have foretold 2,500 years ago that Tyre would be extinct, and Sidon would continue, but suffer tribulation during the succeeding centuries; instead of Tyre enduring sorrows, and Sidon being desolate and deserted during the long period." 12/19, 20

The conclusion seems unnecessary. The point has been made. Ezekiel was so completely sure, so clear in precisely which city would stand and which would fall. Maybe we could compare this today with Los Angeles and San Francisco. Which one would fall, which one would stand? Would either fall? Would either remain? Yet Ezekiel declared with the firmness and assurance of a prophet of God that Tyre would fall and Sidon would have a bloody history (recall the Morris quote above).

3. SAMARIA

1A. SCRIPTURE AND DATING

The prophets Hosea and Micah prophesied against the city of Samaria.

Hosea 13:   (748-690 B.C.)

16.   Samaria will be held guilty, for she has rebelled against her God.
      They will fall by the sword,

Their little ones will be dashed in pieces,
And their pregnant women will be ripped open.

Micah 1:   (738 - 690 B.C.)

6. For I will make Samaria a heap of ruins in the open
    country,
    Planting places for a vineyard.
    I will pour her stones down into the valley,
    And will lay bare her foundations.

2A. PREDICTIONS

1B. Fall violently (Hosea).

2B. Become "as a heap in the field" (Micah).

3B. Vineyards will be planted there (Micah).

4B. Samaria's stones will be poured down into the valley (Micah).

5B. The foundations shall be "discovered" (Micah).

3A. HISTORY

The history of Samaria is relatively brief and very stormy. Samaria was the capital of the northern Hebrew kingdom of Israel and represented the turning away of the Jews from Yahweh. It was captured, as Joseph Free states, by "Sargon, [who] in some of his extant documents, indicates that he captured Samaria. Most recent writers have accepted this indication, and have held that, while Shalmanesser initiated and carried on the siege of Samaria, it was Sargon who completed the capture of the city." [Prediction 1B] 18/199

According to the *International Standard Bible Encyclopaedia*, Sargon took Samaria in 722 B.C. Not only did Samaria fall by the sword in 722, but also in 331 B.C. by Alexander and a third time in 120 B.C. by John Hyrcanus, all conquerors causing great damage and death to the citizens of Samaria. Even the skeptic who would contend that the destruction of Samaria came after the event will not be able to disagree about the rest of the ramifications. [Prediction 1B] 44/2672

John Urquhart records Henry Maundrell's reaction in 1697 to what he witnessed: " 'Sabaste is the ancient Samaria, the imperial city of the ten tribes after their revolt from the house of David. . . . This great city is now wholly converted into gardens, and all the tokens that remain to testify that there has ever been such a place, are only on the north side, a large square piazza encompassed with pillars, and on the east some poor remains of a great church.' " (Prediction 3B) 55/127, 128

Urquhart continues with another, more recent account: "As it was then found, it has since remained, 'The whole hill of Sebastieh,' says Robinson, 'consists of fertile soil; it is now cultivated to the top, and has upon it many olive and fig trees. The ground has been ploughed for centuries; and hence it is now in vain to look for the foundations and stones of the ancient city.' " (Predictions 2B, 3B) 55/128

Predictions 4B and 5B find fulfillment through Van de Velde, who calls Samaria " 'a pitiable hamlet, consisting of a few squalid houses, inhabited by a band of plunderers. . . . The shafts of a few pillars only remain standing to indicate the sites of the colonnades. . . . Samaria, a huge heap of stones! Her foundations discovered, her streets ploughed up, and covered with corn fields and olive gardens. . . . Samaria has been destroyed, but her rubbish has been thrown down into the valley; her foundation stones, those grayish ancient quadrangular stones of the time of Omri and Ahab, are discovered, and lie scattered about on the slope of the hill.' " (Predictions 4B, 5B) 55/128

Floyd Hamilton gives a description also: "To-day the top of the hill where Samaria stood is a cultivated field with the foundations of the columns marking the place where the palaces and mansions stood. At the foot of the hill, in the valley, lie the foundation stones of the city. . . ." (Predictions 4B, 5B) 23/316

4A. FULFILLMENT AND PROBABILITY

John Urquhart presents a final description, noting fulfillment of the predictions: "But the doom has long since fallen, and the prediction which so many ages seemed to mock, has become the most accurate of all descriptions of Samaria." 55/127

He also points out specifically, fulfillment of third, fourth and fifth predictions: "The stones of the great city have been taken up by the cultivators and piled together or thrown down the hill-sides, that its site might be turned into fields and vineyards." 55/128, 129

Israel: An Uncommon Guide, by Joan Comay (New York: Random House, 1969) records: "The remains of magnificent buildings of that period, as well as great circular towers . . . can easily be identified today."

Peter Stoner in *Science Speaks* evaluates the probability thus: "If Micah had considered the city of Samaria and made these five predictions regarding it in human wisdom, his chance of having them come true would thus be about 1 in 4 [chance of predicting the destruction] x 5 [chance of lying as a heap in the field rather than rebuilt] x 100 [chance of it becoming a garden spot] x 10 [chance of the stones being rolled down the hill] x 2 [chance of the foundation stones being removed]. This is 1 in 40,000 or 1 in 4 x 10^4." 53/82

The article in the *Bible Encyclopaedia,* "Samaria," is very good for giving a deeper description of what Samaria was like. Though it was Jewish, it was evil, idolatrous and engaged in sinful rebellion against God. The judgment which fell on this city was thorough, as was the fulfillment. 44/2671

4. GAZA-ASHKELON

There are two cities on the Mediterranean coast west of the Dead Sea, Gaza and Ashkelon, which have been mentioned in prophecy.

1A. SCRIPTURE AND DATING

Amos 1:   (775-750 B.C.)

8. "I will also cut off the inhabitant from Ashdod,
    And him who holds the scepter, from Ashkelon;
    I will even unleash My power upon Ekron,
    And the remnant of the Philistines will perish,"
    says the Lord God.

Jeremiah 47:   (626-586 B.C.)

5. Baldness has come upon Gaza;
    Ashkelon has been ruined.
    O remnant of their valley,
    How long will you gash yourself?

Zephaniah 2:   (640-621 B.C.)

4. For Gaza will be abandoned,
    And Ashkelon a desolation;
    Ashdod will be driven out at noon,

And Ekron will be uprooted.

6. So the seacoast will be pastures,
   With caves for shepherds and folds for flocks.

7. And the coast will be
   For the remnant of the house of Judah,
   They will pasture on it.
   In the houses of Ashkelon they will lie down at evening;
   For the Lord their God will care for them
   And restore their fortune.

(Note that Ashdod is another city apart from Ashkelon, about 10 miles north along the coast from Ashkelon.)

2A. PREDICTIONS

1B. Philistines will not continue (Amos 1:8).

2B. Baldness shall come upon Gaza (Jeremiah 47:5).

3B. Desolation shall come on Ashkelon (Zephaniah 2:4).

4B. Shepherds and sheep will dwell in the area around Ashkelon (Zephaniah 2:6).

5B. Remnant of House of Judah will reinhabit Ashkelon (Zephaniah 2:7).

3A. HISTORY

George Davis' *Bible Prophecies Fulfilled Today* begins the history of Ashkelon: "Judgment fell upon the Philistines precisely as predicted. Sultan Bibars destroyed Ashkelon in 1270 A.D. and filled up its harbor with stones. Since that time, for nearly 700 years, the once mighty city of Ashkelon has lain waste and desolate." (Prediction 3B) 11/46

Peter Stoner expands on this incident: "But in A.D. 1270 Sultan Bibars destroyed it, and it has become the grazing place for many flocks of sheep. It is dotted with shepherds' huts and sheepfolds." (Prediction 4B) 53/83

George Davis continues: "And not only was Ashkelon destroyed but the entire nation of the Philistines was 'cut off' precisely as predicted by the prophet Ezekiel 2,500 years ago. The Philistines have been destroyed so completely that there is not a single Philistine living anywhere in the world today." (Prediction 1B) 11/46

(Note that the Ezekiel reference goes to the whole nation of the Philistines, thus the Ezekiel prediction was not included for study in this section; it is recorded in Ezekiel 25:15-17.)

Floyd Hamilton picks up the story of Ashkelon. "There was a Turkish garrison in Ascalon [Ashkelon] as late as the seventeenth century, but since that time it has been deserted. Portions of the wall with its ruined towers and battlements still remain, although Ascalon alone of all the cities of the plain has walls still standing." (Prediction 3B) 20/314

Hamilton continues with a comment on the fifth prediction: "The walls of the houses still stand in part, so that though now the site is completely deserted (even those who have orchards and gardens inside the walls do not live there), yet at some future time when the Jews return to their own country, it is quite possible that Ascalon may be built once more on the ancient site." 20/314

George Davis gives a good picture of present-day Ashkelon: "Following the establishment of the State of Israel the Jews recognized the splendid location of the old city of Ashkelon on the seacoast of their country. They decided to make it a beautiful city of Israel's new State. The *Jerusalem Post* says the new city of Ashkelon has been 'designed on the lines of a Garden City.' " 11/48

Davis adds that today, "after long centuries of mighty Ashkelon lying waste and desolate, it is now being transformed into a garden city. The coast of the Mediterranean is indeed for 'the house of Judah,' and 'in the house of Ashkelon shall they lie down in the evening.' " (Prediction 5B) 11/48

Eugene Fodor writes: "Today most of Israel's population is concentrated along the shores of the Mediterranean. Tel Aviv and Haifa account for at least ¼ of the total. Many additional towns and cities have been built, or rebuilt on sites both new and ancient." 17/322

Fodor describes Ashkelon's development as a pasture (Prediction 4): "Underground water springs, blithely indifferent to man's comings and goings, continued to pour forth their life-giving waters, gradually transforming the ruins into a virgin forest of lush vegetation." 17/322

Davis presents a good conclusion: "Ashkelon was destroyed exactly as foretold! The Philistines were 'cut off' from the face of the earth till not one Philistine remains in all the world! (Prediction 1B) And lastly, long desolate Ashkelon (Prediction 3B) has been revived from its ruins of centuries, and is becoming a Garden City. And God has visited His people Israel and turned away their captivity and caused them to inhabit once desolate and now restored Ashkelon!" 11/49

The prophecies seem to have been very accurate and have also conformed to the amount of historical data which we have on the cities. The city of Gaza has a more mysterious history.

"A city of Gaza still exists," writes Peter Stoner, "so for a long time, the prophecy with respect to Gaza was thought to be in error. Finally a careful study was made of the location of Gaza, as described in the Bible, and it was found that the new city of Gaza was in the wrong location. A search was made for the old city and it was found buried under the sand dunes. It had indeed become bald. What better description could you give of a city buried under sand dunes than to say that it had become bald?" (Prediction 2B) 53/83

John Urquhart expands on Gaza's total disappearance.

". . . But meanwhile the prophecies had been so fully accomplished that the ancient city of Gaza could lift no protest against the mistake that was being made. The modern town is not built, as Dr. Keith afterwards discovered, on the site of the old, and is not therefore the subject of the prophecies. The great Gaza of the Philistines lay two miles nearer the shore and is now a series of sandhills, covered with minute but manifold remains. It is so forsaken that there is not a single hut resting on its site. It is so bald that neither pillar nor standing stone marks the place where the city stood, nor is there a single blade of grass on which the weary eye can rest." 55/105

"The historical Gaza," writes Comay (*Israel: An Uncommon Guide,* p. 121), "remains buried, awaiting serious archaeological excavation. Above the surface, the vista of sand and red soil and crowded towns and camps is redeemed by sunshine. . . ."

4A. PROBABILITY

Peter Stoner concludes: "Thus the human probability of those four prophecies coming true [concerning Gaza and Ashkelon] would be 1 in 5 [chance of Philistines vanishing] x 100 [chance of Gaza being sand-covered] x 5 [chance of Ashkelon becoming desolate] x 5 [chance of Ashkelon being a sheep country] or 1.2×10^4." 53/84

In other words, 1 in 12,000.

5. MOAB-AMMON

Two small kingdoms, Moab, positioned east of the Dead Sea, and Ammon, north of Moab, were also objects of God's judgment.

1A. SCRIPTURE AND DATING

Ezekiel 25:   (592-570 B.C.)

3. . . . And say to the sons of Ammon, "Hear the word of the Lord God! Thus says the Lord God, 'Because you said, "Aha!"' against My sanctuary when it was profaned, and against the house of Judah when they went into exile, and against the land of Israel when it was made desolate,

4. "Therefore, behold, I am going to give you to the sons of the east for a possession, and they will set their encampments among you and make their dwellings among you; they will eat your fruit and drink your milk.' "

Jeremiah 48:   (626-586 B.C.)

47. "Yet I will restore the fortunes of Moab
In the latter days," declares the Lord.
Thus for the judgment on Moab.

Jeremiah 49:

6. "But afterward I will restore
The fortunes of the sons of Ammon,"
Declares the Lord.

2A. PREDICTIONS

1B. Will be taken by easterners who will live off the fruits of the land (Ezekiel 25:4).

2B. "Men of the east" will make Ammon a site for their palaces (Ezekiel 25:4).

3B. People of old Moab and Ammon will reinhabit their land (Jeremiah 48:47; 49:6).

3A. HISTORY

With this in mind, we will study the background and history of these lands. Howard Vos writes: "A study of the topography of the area demonstrates the impregnable nature of mountain strongholds, and an indication of the military prowess is seen in the fact that Baasha, the Ammonite, sent 10,000 troops to Quargar in 354 B.C. to do battle with Shalmanesser of Assyria. So rich and powerful was the nation when Jeremiah wrote 'Rabbah [Ammon] shall be a desolate heap' that it seemed very unlikely that such a catastrophe would ever occur." (Prediction 1B) 56/131

The first and second predictions have been fulfilled as predicted, according to Howard Vos: "The Emir Abdullah of the East, ruler of Transjordania, built his palace there, fulfilling another prophecy that the men of the East shall possess Rabbah and set dwellings and palaces in her. In recent days the Emir has distinguished himself as director of the Arab Legion, which has taken such an active part in the fighting with the Jews in Palestine. Today the city of Ammon has a population of over 20,000, is a stopping place of the Damascus-Hejaz Railway, and has officials of other nations numbered among its population. The size of the city is significant when one realizes it numbered only a couple of hundred inhabitants in 1920." 56/136

Vos summarizes in a simple manner and states that "men of the east do inherit her (Moab) at the present. . . ."

At present, however, Moab and Ammon are waking up. Keep in mind the third prediction as this quote from Davis is revealed.

George Davis, writing in 1931 concerning Moab and Ammon, says: "Both lands [Moab and Ammon] are making rapid strides forward after their long sleep of centuries. Ammon, the capital of Trans-Jordan, is the Old Rabbath of the Ammonites, that was captured by Joab and the Israelites acting under the direction of King David. Only a dozen years ago Ammon was a mere village of two or three hundred people. Today it is a flourishing city with a population of 20,000 and is the residence of the ruler of Trans-Jordan, the Emir Abdellah." 12/60, 62

Possibly the people inhabiting Moab and Ammon are not the ancient Moabites and Ammonites, but even if this possibility were to be entertained, is it too much of a stretch of the imagination to see it happening in the future?

Howard Vos says: "The impact of this material has been so great that a writer in a purely secular encyclopedia with a tremendous circulation has said: 'But Israel remained a great power while Moab disappeared. It is true that Moab was continuously hard pressed by desert hordes; the exposed condition of the land is emphasized by the chains of ruined forts and castles which even the Romans were compelled to construct. But the explanation is to be found within Israel itself, and especially in the work of the prophets.' " 56/215

Peter Stoner evaluates the probability of this being fulfilled at one thousand-to-one.

"The estimates for the probable fulfillment of these items [relating to] the Moab-Ammon prophecies were given as (1) 1 in 5 for the take-over by men of the east; (2) 1 in 10 [for] palaces in Ammon; (3) 1 in 20 [for the] return of the Moabites and Ammonites. This gives an estimate in the whole prophecy of 1 in 10^3." 53/92

6. PETRA AND EDOM

1A. INTRODUCTION

The prophecies concerning the kingdom of Edom (southeast of the Dead Sea) and its capital, Petra, seemed as simple as the two prophecy areas before this, Gaza-Ashkelon and Moab-Ammon. This study began with three simple predictions from Isaiah and Jeremiah, but the more this was studied, the broader the sources became and the more fascinating grew the whole prophecy. Petra is one of the most mysterious cities on the face of the earth; it must be because of the way people speak of it. When research was finally stopped on this area, the predictions had grown from three to seven and this quote was discovered:

"In all, six prophets heap condemnation upon this nation Edom: Isaiah, Jeremiah, Ezekiel, Joel, Amos, and Obadiah." 56/173

Edom must have been a very evil nation.

"Their prophecies on Edom," writes George Smith, "number so great, they are so exuberant in language, so various, grand, and minute, that many pages might be filled in reciting them, and many more employed in showing their exact and complete fulfillment." 51/217, 218

2A. SCRIPTURE AND DATING

Isaiah 34:   (783-704 B.C.)

    6. The sword of the Lord is filled with blood,

> It is sated with fat, with the blood of lambs and goats,
> With the fat of the kidneys of rams.
> For the Lord has a sacrifice in Bozrah,
> And a great slaughter in the land of Edom.

7. Wild oxen shall also fall with them,
    And young bulls with strong ones;
    Thus their land shall be soaked with blood,
    And their dust become greasy with fat.

10. It shall not be quenched night or day;
    Its smoke shall go up forever;
    From generation to generation it shall be desolate;
    None shall pass through it forever and ever.

13. And thorns shall come up in its fortified towers,
    Nettles and thistles in its fortified cities;
    It shall also be a haunt of jackals
    And an abode of ostriches.

14. And the desert creatures shall meet with the wolves,
    The hairy goat also shall cry to its kind;
    Yes, the night-monster shall settle there
    And shall find herself a resting place.

15. The snake shall make its nest and lay eggs there,
    And it will hatch them and gather its brood under its shade;
    Yes, the hawks shall be gathered there,
    Every one with its kind.

Jeremiah 49:   (626-586 B.C.)

17. And Edom will become an object of horror; everyone who
    passes by it will be horrified and will hiss at all its wounds.

18. "Like the overthrow of Sodom and Gomorrah with its
    neighbors," says the Lord, "no one will live there, nor will a
    son of man reside in it."

Ezekiel 25:   (592-570 B.C.)

13. . . . Therefore, thus says the Lord God, "I will also stretch out
    My hand against Edom and cut off man and beast from it. And
    I will lay it waste; from Teman even to Dedan they will fall by
    the sword.

14. "And I will lay My vengeance on Edom by the hand of My
    people Israel. Therefore, they will act in Edom according to
    My anger and according to My wrath; thus they will know my
    vengeance," declares the Lord God.

Ezekiel 35:

5. "Because you have had everlasting enmity and have delivered
    the sons of Israel to the power of the sword at the time of their
    calamity, at the time of the punishment of the end,

6. "Therefore, as I live," declares the Lord God, "I will give you
    over to bloodshed, and bloodshed will pursue you. . . .

7. "And I will make Mount Seir a waste and a desolation, and I
    will cut off from it the one who passes through and returns."

3A. PREDICTIONS AND EXPLANATION

1B. Become a desolation (Isaiah 34:13).

2B. Never populated again (Jeremiah 49:18).

3B. **Conquered by heathen** (Ezekiel 25:14).

4B. **Conquered by Israel** (Ezekiel 25:14).

5B. **Shall have a bloody history** (Ezekiel 35:5, 6; Isaiah 34:6, 7).

6B. **Make Edom desolate as far as the city of Teman** (Ezekiel 25:13).

7B. **Wild animals will inhabit the area** (Isaiah 34:13-15).

8B. **Cessation of trade** (Isaiah 34:10; Ezekiel 35:7).

9B. **Spectators will be astonished** (Jeremiah 49:17).

There are many additional comments on the Edomites. The following are some of them:

"The awful fate of Edom and its cause," says David Higgins, "are clear. Edom would become a desolate wilderness because she had mistreated Israel (In contrast, verse 20 of Joel 3 predicts the perpetuity of Judah and Jerusalem). All the other prophetic utterances against Edom which followed were but a development of these two verses of Joel" (Joel 3:19,20). 22/47

Higgins continues: "Isaiah 34 predicts that, where once men and their palaces and fortresses were prominent, wild animals and weeds would become conspicuous. Travellers in Edom have marvelled at the fulfillment of this prophecy down to the very details." 22/57

4A. HISTORY

1B. Pre-prophecy Period

The history of Edom opens in a stormy way, and hardly slows down. For further background, what follows is a pre-prophecy history, i.e., the history before the prophecies were declared. George L. Robinson in his *Sarcophagus of an Ancient Civilization; Petra, Edom and the Edomites,* says that "after Saul's death, the Edomites took the first opportunity afforded them of showing their hatred of Israel. While David was occupied in north Syria smiting Hadadezer, king of Zobah, Edom seems to have invaded the southern part of Judah, even threatening Jerusalem. But upon David's return the much older kingdom of Edom was terribly reduced by the younger kingdom of Israel; eighteen thousand of the Edomites being smitten in the Valley of Salt at the south end of the Dead Sea." 49/348

"David conquered Edom, which remained subservient to Judah even during the time of the divided monarchy, until the rule of Jehoram." 56/179

(Note: *The International Standard Bible Encyclopedia* dates the reign of Jehoram at 853-841 B.C., which is prior to most of the prophets.) 44/1580

"Some fifty years," writes David Higgins, "after the death of Jehoram, Amaziah (ca 800-875 B.C.), king of Judah, invaded Edom and captured the stronghold of Sela." (Sela is the Hebrew word for *rock,* while Petra is the Greek word for *rock*). 22/36

"The freedom," says H. Vos, "which Edom gained from Judah proved to be only the preparation for more bondage — this time to Assyria." 56/179

Howard Vos continues that "with the passing of Assyrian virility, Chaldean hordes swept down from Transjordan, gobbling up Edom along with the rest of the nations." 56/180

2B. Post-prophecy Period

The fall of Assyria marked the approximate period of completion of the prophecies against Edom. What follows is the history after the prophecies were completed. "The Nabeans are probably 'the children of the east' mentioned in Ezekiel 25:4. Some time during the sixth century B.C. the Nabethians succeeded in expelling Edom from their rock fortresses and taking the city of Petra." (Prediction 3B) 22/40

Discussing the fulfillment of Prediction 4B, Bernard Ramm explains the Jewish conquest of Petra and Edom: "That the Jews conquered them [Edomites] is proved by reference to I Maccabees 5:3 and to Josephus' *Antiquities* (XII, 18, 1). They were attacked successively by John Hyrcanus and Simon of Gerasa. Therefore, the prediction that the Jews too would conquer them has been fulfilled." 48/103

Around the birth of Christ, Petra was prosperous. Citing Strabo, who lived about that time, George Davis explains, "Petra was also a city of great prosperity. Strabo tells that it was the terminus of one of the great commercial routes of Asia. It was the market of the Arabians for their spice and frankincense." 11/52

Unger's Bible Dictionary, concerning Edom during Roman times, records: "The Edomites were now incorporated with the Jewish nation, and the whole province was often termed by Greek and Roman writers *Idumaea.* Immediately before the siege of Jerusalem by Titus, 20,000 Idumaeans were admitted to the Holy City, which they filled with robbery and bloodshed. From this time, the Edomites, as a separate people, disappear from the page of history." 54/286

When the Jews needed help the most, during the Roman siege (70 A.D.), was when the Edomites hurt the worst. "After the massacre of the Jews," writes David Higgins, "the Idumeans returned home. But with the fall of Jerusalem in 70 A.D. the children of Esau disappear as a separate people from the stage of recorded history." (Prediction 5B) 22/44, 45

The rock fortress of Petra, however, lived on. *Encyclopaedia Britannica* tells us: "It [Petra] was already in decline at the time of the Islamic invasion in the 7th century. (Prediction 3B) In the 12th century the crusaders built a castle there called Sel. Otherwise, the site was occupied only by wandering tribesmen, and it was in this condition when rediscovered for the Western world by the Swiss traveler J. L. Burckhardt in 1812." (Prediction 8B) 15/xvii-751

George L. Robinson says: "Since Burckhardt's discovery of this wild desert metropolis in 1812, only occasional explorers and a comparatively small number of tourists have ventured to run the risk of visiting its ruins." 49/4

Concerning the skepticism over the existence of Edom, Henry Morris explains that "Edom and the Edomites are mentioned time and again in the Bible, but were completely forgotten in secular history until the nineteenth century, when references to them were found in Egyptian and Assyrian monuments. Finally the splendidly preserved remains of their capital city, Petra, 'the rock city,' were discovered. *Thus the critics, who had maintained the Edomites to be legendary, were again routed."* (Italics ours.) 39/93

To the above, Davis adds: "Petra, the capital of the land of Edom, was one of the wonders of the ancient world. It was built out of a mountain of rock. Many of its buildings were hewn out of the solid rock. Petra presents a stupendous sight with its rock-hewn buildings, carved out of the very mountainside itself, of beautiful rose-red stone. It was practically impregnable from the assault of enemies. There was just one long narrow canyon-like entrance, where a small force of soldiers could protect the city from being taken by a large army." 11/50-52

But what does Petra look like today? The description is like something from Edgar Allen Poe's scariest stories, yet it is completely true. George Smith vividly describes Edom by referring to various authors:

"The fulfillment of these prophecies is equally complete, and as minutely exact as the preceding. Captain Mangles, who visited these ruins, says that when surveying the scenery of Petra, 'the screaming of the eagles, hawks, and owls, who were soaring over our heads in considerable numbers, seemingly annoyed at any one approaching their lonely habitation, added much to the singularity of the scene.' It was also declared, 'It shall be a habitation for dragons (or serpents). I laid his heritage waste for the dragons of the wilderness.' Dr. Shaw represented the land of Edom, and the desert of which it now forms a part, 'as abounding with a variety of lizards and vipers, which are very numerous and troublesome.' And Volney relates that 'the Arabs, in general, avoid the ruins of the cities of Idumea, on account of the enormous scorpions with which they swarm.' So plentiful, as observed by Mr. Cory, 'are the scorpions in Petra, that, though it was cold and snowy, we found them under the stones, sometimes two under one stone!' The sheik, and his brother, who accompanied Mr. Cory, assured him that 'both lions and leopards are often seen in Petra, and on the hills immediately beyond it, but that they never descend into the plain beneath.' As the term 'satyr' is known to be usually applied to a fabulous animal, the use of the name in the Scriptures has occasioned some surprise and inquiry. The word signifies 'a rough hairy one'; and may well have been used to designate the wild goat, large herds of which are found on these mountains." (Predictions 1B, 2B, 7B, 9B) 51/221, 222

Higgins ties up the prophecy with the fulfillments:

"Again and again the desolation of Edom is foretold. In the time of the prophets such a prediction seemed most unlikely of fulfillment. Even after the Edomites had been pushed out, the Nabateans developed a flourishing civilization that lasted for centuries. But God had said, 'I will lay thy cities waste.' Today the land stands deserted, a mute testimony to the sure Word of the Lord. Petra is a remarkable example of the literal fulfillment of this prophecy. This great ancient capital with its theatre seating 4000, its temples, its altars and its monuments, is now silent and alone, decaying with the passage of time." (Predictions 1B, 2B, 8B) 22/55

Herbert Stewart gives a further description: "The ground is covered with broken pillars and pavements, heaps of hewn stone, and many other ruins. Scorpions and owls abound among its ruins. Burchardt, one of the boldest and most daring of travellers, says he never knew what fear was until he came near Petra. At nightfall the jackal howl is heard from the top of the rocks, answered by another far up the Wadi. The stone on which the traveller may sit is surrounded by nettles and thistles in what had been in the precincts of noble temples or palaces or beauty, and everything mentioned in the passages quoted [Isa. 34:10-14; Jer. 49:16], during the past centuries have found resting places within the deserted city." (Predictions 1B, 7B, 8B) 52/71, 72

George L. Robinson elucidates the feelings of standing in Petra today:

"Petra is a place which astonishes and baffles, but above all fascinates. Your first visit is an event in your life. Elemental feelings stir; again you know what awe is and humility. You have a sense of God's work through man and without man. If you have never experienced the sensation before, here at last you come under the spell of mystery. The place seems so remote, so unrelated to its surroundings . . . so undiscovered and so undiscoverable. What other city has been lost for a thousand years and at last, when stumbled upon by accident, has had still so much of its glory left with which to astonish the amazed traveler?" 49/9

Another vivid picture of Petra is painted by Alexander Keith in *Evidence of the Truth of the Christian Religion:* "I would that the skeptic could stand as I did, among the ruins of this city among the rocks, and there open the sacred Book and read the words of the inspired penman, written when this desolate place was one of the greatest cities in the world. I see the scoffer arrested, his cheek pale, his lip quivering, and his heart quaking with fear, as the ruined city cries out to him in a voice loud and powerful as that of one risen from the dead, — though he would not believe Moses and prophets, he believes the hand-writing of God Himself in the desolation and eternal ruin around him." 27/339

5A. SPECIFIC FULFILLMENTS

Individual predictions will now be expounded. The first has been dealt with very effectively; Edom is clearly a desolate place. The second has equally been established. The Moslem take-over of Edom of the sixth century A.D. can surely qualify as the "heathen" conquering of the third prediction. The fourth prediction, conquered by Israel: "It was predicted in Ezekial 25:14 that Israel would be used by God to take vengeance on Edom. Considering the fact that Israel was then in the Babylonian captivity, such a prophecy probably seemed ludicrous. Yet, some four centuries later the prediction finds its fulfillment in Judas Maccabeus and John Hyrcanus. Thousands of Edomites were slain and the nation was forced to submit to Jewish circumcision, and for all practical purposes they became Jews." 22/58, 89

The fifth prediction, that of a bloody history, follows: "A study of Edom's history has already borne this out. Assyria invaded the land and reduced Edom to servitude. The coming of Nebuchadnezzar took its toll. The migration of the Nabateans reduced their numbers. Forty thousand Edomites died at the hand of Judas Maccabeus." 22/55

The fulfillment of the sixth prediction, concerning Teman, or Maan, is described by Floyd Hamilton: "And strange as it may seem, Teman, or Maan, as it is called today, is still a prosperous town, on the eastern border of the land of Edom, and the only city in all that land that is not deserted! Could any more marvelous fulfillment of prophecy be found than this? Think what small chance there would be of a mere man picking out only one city in the whole land as the one city that should live down the centuries, while all the other cities shared in the general fate of destruction and desolation! God alone could foretell such a result, and the book which contains such prophecies must be His Book!" 20/312, 313

Raphael Patai explains that "Petra was the key city of the network of caravan routes from Africa to Asia Minor. . . . One could imagine it at the height of its prosperity. . . . Yet strangely enough, for all its importance, Petra was literally a lost city for six hundred years. Nothing whatever is known of it from A.D. 1200 to 1812, when it was rediscovered. . . . Even today, though its fame has spread throughout the world, the number of people who have actually seen it is negligible. It remains hidden and lost, one of the strangest yet most beautiful sights in the world; a vast, colorful necropolis watched over by eagles." 45/121, 122

The seventh prediction, concerning wild animals, has been previously borne out.

The eighth prediction, cessation of trade: "Included in the prophecy concerning the desolation of Edom," says D. Higgins, "is the fact of cessation of trade. Isaiah said that 'none shall pass through it forever and ever' (34:10); to which Ezekiel adds: 'I will cut off from it him that passeth through' (35:7). That the commerce of Edom should cease was unthinkable, for the land was the crossroads of the trade routes. But the prophecy has been literally fulfilled. . . ." 22/56

From William G. Blaikie's *A Manual of Bible History*, regarding the prophecy that "none shall pass through it," we see "the objection that the prophecy . . . has not been literally fulfilled, inasmuch as travelers have passed through Edom, is evidently frivolous. When the vast streams of traffic that used to pass through Edom have been so withdrawn that not a single caravan is ever seen on the route, the prophecy has surely been abundantly verified." 5/141

The ninth prediction, the astonishment of spectators, has also been fully explored. Higgins makes a good summation: "Jeremiah," continues Higgins, "indicated that those who passed through Edom would be astonished at her desolation. . . . The magnificent cities of Edom have been laid waste and curious travellers never cease to wonder at the abandoned fortresses in the mountains." (Prediction 9B) 22/59

Iain Browning points out that ". . . the visitors to Petra were not so much 'astonished' by the sheer scenic wonders which time had wrought, as by the devastation which the Lord was supposed to have brought down." 61/72

"For the early traveller, a visit to Petra was one of the great experiences. . . . The amazing thing is that, even though it is now quite simple and safe to visit this long lost city, the same sense of excited enchantment still pervades the expedition, and visitors still sense all of the same sense of thrills and climaxes about which our forebearers wrote." 61/78

6A. PROBABILITY AND CONCLUSION

Peter Stoner finds a great probability against the accurate human prediction of just three of the prophecies: "The probabilities for the fulfillment of these different items were estimated as follows [for the Edom prophecies]: (1) 1 in 10 [for Edom's being conquered]; (2) 1 in 10 [on the subsequent desolation]; (3) 1 in 100 [on never being reinhabited]. This gives a probability for the whole prophecy of 1 in 10^4." 47/93 It would be 1 in 10,000.

Many probably realize that this estimate of prophecy is difficult to grasp; the best course of action is to bring it closer to home. Edom was about 60 miles wide and 110 miles long; this rectangular-shaped kingdom was roughly 6,600 square miles. The kingdom of New Jersey is about 7,500 square miles. Consider a prediction. (1) New Jersey will become desolate. (2) It will never be reinhabited after it is conquered. (3) It will be invaded by men of the East, across the sea. (4) It will also be conquered by men of the North. (5) It will have an even bloodier and more corrupt future than any other nation in the United Kingdom of America. (6) It will be totally destroyed up to Philadelphia. (7) The site of the old kingdom will be infested with wild animals and beasts.

If one were to predict this today, he would either be mocked, ignored, or locked up. It sounds ridiculous. Three hundred million to one would be conservative, yet that is roughly what happened in real life to Edom. Edom was populous and powerful; Israel was broken and captive in Babylon, and it was Ezekiel who made prophecies too fantastic to be true — yet they *have* come true. The grim reality is staring us in the face. The prophecy is real. God's wrath is real. Ezekiel is real. The ruins of Petra are very real.

7. THEBES AND MEMPHIS

There seem to be few lands more enchanting and fascinating than ancient Egypt. Ezekiel prophesied about many cities in this land, but we will

consider only two: Thebes (ancient "No") and Memphis (ancient "Noph").
John Urquhart's book *The Wonders of Prophecy* is a priceless source in this
study on Egypt.

1A. SCRIPTURE AND DATING

Ezekiel 30:   (592-570 B.C.)

13. Thus says the Lord God,
"I will also destroy the idols
And make the images cease from Memphis.
And there will no longer be a prince in the land of Egypt,
And I will put fear in the land of Egypt.

14. "And I will make Pathros desolate,
Set a fire in Zoan,
And execute judgments on Thebes.

15. "And I will pour out My wrath on Sin [or Pelusium],
The stronghold of Egypt;
I will also cut off the multitude of Thebes."

2A. PREDICTIONS

1B. Destroy the idols of Memphis (Ezekiel 30:13).

2B. Thebes will be destroyed ("broken up") and fired (Ezekiel 30:14).

3B. Thebes: I will cut off the multitude of ... (Ezekiel 30:15).

4B. There will no longer be a native prince from Egypt (Ezekiel 30:13).

3A. HISTORY

The history of Memphis will come first. John Urquhart gives us the initial
information: "This name preserves the designation Pa-Nouf by which the
Egyptians named the ancient city known to us as Memphis. It is said to have
been founded by Menes, and that there the first regulations were made for
the worship of the gods and the service of the temples. It is certain that it was
regarded with the deepest veneration." 55/45

We can see the high value placed on images and idols early in the Memphis
history. The following account is found in *A Commentary: Critical,
Experiential and Practical on the Old and New Testament:* "Memphis, the
capital of Middle Egypt, and the stronghold of 'idols.' Though no record
exists of Nebuchadnezzar's 'destroying' these, we know from *Herodotus* that
Cambyses took Pelusium, the key of Egypt, by placing before his army dogs,
cats, &c., all held sacred in Egypt, so that no Egyptian would use any
weapon against them. He slew Apis, the sacred ox, and burned other idols of
Egypt." 23/iv.318 (Prediction 1B; Urquhart dates this invasion at 525 B.C.,
easily after the prophecy.)

Since idolatry was strongly opposed by Yahweh, it seems particularly ironic
that the fall of an idolatrous city was *because* of this sin. The following is a
paraphrase of John Urquhart's section on Egypt:

To examine Memphis around Christ's time and then see the prophecies
would make the predictions even more impossible. Strabo saw Memphis as
second behind Alexandria in area. However, with the founding of Cairo
nearby, Memphis began to decline about the seventh century A.D. Parts of
Memphis began to be transplanted, even though it seemed the city would
never completely disappear. A thirteenth century traveler, Abdul-Latif,
claimed a hearty portion of Memphis still remained to entertain the eye. A
"collection of wonderful works" was his phrase. 55/46

Urquhart continues with an explanation of the present. A century ago, he explains, even the site was in question. With the settling of this question is also the settlement of the prophecy. 55/46

Many other travelers have passed observations on Memphis. John Urquhart lists Wilkinson, who was surprised that as little of the vast city was left as he saw. Also, Miss Amelia B. Edwards, in her *A Thousand Miles Up the Nile* (pp. 97-99), is recorded to have observed the scattered and sparse relics of ancient grandeur. Much of what remains is hardly worth the effort of observing; and the leftovers are so few, they can be listed with ease. "One can hardly believe that a great city ever flourished on this spot." 55/47, 48

Theban history was different. According to Urquhart, the judgments against Thebes were so strong, historians have unrealizingly presented the fulfillments. Two hammer blows were to beat Thebes into the ground, neither happening before the prediction. Urquhart points out that Ezekiel lived during Nebuchadnezzar's reign, and 13 years after this king was gone and the Persians were the dominant empire, Cambyses (525 B.C.) invaded Egypt and hammered at the defenseless brow of Thebes as much destruction as anyone so crazy could deliver. He burned the temples and tried to destroy the colossal statues. Thebes rose quickly from this but carried a limp she would never shake off. 55/26, 27

Urquhart records the falling of the second blow in the century before Christ. Even then, she remained among the top cities financially in the area. Yet about 89 B.C., a siege was laid to the city which lasted three years. When Thebes finally did fall, it fell into eternal oblivion. It was virtually leveled, thus fulfilling Ezekiel 30: 14, 15. Its multitude was cut off and never returned. 55/27

Urquhart noted Diodorus Siculus of about 50 B.C. who saw the fallen Thebes and admired her because of the religious significance of the city. Even in the fallen condition, Diodorus saw her greatness and grace; her circumference had been 1¾ miles, her walls 24 feet thick and 66 feet high, and her riches were the product of the best quality craftsmanship of many monarchs. 55/25

Strabo is recorded to have observed Thebes in 25 B.C. and claimed that the city was broken up into multiple villages, in which form it has remained even in modern times — broken up and disunited. It seems phenomenal to note that the prophecy stipulated even the condition in which it would forever remain. 55/28

To contrast the two cities, we must remember: Thebes would be broken up and the people cut off; Memphis would have its idols destroyed, which meant virtually the entire city. Floyd Hamilton elucidates this area: "Now if we compare Memphis with Thebes, where the idols are still standing in great numbers, and where the images are still seen on the temple walls, the wonder of the fulfilled prophecy grows even more amazing. How did it happen that the prophecies about the two cities were not interchanged? How did it happen that it was not Thebes where the idols were destroyed, and Memphis which was to exist and yet be broken up? How did it happen that among all the ruined cities of Egypt, Memphis was selected for the peculiar fate of having its idols destroyed?" 20/308

Urquhart, too, found a beautiful comparison in Brugsch Bey's *Egypt Under the Pharaohs,* where Bey sees Memphis as the city of the gods. It is sensible that the God against idolatry would go against Memphis — though at the time, the fall of this city seemed almost impossible. In other places, i.e., Thebes, which was ruined at Memphis' apex, the idols have remained, yet the judgment of Memphis remains also. 55/45

The final prediction has been neglected, but applies even today. The prophecy concerning the absence of a native prince from Egypt has been completely fulfilled. Obviously, the prediction did not claim eternal anarchy, but that her government would be headed by foreigners. The Persians took Egypt in 525 B.C. and she remained a rebellious province for all of 170 years. In 350 B.C., Ochus finally crushed Egypt and from then on, foreigners have controlled the government. 55/42

Finally, John Urquhart teaches that when one keeps these prophecies in context, they tell us of God's judgment toward sin and pride. God is sovereign and He never forgets His warnings or His promises. 55/42

8. NINEVEH

The next two prophetic areas should be remembered together as they are very similar. The two major cities of the ancient world were Nineveh and Babylon. They were both incredibly strong cities, as you will soon see. They were populous and highly militaristic — centers of extremely strong military empires. Yet at around their respective peaks in power and influence, prophecies of doom were cast against their impregnable walls, and soon afterward they were conquered — Nineveh after a three-month (very short) siege and Babylon without a fight.

The first to be investigated will be Nineveh, the evil capital of the Assyrian Empire. Nahum was sent to preach repentance — there was no repentance — and then to prophesy the Lord's will.

1A. SCRIPTURE

Nahum   (661-before 612 B.C.)

> 1:8 But with an overflowing flood
> He will make a complete end of its site,
> And will pursue His enemies into darkness.

> 1:10 Like tangled thorns,
> And like those who are drunken with their drink,
> They are consumed
> As stubble completely withered.

> 2:6 The gates of the rivers are opened,
> And the palace is dissolved.

> 3:10 Yet she became an exile,
> She went into captivity;
> Also her small children were dashed to pieces
> At the head of every street;
> They cast lots for her honorable men,
> And all her great men were bound with fetters.

> 3:13 Behold, your people are women in your midst!
> The gates of your land are opened wide to your enemies;
> Fire consumes your gate bars.

> 3:19 There is no relief for your breakdown,
> Your wound is incurable.
> All who hear about you
> Will clap their hands over you,
> For on whom has not your evil passed continually?

2A. PREDICTIONS AND EXPLANATION

1B. Would be destroyed in a state of drunkenness (Nahum 1:10).

2B. Would be destroyed in "an overflowing flood" (Nahum 1:8, 2:6).

3B. Would be burned (Nahum 3:13).

4B. Would be totally destroyed ("Your wound is incurable") and become desolate (Nahum 3:19).

3A. DATING

For the dating of Nahum, we have George E. Meisinger writing: "The earliest and latest possible dates of Nahum are established by the prophet himself. The earliest date is fixed in 3:8 where the prophet looks at the conquest of Noamon (Thebes) as a past event. One learns from the Assyrian Annals that Asshurbanipal sacked Thebes in 663 B.C. — [John Bright, *A History of Israel* (Philadelphia: Westminster Press, 1960), p. 289.]

"The latest possible date is fixed by the nature of the contents of the book, i.e. it looks at the fall of Nineveh as a future event. The *Babylonian Chronicle* fixes the date of Nineveh's fall as 612 B.C. [D. J. Wiseman, *Chronicles of Chaldean Kings (685-556 B.C.) In the British Museum* (London: Published by the Trustees of the British Museum, 1956), pp. 24-26.]" 37/12

4A. BACKGROUND

As further study will show, the rivers around Nineveh will play an important part in the history.

"Sennacherib, Asshurbanipal's grandfather," writes Walter A. Mair, "complained that the river not only rose above its bank repeatedly during the centuries, but also undermined the foundations of some palaces and probably was the cause of their demolition. In his days the river constituted such a menace that he changed its course, perhaps removing some of the bends in order to expedite its flow. He also strengthened the foundations of the temple with 'mighty slabs of limestone,' so that 'its platform might not be weakened by the flood of high water.' " 34/124

Nineveh's defenses were very impressive. From certain sources (Diodorus 12, I, xxvi-xxvii; II. ii.3, iii.2 [12]; *International Standard Bible Encyclopaedia*, p. 2148-51 [20]) we can get a fair idea of the specifications of Nineveh.

unequaled in size of all the ancient cities
inner wall: 100 feet tall (10-story building)
              50 feet thick (6-7 cars abreast)
              three chariots abreast
              towers 200 feet tall (20-story)
              15 gates
150-foot-wide moat
7-mile circumference

Austen H. Layard, a specialist on Nineveh and Babylon, made this comment in his book *Discoveries Among the Ruins of Nineveh and Babylon:* "An enemy coming from the east, the side on which the inclosure was most open to attack, had consequently first to force a stupendous wall strengthened by detached forts. Two deep ditches and two more walls, the inner being scarcely inferior in size to the outer, had then to be passed before the city could be taken.

(According to Mr. Rich, the distance from the inside of the inner wall to the inside of the outer wall was 2,007 feet. Allowing 200 feet for the outer, the breadth of the whole fortifications would be about 2,200 feet, or not far from half a mile.)

"The remains still existing of these fortifications almost confirm the statements of Diodorus Siculus, that the walls were a hundred feet high, and that three chariots could drive upon them abreast; and lead to the conclusion that in describing the ramparts forming the circuit round the whole city, ancient historians were confounding them with those which inclosed only a separate quarter or a royal residence, as they have also done in speaking of Babylon. Whilst the inner walls werè constructed of stone and brick masonry, the outer appear to have consisted of little else than of the earth, loose pebbles, and rubble dug out from the ditches, which were cut with enormous labor in the solid conglomerate rock." 32/660

5A. HISTORY

The history will begin with an eerie analysis by George Meisinger (*The Fall of Nineveh*, Master's Thesis presented to the faculty of Dallas Theological Seminary, 1968): "Psammetichus [an Egyptian revolutionary against Assyrian rule] soon began a minor rise in power that forever thwarted Assyrian aspirations in Egypt. The Elamite territory was lost before Asshurbanipal's death. Though minor losses, as they had been minor gains, they were indicative of the fact that the wheels of Providence were now turning against Assyria. Her last act on the stage of history was in process. One of the bewildering riddles of history is that this nation — at her apex in 663 B.C. — fell to oblivion in just fifty-one years, never to be heard from again." 37/65

Assyria seemed to crumble, even though the Nineveh walls were good.

"In the summer of 614 B.C.," continues Meisinger, "Cyaxares marched against Nineveh itself, and though the text becomes defective, it is clear he was unable to breach the walls. He then turned to greener pastures. Tarbis, a few miles northwest of Nineveh, was sacked. Then Cyaxares marched south. Nimrud was sacked. [M. E. L. Mallowan, *Nimrud and Its Remains* (London: Collins St. James Place, 1966), II, 388, 389, 391.]" 37/82

And further, "Granted that national and/or military reverses in recent years had trod down the morale of the army, yet one still is unable to explain the wholesale terror exhibited in the 612 debacle by the Assyrian army on that basis. Something extraordinary must account for Nineveh's emotional reaction." 37/88

Meisinger builds his case: "Overwhelming military might cannot satisfy the requirements of Nahum's picture. Allowing that the coalition had *all* the most advanced techniques, military savvy, and armaments of its era, it still would not be able to penetrate Nineveh's walls with 'ease.' Walls that are one hundred feet high, with towers manned by a veteran army, plus a hundred and fifty foot wide moat do not succumb easily within three months." 37/88

And then, the final blow. "At the conclusion of Asshurbanipal's reign, the Medes and the confederated tribes of the Umman-Manda 'were fast gathering . . . like vultures awaiting the last moments of their victim [H. R. Hall, *The Ancient History of the Near East* (London: Methuen and Co. L.T.D., 1932), p. 511].' The vultures swooped upon their victim in 612 B.C., and thoroughly devoured it." 37/97

A three-month siege is incredible. "When one considers that Psammetichus besieged Ashdod for twenty-nine years [Herodotus, II, 157 (Axotus=Ashdod)], a city of considerably lesser dimensions than Nineveh, it is amazing that Nineveh fell in just three months. However, the prophet Nahum predicted that this great city would fall with ease. He prophesied that as a ripe fig falls off a tree when shaken, so Nineveh will fall" (Nahum 3:12). 37/87

We now switch from Meisinger to Gleason Archer (*A Survey of Old Testament Introduction*, Moody Press, 1964): "Nahum 2:6 contains a remarkably exact prediction, for subsequent history records that a vital part of the city walls of

Nineveh was carried away by a great flood, and this ruin of the defensive system permitted the besieging Medes and Chaldeans to storm the city without difficulty." (Prediction 2B) 1/341

Nineveh fell hard. The following is a paraphrase from *Diodorus of Sicily II*, 26 and 27. 50

Camped outside the city walls, the king of Assyria, who had been unaware of his deteriorating position militarily and over-aware of his victories against the enemy, became lax in his vigilance and began to indulge with his soldiers in a feast of animals and much wine and drinking (Prediction 1B). This fact of decline in the Assyrians' defenses reached the enemy general, Arbaces, through deserters, and a night attack was pursued. With great success, Arbaces' organized troops routed the disorganized camp of the Assyrians and sent them back in flight to their city with great losses. This battle, decided apparently entirely by the Assyrian drunkenness and disorganization, was the final scene before the actual battle for the city itself — the siege. Realizing the precarious situation he was in, the Assyrian leader, Sardanapallus, made preparations for the defense of his city as well as his kingdom. A prophecy was in the land which stated, "No enemy will ever take Nimus by storm unless the river shall first become the city's enemy." Sardanapallus decided this would never be and therefore felt secure.

The enemy of the Assyrians was very happy with its successes to this point, but could not break down the mighty city walls. The inhabitants had great amounts of food stored away, and as a result, the city remained a resistance to the attackers for three years; but after three years and heavy rains, the river, swelling wide, broke down a distance of the city walls and flooded a portion of the city. The king panicked, believing the forementioned prophecy had been completed. He gave up hope and ordered his kingly possessions as well as concubines, etc., into a portion of his palace and sealing off that palace, burned the whole thing down (Prediction 3B). The siegers, learning of the break in the wall, attacked this point, forcing entry into the city, and took over as victors of the whole city. Arbaces was crowned its king and given supreme authority.

"Extensive traces of ash which represent the sack of the city by Babylonians, Scythians, and Medes in 612 B.C. have been observed in many parts of the Acropolis. Thereafter the city ceased to be important."

We now reach the present.

Joseph P. Free states: "A century ago such familiar Biblical cities as . . . Nineveh . . . and many others were shapeless mounds, the very identity of which, in some cases, had been forgotten." (Prediction 4B) 18/5

Edward Chiera adds: "If the tourist of today, after all that has been written about the ancient civilizations of Babylon and Assyria, fails to get an accurate conception of what the past was, one can easily imagine that the first travelers crossed and recrossed the land without suspecting that they were close to the historical sites of Babylon and Nineveh. Even scientifically-minded travelers who knew from the Bible of the existence of these two cities, and attempted to find them, several times passed over their very ruins without knowing it." (Prediction 4B) 8/40

Merrill Unger records the devastation of Nineveh: "In 612 B.C. the ancient splendid city and capital of the Assyrian Empire was so completely obliterated, according to its prophesied decimation by Hebrew prophets, that it became like a myth until its discovery by Sir Austen Layard and others in the 19th century. The site has now been extensively excavated." 54/795

George Meisinger speaks to the critics who jeered at even the prior existence of Nineveh: "The priceless records of this once dauntless empire had been withheld from the annals of world history until the nineteenth century A.D. Sir Henry Layard, that indefatigable, English pioneer archaeologist, was the first to unlock the mysteries of this nation — a nation which had refused to yield her secrets to mankind for so long. Yet, almost from the first turn of Layard's spade, the city [Nineveh] began to surrender hundreds and then thousands of informative clues to the past. For centuries the only knowledge that such an empire existed was to be found in the direct and indirect statements of Scripture. As the centuries rolled by, and as no archaeological evidence turned up to "substantiate" the Biblical record, doubt began to grow as to whether such a people ever existed. The historian puzzled; the skeptic jeered the scriptural accounts. So complete was Assyria's extinction!" 37/4, 5

Archaeologists face a predicament, writes Merrill Unger: "Nineveh is a site so huge that perhaps it never will be completely excavated. A modern village covers one of the larger palaces. Cemeteries which cannot be disturbed cover other areas. Excavators have to bore through 30-45 feet of debris before Assyrian strata are reached." 54/796

M. E. L. Mallawan vividly records the destruction of Assyria. His description of the downfall is similar to the disaster in Nineveh. "The condition in which we found it [throne room at Fort Shalmanessar] was a dramatic illustration of the final sack: the wall plaster had been packed hard and burnt yellow by the flames and then blackened with soot which had penetrated into the brickwork itself. The intense heat had caused the south wall to bend inwards at a dangerous angle and the floor of the chamber itself was buried under a great pile of burnt debris over a metre and a half in depth, filled with ash, charcoal, small antiquities . . . there were also many hundreds of mutilated fragments of ivory carvings burnt black and gray, sometimes to a high polish from the heat. This debris was mixed with inflammable cereals which consisted of millet, barley, wheat, and emmer. I have in my time witnessed the debris of many an ancient fire — at Ur of the Chaldees, at Nineveh, at Arpachiyah, on sites in the Habur and Balih valleys — but never have I seen so perfect an example of a vengeful bonfire, loose-packed as bonfires are, the soot still permeating the air as we approached. After this great holocaust parts of the walls toppled over into the chamber, which was filled to a total height of three metres in all with mud brick. The hard upper packing, amounting to another metre and a half of debris over that of the bonfire, thus finally sealed the contents which were left undisturbed [sic] until we reached them in 1958." 35/ii.434

6A. SPECIFIC FULFILLMENTS

The prophecy mentioned a flood. What follows by Walter Maier is strong evidence supporting the flood. "Three times Nahum predicts that Nineveh is to be destroyed by a flood . . . (1:8) . . . (2:7) . . . (2:9). This triple emphasis on inundation is more than figurative, and the expressions 'gates of the rivers,' 'overrunning flood,' 'pool of water' cannot be described away as poetic imagery." 34/118

George Meisinger says: "It was further shown that even the coalition was unable to account for all the details involved in Nineveh's fall. For this reason, the traditions of a flood were pursued. Sufficient evidence — this paper contends — was presented to demonstrate that a flood solution to Nineveh's collapse is the only satisfactory answer, accounting for all details. A flood that destroyed a degree of Nineveh's defense system permitted the coalition to sack and vent its vengeance on Nineveh." 37/96

Walter Maier states: "The Babylonian tablet inferentially offers an acceptable background for the fulfillment of Nahum's prophecy. According to its chronology Nineveh fell in the month of Ab. The season of the heavy rainfall in Nineveh occurs normally in March, while the rivers attain their greatest height in the months of April and May, the period roughly parallel to Ab." 34/118, 119

Meisinger refers to Gadd (*The Fall of Nineveh: The Newly Discovered Babylonian Chronicle*, No. 21, 901, In the British Museum, London: Oxford University Press, 1923, pp. 27-30) when he says, "The most famous of the ancient accounts is that of Diodorus who quotes the much earlier Ctesias. He related that assaults were continually made upon the walls without success, but that in the third year (This evidently figures from 614 B.C. when Cyaxares made his abortive attempt to breach the walls of Nineveh. It was not a three-year *continual* siege, for the *Babylonian Chronicle* is clear that the Medes were absent from Assyria in 613, and that the Assyrian army was on offensive maneuvers against the Babylonian army that same year.) a succession of heavy downpours swelled the Euphrates [sic], flooded part of the city, and cast down the wall to a length of 20 stades." 37/89, 90

George Badger records: "The fact [of the flood] here recorded [Nahum 1:8; 2:7] literally fulfills the prophecy of Nahum and accounts for a stratum of pebble and sand which has been found a few feet below the surface [of the river] in the mounds of Koyoonjuk and Nimrud." 3/1, 78, 79

Some scholars believe the Tigris didn't even flow past ancient Nineveh since it does not at present.

Walter Maier answers these critics and gives reference for further checking: ". . . the majority of scholars have held that the Tigris flowed directly past the city on the west. (Karl Ritter, *Die Erdkunde* (1822-59), p. 224. Sir Austin Henry Layard, *Nineveh and Babylon* (1875), p. 77. Felix Jones, "Nineveh's Location," *Journal of Royal Asiatic Society* (1855), XV, 316, 323. F.E. Peiser, "Tigris to the East of Nineveh," *Mitteilungen der Vorderasiatischen Gesellschaft*, III, 277, 278. C. F. Lehmann and Paul Haupt, *Israel, seine Entwickelung im Rahmen der Weltgeschichte*, 1911, p. 149. Claude Hermann and Walter Johns, "Location of Tigris," in *Encyclopaedia Britannica*. 11th ed., 1911, XIX, Col. 3, 421.)" 34/120

Meisinger adds: "Debate is waning to the effect that this river (Tigris), at high flood level, could not destroy a river gate." 37/93

Not only could the Tigris River have done it, but also there are two other possibilities:

Walter Maier continues:

"The second river which could have caused the overrunning flood was the Khosr . . . At both of these dams [to hold out the high-water from the Khosr], constructed in the typical Assyrian style, the investigators believe, there was originally a gate or sluice to regulate the water flow. How easy, then, for the besieging army to impound the Khosr River at this place, close the sluices of the *agammu*, cut off this source of water supply (the water of the Tigris was not drinkable), and then, open the river gates, let the mass of dammed waters sweep down on the doomed city, carry the river gates away, flood the lower sections of the city, and thus help spell the beginning of Nineveh's end! Even today, at the supposed site of the Ninlil Gate in the city's walls, the Khosr broadens to recall the prophet's words: 'Nineveh is like a pool of water' " (2:9). 34/121, 122

"The third river, whose gates could have been opened or whose waters could have produced the overrunning flood, is the Tebiltu. This stream, as its name implies (it is significantly derived from the Assyrian verb *tabalu*, 'to take away,' 'to tear away') could become a raging torrent." 34/123

By way of review, the predictions have been fulfilled.

1. **Nineveh fell in a state of drunkenness.**
   Bernard Ramm states: "Part of the success of the Medes was due to the optimism of the Ninevites who assumed the enemy was permanently repulsed and gave themselves to drinking and feasting." 48/107

We can honestly assume that:

2. **Nineveh was destroyed in a flood.**

3. **Nineveh was burned.**

4. **Nineveh was totally destroyed and became desolate.**

In *The Road to Nineveh*, Kubie writes: "Here at Nineveh — if it was Nineveh — were none of the graceful columns, the carvings, the legible inscriptions. . . . Here, in the Land between the Rivers, were no trees and blossoming vines among the ruins, no running streams and aquaducts. . . . It was a cruel land, desolate even in spring. . . . Here there was *nothing* to indicate what might lie beneath those man-made hills rising abruptly from the flat plane. Layard could not conceive the shape of the buildings — if there were any buildings. He was somehow sure that there must be: 'It was believed that the great edifices and monuments which had rendered Nineveh one of the most famous and magnificent cities of the world had perished with her people, and like them had left no wreck behind. But even then, as I wandered over and among the great mounds, I was convinced that they must cover some vestiges of the great capitol, and I felt an intense longing to dig into them.' " 30/56

9. BABYLON

The mysterious city of Babylon, capital of the ancient world, head of the Babylonian empire, the center of trade, culture, learning and a dozen other things, was also the center of certain prophecies.

1A. SCRIPTURE AND DATING

Isaiah 13:   (783-704 B.C.)

19. And Babylon, the beauty of kingdoms, the glory of the
    Chaldeans' pride,
    Will be as when God overthrew Sodom and Gomorrah.

20. It will never be inhabited or lived in from generation to
    generation;
    Nor will the Arab pitch his tent there,
    Nor will shepherds make their flocks lie down there.

21. But desert creatures will lie down there,
    And their houses will be full of owls,
    Ostriches also will live there, and shaggy goats will frolic
    there.

22. And hyenas will howl in their fortified towers
    And jackals in their luxurious palaces.
    Her fateful time also will soon come
    And her days will not be prolonged.

Isaiah 14:

23. "I will also make it a possession for the hedgehog, and
    swamps of water, and I will sweep it with the broom of

destruction," declares the Lord of hosts.

Jeremiah 51:   (626-586 B.C.)

26. "And they will not take from you even a stone for a corner
     Nor a stone for foundations,
     But you will be desolate forever," declares the Lord.

43. Her cities have become an object of horror,
     A parched land and a desert,
     A land in which no man lives,
     And through which no son of man passes.

2A. PREDICTIONS

1B. Babylon to be like Sodom and Gomorrah (Isaiah 13:19).

2B. Never inhabited again (Jeremiah 51:26; Isaiah 13:20).

3B. Tents will not be placed there by Arabs (Isaiah 13:20).

4B. Sheepfolds will not be there (Isaiah 13:20).

5B. Desert creatures will infest the ruins (Isaiah 13:21).

6B. Stones will not be removed for other construction projects (Jeremiah 51:26).

7B. The ancient city will not be frequently visited (Jeremiah 51:43).

8B. Covered with swamps of water (Isaiah 14:23).

3A. THE HISTORY

As for the history, the *Encyclopaedia Britannica* writes that "until the 19th century the knowledge of Babylonia and Assyria was based on the Old Testament and a few Greek writers. Not until after the discovery of ancient monuments and written documents in the two countries, and especially after the decipherment of the cuneiform script and the languages written in this script, did the history and civilization of Babylonia and Assyria become known." (Predictions 1B, 2B) 15/ii. 950

Babylon was a rich city. "Long before Babylon had overcome her rival Nineveh," writes Austen Layard, "she was famous for the extent and importance of her commerce. No position could have then been more favourable than hers for carrying on a trade with all the regions of the known world. She stood upon a navigable stream that . . . approached in one part of its course within almost one hundred miles of the Mediterranean Sea, and emptied its waters into a gulf of the Indian Ocean. Parallel with this great river was one scarcely inferior in size and importance. The Tigris . . . flowed through the fertile districts of Assyria, and carried their varied produce to the Babylonian cities. Moderate skill and enterprise could scarcely fail to make Babylon not only the emporium of the Eastern world, but the main link of commercial intercourse between the East and the West." 32/455

Babylon was a busy city. Joseph Free speaks of the great buildings: "The archaeological excavations in Babylon have brought forth inscriptions which tell of Nebuchadnezzar's great building activities. The East India House inscription, now in London, has six columns of Babylonian writing telling of the stupendous building operations which the king carried on in enlarging and beautifying Babylon." 18/228

And it all began with Nabopolassar. Charles Feinberg in *The Prophecy of Ezekiel* adds: "In the late 7th and early 6th centuries B.C. Nabopolassar and his son Nebuchadnezzar rebuilt the city whose remains have survived until today; and it was at this time that Babylon attained its greatest fame." 15/ii. 948

It was surrounded with marshes. "According to the united testimony of ancient authors," writes Austen Layard, "the city was divided by the Euphrates into two parts. The principal existing ruins are to the east of the river; there are very few remains to the west, between Hillah and the Birs Nimrud. Indeed, in some parts of the plain, there are none at all. This fact might, to a certain extent, be explained in the following manner. To this day the Euphrates has a tendency to change its course and to lose itself in marshes *to the west* of its actual bed. We find that the low country on that side was subject to continual inundations from the earliest periods, and that, according to a tradition, Semiramis built embankments to restrain the river, whilst a later queen seems to have taken advantage of the overflowing of its waters to dig a great lake outside the walls. (Herod. l.i.c. 184, 185.) We know, too, from Arrian (Lib. vii.c. 17. and Diod. Sic. ii. 7.) that the western quarter of the city was surrounded and defended by enormous marshes, which prevented all access to it. These swamps were fed by the Euphrates." 32/420

Based on the *International Standard Bible Encyclopaedia* and Herodotus (1.178,.179,.180,.181), we can begin to see that the specifications of Babylon are quite astonishing:

> 196 square miles
> 14-mile sides
> 56-mile circumference
> surrounded by a 30-foot-wide moat
> double walls
>> outer wall:
>> 311 feet high — appx. the height of a 30-story building
>> 87 feet wide — park 11 cars abreast across the top
>>> 8 chariots abreast
>> 100 gates of solid brass, as also were the hinges and lintels
>> 250 watchtowers 100 feet higher than the outer walls
>>>>>> 44/350; 18

Many scholars believe that Herodotus' measurements are exaggerated, and that one should be more conservative in calculating the dimensions of Babylon. Herodotus and especially Xenophon in his *Cyropaedia* (English translation by Walter Miller, The Macmillan Co., 1914, pp. 261-285, found in the Loeb Classical Library edited by T. E. Page and W. H. D. Rouse) give the following description of the fall of Babylon the Great. The Persians, after laying siege to Babylon, saw they could in no way storm the massive walls or break down their gates. They had two Babylonian deserters, Gobryas and Gadatas, enter their camp. At this time, Chrysantas, a counsellor to Cyrus, made the observation that the Euphrates river ran underneath these gigantic walls and was deep enough and wide enough to march an army under. Cyrus ordered his troops to dig huge ditches and the two deserters to lay plans for attacking Babylon from within her walls. While the Persians were building canals to divert the course of the river, the Babylonians were laughing and mocking their seemingly helpless enemy outside their walls. The Babylonians were carousing at an annual feast to their gods and celebrating their victory over the Persians (as recorded in Daniel 8) without realizing that Cyrus had diverted the Euphrates river from underneath the walls of Babylon and was at that very time entering the city with his troops. One might say that the city was taken without a fight, thanks to two deserters and the drunkenness of the Babylonians. (See also Isa. 21:5; 44:27;

Jer. 51:36. Concerning Belshazzar's death see Isa. 14:18-20; Jer. 51:57.)

Thus Babylon the Great fell in a peaceful manner as recorded by Merrill Unger, *Unger's Bible Dictionary:* "On October 13, 539 B.C., Babylon fell to Cyrus of Persia and from that time on the decay of the city began. Xerxes plundered it. Alexander the Great thought to restore its great temple, in ruins in his day, but was deferred by the prohibitive cost. During the period of Alexander's successors the area decayed rapidly and soon became a desert." (Prediction 1B) 54/116

(Note: I.S.B.Ency. p. 3126 lists the reign of Xerxes at 485-465 B.C.)

Alexander's death was unfortunate. Gerald A. Larue writes: "Immediately the struggle for portions of the empire began among Alexander's generals. Babylon was wracked by political struggles and battles for control and by the plundering activities of the troops of the contending parties. Possession of the city was shuttled back and forth until finally it became the property of the Seleucids. So badly shattered was the once beautiful city that it was apparent that reconstruction would be as costly as building a new city and the Seleucids decided on the latter course. The city of Seleucia was constructed on a site forty miles north of Babylon on the Tigris river and one by one business establishments and commercial interests moved out of Babylon to Seleucia." 31/79

It died a slow death, continues Larue: "During the reign of Augustus (27 B.C.-14 A.D.) Strabo visited the site and commented, 'The great city has become a desert' " (xvi:i). 31/79, 80

"Trajan visited Babylon in A.D. 116 during his campaign against the Parthians and found, according to Dio Cassius, 'mounds and legends of mounds' " (lxviii.30). 31/80

"In A.D. 363, the Emperor Julian engaged in war with the Sassanian rulers of Persia and during one campaign destroyed the walls of Babylon which had been partially restored by the Sassanians who used the enclosed area as a hunting preserve." 31/80 (Prediction 5B)

"Fifty-four miles south of modern Baghdad lie the desolate, sand-swept ruins of the once proud city of Babylon." 31/11 (Predictions 1B, 2B; see pictures at end of this prophecy area.)

Modern scientists stand amazed. George Davis records: "Professor Kerman Kilprect, the well-known archaeologist, in his book, *Explorations in Bible Lands in the Nineteenth Century,* says: '. . . What a contrast between the ancient civilization and the modern degradation. [Prediction 1B] Wild animals, boars, and hyenas, jackals, and wolves, and an occasional lion infest the jungle.' " (Prediction 5B) 11/78, 79

Excavators stand in awe before the gigantic task of excavation.

Robert Koldewey, author of *The Excavation at Babylon,* is well known for his finds at Babylon. He says that "the city walls, for instance, which in other ancient towns measure 3 meters, or at most 6 or 7 meters in Babylon are fully 17 to 22 meters thick. On many ancient sites the mounds piled above the remains are not more than 2 or 3 to 6 meters high, while here we have to deal with 12 to 24 meters, and the vast extent of the area that was once inhabited is reflected in the grand scale of the ruins." 29/v

Werner Keller in his *The Bible as History* explains: "The German archaeologists had to clear away over a million cubic feet of rubble before they exposed part of the temple of Marduk on the Euphrates, which had been rebuilt under Nebuchadnezzar. The structure, including its outbuildings, measured approximately 1500 by 1800 feet. Opposite the temple rose the ziggurat, the tower of Marduk's sanctuary." 28/299, 300

The size means it is five football field lengths (500 yards) by six football field lengths:

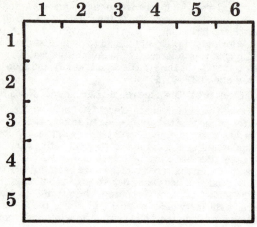

4A. SPECIFIC FULFILLMENTS

The specific fulfillments can be seen from the above history of Babylon: Prediction 1B says that Babylon would be destroyed and become as Sodom and Gomorrah (Isa. 13:19). Notice, it does not predict destruction in the same manner as Sodom and Gomorrah.

Austen H. Layard in *Discoveries Among the Ruins of Nineveh and Babylon* writes vividly of the remains of the destruction of Babylon in comparison with Sodom and Gomorrah. He also touches on the specific fulfillments of Predictions 2B, 3B, 4B and 5B (no Arab tents, no sheepfolds and the city would be overrun by desert creatures): ". . . the site of Babylon a naked and hideous waste. Owls start from the scanty thickets and the foul jackal skulks through the furrows. Truly, 'the glory of kingdoms and the beauty of the Chaldees' excellency is as when God overthrew Sodom and Gomorrah. Wild beasts of the desert lie there; and their houses are full of doleful creatures; and owls dwell there, and satyrs dance there. And the wild beasts of the island cry in their desolate houses, and dragons in their pleasant palaces,' for her day has come." (Isaiah 13:19-22) 32/413

Layard adds: "A large gray owl is found in great numbers, frequently in flocks of nearly a hundred, in the low shrubs among the ruins of Babylon." 32/414

A mention of the animals seems to be one of the major comments of modern travelers and archaeologists to Babylon.

Floyd Hamilton clarifies the above: "Travelers report that the city [Babylon] is absolutely uninhabited, even [by] Bedouins. There are various superstitions current among the Arabs that prevent them from pitching their tents there, while the character of the soil prevents the growth of vegetation suitable for the pasturage of flocks." 20/310

Peter Stoner states, "There are no sheepfolds about Babylon." 53/93,94

Edward Chiera wrote a letter from the site of Babylon:

"The sun has just now disappeared, and a purple sky smiles, unmindful of the scene of desolation. . . .

"A dead city! I have visited Pompeii and Ostra, but those cities are not dead: they are only temporarily abandoned. The hum of life is still heard and life blooms all around. . . .

"Here only is real death. . . .

"I should like to find a reason for all this desolation. Why should a flourishing city, seat of an empire, have completely disappeared? Is it the fulfillment of a prophetic curse that changed a superb temple into a den of jackals?" 7/xii-xiv

Nora B. Kubie writes: "The owl's hoot and the lion's roar were still heard in the ruins of Babylon." 30/272

Kubie continues that the workmen for Austen Layard "refused to set up camps near the abandoned ruins of Babylon. A sense of mystery and dread hung over the crumbling heaps of brick and sand." 30/272

Stoner expounds on the prediction that "stones will not be taken away" (Prediction 6B): "Bricks and building materials of many kinds have been salvaged from the ruins for cities round about, but the rocks, which were imported to Babylon at such great cost, have never been moved." 53/94

This sixth prediction (6B) is a tricky one. In Jeremiah 51:26, the pronoun "they" has no direct receiver, therefore this could refer to the conqueror. If so, then Cyrus the Great, the conqueror of Babylon, fulfilled the prophecy as you have seen. The fact is that Babylon's building bricks have been found elsewhere. One question to keep in mind is whether a brick would qualify as a "stone" or is Jeremiah referring to the literal foundation stones?

Prediction 7B, that "men will not pass by the ruins," is explained by Peter Stoner: "Though nearly all ancient cities are on prominent tourist routes, Babylon is not, and has very few visitors." 53/94

The fulfillment of Prediction 8B, "covered with swamps of water" is seen in the *Encyclopaedia Britannica:* "A large part of the old city buried under a deep bed of silt remains to be found, and the Babylon of Hammurabi, of which only the slenderest traces have been detected, now lies beneath the water table." 15/ii.950

Austen Layard continues: "The great part of the country below ancient Babylon has now been for centuries one great swamp. . . . The embankments of the rivers, utterly neglected, have broken away, and the waters have spread over the face of the land." (See Isa. 21:1.) 32/480

Kubie comments about part of Babylon being under water: "Not a blade of grass would grow in the peculiar soil, blanched as if with a deadly poison, and the reedy swamps round about breathed a miasma of fever" (referring to Layard's explorations around the site of Babylon).

". . . Layard looked out over the malarial swampland called by the Arabs '*the desert of waters*.' . . . After the city's fall, the great engineering works of Babylonia were neglected, the irrigation canals became choked up, and the rivers overflowed." 30/272, 274-275

5A. CONCLUSION AND PROBABILITY

All eight predictions have been fulfilled. Floyd Hamilton challenges us to "notice the difference between the prophecies concerning Babylon and those concerning Egypt! The Babylonian nation was to disappear, Egypt to continue a base nation and *has continued* as a base nation. How did it happen that both of these unlikely events came to pass exactly according to the way in which the prophecy was worded, and that the names were not exchanged?" 20/311

Werner Keller brings out an interesting observation: "Babylon was not only a commercial metropolis but a religious one, as can be seen from an inscription: 'Altogether there are in Babylon 53 temples of the chief gods, 55 chapels of Marduk, 300 chapels for the earthly deities, 600 for the heavenly deities, 180 altars for the goddess Ishtar, 180 for the gods Nergal and Adad and 12 other altars for different gods.' " 28/299

There were many centers of religious worship in the ancient world: Memphis-Thebes, Babylon, Nineveh, and Jerusalem were among them. The pagan deities which men said claimed an equal footing with the One-God, Yahweh, never did last, especially after Jesus Christ. Yet Yahweh refused to even consider Himself on equal terms with these pagan gods, and even went further by condemning the cities in which these gods flourished. It is one thing to issue threats, but the point here is to look at history. Which city out of the above listed has remained?

Peter Stoner evaluates the first seven predictions and comes up with an unbelievable one-in-five-billion chance of completion: "The probable fulfillment of each item in the Babylonian prophecy was estimated as follows: (1) 1 in 10 [it will be destroyed]; (2) 1 in 100 [never be reinhabited]; (3) 1 in 200 [Arabs will not pitch their tents there]; (4) 1 in 4 [no sheepfolds there]; (5) 1 in 5 [wild beasts occupy the ruins]; (6) 1 in 100 [stones will not be removed for other buildings]; (7) 1 in 10 [men will not pass by the ruins]. This makes a probability for the whole prophecy of 1 in 5×10^9." This is 1 in 5,000,000,000. 53/95

There are two small observations to be made on the Nineveh and Babylon prophecies as a pair. The first involves defenses. Even during World War I, defenses of the magnitude of these two cities would have stopped an entire army cold. Only since development of the airplane and sophisticated artillery has the technique of walled-city defense been completely outdated.

Babylon	Nineveh
14 square miles	150-foot-wide moat
moat all around	towers 200 feet tall
double walls	(20-story bldg.)
311 feet tall (30-story building)	walls
87 feet wide (11 cars abreast)	100 feet tall (10 stories)
100 gates: solid brass	50 feet wide (6 cars)
adequate land within for cultivation	3 chariots abreast

We can assume one thing from this. There is not one wall high enough or thick enough and no moat deep enough and no defense strong enough to keep out God or His judgment. Men cannot ignore Him with walls, no more than they can with rationalism or anything else.

The second observation involves probability of the two cities falling. Though Nineveh and Babylon were similar in some ways, they were different in others, just like any two cities of today are different (New York and Los Angeles). If someone were to be asked today which city would be destroyed, New York or Los Angeles, he would think that neither would or maybe choose one of them, but never choose both. The complete desolation of ancient Nineveh and Babylon stand as miraculous then as would the destruction of New York and Los Angeles and all their suburbs today. Yet they slowly died — never to be reinhabited.

6A. CONCLUSION

The following passage is a proper conclusion to this area. It includes parts of a letter, published in the prologue to *They Wrote on Clay: The Babylonian Tablets Speak Today* by Edward Chiera. Chiera was writing to his wife as he was excavating Kish, an ancient city very close to Babylon (eight miles east of Babylon). This is the archaeologist's personal view: "This evening I made my usual pilgrimage to the mound covering the ancient temple tower. . . .

"Seen from below, it does not look so high as might be expected of a Babylonian temple tower. Did not that of Babylon pretend to reach to heaven? One gets the answer after ascending it. Though rather low (it can hardly be more than five hundred feet), still from the top the eye sweeps over an enormous distance on the boundless, flat plain. . . . The ruins of Babylon are nearer. All around the tower small heaps of dirt represent all that remains of Kish, one of the oldest cities of Mesopotamia.

". . . The large network of canals, which in ancient times distributed the waters of the Euphrates over all this land, is now represented by a series of small mounds of dirt, running in all directions. Even the Euphrates has abandoned this land by changing its course. . . .

"A dead city! I have visited Pompeii and Ostia, and I have taken walks along the empty corridors of the Palatine. But those cities are not dead: they are only temporarily abandoned. The hum of life is still heard, and life blooms all around. They are but a step in the progress of that civilization to which they have contributed their full share and which marches on, under their very eyes.

"Here only is real death. Not a column or an arch still stands to demonstrate the permanency of human work. Everything has crumbled into dust. The very temple tower, the most imposing of all these ancient constructions, has entirely lost its original shape. Where are now its seven stages? Where the large stairway that led to the top? Where the shrine that crowned it? We see nothing but a mound of earth — all that remains of the millions of its bricks. On the very top [are] some traces of walls. But these are shapeless: time and neglect have completed their work.

"Under my feet are some holes which have been burrowed by foxes and jackals. At night they descend stealthily from their haunts in their difficult search for food, and appear silhouetted against the sky. This evening they appear to sense my presence and stay in hiding, perhaps wondering at this stranger who has come to disturb their peace. The mound is covered with white bones which represent the accumulated evidence of their hunts.

". . . Nothing breaks the deathly silence. . . .

"A jackal is now sending forth his howl, half-cry and half-threat. All the dogs of the Arab village immediately take up his challenge, and for a moment the peace is upset by howling and barking.

". . . But a certain fascination holds me here. I should like to find a reason for all this desolation. Why should a flourishing city, the seat of an empire, have completely disappeared? Is it the fulfillment of a prophetic curse that changed a superb temple into a den of jackals? Did the actions of the people who lived here have anything to do with this, or is it the fatal destiny of mankind that all its civilizations must crumble when they reach their peak? And what are we doing here, trying to wrest from the past its secrets, when probably we ourselves and our own achievements may become an object of search for peoples to come?" 8/xi-xiv

10. CHORAZIN, BETHSAIDA, CAPERNAUM

A fulfilled New Testament prophecy is unique indeed, yet this is what will now be investigated. By way of introduction, we have George T. B. Davis: "We read in the New Testament of four ancient cities which were beautifully situated near or in the shores of the Sea of Galilee. These four cities were Capernaum, Chorazin, Bethsaida, and Tiberias. Three of these cities have perished. Only the last named is standing today." 11/33

The prophecy, recorded in Matthew, was given by Jesus of Nazareth.

1A. SCRIPTURE AND DATING

Matthew 11:   (50 A.D.)

20.   Then He began to reproach the cities in which most of His miracles were done, because they did not repent.

21.   "Woe to you, Chorazin! Woe to you, Bethsaida! For if the miracles had occurred in Tyre and Sidon which occurred in you, they would have repented long ago in sackcloth and ashes.

22.   "Nevertheless I say to you, it shall be more tolerable for Tyre and Sidon in the day of judgment, than for you.

23.   "And you, Capernaum, will not be exalted to heaven, will you? You shall descend to hades; for if the miracles had occurred in Sodom which occurred in you, it would have remained to this day.

24.   "Nevertheless I say to you, that it shall be more tolerable for the land of Sodom in the day of judgment, than for you."

Though there is recorded no specific prophecy on how the cities were to be destroyed, the unmistakable mark of God's judgment and displeasure is on the brow of the three cities. History records a distinct story for these cities.

2A. HISTORY

Encyclopaedia Britannica mentioned Capernaum briefly: ". . . an ancient city on the northwest shore of the Sea of Galilee in Israel, identified with the ruined site at Tell Hum. . . . Its fame did not prevent the complete disappearance of the name and a long dispute over its location." 15/iv. 826

George Davis in his *Bible Prophecies Fulfilled Today* records that "an earthquake destroyed Capernaum about 400 A.D. and doubtless Chorazin and Bethsaida perished at the same time." 11/36

Davis expands: "Ancient Bethsaida's situation on the shore of the Sea of Galilee had been so beautiful that about 700 A.D., King Albalid I of Damascus decided to build a magnificent winter palace on the site of the ruined city. For fifteen years his workmen labored erecting the palace. Then King Albalid died, and the great palace was never completed. As the centuries rolled by, the palace became mere ruins. Today about all that remains of its former grandeur are some foundation stones and some unfinished mosaic flooring. Archeologists have covered up this mosaic with sand, lest it too should be carried away by vandals, and thus all traces of the palace should be lost." 11/36, 37

Samuel Clemens notes in his *Innocents Abroad* a description of Lake Tahoe. "The lake is solitude, for birds and squirrels on the shore and fishes. In the water [Lake Tahoe] are all the creatures that are near to make it otherwise, but it is not the sort of solitude to make one dreary. Come to Galilee for that. If these unpeopled deserts, these rusty mounds of barrenness, that never, never do shake the glare from their harsh outlines and fade and faint into vague perspective; that melancholy ruin of Capernaum; this stupid village of Tiberias. . . ." 9/238f.

Davis explains the situation of Capernaum: "For long centuries the synagogue lay buried under the earth like the rest of the destroyed city. . . . A man conceived the idea of restoring the ancient synagogue from its ruins. At length part of the walls of the building were re-erected, and a number of the pillars were put in their places.

"Then the unexpected happened. The architect of the partly restored synagogue suddenly died — just as King Albalid had died centuries ago before his palace in Bethsaida was completed." 11/38

Unger's Bible Dictionary sums up the plight of the three doomed cities: "The doom pronounced against Capernaum and the other unbelieving cities (Matt. 11:23) has been remarkably fulfilled. Tell Hum, its now generally accepted site, is a mass of ruins adjacent to Bethsaida and Tabgha, and yielded a 3rd century A.D. synagogue when excavated." 54/180

Davis concludes the prophecy with comments on Tiberias: "Not one word of judgment was pronounced on the city of Tiberias by our Lord. It has been partly destroyed several times but it has always been rebuilt." 11/40

Davis adds: "Each time we have visited Tiberias and the area around the Sea of Galilee we have been impressed anew with the truthfulness and the supernatural inspiration of the Word of God. There are the ruins of three cities, destroyed exactly as foretold by our Lord, and one city, Tiberias, upon which no word of judgment was uttered, still standing and flourishing after nineteen long centuries." 11/41

11. JERUSALEM'S ENLARGEMENT

Jeremiah, living in 626 to after 586 B.C., made a surprising prediction in 31:38-40. He plotted the future growth of the city of Jerusalem.

1A. SCRIPTURE AND DATING

Jeremiah 31:   (626-586 B.C.)

38. "Behold, days are coming," declares the Lord, "when the city shall be rebuilt for the Lord from the tower of Hananel to the Corner Gate.

39. "And the measuring line shall go out farther straight ahead to the hill Gareb; then it will turn to Goah.

40. "And the whole valley of the dead bodies and of the ashes, and all the fields as far as the brook Kidron, to the corner of the Horse Gate toward the east, shall be holy to the Lord; it shall not be plucked up, or overthrown any more forever."

2A. FULFILLMENT

This prophecy could sound vague unless one checks the map toward the end of this section. George T. B. Davis' book, *Fulfilled Prophecies That Prove the Bible*, bases fulfillment of this prophecy on Mr. G. Olaf Matson's booklet, "The American Colony Palestine Guide." What follows is a paraphrase and quotes from Mr. Davis' book. 12/88-104.

"It would be difficult to quote a Bible prophecy that is more definite and graphic than is this forecast by Jeremiah of the oft-destroyed city of Jerusalem." 12/90

Jeremiah uses clear landmarks to chart the route of the unusual growth of this city. These guide posts have remained many centuries until some of them were destroyed due to city growth, i.e., the fulfillments of the prophecy.

Zechariah has another passage that expands on Jeremiah in one area. Zechariah 14:10 reads:

"All the land will be changed into a plain from Geba to Rimmon south of Jerusalem; but Jerusalem will rise and remain on its site from Benjamin's gate as far as the place of the First Gate to the Corner Gate, and from the Tower of Hananel to the king's wine presses."

What will now be done is a tracing of the prophecy from point to point.

Modern terms will be expressed for some of the landmarks of Jerusalem and a proper context of ancient Jerusalem should be kept. Jeremiah's Jerusalem was farther south than the modern city. Most maps will show that it has been growing mainly northward.

The northwest corner of the Mosque of Omar vicinity is where the Tower of Hananel stood, and the present Jaffa Gate is where the ancient "Gate of the Corner" stood. The area between these two points is inside the walls and was built up before this present generation, yet some time after Jeremiah. The next move will be outside the city walls to the hill of Gareb which stands to the northeast of the corner gate. This area has been sold, and bought largely by Jews, in this generation. The hill Gareb is where presently the Russian Compound rests, and modern growth has followed the line.

Present-day Schneller's Orphanage, a German industrial school, is where the Hill Goah is. This begins the northerly hook of the city growth and is point 4 on the map prepared by Stoner, found at the end of this section. This has been until recently the limit of suburbs to the northwest. The city has grown along this line in an easy manner since the Jaffa Road has become a major thoroughfare. This is point 3 on the Stoner map, the area populated prior to the growth of the Goah Hill area.

The "Valley of Dead Bodies," place of the government tree nursery, is point 5 on the map. This valley was formerly a cemetery. This is where the Zechariah prophecy fits in. The king's wine presses are found north of the Valley of Dead Bodies. Very recently in this area, a new sub-division of Yemenite Jews has grown since about 1925. This is not numbered on Peter Stoner's map. We now continue with Jeremiah's prophecy. We would have seen "ash heaps" (southeast of Goah) had we been around until recently. But they gradually disappeared between about 1900 and 1930 due to construction; they were real ashes, supposed to be remains of temple sacrifices. This ash was a good ingredient for building mortar; therefore it was carried away in small quantities. This area was populated, thus filling in the hook of growth illustrated on the maps; this is number 6 on the Stoner map.

For a while, this was the extent of growth. Points 7, 8 and 9 were the "fields" of the brook Kidron of Kidron Valley. This is doubtless the direction in which growth will follow, since in 1931 (copyright of Davis' book) very new houses were springing up throughout this area. The "Horse Gate" is in the eastern wall of the old city and has disappeared but is not far from the walled-up Golden Gate.

The growth of the city has not covered the prescribed route of growth, but has *followed*, point by point, the line set down in Jeremiah. The prophet told a step-by-step progression of the growth of Jerusalem, and this process has been followed in actual fact with closeness. There are other prophecies dealing with southward trends of growth which have also been systematically fulfilled.

Jeremiah (31:40) summed up the prophecy which has been fulfilled from about 1880 to 1935 in the following manner: ". . . shall be holy unto the Lord; it shall not be plucked up, or overthrown any more forever."

Mr. Davis sums up this passage in his book (remember the pre-1948 copyright) in the following manner:

"How soon this latter part, that is, that it shall be holy unto the Lord, will become fact, or just how it will come about, is a question more easily asked than answered at the present time of political and racial antipathies and strife; but doubtless it will come in the right time, just as the more material part of the prophecy has come; and when it does, it will be in just as natural a manner as the other." 12/104

In her book, *Israel: An Uncommon Guide,* Joan Comay writes: "Nothing about the serene air of Jerusalem today recalls its 33 centuries of turbulent history, including earthquakes, nineteen military sieges, two total destructions by conquerors and many rebuildings. The existence and stubborn survival of an important city at this spot at first seem to defy reason. It is far from the seacoast or any river basin, and off the great caravan routes of early times. Surrounded by bleak hills, it is difficult to reach and in past ages had scanty water resources. . . .

"But throughout the flux of these thousands of years there runs one constant thread — the unique attachment of the Jewish people to Jerusalem. . . . Through all the centuries of dispersion, in the farthest corners of the earth, Jews have prayed for the return to Zion. . . . History has no parallel to this mystic bond; without it there would have been no state of Israel."

Below is a map including certain landmarks which are included in the prophecies. (Also notice that the Scripture reference has been divided into phrases, showing the steps of the prophecy.)

"Behold, the days come," saith the Lord, "that the city shall be built to the Lord from the *tower of Hananel* unto the *gate of the corner.*"

"And the measuring line shall yet go forth over against it upon the *hill Gareb,* and shall *compass about Goah.*

"And the whole valley of the dead bodies

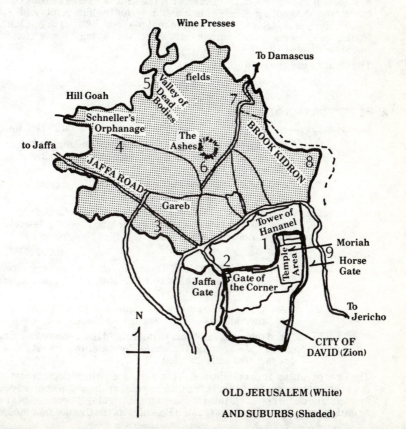

OLD JERUSALEM (White)

AND SUBURBS (Shaded)

and of the ashes

and all the fields *unto the brook of Kidron,*

unto the *corner of the Horse Gate* toward the east,

shall be holy unto the Lord; it shall not be plucked up, nor thrown down any more forever" (Jeremiah 31:38-40).

"The early growth of the city [Jerusalem]," writes Stoner, "covers numbers 1 and 2 [see map]; these are inside the Suleiman's wall. Fifty years ago Jerusalem overflowed the wall and started out in the direction of number 3." 53/88

"Thus nine items were named in the expansion of the city of Jerusalem. First, it was prophesied that it would expand, then the order of expansion." 53/88

Peter Stoner gives the following explanation of the probability of this prophecy's fulfillment:

"It is rather easy to find the number of ways in which the city of Jerusalem might have grown in its first nine steps. There are six definite corners to the old city. Certainly the growth might have started from any one of these corners, to say nothing of the sides. Let us say then, that the first development could have come at any of these six corners. Having built at point number 1 it could have next built at any of the old corners, or gone on in any one of these directions from number 1; thus, the second expansion could have come at any of 8 places. Continuing this on for the nine points and multiplying the results together, we find that the probability of Jeremiah writing this prophecy, from human knowledge, and having it come true would be about 1 in 8 x 10^{10}." 53/88

The chances are one in 80 billion.

12.   PALESTINE

1A. SCRIPTURE AND DATING

Leviticus 26:   (1520-1400 B.C.)

31.   "I will lay waste your cities as well, and will make your sanctuaries desolate; and I will not smell your soothing aromas.

32.   "And I will make the land desolate so that your enemies who settle in it shall be appalled over it.

33.   "You, however, I will scatter among the nations and will draw out a sword after you, as your land becomes desolate and your cities become waste."

Ezekiel 36:   (592-570 B.C.)

33.   Thus says the Lord God, "On the day that I cleanse you from all your iniquities, I will cause the cities to be inhabited, and the waste places will be rebuilt.

34.   "And the desolate land will be cultivated instead of being a desolation in the sight of everyone who passed by.

35.   "And they will say, 'This desolate land has become like the garden of Eden; and the waste, desolate, and ruined cities are fortified and inhabited.' "

The final prophecy area is Palestine. This is one area where documentation is virtually unnecessary because the fulfillments are happening before our eyes, yet the deeper one digs into this, the more intriguing it becomes. As far as dating goes, Leviticus is a part of the Pentateuch, the five books of Moses.

Unger's Dictionary places the writing somewhere between 1520-1400 B.C. (the lifetime of Moses). The last reference, Ezekiel, is dated 592-570 B.C. Actually, however, when you examine the fulfillments, it is ridiculous to try to post-date them. The predictions follow:

2A. PREDICTIONS

1B. Palestinian cities will resemble waste (Leviticus 26:31, 33).

2B. Desolation will come over the sanctuaries (Leviticus 26:31).

3B. Desolation will come over the land (Leviticus 26:32, 33).

4B. Palestine will be inhabited by enemies (Leviticus 26:32).

5B. People of Israel will disperse (Leviticus 26:33).

6B. Jews will be persecuted (Leviticus 26:33).

7B. Palestine will become reinhabited by Jews, cities will revive and the land will be farmed (Ezekiel 36:33-35).

3A. FULFILLMENTS

Fulfillments do not begin until after Christ. John Urquhart is a phenomenally good source. In *The Wonders of Prophecy,* he went into depth on the fate of Palestine and the Israelites.

The warning, John Urquhart begins, has been with the Jews ever since they first entered the Promised Land. Moses in Leviticus warned that if they completed the sin against the Divine Plan of Yahweh, the horrible fate would fall upon them as listed in Leviticus 26: 31-33.

This became a reality when, in 70 A.D., the Roman legions smashed, tore and ripped at the marrow of the land, and the inhabitants fanatically resisted the invaders. Consequently, the Romans showed even less mercy, and everything that stood for Judaism was destroyed. (Prediction 2B) The temple was smashed and burned. The abominable figure of a pig rested over the gate of Bethlehem. Since that time, the Jew has never sacrificed and the old practice was brought to an abrupt halt. (Prediction 2B) The Jewish dispersion is a well-known fact of history. They were dug up and gutted out, but this did not happen completely with the first Roman destruction of Palestine. In this, the Jews were crushed and trounced, but not really dispersed. This prediction was totally fulfilled in 135 A.D., when all of the land was confiscated and sold to Gentiles by Hadrian. From then on, Gentiles, the Jews' enemy, have been in control of Palestine and though the land has changed hands often, the owners have held two characteristics, Gentile background and hostility to Jews. (Predictions 4B, 5B)

The fulfillment, however, of the Jewish scattering seemed to impair fulfillment concerning the cities' desolation. The new landowners rebuilt the cities and the land was far from desolate. With Constantine on the throne, new churches grew on famous spots of Bible history. The land became so strong that the Persian invasion (seventh century) under Chosroes was delayed when going through this. Later, Jerusalem held out four months against Arab attackers. The Crusaders (eleventh century) still saw the strength of the cities in Palestine, yet the prophecy concerning the cities was no empty threat, and long since has been recognized as fulfilled. (Prediction 1B) 55/114-119

Werner Keller expands on the incident which happened in 70 A.D.:

"Archaeologists have found no material evidence of Israel's existence in Palestine after the year 70, not even a tombstone with a Jewish inscription.

The synagogues were destroyed, even the house of God in quiet Capernaum was reduced to ruins. The inexorable hand of destiny had drawn a line through Israel's part in the concert of nations." (Predictions 1B, 2B, 5B) 28/408

Mark Twain (Samuel L. Clemens) mentions Palestine in his *Innocents Abroad,* and he definitely wrote the way he saw it in 1869: "There is not a solitary village throughout its whole extent — not for 30 miles in either direction. There are two or three small clusters of Bedouin tents, but not a single permanent habitation. One may ride ten miles here-abouts and not see ten human beings." (Prediction 3B) 9/213

There are some authors who try to build beauty from desolation. Clemens comments: "I have given two fair, average specimens of the character of the testimony offered by the majority of the writers who visit the region. One says, 'Of the beauty of the scene I cannot say enough,' and then proceeds to cover up with a woof of glittering sentences a thing which, when stripped for inspection, proves to be only an unobtrusive basin of water, some mountainous desolation, and one tree. The other, after a conscientious effort to build a terrestrial paradise out of the same materials, with the addition of a 'grave and stately stork,' spoils it all by blundering upon the ghastly truth at the last. . . . The veneration and the affection which some of these men felt for the scenes they were speaking of heated their fancies and biased their judgment; but the pleasant falsities they wrote were full of honest sincerity, at any rate." 9/242

Clemens gives a great description of a vicious enemy: "We rested and lunched, and came on to this place, Ain Mellahah (the boys call it Baldwinsville). It was a very short day's run, but the dragoman does not want to go further, and has invented a plausible lie about the country beyond this being infested by ferocious Arabs, who would make sleeping in their midst a dangerous pastime. Well, they ought to be dangerous. They carry a rusty old weather-beaten flintlock gun, with a barrel that is longer than themselves; it has no sight on it; it will not carry farther than a brickbat, and is not half so certain. And the great sash they wear in many a fold around their waists has two or three absurd old horse-pistols in it that are rusty from eternal disuse — weapons that would hang fire just about long enough for you to walk out of range, and then burst and blow the Arab's head off. Exceedingly dangerous these sons of the desert are." (Prediction 4B) 9/210

This gruff old author was moved to quote the Leviticus passage (26:32-34), and then confessed that no one could stand by Ain Mellahah in 1869 and refuse to say the prophecy was fulfilled. 9/214

John Urquhart quotes Rabbi-Nowitz who investigated the area for possible Jewish re-populating: "But meanwhile the doom remains. Rabbi-Nowitz, who went in 1882 to Palestine with the view of determining whether the 'tribes of the wandering foot and weary breast' might not find a refuge in their ancient home, had to abandon the idea. He was compelled to admit that the poverty of the soil and the oppression of the Turkish government make return an impossibility." 55/116, 117

Even as late as 1927, "a land of ruins."

"According to that prophecy," writes Floyd Hamilton, "the cities of the land should be a waste and the land a desolation. Palestine today is a land of ruins. In almost no other land are the ruins of cities and villages so numerous as they are in Palestine today. The land that formerly supported such a large population, is now barren and capable of supporting only a mere fraction of its former population." 20/316

And finally, as George Davis points out: "The return of more than a million Jews to the land of Israel, after being away from their ancient homeland for nearly 2,000 years, is one of the most amazing and remarkable miracles of all time. And the astonishing thing about this modern return of the Jews to their homeland is this — it was foretold in detail by the prophet Jeremiah 2500 years ago." (Prediction 7B) 11/1

The land shall be tilled: "For many generations the Negev, in the southern part of Israel, has been largely a dry and isolated wilderness. There were some towns and villages in the Negev, but a large proportion of the inhabitants were roving bands of Bedouin. Today, portions of this long-barren land of the Negev are being cultivated, and are gradually being transformed from desert to fruitfulness and fertility." 11/80

And the cities shall be rebuilt: "For years," writes Davis, "Beersheba was a sleepy Arab town with crude buildings and homes. But not long after the winning of the Nageb by the Jews in the Arab-Jewish War, there began to be a change in Beersheba. It came slowly at first. When I visited Beersheba in 1950, two years after the war, there were few visible signs of progress. Three years later when I was again in Beersheba, the transformation of the city was in full swing. Modern houses were replacing the old tumbled-down dwellings, as large numbers of Jews began to make their homes in Beersheba. They showed me an area outside the old city which was to be the business center of Beersheba; and a district that was to be set apart for building factories. The population of the city has now increased to more than 20,000, and it is still growing and flourishing." 11/85

4A. SPECIFICS AND PROBABILITIES

Palestine is a bustling place, and it is growing. After 1,900 years of oppression, it is remarkable how suddenly, just since 1948, the Jews have built the nation which they have. Before that, they roamed from place to place; yet give them a place to stand and they move the world.

Peter Stoner evaluates the Palestine Prophecy Area at a 20,000 to 1 chance of fulfillment. A short review as well as a breakdown of this probability will follow. 53/90, 91

1B. The cities have resembled waste (1 in 10).

2B. The sanctuaries have been desolate (1 in 2).

3B. The land has been desolate (1 in 10).

4B. Enemies have inhabited Palestine (1 in 2).

5B. The Jews have been dispersed (1 in 5).

6B. The Jews have been persecuted (1 in 10).

7B. The Jews are regathering, rebuilding and retilling (1 in 10).

What follows is a paraphrase from John Urquhart in *The Wonders of Prophecy,* which is precisely why this prophecy was chosen to end 12 Prophecy Areas. This involves Prediction 6B, "a sword shall go out after the Jews" (Lev. 26: 33). 55/233-235

The Jewish persecution is clearly the picture of man at his worst. The second century saw revolts of these people in Cyprus, Egypt, Babylon and Cyrene which were bitterly crushed. They were outlawed under penalty of death from Cyprus, and even shipwreck on the island was no excuse. Egypt ripped them apart so fiercely that some believe fewer escaped from that place with Moses than were slaughtered there (600,000 men).

The history of the Jews is persecution. But the fire poured on their heads was also, in some measure, caused by their own brutality. They helped the Persians capture Jerusalem (7th century) and massacred their Christian prisoners, as well as the Persian Christian captives. This move backfired. It was not much later that Peter the Hermit began the first Crusade — not in the Holy Land but in Germany where, to protect their "Christian" homeland, Gentiles furiously slaughtered all Jews in sight all along the route. No one learned anything from this because 50 years later the same craze swept through the Rhineland. Jews suffered in every popular uprising of that land.

Milman, in *History of the Jews* (pp. 222, 223), points out that these periods of insanity seem not to be sparked by any special incident, but appear to seep up to the surface from some deep, hidden hate which knows no bounds. Milman further states that the Jews were blamed for the black plague. Also, the Flagellants, a crazed movement of enthusiasts, marched behind a crucifix and tortured themselves for their sins and, as blind fanatics will, mis-reasoned that, to the glory of God and atonement for sin, they plundered and massacred Jews of Frankfurt and elsewhere. Other rumors, fiercely "rectified," were spread of "fountains poisoned, children crucified, the Host stolen and outraged." The Jews could find no fair protection under the law. They spread around and wandered from place to place: Germany, Brunswick, Austria, Franconia, Rhineland, Silesia, Brandenberg-Prussia, Bohemia, Lithuania and Poland. These people were hated aliens in a sin-filled world.

Urquhart picks up again from Milman with the ability of even a progressive despot like Frederick the Great to inflict shameful despotism over the head of the life of the Jews.

England was little better; robbed and hazed by commoner and noble, 500 to 1,500 Jews died in one incident in York. All their property was taken at the end of the 1200's, and they were brutally expelled from the kingdom and not readmitted until Charles II.

For a period, France was an Eden for them. They held offices and high positions, were very literate and learned; yet this high position singled them out for greater oppression and robbery than when they were down. They were enslaved and looted by the heirs of the nobles they originally advised. Philip Augustus had them banished after he robbed them. For a price, they were allowed to return; but too late they found this was a trap. Louis VIII cancelled all interest to debts owed them and condemned them to serfdom. Mobs in Paris rose against them in 1239 and acted very similarly to Germans. Between about 1400 and 1794, the Jews were outlawed from all of France.

Their story in Spain is even worse.

Well known is the hatred in many other unmentioned countries.

"The contempt and hatred with which the Jews are still regarded there and elsewhere on the continent are well known, and the trembling of heart of which the prophet spoke has not ceased even now." 55/235, 236

At this point one may remember what a Pharisaic Jew wrote about, prior to the fall of Jerusalem:

". . . For all have sinned and fall short of the glory of God" (Romans 3:23).

It seems that out of all this world's hate and injustice, there must be a God somewhere who knows love and justice and who will level the scales and wipe out the hate; in short, there must be a righteous God to balance out all of man's unrighteousness. Thank God that there is!

PROPHETIC PROBABILITY

An excellent source here is Peter Stoner's *Science Speaks.* 53/95-98

Listing eight prophecies which we have considered and three by Stoner, the probabilities of their fulfillment are:

Tyre	1 in 7.5 x 10^7
Samaria	1 in 4 x 10^4
Gaza and Ashkelon	1 in 1.2 x 10^4
Jericho	1 in 2 x 10^5
The Golden Gate	1 in 10^3
Zion Plowed	1 in 10^2
Jerusalem Enlarged	1 in 8 x 10^{10}
Palestine	1 in 2 x 10^5
Moab and Ammon	1 in 10^3
Edom	1 in 10^4
Babylon	1 in 5 x 10^9

The probability of these 11 prophecies coming true, if written in human wisdom, is now found by multiplying all of these probabilities together, and the result is 1 in 5.76 x 10^{59}.

Some will say that the estimates given in some of these prophecies are too large and should be reduced. Others may say that some of the prophecies are related and should have smaller estimates. That may be true, so I would suggest that such a person go back over the prophecies and make his own estimates. They will be found to be still large enough to be conclusive. He may add to the consideration other prophecies and estimate their probability of fulfillment. Use, for example, such prophecies as those referring to the city of Sidon (Ezekiel 28:20-23); Capernaum and Bethsaida (Luke 10:13, 15); the desolation of Egypt (Ezekiel 29:12-14; 30:13); etc. I am sure there are more than enough fulfilled prophecies to establish the probability number given above even when the estimates are taken from the conservative critic.

Others may say that these accounts in the Bible are not prophecies, but historical accounts written after the events happened. This is absurd, for all of these prophecies are found in the Old Testament, and everyone will date its writing before Christ. One of these prophecies was completely fulfilled before Christ. Two had small parts fulfilled before Christ, and the remaining parts after Christ. All other prophecies considered were completely fulfilled after Christ. If we were to strike out all estimates given for parts of prophecies fulfilled before Christ, our probability number would still be so large that the strength of its argument could not be comprehended.

Let us try to visualize our probability of 1 in 5.76 x 10^{59}. Let us round this off to 5 x 10^{59}. Let us suppose that we had that number of silver dollars. What kind of a pile would this be?

The volume of the sun is more than 1,000,000 times that of the earth, yet out of 5 x 10^{59} silver dollars we could make 10^{28} solid silver balls the size of the sun.

Our group of stars, called our galaxy, comprises all of the stars which stay together in this one group. It is an extremely large group of at least 100,000,000,000 stars, each star averaging as large as our sun. At great distances from our galaxy are other galaxies similar to ours, containing about the same number of stars. If you were to count the 100,000,000,000 stars, counting 250 a minute, it would take you 750 years, counting day and night, and you would have counted only the stars in a single galaxy.

(Note: All computations are only approximate, and all numbers are expressed with only one or two digits.)

It has been estimated that the whole universe contains about two trillion galaxies, each containing about 100 billion stars. From our 5 x 10^{59} dollars we could make all of the stars, in all of these galaxies, 2 x 10^5 times.

Suppose we had marked one of these silver dollars, and had stirred it into the whole pile before we had made them into balls the size of the sun. Then suppose we had blindfolded a man and told him to go over all of these great balls and pick up the dollar which he thinks is the right one. What chance would he have of finding the right one? It would be a very great task to look over this mass of dollars. If our blindfolded man were to travel 60 miles per hour, day and night, it would take him five years to go once around a star. This would give him a very poor chance to select what might be the marked dollar from that star, but this amount of time per star would take 500 billion years for each galaxy. Let us suppose our man were extremely speedy, able to look over all of the dollars contained in 100 billion stars each second (instead of 500 billion years); it would still take him about 3×10^9 years (three billion years) to look over the whole mass. It is absurd to think that he would have any conceivable chance of picking up the right dollar.

The chance of these 11 prophecies being written in human wisdom, and all coming true, is a similar chance to that which the blindfolded man had of finding the right dollar. But these prophecies, and many more, all came true. We can then draw only one conclusion, and that is that God inspired the writing of every one of these prophecies. What stronger proof can any man ask for the inspiration of the Bible?

In Isaiah 41:23 the prophet hurled out the challenge to heathen gods: "Show the things that are to come hereafter, that we may know that ye are gods."

God has accepted this challenge. He has predicted multitudes of events to happen in the future. They have come true exactly as predicted, even though in some cases thousands of years were involved for the fulfillment. God has proven that He is our supernatural God with all wisdom. We have no alternative but to believe.

CONCLUSION

What seemed to be a great blow to the Christian faith, the Moslem invasion of the Holy Land and eventual military failure of the Crusades, is in reality a great victory for the Christian. The Moslems catalyzed the final sealing of many prophecies. How many condemned cities in this study alone fell during or directly because of the Crusades and the Moslem invasions? (Tyre, Petra, Samaria, Ashkelon) It is rather ironical that the apparent enemy of Christianity is, after closer study, the principal pawn used by the Lord to complete His purpose in the Church Age.

The overwhelming truth, which is becoming clear as a direct result of this study, is that God has a direct hand in history. These prophets had no control over the fulfillments, and never claimed to be speaking on their own authority. They claimed to be prophets of the living God, and consequently, the living God is directly responsible for fulfilling these judgments.

BIBLIOGRAPHY

1. Archer, Gleason L. *A Survey of Old Testament Introduction*. Chicago: Moody Press, 1964. Used by permission.
2. Arrian. *History of Alexander and Indica*. Translated by E. Iliff Robson (with an English translation from the Loeb Classical Library, edited by T. E. Page), 2 vols. Cambridge: Harvard University Press, 1954.
3. Badger, George Percy. *The Nestorians and Their Rituals*. London: n.p., 1852.
4. Beck, John Clark, Jr. *The Fall of Tyre According to Ezekiel's Prophecy*. Unpublished Master's Thesis, Dallas Theological Seminary, 1971.

5. Blaikie, William G. *A Manual of Bible History.* London: Thomas Nelson & Sons, 1904.

6. Browning, Iain. *Petra.* Parkridge, N.J.: Noyes Press, 1973.

7. Chiera, Edward. *They Wrote on Clay: The Babylonian Tablets Speak Today.* Chicago: University of Chicago Press, 1938.

8. Chiera, Edward. *They Wrote on Clay: The Babylonian Tablets Speak Today.* Edited by George C. Cameron. Rev. ed. Chicago: University of Chicago Press, 1966.

9. Clemens, Samuel L. (Mark Twain). *Innocents Abroad or The New Pilgrim's Progress.* Vol. II. New York: Harper & Brothers Publishers, 1869.

10. Curtius, Quintus. *History of Alexander.* Translated by John C. Rolfe (from the Loeb Classical Library, edited by T. E. Page), 2 vols. Cambridge: Harvard University Press, 1946.

11. Davis, George T. B. *Bible Prophecies Fulfilled Today.* Philadelphia: The Million Testaments Campaigns, Inc., 1955.

12. Davis, George T. B. *Fulfilled Prophecies that Prove the Bible.* Philadelphia: The Million Testaments Campaign, 1931.

13. Delitzsch, Franz. *Biblical Commentary of the Prophecies of Isaiah.* Translated from the German by James Martin, 2 vols. Grand Rapids: William B. Eerdmans Publishing Company, 1963. Used by permission.

14. Douglas, J. D. (ed.). *The New Bible Dictionary.* Grand Rapids: William B. Eerdmans Publishing Company, 1962. Used by permission.

15. *Encyclopaedia Britannica.* Reprinted by permission, copyright, Encyclopaedia Britannica, 1970.

16. Feinberg, Charles Lee. *The Prophecy of Ezekiel.* Chicago: Moody Press, 1969.

17. Fodor, Eugene. *Fodor's Israel.* New York: David McKay Co., Inc., 1974.

18. Free, Joseph P. *Archaeology and Bible History.* Wheaton: Scripture Press Publications, 1950.

19. Gillett, E. H. *Ancient Cities and Empires.* Philadelphia: Presbyterian Publication Committee, 1867.

20. Hamilton, Floyd E. *The Basis of Christian Faith.* New York: George H. Doran Company, 1927.

21. *Herodotus.* Translated by Henry Cary (from the Bohn's Classical Library). London: George Bell and Sons, 1904.

22. Higgins, David C. *The Edomites Considered Historically and Prophetically.* Unpublished Master's Thesis, Dallas Theological Seminary, 1960.

23. Jamieson, Robert, A. R. Fausset and David Brown. *A Commentary: Critical, Experiential and Practical on the Old and New Testaments.* Grand Rapids: William B. Eerdmans Publishing Co., 1961. Used by permission.

24. Jidejian, Nina. *Tyre through the Ages.* Beirut: Dar El-Mashreq Publishers, 1969.

25. Josephus, Flavius. *Jewish Antiquities.* Translated by Ralph Marehus (from the Loeb Classical Library, edited by T. E. Page), 5 vols. Cambridge: Harvard University Press, 1963.

26. Keil, C. F. *Biblical Commentary on the Old Testament: The Prophecies of Jeremiah.* Translated by David Patrick. Vol. I. Grand Rapids: William B. Eerdmans Publishing Co., 1964. Used by permission.

27. Keith, Alexander. *Evidence of the Truth of the Christian Religion.* London: T. O. Nelson and Sons, 1861.

28. Keller, Werner. *The Bible as History.* Translated by William Neil. New York: William and Company, 1956.

29. Koldewey, Robert. *The Excavations at Babylon.* Translated by Agnes S. Johns. London: Macmillan and Company, Ltd., 1914.

30. Kubie, Nora Benjamin. *Road to Nineveh*. New York: Doubleday and Company, 1964.

31. Larue, Gerald A. *Babylon and the Bible*. Grand Rapids: Baker Book House, 1919.

32. Layard, Austen H. *Discoveries Among the Ruins of Nineveh and Babylon*. New York: Harper and Brothers, 1853.

33. Luckenbill, Daniel David. *Ancient Record of Assyria and Babylonia*. 2 vols. Chicago: University of Chicago Press, 1926.

34. Maier, Walter A. *The Book of Nahum: A Commentary*. St. Louis: Concordia Publishing House, 1959.

35. Mallowan, M. E. L. *Numrud and Its Remains*. 3 vols. London: Collins, St. James Place, 1966.

36. Maurice, Thomas. *Observations on the Ruins of Babylon, Recently Visited and Described by Claudius James Rich, Esq*. London: John Murray of Albermarle St., 1816.

37. Meisinger, George E. *The Fall of Nineveh*. Unpublished Master's Thesis, Dallas Theological Seminary, 1968.

38. Michaud, Joseph Francois. *History of the Crusades*. 2 vols. Philadelphia: George Barrie.

39. Morris, Henry M. *The Bible and Modern Science*. Rev. ed. Chicago: Moody Press, 1956.

40. Myers, Philip Van Ness. *General History for Colleges and High Schools*. Boston: Ginn and Company, 1889.

41. Nasir-i-Khurran. *Diary of a Journey Through Syria and Palestine in 1047 A.D.* London, n.p., 1893.

42. Nelson, Nina. *Your Guide to Lebanon*. London: Alvin Redman, Ltd., 1965.

43. Newton, Benjamin Wills. *Babylon: Its Future History and Doom*. London: Wertheimer, Lea and Co., 1890.

44. Orr, James (ed.). *International Standard Bible Encyclopedia*. Grand Rapids: William B. Eerdmans Publishing Co., 1960. Used by permission.

45. Patai, Raphael. *The Kingdom of Jordan*. Princeton, N.J.: Princeton University Press, 1958.

46. Pliny the Elder. *Natural History*. Translated by H. Rackham and W. H. S. Jones (from the Loeb Classical Library, edited by T. E. Page). Cambridge: Harvard University Press, 1951.

47. Rackl, Hans-Wolf. *Archaeology Underwater*. Translated by Ronald J. Floyd. New York: Charles Scribner's Sons, 1968.

48. Ramm, Bernard. *Protestant Christian Evidences*. Chicago: Moody Press, 1957. Used by permission.

49. Robinson, George Livingston. *The Sarcophagus of an Ancient Civilization*. New York: Macmillan Company, 1930.

50. Siculus, Diodorus. *Bibliotheca Historica*. Translated by Francis R. Walton, C. H. Oldfather, C. L. Sherman, C. Bradford Welles, Russel M. Greer (from the Loeb Classical Library, edited by T. E. Page). Cambridge: Harvard University Press, 1957.

51. Smith, George. *The Book of Prophecy*. London: Longmain, Green, Reader, and Dyer, 1865.

52. Stewart, Herbert. *The Stronghold of Prophecy*. London: Marshall, Morgan and Scott Publications, Ltd., 1941.

53. Stoner, Peter W. *Science Speaks: An Evaluation of Certain Christian Evidences*. Chicago: Moody Press, 1963. Used by permission.

54. Unger, Merrill F. *Unger's Bible Dictionary*. Rev. ed. Chicago: Moody Press, 1966.

55. Urquhart, John. *The Wonders of Prophecy.* New York: C. C. Cook, n.d.
56. Vos, Howard Frederick. *Fulfilled Prophecy in Isaiah, Jeremiah, and Ezekiel.* Unpublished Doctoral Dissertation, Dallas Theological Seminary, 1950.
57. Ward, Philip. *Touring Lebanon.* London: n.p., 1971.
58. Wright, Thomas. *Early Travels in Palestine.* London: Henry G. Bohn, 1848.
59. Xenophon. *The Anabasis of Cyrus.* Translated by Carleton L. Brownson (from the Loeb Classical Library, edited by T. E. Page). Cambridge: Harvard University Press, 1950.
60. Young, E. J. *Introduction to the Old Testament.* Grand Rapids: William B. Eerdmans Publishing Company, 1956. Used by permission.

chapter 12

the
uniqueness
of the
Christian
experience

The following is an outline designed to aid you in effectively using this material.

1A.   INTRODUCTION

    1B.   Definition of Christian Experience

    2B.   Need for Christian Experience

2A.   UNIQUE CONTENT OF CHRISTIAN EXPERIENCE

    1B.   Its focal point — Jesus Christ

    2B.   Its Objective Reality

    3B.   Its Universality

3A.   TESTIMONIES OF CHRISTIAN EXPERIENCE

1A.   INTRODUCTION

1B.   What Is the Christian Experience?

Christian experience is the state or condition produced in the mental, moral and spiritual nature of man, through the power of the Holy Spirit, as a result of the establishment of a personal relationship with the risen Christ.

2B.   Need for Christian Experience

Christian experience must be relevant to all phases of human life.

Bernard Ramm in *Protestant Christian Evidences* states that "whatever passes as true must have direct tangency with life and experience. . . . It is to be questioned if Christianity would have had the hold it has had, and does have on hundreds of thousands of people if it lacked direct tangency with life and experience even though it created such an imposing theological and philosophical edifice. Because Christianity is true, it must have relevancy to every significant aspect of the universe and human experience. It must not only provide us with the material of a great philosophy — Christian trinitarian theism — and a great theology; but it must have a relevancy or tangency to human experience." 38/208

Christianity fails if it is not applicable to life on this earth. Conversely, Christian experience is of no significance if the life, death and resurrection of Christ are not factual events in history. The two are interdependent and inseparable. However, evidence for the validity of both is overwhelming. As Kenneth Scott Latourette, noted historian at Yale University states, "Never has Jesus had so wide and so profound an effect upon humanity as in the past three or four generations. Through Him millions of individuals have been transformed and have begun to live the kind of life which He exemplified." 25/227

Kenneth Scott Latourette goes on to say, "Through Him movements have been set in motion which have made in society for what mankind believes to be its best — in the inward transformation of human lives, in political order, in the production and distribution of goods to meet the physical needs of men, in healing physical ills, in the relations between races and between nations, in art, in religion and in the achievements of the human intellect. Gauged by the consequences which have followed, the birth, life, death, and resurrection of Jesus have been the most important events in the history of man. Measured by His influence, Jesus is central in the human story." 26/227

2A. UNIQUE CONTENT OF CHRISTIAN EXPERIENCE

1B.   The Focal Point of Christian Experience — Jesus Christ

Many people have the impression that Christian conversion is a psychologically induced experience brought about by brainwashing the subject with persuasive words and emotional presentations of Christian "myths." An evangelist is thought of as a psychologist manipulating weak, helpless minds into conformity with his own views.

Some have even suggested that the Christian experience can be explained on the basis of conditioned reflexes. They claim that anyone, after repeated exposure to Christian thought, can be caught in a type of "spiritual hypnosis" in which he will mechanically react in certain ways under certain conditions.

Paul Little in *Know Why You Believe* concludes that "to attempt to explain all Christian experience on a psychological basis does not fit the facts." He adds that "Christian experience can be described psychologically, but this does not explain why it happens or negate its reality." 29/178

The "why" of Christian experience is the person of Jesus Christ. This fact distinguishes Christianity from all other religions, for it is only Christianity that provides a totally new source of power for living.

Robert O. Ferm comments on the uniqueness of Christian conversion: "For the Christian this new center of energy is the person of Christ. The difference between the Christian and the non-Christian turns out to be, not difference in psychological symptoms, but rather in the object about which the new personality is integrated. The thing that makes Christian conversion different, then, is Christ." 16/225

Furthermore, this "object" of our faith is not some philosophical invention of man's mind, but a physical, historical reality. The previous sections set forth overwhelming evidence to support this point.

The God of Christianity is not an imperceptible, unknown God, but one who has specific attributes and characteristics, which are revealed in the Scriptures. Unlike some of the religions devoted to a mystical god, Christians put their faith in a God who may be identified and who made Himself known in *history* by sending His Son, Jesus Christ. Christians can believe that their sins have been forgiven because forgiveness was accomplished and recorded in *history* by the shedding of Christ's blood on the cross. Christians can believe that Christ is now living within them because He was raised from the dead in *history*.

2B. Significance of an Objective Reality Behind the Subjective Experience

I was giving my testimony during a debate in a history class recently, and just as I was finishing, the professor spoke up and remarked, "Look, McDowell, we're interested in facts, not testimonies. Why, I have met scores of people around the world who have been transformed by Christ." I interrupted and said, "Thank you, let me wrap up what I am sharing, and then I will concentrate my remarks on your statement."

After my testimony of how Christ changed my life, I outlined the following to the class: "Many of you are saying, 'Christ changed your life, so what?' One thing that has confirmed to me the resurrection of Jesus Christ 2,000 years ago is the transformation of the lives of millions of people when they become related by faith to the person of Jesus. Although they are from every walk of life and from all the nations of the world, they are changed in remarkably similar ways. From the most brilliant professor to the most ignorant savage, when one puts his trust in Christ, his life begins to change.

"Some say it is just wishful thinking, or they simply excuse it by saying it doesn't prove a thing. For a Christian, behind his subjective experience there is an objective reality as its basis. This objective reality is the person of Jesus Christ and His resurrection.

"For example, let's say a student comes into the room and says, 'Guys, I have a stewed tomato in my right tennis shoe. This tomato has changed my life. It has given me a peace and love and joy that I never experienced before, not only that, but I can now run the 100-yard dash in 10 seconds flat.'

"It is hard to argue with a student like that if his life backs up what he says (especially if he runs circles around you on the track). A personal testimony is often a subjective argument for the reality of something. Therefore, don't dismiss a subjective experience as being irrelevant.

"There are two questions or tests I apply to a subjective experience. First, what is the objective reality for the subjective experience, and second, how many other people have had the same subjective experience from being related to the objective reality? Let me apply this to the student with the 'stewed tomato' in his right tennis shoe.

"To the first question he would reply: 'a stewed tomato in my right tennis shoe.' Then the second question would be put this way: 'How many people in this classroom, in this university, in this country and on this continent, etc., have experienced the same love, peace, joy and increased track speed as the result of a stewed tomato in their right tennis shoes?' "

At this point, most of the history students laughed. I didn't blame them, for it was obvious that the answer to the second question was "No one!"

Now I had to apply these same two questions to my own subjective experience:

1. What is the objective reality or basis for my subjective experience — a changed life?

   Answer: the person of Christ and His resurrection.

2. How many others have had this same subjective experience from being related to the objective reality, Jesus Christ?

The evidence is overwhelming, as brought out in the following pages of this section, that truly millions from all backgrounds, nationalities and professions have seen their lives elevated to new levels of peace and joy by turning their lives over to Christ. Indeed, the professor confirmed this when he said, "I have met scores of people around the world who have been transformed by Christ."

To those who say it is a delusion, then WOW! What a powerful delusion. *E. Y. Mullins* writes: "A redeemed drunkard, with vivid memory of past hopeless struggles and new sense of power through Christ, was replying to the charge that 'his religion was a delusion.' He said: 'Thank God for the delusion; it has put clothes on my children and shoes on their feet and bread in their mouths. It has made a man of me and it has put joy and peace in my home, which had been a hell. If this is a delusion, may God send it to the slaves of drink everywhere, for their slavery is an awful reality.' " 34/294, 295

For further development of the subjective argument, see Paul Little's excellent chapter, "Is Christian Experience Valid?" in his book, *Know Why You Believe.*

3B. Universality of the Christian Experience

The claims of great numbers of people confessing Christ are amazingly similar regardless of place, time, environment or background. They confirm that Christ satisfies the deepest mental and spiritual needs of all intellects, ages, races and nationalities. The following quotes support these points.

Bernard Ramm: "We Christians feel that we have had the same essential experiences. . . . We not only say similar things, but we feel the same way about them, and we value them the same way. It is spirit bearing witness to spirit. The underlying reason is that we have been saved by the same God, through the same Savior, and by the same Gospel." 38/214

E. Y. Mullins: "I have, for me at least, irrefutable evidence of the objective existence of the Person so moving me. When to this personal experience I add that of tens of thousands of living Christians, and an unbroken line of them back to Christ, and when I find in the New Testament a manifold record of like experiences, together with a clear account of the origin and cause of them all, my certainty becomes absolute. One of the most urgent of all duties resting upon modern Christians is to assert with clearness and vigor the certainties of Christian experience." 34/284, 285

Gordon Allport: Christianity ". . . has everything. For the theoretical mind it can accommodate all that science can discover and still challenge science to dig deeper and deeper. For the social mind it contains the high-road to all successful and just social relations, even a solution to the problems of war. For the aesthetic mind it gives an absolutely satisfying conception of harmony and beauty. For economic and political minds, it gives a meaning to production and power, and a guide to conduct."

Allport goes on to say that "its goals and ideals are always ahead of what any human being can fully achieve. Christianity can never cloy because even for the most saintly, Christian perfection lies ahead. Christian objectives are too high to make complete achievement possible. Having once experienced the blessedness of certitude, though but for a moment, you will never be satisfied but will be impelled to seek to regain and extend this experience all your life long." 39/20, 21

In the final analysis, it is clear that it is the content of the Christian faith which makes it unique. Robert O. Ferm concludes: "It is for this reason that it must be insisted that the entire phenomenon of conversion must be studied, not from the point of view of psychologist, but from that of the student of the Scriptures, for the psychologist as such, has no means by which to judge its genuineness. He must, therefore, himself become a student of the Scriptures, and fully informed therein, and born anew by the Spirit of God, if he would be equipped to study the phenomenon as it applies to the evangelical." 17/225

3A. A MULTITUDE OF CONVERSIONS AND CHANGED LIVES

The following testimonies of men and women from all walks of life demonstrate the unity of Christian experience. While each one embraces a different background, profession or culture, each points to the same object as the source of new power for transformed lives — Jesus Christ. Multiply these testimonies by the hundreds of thousands and you would begin to approach something like the impact Christ has had on the world in the past 2,000 years.

Is the Christian experience valid? These and millions more believe so, and have new lives to back up their statement.

In reading the following 58 testimonies, you will find that God revealed Himself to man in many different ways. God reveals Himself adequately to every man.

DIFFERENT OCCUPATIONS

1.   COMPUTER EXPERT

"When Christian conversion comes, God forgets our sins, but He does not erase our memory of them; we remain 'readable.' But through Jesus Christ we are given the ability to say to God, 'You take over.' This means the blocking of certain information and the releasing of other information. Men and computers are not the same, for there is no love in a computer, and no sin. But we are similar in this, that *instructions are formed only by decisions.* We are controlled by instructions; but such human instructions, controlling man's behavior and reaction patterns, are conditioned by decisions formerly experienced. The game of golf, for example, does not become a part of us until we begin to swing the club. The decisions we make open avenues of activity which were previously unavailable.

"It is a real miracle when a spiritual rebirth happens. Such an event has occurred in my life. Now, even the most perfect computer gives poor results if there is garbage information stored undetected in certain areas. Most complex computer programs must be debugged. Human instructions are formed over a lifetime by experiences received and decisions made (very complex). A human being cannot intentionally erase any previous decisions no matter how much he may wish to do so, just as a computer cannot free itself. In order to make the system operative, wrong past instructions have to be made ineffective and new instruction patterns stored. And that is exactly what happened in my life when I asked Jesus Christ to come in and prevent me from doing what He didn't want me to do." 43/8, 9

Dr. Gerhard Dirks was management consultant in research and development for International Business Machines. Born in Herbsleben, Germany, he holds a Ph.D. in law from the University of Leipzig. Today he holds a number of basic patents for the memory structures of modern electronic computers.

2. POLICEMAN

"I've been on both sides of the fence: a gang member as well as a policeman. I have seen tragedy, permanent injury, property damage, wasted lives and even death as a result of sin.

"My whole outlook on life has changed since Christ came into my life and, being a Christian policeman, I view things much differently. In all my duties I am constantly aware that I must share God's wonderful plan of salvation with others as I continue 'on patrol for God.' "

Melvin Floyd was voted by the National Jaycees as one of 1969's "Ten Outstanding Young Men in America." 35

3. FORMER PROSTITUTE

Excerpt from Arthur Blessitt's *Turned On To Jesus:*

"On a night when business is lagging I find Linda in a bikini coiled in a lounge chair at Al's place.

" 'Things are going great,' she volunteers. 'No hangups. No hangups at all.'

" 'You're lying and you know it,' I say. 'You're not happy. You're miserable. If you were really happy, you wouldn't have to take all the dope to rid yourself of guilt.'

" 'Arthur Blessitt, I can handle anybody except you. You're right. I am miserable. Today I tried to jump out of Al's car on the freeway. He grabbed my arm and held me back.'

"I shared Christ with Linda for more than an hour.

"It takes! It is one of the most unexpected turnabouts I have ever encountered. Linda gets down on her knees with me and prays, her tears washing her mascara in streaks down her face. After we pray she looks up and her eyes sparkle.

" 'I'm saved!' she says joyously. 'Jesus has found me and I'm going back to my baby.'

"Still on our knees, we hear the buzzer sound. I get up and go to the door.

" 'Are you open for business?' the customer, a fiftyish man with a crew cut and horn-rimmed glasses, asks.

" 'Yes, sir, come right in.'

"When he enters, I give him one of my Big Question tracts. He brings it close to his face and seems disturbed as he reads it. Then he looks at Linda, still on her knees. He starts backing off toward the door. 'I must be in the wrong place.' " 3/128

4. NAZI PILOT IN WORLD WAR II

"Moelders was a colonel in the Luftwaffe, ace of all Germany's aces, holder of the highest decoration his country awards her fighters — the Knight's Cross of the Iron Cross, with Oak Leaves and Diamonds.

"He climbed from his riddled plane; his eyes were glassy; his frozen hands trembled; his body still shook with emotion. Werner Moelders had looked on the face of Death, and he was changed. In those terrible moments, almost unknown to himself, he had whispered: 'God, God Almighty in heaven — help me out of this. YOU alone can save me!' His words had echoed in the cockpit of the plane — 'Only God can help . . .'

"Back in his quarters, Moelders shut himself up alone. He had to have time to think. Clearly, faith in Hitler and Naziism could not sustain him. His mind flew back to his home in Stettin, to his godly parents, to the kindly pastor. He remembered the story of the Cross and the redeeming love of God in Christ Jesus, who died for sinners like him. And he knew he could never have survived that dreadful danger out there if he had not called on the everlasting God. Fear had taught him faith.

"Now, freed forever from the nightmare of Naziism, he felt relieved, happy; a sense of the reality of God filled his heart with peace. He sat down and wrote out his thoughts in a letter to the Stettin pastor. . . .

"Day after day Moelders spoke with his comrades about his faith and about the love of God in Christ Jesus. But that did not suit his masters. In a mysterious accident Germany's famous Number 1 ace was killed — silenced forever, the Nazi leaders thought. . . .

"The Gestapo went into action against the faithful friends of Moelders who copied and distributed his letter. A reward of $40,000 was offered to anyone who would denounce a friend who believed what Moelders believed and passed on his letter." 10/22-25

5. FORMER CRIMINAL

"Pacing back and forth in his prison cell, Leo D'Arcangelo was deeply disturbed. Who wouldn't be, facing what was ahead of him?

"As a boy of eleven, he had picked a lady's handbag on a crowded trolley car. That was the start.

"Five years of stealing followed before his first arrest at sixteen in a Philadelphia department store.

"Shortly after release he started mainlining heroin. Then began the seemingly endless arrests: November, 1954, for use and possession of drugs, January, 1955, for picking pockets. Shortly after, in Los Angeles, Leo was arrested for jumping bail.

". . . As he paced his cell he noticed a few lines crudely scrawled on the wall.

" 'When you come to the end of your journey and this trouble is racked in your mind, and there seems no other way out than by just mourning, turn to Jesus, for it is Him that you must find.'

"This started him thinking.

"This is the end of my journey. What have I got to show for it? Nothing except a lousy past and a worse future.

"Jesus, I need Your help. I've made a mess of my life and this is the end of the journey, and all the crying isn't going to change my past. Jesus, if You can change my life, please do it. Help me make tomorrow different.

"For the first time Leo felt something besides despair.

". . . Released from prison in September, 1958, Leo earned his high school diploma and then went on to graduate from West Chester State College and the Reformed Episcopal Seminary in Philadelphia.

"He is presently active in prison work and as a speaker in church and youth meetings." 25

6. MINISTER

"In my first two churches I preached all that I knew, honesty, faith (not knowing what it meant), good habits, church attendance, honor, and a continual exhortation to be 'good,' to serve God. I talked about the fruits without knowing the roots. Enthusiasm carried me in those days — enthusiasm and youth. These two proved not to be enough.

"My wife's religion consisted of a belief in God, worship of beauty, and social and personal ethic, aesthetics, lovely music, sunsets, and nature appreciation. I believed in conversion, preached it, but did not know it.

"The marriage was getting difficult. My wife believed one thing. I believed another. We decided to study Jesus, without any helps of any kind, which we did with a small group for seven weeks in Canada. . . . It began to dawn upon me that if I would put my will into God's hands . . . that this would be equal to doing God's will. . . . I was committing myself to all of God I could see in Jesus, plus all of God that would be revealed tomorrow and the next day and the next. . . . The light broke upon me. I wept like a child calling out to my wife: 'I have missed it. Utterly missed it.' All these years I have preached only ethics, social and personal, but not the gospel. . . . The gospel was the living Christ who has come to dwell in me. He has liberated me. He assured me my sins were forgiven. . . . There was a new center for all my social passion — it was not centered in human striving — it was centered in Christ. . . . Power in some measure has come."
23/125-127

Dr. Don E. Schooler

7.   COACH — DALLAS COWBOYS

"St. Augustine said, 'Thou hast made us for Thyself, O God, and our hearts are restless until they find their rest in Thee.'

"Well, I discovered that truth at the age of 33. The most disappointing fact in my life, I believe, is that I waited so long before I discovered the fellowship of Jesus Christ. How much more wonderful my life would have been if I had taken this step many years earlier!" 18

Tom Landry

8.   GOLFER

In 1974, professional golfer Rik Massengale was ready to exchange his clubs for farmer's overalls. Life, like his golf game, had lost its zip. Massengale contemplated leaving the sport to go into the dairy business.

Thin from the strain of the Professional Golfers Association tour, his marriage beginning to sour, Massengale suffered through his fifth season, a year in which his earnings dipped to $14,193.

But one night at home with his wife, Cindy, Rik began to watch *The Greatest Story Ever Told,* a movie on the life of Christ. The Massengales' lives — and Rik's erratic golf game — underwent a dramatic change thereafter.

"We started questioning and decided to go to the Bible study on the tour," recalls Massengale, a former University of Texas star. Evangelist Billy Graham was the guest speaker the first night they attended.

"I realized afterward that intellectually I had always believed Christ was the Son of God," Rik says. "That week, after Graham spoke, I asked Christ to come into my life."

With a new outlook on life, Massengale began to play like a new golfer. "If I blew a shot, I'd be torn up inside. Now Christ has given me self-control and peace. A bogey is no longer the end of the world."

Since Massengale's spiritual and mental turnabout, he has captured several tournament titles, including the 1977 Bob Hope Desert Classic. In the Hope Classic, he broke Arnold Palmer's longstanding record by one stroke with a 23-under-par-337. The win boosted him high among the tour's top money winners.
31/38

Rik Massengale

9. TENNIS PLAYER

Reminiscing about a tennis match, Stan Smith says, "I wondered where my confidence had gone. Hadn't I always been confident about my game?

"Not always. At least not until I got into my sophomore year in college. Before that, I had always considered myself a mediocre player. That year, though, I began meeting with a group of athletes at the University of Southern California. These were different guys than I had known before — and they told me about a Person who was very new and exciting to me — Jesus Christ. Toward the end of that year, I put my life into His hands. I asked Him to give my life more meaning. He helped me find myself and He gave me self-confidence.

"My frustration seemed to drain off. I was confident again.

"Christ helped me win over myself. It's so clear to me now why in all things I must be a mirror of His teachings." 46

Stan Smith

10. FOOTBALL PLAYER

"My future reaches far beyond football, of course, and this is what really excites me. Christianity is the most important part of my life and I'll always speak out about it. I am fortunate to have been blessed with certain talents and skills and they are the reason I have become a public figure, in a position to attract attention and be heard. I would be rejecting God's love and blessings if I didn't use my opportunities to the utmost, to talk about my faith, why it is precious to me. To enjoy something beautiful like this to the fullest, you must share it. . . .

"Ours is a very dynamic, fast-paced world. It can become terribly hectic. Sometimes your mind seems to spin when you consider everything that is happening. It seems that it's just one thing after another, that you just can't enjoy peace of mind. To me, there is a very simple solution to these problems. If you have a relationship with Christ, He will give you peace of mind. If only we try to live beyond the earthly life we're involved in every day there won't be problems like Watergate, war, adultery, prejudice, and crime. If we look beyond this we can withstand anything in our own lives because we are living for God and not ourselves. . . ." 47/274, 275, 279

Roger Staubach

11. MISS AMERICA 1973

"From the time I was a small child, I dreamed of being a professional singer and actress and seeing my name up on a marquee. After a year of college, I had my first chance to sing with a small group in nightclubs throughout the Midwest. On the road I was hit with a lot of things that I wasn't prepared to handle: alcoholism, bad marriages and a lot of lonely people who were trying to escape reality.

"Then in 1970, I joined the New Christy Minstrels. But I was disillusioned with this experience, too, as we performed 50 weeks out of the year under all kinds of conditions. Still, I became increasingly determined that, if I had to scratch my way to the top, I would.

"This all changed after a performance at a Baptist college in Kansas. During the concert, the kids would clap every time we mentioned anything about God or Jesus Christ. I thought they were crazy at the time, but afterward, at a drive-in, one of the Christian students came up and started talking to me.

"We small-talked about show business and life on the road for awhile. Then she asked me a question that no one had ever asked me in my 22 years: 'Are you a Christian?' When I replied that I believed in God, she said, 'No, you don't understand,' and briefly explained about God's love and His desire to have a relationship with me through Jesus Christ.

"She gave me a Four Spiritual Laws booklet and told me to read it that night so we could talk about it over breakfast the next morning. I was willing to do that because I saw that she had a peace that I didn't have and was looking for. I started to just skim the booklet until I noticed how brief and to the point it was. Before I knew it, I was reading the suggested prayer at the end and asking God to forgive me and give me the peace that I'd never found in show business.

"The next day, the Christian girl showed genuine excitement about my decision and more love for me personally than I'd seen in a long time. And as our group was about to leave, she gave me a Bible and said, 'I don't care how busy you get — if you read a chapter a day, I promise you your life will change.'

"And it did. I began to realize that Jesus was someone who understood me and my insecurities and feelings about show business. Specific things changed in my life, too. I was very overweight at the time and smoked a pack-and-a-half of cigarettes a day. That changed, and with it changed the low self-image that I'd always had of myself.

"Soon after I left the Christies, I found myself back home in DePere, Wisconsin, with no money and no way to get the professional training I needed to sing and act. That's when a friend of mine encouraged me to enter the Miss America pageant — even though I was feeling 'old' at 22. She argued that, because it was a good, clean program, I wouldn't have to compromise what I believed in and might even win the scholarship I needed.

"From that point on, God began opening doors, working out His plan for my life. That plan included becoming Miss America 1973. Then, during my reign, God worked more changes — in my outlook on my career and future. I realized that, though I'd been praying for God's direction in my career, I wasn't really listening for *His* answers. Now I understand that my first responsibility is to God, my second is to my husband (Tom) and children as they come. After that I can begin to think about a career.

"It's funny how God has also given me a desire to conform to His will. He still may lead me into a full-time career — just as He's led me to put out a gospel album and begin writing a book. Only now my motivation is different. I don't care about being in the limelight anymore — because I've found that the only lasting things we do are the things we do for Christ." 6/15, 16

Terry Meeuwsen Camburn

12. BILLIONAIRESS

"Outwardly plain and almost conspicuous by her simple taste in clothes, June is surrounded by her father's Dallas-based empire with assets estimated in the billions in oil, cattle, electronics, real estate, investments, pharmaceuticals and cosmetics.

"What is it like to be the daughter of one of the richest men in the world? June answers in her soft, southern drawl, 'Growing up was an experience of being able to do many things. Now I have the opportunity to do the things for which I'm best suited.'

"June traces the beginning of her active Christian life to one day during her teenage years when she came to know the Lord. She explains, 'I was raised in a denomination that did not explain the true meaning of salvation. Then my father had us join a Bible believing church. At fifteen, I became aware that some people at church had a quality of life that was different, and I tried to determine what it was. I thought I could reproduce that quality simply by watching them. When they asked if I were a Christian, I said 'yes' without realizing the vast difference between religion and a relationship with Jesus Christ. Because you go into a garage doesn't make you a car. My going to a Christian church didn't make me a Christian.'

" 'Someone explained Revelation 3:20 to me: "Behold, I stand at the door and knock; if any one hears My voice and opens the door, I will come in . . ."! I am a very analytical person, so I weighed the pros and cons of becoming a Christian:

what I would gain and what I would lose. I decided it was worth every risk if He could give me the quality of life I was seeking, so at the age of fifteen I invited Christ into my life.'

"At the time, little did June realize this was only the first step toward her present purpose of serving the Lord.

"Singing message music is what the guitar-playing Dallasite really enjoys, and sing she does at conventions, crusades, youth rallies and Christian women's clubs.

" 'I want to share the positive life that Jesus Christ offers to each person who will accept Him.'

"And that's worth much more than a billion dollars." 50

June Hunt

13. CARTOONIST

"I grew up an only child, and my mother died the very week I was drafted.

"Before going into the armed forces I met a minister from a local congregation. . . . I began to attend services at his church.

". . . The more I thought about the matter during those Bible studies, the more I realized that I really loved God.

". . . I cannot point to a specific time of dedication to Christ; I was just suddenly 'there,' and did not know when it happened that I arrived.

"I feel a constant gratefulness to God for His patience with me and with all of us. I cannot fail to be thrilled every time I read the things that Jesus said, and I am more and more convinced of the necessity of following Him. What Jesus means to me is this: in Him we are able to see God and to understand His feelings toward us." 42

Charles Schulz

14. MOVIE ACTOR

"I had attained many of my goals. I had a beautiful lady who loved me; three wonderful kids; a $23,000 Ferrari; a garage, crowded with four racing motorcycles; a California avocado ranch; and made between $15,000 and $20,000 a week when I was working on films. Yet there was no sense of fulfillment.

"In frustration I had driven my Ferrari at 100-plus miles per hour over the winding Malibu Canyon roads at night, not with any desire to kill myself, but with a feeling that if I did lose control of the car, so what? No great loss. I really played with the line at which the car could stay glued to the pavement around the curves."

He once took a motorcycle trip with two friends into Mexico's Baja Peninsula, miles from civilization. They stopped to buy some beer from an incredibly poor Mexican family. Dean gave a machete to an old man and a pair of levis to one of the young men. But what really shook him was a little girl with open sores on her face. Flies were all over her, picking at the sores.

"I was so angry that I jumped on my bike and opened up the throttle wide — too wide for the rough terrain," Dean says. "With total abandon, I cursed God and screamed out at the wind, 'God, if You exist, which I doubt, why do You let little children go through that kind of misery?'

"Tears blinded my eyes. The last thing I remember was a small gully ahead of me. It triggered the thought, *Twist that throttle and get that front wheel up!*

"I didn't make it. When I came to, one of my friends had his fist in my hip, trying to stop me from bleeding to death. The rear foot peg of the cycle had shot through my hip, shattering my pelvis in 13 places. I had a brain concussion (with partial amnesia) and a separated right shoulder. In addition, almost every inch of my body was sandpapered by the desert floor. I lay there in shock for a day and a half before arrangements could be made to transport me to a hospital in Burbank."

All of this hopelessness came to a head the summer of 1973 in Cherry Hill, N.J., when Dean was doing a stage production of *1776*.

"I felt so empty that I went to the lodge one night and stood at the window gazing out at the sumptuous landscape," he says.

"I realized I had been motivated by self all my years. But I had come to the point where self could no longer carry me through life. There would come a time when I would not have enough motivation to stay alive. I might even take a shotgun to the top of my head like Ernest Hemingway. I turned from the window, walked to the edge of the bed, knelt and began to pray.

" 'God, You probably don't exist. I'm probably just talking to the walls here, but. . . .' " I began to pour out my doubts, weaknesses, failures to God. I wept like a child.

"Finally I said something like, 'If You do exist, if You are real, and if You will make Yourself known to me in some way, I'll serve You the rest of my life.' It was a total commitment.

"Suddenly my soul was flooded with a peace that passed understanding. It filled that emptiness. It was as though Bambi, the little deer in the forest, heard everything go silent. The birds stopped singing, the crickets stopped chirping, and all the other sounds just ended. There was such a silence that it became something I listened to. I listened to the calm. I had an inner spirit without agitation or anxiety."

At the time, Dean didn't fully understand what had happened to him, but he and Lory . . . began searching for a church. Finally God led them to one in the San Fernando Valley, and February 10, 1974, both he and Lory publicly confessed their faith in Jesus Christ. 52/16ff

Dean Jones

15. SINGER

. . . By 1970 he had made $13 million. By 1976, despite his success in selling more than 32 million records, including the hit recording, "Raindrops Keep Falling On My Head," B.J. Thomas was $800,000 in debt.

His life was bankrupt in more ways than a financial one. In spite of his successful singing career, for years B.J. was about as miserable as a man could be. He was a drug addict with a $3,000-a-week cocaine habit. In addition, he was so hooked on uppers and downers that he was taking 40 to 50 pills at a time just to keep going.

"At 15, I started in music and almost immediately I got involved with drugs," Thomas said.

"Eleven years later," Thomas added, "I was an addict. I couldn't go to sleep without it. I couldn't do anything without it."

Thomas was so doped up he barely remembers recording his 1969 hit, "Raindrops." And its success helped catapult him even deeper into drugs. Cocaine was ruling his life. His marriage was broken and he could barely function.

Once he took 80 pills and was taken unconscious off a plane in Hawaii. He was rushed to a hospital. He almost died of the overdose, and at the time he didn't care if he died or not.

When he came to he asked the sister attending him in the Catholic Hospital if "it had been close." She said, "Very close" and told him he had been on the machine for an hour and 40 minutes, which was the only reason he pulled through. "I don't understand why I made it," he told the nurse. "I really didn't want to make it."

She asked him to bow his head and she prayed for him. She said, "God must have something He wants to do with your life."

On a later tour he realized that he was losing his mind. When his brother and his road man — the people who loved him — looked at him in pity he hated them. "I wanted to kill them," said Thomas. "In fact, I was afraid I would."

B.J. became so saturated with drugs he couldn't sleep for days. He could not get high. There was nothing he could do to get that euphoric feeling any more. In desperation he called his wife, Gloria. He thought maybe if he went home he could get a little sleep there.

"We had separated several times over the years," Thomas explained, "because I was acting so crazy." But lately when he had called he had sensed a peace and calmness coming from Gloria on the phone. She had asked him to come home, saying, "There's help here," but she would not explain what the help was. . . .

When he arrived he found his wife had become a Christian and that there were a lot of people praying for him and wanting to talk to him about the Lord.

"That was the last thing I wanted to do," Thomas said. But one evening his wife got him to drop by the home of the friends who had led her to the Lord.

The husband, Jim Reeves, was gone, but the wife asked them to stay for dinner. With the husband away B.J. felt safe from religious talk, and they stayed. "I felt such peace in that home," B.J. said, "that I knew they must know God. When Jim came home I asked him about it, and he began to tell me about the Lord."

"Jim Reeves told me that as he talked with me there was something about me, or about my face or eyes that frightened him," B.J. said. "He could tell I wanted to listen, but one minute I was receptive and the next minute I was not. The strangeness startled him. He asked if he could pray for a minute. He bowed his head right there at the dining room table, and asked that if there were any forces of Satan or any power of Satan in that room that were interfering with B.J. hearing the word of God that by the shed blood of Jesus Christ they would leave."

"As he prayed," B.J. related, "there was a disturbance in my chest. I felt for a minute a sharp pain and I thought I might have a broken rib. Then I had the illusion that something was 'just going' and a peace came over me. I had a receptive attitude and I listened intently to all they told me. Then I put my head down and began to pray. I prayed for about 20 minutes, and I prayed all the good things they told me I should pray.

"When I raised my head these guys were crying, and I was so happy I was just jumping around. That conversion experience to me was just a miraculous thing. I had been such a bad person."

What happened that night caused a mental change and a physical change in B.J. Thomas. He had some marijuana, but he went home and threw it away. He had been dependent upon valium for years. He needed that more than all the other pills. But that very night he stopped taking it.

B.J. expected terrible withdrawal pains. He was willing to go through it. He had done so before, but had always gone back to drugs. But this time he went through no withdrawal symptoms: no shakes, no bad illusions or dreams. His deliverance from drugs was just as miraculous as his salvation and from that day, January 29, 1976, to this, he has never doubted his experience with the Lord or that his salvation was real. . . . 53/1, 34

B.J. Thomas

16. AUTHOR

"At the age of thirty-three, I had almost lost interest in finding the key to why I am here. My study of the philosophies had stimulated my mind but had left my heart empty. My study of many of the religions of the world left me exhausted. I knew that somehow I didn't have enough desire to 'know righteousness' to go through the elaborate intellectual and spiritual gyrations required by them to 'reach God.'

"My life was won by Ellen Riley, a childhood friend whom I saw again while in Charleston after those 18 years. Ellen had become a dynamic Christian. Christ was a Person to her. She was home from New York City on her vacation at the same time I was there from Chicago. When she saw me again she was horrified to see the girl she had known as a bubbling, happy teenager, now a tired, bored, would-be sophisticate. She said I looked as though I was warding off a blow.

" '. . . What do you really believe about God?' I asked her. 'I believe God came to earth in the Person of Jesus Christ to show us what He is really like and to save us from sin.'

". . . And so, on Sunday afternoon, October 2, 1949, after quite an argument on my part I just suddenly looked at her and said: 'Okay, I guess you're right.' And that was it. God doesn't require any big, formal introduction.

"Since then, day by day, life with Christ has been a continuous experience of one new discovery after another. Now I like to get up in the morning. He is my reason for waking up!" 37

Eugenia Price

17. BUSINESSMAN

"There is one fundamental concept I have learned very clearly from my business experience. There is need for a definite and clearly understood charter for one's operations. Having established that charter, there is need for complete belief in it and in the program which it provides.

"In the Christian life the Bible is our charter. It is the supreme authority for our lives and it is sufficient for our needs. I believe it is a requirement of paramount importance that Christ be the Lord of our whole life, and that our allegiance to Him be in no way divisible.

". . . He has provided the way through Jesus Christ so that by our commitment to Him we may meet God's requirements and be acceptable.

". . . One's relationship to God and to Jesus Christ is strictly a personal relationship. . . . One cannot remain neutral about Him." 11

Dr. Elmer W. Engstrom is Chairman of the Executive Committee of the Radio Corporation of America. He was graduated from the University of Minnesota and holds honorary Doctor of Science, Doctor of Laws and Doctor of Engineering degrees from 10 different schools.

Elmer Engstrom

18. MEDICAL DOCTOR

"After the war, I started general practice in the Harrisburg, Pennsylvania, area. I was introduced to a social life that I thought necessary to be successful. This included frequent cocktail parties and country club dances. I thought this was fine, because I relaxed from the problems of the day and got away from reality for short periods.

"By 1952 I had to do more relaxing by attending parties two and three times a week. Before this time I would have considered myself a heavy drinker, but now my drinking became uncontrollable.

"I suffered a decline in my medical practice, and worst of all, the loss of the respect of my wife and family. I finally admitted my desperate need of help.

". . . A brother of mine had trusted Christ as his Saviour a year earlier. He invited me one day to go along with him to a banquet of the Christian Business Men's Committee. At this meeting I heard testimonies in which men told how their lives had been changed. One man had had a life quite similar to mine, until Christ transformed him.

". . . These men were different from the men I was associating with, and they were willing to help me when I was in serious trouble. Greatest of all, they told me my need was knowing the Lord Jesus Christ.

". . . On May 21, 1959, while on a business trip, I was under deep conviction as I drove along. I prayed to God to save me. I realized that I was lost and needed God's help. But it was not until I said, 'Anything You want me to do, Lord, I will do,' that I could believe, and the indescribable experience occurred. Tears of joy ran down my cheeks as the tremendous load of sin was lifted. God gave me the assurance that I was a new creature in Christ Jesus. I have not been tempted since to take another drink of alcohol. My main problem was not alcoholism, but that I did not know Jesus Christ." 12/65-69

Vernon R. Phillips

19. FARMER

"My ambition as a young man was to be a successful farmer. I decided not to go to college because I liked farm work so well and was needed there.

"Any way you look at it, I thought I was doing quite well. I didn't really look at myself as being bothered with any kind of problems. I wasn't too aware that I had a disease that no one could cure with medicine — the disease of sin.

"It wasn't until I heard the Bible words from Romans 3:23 that I realized that all my church-going and community respectability couldn't keep me free from the consequences of sin. That verse says: 'For all have sinned, and come short of the glory of God.' There is none righteous, no, not one (Rom. 3:10).

"That made it quite clear, I needed more than what I could do for myself. I needed to be cleansed by the power of God. This could only come as I trusted in Jesus Christ.

"Of course I've been plagued by the disease of sin since then. What man isn't? But I thank the Lord I can go to Him for the cure. Christ, by forgiving me each time, arrests the disease of sin.

"And just as I can get excited about my Specific Pathogen Free Yorkshires, I can get excited about telling other men about Jesus Christ. That's why I'm a part of the Christian Business Men's Committee of Barrie. I want to be able to invite other men to share in the disease-freeing power of Jesus Christ." 16

Murray G. Faris

20. FORMER WHITE HOUSE AIDE

"I felt a strange deadness when I left the White House. I should have been exhilarated because I'd done all the things I'd ever set out to do, and in a hurry. I'd gone to law school nights, worked days, earned scholarships, been the youngest company commander in the Marine Corps, and the youngest administrative assistant on Capitol Hill. I had gotten to the top of the mountain and I couldn't think of any other mountains.

"And then I saw Tom Phillips, an old friend. He's a guy much like myself in that he was born to immigrant parents, he went to school nights, he became an engineer at Raytheon when he was twenty-five and by age thirty-six was executive vice president. By age forty, he was president — a tremendous success story. A busy, frantic worker, barking orders, very aggressive, very dynamic.

"When I saw him in the Spring of '73, he seemed totally different. He was smiling, he was radiant, caring about me. I asked him what had happened. He told me he'd committed his life to Jesus Christ.

"I'd . . . learned about Jesus Christ as an historical figure, a prophet, a cut above

His time. But the whole idea of an intelligent, educated, successful businessman saying, 'I've accepted Him and committed my life,' just threw me. I thought Tom had had some sort of strange experience — I changed the subject.

"The months went by, very tough months in Washington. And everything that Tom represented, Washington wasn't. I marveled at it and wanted to find out for myself, so I called him and spent an evening on his porch. He read to me from C. S. Lewis' *Mere Christianity,* the chapter on pride. It was a torpedo. I could just see my whole life. I felt unclean. Then Tom told me he had had a real spiritual longing until he went to a Billy Graham rally in New York and accepted Christ.

"It was such a beautiful story, but I wouldn't admit it to him. I was the big time Washington lawyer.

"That night I couldn't get the keys into the ignition because I was crying so hard. I didn't like to cry because I never liked to show weakness. I prayed in the car, and thought. It was sort of an eerie feeling sitting by the side of the road alone, and yet not alone now. There was a tremendous cleansing feeling that night. Then I spent a week on the Maine Coast, and later that week, the case for Christ became obvious to me.

"My biggest problem had always been the intellectual reservations. I knew there was a God, but I could never see how man could have a personal relationship with Him. But the intellectual case for Christianity became powerful to me after reading *Mere Christianity.* At the end of the week I could not imagine how you could not believe in Jesus Christ." 45

Charles Colson

21.   U.S. SENATOR

"It is my belief that unless we as Americans begin to follow Christ and love Him with every facet of our being, we can never meet the grave challenges of our time. For it is impossible to equate mediocrity with the things of Jesus Christ. Personally, I would like to come more and more to the place where everything I do is for Him.

"I saw that for 31 years, I had lived for self. I decided I wanted to live the rest of my life for Jesus Christ alone. I asked God to forgive me and to make my life His own. I was assured by God's Word, 'If any man be in Christ, he is a new creature: old things are passed away; behold, all things become new.'

"In this day of uncertainty we need peace on an individual basis, for each family, each city, state, nation and the world. The fact that 'God was in Christ, reconciling the world unto Himself,' still holds true. Serving Christ is God's method of granting us peace and purpose and allowing us to become ambassadors for Him.

"Following Jesus Christ has been an experience of increasing challenge, adventure and happiness. He is totally worthwhile. How true are His words: 'I am come that they might have life, and that they might have it more abundantly.'

"It is not to a life of ease and mediocrity that Christ calls us, but to the disciple-like, Christ-empowered life. No matter what our mission in life, we are called to give our complete allegiance to Him. He becomes our standard of excellence. No cause, noble as it may seem, can be satisfying or purposeful without the personal direction of Jesus Christ. I can say with all sincerity that being committed to Him is truly satisfying." 19

Mark Hatfield, Senator from Oregon

22.   FORMER PRESIDENT OF THE U.N. GENERAL ASSEMBLY

"Having fully realized that the whole world is as it were dissolving before our very eyes, it is impossible then to ask more far-reaching questions than these three: What is then emerging? Where is Christ in it? And what difference are we making to the whole thing?

"In one word: the life of the spirit is life in Jesus Christ. In Him and through Him we can raise and answer these three fundamental questions. In Him and through Him we can be saved from the universal dissolution of the world.

"These are great days and what is being decided in them is absolutely historic. But all these things are going to pass, and with them life itself. What, then, is the life that does not pass?; what, then, is life eternal?: This is the first and last question. I believe that 'this is life eternal, that they might know Thee the only true God, and Jesus Christ, whom Thou has sent.' (John 17:3) . . . Faith in Jesus Christ is the first and last meaning of our life. I do not care who or what you are; I put only one question to you: Do you believe in Jesus Christ?" 30

Dr. Charles Malik served as President of the United Nations General Assembly in 1959. He is now a professor at The American University in Beirut, Lebanon.

Charles Malik

23.   CITY PLANNER

"I had a fairly good education. I had economic security rather early in life. I had a good home environment as a child. Yet, I had an ego problem; I thought I was the Master of everything.

". . . It seemed as though everything I found myself in ultimately was a success.

". . . Actually, I had become an ego-maniac and a 'social drinker.'

". . . I played basketball on an athletic scholarship. . . . I was an all-conference selection.

". . . For the next 10 years I was a social derelict. During this period I had all kinds of jobs. Due to excessive use of alcohol, I would usually quit before being fired for absenteeism. I also vividly remember my first bout with the 'DTs' (delirium tremens). I thought I was losing my mind. During short intervals of sleep I saw visions of heaven or hell. Upon recovery from my first attack, I began to research books dealing with alcoholism. When I found that I really wasn't crazy, I started drinking all over again. After each bout with the DTs, my alcoholic intake increased. Subsequently, I left my family.

"One evening an old friend stopped by to see me. It was evident that a change had taken place in his life. I attended several Christian Business Men's Committee prayer breakfasts and an annual banquet.

". . . He sent me a tract entitled, 'Manna from Heaven.' This made me furious. Who did this self-righteous person think he was?

". . . It [the tract] placed me on the path leading to an ultimate, 'personal encounter' with Christ.

". . . [Since then] I have had many occasions to speak about model cities. These ventures afford a wonderful opportunity to speak a few words about Christ who changed my ego-blighted life." 36

Charles H. Penn

24.   PHILOSOPHER

"Dr. Cyril E. M. Joad, head of the philosophy department of the University of London . . . believed that Jesus was only a man, that God was a part of the universe and that, should the universe be destroyed, God would be destroyed. He believed that there is no such thing as sin, that man was destined for a Utopia; that given a little time, man would have heaven on earth.

"In 1948, in the magazine section of the Los Angeles Times, there was a picture of that venerable old scholar, and with it was a statement concerning the dramatic change that had taken place in his life. He told how for many years he had been antagonistic toward Christianity. Now he had come to believe that sin was a reality.

"Two world wars and the imminence of another had demonstrated conclusively to him that man was sinful. Now he believed that the only explanation for sin was found in the Word of God, and the only solution was found in the cross of Jesus Christ. Before his death, Dr. Joad became a zealous follower of the Savior." 4/2, 3

25. PSYCHOLOGIST

"The professor was too polite to say that the landlord had warned him about his Protestant neighbor. 'He is a very zealous Protestant,' the owner of the apartment building had said. 'He will try to convert you.'

"Professor Ruda's face then had creased with a soft Latin smile. 'Let him. I will match wits with him. Perhaps I can convert him to be a freethinker like me. No?'

"The Professor felt that he had little to fear from a zealous Protestant. He knew something about religion and psychology himself. Had he not been raised in the Catholic faith, even though he no longer accepted the old dogmas? He had his doctorate in psychology and was professor of logic and researcher in psychology in the Argentine University of the South. His major field of study and teaching was in personality development. Perhaps, he thought, I will learn something by analyzing the personality of a Protestant missionary.

"After attending the missionary's church and after exchanging beliefs hoping to show him his error, Ruda finally made the decision for Christ. He explains it this way:

" 'As a research psychologist in the field of personality development I analyzed hundreds of people. I sought to discover the inner motivation which governs the basic attitudes of living.

" 'But when I met Charles Campbell I knew that here was someone whose personality I could not rationally explain. Then when I became a Christian I understood that the life-changing ingredient in his life was Christ. Today, the most important proof to me of Christianity is the amazing change that has come into my own life. Peace and confidence in God have taken the place of anxiety and worry. My troubles increased when I became a Christian, but Christ gave me power to have victory over all of them.' " 20/59-64

26. UNIVERSITY LECTURER

"From the beginning of my time at school I was very interested in religion. I read many of the major religious writings of mankind, including the Bible, the Koran, the Bhagavad-Gita (Hindu) and the Tao Te Ching (Taoism), wanting to make up my own mind, to form my personal opinion from an intellectual point of view as to what I would believe.

"In 1966 Billy Graham held a Crusade in Berlin, and along with 10,000-15,000 other people, I sat in a large hall and listened as he explained the Jesus Christ of the Bible. As he spoke, I realized that all of my attempts to form a personal opinion were a preparation for this very moment when I needed to confess my sins and give myself to Christ. From my own readings and Dr. Graham's message, I was able to judge that the gospel of Jesus Christ was the real truth for me.

"At first I did not regard the other religions as false, believing that they might have *part* of the truth or have another way of expressing the truth. But later, as I continued my studies in comparative literature at the Universities of Berlin and Geneva, I realized that there is *no* alternative to the historical truth of the resurrection of Jesus Christ. Under the most careful scrutiny, no scientist, no historian, no literary critic, if he is honest to his science, will be able to deny the basic truth of the gospel of the New Testament. No other religion or philosophy of mankind can claim this kind of historical support.

"Of course, Christianity involves not only the intellect, but the spirit and emotions as well. It is a way of living, and a way of living means that it occupies your whole being and your whole time. My belief is a personal affair — within myself. But when I talk to someone else about my faith, I have to do it with intellectual discussion, for the basis of a person's belief is the historicity of the resurrection.

"There are hardly any universities now where true Christian belief is taught. Modern German theologians and philosophers claim to use objective methods of literary analysis in determining that much of the New Testament is legendary. But as I compare the writings of these critics, I find that they are working with pre-formed biases, leaving out any historical truth which might contradict their own beliefs.

"I believe it can be shown that everything written in the New Testament has historical and literary proof to back it up. I would like to introduce a Christian method of analyzing literature, mainly to provide students with an alternative to common methods of interpreting literature (positivism, structuralism, new criticism, existentialism, etc.). It seems like a mammoth task, but it is not merely I trying to do it, but Christ working in me, giving me the ideas.

"Through the years I have grown stronger and more certain of my beliefs. My desire to find the truth through the examination of various religions and philosophies was satisfied in the words and person of Jesus Christ. Within myself I am certain that my faith is based on facts that can never be proved false." 48/11

Carsten Thiede is assistant lecturer in German and Comparative Literature at the University of Geneva.

Carsten Thiede

27. FORMER GANG LEADER

This excerpt from Nicky Cruz's autobiography, *Run Baby Run*, tells of his conversion:

"Wilkerson was speaking again. He said something about repenting for your sin. I was under the influence of a power a million times stronger than any drug. I was not responsible for my movements, actions or words. It was as though I had been caught in a wild torrent of a rampaging river. I was powerless to resist. I didn't understand what was taking place within me. I only knew the fear was gone.

"Wilkerson was speaking again. 'He's here! He's in this room. He's come especially for you. If you want your life changed, now is the time.' Then he shouted with authority: 'Stand up! Those who will receive Jesus Christ and be changed — stand up! Come forward!'

"I felt Israel stand to his feet. 'Boys, I'm going up. Who's with me?'

"I was on my feet, I turned to the gang and waved them on with my hand. 'Let's go.' There was a spontaneous movement out of the chairs and toward the front. More than 25 of the Mau Maus responded. Behind us about 30 boys from other gangs followed our example.

". . . I wanted to be a follower of Jesus Christ.

". . . I was happy, yet I was crying. Something was taking place in my life that I had absolutely no control over . . . and I was happy about it."

Since his conversion and subsequent college training, Nicky has spent almost every weekend criss-crossing the United States, sharing his faith in Jesus Christ with the youth of America.

One year in city-wide crusades, church services, high school and college assemblies and other meetings, Nicky spoke to over 200,000 young people. 9/126, 127

28.   PRISONER

"I'm a Negro, just 23 years of age, but I'm ready to go, you see. Why, if my number were up this very minute, I'd be ready to meet God. I'm really happy. Just this week I had a dream that I'll carry with me to the chair. I was on my way to heaven. Jesus was with me. But I was taking four steps to His two. He asked me why I was going so fast. I told Him I was eager to get there. Then I was there, surrounded by numerous angels.

"Some folks might think that's strange talk from a man who came to jail an atheist. But that's just the way I feel. You'll understand better when I tell you how I met God early one morning.

"Not long after I was placed behind the bars last March 23, a woman of my own race — Mrs. Flora Jones, of Oliver Baptist Church — invited me to attend a prisoner's gospel service. I was playing cards with some other fellows at the time and laughed at her. 'Why, I don't even believe there's a God,' I boasted, and went on playing cards, the woman still pleading with me. Actually I felt so sinful, that I didn't want to know about God even if He existed — so I ignored her.

"Suddenly, something she was saying caught my attention. 'If you don't believe in God,' she called from outside the bars, 'just try this little experiment. Before you go to sleep tonight ask Him to awaken you at any time; then ask Him to forgive you your sins.' She had real faith. It got a hold of me.

"I didn't go to the service but I remembered the experiment. 'God,' I mumbled as I lay on my cot, 'wake me up at 2:45 if You're real.'

"Outside it was wintery. Windows on the inside were frosted. For the first few hours I slept soundly, then my sleep became restless. Finally, I was wide awake. I was warm and sweating, although the cell was cool. All was quiet except for the heavy breathing of several prisoners and the snoring of a man near by. Then I heard footsteps outside my cell. It was a guard, making his regular check. As he was passing, I stopped him. 'What time is it?' I asked.

"He looked at his pocket watch. 'Fifteen to three —'

" 'That's the same as 2:45, ain't it?' I asked, my heart taking a sudden leap.

"The guard grunted and passed on. He didn't see me climb from my cot and sink to my knees. I don't remember just what I told God but I asked Him to be merciful to me, an evil murderer and sinner. He saved me that night I know. I've believed on His Son Jesus ever since.

"I'd promised a whipping to another prisoner the next day. That morning I went to him. He backed off. 'I don't want to fight you; you used to be a boxer,' he said.

" 'I don't want to fight,' I said. 'I just came to see you.' Several prisoners had gathered for a fight and were disappointed.

"But God had saved me from my sins — why should I want to fight? Later it was whispered around that I was putting on an act, trying to get out of going to the chair.

"My case did later come up before the Illinois Supreme Court, but they upheld the death sentence. Sure, that jolted me some, but I haven't lost faith in God. I know He will go with me. So, you see, I'm really not afraid."

(Pete Tanis, then a prison-gate missionary from Chicago's Pacific Garden Mission, takes up the story here and describes Ernest Gaither's last hours on earth.)

"I was admitted to Ernest's cell about an hour before midnight. The atmosphere seemed charged and guards who stood about his cell kept talking to keep his mind off the midnight journey. But things they said were strained and meaningless, like the things you say when you don't know what to say.

"As I entered, Ernest smiled and greeted me. A Negro chaplain was reading with him from the Bible. He gave me the Book and asked me to read. I selected the first chapter of Philippians. Ernest leaned forward intently as I read:

" 'For to me to live is Christ, and to die is gain. . . . For I am in a strait betwixt two, having a desire to depart, and to be with Christ; which is far better.'

". . . A moment later a black hood was slipped over his head and he began the last mile. At each side were guards, both noticeably nervous. Ernest sensed it: 'What are you fellows shaking for? I'm not afraid.'

". . . Finally, at 12:03 A.M., the first of three electrical shocks flashed through his body.

"By 12:15 five doctors had paraded up, and one by one, confirmed the death.

"But I knew that the real Ernest Gaither still lived — only his body was dead. As I left the jail, I thought of the verse he liked so well: 'For to me to live is Christ, but to die is gain.' " 1/149-155

DIFFERENT NATIONALITIES

29. HONG KONG

"I was born in a family that worshipped idols, so I worshipped idols, too. For this reason, jeering at my schoolmates who are Christians was my favorite job.

"One night, I was given a World Literature Crusade Gospel tract, entitled 'The Almighty.' While I was reading it my heart was moved, so I wrote down my name and address on the decision card and sent it in.

"I know Jesus and now I am a Christian." 44

Kane Dju Lie

30. JAPAN

"A graduate in engineering physics (Tokyo University), Kosuke Maki received the coveted government prize for excellent research, after which he studied at several universities and seminaries. Later he joined the faculty of famous Tokyo University.

"His steward, the leading general of the Japanese-Russian war, reared him for an extremely strict and disciplined life.

" 'I received Jesus Christ into my life as a child. Later I was sent to war against Russia. After Japan's defeat, I lost my peerage and property. Living became very difficult. I became skeptical toward God.'

" 'Two years later my best friend lay dying. He spoke to me. "Maki! I feel hopeless, without peace. I have studied medical science, but science and money are not absolute. Help me!" How I cursed myself. I was unable to do anything. In deep repentance, I received God's wonderful forgiveness. The one Person with the answer we long for, in our secret thoughts, is Jesus Christ. Christ is the only true hope to live by and to die by.' " 22

31. BRAZIL

"His name was Papa and in 1954 he had never seen a white man before.

"From Chavante kinsmen he heard tales of intruders from the awesome outside world, but Papa was never really sure he believed them. They told him of people with pale faces. A hunting party had surprised them beside the Kuluene River — and called them gods. Arrows that could kill a parakeet at 20 paces somehow failed to find their target when the Chavantes fired point-blank at the missionaries.

"With a surge of courage, Papa went to Batovi with two other Indians to see for himself these strange creatures. From some unknown source he summoned the bravery to touch the arm of Tom Young and determine once for all if he was a flesh and blood human being.

"Little by little, the language barrier fell. Papa helped the Youngs learn the complicated Chavante language — and proudly acquired a simple vocabulary of Portuguese words. More than that, he listened.

"Then one day Papa spoke quietly in Chavante to the Son of God and said, 'Jesus, You are good. I am bad. Come into my heart and make me good, too.'

"Papa became the first Chavante preacher — the first of his tribe to speak to others about Jesus Christ.

"His shining face bears eloquent testimony to the work of grace done in his heart. Many Chavantes have followed in his steps. More than 300 of his fellow tribesmen are believers in Jesus Christ." 49

32.   ZAIRE (CONGO)

"One night I became involved in a fight over another man's wife. I was thrown into prison. . . . I was so blinded with rage over the betrayal of my firm friend that I grabbed a big stick like a mad man and struck my friend with such powerful force that I killed him instantly. I was given life imprisonment and was chained to another prisoner, also guilty of murder. At night he would tell me of his Savior. He was transferred after ten months. I acquired a Bible but it was discovered and burned. . . . Two other prisoners who had become interested in knowing about Christ helped me daily by carrying their portion of the Scriptures under their prison pullovers, just under the belt. . . . I surrendered to Him. Paul began to be my example. . . . I can do nothing but serve Him and praise Him whose willing prisoner I am forever." 23/90, 91

Appollo Maweja

33.   AMERICAN INDIAN

"Born on the Klamath Indian Reservation in Southern Oregon, June Wright Poitras cared little for Indian life and had no pride in her racial heritage.

"She was to christen the Modoc Point, a Liberty ship which went down the ways at Portland, Oregon. . . . She was presented with a recording of the proceedings, and as she played it over, she was impressed by the invocation, delivered by a Portland pastor, Rev. Kenneth Dunkelberger. . . . She accepted Jesus Christ as her Savior and Lord.

"The joy of knowing Jesus Christ not only as Savior but as Friend has given her a fresh appreciation for the Indian ways and traditions." 21

34.   CZECHOSLOVAKIA

"At 16 I was an atheist. At 18 I was organizer of Communist Youth in our factory. Now today I had been elected national president of the Communist Youth. I drifted off to sleep and dreamed.

". . . Out of the sky came a voice: 'Take heed that ye be not deceived; for many shall come in my name, saying, I am Christ . . . and then shall they see the Son of Man coming in a cloud with power and great glory.'

". . . I awoke with a start. My heart was pounding fiercely. I tried to tell myself it was only a dream. But God's presence was there in the room. Dropping off the side of the bed onto my knees, I prayed, 'Oh Lord, forgive me. Accept me.'

"I spent the rest of the night in prayer. Then as the first light of dawn appeared, another voice spoke inside me. 'What have you done? You will have to give up everything you worked for. Your former friends will mock you, despise you, persecute you. Turn back now before it is too late.'

"I was full of fear, but inside God said, 'Have no fear; my Spirit shall witness for you.'

" '. . . I am resigning my functions as your leader for I can no longer be a Communist,' I said.

" 'You are a fool,' they replied. 'Why do you wish to take such stupid action?'

" 'I can no longer follow Marx and Lenin,' I said. 'Because I am now a follower of Jesus Christ.'

". . . Today I am pastor of a small church near the Russian border. If I go to prison, it matters not; for wherever I am I serve Him, and He strengthens me.

"Lenin taught that you change man by changing society. Jesus, however, teaches that you change society by changing man. I serve in God's 'new world order,' introduced by the greatest revolutionary of all time — Jesus Christ." 7

Jan Chelcicky

35.   VIETNAM

"A delegation of Halang tribal elders made their way recently to the provincial capital of Kontum in the Vietnamese highlands. They sought out a Vietnamese pastor and announced the purpose of their visit. Their entire Halang village wanted to study the way of God. They had observed, they said, that the Christian way made for a happier and better way of life. So, please, could teachers come right away?

"Din . . . was the headman of the Halang village where Jim and Nancy Cooper, with Wycliffe Bible Translators, settled in 1963 to learn the Halang Language. Most of the Coopers' language learning came from the stories Din told them.

"Many of Din's stories had had to do with sacrificing to the spirits, and about the taboos with which the people had to contend. It seemed there was nothing that could be done without appeasing the spirits. Din was himself extremely conscious of this. His wife became ill; then his house burned down. People began to say the spirits were angry with him for revealing Halang customs to the Coopers. Still he kept working with them.

"Before long, Din began to show an interest in the Gospel he was helping to translate. He had a habit of writing notes to Jim and leaving them on his desk or typewriter. Usually they had to do with nothing more than that he would have to leave on Friday this week, or perhaps that he needed an advance in wages. But one morning the message read: 'Teach me about your religion.'

"Jim explained that the Christian religion is contained in God's Word, which is in the Bible. Din had already helped translate the story about Jesus dying for men so that they might be free of sin and could become God's children. There were a lot of questions still to be answered, but a fundamental change came to Din's life. He became fully engrossed in getting to know God and God's Word. He once sat in a jeep at an airstrip, so engrossed in reading God's Word that he could not be disturbed by a near-aircrash that took place right in front of him.

"Then one day another note appeared on Jim's typewriter. This time it read: 'What makes me happy? Jesus makes me happy.' *And right there is the explanation of the delegation of tribal elders who came in to Kontum to ask for a teacher.*" 51

INTERNATIONAL STUDENTS

36.   ONTARIO, CANADA

"In high school I thought of myself as the kind of kid everyone took to the locker room to wipe the floor with. My mental image of myself didn't change when I went to college.

"By my second year, I had resorted to tranquilizers because I couldn't hang together without them.

". . . So I gave Him every part of myself — my intellect, my will, my emotions.

". . . I became aware of how God was changing me. I found myself leading people instead of following others. I found I could have confidence, not in myself, but in God working in me. This gave me the ability to approach my studies with a new attitude.

". . . God changed me from a totally defeated person to one serving Him with confidence in His ability to run my life." 8/10

David Cale

37.   THAILAND

"Although I was raised in a Buddhist family, I believed that somewhere in the universe there was a supreme being, only I did not know who He was.

". . . Fear, loneliness and emptiness still remained in my heart.

". . . I invited Him to come into my heart and life to be my Savior and Lord.

". . . My boss asked me a question, he looked at me and said, 'What happened to you?'

"Christ made a difference in my attitude toward my family, too. I had always worried about my family, but after trusting Christ, I turned them over to God.

". . . God has given me a new heart and life." 8/21

Valaiporn Viriyakovint

38.   KENYA

"It should be obvious that there is a difference between a person and an activity. Yet I never considered Jesus as a person, but rather as something around which to center activities.

". . . For the first time I clearly saw that merely being active in Christian things was not enough. To really know God I needed to ask Jesus Christ into my heart.

". . . Christ made several very important changes in my life. I found more meaning in life. God changed my orientation from activities to getting to know Jesus better." 8/17

Samson Nginyo Karugo

39.   ONTARIO, CANADA

"I didn't like being selfish, but there was nothing I could do about it.

". . . I went away to college. I started exploring many different things. I began to doubt God's existence. I attended a conference just to please my parents.

". . . When I got there I was really hit hard by the happiness of the kids there and their love for each other, since most of the people I knew were trying to be happy but were not succeeding.

". . . I just had to accept Him right then.

". . . Since that time my life has never been the same. I've found so much joy that I want to tell everybody about Christ.

"God has also changed my attitude toward my family.

". . . Rather than doing all I can to selfishly satisfy myself, I want to reach out and help others." 8/10, 11

Beth Cale

40. FINLAND

"At one time in my life I really didn't think anything in particular about God.

". . . I started at the university back in Finland.

"There I met a bunch of students who were so excited about their personal relationship with God that I wondered why I couldn't have the same kind of assurance they had. When they told me that all I had to do to know God personally was ask Jesus Christ into my heart as Lord and Savior, I readily gave myself over to His loving control.

". . . Perhaps the biggest change God has made in my life is in my attitude toward other people. Now the most important thing I can do for others is to tell them how they can have a personal relationship with God through His Son, Jesus Christ, because people all over are just ready and waiting to hear the good news about God's individual love for them." 8/5

Olli Valtonen

41. PANAMA

"I could not put my ideas in order, they were so abstract and empty.

". . . I received Christ into my life.

"I began to see my life changing. One of the first evidences of the presence of God in my life was that at the moment I received Christ, I felt I could become a good nurse with the help of God." 8/29

Maria Rodriquez

42. SUSSEX, ENGLAND

"Forget God. That's the attitude I developed by the time I was 14.

". . . But when I was in college, I felt that life was nothing more than growing old and dying.

". . . One night I started to read the New Testament.

". . . That night I prayed, 'Jesus, if You are out there and this is the story of You, come to me because I want to know You.'

". . . The peace and the joy that swept into my life then are hard to describe. God began to change my life.

"I know, through the big and little changes, that I've found the reality of God. I'm in touch with Him." 8/4

David Taylor

43. INDIA

"I was leading a life concerned with social and economic problems and their solutions. I was frustrated and worried about almost everything.

". . . I came to the conclusion that God was a product of the imagination and the servant of abnormal people.

". . . I became a radical Marxist. I had an opportunity to attend a College Life meeting.

". . . The speaker put forward the claims of Jesus of Nazareth for the whole human race. I felt that the philosophies I had believed were proved wrong.

". . . Since Jesus Christ entered into my life, I have found purpose and meaning for my life. The frustration is gone.

". . . It was election time when I became a Christian. Candidates for election were allowed five minutes to speak in their classes.

"So I went into the classrooms and said, 'I am going to introduce one of the greatest candidates for whom you can vote.' Then I talked about the uniqueness of this person and I finally said, 'He is the only One who is worthy of your vote, and His name is Jesus of Nazareth.' " 8/20

Charlie Abero

44. GUATEMALA

"A misconception is defined as a misunderstanding. That pretty well describes the problem I had with God.

". . . Some friends and I started studying books on philosophy and psychology.

". . . I arrived at this conclusion: the world's problems were God's fault.

". . . A Campus Crusade staff member told me how I could know God better by asking Christ into my life as personal Savior, and so I did.

"I see now how God really is love." 8/29

Arturo Jimenez

45. BERLIN, GERMANY

"Suicide seemed to be the only solution. When big problems began to come, I couldn't solve them. My life became so meaningless I decided that either there was no God or else He was making fun of me. In my despair I began to read Neitzsche, Sartre and other philosophers who believed that God is dead, but this didn't satisfy me either.

"A girl friend began to tell me about a new relationship she had with Jesus Christ.

". . . Through prayer I invited Him to come into my heart and take over.

". . . Christ did come into my life. My life has meaning. I still have the same problems, but through Christ I can face and solve them.

". . . I'm glad I committed my life to Him." 8/4, 5

Christa Nitzschke

CONVERTS FROM OTHER RELIGIONS

46. JUDAISM

"But, as I went to the synagogue, I had other questions. . . .

"Does it really matter to God what type of dishes I eat off? How important is it if I fast and observe certain traditions? Is all there is to life — money, materialism, sex and popularity?

". . . I read in the Scriptures that God would send a perfect sacrifice to atone for my sins, one called The Messiah.

"But, how could I know who this Messiah would be? Then, in the Jewish Bible, I saw all the prophecies which identified Him; such as, — that He would be born in Bethlehem of Judea, that He would be born of a young maiden who was a virgin, that He would die by crucifixion and that He would arise from the dead!

"I knew that only One Person in all of history could seriously be considered — Yeshua, known to the Gentiles as Jesus!

"And this Jewish boy, not being very religious — in the privacy of my own room, I prayed . . . 'Messiah, if you're there, COME INTO MY HEART AND LIFE AND CLEANSE ME WITH YOUR PRECIOUS BLOOD OF ATONEMENT!'

"It was like being in a dark room and somebody suddenly turned on the lights!!

"God, who had been a million miles away, all of a sudden came closer than my mother, my sister, my hands or even my breath! I FINALLY FOUND THE

PEACE AND THE PURPOSE AND THE JOY AND THE REALITY FOR
WHICH I HAD BEEN SEEKING!!!" 5

Manny Brotman
President, Messianic Jewish
Movement, International

47. ISLAM

"Bishop John A. Subhan of the Methodist Episcopal Church at Hyderabad was a convert from Islam. He was born in Calcutta into a well-to-do Muslim family whose ancestors were of the Moghul race and who had served at the Great Moghul's court.

"The new stage originated in a simple event; a Muslim friend gave him a copy of the Gospel. When the same thing had happened a few years earlier, he had torn it to pieces in spite of an unsatisfied longing. This longing, to know and understand the revelation given in Jesus, had never subsided. On the contrary, his close acquaintance with Sufism had intensified it. Now, he decided to study the book. He still considered it corrupt, but he argued that it must contain at least parts of the original revelation. As for its blasphemous contents, surely they could be easily detected and discarded as interpolations or inventions by wicked Christians!

"The result of his initial reading was startling. First, he did not find a single blasphemous or Satanic clause, though he had read it with vigilance. Second, his common sense told him that the deliberate corruption of sacred books must have a sufficient motive behind it. His close examination of the Gospel yielded no adequate ground for such an act. The high ethical teaching of the Gospel, for example, bore no mark of tampering; there was no ethic of convenience here. He reached the same conclusion in the study of the Gospel narratives. No disciple would have invented the crucifixion story with its shameful treatment of the founder of Christianity. Even if true, the crucifixion would have been the first thing to be removed or modified. How plainly it refuted the claim that Jesus was the Son of God! This wrestling of the young Muslim with his preconceived ideas of the New Testament is revealing.

"His second reading of the Gospel produced a deep conviction that it was the true *Injil,* that it was God's word and His revelation. The effect of reading the Gospel was markedly different from that produced by the recitation of the Quran.

"Upon this second reading Subhan decided to become a Christian. He was convinced that Christianity was the only true religion. The conviction and decision are remarkable, for apart from the Gospel he had no knowledge of the Christian faith. All the time he had been moving within Islam. He had no Christian friends; the Gospel was given to him by a Muslim.

"He sums up his experience of Christianity in these words: 'It is not a mere acceptance of certain beliefs and dogmas, though they are necessary, but essentially it is living in close fellowship with Christ. It is not only a religion to be practiced, but also a life to be lived.' " 14/51-61

48. HINDUISM

"Anath Nath Sen was born in Calcutta. . . .

"As a youth Anath Nath took ancestral religion very seriously. He strictly observed all the laws, manners and customs of Hindu society. He became a zealous Hindu, and was particularly devoted to Krishna. This was accompanied by a glowing hatred of Christianity because he considered it a foreign religion. Together with other boys, Anath Nath used to make determined efforts to obstruct the meetings of Christians. Sometimes, they made a terrible noise, sometimes they threw missiles. When these attempts failed, Anath Nath organized bands of young men to purchase Gospel portions, hymn sheets and tracts and then burnt them before the missionaries.

"One year, Anath Nath and his companions planned to burn the thatched hut which the missionaries used as a reading room and book store. On the previous night Anath Nath stole into the reading room and, out of curiosity, took away a Bible. When alone in his bedroom, he began to read it, first the Sermon on the Mount, then stories of Christ's call to sinners, and finally, after midnight, St. Luke's account of the Crucifixion. The non-violence and non-resistance taught and practiced by Christ stirred the conscience of Anath Nath. Accordingly, he cancelled the plan, much to the astonishment of his fellow conspirators. They took him to be a coward, though they dared not oppose him.

"Yet he still hoped to find the truth he was longing for in his ancestral religion. He went on pilgrimages, to Benares, Prayag, Gaya, Brindaban, Hardwar and Rishikesh, among other places. He associated with *sanyasis* or ascetics, and *fakirs,* but still satisfaction eluded him. A missionary befriended Anath Nath and through him he realized that Jesus was a historic person, 'the true Savior of the world.'

"Already he was on the way to full surrender to Christ. He describes his experiences at that time in detail. 'I heard the voice of Jesus: "I am the way, and the truth, and the life: no man cometh unto the Father, but by Me." ' It is not quite clear whether it was an audible or an inner voice he heard, but he says: 'This was a wonderful revelation to me, and from that moment I understood that Jesus Christ was the Teacher of the world and decided to seek Him, to find Him and to worship His Father as the true God.' " 14/41-45

49. HINDUISM

"I was born in a family that was considered Sikh by caste, and in which the teaching of Hinduism was considered most essential. My dear mother was a living example and faithful exponent of its teaching. She used to rise daily before daylight, and, after bathing, used to read the Bhagavad Gita.

"I often used to read the Hindu scriptures till midnight that I might in some way quench the thirst of my soul for peace.

"I frequently asked the pundit to explain my spiritual difficulties for me.

" 'You cannot get to this grade of spirituality all at once. To get to it, a long time is essential. Why are you in such a hurry? If this hunger is not satisfied in this life it will be satisfied in your next re-births, provided that you keep on trying for it,' he said.

"The loss of my mother and my elder brother within a few months of each other was a great shock to me. The thought that I should never see them again cast me into despondency and despair, for I could never know into what form they had been reborn, nor could I ever even guess what I was likely to be in my next re-births.

"In the Hindu religion, the only consolation for a broken heart like mine was that I should submit to my faith and bow down to the inexorable law of *karma,* which is the law of works and retribution.

"Now another change came into my life. I was sent, for my secular education, to a small primary school that had been opened by the American Presbyterian Mission in our village of Rampur. At that time I had so many prejudices about Christianity that I refused to read the Bible at the daily lessons. My teachers insisted that I should attend, but I was so opposed to it that the next year I left that school and went to a government school at Sanewal three miles away, and there I studied for some months.

"To some extent the teaching of the Gospel on the love of God attracted me, but I still thought it was false. So firmly was I set in my opinions that one day, in the presence of my father and others, I tore up a Gospel and burned it.

"According to my ideas at that time, I thought I had done a good deed in burning the Gospel, yet my unrest of heart increased, and for two days afterward I was very miserable. On the third day, when I felt I could bear it no longer, I got up at three o'clock in the morning and after bathing, I prayed that if there was a God at all He would reveal Himself to me, show me the way of salvation, and end this unrest of my soul. I firmly made up my mind that, if this prayer was not answered, I would before daylight go down to the railway tracks and place my head on the rail before the oncoming Ludhiana express.

"I remained until about half past four, praying and waiting and expecting to see Krishna, or Buddha, or some other *avatar* of the Hindu religion, but they did not appear. A light seemed to be shining in the room, and I opened the door to see where it came from, but all was dark outside. I returned inside, and it seemed that the sphere of light increased in intensity. In this light there appeared not the form I expected, but the living Christ whom I had counted as dead.

"To all eternity I shall never forget His glorious and loving face, nor the few words which He spoke: 'Why do you persecute Me? See, I have died on the cross for you and the whole world.' These words were burned into my heart as by lightning, and I fell on the ground before Him. My heart was filled with inexpressible joy and peace, and my whole life was entirely changed. Then the old Sundar Singh died and a new Sundar Singh, to serve the living Christ, was born.

"It is characteristic of this new life that it constrains one to bring others to Christ, not by compulsion, but from the desire to let others share in the joy of this wonderful experience. During the summer holidays I went to Subathu and Simla, and, instead of returning to school, I was baptized and began to go about as a sadhu and preach the Gospel.

"Without Christ I had been without hope and full of fear about the future life. Now, by His presence, He has turned fear into love, and hopelessness into realization. Fear is transitory, but love is eternal. Faith and love are the tendrils of the soul, which, in the light and heat of God's sun, grow towards heaven, and cling around the Lord of love; but without Him, hopeless and in the dark, they wither away and die."

Sundar Singh, probably the most unusual convert from Hinduism, thereafter preached the saving gospel of Jesus Christ among his people. He made several dangerous missionary trips to Tibet, from the last of which he never returned. 40

50. SATANISM

"My parents were church members, and I had gone to church fairly regularly with them. But it was an empty thing. Jesus Christ was some vague, far-off figure, with little meaning for me. When I asked my parents questions about God, they turned them aside. 'You're a regular question box,' they'd say. 'Just accept it as we do.' I couldn't do that, and as far as I was concerned the church offered nothing.

"I was constantly searching, however, for something to fill the void in my life. At the age of 17 I met a spiritist medium.

" 'The only way to live,' said my new friend, 'is by the cards and your horoscope. Come, let me show you.'

"I was fascinated. She seemed ruled by a strange spirit, and in a trance-like vision she laid out my cards and unfolded to me past happenings with an eerie accuracy. She also demonstrated a strange ability to cure diseases. Often doctors sent patients to her.

" 'Here's a deck of cards,' she offered one day. 'You must always start your day off by laying the cards.' Deftly she laid my cards and showed me how to interpret them. I learned the different combinations and their meanings. Soon I was able to spell out future events, it appeared.

"In months that followed I found myself controlled more and more by this mysterious woman. Step by step she led me into the spirit world until one day she declared, 'You're one of us now. Will you take the oath?'

"Powerless, I nodded agreement. Hardly knowing what I was doing, I cut my finger and with my own blood wrote, 'I give to thee, O Satan, my heart, body and soul.'

"I now lived completely by the cards and my horoscope. I hardly dared to breathe without first consulting them.

"The devil, who now had claim to my soul, tormented me incessantly. I did things that can't be told publicly. By the age of 19 I was utterly demoralized.

"Melancholy and depression filled me. I had fits of temper. I couldn't concentrate on my nursing work because of the turmoil of soul, and my job suffered.

"In March, 1960, I signed the horoscope chart that forecast I would take my life on July 26. According to the horoscope, my life was no longer of any use. And so on the night of July 25 I wandered the dark streets searching for a way out. I was terrified at the thought of dying.

"Beautiful music penetrated my troubled soul, and I was drawn toward a religious meeting being held in a large tent. Furtively I entered the tent. The music ended and the speaker, Leander Penner of the Greater Europe Mission, stood up. 'Tonight I'm going to tell you about the wonderful power of the Gospel,' he said.

"I wanted to run, but I was drained of energy. In all my years of churchgoing I had never heard of this Christ — a personal Saviour who had died for me personally. Oh, how I longed to break Satan's hold.

" 'Only Christ can break the power of Satan,' the preacher said. He invited the hearers to come forward and confess Christ. I pushed myself to the front and asked: 'Is there hope for a sinner such as I? Preacher, if what you say is true, I want deliverance. Pray for me.'

"The evangelist prayed, and then assured me that Christ could and would forgive the greatest of sinners if only He is asked. 'For him that cometh to Me I will in no wise cast out,' he quoted from John 6: 37.

"But I couldn't ask Christ for help. Each time I tried I felt an invisible hand clutching my throat.

" 'Go home,' the preacher advised me, 'and we'll have a special prayer group for you. Come back tomorrow night.' "

"I wanted to cry: 'But that will be too late!' Fearfully I went home.

"The long night of terror passed. I couldn't sleep; I could only dread the approaching day. Slowly daylight seeped into my room, and I mechanically laid my cards and got ready for work.

"I shuddered as I crossed the river on my way to the hospital; I would soon be down there. I arrived at work and tried once more to escape my tormentor. With trembling finger I dialed the evangelist's number. 'Can you come right over?' I asked. 'It's a matter of life and death.'

"When he came hurrying in I demanded, 'Does your Christ really have power over Satan?'

" 'Yes, of course,' he assured me.

"I handed him the box with my horoscope and the neatly folded pledge of death inside. 'Read it,' I urged. 'If your Christ can't rescue me now, I'll have to jump in the river this afternoon. The time, place, and method have already been picked out for me.'

"Fervently he prayed, and I felt as if I were being torn apart. I twitched and shook uncontrollably. Tears cooled my cheeks. In vain I tried to reach out for Christ. I tried to pray, but an invisible power choked me just as before. 'It's no use, I can't do it,' I cried.

" 'You can't, but Christ can,' came the earnest reply. For a half-hour the preacher prayed, and the battle within me raged. With a violent twist I suddenly threw myself on my knees and beseeched the Lord to take this awful devil obsession from me. Christ's power won, and a feeling of peace flooded my soul. I knew that I could live.

"For a week after that I struggled to get up the courage to live without my occult crutches. At last I apprehensively put them all in a bag and surrendered them to Mr. Penner. Then I began climbing the long road to spiritual stability and serenity. I have had setbacks along the way, and sometimes I feel a sinister presence, but Christ's strength is always sufficient when I ask for it.

"Today, thanks to God's grace, I'm working in a Bible conference center, helping to print and distribute Gospel tracts. My daily prayer is, 'Please, Lord, let me be a blessing to someone who is still bound by Satan.' " 2/68-71

Anonymous

CONVERTED SKEPTICS

51. FRANK MORISON

Frank Morison was an English journalist who set out to prove that the story of Christ's resurrection was nothing but a myth. However, his probings led him to the point where he placed his faith in the risen Christ. Morison went on to write a book on his findings titled, *Who Moved the Stone?*

"I wanted to take this Last Phase of the life of Jesus, with all its quick and pulsating drama, its sharp, clear-cut background of antiquity, and its tremendous psychological and human interest — to strip it of its overgrowth of primitive beliefs and dogmatic suppositions, and to see this supremely great Person as He really was.

"I need not stay to describe here how, fully 10 years later, the opportunity came to study the life of Christ as I had long wanted to study it, to investigate the origins of its literature, to sift some of the evidence at first hand, and to form my own judgment on the problem which it presents. I will only say that it affected a revolution in my thought. Things emerged from that old-world story which previously I should have thought impossible. Slowly but very definitely the conviction grew that the drama of those unforgettable weeks of human history was stranger and deeper than it seemed. It was the strangeness of many notable things in the story which first arrested and held my interest. It was only later that the irresistible logic of their meaning came into view." 33/11, 12

52. C. S. LEWIS

C. S. Lewis, British author and teacher noted for his wit, imagination and clarity of expression, was a skeptic until he was converted in 1931. The following excerpts from *The Letters of C. S. Lewis* tell his story.

From a letter of C. S. Lewis to his father, March 31, 1928:

"There is a religious revival going on among our undergraduates . . . run by a Dr. Buchman. He gets a number of young men together (some reports say women too, but I believe not) and they confess their sins to one another. Jolly, ain't it? But what can you do? If you try to suppress it you only make martyrs. . . ." 29/126

To Owen Barfield, undated, 1930:

"'Terrible things are happening to me. The 'Spirit' or 'Real I' is showing an alarming tendency to become much more personal and is taking the offensive, and behaving just like God. You'd better come on Monday at the latest or I may have entered a monastery." 25/141

His brother tells of Lewis' decision:

"'I well remember that day in 1931 when we made a visit to Whipsnade Zoo. . . . It was during that outing that he made his decision to rejoin the Church. This seemed to me no sudden plunge into a new life, but rather a slow, steady convalescence from a deep-seated spiritual illness of long standing. . . ." 29/19

To Owen Barfield, undated, 1933:

"Since I have begun to pray, I find my extreme view of personality changing. My own empirical self is becoming more important, and this is exactly the opposite of self love. You don't teach a seed how to grow into treehood by throwing it into the fire: and it has to become a good seed before it's worth burying. . . ." 29/155

Before he died in 1963, Lewis authored a number of Christian books including *Miracles, The Problem of Pain* and *Mere Christianity.*

In *Mere Christianity* he makes this statement:

"A man who was merely a man and said the sort of things Jesus said would not be a great moral teacher. He would either be a lunatic — on a level with the man who says he is a poached egg — or else he would be the Devil of Hell. You must make your choice. Either this man was, and is, the Son of God: or else a madman or something worse. You can shut Him up for a fool, you can spit at Him and kill Him as a demon; or you can fall at His feet and call Him Lord and God. But let us not come with any patronizing nonsense about His being a great human teacher. He has not left that open to us." 39/40, 41

53. LEW WALLACE

Lew Wallace became convinced of Christ's divinity after studying the Bible in preparation for writing *Ben-Hur,* a work that was initially to present Christ as a mere man.

"It is not strange that he regarded Ben-Hur as his best work. It marked a crisis in his own spiritual experience. He became a Christian through his study of the life of Christ, in preparing to write the story. It has been related that an atheistic friend once predicted to him that within a few years the little white churches of his beloved Indiana countryside would be only a memory buried in the general crash of all religion. He was too ignorant to answer the assertion with Christian arguments. He had no convictions in regard to God and Christ. In his fascinating account of how he came to write Ben-Hur, he tells us he was painfully ignorant of the theme of that discussion with his friend, 'such elemental themes as God and life hereafter and Jesus Christ and his divinity.' He then and there determined to study them until he had firsthand convictions of his own. He went to the Bible itself as his source book. He would trust his lawyer-training in logic to lead him to proper conclusions and he would enliven what he thought would be a somewhat dreary study by embodying in a story of the Christ such material as he might find. But he was working with the supernatural factors of which he did not dream. No man can read the Bible with an open mind desiring to know the truth in regard to Jesus Christ without becoming convinced of His divinity. As he studied the historic background of the condition of the world at the time of his story, the evils of society and the very need of men for a divine Saviour seemed an argument in favor of accepting the Saviour who had come. His purpose in writing the story of the years between Bethlehem and Calvary was to make readers see that argument." 13/116, 117

54. GIOVANNI PAPINI

"Although Giovanni Papini was one of the foremost Italian men of letters, the publication of his *Life of Christ* in 1921 came as a stunning surprise to many of his friends and admirers. For Papini had been an atheist, a vocal enemy of the Church and a self-appointed debunker of any form of mysticism. A more unlikely source for a reverent portrait of Jesus could hardly be imagined.

"What brought about his sudden conversion — so reminiscent of Saul's on the road to Damascus? Like many cynics he was, under the surface, a tormented soul, disgusted with a humanity that could accept the first World War, unable to see hope for better things unless, somehow, the hearts of men could be changed. And he craved, as he later said, 'a crumb of certitude.'

"During that war he took his family to live in a mountain village. There, living with the peasants, observing their devotions, something began to happen to him. Sometimes in the evenings, he was asked to read aloud stories from the New Testament. This rediscovery of the Bible, against the background of his own uncertainties, became a revelation to him, and soon he determined to write his own version of the life of Christ. Before long he became convinced that the only power that could change the hearts of men was the teaching of Jesus.

"This conviction pervades *The Life of Christ,* a book which, in the words of a distinguished critic, 'will stand for many years as a rallying sign for thousands making their way painfully to a less inhuman, because a more Christlike, world.' " 15/8

EXAMPLES OF SUFFERING FOR THE GOSPEL
55. THE REV. RICHARD WURMBRAND

"The Rev. Richard Wurmbrand is an evangelical minister who spent 14 years in communist imprisonment and torture in his homeland of Rumania. He is one of Rumania's most widely known Christian leaders, authors and educators. Few names are better known in his homeland.

"In 1945, when the communists seized Rumania and attempted to control the churches for their purposes, Richard Wurmbrand immediately began an effective, vigorous 'underground' ministry to his enslaved people and the invading Russian soldiers. He was eventually arrested in 1948, along with his wife Sabina. His wife was a slave-laborer for three years. Richard Wurmbrand spent three years in solitary confinement — seeing no one but his communist torturers. After three years he was transferred to a mass cell for five years, where the torture continued.

"Due to his international stature as a Christian leader, diplomats of foreign embassies asked the communist government about his safety. They were told he had fled Rumania. Secret police, posing as released fellow-prisoners, told his wife of attending his burial in the prison cemetery. His family in Rumania and his friends abroad were told to forget him since he was now dead.

"After eight years he was released and promptly resumed his work with the Underground Church. Two years later, in 1959, he was re-arrested and sentenced to 25 years in prison.

"Mr. Wurmbrand was released in a general amnesty in 1964, and again continued his underground ministry. Realizing the great danger of a third imprisonment, Christians in Norway negotiated with the communist authorities for his release from Rumania. The communist government had begun 'selling' their political prisoners. The 'going price' for a prisoner was $1,900. Their price for Wurmbrand was $10,000.

"In May, 1966, he testified in Washington before the Senate's Internal Security Subcommittee and stripped to the waist to show 18 deep torture wounds covering his body. His story was carried across the world in newspapers in the U.S.,

Europe and Asia. Wurmbrand was warned in September, 1966, that a decision had been made by the communist regime of Rumania to assassinate him. Yet he is not silent in the face of these death threats. He has been called 'the voice of the Underground Church.' Christian leaders have called him 'a living martyr' and 'the Iron Curtain Paul.' " 54/5, 6

The following is an excerpt from Wurmbrand's book, *Tortured for Christ.*

"A pastor by the name of Florescu was tortured with red-hot iron pokers and with knives. He was beaten very badly. Then starving rats were driven into his cell through a large pipe. He could not sleep, but had to defend himself all the time. If he rested a moment, the rats would attack him.

"He was forced to stand for two weeks, day and night. The communists wished to compel him to betray his brethren, but he resisted steadfastly. In the end, they brought his 14 year-old son and began to whip the boy in front of his father, saying that they would continue to beat him until the pastor said what they wished him to say. The poor man was half mad. He bore it as long as he could.

"When he could not stand it any more, he cried to his son; 'Alexander, I must say what they want! I can't bear your beating any more!' The son answered, 'Father, don't do me the injustice to have a traitor as a parent. Withstand! If they kill me, I will die with the words, "Jesus and my fatherland." ' The communists, enraged, fell upon the child and beat him to death, with blood spattered over the walls of the cell. He died praising God. Our dear brother Florescu was never the same after seeing this." 54/36

56. MARTYR IN VIETNAM

"Gaspar Makil, with Wycliffe Bible Translators, was shot by communist guerrillas on March 4, 1963, in full view of his wife, Josephine. Also killed at the same time was their little four-month-old Janie, another missionary and a Vietnamese soldier. The Makils' three-year-old Tommy was critically injured. The Makil family and another missionary family were traveling in a jeep-like Land Rover along South Vietnam's most heavily traveled highway, Route 20. They were stopped by communist guerrillas, about 20 in number. When a government army truck appeared on the highway, the Viet Cong opened fire with their machine guns. Gaspar was a Philippine national and was converted while he was an engineering student here in the United States. A few days before sailing to South Vietnam, he wrote, 'We cannot tell what awaits us in South Vietnam, but we know that the Lord is with us, having commissioned us into this ministry. Our times are in God's hands and He brings all things to pass in His own time, which is the right time. The Lord is interested in every single detail of our lives.' " 32

57. MISSIONARIES TO THE AUCA INDIANS

"On January 8, 1956, the whole world was stunned by the word that a band of Auca Indians, the fiercest of Ecuador's aborigines, had fatally speared an American missionary pilot, Nate Saint, and his four co-workers, Jim Elliot, Roger Youderian, Ed McCully and Peter Fleming. After official investigation confirmed the tragedy, Ecuadorian troops and missionaries serving adjoining tribes formed an expedition upriver to bury the victims. They found the plane demolished, its fabric torn to shreds.

"The pilot was my brother. He and his companions were engaged in what has since become known as 'Operation Auca,' a mission to carry the Gospel of Jesus Christ to this unlettered, Stone Age tribe in the fastnesses of the Amazon.

"Through one miracle after another, as told in *The Dayuma Story,* all five killers confessed Christ as Saviour. I believe it is significant that the first to believe among the Auca men were the five living killers — Kimo, Minkayi, Gikita, Dyuwi and Nimonga. When the first baptismal service was held in Tiwaeno, a little more than two years after our entry into the tribe, four of the five were baptized. The fifth was in the second group of baptisms. In this case my brother Phil did the baptizing. Each of the wives also opened her heart to the Lord Jesus Christ and received baptism." 41

Rachel Saint

58. THE REV. JOON GON KIM

The Rev. Joon Gon Kim is director of Korean Campus Crusade for Christ.

"Dr. Kim's experience with the communists has been personal and tragic. When campus strikes broke out in Korea in 1950, communists swept over all the colleges except one Christian university. Well over 70% of the students were in favor of communism. Thousands of them were financially supported on the campuses by the Russian communists. These turned out to be the active leaders during the Korean War.

"Dr. Kim says, 'One night I was awakened by the noise of men calling my name. My family and I were taken where 60 human beings, including the old, and women and children, were being killed. Ten military men, all familiar villagers, were assigned to execute my family. My wife and father were slaughtered before my eyes. I was beaten and left for dead.'

"Kim survived the savage beating of the communists, and asked God to give him a love for the souls of his enemies. Kim led 30 of the communists to Christ, including the leader responsible for the death of his loved ones.

"Dr. Kim knows from first-hand knowledge that Jesus Christ is the answer to communism, as He is the answer to every other problem in life." 24

BIBLIOGRAPHY

1. Adair, James R. *Saints Alive.* Wheaton: Van Kampen Press, 1951.

2. Adair, James R. and Ted Miller (eds.). *We Found Our Way Out.* Grand Rapids: Baker Book House, 1964.

3. Blessitt, Arthur. *Turned on to Jesus.* New York: Hawthorne Books, Inc., 1971.

4. Bright, Bill. *Jesus and the Intellectual.* Campus Crusade for Christ International, 1968.

5. *But You Don't Look Very Jewish.* (pamphlet) The Messianic Jewish Movement International, 1971. Used by permission.

6. Camburn, Terry Meeuwsen. "Miss America 1973." *Worldwide Challenge.* Vol. 3, No. 2, pp. 15,16. San Bernardino: Campus Crusade for Christ, Inc., Feb., 1976.

7. Chelcicky, Jan. "My Last Days as a Communist." *Guideposts.* Carmel: Guideposts Associates, Inc., 1971. Used by permission.

8. *Collegiate Challenge.* Vol. 11, No. 2, pp. 4,5. San Bernardino: Campus Crusade for Christ, Inc., 1972.

9. Cruz, Nicky. *Run Baby Run.* Plainfield, N. J.: Logos Books, 1968.

10. Dennis, Clyde H. (ed.). *These Live On.* Westchester, Ill.: Good News Publishers, 1966.

11. Engstrom, Elmer W. "Christ and the Century of Change." *Collegiate Challenge.* Vol. 5, No. 2, pp. 12, 13. San Bernardino: Campus Crusade for Christ, Inc., 1966.

12. Enlow, David R. *Men Made New.* Grand Rapids: Zondervan Publishing House, 1964. Used by permission.

13. Erdman, Walter C. *More Sources of Power in Famous Lives.* Nashville: Cokesbury Press, 1937.

14. Estborn, S. *Gripped by Christ.* London: Lutterworth Press, 1965.

15. *Family Treasury of Great Biographies.* Vol. III. Pleasantville, N. J.: Reader's Digest Association, 1970.

16. Faris, Murray G. "Disease Free." *Contact.* March, 1972, p. 9. Glen Ellyn: Christian Business Men's Committee, Int.

17. Ferm, Robert O. *The Psychology of Christian Conversion.* Westwood, N. J.: Fleming H. Revell Company, 1959.

18. *Football Was the Name of the Game.* (tract) Oradell, N. J.: American Tract Society. Used by permission.

19. Hatfield, Mark O. "Excellence: The Christian Standard." *Collegiate Challenge.* Vol. 4, No. 3, pp. 6, 7. San Bernardino: Campus Crusade for Christ, Inc., 1965.

20. Hefley, James C. *Living Miracles.* Grand Rapids: Zondervan Publishing House, copyright 1964. Used by permission.

21. "How June Poitras Found God." *Indian Life.* Vol. 6, No. 2, p. 7. Rapid City: American Indian Mission.

22. "Japanese Feudal Lord Finds the Answer." *Collegiate Challenge.* Vol. 1, No. 8, p. 7. San Bernardino: Campus Crusade for Christ, Inc., 1962.

23. Jones, E. Stanley. *Conversion.* New York: Abingdon Press, copyright 1959.

24. Joon Gon Kim. Xerox copy of personal testimony from International Office, Campus Crusade for Christ International.

25. *Journey's End.* (tract) Oradell, N. J.: American Tract Society. Used by permission.

26. Latourette, Kenneth Scott. *Anno Domini.* New York: Harper and Brothers, 1940.

27. Lewis, C. S. *Mere Christianity.* New York: The Macmillan Company, 1952.

28. Lewis, W. H. *Letters of C. S. Lewis.* London: Geoffrey Bles Ltd., 1966.

29. Little, Paul E. *Know Why You Believe.* Wheaton: Scripture Press Publications, Inc., 1967.

30. Malik, Charles. "Hope for a World in Crisis." *Collegiate Challenge.* Vol. 7, No. 2, pp. 32-35. San Bernardino: Campus Crusade for Christ, Inc., 1968.

31. Massengale, Rik. *Athletes in Action.* p. 38. San Bernardino: Arrowhead Springs Publications, 1977.

32. *Moody Alumni Martyrs.* Chicago: Moody Bible Institute.

33. Morison, Frank. *Who Moved the Stone?* London: Faber and Faber, 1958.

34. Mullins, E. Y. *Why Is Christianity True?* Chicago: Christian Culture Press, 1905.

35. *On Patrol for God.* (tract) Oradell, N. J.: American Tract Society. Used by permission.

36. Penn, Charles H. "A Blighted Life Can Be Changed." *Contact.* September, 1971. Glen Ellyn: Christian Business Men's Committee, Int.

37. Price, Eugenia. "Personally Involved . . . and Transformed." *Collegiate Challenge.* Vol. 1, No. 4, pp. 6, 7. San Bernardino: Campus Crusade for Christ, Inc., 1962.

38. Ramm, Bernard. *Protestant Christian Evidences.* Chicago: Moody Press, 1953. Used by permission.

39. "The Roots of Religion." *Pastoral Psychology.* Vol. V, No. 43, April, 1954.

40. Sadhu Sundar Singh. *With and Without Christ.* New York: Harper and Row Publishers, 1929.

41. Saint, Rachel. "Ten Years After the Massacre." *Decision.* January, 1966. Minneapolis: The Billy Graham Evangelistic Association.

42. Schulz, Charles. *Collegiate Challenge.* Vol. 4, No. 3, pp. 3-5. San Bernardino: Campus Crusade for Christ, Inc., 1965.

43. "A Scientific Approach." *Decision*. November, 1966. Minneapolis: The Billy Graham Evangelistic Association.

44. "She was an Atheist Until She Met a God of Love." *Pray*. World Literature Crusade, February, 1969.

45. Short, Shirl. (excerpt from) "Exclusive Interview with Charles Colson." *Moody Monthly*. Feb., 1976. Chicago: Moody Bible Institute. Used by permission.

46. Smith, Stan. "My Way of Playing." *Guideposts*. pp. 22,23, 1972. Carmel: Guideposts Associates, Inc.

47. Staubach, Roger. *Staubach: First Down, Lifetime to Go*. pp. 274, 275, 279. Waco: Word Incorporated, 1974. Used by permission.

48. Thiede, Carsten. *Collegiate Challenge*. Vol. 16, p. 11. San Bernardino: Campus Crusade for Christ, Inc., 1977.

49. *Three Steps from Darkness*. (tract) Lake Worth, Florida: South America Mission.

50. Wells, Ginny. "Worth More than a Billion." *Moody Monthly*. Chicago: Moody Bible Institute, 1972. Used by permission.

51. *What Is Happiness for a Vietnamese Tribesman?* Wycliffe Bible Translators. (Xerox copy of personal testimony.)

52. White, Lona A. "How the Shaggy D.A. Became a Lamb," *Christian Life*. Vol. 39, No. 9, January, 1978. Wheaton: Christian Life, Inc. Used by permission.

53. Willems, Betty. "B. J. Thomas: Home Where He Belongs," *Contemporary Christian Acts*. pp. 1,34. January, 1978. Santa Ana: Contemporary Christian Acts, Inc. Used by permission.

54. Wurmbrand, Richard. *Tortured for Christ*. Glendale, Calif.: Diane Books, 1967.

HE CHANGED MY LIFE
by
Josh McDowell

Jesus Christ is alive. The fact that I'm alive and doing things I do is evidence that Jesus Christ is raised from the dead.

Thomas Aquinas wrote: "There is within every soul a thirst for happiness and meaning." As a teen-ager I wanted to be happy. There's nothing wrong with that. I wanted to be one of the happiest individuals in the entire world. I also wanted meaning in life. I wanted answers to questions. "What am I?" "Why in the world am I here?" "Where am I going?"

More than that, I wanted to be free. I wanted to be one of the freest individuals in the whole world. Freedom to me is not going out and doing what you want to do. Anyone can do that, and lots of people are doing it. Freedom is "to have the power to do what you know you ought to do." Most people know what they ought to do, but they don't have the power to do it. They're in bondage.

So I started looking for answers. It seems that almost everyone is into some sort of religion, so I did the obvious thing and took off for church. I must have found the wrong church though. Some of you know what I'm talking about: I felt worse inside than I did outside. I went in the morning, I went in the afternoon, and I went in the evening.

I'm always very practical, and when something doesn't work, I chuck it. I chucked religion. The only thing I ever got out of religion was the 25 cents I put in the offering and the 35 cents I took out for a milkshake. And that's about all many people ever gain from "religion."

I began to wonder if prestige was the answer. Being a leader, accepting some cause, giving yourself to it, and "being known" might do it. In the first university I attended, the student leaders held the purse strings and threw their weight around. So I ran for freshman class president and got elected. It was neat knowing everyone on campus, having everyone say, "Hi, Josh," making the decisions, spending the university's money, the students' money, to get speakers I wanted. It was great, but it wore off like everything else I had tried. I would wake up Monday morning, usually with a headache because of the night before, and my attitude was, "Well, here goes another five days." I endured Monday through Friday. Happiness revolved around three nights a week: Friday, Saturday and Sunday. Then the vicious cycle began all over again.

Oh, I fooled them in the university. They thought I was one of the most happy-go-lucky guys around. During the political campaigns we used the phrase, "Happiness is Josh." I threw more parties with student money than anyone else did, but they never realized my happiness was like so many other people's. It depended on my own circumstances. If things were going great for me, I was great. When things would go lousy, I was lousy.

I was like a boat out in the ocean being tossed back and forth by the waves, the circumstances. There is a biblical term to describe that type of living: hell. But I couldn't find anyone living any other way and I couldn't find anyone who could tell me how to live differently or give me the strength to do it. Everyone was telling me what I ought to do, but none of them could give me the power to do it. I began to be frustrated.

I suspect that few people in the universities and colleges of this country were more sincere in trying to find meaning, truth and purpose of life than I was. I hadn't found it yet, but I didn't realize that at first. In and around the university I noticed a small group of people: eight students and two faculty members, and there was something different about their lives. They seemed to know why they believed what they believed. I like to be around people like that. I don't care if they don't agree with *me*. Some of my closest friends are opposed to some things I believe, but I admire a man or woman with conviction. (I don't meet many, but I admire them when I meet them.) That's why I sometimes feel more at home with some radical leaders than I do with many Christians. Some of the Christians I meet are so wishy-washy that I wonder if maybe 50% of them are masquerading as Christians. But the people in this small group seemed to know where they were going. That's unusual among university students.

The people I began to notice didn't just *talk* about love. They got involved. They seemed to be riding above the circumstances of university life. It appeared that everybody else was under a pile. One important thing I noticed was that they seemed to have a happiness, a state of mind not dependent on circumstances. They appeared to possess an inner, constant source of joy. They were disgustingly happy. They had something I didn't have.

Like the average student, when somebody had something I didn't have, I wanted it. That's why they have to lock up bicycles in colleges. If education were really the answer, the university would probably be the most morally upright society in existence. But it's not. So, I decided to make friends with these intriguing people.

Two weeks after that decision we were all sitting around a table in the student union, six students and two faculty members. The conversation started to get around to God. If you're an insecure person and a conversation centers on God, you tend to put on a big front. Every campus or community has a big mouth, a guy who says, "Uh . . . Christianity, ha, ha. That's for the weaklings, it's not intellectual." (Usually, the bigger the mouth, the bigger the vacuum.)

They were bothering me, so finally I looked over at one of the students, a good-looking woman (I used to think all Christians were ugly); and I leaned back in my chair because I didn't want the others to think I was interested, and I said, "Tell me, what changed your lives? Why are your lives so different from the other students, the leaders on campus, the professors? Why?"

That young woman must have had a lot of conviction. She looked me straight in the eye, no smile, and said two words I never thought I'd hear as part of a solution in a university. She said, "Jesus Christ." I said, "Oh, for God's sake, don't give me that garbage. I'm fed up with religion; I'm fed up with the church; I'm fed up with the Bible. Don't give me that garbage about religion." She shot back, "Mister, I didn't say religion, I said Jesus Christ." She pointed out something I'd never known before, Christianity is not a religion. Religion is humans trying to work their way to God through good works. Christianity is God coming to men and women through Jesus Christ, offering them a relationship with Himself.

There are probably more people in universities with misconceptions about Christianity than anywhere else in the world. Recently I met a teaching assistant who remarked in a graduate seminar that "anyone who walks into a church becomes a Christian." I replied, "Does walking into a garage make you a car?" There is no correlation. A Christian is somebody who puts his trust in Christ.

My new friends challenged me intellectually to examine the claims that Jesus Christ is God's Son; that taking on human flesh, He lived among real men and women and died on the cross for the sins of mankind, that He was buried and He arose three days later and could change a person's life in the 20th century.

I thought this was a farce. In fact, I thought most Christians were walking idiots. I'd met some. I used to wait for a Christian to speak up in the classroom so I could tear him or her up one side and down the other, and beat the insecure professor to the punch. I imagined that if a Christian had a brain cell, it would die of loneliness. I didn't know any better.

But these people challenged me over and over. Finally, I accepted their challenge, but I did it out of pride, to refute them. But I didn't know there were facts. I didn't know there was evidence that a person could evaluate.

Finally, my mind came to the conclusion that Jesus Christ must have been who He claimed to be. In fact, the background of my first two books was my setting out to refute Christianity. When I couldn't, I ended up becoming a Christian. I have now spent 13 years documenting why I believe that faith in Jesus Christ is intellectually feasible.

At that time, though, I had quite a problem. My mind told me all this was true but my will was pulling me in another direction. I discovered that becoming a Christian was rather ego-shattering. Jesus Christ made a direct challenge to my will to trust Him. Let me paraphrase Him. "Look! I have been standing at the door and I am constantly knocking. If anyone hears Me calling him and opens the door, I will come in" (Revelation 3:20). I didn't care if He did walk on water or turn water into wine. I didn't want any party pooper around. I couldn't think of a faster way to ruin a good time. So here was my mind telling me Christianity was true, and my will was somewhere else.

Every time I was around those enthusiastic Christians, the conflict would begin. If you've ever been around happy people when you're miserable, you understand how they can bug you. They would be so happy and I would be so miserable that I'd literally get up and run right out of the student union. It came to the point where I'd go to bed at 10 at night and I wouldn't get to sleep until four in the morning. I knew I had to get it off my mind before I went out of my mind! I was always open-minded, but not so open-minded that my brains would fall out.

But since I was open-minded, on December 19, 1959, at 8:30 p.m. during my second year at the university, I became a Christian.

Somebody asked me, "How do you know?" I said, "Look, I was there. It's changed my life." That night I prayed. I prayed four things to establish a relationship with the resurrected, living Christ which has since transformed my life.

First, I said, "Lord Jesus, thank You for dying on the cross for me." Second, I said, "I confess those things in my life that aren't pleasing to You and ask You to forgive me and cleanse me." (The Bible says, "Though your sins be as scarlet, they shall be as white as snow.") Third, I said, "Right now, in the best way I know how, I open the door of my heart and life and trust You as my Savior and Lord. Take over the control of my life. Change me from the inside out. Make me the type of person You created me to be." The last thing I prayed was, "Thank You for coming into my life by faith." It was a faith based not upon ignorance but upon evidence and the facts of history and God's Word.

I'm sure you've heard various religious people talking about their "bolt of lightning." Well, after I prayed, nothing happened. I mean nothing. And I still haven't sprouted wings. In fact, after I made that decision, I felt worse. I literally felt I was going to vomit. I felt sick deep down. "Oh no, what'd you get sucked into now?" I wondered. I really felt I'd gone off the deep end (and I'm sure some people think I did!).

I can tell you one thing: in six months to a year and a half I found out that I hadn't gone off the deep end. My life *was* changed. I was in a debate with the head of the history department at a midwestern university and I said my life had been changed, and he interrupted me with, "McDowell, are you trying to tell us that God really changed your life in the 20th century? What areas?" After 45 minutes he said, "Okay, that's enough."

One area I told him about was my restlessness. I always had to be occupied. I had to be over at my girl's place or somewhere else in a rap session. I'd walk across the campus and my mind was like a whirlwind with conflicts bouncing off the walls. I'd sit down and try to study or cogitate and I couldn't. But a few months after I made that decision for Christ, a kind of mental peace developed. Don't misunderstand. I'm not talking about the absence of conflict. What I found in this relationship with Jesus wasn't so much the absence of conflict but the ability to cope with it. I wouldn't trade that for anything in the world.

Another area that started to change was my bad temper. I used to blow my stack if somebody just looked at me cross-eyed. I still have the scars from almost killing a man my first year in the university. My temper was such a part of me that I didn't consciously seek to change it. I arrived at the crisis of losing my temper only to find it was gone! Only once in 20 years have I lost my temper — and when I blew it that time, I made up for about six years!

There's another area of which I'm not proud. But I mention it because a lot of people need to have the same change in their lives, and I found the source of change: a relationship with the resurrected, living Christ. That area is hatred. I had a lot of hatred in my life. It wasn't something outwardly manifested, but there was a kind of inward grinding. I was ticked off with people, with things, with issues. Like so many other people, I was insecure. Every time I met someone different from me, he became a threat to me.

But I hated one man more than anyone else in the world. My father. I hated his guts. To me he was the town alcoholic. If you're from a small town and one of your parents is an alcoholic, you know what I'm talking about. Everybody knows. My friends would come to high school and make jokes about my father being downtown. They didn't think it bothered me. I was like other people, laughing on the outside, but let me tell you, I was crying on the inside. I'd go out in the barn and see my mother beaten so badly she couldn't get up, lying in the manure behind the cows. When we had friends over, I would take my father out, tie him up in the barn, and park the car up around the silo. We would tell our friends he'd had to go somewhere. I don't think anyone could have hated anyone more than I hated my father.

After I made that decision for Christ — maybe five months later — a love from God through Jesus Christ entered my life and was so strong it took that hatred and turned it upside down. I was able to look my father squarely in the eyes and say, "Dad, I love you." And I really meant it. After some of the things I'd done, that shook him up.

When I transferred to a private university I was in a serious car accident. My neck in traction, I was taken home. I'll never forget my father coming into my room. He asked me, "Son, how can you love a father like me?" I said, "Dad, six months ago I despised you." Then I shared with him my conclusions about Jesus Christ: "Dad, I let Christ come into my life. I can't explain it completely, but as a result of that relationship I've found the capacity to love and accept not only you but other people just the way they are."

Forty-five minutes later one of the greatest thrills of my life occurred. Somebody in my own family, someone who knew me so well I couldn't pull the wool over his eyes, said to me, "Son, if God can do in my life what I've seen Him do in yours, then I want to give Him the opportunity." Right there my father prayed with me and trusted Christ.

Usually the changes take place over several days, weeks, or months, even a year. My life was changed in about six months to a year-and-a-half. The life of my father was changed right before my eyes. It was as if somebody reached down and turned on a light bulb. I've never seen such a rapid change before or since. My father touched whiskey only once after that. He got it as far as his lips and that was it. I've come to one conclusion. A relationship with Jesus Christ changes lives.

You can laugh at Christianity, you can mock and ridicule it. But it works. It changes lives. If you trust Christ, start watching your attitudes and actions, because Jesus Christ is in the business of changing lives.

But Christianity is not something you shove down somebody's throat or force on someone. You've got your life to live and I've got mine. All I can do is tell you what I've learned. After that, it's your decision.

Perhaps the prayer I prayed will help you: "Lord Jesus, I need You. Thank You for dying on the cross for me. Forgive me and and cleanse me. Right this moment I trust You as Savior and Lord. Make me the type of person You created me to be. In Christ's name. Amen."

(Taken from Josh McDowell's *More Than a Carpenter.* Wheaton: Tyndale House Publishers, Inc., 1977. Used by permission.)

ADDITIONAL HISTORICAL SOURCES OF CHRISTIANITY

The following are additional secular references to Christ and Christianity:

(1) Josephus, *Antiquities,* Book 18, ch. 5, par. 2. This is an interesting reference to John the Baptist and his execution at Macherus at the hands of Herod Antipas.

(2) Trajan, Roman Emperor (Pliny the Younger, *Epistles* 10:97). This is a letter from the Emperor to Pliny, telling him not to punish those Christians who are forced to retract their beliefs by the Romans. He tells Pliny that anonymous information about the Christians is not to be accepted by the Roman officials.

(3) Macrobius, *Saturnalia,* lib. 2, ch. 4. Pascal *(Pensees,* 753 in the Penquin edition) mentions this quote of Augustus Caesar as an attestation of the slaughter of the babes of Bethlehem.

(4) Hadrian, Roman Emperor (Justin Martyr, *The First Apology,* ch. 68,69). Justin quotes Hadrian's letter to Minucius Fundanus, Proconsul of Asia Minor. The letter deals with the accusations of the pagans against the Christians.

(5) Antoninus Pius, Roman Emperor (Justin Martyr, *The First Apology,* ch. 70). Justin (or one of his disciples) quotes Antoninus' letter to the General Assembly of Asia Minor. The letter basically says that the officials in Asia Minor are getting too upset at the Christians in their province, and that no changes will be made in Antoninus' method of dealing with the Christians there.

(6) Marcus Aurelius, Roman Emperor (Justin Martyr, *The First Apology,* ch. 71). This letter from the Emperor to the Roman Senate was added to the manuscript by one of Justin's disciples. The Emperor describes Christians in fighting action in the Roman army.

(7) Juvenal, *Satires,* 1, lines 147-157. Juvenal makes a veiled mention of the tortures of Christians by Nero in Rome.

(8) Seneca, *Epistulae Morales,* Epistle 14, "On the Reasons for Withdrawing from the World, par. 2. Seneca, like Juvenal, describes the cruelties of Nero dealt upon the Christians.

(9) Hierocles (Eusebius, *The Treatise of Eusebius,* ch. 2). This quote by Eusebius preserves some of the text of the lost book of Hierocles, *Philalethes,* or *Lover of Truth.* In this quote, Hierocles condemns Peter and Paul as sorcerers.

In discussing Christ as a man of history, one of the most important collections of material is a volume published in Cambridge in 1923 by C. R. Haines entitled *Heathen Contact with Christianity During Its First Century and a Half.* The subtitle reads as follows: "Being all References to Christianity Recorded in Pagan Writings During That Period."

BIOGRAPHICAL SKETCHES OF AUTHORS

Albright, W. F., PhD, LittD, was the W. W. Spence Professor of Semitic Languages and Chairman, Oriental Seminary at Johns Hopkins University. He taught at Johns Hopkins from 1929 to 1958. He was president of the International Organization of Old Testament Scholars, director of the American School of Oriental Research in Jerusalem, and led a number of archaeological expeditions in the Middle East. He is the author of more than 800 publications on archaeological, biblical and Oriental subjects. In 1933 he described his position as "neither conservative nor radical in the usual sense of the terms" (*Bulletin of the American Schools of Oriental Research,* No. 51, September, 1933, pp. 5,6).

Anderson, J. N. D., OBE, LLD, FBA, has lectured in Islamic law for many years. He is Professor of Oriental Laws and Director of the Institute of Advanced Legal Studies at the University of London.

Archer, Gleason L., Jr., is chairman of the division of Old Testament at Trinity Evangelical Divinity School, Deerfield, Ill. He holds a BA, MA and PhD from Harvard; an LLB from Suffolk University Law School, Boston; and a BD from Princeton Seminary.

Bruce, Alexander Balmain, DD, 1831-1899, was Professor of Theology (Apologetics and New Testament Exegesis) in the Free Church College, Glasgow (now Trinity College).

Bruce, F. F., MA, DD, was Rylands Professor of Biblical Criticism and Exegesis at the University of Manchester.

Delitzsch, Franz Julius, 1813-1890, studied at the University of Leipzig, Professor of Theology at Rostock in 1846, at Erlangen in 1850.

Earle, Ralph, is head of the Department of New Testament at Nazarene Theological Seminary at Kansas City.

Edersheim, Alfred, 1825-1889, attended the University of Vienna; a teacher of languages of Pest, Hungary. He was Warbutonian Lecturer at Lincoln's Inn (Oxford); Grinfield Lecturer on the Septuagint.

Free, Joseph P., PhD, is Professor of Archaeology and History, Bemidji State College; formerly Director of Archaeological Studies, Wheaton College.

Geisler, Norman L., is a graduate of Wheaton College (BA) and Wheaton Graduate School (MA), majoring in philosophy and theology respectively. He also attended Detroit Bible College (ThB). At present Mr. Geisler is Assistant Professor of Bible and Philosophy at Trinity College, Deerfield, Illinois.

Green, Canon E. M. B., is Principal of St. John's College, Nottingham. He read Classics at Exeter College, Oxford, and Theology at Queens' College, Cambridge.

Greenlee, J. Harold, is Professor of New Testament Greek, Oral Roberts University.

Hengstenberg, Ernst Wilhelm, 1802-1869, was qualified at 17 to enter the University of Berlin. There he laid such an excellent foundation in Oriental languages and philosophies that he was able to issue an edition of an Arabic work in German when he was only 21.

Hort, Fenton John Anthony, 1828-1892, was educated at Rugby and Trinity College, Cambridge. In 1857 he became vicar of St. Ippolyts near

Cambridge. Cambridge frequently called upon him to serve as examiner, lecturer and professor. For six years he lectured on New Testament and patristic subjects at Emmanuel College (Cambridge). In 1878 he was made Hulsean Professor of Divinity.

Kenyon, Sir Frederic George, was a British scholar and administrator. He was assistant keeper of manuscripts in The British Museum (1898-1909). He then became director of the museum, an office he held until 1930. He published numerous works including: *The Palaeography of Greek Papyri; Our Bible and Ancient Manuscripts; Handbook to the Textual Criticism of The New Testament;* and *The Bible and Archaeology.*

Kevan, Ernest F., is principal of London Bible College in England. He holds the BD and MTh degrees from the University of London.

Lewis, C. S., was, until his death in 1963, Professor of Medieval and Renaissance Literature at Cambridge University.

Little, Paul, was Director of Evangelism for Inter-Varsity Christian Fellowship. He spoke on more than 180 college campuses throughout the United States and in 29 countries of Europe and Latin America. Mr. Little served periodically as Assistant Professor of Evangelism at Trinity Evangelical Divinity School, Deerfield, Illinois.

Metzger, Bruce M., is Professor of New Testament Language and Literature, Princeton Theological Seminary.

Montgomery, John Warwick, was Professor and Chairman, Division of Church History and History of Christian Thought, and Director of the Library at Trinity Evangelical Divinity School, Deerfield, Illinois. He is currently Professor-at-large, Melodyland School of Theology, Anaheim, California.

Morris, Henry M., attended the University of Minnesota (MS, PhD), and Rice University (BS). He was Professor of Hydraulic Engineering and Head of the Department of Civil Engineering, Virginia Polytechnic Institute. At the present time he is Director of the Christian Research Science Center and Academic Vice President of Christian Heritage College, San Diego, California.

Nix, William, taught at Detroit Bible College, LeTourneau College, Kilgore College and Trinity College. He holds a PhD from the University of Oklahoma.

Ramm, Bernard, is currently Professor of Theology at Eastern Baptist Theological Seminary. He holds a PhD from the University of Southern California and has authored such books as *Protestant Christian Evidences, The Christian View of Science and Scripture* and *Protestant Biblical Interpretation.*

Ramsay, Sir William, was a British archaeologist; Professor of Classical Archaeology and Art at Oxford (1885-1886); Professor of Humanity at Aberdeen University (1886-1911). He made discoveries in geography and topography of Asia Minor and its ancient history. He is the author of *The Historical Geography of Asia Minor; The Cities of St. Paul;* and *The Letters to the Seven Churches in Asia.*

Smith, Wilbur, DD, was Professor of English Bible at Fuller Theological Seminary and Trinity Evangelical Divinity School. His writings include *The Supernaturalness of Jesus* and *Therefore Stand: Christian Apologetics.*

Sparrow-Simpson, W. J., served as chaplain of St. Mary's Hospital of Ilford, England, and was highly respected in Great Britain. He was one of the contributors to the Oxford Library of Practical Theology.

Stauffer, Ethelbert, was a student and professor at several German universities. He was assistant professor at the Universities of Halle and Bonn and a professor of New Testament studies and ancient numismatics at Erlangen University. He has also authored six books on Christ and Christian theology.

Stoner, Peter W., MS, was Chairman of the Departments of Mathematics and Astronomy at Pasadena City College until 1953; Chairman of the Science Division, Westmont College, 1953-1957; now Professor Emeritus of Science, Westmont College.

Stott, John R. W., is Rector of All Souls Church, London.

Tenney, Merrill C., is Dean of the Graduate School and Professor of Bible and Philosophy at Wheaton College, Wheaton, Illinois. He holds the PhD degree from Harvard University.

Unger, Merrill F., received AB and PhD degrees at Johns Hopkins University and his ThM and ThD degrees at Dallas Theological Seminary. He is a professor at Dallas Theological Seminary.

Vos, Howard F., obtained his education at Wheaton College (AB), Dallas Theological Seminary (ThM, ThD), Northwestern University (MA, PhD), Southern Methodist University and the Oriental Institute of the University of Chicago. He is Professor of History at Trinity College, Deerfield, Illinois.

Warfield, Benjamin, is an instructor in New Testament Language and Literature at Western Theological Seminary in Pittsburgh. He received the Doctor of Laws from both the College of New Jersey and Davidson College in 1892; Doctor of Letters from Lafayette College in 1911; and Sacrae Theologiae Doctor from the University of Utrecht in 1913. In 1886 he was called to succeed Archibald Alexander Hodge as Professor of Systematic Theology at Princeton Theological Seminary — a position which he occupied with great distinction until his death in 1921.

Westcott, Brooke Foss, 1825-1901, was educated at King Edward VI's school at Birmingham and at Trinity College, Cambridge, graduating with highest honors.

Wiseman, Donald J., has served since 1948 as Assistant Keeper of the Department of Egyptian and Assyrian (now Western Asiatic) Antiquities of the British Museum. Educated at King's College, London, and Wadham College, Oxford, he has excavated at Nimrud, Iraq, and Harran, South Turkey, and has served on archaeology survey teams in other Near Eastern countries. He is Professor of Assyriology at London University.

Young, E. J., is a graduate of Stanford University. He received his PhD degree from the Dropsie College for Hebrew and Cognate Learning, Philadelphia. He spent two years in Palestine, Egypt, Italy and Spain in the study of ancient languages, and studied at the University of Leipzig while in Germany. Since 1936 he has served as Professor of Old Testament at Westminster Seminary, Philadelphia.

AUTHOR INDEX

A

Aitken, P. Henderson, 215
Albright, William Foxwell, 23,62f., 65ff.,69f.
Alford, Henry, 93,203,209
Allnutt, Frank, 136
Allport, Gordon, 328f.
Althus, Paul, 217
Anderson, J. N. D., 2,60,183f.,188f., 194,217,219f.,224,228,232ff.,245ff.,257
Anderson, Robert, 92
Archer, Gleason L., 45,53f.,58,298f.
Aristides, 115f.
Arnold, Thomas, 190f.
Arrian, 275
Ash, Sholem, 129
Athanasius, 37

B

Badger, George, 301
Ballard, Frank, 128
Bancroft, George, 134
Beattie, F. R., 2,4
Beck, John C., 276ff.
Betz, Otto, 81
Biederwolf, William, 97
Blaikie, William G., 293
Blaiklock, E. M., 73
Blinzler, Josef, 161
Broadus, John A., 126
Brooks, Phillips, 128
Brown, David, 241ff.
Browning, Iain, 293
Bruce, Alexander Balmin, 207,209,211, 239,241f.,244f.
Bruce, F. F., 17,25f.,32,37f.,41f.,50,56, 58,62,64,66,73,81,84f.,93
Burrows, Millar, 46,58,66ff.
Buttrick, George, 134

C

Campbell, A. G., 93f.
Carlyle, Thomas, 129
Chafer, Lewis Sperry, 23,98f.
Chandler, Samuel, 199f.,208
Channing, William E., 106f.,122,126,134
Chase, F. H., 124
Chiera, Edward, 299,306ff.
Christlieb, Theodore, 249f.
Chrysostom, John, 210,238,240,243
Clark, G. W., 215
Clarke, Edward, 190

Clemens, Samuel (Mark Twain), 136, 310,316
Collett, Sidney, 20
Comay, Joan, 283,285,313
Cooper, David L., 145
Copley, John Singleton, 191
Currie, George, 212f.
Curtius, 275
Cyril of Alexandria, 220

D

Dalrymple, David, 50f.
Davidson, Samuel, 53
David, George, 280f.,284f.,287,290f., 305,309ff.,316f.
Day, E. Hermitage, 198,217,220,225f., 235ff.,253
Delitzsch, Franz, 148,152
Denney, James, 227
Diocletian, 20
Diodorus Siculus, 299
Dodd, C. H., 188
Driver, S. R., 149

E

Eager, George B., 206
Earle, Ralph, 33,57
Edersheim, Alfred, 186,205,208, 214ff.,253f.
Edgar, R. M'Cheyne, 182
Emerson, R. W., 122,128
Estborn, S., 5
Ethridge, J. W., 163
Eusebius, 31,63,196

F

Fairbairn, A. M., 126,134,225
Fallow, Samuel, 241
Farrar, Frederic W., 197
Fausset, A. R., 146,152ff.
Feinberg, Charles, 303f.
Felder, Hilarin, 91f.,100f.
Ferm, Robert O., 326f.,329
Fleming, Ambrose, 189f.
Fodor, Eugene, 285
Free, Joseph, 271,278,282,299,303

G

Garstang, John, 69
Garvie, A. E., 119,121,124,126
Geisler, Norman L., 17,20,28,35f.,43f., 52,59

Glueck, Nelson, 22,65
Godet, F., 233
Goethe, 128
Green, Michael, 11,102,182f.,187,193f.,
   197ff.,205,218,231
Green, William Henry, 56
Greenleaf, Simon, 91,191f.,227,243f.,259
Greenlee, J. Harold, 26,41,50,52
Gregg, W. R., 126
Gregory of Nyssen, 243
Gromacki, Robert, 113f.
Gruenler, Royce Gordon, 130,133

H

Hamilton, Floyd, 175,279,281,283f.,292,
   295,306f.,316
Hanson, George, 216,237,247,259
Hardy, G. B., 259
Harnack, Adolf, 181
Harnack, Theodosus, 180
Hartzler H. Harold, 167,272
Hastings, H. L., 21
Hastings, James, 206
Hausrath, 126
Hearn, Walter, 136
Heinisch, Paul, 147
Hengstenberg, E. W., 146ff.,151
Henry, Matthew, 146f.,150,160,162
Herodotus, 304
Higgins, David, 289ff.
Hinisie, L. E., 250
Hobbs, Herschel, 91f.
Hoehner, Harold, 173
Holloman, H. W., 207
Hopkins, Mark, 131
Horn, Robert M., 9,61
Hort, Fenton John Anthony, 41,103,130
Houghton, Samuel, 198f.
Huxley, Aldous, 11

I-J

Ignatius, 37,64,115,185f.,194f.
Irenaeus, 54,63f.
Ivy, A. C., 193
Jefferson, Charles Edward, 98,121
Jerome, 37
Jidejian, Nina, 274,276ff.
Johnson, Paul H., 136
Josephus, Flavius, 31,55,64f.,82f.,
   99f.,169,187,206
Julian the Apostate, 125
Justin Martyr, 37,85,116,186,195,238

K

Keith, Alexander, 292
Keller, Werner, 305,307f.,315f.

Kenyon, Frederic G., 40,46ff.,55,66
Kevan, Ernest F., 182,187f.,218f.,232,
   236,239,245,255
Kierkegaard, Soren, 10
Kilprect, Kerman, 305
Klausner, Joseph, 86f.,127
Kligerman, Aaron Judah, 153
Kluerer, Heinrich, 249
Knott, H. W., 191
Knox, John 237
Koldewey, Robert, 305
Kreyssler, Henry, 95f.,100ff.
Kubie, Nora Benjamin, 302,307

L

Laetsch, Theodore, 150,159,165f.
Lake, Kirsopp, 25,255ff.
Lamb, Charles, 127
Larue, Gerald A., 305
Latham, Henry, 201,206f.,221f.,244
Latourette, Kenneth Scott, 24,103f.,
   121,132,230,325f.
Layard, Austen H., 297f.,303f.,306f.
Lea, John W., 19,21
LeCamus, Bishop E., 200,211,215,234,
   237,239
Lecky, William, 105,122,132f.
Lenski, R. C. H., 239
LeStrange, 277
Lewis, C. S., 103,106,123,223f.,247f.,254
Liddon, H. P., 181
Linton, Irwin, 90f.
Little, Paul E., 2,4,123,126,227,230,233,
   237,241f.,245f.,253f.,256f.,326
Locke, John, 183,192
Lucian, 82
Luke, 71f.

M

Machen, J. Gresham, 115,118,248
Maclean, G. F., 131
Magath, 168
Maier, Walter A., 297,300ff.
Maimonides, 152,169,207
Maine, Henry Sumner, 209
Major, H. D. A., 230
Mallawan, M. E. L., 300
Mara Bar-serapion, 84f.
Marcion, 37
Martin, J. C., 137
Matheson, George, 227
Matson, E. J., 136
Mattingly, John, 196f.
McAfee, Cleland B., 23
Meisinger, George, 297ff.
Meldau, Fred John, 90

Metzger, Bruce M., 27,42f.,46f.,52
Michaud, Joseph, 277
Mill, John S., 105,122
Milligan, William, 180,182,235,237,253
Minkin, Jacob S., 149
Mixter, R. L., 136
Montefiore, C. G., 91,102
Montgomery, John Warwick, 5,7ff.,19, 40,60f.,65,81,224,259
Moore, Clifford Herschel, 193
Morison, Frank, 91,190,208f., 217ff.,256ff.
Morris, Henry, 70,112,118,121,130,138, 273,281,290
Morris, Leon, 231
Motyer, J. A., 269f.
Moyer, Elgin S., 64,85,195
Mullins, E. Y., 133,328
Myers, Philip, 276

N-O

Napoleon Bonaparte, 106,127,133
Nelson, Nina, 278f.
Nicholi, Armand, 194
Nicoll, W. Robertson, 182,252
Nix, William E., 17,20,28,35f.,43f.,52,59
Origen, 29,116f.
Orr, James, 113,115,252

P-Q

Paley, William, 242,246f.
Pannenberg, Wolfhart, 188,225
Papias, 63
Parker, Joseph, 127,130
Parker, Theodore, 127
Pascal, 126
Patai, Raphael, 292
Peake, W. S., 131
Peters, F. F., 39
Phelps, William Lyon, 189
Phillips, J. B., 5
Philo, 99
Phlegon, 84
Pinnock, Clark H., 2ff.,100,187
Pliny the Elder, 277
Pliny the Younger, 83
Polycarp, 37,64,195

R

Rabbi Aquiba, 56
Rackl, Hans-Wolf, 278f.
Radmacher, Earl, 22
Ramm, Bernard, 19,21,24,67,111,121ff., 125,129f.,134,136,138,184,187f.,194f., 224,272ff.,290,302,325,328

Ramsay, Sir William, 70f.
Rauk, Otto, 136
Renan, Ernest, 129,134
Rice, John R., 114
Robertson, Archibald T., 90,92f.,209, 211,222
Robinson, George L., 289ff.
Robinson, John A. T., 63
Robinson, William Childs, 90f.,100, 113,137
Rogers, Clement F., 114ff.,118
Romanes, G. J., 130
Rober, Albert, 200,210f.,216,223, 240f.,243
Ross, G. A. Johnston, 129
Rosscup, James R., 171,236,245
Rousseau, 122,129
Rowley, H. H., 33,65,272
Russell, Bertrand, 11

S

Sanders, C., 39
Schaff, Philip, 9,24,44f.,105ff.,120ff., 131f.,136,183
Scheffrahn, Karl, 95f.,100ff.
Schonfield, Hugh, 116
Schultz, Thomas, 89,97
Schweitzer, George, 136
Scott, Martin J., 126,132
Scott, Walter, 74
Selwyn, Edwin Gordon, 190,242
Shatsky, J., 250
Simpson, Carnegie P., 2,127
Smith, George, 287,291
Smith, Harold, 212,214
Smith, Wilbur M., 22,121f.,128,180ff., 190f.,193,200,204f.,230,239ff.,244ff., 248,250,256ff.
Smith, William, 214
Sparrow-Simpson, W. J., 181ff.,189, 194f.,200f.,216,218f.,232,250f.,253
Spurr, Frederick, 93
Stauffer, Ethelbert, 9,116f.,124f.
Stevenson, Herbert F., 99f.102
Stewart, Herbert, 291
Stonehouse, N. B., 36
Stoner, Peter W., 167,272,279f.,283ff., 287,293,306ff.,314,318ff.
Stott, John R. W., 96,98f.,121,184,198, 220f.,225,227,234,246,248f.,252,255,258
Straton, Hillyer H., 248
Strauss, David Frederick, 122,134,234f.
Streeter, Burnett Hillman, 46
Suetonius, 83
Swete, Henry Barclay, 90

T

Tacitus, Cornelius, 81f.,168
Tenney, Merrill C., 94,98,206,235f.,
    243,258
Tertullian, 51,83f.,186f.,195,238
Thallus, 84
Thiessen, 95f.
Thomas Aquinas, 136
Thomas, W. H. Griffith, 118,121f.,
    124ff.,130ff.,137
Thorburn, Thomas James, 207f.,211,
    223,233,238,249,254f.
Tischendorf, 47f.
Tucker, T. G., 213f.,223
Tyndale, William, 3

U-V

Unger, Merrill F., 66,70,100,145f.,
    268ff.,290,299f.,305,311
Urquhart, Thomas, 273,282f.,285,
    294ff.,315ff.
Van Ness Myers, Philip, 280

Vincent, Marvin R., 93,209
Voltaire, 20
Von Herder, Johann Gottfried, 127
Vos, Howard, 286f.,289

W

Ward, Philip, 279
Warfield, Benjamin B., 43ff.,182,193
Wells, Albert, 89
Wells, H. G., 128f.
Westcott, B. F., 137f.,192f.
Whedon, D. D., 209f.,214,222
Whitworth, John F., 244,247
Wilson, Joseph D., 162,172ff.
Wilson, Robert Dick, 22,55f.
Wordsworth, 94
Wright, Thomas, 121

X-Y-Z

Young, Edward J., 271f.
Young, John, 126f.

SUBJECT INDEX

A

Ammon, 286ff.,319
Apocrypha
    N. T., 38
    O. T., 33ff.
Apostles
    Eyewitnesses, 5f.,61f.,189ff.
    Firsthand knowledge, 7,191f.
    Resurrection, 216ff.,227f.
Archaeology, 65ff.
Artemis, Statues of, 72
Ashkelon, 284f.,319
Assyrians, 289,292,296ff.

B

Babylon, 302ff.,319
    Size, 304,308
Bethsaida, 309ff.
Bible, Destruction of
    Criticism, 21f.
    Persecution, 20
Bible, Unique, 19ff.
    Authors, 17
    Circulation, 17ff.
    History, 22f.
    Influence, 23f.
    Languages, 16
    Survival, 19ff.
    Translations, 19
Bodmer Papyri, II, 46f.
Books, Divisions, 27f.,30

C

Canon
    Christ's Witness to O. T., 30f.
    Definition, 29
    Hebrew, 30
    N. T., 36ff.
    O. T., 29ff.
    Tests, 29
Capernaum, 309ff.
Chester Beatty Papyri, 47
Chorazin, 309ff.
Christ (See Jesus)
Christ, The Incomparable, 135
Christian Experience
    American Indian, 346
    Aucas, 358f.
    Author, 337f.
    Billionairess, 334f.
    Brazil, 345f.
    Businessman, 338
    Canada, 347f.
    Cartoonist, 335
    City-Planner, 341
    Computer Expert, 329f.
    Criminal, 331
    Czechoslovakia, 346f.
    England, 349
    Farmer, 339
    Finland, 349
    Football Coach, 332
    Football Player, 333
    Former White House Aid, 339f.
    Gang Leader, 343
    Germany, 350
    Golfer, 332
    Guatemala, 350
    Hinduism, 351ff.
    Hong Kong, 345
    India, 349f.
    Islam, 351
    Japan, 345
    Judaism, 350f.
    Kenya, 348
    Korea, 359
    Martyr, 358
    Medical Doctor, 338f.
    Minister, 331f.
    Miss America, 333f.
    Movie Actor, 335f.
    Nazi Pilot, 330f.
    Panama, 349
    Philosopher, 341f.
    Policeman, 330
    President, U. N. General
        Assembly, 340f.
    Prisoner, 344f.
    Prostitute, 330
    Psychologist, 342
    Rumania, 357f.
    Satanism, 353ff.
    Singer, 336f.
    Skeptics, 335ff.
    Tennis Pro, 333
    Thailand, 348
    University Lecturer, 342f.
    U. S. Senator, 340
    Vietnam, 347
    Zaire, 346
Church
    Witness of Resurrection, 228ff.
Church Fathers, 50ff.,63ff.,81,115f.
    Resurrection, 194f.
Codex, 27

Crucifixion, 160ff.

D

Dead Sea Scrolls, 52f.,56ff.
Defense, 1,2
Delphi Inscription, 73
Diatessaron, 47
Documentary Hypothesis, 21f.,68

E

Ebla, 68
Edom, 287ff.,319
Egypt, 293ff.,307f.
Euphrates River, 304
Evidence, Historical,2ff.,81ff.,
    185ff.,189ff.
Excuses for Rejecting, 10ff.
Ezekiel, Dating of, 271f.

F

Faith
    Blind, 3f.
    Factual, 2,4f.
    In Resurrection, 4
    Leap, 10
    Objective, 4f.,327f.

G

Gaza, 283ff.,319
Gemaras, 60
Genesis, 68ff.
Guard
    Roman, 210ff.,223,239ff.
    Temple, 211f.

H

Hexapla, 60
History
    Approach, 7ff.
    Definition, 7ff.
    Prejudices, 7ff.
    Resurrection, 185ff.
    Skepticism, 7ff.
Horites, 69

I-J

Idumeans, 290
Jamnia, Council of, 32f.
Jericho, 69
Jerusalem, 170ff.,311ff.,319
Jesus, Direct Claims to Deity
    Equality With the Father, 92f.
    "I AM," 93f.
    Received Worship, 95

    To Believe as the Father, 94
    To Honor as the Father, 94
    To Know as the Father, 94
    To See as the Father, 95
    Witnesses of Others, 5ff.,96f.
Jesus, Indirect Claims to Deity
    Authority, 99
    Forgives sins, 98
    Immutable, 98
    Life, 98
    Son of God, 100f.
    Son of Man, 101f.
    Titles Given, 99ff.
Jesus, the Character of
    Different from Other Men, 126ff.
    Sinless, 118ff.
Jesus, the Person of
    Death, 137,195ff.
    Deity, 89ff.
    Historical, 81ff.
    Impact on Lives, 325ff.
    Lord, Liar, Lunatic, 103ff.
    Post-resurrection
        Appearances, 223f.
    Resurrection, 179ff.
    Trial, 90ff.
    Virgin Birth, 112ff.
John Ryland MSS, 46

M

Mahaparinibbana Sutta, 180
Manuscripts (MSS)
    Bibliographical Test,
        New Testament, 39ff.
        Old Testament, 52ff.
    Comparison with Secular MSS,
        41ff.
    Dating, 46
    External Evidence Test, 63ff.
    Hebrew, 56ff.
    Internal Evidence Test, 60ff.
    Number of, 39ff.
    Preparation, 25ff.
    Reliability, 39ff.
Marduk, 305,308
Mari, 70
Massoretes, 54f.
Medes, 302
Memphis, 293ff.
Messiah-Messianic Prophecy,
    141ff.,183ff.
Midrash, 60,151
Miracles, 122ff.
Mishnah, 60,86,214f.
Moab, 286ff.,319
Myth, 5,81,326

N

Nabeans, 290
Nazarene Inscription, 218
Nineveh, 296ff.
    Size of, 308
Nuzu, 70

O

Old Syriac, 49
One Solitary Life, 134f.
Ostraca, 26

P

Papyrus, 25f.
Parchment, 26
Pavement, 73
Persians, 296,304f.
Peshitta, 49
Petra, 287ff.
Philistines, 283ff.
Pool of Bethesda, 73
Presuppositions, 7ff.,273
Progressive Labor Party, 81
Prophecies, Messianic
    Anointment of the Holy Spirit, 154
    Ascension, 157
    Betrayed, 158
    Bones not Broken, 165
    Born at Bethlehem, 149f.
    Born of a Virgin, 145f.
    Called Lord, 151f.
    Committed to God, 165
    Crucified Between Thieves, 161f.
    Darkness, 166
    Donkey, 156
    Dumb Before Accusers, 159
    Enter the Temple, 156
    Fall Under Cross, 161
    False Witnesses, 159
    Family Line of Jesse, 148
    Forsaken, 159
    Forsaken Cry, 164
    Friends Stood Afar Off, 163
    Galilee, 155
    Gall and Vinegar Offered, 164
    Garments Parted and
        Lots Cast, 163
    God's House, 158
    Hands and Feet Pierced, 161
    Hated, 162
    Heads Shaken, 163
    Heart Broken, 165
    Herod Kills Children, 150
    House of David, 149
    Immanuel, 152
    Intercession, 162
    Judge, 153f.
    King, 154
    Light to Gentiles, 157
    Miracles, 156
    Mocked, 160
    Parables, 156
    Potter's Field, 159
    Preceded by Messenger, 155
    Pre-existence, 151
    Presented With Gifts, 150
    Priest, 153
    Prophet, 152f.
    Rejected, 162
    Resurrection, 157
    Rich Man's Tomb, 166
    Seated at the Right Hand
        of God, 158
    Seed of Abraham, 146f.
    Seed of the Woman, 144f.
    Side Pierced, 165f.
    Son of God, 146
    Son of Isaac, 147
    Son of Jacob, 147f.
    Spit Upon, 160
    Stared Upon, 163
    Stumbling Stone, 156f.
    Thirst, 164
    Thirty Pieces of Silver, 158
    Tribe of Judah, 148
    Wounded and Bruised, 160
    Zeal for God, 155
Prophecy
    Dating, 270f.
    Definition, 267ff.
    Probability, 166f.,283,285,293,
        307f.,317ff.
    Unique, 22
Prophets
    Test of, 269f.

R

Resurrection, 137f.,328
    Burial, 137,202,204ff.
    Church, 228ff.
    Claims of Christ, 183ff.
    Death, 137,195ff.
    Empty Tomb, 180,200ff.,
        216ff.,226f.
    Guard, 210ff.
    Importance of, 180ff.
    Post-resurrection
        Appearances, 223f.
    Sacraments, 231
    Seal, 209f.
    Stone, 207ff.
    Sunday, 230f.
    Witness of Law, 189ff.

Resurrection Theories, 232ff.
    Hallucination Theory, 247ff.
    Swoon Theory, 232ff.
    Theft Theory, 238ff.
    Wrong Tomb Theory, 255ff.

S

Samaria, 281ff.,319
Samaritan Text, 59
Sanhedrin, 168ff.
Scrolls, 27
Septuagint, 58f.
Sidon, 280f.
Sinaiticus, Codex, 24,27,47
Synagogue of the Hebrews, 72

T

Talmud, 54,85ff.,154,157,168f.
Talmudists, 53f.
Targums, 59f.
    Isaiah, 148,151ff.,157,160
    Jonathan, 147f.

    Onkelos, 145,147
    Pseudo Jonathan, 145,148
Teman, 289
Textual Variations, 43ff.
Thebes, 293ff.
Theories of the Resurrection
    (See Resurrection Theories)
Tiberias, 311
Tower of Antonia, 73
Tower of Babel, 69
Tyre, 274ff.,319

U-V-W

Ugarit, 70
Vaticanus, Codex, 27,47
Vellum, 26
Versions, 48ff.
Virgin Birth, 112ff.,145f.
Writing
    Instruments, 26
    Material, 25f.
    Types of, 27

HAVE YOU HEARD

OF THE

Four Spiritual Laws?

Just as there are physical laws that govern the physical universe, so are there spiritual laws which govern your relationship with God.

LAW ONE

GOD **LOVES** YOU, AND OFFERS A WONDERFUL **PLAN** FOR YOUR LIFE.

GOD'S LOVE

"For God so loved the world, that He gave His only begotten Son, that whoever believes in Him should not perish, but have eternal life" (John 3:16).

GOD'S PLAN

(Christ speaking) "I came that they might have life, and might have it abundantly" (that it might be full and meaningful) (John 10:10).

Why is it that most people are not experiencing the abundant life?

Because . . .

LAW TWO

MAN IS **SINFUL** AND **SEPARATED** FROM GOD. THEREFORE, HE CANNOT KNOW AND EXPERIENCE GOD'S LOVE AND PLAN FOR HIS LIFE.

MAN IS SINFUL

"For all have sinned and fall short of the glory of God" (Romans 3:23).

Man was created to have fellowship with God; but, because of his stubborn self-will, he chose to go his own independent way and fellowship with God was broken. This self-will, characterized by an attitude of active rebellion or passive indifference, is evidence of what the Bible calls sin.

MAN IS SEPARATED

"For the wages of sin is death" (spiritual separation from God) (Romans 6:23).

This diagram illustrates that God is holy and man is sinful. A great gulf separates the two. The arrows illustrate that man is continually trying to reach God and the abundant life through his own efforts, such as a good life, philosophy or religion.

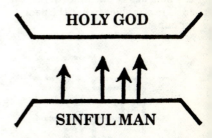

The Third Law explains the only way to bridge this gulf . . .

LAW THREE

JESUS CHRIST IS GOD'S
ONLY PROVISION FOR
MAN'S SIN. THROUGH HIM
YOU CAN KNOW AND
EXPERIENCE GOD'S LOVE
AND PLAN FOR YOUR LIFE.

HE DIED IN OUR PLACE

"But God demonstrates His own
love toward us, in that while we
were yet sinners, Christ died for us"
(Romans 5:8).

HE ROSE FROM THE DEAD

"Christ died for our sins . . . He
was buried . . . He was raised on
the third day according to the
Scriptures . . . He appeared to
Peter, then to the twelve.
After that He appeared to more
than five hundred . . ."
(I Corinthians 15:3-6).

HE IS THE ONLY WAY

"Jesus said to him, 'I am the way,
and the truth, and the life; no one
comes to the Father, but through
Me'" (John 14:6).

This diagram illustrates that God
has bridged the gulf which
separates us from Him by sending
His Son, Jesus Christ, to die on the
cross in our place to pay the penalty
for our sins.

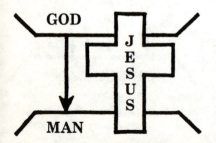

**It is not enough just to know these
three laws . . .**

LAW FOUR

WE MUST INDIVIDUALLY
RECEIVE JESUS CHRIST AS
SAVIOR AND LORD; THEN
WE CAN KNOW AND
EXPERIENCE GOD'S LOVE
AND PLAN FOR OUR LIVES.

WE MUST RECEIVE CHRIST

"But as many as received Him, to
them He gave the right to become
children of God, even to those who
believe in His name" (John 1:12).

WE RECEIVE CHRIST
THROUGH FAITH

"For by grace you have been saved
through faith; and that not of
yourselves, it is the gift of God; not
as a result of works, that no one
should boast" (Ephesians 2:8,9).

WE RECEIVE CHRIST BY
PERSONAL INVITATION

(Christ is speaking): "Behold, I
stand at the door and knock; if any
one hears My voice and opens the
door, I will come in to him"
(Revelation 3:20).

Receiving Christ involves turning
to God from self, (repentance) and
trusting Christ to come into our
lives, to forgive our sins and to
make us the kind of people He
wants us to be. Just to agree
intellectually that Jesus Christ is
the Son of God and that He died on
the cross for our sins is not enough.
Nor is it enough to have an
emotional experience. We receive
Jesus Christ by faith, as an act of
the will.

These two circles represent two kinds of lives:

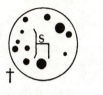

SELF-DIRECTED LIFE

S — Self is on the throne

† — Christ is outside the life

● — Interests are directed by self, often resulting in discord and frustration

CHRIST-DIRECTED LIFE

† — Christ is in the life and on the throne

S — Self is yielding to Christ

● — Interests are directed by Christ, resulting in harmony with God's plan

Which circle best represents your life?

Which circle would you like to have represent your life?

The following explains how you can receive Christ:

YOU CAN RECEIVE CHRIST RIGHT NOW THROUGH PRAYER

(Prayer is talking with God)

God knows your heart and is not so concerned with your words as He is with the attitude of your heart. The following is a suggested prayer:

"Lord Jesus, I need You. Thank You for dying on the cross for my sins. I open the door of my life and receive You as my Savior and Lord. Thank You for forgiving my sins and giving me eternal life. Take control of the throne of my life. Make me the kind of person You want me to be."

Does this prayer express the desire of your heart?

If it does, pray this prayer right now, and Christ will come into your life, as He promised.

HOW TO KNOW THAT CHRIST IS IN YOUR LIFE

Did you receive Christ into your life? According to His promise in Revelation 3:20, where is Christ right now in relation to you? Christ said that He would come into your life. Would He mislead you? On what authority do you know that God has answered your prayer? (The trustworthiness of God Himself and His Word.)

THE BIBLE PROMISES ETERNAL LIFE TO ALL WHO RECEIVE CHRIST

"And the witness is this, that God has given us eternal life, and this life is in His Son. He who has the Son has the life; he who does not have the Son of God does not have the life. These things I have written to you who believe in the name of the Son of God, in order that you may know that you have eternal life" (I John 5:11-13).

Thank God often that Christ is in your life and that He will never leave you (Hebrews 13:5). You can know on the basis of His promise that Christ lives in you and that you have eternal life, from the very moment you invite Him in. He will not deceive you.

An important reminder...

DO NOT DEPEND UPON FEELINGS

The promise of God's Word, not our feelings, is our authority. The Christian lives by faith (trust) in the trustworthiness of God Himself and His Word. This train diagram illustrates the relationship between **fact** (God and His Word), **faith** (our trust in God and His Word), and **feeling** (the result of our faith and obedience) (John 14:21).

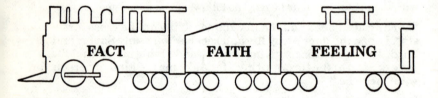

FACT   FAITH   FEELING

The train will run with or without the caboose. However, it would be useless to attempt to pull the train by the caboose. In the same way, we, as Christians, do not depend on feelings or emotions, but we place our faith (trust) in the trustworthiness of God and the promises of His Word.

NOW THAT YOU HAVE RECEIVED CHRIST

The moment that you received Christ by faith, as an act of the will, many things happened, including the following:

1. Christ came into your life (Revelation 3:20 and Colossians 1:27).
2. Your sins were forgiven (Colossians 1:14).
3. You became a child of God (John 1:12).
4. You received eternal life (John 5:24).
5. You began the great adventure for which God created you (John 10:10, II Corinthians 5:17 and I Thessalonians 5:18).

Can you think of anything more wonderful that could happen to you than receiving Christ? Would you like to thank God in prayer right now for what He has done for you? By thanking God, you demonstrate your faith.

Now what?

SUGGESTIONS FOR CHRISTIAN GROWTH

Spiritual growth results from trusting Jesus Christ. "The righteous man shall live by faith" (Galatians 3:11). A life of faith will enable you to trust God increasingly with every detail of your life, and to practice the following:

G Go to God in prayer daily (John 15:7).

R Read God's Word daily (Acts 17:11) — begin with the Gospel of John.

O Obey God, moment by moment (John 14:21).

W Witness for Christ by your life and words (Matthew 4:19; John 15:8).

T Trust God for every detail of your life (I Peter 5:7).

H Holy Spirit — allow Him to control and empower your daily life and witness (Galatians 5:16,17; Acts 1:8).

FELLOWSHIP IN A GOOD CHURCH

God's Word admonishes us not to forsake "the assembling of ourselves together . . ." (Hebrews 10:25). Several logs burn brightly together; but put one aside on the cold hearth and the fire goes out. So it is with your relationship to other Christians. If you do not belong to a church, do not wait to be invited. Take the initiative; call the pastor of a nearby church where Christ is honored and His Word is preached. Start this week, and make plans to attend regularly.